INSIDE THE TRANSFORMING URBAN ASIA

Processes, Policies and Public Actions

By the Same Author

Solid Waste Management in Indian Cities: Status and Emerging Practices

---

About the Editor

Prof. Darshini Mahadevia, teaches at Faculty of Planning and Public Policy, CEPT University, Ahmedabad and is a Visiting Faculty at Centre for Development Alternatives, Ahmedabad. She is a PhD from Jawaharlal Nehru University, New Delhi, and has been a visiting scholar at Graduate School of Architecture and Urban Planning, University of California, Los Angeles; at School of Urban Planning, McGill University and Visiting Fellow at Tsinghua University, Beijing and Tianjin University of Finance and Economics, Tianjin. She has been researching on urban poverty, urban development, human and gender development. Has published extensively on these subjects. Has wide experience of working with NGOs in India.

INSIDE THE TRANSFORMING URBAN ASIA

Processes, Policies and Public Actions

Edited by

Darshini Mahadevia

CONCEPT PUBLISHING COMPANY, NEW DELHI-110059

Cataloging in Publication Data—DK
Courtesy: D.K. Agencies (P) Ltd. <docinfo@dkagencies.com>

Inside the transforming urban Asia : processes, policies and public actions / edited by Darshini Mahadevia.

p. cm.

Contributed articles and seminar papers.
Includes bibliographical references (p.).
Includes index.
ISBN 13: 9788180695742
ISBN 10: 8180695743

1. Urban policy—India. 2. Urban policy—China. 3. Urban policy—Asia. 4. Urbanization—India. 5. Urbanization—China. 6. Urbanization—Asia. 7. Globalization—Social aspects—Asia. I. Mahadevia, Darshini, 1959-

DDC 307.141 609 5 22

ISBN-13: 978-81-8069-574-2
ISBN-10: 81-8069-574-3

First Published 2008

Published and Printed by
Ashok Kumar Mittal
Concept Publishing Company
A/15-16, Commercial Block, Mohan Garden
New Delhi-110059 (INDIA)

Phones : 25351460, 25351794
Fax : 091-11-25357103
Email : publishing@conceptpub.com

PREFACE

This book is collection of articles on the rapid ongoing transformations within the Asian cities in the period when Asia is rising economically. It is about the processes of these transformations, State Policy in support of these transformations, exclusions and inclusions therein and contestations and resistance by those getting adversely affected by the changes in urban space. This volume is different than many earlier publications on Asian megacities that look at the changing economic base and increase in incomes, real estate development and many other growth related changes as a consequence of globalisation of their national economies. This book is among those few that look at exclusions and inclusions within the Asian cities as a consequence of globalisation.

The book has 11 articles on Indian cities; eight of them are from the research carried out under the project titled 'Inclusive Mega Cities in Asia in a Globalising World', funded by the Indo Dutch Programme on Alternatives in Development (IDPAD)—a joint Programme on Development Research of the Indian Council of Social Science Research (ICSSR), New Delhi and Science for Global Development (WOTRO), The Hague. The research project was anchored at Centre for Development Alternatives (CFDA), Ahmedabad and Institute of Social Studies (ISS), The Hague. The IDPAD research funding came in at the right time when large scale changes were taking place in the Indian cities.

The megacity theme under the Fifth Phase of IDPAD projects announced in 2002 proposed to deal with the issues such as relationship between globalisation and megacities, shifting economic base of the megacities and resulting processes of development, shifting urban policies to deal with challenges of globalisation posed to the megacities, impacts of such policy changes and processes on the marginal populations within the city, and construction of ethnic and religious identities as well as new movements in megacities in such times. We, my project partner from the ISS, the Hague, Dr. Erhard Berner and myself, decided to focus on two concerns, emerging dualisms within the cities and marginalities and contestations emerging from shifting economic base of the megacities. We decided to take up three Indian megacities Mumbai, Bangalore and Ahmedabad and Dhaka from Bangladesh for in-depth research; addressing the issues such as what type of transformations are taking place, who is driving these transformations, what is the politics of it, how the public opinion is being manufactured in support of a particular model of urban development, what is the funding of such transformations, are the poor and the marginal groups being included in these changes at the policy level or the process level? However, due to some reasons beyond our control; we were unable to complete our research on Dhaka.

Other papers in the book were presented at the final Conference held under the project in June 2006 in New Delhi, when participants from other Asian countries and other than the project-cities were invited to share their research on the subject. Of these, two were on Chinese cities and rightly so as the Chinese experience of city transformation is very important on many counts; one the sheer size of the country, massive changes observed in the Chinese cities in last decade and a half and deep interest in Indian policy circles on the transformation of Chinese cities, represented by the incumbent Prime Minister of India Dr. Manmohan Singh's wish of 'making Mumbai like Shanghai'. Subsequently, two more chapters on Chinese cities were added from my own research on China undertaken through the funding from Asian Scholarship Foundation, Bangkok.

The publication of this volume is with the grant from IDPAD. I am extremely grateful to IDPAD for funding the main research, final review conference and publication of this volume. In particular, I am grateful to the IDPAD secretariat in India and the Netherlands for facilitating the project and the publication. My deep gratitude to Dr. Sanchitta Dutta, ICSSR, IDPAD secretariat in India and Dr. Cora Govers, WOTRO, IDPAD secretariat in the Netherlands for the same.

The research in Bangalore was carried out by Dr. Solomon Benjamin and his team. Over the period of this project we had some rich discussions over the processes observed in Bangalore. I am thankful to Solly and his team for participating in this project and bringing to fore the dimension of politics in city transformation in such an internationally integrated city such as Bangalore, the articulation of India in the global economy.

Research in Mumbai and Ahmedabad was carried out by us at the

CFDA, with a research team of Harini Narayanan and Riby Rachel Mathews working on Mumbai and Harpreet Singh Brar working on Ahmedabad. Workers of the NGO YUVA supported us for the primary survey in Mumbai slums and we would like to express our thanks to Chandan, Amrita, Kaushalya, Reshma and Chitra of YUVA. NGO Saath in Ahmedabad collaborated with us for the primary surveys in Ahmedabad slums and I would like to thank Mr. Rajendra Joshi and Chiranjivbhen for this participation.

For our first workshop in Mumbai, we got support from Mr. Rahul Srivastava of PUKAR, Mr. Naresh Fernandes of Time-out magazine, and Arvind and Neera Adarkar of Mumbai Study Action group. On behalf of our team, I would like to thank large many individuals who spared their time for discussions with us and made their reports available to us; from Mumbai, Dr. Amita Bhide (TISS & CRH), Prof. Sharit Bhowmick (Bombay University), Dr. Uday Mehta, Simpreet (NAPM), Shweta Tambe (CRH), Deepika D'Souza (Centre for Human Rights and Law), Ms. Qudsiya Contractor (CEHAT), Mr. Praksh Reddy (Gen Sec CPI), Dr. Adsule, Rupa Mathew and Alphonsa (Nirmala Nikethan), Mr Phatak and Mr. Ghorpade (MMRDA) and from Ahmedabad, Mr. Himanshu Thakker of AUDA and Captain Dileep Mahajan from AMC.

Two students of School of Planning, CEPT University also assisted in this research, Mr. Subhankar Mitra for Mumbai and Mr. Chandra Kant Yadav for Ahmedabad. Ms. Sharda Srinivasan, a Masters student at Institute of Social Studies, The Hague assisted in secondary information collection.

Our final review conference was held in collaboration with the Institute of Human Development (IHD), New Delhi and CEPT University, Ahmedabad. My deep gratitude to Prof. A.N. Sharma for agreeing to collaborate with his characteristic enthusiasm and Aseem Prakash of IHD for taking on many responsibilities of organising this event and Dr. R. N. Vakil, Director, CEPT for partial financial support for the final review conference. Support of Prof. Indira Hirway, Director CFDA throughout the project has been very valuable.

My thanks to all the researchers who contributed papers and presentations at different workshop consultations and the final review conference. I am particularly grateful to the contributors of this volume. The research team is also grateful to the respondents of all our primary surveys. Lastly, warm gratitude to Erhard for support throughout the project.

This volume has larger representation of cases of India followed by

China than other Asian countries. This is primarily so because the IDPAD research was based on Indian cities and my own other independent interest has been on Chinese cities. On the other hand, the countries of the west Asia are not represented here at all. On a logical note, one may say that India and China together make up 40 per cent of the world and 63 per cent of Asia's population and both undergoing rapid urbanisation, it is justifiable to have more articles on these two countries than other Asian countries. The final chapter selection did not emerge out of any such logical decision, I must admit. This limitation of this volume is primarily because of resource persons one could identify to write articles. And for this, the responsibility is entirely mine.

I am very happy to put forward these articles to the larger community interested in urban policies and processes within the Asian cities. I hope that these articles would greatly contribute to the concerns about need for 'Inclusive' development paradigm for the urban areas in general and urban areas of Asia in particular.

Darshini Mahadevia

CONTENTS

PUBLIC ACTION

LIST OF TABLES

LIST OF BOXES, FIGURES AND MAPS

List of Boxes

List of Figures

List of Maps

LIST OF PHOTOGRAPHS

ACRONYMS

AC	:	Asbestos Cement
ADB	:	Asian Development Bank
ADD	:	Acute Diarrhoea Disease
AGR	:	Annual Growth Rate
ALM	:	Advance Locality Management
AMC	:	Ahmedabad Municipal Corporation
AMTS	:	Ahmedabad Municipal Transport Services
ASEAN	:	Association of South East Asian Nations
ASF	:	Asian Scholarship Foundation
AUA	:	Ahmedabad Urban Agglomeration
AUDA	:	Ahmedabad Urban Development Authority
BATF	:	Bangalore Agenda Task Force
BCG	:	Beijing Capital Group
BDA	:	Bangalore Development Authority
BEST	:	Bombay Electric Supply and Transport
BHEL	:	Bharat Heavy Electical Ltd
BIIC	:	Beijing Infrastructure Investment Co. Ltd.
BINGO	:	Big International Non-Government Organisation
BJP	:	Bharatiya Janata Party
BKC	:	Bandra-Kurla Complex
BMC	:	Bombay Municipal Corporation
BMP	:	Bangalore Mahanagar Palike
BMRDA	:	Bangalore Metropolitan Regional Development Authority
BOT	:	Build Operate Transfer
BOOT	:	Build Own Operate Transfer
BPO	:	Business Process Outsourcing
BRPL	:	BSES Rajdhani Power Ltd
BRT	:	Bus Rapid Transit

BRTS	:	Bus Rapid Transit System
BSE	:	Bombay Stock Exchange
BSP	:	Bahujan Samaj Party
BSSIA	:	Bombay Small Scale Industries Association
BT	:	Bio Technology
BTS	:	Bangalore Transport Services
BUTP	:	Bombay Urban Transport Project
BWSSB	:	Bangalore Water Supply and Sewerage Board
BYPL	:	BSES Yamuna Power Ltd
CAG	:	Citizen's Action Group
CAGR	:	Compound Annual Growth Rate
CBD	:	Central Business District
CBO	:	Community Based Organisation
CCC	:	Citizens' Consultative Committee
CCF	:	City Challenge Fund
CCP	:	Chinese Communist Party
CDP	:	City Development Plan
CEHAT	:	Centre for Enquiry Into Health and Allied Themes
CEO	:	Chief Executive Officer
CEPA	:	Closer Economic Partnership Arrangement
CIF	:	Chief Inspector of Factories
CII	:	Confederation of Indian Industries
CL	:	Casual Labour
CM	:	Chief Minister
CMCs	:	City Municipal Councils
CMIE	:	Centre for Monitoring of Indian Economy
CMP	:	Common Minimum Programme
CMTF	:	Chief Minister's Task Force
COHRE	:	Centre on Housing Rights and Evictions
CPF	:	Central Provident Fund
CPI (M)	:	Communist Party of India Marxist
CPPCC	:	Chinese People's Political Consultative Committee
CPRGS	:	Comprehensive Poverty Reduction and Growth Strategy
CPV	:	Communist Party of Vietnam
CRES	:	Centre for Natural Resources and Environmental Studies
CRH	:	Committee for Right to Housing
CRSUD	:	Council of China Research Society of Urban Development
CRZ	:	Coastal Regulatory Zone

CTG	:	Capital Tree Group
CUA	:	Chennai Urban Agglomeration
CV	:	Coefficient of Variation
DA	:	Development Authority
DC	:	District Collector
DCB	:	Delhi Cantonment Board
DCR	:	Development Control Regulations
DDA	:	Delhi Development Authority
DERC	:	Delhi Electricity Regulatory Commission
DESU	:	Delhi Electric Supply Undertaking
DF	:	Democratic Front
DJB	:	Delhi *Jal* Board
DM	:	District Magistrate
DMC	:	Delhi Municipal Corporation
DMRC	:	Delhi Metro Railway Corporation
DP	:	Development Plan
DPCL	:	Delhi Power Supply Company Limited
DSS	:	Dalit Sangharsh Samiti
DTC	:	Delhi Transport Corporation
DTL	:	Delhi Transco Ltd
DTU	:	Delhi Transport Undertaking
DUA	:	Delhi Urban Agglomeration
DVB	:	Delhi Vidyut Board
DWSSDU	:	Delhi Water Supply and Sewage Disposal Undertaking
DyCM	:	Deputy Chief Minister
EIUS	:	Environmental Improvement of Urban Slums
EPIP	:	Export Promotion Zone
EWS	:	Economically Weaker Section
FAR	:	Floor Area Ratio
FBAS	:	Fund Based Accounting systems
FDI	:	Foreign Direct Investment
FICCI	:	Federation of Indian Chamber of Commerce and Industry
FRL	:	Full Reservoir Level
FSI	:	Floor Space Index
GDCR	:	Gujarat Development Control Regulations
GDP	:	Gross Domestic Product
GI	:	Galvanized Iron
GIS	:	Geographic Information System
GNCTD	:	Government of National Capital Territory of Delhi

GOC	:	General Officer Commanding
GoK	:	Government of Karnataka
GoM	:	Government of Maharashtra
GP	:	Gram Panchayat
GPCB	:	Gujarat Pollution Control Board
GSDMA	:	Gujarat State Disaster Management Authority
GTPS	:	Gas Turbine Power Station
HACI	:	Hanoi Association of Commerce and Industry
HCR	:	Head Count Ratio
HDB	:	Housing and Development Board
HDR	:	Human Development Report
HMWSSB	:	Hyderabad Metropolitan Water Supply and Sewerage Board
HSDC	:	Hanoi Sewerage and Drainage Company
HUA	:	Hyderabad Urban Agglomeration
HUDA	:	Hyderabad Urban Development Authority
HUDCO	:	Housing and Urban Development Corporation
ICICI	:	Industrial Credit and Investment Corporation of India
ICT	:	Information and Communication Technologies
ID	:	Identity Card
IDPAD	:	Indo Dutch Programme of Alternatives in Development
IFC	:	International Finance Corporation
IIMB	:	Indian Institute of Management
IL&FS	:	Infrastructure Leasing and Financial Services
IMC	:	Indian Merchants' Chamber
IMF	:	International Monetary Fund
IMR	:	Infant Mortality Rate
IPGCL	:	Indraprastha Power Generation Company Ltd
IPHRC	:	Indian People's Human Rights Commission
IPHRT	:	Indian Peoples Human Rights Tribunal
IPT	:	Indian People's Tribunal
IPTEHR	.	Indian Peoples Tribunal on Environment and Human Rights
ISB	:	Indian School of Business
IT	:	Information Technology
ITCDC	:	IT Corridor Development Corporation
ITES	:	Information Technology Enabled Services
ITPL	:	International Technology Park Ltd.
JBIC	:	Japanese Bank of International Cooperation
JJ	:	Jhugghi Jhumpri

JNNURM	:	Jawaharlal Nehru National Urban Renewal Mission
JNP	:	Jawaharlal Nehru Port
JTC	:	Jurong Town Corporation
KEB	:	Karnataka Electricity Board
KHB	:	Karnataka Housing Board
KIADB	:	Karnataka Industrial Area Development Board
KJS	:	Karnataka Janandolana Sangatane
KKNSS	:	Karnataka Koligeri Nivasa Sangathana
KSCB	:	Karnataka Slum Clearance Board
KUA	:	Kolkata Urban Agglomeration
KUIDFC	:	Karnataka Urban Infrastructure Development and Finance Corporation
LIC	:	Life Insurance Corporation
LIG	:	Low Income Group
LOA	:	Land Owning Agency
LPCD	:	Litres Per Capita Per Day
LRT	:	Light Rail Transit
MC	:	Municipal Commissioner
MCD	:	Municipal Corporation of Delhi
MCGM	:	Municipal Corporation of Greater Mumbai
MCH	:	Municipal Corporation of Hyderabad
MCOCA	:	Maharashtra Control of Organised Crime Act
MDG	:	Millennium Development Goals
MES	:	Military Engineering Services
MGD	:	Million Gallons per Day
MHADA	:	Maharashtra Housing and Area Development Authority
MIG	:	Middle Income Group
MLA	:	Member of Legislative Assembly
MLPD	:	Million Litres Per Day
MMR	:	Mumbai Metropolitan Region
MMRDA	:	Mumbai Metropolitan Regional Development Authority
MMSEZ	:	Maha Mumbai Special Economic Zone
MNC	:	Multi National Companies
MOC	:	Ministry of Construction
MoU	:	Memorandum of Understanding
MP	:	Member of Parliament
MPC	:	Metropolitan Planning Committee
MPD	:	Master Plan of Delhi
MRT	:	Mass Rapid Transit

MRVC	:	Mumbai Rail Vikas Corporation
MSRDC	:	Maharashtra State Road Development Corporation
MT	:	Metric Tonnes
MTA	:	Merchants and Traders Association
MU	:	Million Unit
MUA	:	Mumbai Urban Agglomeration
MUIP	:	Mumbai Urban Infrastructure Project
MUTP	:	Mumbai Urban Transport Project
NABARD	:	National Bank for Agricultural and Rural Development
NAC	:	National Advisory Council
NAPM	:	National Alliance of People's Movement
NASVI	:	National Alliance of Street Vendors of India
NBS	:	National Bureau of Statistics
NCHR	:	National Campaign for Housing Rights
NCO	:	National Classification of Occupation
NCP	:	Nationalist Congress Party
NCR	:	National Capital Region
NCRPB	:	National Capital Region Planning Board
NCT	:	National Capital Territory
NCU	:	National Commission on Urbanisation
NDA	:	National Democratic Alliance
NDMC	:	New Delhi Municipal Council
NDPL	:	North Delhi Power Limited
NDZ	:	No Development Zone
NGEF	:	New Government Electric Factory
NGO	:	Non Governmental Organisations
NHSS	:	Nivara Hakk Suraksha Samiti
NIC	:	National Industrial Classification
NIE	:	Newly Industrialising Economies
NIURP	:	National Institute of Urban and Rural Planning
NMSEZ	:	Navi Mumbai Special Economic Zone
NOIDA	:	New Okhla Industrial Development Area
NP	:	Nagar Panchayat
NPC	:	National People's Congress
NR	:	No Reply
NRI	:	Non Resident Indians
NSDP	:	Net State Domestic Product
NSE	:	National Stock Exchange
NSM	:	New Social Movement
NSS	:	National Sample Survey

NURM	:	National Urban Renewal Mission
OBC	:	Other Backward Castes
ODA	:	Overseas Development Assistance
P.A.	:	Per Annum
PAP	:	Peoples' Action Party
PCNSDP	:	Per Capita Net State Domestic Product
PIL	:	Public Interest Litigation
PIO	:	People of Indian Origin
PPCL	:	Pragati Power Corporation Ltd
PPP	:	Public Private Partnership
P.P.P.	:	Purchasing Power Parity
PRC	:	People's Republic of China
PROOF	:	Public Record of Operations and Finance
PUCL	:	People's Union for Civil Liberties
PUDR	:	People's Union of Democratic Rights
PVC	:	Praja Vimochana Cheluvali
PWD	:	Public Works Department
R&R	:	Rehabilitation and Resettlement
RBI	:	Reserve Bank of India
RC	:	Residents' Committee
RCC	:	Reinforced Cement Concrete
RE	:	Regular Employed
RFC	:	Regional Financial Centre
RMB	:	Renminbi
RMP	:	Registered Medical Practitioner
ROB	:	Rail Over Bridges
Rs.	:	Indian Rupees
RWA	:	Resident Welfare Associations
SAR	:	Special Economic Region
SARS	:	Severe Acute Respiratory Syndrome
SC	:	Scheduled Caste
SDP	:	State Domestic Product
SE	:	Self Employed
SEWA	:	Self Employed Women's Association
SEZ	:	Special Economic Zone
SG	:	Sarkhej - Gandhinagar
SLDC	:	State Load Dispatch Centre
SOE	:	State Owned Enterprises
SP	:	Sardar Patel
SPARC	:	Society for the Promotion of Area Resource Centres

SPV	:	Special Purpose Vehicle
SRA	:	Slum Rehabilitation Authority
SRD	:	Slum Redevelopment Scheme
SRFDCL	:	Sabarmati Riverfront Development Corporation Limited
SRFDP	:	Sabarmati Riverfront Development Project
SRS	:	Slum Rehabilitation Scheme
SS	:	Shiv Sena
SSI	:	Small Scale Industries
ST	:	Scheduled Tribe
STU	:	State Transmission Utility
SUV	:	Sports Utility Vehicles
TCPO	:	Town and Country Planning Organisation
TDR	:	Transfer of Development Rights
TEDA	:	Tianjin Economic Development Area
TISS	:	Tata Institute of Social Sciences
TMC	:	Town Municipal Council
TMCF	:	Thousand Million Cubic Feet
TNC	:	Transnational Corporation
TP	:	Town Planning
TPO	:	Town Planning Organisation
TUFE	:	Tianjin University of Finance Economics
UCMF	:	Urban Construction and Maintenance Fund
UCMT	:	Urban Maintenance and Construction Tax
UE	:	Unemployment Rate
ULB	:	Urban Local Bodies
ULCRA	:	Urban Land Ceiling and Regulation Act
UNCTAD	:	United Nations Conference on Trade and Development
UNDP	:	United Nations Development Programme
UNESCO	:	United Nations Educational, Scientific and Cultural Organisation
UNFPA	:	United Nations Population Fund
UPA	:	United Progressive Alliance
URA	:	Urban Redevelopment Authority
URIF	:	Urban Reform Initiative Fund
US	:	United States
USAID	:	United States Agency for International Development
USSR	:	United Soviet Socialist Republic
UT	:	Union Territory
UTI	:	Urinary Tract Infection

VAMBAY	:	Valmiki Ambedkar Awas Yojana
VHP	:	Vishwa Hindu Parishad
VIP	:	Very Important Person
VND	:	Vietnamese Dong
VUPDA	:	Vietnam Urban Planning and Development Association
WPR	:	Work Participation Rate
WSF	:	World Social Forum
WTO	:	World Trade Organisation
YUVA	:	Youth Unity for Voluntary Action

CONTRIBUTORS

Lalit Batra is independent researcher and activist working on urban issues in Delhi and other Indian cities and is currently a Visiting Fellow at the Centre for the Study of Law and Governance, Jawaharlal Nehru University, New Delhi. Email: lalitbatra@gmail.com.

Dr. Amita Bhide, is Professor, Tata Institute of Social Sciences, Mumbai, a fellow of India China Institute and researches on urban housing and poverty, slum, education. Email: amita@tiss.edu

Dr. Solomon Benjamin, with a PhD from MIT, Department of Urban Studies and Planning, is faculty at the Department of Political Science University of Toronto with an interest on city politics, economy and land issues. Email: sollybenj@yahoo.co.in .

Bhuvaneswari Raman is an architect-planner by training, is finishing doctoral dissertation at the London School of Economics and researches on urban poverty, governance, politics, economy and land issues. Email: B.Raman1@lse.ac.uk.

Harpreet Singh Brar, Masters in Urban and Regional Planning and Research Associate at Centre for Development Alternatives, Ahmedabad at the time of this research work. Email: harpreetsingh_brar@yahoo.co.in.

Dr. Lim Lan Yuan, is Professor at Faculty, Real Estate Department, National University of Singapore. Email: rstlimly@nus.edu.sg or limkly@singnet.com.sg

Lim Pohim, is a PhD candidate at Faculty of Design and Environment, National University of Singapore. Email: poim_lim@yahoo.com.

Prof. Darshini Mahadevia, teaches at Faculty of Planning and Public Policy, CEPT University, Ahmedabad and is Visiting Faculty at Centre for Development Alternatives, Ahmedabad. She is a PhD from Jawaharlal Nehru University, New Delhi, and has been a visiting scholar at Graduate School of Architecture and Urban Planning, University of

California, Los Angeles; at School of Urban Planning, McGill University and Visiting Fellow at Tsinghua University, Beijing and Tianjin University of Finance and Economics, Tianjin. She has been researching on urban poverty, urban development, human and gender development. Has published extensively on these subjects. Has wide experience of working with NGOs in India. Email: darshini@cept.ac.in

Dr. Shipra Maitra, Senior Fellow at Institute of Human Development at the time of writing the paper. Now, a Professor of Economics at Amity School of Urban Management, New Delhi. Dr. Maitra has been writing on urban issues. Email: shipra_maitra@hotmail.com.

Manjunath has master's degree in sociology and is working on self help groups, women's development, land rights, livelihood and poverty.

Riby Rachel Mathew, Masters in Urban and Regional Planning and Research Associate at Centre for Development Alternatives, Ahmedabad at the time of this research work. Email: ribymathew@gmail.com.

Diya Mehra is a PhD candidate in the Department of Anthropology at the University of Texas at Austin.

Harini Narayanan, is an independent researcher based in New Delhi and has research interests on various urban issues. Email: narayananharini@gmail.com

P. Rajan is a lawyer by training and has been working on the issues of human rights, urban poverty, urban livelihoods, and urban politics. Email: advtrajan@gmail.com

Dr. C. Ramachandraiah is an Associate Professor in Geography at Centre for Economic and Social Studies, Hyderabad, with main research interests in urban environment, drinking water, public transport, and information technology and also interest in advocacy and social activism. E-mail: crchandraiah@gmail.com

Dr. Supriya Roychowdhury, educated in Kolkata and Princeton, is Professor at the Centre for Political Institutions, Governance and Development, Institute for Social and Economic Change, Bangalore and has research interests and publications in the area of impact of globalisation on labour, trade unions and urban governance. Email: supriya@isec.ac.in.

David G. Westendorff is the founder and CEO of urbanchina partners, a consulting firm in Shanghai, China that assists policy makers, local authorities, and international and local civil society organisations expand notions and practices of participatory urban governance. Formerly was working at UNRISD, Geneva. Email: urbanchina@att.net

1

INSIDE URBANISING ASIA

DARSHINI MAHADEVIA

The Asian Century

The 21st century belongs to Asia, goes the popular aphorism. This has been followed by writings on shift in economic balance towards Asia, commonality of Asian values and culture and Asian Renaissance. It is true, as the statistics in this section would indicate that Asia has economically emerged globally. Nonetheless, in general the concepts of 'Asian rise', one Asia and so on have been contested with the argument that much of Asian values are authoritarian (as emerging from the functioning of the 'Developmental State'); the dynamics of Asian mobility are sprawl of Chinese and Indian Diaspora across the globe; the Renaissance does not have purely Asian lineage as European Renaissance extended well beyond Europe; economic emergence of Asia including that of Japan is dependent on technology imports/transfers from outside the region; the economic growth in Asian countries is dependent on the exports of their economies to the markets of Europe and North America and the intercultural exchange between Asia and the West (North America and Europe) has been long and historically layered to make any special sense of the concept of Asian culture (Pieterse 2000: 4). Further, inspite of rise of Asian economies, the global division of labour remains, with the developed economies of North America and Europe continuing to dominate the services, finance and technology sectors, whereas the developing economies of Asia emerging as manufacturing and low-end services centres because of their advantage of low labour costs and relaxed environmental laws. The shift of manufacturing to Asia has led to increase in pollution and green house gas emissions from these countries. Growth process has also led to increase in inequalities within the countries. In all, the economic growth process in these countries is not sustainable, environmentally or politically.

Inspite of these contentions, there is no doubt that Asia has emerged as an important player in the global economy, that has experienced a series of structural adjustments during the decades of the 1980s and 1990s, when once powerful industrial centres, the United States, the European Union, and more recently Japan experienced relative decline and several developing countries, particularly in Asia, experienced growth through rapid industrialization (Lo and Yeung 1996). With this, the production, investments and economic growth shifted out of US-Europe circuit to Asia. Japan was the first Asian country to register rise at the global level in the decade of 1960s. With this increased the importance of Tokyo as a World City, an economic magnet for Japanese economy and financial, telecommunications, and Transnational Corporation (TNC) centre. Simultaneously emerged growing importance of the South Korea and Taiwan; all three together termed as Newly Industrialising Economies (NIEs). During the 1970s and the 1980s, ASEAN (Association of South East Asian Nations) countries emerged as manufacturing centres, and investments came in from the NIEs, particularly from Japan. From 1980 onwards came China on the global scene of economic growth with its gradual opening-up policies from 1978 onwards. And China being a large country, with very large economic development needs, investments and manufacturing activities shifted in a big way to Asia. China has fuelled the world economic growth for now two decades and has also sustained the story of 'Asian ascent' for long. From 2000 onwards, India is emerging on the global economic scene and she is expected to continue this Asia-ward shift of global economic growth for now next two decades. In the rise of China, finance capital came not just from US and European countries but also from Japan, Taiwan, Hong Kong and Singapore. These countries are expected to be important investors in India as well[1].

The Economic Growth Engine of the World

In 2006, on the whole, the total exports from Asia as a proportion of the total world exports stands at 34.1 per cent (US$ 4080.46 billion)[2], as compared to 24.7 per cent in 1980 and 25.5 per cent in 1990. Thus, noticeable shift of global trade towards Asia begins from the decade of 1990s. In this 34.1 per cent exports from Asia, 28.3 per cent (US$ 3,389.48 billion) is from the Developing Asia. Further, in the Developing Asia, the largest share of exports is of East Asia (15.4% of the global exports—US$ 1847.81 billion) and in East Asia of China (8.1% of global exports—US$ 969.10 billion). The exports from East Asia have increased from 3.7 per cent of the global share in 1980 to 8.1 per cent in 1990 to 12.0 per cent in 2000 to what it is today. From 1990s onwards, share of East Asia in the total exports has increased because the global manufacturing has shifted somewhat to China, whose share in the total exports was just 0.9 per cent in 1980, which increased to 1.8 per cent in 1990, to 3.9 per cent in 2000 to what it is today. In 1980 and 1990, the leading East Asian exporters were Hong Kong and Taiwan, the former since 1997 a part of China with special status. The fourth leading exporter of East Asia is South Korea. These three geographic units fill up the gap between exports from East Asia and China.

The Southeast Asia's share has also increased post 1990s and stands at 6.3 per cent in 2006 from 3.6 per cent in 1980 and 4.1 per cent in 1990 in the total global exports. South Asia does not have much presence on the global exports scene (1.9% of the total exports in 2006) and India the leading country in South Asia had just 1 per cent of the global exports share in 2006. If India's economic growth sustains as it is now for the next decade at the least, the share of Developing Asia in world exports would go up further. Lastly, Developed Asia, that includes Israel and Japan has a share of 5.8 per cent in global exports in 2006, which is a decline from 7.9 per cent in 2000, 8.6 per cent in 1990 and 6.7 per cent in 1980. This indicates that indeed Developing East Asia and Southeast Asia are the manufacturing hubs of Asia.

We say that these two regions have become manufacturing hubs of Asia because only 15 per cent of the total exports from Developing Asia are in the services sector in 2006. These figures for East Asia, China and Southeast Asia are 13.4 per cent, 8.9 per cent and 16.9 per cent respectively when globally the services formed 20.8 per cent of the total exports. Interestingly, in South Asia, services comprised of 39.2 per cent of its total exports and this is because of India emerging as a global back-office and Information Technology (IT) services centre.

These services exported are by no means low-end services. These are relatively high end services that require basic graduate level education and working knowledge of English language. Since, on the whole the total exports from South Asia is still miniscule, the employment generated by the high end service exports would also be quite less. This is what is shown by Mahadevia (Chapter 2) for Indian cities, where the vast majority continue to be employed in either traditional manufacturing sectors or in low wage informal service sector. This has created a great divide between those integrated with the global economy and those not, illustrated by the example of Bangalore in Mahadevia's article (Chapter 2).

Table 1.1: FDI Inflow and Outflows

	Percentage share in global FDI Inflow				*Percentage share in global FDI Outflow*			
	1980	*1990*	*2000*	*2005*	*1980*	*1990*	*2000*	*2005*
Developed Asia*	0.5	0.9	0.9	0.9	4.4	21.0	2.8	6.2
Developing Asia	1.2	11.2	10.5	21.8	2.1	4.8	6.6	10.7
—Eastern	1.7	4.4	8.2	12.9	0.3	4.2	5.8	7.0
—China	0.1	1.7	2.9	7.9	—	0.4	0.1	1.5
—Southern	0.5	0.1	0.3	1.1	0.0	0.0	0.0	0.2
—India	0.1	0.1	0.3	0.7	0.0	0.0	0.0	0.2
—South-eastern	5.0	6.4	1.7	4.1	0.7	1.0	0.7	1.5
Global (billion US$)	55.27	201.61	1409.57	916.28	53.83	229.89	1244.47	778.73

* Includes Israel and Japan.

Source: United Nations Conference on Trade and Development (2007).

The export-based manufacturing has increased in Developing Asia because of increased Foreign Direct Investment (FDI) to the region in the two and a half decades. In 1980, this region received just 1.2 per cent of the total FDI in the world. The overall Developing Asia's figure is lower than the FDI received by East Asia and Southeast Asia because of massive negative value (-3,328 million US$) of the FDI for Western Asia (Table 1.1). If western Asia's FDI flows are deducted then, in 1980, 7.2 per cent of the global FDI was flowing to the three developing regions of Asia (Table 1.1). In 2005, the total global FDI flow to these three regions of Asia went up to 18.1 per cent. On the whole, the total FDI to Developing Asia went upto 21.8 per cent in the same year, indicating improvement in the situation in West Asia. Once again, it is China that has been getting the largest share of the global FDI after 1990s.

The improvement in share of China would be from 1992-93 onwards when Pudong was developed to induce economic growth in Shanghai (Yeung 1996) and hence the rest of the country. East Asia's share in the total FDI has increased from 1.7 per cent in 1980 to 4.4 per cent in 1990 to 8.2 per cent in 2000 and to 12.9 per cent in 2005. In this, in 2005, China's share in the total global FDI is 7.9 per cent. Even Hong Kong SAR has been receiving large share of FDI but not as large as China. The share of Southeast Asia in the total FDI received has gone down over the period from 5.0 per cent in 1980 to 4.1 per cent in 2005. South Asia continues to get the least amount of FDI in Asia, a situation that may change if the Special Economic Zone (SEZ) policy of India works out to attract FDI.

With the increase in FDI inflow to the region, the FDI outflow from the region has also increased. This shows increasing integration of Asia with the global economy. But, on the whole, FDI inflow to Asia as well as Developing Asia is far higher than the FDI outflow in nominal as well as percentage terms (Table 1.1). Part of the FDI outflow from the region is because some Asian countries are themselves investing abroad; for example, China's public investment fund acquiring oil companies in Africa and Indian private companies taking over companies in Europe and USA. This new emerging trend however does not negate the one set in for a long time; the economies of Developing Asia being manufacturing hub as well as service hub for the globe. Also, inspite of the new trend of export of capital from China and India, the global unequal division of labour between the developed and developing economies of the world would remain for a long time to come.

Table 1.2: GDP Contribution of Asia

	Percentage share in global GDP				*Per Capita GDP Ratio (Region/World)*			
	1980	*1990*	*2000*	*2005*	*1980*	*1990*	*2000*	*2005*
Developed Asia*	9.0	13.8	15.1	10.5	3.3	5.7	6.9	5.1
Developing Asia	11.2	9.8	12.7	14.6	0.2	0.2	0.2	0.3
—Eastern	3.8	4.1	6.6	7.4	0.2	0.2	0.3	0.3
—China	2.6	1.7	3.4	4.5	0.1	0.1	0.2	0.2
—Southern	2.9	2.4	2.3	2.8	0.1	0.1	0.1	0.1
—India	1.5	1.5	1.5	1.8	0.1	0.1	0.1	0.1
—South-eastern	1.6	1.6	1.9	2.0	0.2	0.2	0.2	0.2
Global GDP (billion US$)	11858.5	22059.8	31678.6	44475.2	—	—	—	—

* Includes Israel and Japan.

Source: United Nations Conference on Trade and Development (2007).

Inspite of increase in exports share as well as FDI flow to Developing Asia in the last two and a half decades, the Gross Domestic Product (GDP) generated from the region is relatively low (Table 1.2). While the exports from the Developing Asia were 28.3 per cent of the total (in 2006), the GDP generated from the region was just 14.6 per cent of the global GDP (in 2005) (Table 1.2). In 1980, when the exports from the region were 18.0 per cent, the GDP from the region was 11.2 per cent. Thus while the exports share from Developing Asia has increased by 10 percentage points, the GDP from the region has increased by just 3.4 percentage points.

Nonetheless, the GDP has increased and the validity of export-led strategy of inducing economic growth in the Asian economies still remains.

The concomitant improvement in the GDP share of Developing Asia is also not observed in comparison to the region's FDI share. For example, 7.2 per cent of the FDI came to Developing East, South and Southeast Asia in 1980, whereas the GDP generated from the three regions together was 8.3 per cent, not much of a difference. But, in 2005, while the FDI to the three regions of Asia was 18.0 per cent of the total global FDI, the GDP generated in these regions was much less; 12.2 per cent. In 1980, the situation was reverse; GDP share was higher than the FDI share. Thus, the FDI to the region has increased the region's export share and total and per capita GDP over time; inequality between the Developing Asia and Developed countries of the world has increased.

Also, the ratio of per capita GDP in the Developing Asia and the sub-regions of Asia to the per capita global GDP remain very low, increasing from 0.2 in 1980 to 0.3 in 2005. In other words, the global income inequalities have slightly increased in these 25 years. If the per capita incomes are adjusted for the Purchasing Power Parity (PPP), the gap would narrow down but the ratios would be far from being equitable.

Developing Asia has registered real GDP growth rates of 5.7 per cent, 6.2 per cent and 6.3 per cent respectively during 1980-90, 1990-2000 and 2000-05 periods, East Asia registered real GDP growth rates of 9.1 per cent, 7.9 per cent and 7.1 per cent respectively (Table 1.3). And China has registered real GDP growth rates of 10.3 per cent, 10.6 per cent and 9.6 per cent in the three periods respectively. The economic growth rates have accelerated and so has per capita income growth in the Asia but the inequality has also increased between the developed world and developing Asia.

Table 1.3: GDP and Per Capita GDP Growth Rates

	Real GDP growth rate			*Real per capita GDP growth rate*		
	1980-90	*1990-2000*	*2000-05*	*1980-90*	*1990-00*	*2000-05*
Developed Asia*	3.9	1.1	2.8	3.3	0.7	1.2
Developing Asia	5.7	6.2	6.3	3.7	4.5	5.0
—Eastern	9.1	7.9	7.1	7.6	6.9	6.4
—China	10.3	10.6	9.6	8.8	9.5	8.8
—Southern	4.7	5.1	6,5	2.3	3.0	4.7
—India	5.8	6.0	6.7	3.4	3.9	6.0
—South-eastern	5.3	5.0	5.0	3.1	3.3	3.5
World	3.1	2.8	2.8	1.3	1.3	1.5

*Includes Israel and Japan.

Source: United Nations Conference on Trade and Development (2007).

The existing global income inequalities can be well summed up by the presentation of Ohmae (2001), in the plenary address to the Conference on Global City Regions held in 1999 at the School of Public Policy and Social Research, University of California, Los Angeles (pp. 37-8):

> "Let us now turn to one of the poorest countries on earth: India, three hundred dollars per capita GNP—excuse me, it has now improved to six hundred. Go straight to Bangalore and you will see a cybercity with a future. Bangalore has more IQ-based, mathematically competent people, in absolute numbers, than anywhere else on earth. Hyderabad in Andhra Pradesh is close behind, and Chandrababu Naidu, the Chief Minister of Andhra Pradesh, was re-elected, thank goodness, in this month's election (October 1999)[3]. Pune in Maharashtra, is third in the cybereconomies of India. So although you may be born in one of the poorest nations on earth there is opportunity to be quite prosperous—by linking through satellite communications to the cybereconomy of the rest of the world.
>
> One of the companies in Bangalore, Infosys Technologies, has just listed their stock on NASDAQ. First they achieved a $[4]2.5 billion market capitalization. More than one hundred out of three thousand of their employees became instant millionaires. .... This means Infosys has created over two hundred millionaires and its founder, Narayan Murthy, has become the richest Indian. This defies and disables the traditional caste system. Nowadays, therefore, if you are competent, you can work for GE or Bell Atlantic using satellite communications. You may also continue to live in Bangalore and enjoy a cost of living one-fiftieth of the cost of living in Japan. You will live like royalty."

The quotation suggests that even though some companies of the developing world—cited here are the 11 companies of India—would become global, the cost of living in certain developing countries such as India where these countries are located would be so low that one can have a better life in cities such as Bangalore, Pune, etc. of India than in New York etc, at the same incomes.

Two simultaneous paradoxical situations exist in the developing Asia's cities. One is low cost of living in general, primarily because of low wage rates in the entire economy. Low wages would mean continuing global income inequality on one hand. On the other, it also means lower capability of governments and the households to pay for all the services and hence lower level of all the services of life, including smaller housing, low per capita water consumption, low per capita road space etc. on an average. It would also mean that the citizens in these cities would have to pay for these services themselves than the State. The other situation is that quality of life at par with that in the developed economies means real estate development of such type, often at the same costs as in the developed economies. Combined with low wage rates, a large section of the population of Asian cities would get priced out of the housing markets. Both the paradoxical situations together can cause multiple marginalisations unless there is a State policy to address the paradoxes. This is the theme that keeps coming up in many of the articles in this book; the costs that the 'legal' and 'illegal' citizens of the Asian cities are paying for the emergence of dual economic order globally and their living spaces getting tied up to such an economic order.

Urban Asia

Economic growth leads to urbanisation. Conversely is also strongly believed; "no country in the industrial age has ever achieved significant economic growth without urbanization" (UNFPA 2007: 1). Cities are Engines of Economic Growth goes the popular policy saying, but for the first time articulated clearly by Jane Jacobs (1984). Cities are places of hope; in India, they provide opportunities for the under-class to escape exclusions and poverty. Cities can be great equalisation place, particularly in a caste fragmented society as India. Cities, especially the 'World Cities' or 'Global Cities' articulate their country's economic aspirations in the global economy. The performance of cities in a country has a great bearing on the overall economic success of a country. Cities attract investments needed for the economic growth of a country. In globalising economies, cities are the places where the global capital and global migrants locate.

It is argued, particularly by the multilateral agencies such as the World Bank, that increasing global trade would lead to increased urbanisation in the developing countries in particular. This is because the trading firms and the TNCs seek locations near transport infrastructure and trained/ skilled labour, which is available only in urban areas. And in the process the cities benefit as they would be able to market their outputs and get capital to finance industry infrastructure and services. Cities would also be able to attract skilled migrants. Hence, globalisation and urbanisation support each other towards virtuous cycle of development (World Bank, 1999).

Economic growth and shifting of global trade towards Developing Asia has led to increase in urban population and urbanisation rates across Developing Asia. Cities are the main beneficiaries of globalisation, the progressive integration of the world's economies. People follow jobs, which follow investment and economic activities. Increase in manufacturing sector, as the economic growth in Developing Asia has been largely because of export-led growth, has led to development of manufacturing enclaves, away from the megacities, but, nonetheless inducing urbanisation. China is now a major world manufacturing centre, and almost all of its factories are located in or near cities. Cities have become the engine of China's rapid economic growth (UNFPA 2007: 12).

Table 1.4: Total and Urban Population Share of Asia

	Percentage share to world population			*Percentage share to world urban population*		
	1990	*2000*	*2006*	*1990*	*2000*	*2006*
Developed Asia*	2.4	2.2	2.0	3.6	3.1	2.8
Developing Asia	56.4	57.1	57.2	39.4	43.5	45.4
—Eastern	23.0	22.0	21.3	16.1	17.9	18.9
—China	21.3	20.4	19.7	13.8	15.9	16.9
—Southern	22.5	23.9	24.5	13.6	14.5	14.9
—India	16.2	17.1	17.5	9.5	9.9	10.0
—South-eastern	8.3	8.5	8.6	6.1	7.2	7.7
World population (million)	5294.9	6124.1	6592.9	2282.1	2866.1	3243.7

* Includes Israel and Japan.

Source: (a) United Nations Conference on Trade and Development (2007).
(b) United Nations Population Fund (2007) for Urbanisation level data only.

Table 1.5: Urbanisation Level and Urban Population Growth Rates, Asia

	Urbanisation level		*Urban Population Growth Rate (% p.a)*	
	1990	*2007*	*1990-2000*	*2000-06*
Developed Asia	64.0	67.4	0.70	0.43
Developing Asia	30.1	39.7	3.32	2.81
—Eastern	30.1	44.2	3.42	2.94
—China	28.0	42.0	3.72	3.17
—Southern	26.1	31.0	2.92	2.60
—India	25.2	29.0	2.60	2.35
—South-eastern	31.5	45.0	4.00	3.35
World	43.1	50.0	2.30	2.00

Overall rate of total population and hence urban population growth have declined over time in the world as well as in Developing Asia. But, there is a slight increase in the share of Developing Asia in the total world population from 56.4 per cent in 1990 to 57.2 per cent in 2006 (Table 1.4). With this, however, there is substantial increase in Developing Asia's urban population share from 39.4 per cent in 1990 to 45.4 per cent in 2006. At the same time, there is increase in urbanisation level (percentage population living in urban areas) in Developing Asia from 30.1 per cent in 1990 to 39.7 per cent in 2007 (Table 1.5). Once again, China, whose urbanisation level has increased from 29.0 per cent in 1990 to 42.0 per cent in 2007, is the largest contributor to Developing Asia's urbanisation process. Although, urbanisation level in Southeast Asia too has increased substantially from 31.5 per cent in 1990 to 45.0 per cent in 2007, this region having small population has not impacted Asian urbanisation in a big way. Another country that has potential of impacting significantly the urbanisation process in Asia is India, where, however, the urbanisation process has slowed down since 1990s as observed in Tables 1.4 and 1.5 as well as Sivaramakrishnan *et al.* (2005).

In the whole world, the urbanisation rate (growth rate of urban population), has reduced to 2.08 per cent per annum (p.a.) in 2000-06 period as compared to 2.30 per cent p.a. in the 1990s, and in Developing Asia too the urbanisation rate has declined to 2.81 per cent (p.a.) in the 2000-06 period from 3.32 per cent (p.a.) in the 1990s (Table 1.5). In all the regions of Asia, urbanisation process has slowed down. But, that in East Asia remains high because of China registering more than 3 per cent (p.a.) urbanisation rate through the 1990s and even post 2000.

The UNFPA's State of the World Population, 2007 with a focus on the process of urbanisation, states that between 2000 and 2030, Asia's urban population will increase from 1.36 billion to 2.64 billion when overall urban population in the world is going to be about 5 billion, indicating that more than half the urban population of the world is going to be living in the cities of Asia by 2030 (UNFPA, 2007: 8). Hence, what goes in within the cities of Asia is of great importance to the world urbanisation process.

Of the total 10 million plus cities (megacities) in the world, 12 are in Asia today as per one source[5]. But, as per Table 1.6, there are 10 megacities in Asia and other 16 are half-million plus citics. Except Dhaka, Delhi, Jakarta, Karachi, Chennai, Lahore and Ahmedabad in South Asia; Wuhan and Chongqing in China (East Asia) and Riyadh in West Asia, all other large cities of Asia have witnessed an annual population growth rate of less than 3 per cent. Shanghai and Seoul have witnessed population decline.

Table 1.6: Population and Population Growth Rates in Asian Megacities

City		Country	Population (millions)			Growth rate per annum (%)	
			1990	2000	2005*	1990-00	2000-05
1.	Tokyo	Japan	25.08	26.44	26.85	0.53	0.30
2.	Mumbai	India	12.31	16.09	18.34	2.71	2.65
3.	Dhaka	Bangladesh	6.62	12.52	15.92	6.58	4.93
4.	Delhi	India	8.21	12.44	15.34	4.25	4.27
5.	Kolkata	India	10.89	13.06	14.30	1.83	1.83
6.	Jakarta	Indonesia	7.65	11.02	13.16	3.72	3.61
7.	Shanghai	China, Peoples Republic	13.34	12.89	12.67	-0.35	-0.35
8.	Karachi	Pakistan	7.15	10.03	11.83	3.45	3.35
9.	Beijing	China, Peoples Republic	10.82	10.84	10.85	0.02	0.02
10.	Manila	Philippines	7.97	9.95	10.68	2.24	1.43
11.	Istanbul	Turkey	6.54	8.95	9.95	3.18	2.13
12.	Seoul	South Korea	10.54	9.89	9.89	-0.64	0.00
13.	Tianjin	China, Peoples Republic	8.79	9.16	9.35	0.41	0.41
14.	Bangkok	Bangkok	5.90	7.37	8.14	2.25	2.00
15.	Teheran	Iran, Islamic Republic	6.36	6.98	7.29	0.93	0.86
16.	Hong Kong	China, SAR	5.70	6.86	7.27	1.87	1.17
17.	Chennai	India	5.34	6.35	6.92	1.76	1.71
18.	Bangalore	India	4.04	5.57	6.53	3.27	3.25
19.	Lahore	Pakistan	3.97	5.45	6.38	3.22	3.19
20.	Hyderabad	India	4.19	5.45	6.15	2.65	2.45
21.	Wuhan	China, People's Republic	3.83	5.17	6.00	3.04	3.04
22.	Chongqing	China, People's Republic	3.12	4.90	5.70	4.61	3.05
23.	Riyadh	Saudi Arabia	2.33	4.55	5.59	6.94	4.20
24.	Baghdad	Iraq	4.04	4.87	5.36	1.88	1.95
25.	Ahmedabad	India	3.26	4.43	5.17	3.12	3.16
26.	Ho Chi Minh City	Vietnam	4.00	4.62	5.02	1.46	1.68
27.	Hanoi	Vietnam	3.13	3.75	4.14	1.84	1.99

Note: The population figures are of urban agglomerations, which ever way these are defined in each of the country.

* Estimated

Source: UN-Habitat (2003).

The megacities tend to be the base of corporate sector and finance and trading companies when manufacturing shifts away. Thus, growth rates have declined or stabilised in the megacities (Table 1.6) but that of the small and medium sized cities have picked up and that is driving urbanisation in the world and also in the Asian economies (UNFPA, 2007).

Except China, where the birth rates are controlled, in all other countries, urban population growth is driven by natural increase in population. In India, the share of growth attributable to urban natural increase ranged from 51 per cent to about 65 per cent over 1961-2001 period (Sivaramakrishnan *et al.*, 2005). In contrast, in China, urbanisation is driven solely by rural to urban migration.

Globalisation has some good news for the cities. Prosperity has increased, particularly in the metropolitan cities. In general, urbanisation has led to economic growth and increased prosperity, except in Sub-Saharan Africa. Countries of East Asia and Southeast Asia are good examples of this process. Global cities have emerged on the world scene. Globalisation has also led to information explosion and this has portent for promoting democracy, pluralism and greater accountability (Savitch, 2002). Infrastructure has improved in many cities and along with it has improved the quality of life of the residents in them. This is true of East Asian and Southeast Asian cities in particular in Asia. However, as the articles in this volume point out, not all urban residents have benefited from such positive achievements of the cities in the period of increasing global integration, although the national, and even city GDPs (wherever they are measured) have increased.

The Visions of 'World Class City'

With increasing globalisation of the world economy, the ideas of 'City development' are also getting globalised. The processes that shape globally linked cities are also getting globalised, something that was articulated for the first time through the studies of what are called the 'World Cities' or Global Cities'. Much has been written about the emergence of 'World Cities' and 'Global Cities' in the world system as distinguished from other cities performing different functions at local and sub-national level. (See Sassen, 1991, 2001; Friedmann and Wolff 1982, Friedmann 1986, 2001, Shachar 1997, Lever 1997, Cai and Sit 2003, Chua 1998, Douglass 2000, Lo and Yeung 1996, Sorensen 2003). We are not going into these discussions but presume that the cities have begun to change their form and appearance to appear to be 'global' in character. This pressure to change is quite high within Asian cities with the emergence of Asian countries on the global economic scene and the national and local governments forced to respond to these pressures. Through transforming some of their respective cities, the Asian countries are sending out a message of being open and welcoming to the global community. They are sending out the message that inspite of low per capita incomes, the quality of life they would offer could be at par with the global standards.

In India, the vision of a city becoming global or welcoming global economic activities is represented by the term 'World Class City'. A document named 'Making of a World Class City', was prepared by a business lobby group for Mumbai (Chapter 3 by Mahadevia and

Narayanan). The general vision of the cities in the present context is well represented by some of the incumbent India's national government proclamations:

> "If the NDA[6] poll campaign was 'India Shinning', then that's just what the UPA[7] government is going to do. The government has made elaborate plans to make all towns and cities shine, literally...... So will traffic jams, water-logging and garbage dumps be a thing of the past? It seems so—they will be replaced by high-speed expressways, flyovers, overbridges with escalators, better roads, by-passes, subways, malls and commercial complexes.
>
> Urban development minister, says the government wants to upgrade the capital with modern roads and integrated transport system keeping in view the 2010 Common Wealth Games.
>
> There's more: water supply will be improved, new sewage systems will be put in place to prevent water-logging during monsoons and state-of-the art traffic signals, tourist complexes and convention centres will come up. There will be special focus on improvement of slums, rehabilitation projects and city beautification (in Delhi)"[8].

In China, the term used is 'World City or Future World City' or 'the 21st Century City' as used for Shanghai by her municipal government in 1994 (Cai and Sit 2003). Term modernization of cities is also used in China, which means a harmonious and attractive city (China Research Society of Urban Development, 2005: 13). "Urban development is symbol of a country's strength and competitiveness"[9]. A city developed in such a mould improves investment environment in the city and leads to overall economic and social development[10]. The current visions of Chinese cities are framed within the paradigm of 'Harmonious Society' of the incumbent President Hu Jintao, which stands for "democracy, rule by law, fair and justice, honesty and love, full of vigour, stability and orderliness, and in harmony with nature".

Going by what other Asian cities have done; a World Class City's structure includes construction of various infrastructure projects and real estate projects. These include: (i) large transport nodes, mainly new airports to increase global connectivity— globalisation entails increased movement of people and also migration—as Shanghai (Pudong airport), Beijing, proposed airports in Mumbai and New Delhi, Kuala Lumpur, Singapore, etc; (ii) inter-urban and intra-urban high speed trains with associated bridges and tunnels, as in Hong Kong, Osaka, Seoul and Shanghai; (iii) Light Rail Transit (LRT) as in Bangkok, Tianjin, Chongqing, Kuala Lumpur, Beijing-Tianjin (to open up by 2007 end), Mumbai (proposed) and/or subway as in Hong Kong, Beijing, Shanghai, Guangzhou, Tianjin, Xian and 15 other cities of China (proposed)[11] , New Delhi, Kolkata, Mumbai, Hyderabad and Bangalore (proposed in all three), (iv) either elevated or on ground high speed roads (freeways/ expressways) (tolled or free) within the city as in Bangkok, Kuala Lumpur, Singapore, Beijing, Shanghai, Tianjin, Guangzhou and most large cities of China; (v) communication infrastructure; (vi) commercial and service infrastructure for activities such as banking and finance—globalisation also entails free glow of capital—consultancy firms and IT enabled services and Business Process Outsourcing (BPO) firms; (vii) industrial parks/hi-tech parks or SEZs, and operated by either public or private sectors, mainly on the urban periphery where large land parcels are available as in Singapore, Taipei, Bangkok, New Delhi, Mumbai, Bangalore, Pune, Hyderabad, Beijing, Shanghai and large number of cities of China; (viii) prestige buildings—some as a part of inner city development and some in the new zones—whose architecture is glass such as Jin Mao tower and Pearl tower in Shanghai, Petronas tower in Kuala Lumpur; (ix) public squares in city centres as in Singapore and most large cities of China; (x) heritage conservation and declaration of heritage districts and development of pedestrian shopping streets for local culture exposure; as in most cities in China and in particular in Beijing that has declared 27 conservation areas and now in Indian cities; (xi) high-end housing projects in all the large and mega Asian cities including those in India, (xii) malls for new form of retailing outlets, and (xiii) in some cities construction of public buildings such as convention centres, opera halls, etc. as in Shanghai, Beijing, and many cities in China. (See Marcotullio, 2003, Dick and Rimmer 1998, Lo and Marcotullio 2000, Lo and Yeung 1996, Mahadevia 2003b, Mahadevia and Narayanan on Mumbai's vision in this book, and photographs in China Research Society of Urban Development, 2005). This is ostensibly the vision of a World Class City.

The vision of a city that promotes rapid global integration of the country is a city which creates environment that attracts foreign investment. For this, the city should be able to provide good living standards, which means cities with adequate infrastructure and low incidence of crime and poverty; should have good governance and be able to mobilise domestic resources to improve physical and human capital base; should offer an environment that reduces the cost of doing business; should have some comparative advantage in producing tradable goods and should have diversified economic base to reduce vulnerabilities (World Bank, 1999).

In the mid-1990s, the Asian Development Bank (ADB) came up with a set of policy recommendations for Asian Megacities (Stubbs and Clarke, 1996), with a clear articulation that the urban productivity improves with the increase in city size due to the presence of capital-intensive technologies in manufacturing and location of financial and managerial services. The policy document presents a long discussion on how to improve the urban productivity. It also points out that there is a scope for improving the productivity of the megacities in Asia.

> "Governments in the region (Asia Pacific) have almost universally recognized the need to make their cities more productive, efficient, and sustainable, and are doing this through measures that include:
>
> - *improved governance through greater community participation, accountability and transparency;*
> - *enhanced efficiency of urban infrastructure services through improved management of public sector institutions and development of public-private partnerships; and*
> - *sharply increased investment levels in urban infrastructure through enhanced cost recovery and access to the resources of private investors, financial institutions, and capital markets."*

This statement of Mitsuo Sato, the then President of the ADB succinctly summarises the approach to megacity development in the twenty first century to meet the expectations of coming 'urban revolution' (Stubbs and Clarke, 1996, v).

The ADB document also gives sector specific policy prescriptions. For the Brown Agenda, it states that there should be comprehensive urban and environmental planning to address the environmental issues. Further, it asks for private sector participation in environmental management. It also states that instead of relying on external funding, there should be local mobilisation of resources for financing of water supply, waste water disposal, power development, and management of solid wastes and toxic and hazardous wastes (Stubbs and Clarke, 1996) and that the principle of cost recovery, appropriate standards and improving operations and maintenance should be part of the practice of the local governments. Lastly, urban environmental goals should be achieved through community participation.

The other sector that gets great attention in this book is urban transport, which it is argued is central to improving economic efficiency of the megacities and health status of the population living in it. The suggestions for this sector include need for expressways and fast connectivity of the city with the airports; increased role of the private sector in urban transport; appropriate city planning such as high density city centre, development of arterial roads, planned laying of roads to guide the development to suit efficient transport system and discouraging urban sprawl; good alternatives to car, such as rail-based mass transit systems, which is affordable to the poor on one hand and ensures full cost recovery on the other; and discouraging use of car at the peak times through measures such as road pricing, parking costs and car-sharing. Other traffic management solutions proposed are; segregating slow and fast vehicles, creating dedicated bus ways or lanes on the big city corridors, and creating ways for pedestrians and non-motorized vehicles.

The policy on urban land focuses on its management. The inventory of suggestions are to: (i) make land market more efficient, (ii) increase the role of the private sector in enhancing land supply, (iii) make government act as an enabler for the housing of the urban poor by making tenured land available to them at affordable price, (iv) deregulate land to increase the land supply and reduce its cost, (v) minimize planning and building regulations, (vi) promote land sharing, and (vii) put in place a credit policy to encourage small loans for small houses. The rental housing supply is recommended to be increased by doing away with the rent control law. The ADB book also suggests that short-term decisions of the private sector be corrected through market mechanisms such as fiscal policies (taxing of vacant land), structural planning instead of comprehensive master plan and public participation in land development. It is also recommended that housing and infrastructure standards be reduced to make them affordable for compliance of regulatory policies. For providing land to the poor it is suggested that besides subsidised public land for housing, sites and services, slum upgradation programmes and innovative housing credit schemes for the urban poor, certain innovative policies, such as land sharing, which have been tried need be encouraged. It has been suggested that new methods to involve private formal and community organisations in the process of land management to be evolved.

With regards to financial resources, the ADB policy proposes that the growing infrastructure needs of the megacities should be financed through new initiatives such as raising private equity finance, using build-operate-transfer (BOT) system, other variations of private sector participation, borrowing at commercial rates from apex financial institutions and borrowing form the external agencies. It also proposes that the local governments become highly proactive to improve financial health of the cities, through exploring all possible local resource bases such as property taxation, user charges, and vehicle taxation. It also proposes to introduce the policy of full cost recovery for private goods and services, such as water supply, sewerage, etc. through user charges and cross subsidies to be used with care, avoid allocational distortions, as it rarely works. It suggests that for the poor emphasis should be best quality that can be given for the price the poor are ready to pay! The document is conscious of the political sensitivity to such policies' operationalisation.

It is also proposed that the mega cities should aggressively negotiate with the higher governments to get their due share of transfers/grants and shared taxes and surcharges. Local governments should seek fiscal transfers from higher levels of government where it's expenditure responsibilities exceed scope for efficient mobilisation from local sources. It argues that the local governments have entitlement to the central taxes and hence the transfers should not be discretionary. Formula of shared tax should be worked out. Whenever entitlement formula is insufficient to meet capital requirements, loans from higher level of government, international funding and capital markets be made available. Such loans however should be only used to leverage private sector funding.

These ADB policy document is very important as urban development policies in some of the countries have followed the suggestions laid down here. A good example of this is a major urban development initiative in India named Jawaharlal Nehru National Urban Renewal Mission (JNNURM) of the Government of India (See Mahadevia 2006b for details and its critique).

This uniform vision of the World Class City has come not only from the multilateral institutions but also from the action of the elite classes in the cities of the developing economies, supported by media. For example, in India, a leading daily carried a series of articles under the title 'Crumbling of Bangalore' and this coincided with the IT professionals going on a *dharna*[12] on Bangalore roads to highlight the state of poor roads in the city.

> "They are the creme de la creme of the country; the would-be techie czars. And yet, they had no option, but take to the streets on Monday. ... Reason? The Bannerghatta Main Road, which is nothing short of

> a glaring blot on the face of India's Silicon capital. Forget tech-gizmos: it is endless bumpy rides on an almost non-existent road, ended up pulling IIMB[13] students on to the streets. ... Can this bunch of techno hopefuls achieve a bit of this success? Over 5,000 residents of the area and even the local version of the powers-that-be, Uttarahalli MLA[14] ..... have pinned their hopes on it: they staged a three-hour dharna with the students, stopping all traffic on the 'non-existent' road. .... The students have cause to be angry: the road is an absolute embarrassment for the IT city and particularly the top-tech campus of the IIMB, which is a must-visit for all top business and IT guns."[15]

> "... top IT firms announced that they will boycott this year's Bangalore IT.Com, the government's flagship event, to be held next month. ... Disgusted by the government's continued indifference to bad roads, the IT firms want to give a wake-up call to the "Kumbhakarna[16]-like" government. ... (A) CEO (of IT firm says): 'This is meant as a wake-up call to the government to take some kind of an action and improve the infrastructure of our city. We have invested millions of dollars in our facilities here and unlike the services companies, we just cannot move out of Bangalore and expand."[17]

There is some common imagery of the World Class cities emerging. In India, often, the imagery of the most promising 'contemporary' city of the time is evoked to indicate the paradigm of urban development. For example, the article by Mahadevia and Narayanan (Chapters 3 and 18) in the book shows that Mumbai (then Bombay) was to be Paris of India in late 1960s, then Hong Kong and Singapore in early and late 1990s, and then Shanghai in mid 2000s. Ahmedabad's image is to be of a 'Mega City', whatever that means (See Chapter 4 by Mahadevia and Brar). Bangalore is called 'Silicon Valley' and vision is to be Singapore (See Chapter 5 by Benjamin). Often, it is not known what the image means except a change from the present, and development of high value properties and freeways.

But, these policy prescriptions and vision are besotted with problems. For example, in the idea about public transport, the question of how to address the requirements of the poor is not explicitly addressed in either the ADB policy or the city specific transport visions and plans. This is because these have to be moored in the urban realities of the particular time. And the reality is that the new transport projects such as underground metros or LRTs are capital intensive projects and have the same costs all over the world but a very large section of the urban population in the developing countries have low incomes and hence cannot afford to pay for such capital intensive transport options and hence the poor largely walk or bicycle (Badami *et al.* 2007; Peng and Zhu 2007). The third most used mode of transport for the poor is bus. Thus, wherever the local governments/sub-national governments permit, the poor tend to live near their place of work (Peng and Zhu, 2007, Haider and Badami, 2007; Wang and Chan, 2007). Their situation worsens when they are pushed out of the city because of various urban redevelopment projects.

Preoccupation with increasing city's financial resources for improving the living conditions in general has also been questioned. Assumption that improved financial position would increase the provision of services, which would then improve urban poors' access to these services has also been questioned (Mahadevia, 2008). Assumption that efficiency of the cities would naturally follow mobilisation of financial resources has also been questioned. " ... successful urban management is not just a technical question. The financial arrangements are necessary but not sufficient conditions" (Amis, 1997: 101), whereas political conditions and commitment are more important than anything else in better urban management (Amis, 1997).

Lastly, some scholars have contested the idea that there are similarities among the cities that are globalising. "While some similarities are growing between cities, the experiences of the developing world cities in the Asia-Pacific region are increasingly different from their counter parts in the developed world" (Marcotullio, 2003: 227). Marcotullio (2003) suggests that the aspects of globalisation that are forcing cities into different development paths are: (i) intensely competitive markets within a global economic system that are forcing specialisations upon the cities; individual cities finding their economic and social niche in the regional hierarchy; (ii) low income cities are being increasingly asked to meet the global environmental standards—as Beijing is being asked to meet atleast during the forthcoming (2008) Olympics; and (iii) 'nested' response to globalisation, which is due to differences in national and local policies. In fact, the differences in the nature of the State in each of the Asian countries are creating different responses of their respective cities to globalisation.

Idea of Competitive Cities

The vision of the city in the globalising economies also includes idea of a competitive city. Based on her research on Chinese cities, Weiping Wu

(1996) states that in the global market place, cities have become independent actors competing with each other for investment and capital in order to create employment opportunities for their residents Cities do not compete to maximise profits like the commercial enterprises do, but, they compete for mobile investment, population, tourism, public funds and hallmark events such as the Olympic Games (Lever and Turok, 1999: 5). They compete by, for example, assembling a skilled and educated labour force, efficient modern infrastructure, a responsive system of local governance, a flexible land and property market, high environmental standards and a high quality of life (Porter 1995, 1996). Porter further argues that economically successful cities have concentration of specialised knowledge, support institutions, rival firms, related enterprises and sophisticated customers and many assets of such cities are products of public and private sector co-operation, sometimes with the third sector involvement as well (Lever and Turok, 1999: 5). Krugman (1996a, 1996b), on the other hand, argues that cities as such do not compete with one another: they are merely the locus for firms and enterprises which compete. He further adds that the assets that cities develop do not facilitate inter-firm competition, which is fundamentally based on cost-efficiency, innovation, marketing and other factors internal to the firm, but are at best basic requirements or necessary conditions for competitive success, not sufficient conditions (Level and Turok, 1999: 5).

With the belief that the cities compete, constant attempts are made to measure the competitive performance of the cities through use of various indicators and computing of composite index using these. What indicators are used depend on the perception of what factors would attract investment. Such exercises are carried out at global, national and sub-national level by the independent researchers and research organisations, governments and multilaterals, business and industry associations, and so on. Cai and Sit (2003) have prepared a World City Index using five criteria: politico-economic circumstances, population and its skills, economic vitality, enabling infrastructure and overall urban image.

Cities compete to attract international events such as Olympics (Beijing 2008), Common Wealth Games (Delhi 2010), World Expo (Shanghai 2010), Asian Games (Guangzhou 2010) and so on. But, then when such international events get located in a city, that city attracts new investments and by that they become further more competitive. In particular, this route of city transformation is selected by some important megacity (ies) of a country.

There is no one estimate of how much Beijing City would benefit from the 2008 Olympics. In 2002, March, the Beijing Organising Committee for the Games expected that the city would spend 3.4 billion US dollars on sport venues and other related facilities for the 2008 summer Olympic Games[18]. As per pronouncements in 2006, Olympics was expected to add US$ 680 million to the city's finance and insurance sector in five years from 2004, US$ 2.16 billion to the construction industry and in general US$ 13.2 billion to the city's total economic output between 2004 and 2008 with the result that 1.82 million new jobs would be created in the city, especially in the construction (430,000) and retail and wholesale (130,000) trade during the period[19]. The 2010 Commonwealth Games will cost the Indian government around Rs.230 billion ($ 5.70 billion)[20]. Shanghai Expo 2010, is expected to get investment of US$ 3 billion, of which 43 per cent would come from government sources, 36 per cent from companies and 21 per cent from banks. Evidently, the investment figures are huge and city transformation expected is also very large (for Beijing see Chapter 6 by Mahadevia).

In competition or not, the cities embark on programmes to improve urban liveability through various policies. This is the activity of the urban local governments. A variety of supply side incentives such as tax and other financial inducements, infrastructure improvements, land assembly and development (Wassall and Hellman, 1985) and improvement in local environment are offered by the local governments in a competitive spirit. Public resources are used for boosting private investment, directly or for underwriting the cost of private investment (Fasenfest, 1993).

Some disagree with the need of competition among cities for capital and investments. Laying down neo-liberal vision of cities, Savitch (1996) states that the cities can come out of depression through private capital and self-help; the latter indicating decentralisation and more power to the cities by the national governments. Savitch (1996: 55) further states that the globalising cities need to balance between competition and co-operation, which means that the cities need to increase their local productivities while collaborating with their counter parts to avoid destructive practices. The objective should be to optimize opportunities and convert them into relationships in which cities view prosperity of others as good for themselves. In the whole scheme of things, Savitch (1996: 56) lays down role of government as facilitator that fosters conditions for success and important condition here is to rebuild local infrastructure, particularly mass transit facilities, highways, streets, utilities and other modes of access. Cox (1995: 214) has cautioned that in the competition for investments among the cities, the investors have considerable leverage and hence if it is believed that the competition among the cities would turn around the fortunes, it may be easier said than happened.

Term Entrepreneurial City is also used in the context of cities that compete for economic supremacy through innovation (Hall and Hubbard, 1998, Jessop and Sum, 2000) and as a wealth creating machine (Jacobs, 1984). Jessop and Sum (2000) differentiate between entrepreneurial city and city that is a growth machine. According to them, the latter cities only adopt suitable local developmental strategies. But, the former pursues innovative strategies intended to maintain or enhance its economic competitiveness vis-à-vis other cities and economic spaces (2289). They also state that these are explicitly formulated and pursued strategies, leaving no scope of any 'ifs' and the cities are clearly marketed as entrepreneurial. The concept of entrepreneurial city comes from Schumpeterian concept of entrepreneurship, which he defined as creation of opportunities for surplus profits through 'new combinations' or innovations (Schumpeter 1934 in Jessop and Sum 2000: 2289). Jessop and Sum (2000) have attempted to apply this framework to Hong Kong, but, with mixed results. Indeed, as the case studies in this volume indicate, many cities have taken to the idea of becoming competitive city or an entrepreneurial city and are attempting to direct investments in that direction.

Infrastructure Development and Investments

Infrastructure development is the first change observed in the cities globalizing or attempting to attract global capital. The first major infrastructure that gets the local and national government attention is the transport system that is sought to be modernised to reach international standards of speed and efficiency and even costs (Harris 1996). At the least 15 cities in China are going for subway system and/or LRT system. Many, Beijing, Shanghai, Tianjin, Guangzhou and Chongqing already have both or either of them. Beijing is expanding the subway network and is expected to spend US$ 526m to upgrade subway system for the 2008 Olympics[21]. Shanghai's Pudong airport has a meglev (magnetic levitation train), the first of its kind within a city. Delhi and Kolkata in India already have subways, which are being expanded. Contract bid has already been awarded in case of Mumbai. Metros (as the subways are called in India) are being considered for Hyderabad and Bangalore.

Jenks (2003) shows that 'Skytrain' or elevated mass rapid transit system introduced in Bangkok in 1999, has become a metaphor of a Global

City. This has been built on the existing streets, some 3-4 stories above ground level and has stops that link with prestigious shopping malls, hotels and commercial areas at the top level, while the vibrant chaos of the city (and Thailand itself)—traffic jams, footpaths with street vendors and food stalls, night markets teeming with people—exist on the streets below. The expensive Skytrain, like subways as already mentioned earlier, is unaffordable to the most populace, who use cheaper modes such as buses and motorcycles. The city is divided by this means of transport, into local and global cities.

The opening up and desire to push for rapid economic growth has inevitably led to expansion of auto industry in most Asian countries. Private vehicle ownership therefore increases and depending on the city size, it is either two wheelers or four wheelers that register increase. Opening up also creates a class of people with large disposable incomes on hand who would prefer travelling using private vehicles than using public transport. For example, Beijing has estimated more than 3 million cars in the middle of 2007[22]. In 2006-07, the city ordered all the old taxis (about 50,000 in number[23]) to be replaced by new ones. Indian cities too have seen expansion of private vehicle ownership; of 2-wheelers as well as 4-wheelers. Delhi registered increase of motor vehicles from 2.4 million in 1996 to 4 million in 2002 (Badami *et al.*, 2007: 100). Reduction in import duties for automobile parts and automobiles has brought private vehicles within affordable range of large number of urban households. This has resulted in pressure on the local governments to build wide roads and expressways within the city to reduce travel time on the roads for daily commuting as well as connecting the airport and other long distance transport hubs. Road improvement and cutting down on travel time is articulated more frequently by the business classes, as can be seen from the media campaign on the bad roads in Bangalore mentioned earlier. The simultaneous improvement in public bus system, the most affordable means of transport for the urban poor is rarely an aspect of public policy or media campaign; certainly not the latter. Mahadevia and Narayanan (Chapter 3) have discussed various road projects envisaged under Mumbai's Vision Plan and the ones that are under construction now.

While, the tendency of the cities is to go for road improvement projects, as budgets of some cities reflect (Mahadevia and Mukherjee, 2003 for Bangalore and Ahmedabad, Mahadevia and Brar Chapter 4, Chapter 6 on Beijing and Dongguan and Chapter 8 on Tianjin and Chongqing by Mahadevia in this volume, Mahadevia 2006a and

2007a), there are also some corrective mechanisms put in place in some countries. For example, the only exception to the above trend is Singapore, which has strict penalties for private vehicle use pushing majority to use public transport for daily commuting. In India, although the city and state governments are inclined towards such capital intensive transport projects the national government has come up with the National Urban Transport Policy[24], that lays emphasis on the public transport system. The transport policy states that all road widening projects should make provisions for bicycle lanes and wide footpaths. The policy also lays emphasis on improvement of public bus system through developing dedicated bus lanes, in particular, Bus Rapid Transit System (BRTS). In China, the national government has asked the cities to stop the subway projects, as they are highly capital intensive on one hand and unaffordable to a large section of population on the other. Beijing City government is considering reducing the fares of Beijing subway and this cut to be supported by the subsidy from the Beijing city government.

Besides the road project and public transport projects, the other important infrastructure that comes up in globalising cities is a modern airport, largely through private sector participation. In India, airports of Mumbai and Delhi, two major international airports have been given for modernisation to private sector consortiums through a bidding process and those in Hyderabad and Bangalore have also been privatised. Mumbai is expected to develop another airport. In China, all major cities have a modern airport. Shanghai has two airports, one of them in Pudong, new development zone, which is connected to Pudong centre through a meglev. Beijing's existing airport has been expanded.

Every city in China, besides the airport, expressways and subways, also lays emphasis on development of open squares, opera houses, convention centres, city planning exhibition facility, and other such city level facilities, often designed by foreign architects and firms. Shanghai has an opera house and city planning exhibition building in the central park called Renmin Park. This park also has large green space with sculptures. Beijing's Tiannanmen square historically had the National Museum and National People's Congress Building, with Mao's Mausoleum in the centre and Forbidden City. It now has built City Planning Museum and an egg-shaped Convention Centre near the square. Dongguan city in Guangdong province in the south, too has developed a central square with an opera house and a library. In Indian cities, as yet, these city level facilities are not yet into the planning horizon as the cities are battling with road improvements and water supply and sanitation improvements.

Urban solid waste management is increasingly through either community participation and/or private sector participation. For case studies on seven Indian cities see Mahadevia and Wolfe (2008). In Chinese cities too, the solid waste is managed by the Neighbourhood Committees through contributions of the community members of the committee itself raising its own resources (Mahadevia, 2006a, 2007a).

Financing

Following from the above discussion, financing of cities has become an important aspect, albeit not very simple for the purpose of research. City level financing systems are embedded in the national level financing systems and regulations (See Peterson and Annez, 2007). However, in general, the cities are increasing private sector participation in the provision of even basic services, airports are being privatised, toll-roads and bridges working on the principle of BOT or BOOT (Built Own Operate Transfer) have come up and there is increase in rates of cost recovery from various public services.

Five articles in this volume are research on financing in Asian cities. Two articles on China, both by Mahadevia (Chapters 6 and 8) are about inter-city and intra-city inequalities in financing capabilities and level of infrastructure in the cities of China, a situation emanating from high level of fiscal decentralisation in the country. But, Chapter 6 compares Beijing, the national capital and a national level city with a provincial level city, Dongguan located in the most globally linked province of China, Guangdong. The chapter finds high levels of inequality in per capita incomes, per capita revenues and per capita expenditures in the two cities, primarily because of their size. It also shows that Beijing is able to attract more debt financing than Dongguan because of its sheer economic size whereas Dongguan has been able to attract FDI because of its location and close association with Hong Kong and Taiwan.

Chapter 8 compares two national level cities of China, Tianjin, which has been left to itself for financing urban infrastructure and Chongqing, which has received transfers from the central government to induce economic growth in the western region of China. Nonetheless, Tianjin, which has historic advantage in terms of economic development, has far higher levels of infrastructure development and investments than Chongqing. Both these chapters however show that with regards to social infrastructure, there is fair amount of equalisation across Chinese cities compared, which could be an outcome of prioritisation of public investment at the city level.

Shipra Maitra's article (Chapter 9) on Delhi has described at length the multiple public agencies involved in service delivery within the city. It also shows that the city of Delhi has three Urban Local Bodies (ULBs), a state government along with many sector specific parastatal agencies. The sector specific parastatals have been established precisely because the city has three local governments and it would have been difficult to co-ordinate provision and operating of the trunk infrastructure at the entire city level. The analysis gets further complicated by changing responsibilities of the ULBs vis-à-vis the state government and the parastatals over time. At the end, given very high deficits in the level of infrastructure within the city, one is not sure what institutional system would have been best suited and what the financing strategies should have been for equitous development in such a megacity.

Two Chapters (4 and 10) on municipal finances and benefit incidence analysis of municipal expenditures in Ahmedabad are by Mahadevia and Brar. Chapter 4 shows that where the ULB as well as the parastatal body are dealing with developments in the peri-urban areas, the latter has been more efficient, but has also been more discriminatory (investing in the globalising parts of the city). The chapter, after looking at the overall development trends in the city and the municipal corporation's response through expenditure priorities and revenue collection sources shows that the exclusive development paradigm has kicked in Ahmedabad in the last few years, particularly since 2003-04, that has led to public capital being diverted to mega projects to globalise the city. It further shows that the parastatal is able to deliver the exclusive development model more efficiently than the ULB. The ULB and parastatal are now using lands to raise new capital.

Chapter 10 on Ahmedabad, which is benefit incidence analysis of public expenditures from the perspective of slum dwellers of the city shows that inspite of the local government's significant allocation of its revenue and capital investments on basic infrastructure such as water supply and sanitation, the proportion that reaches the slum dwellers on per capita basis is less than 40 per cent. If the local government spends Re. 1 per capita on water supply, then the per capita expenditure that a slum dweller enjoys is 31 paise only and if per capita expenditure on Sanitation is Re. 1 then the same for slum dweller is 38 paise only. This is because either the slum is not plugged into the infrastructure network or if it is then the quality of service is very poor. This calls for improved governance and also improved willingness of the local authorities to reach the slum localities. Increased financial allocations may not be sufficient to bring equity.

The Spatial Segmentation and Land Politics

The predominant form of a World City is a Segmented City (Friedmann and Wolff 1982). With the increasing inequality in the cities, the rich begun to live in isolated, enclosed, protected and insulated neighbourhoods, which Friedmann calls 'citadels' (1986). Such 'citadels' emerged amidst the cities, in the developed world. The examples of these are La Défense in Paris, Battery Park in New York (Marcuse and van Kempen (2000: 13) and in the developing countries such as India and China are various gated communities on the city periphery, special development areas such as Pudong in Shanghai and now large number of SEZs coming up even on the city periphery in India.

In the developing world, the contrast between the very rich and the poor is starker than in the developed countries. In the latter, while the citadels for the rich emerge, poor tend to live in slums or ghettos (that are more excluded communities). Relative segmentation of cities has been noticed in India (see Mahadevia 1998 and Mahadevia and Narayanan Chapter 3 on Mumbai; Mahadevia 2002a and Mahadevia and Brar Chapter 4 on Ahmedabad). The segmentation continues in Mumbai, with most Slum Rehabilitation Schemes (SRS) in the city are concentrated in a particular ward of the city (Mahadevia and Narayanan Chapter 3).

North and west segments of Bangalore City are industrial areas with housing of the industrial workers. About 30 per cent of the male workers in the city were employed in manufacturing sector in 1999-2000 and less than 5 per cent of the male workers were employed in the Information Technology (IT) and computer services (Chapter 2 by Mahadevia). Even then the city has an international image of 'Silicon Valley', given that the major software developing companies are located in the city, but in the eastern and southern segments only, near the existing airport, along with the high-end residential areas. Part of the northern industrial areas are being converted into IT enclaves with the support of the state government's industrial development agency, that is transferring the lands to these new enclaves and has also given away land for the new airport (See Chapter 7 by Benjamin *et al.*).

Mactan, the dynamic locality in the Cebu Metropolitan Area, is one such citadel, that has won the global competition of local economic development. On the other hand, Metro Cebu has been sharply divided between the citadels (included) and the ghettos (excluded) in the globalisation process (Berner 2001). Thus, the story of many developing countries of Asia has been segmentation and emergence of ghettos and citadels.

The new developments on the periphery of many Chinese cities are gated communities either as independent communities or in the new townships on the city periphery. For example, Meijiang development area in Hexi district of Tianjin, has large number of gated communities. In fact, all the new residential developments in Tianjin, Beijing, Shanghai and all other cities, which are recorded as commercial residential development in the Chinese statistical system, are gated communities. The new townships coming up on the periphery of large cities are also developed through gated communities[25]. Girior (2006) describes the Purple Jade Villas on the periphery of Beijing as a gated community, a phenomenon that the author state was born in the 1990s. However, one could argue that the urban housing system in China has always been through 'gated communities', as the entire urban life in socialist China was organised around '*danweis*', work units; each work unit functioning as a gated community. Galsze et al (2006) call such developments as private cities.

Special development zones take the form of Special Development Areas such as Pudong and Minhang Industrial Development Zone, etc. in Shanghai, Haidian Hi-Tech Park, in Beijing, Binhai New Area in Tianjin on Bohai Bay and in it Tianjin Economic Development Area (TEDA), Huayuan Hi-tech Economic Development Zone in Tianjin, etc. In China, these have come up even in the second tier cities such as Hangzhou, Suzhou, etc.—the list is endless. They also come up in the form of SEZs or High-Tech zones. The SEZ as a form of new economic enclaves for selective development became popular with China experimenting her reform process through these. But, since then, they have become synonymous with rapid economic growth and export-led growth. SEZs in China finally became large cities by themselves. There are also industrial parks that have come up in many Chinese cities. In India, these were industrial estates for concentrating manufacturing activities. Most of these estates had come up before the reforms. Since, most metropolitan cities are displacing manufacturing activities; such estates are being converted into high-tech parks.

China, in fact, popularised the idea of SEZ with setting up four such zones in 1980, to begin experimenting with market economy and FDI. The country finally developed through the SEZs, maintaining about 10 per cent real Gross Domestic Product (GDP) growth rate since 1989 (United Nations Conference on Trade and Development, 2007). But, with all types of new technological zones developed, all over the country, the number of SEZs in the country has reach 54 in 2006 (Gopalakrishnan, 2007: 1493). Over time, each of the local and provincial governments have declared their own special zones, providing incentives and land to industries and real estate firms, whom Gopalakrishnan calls speculators. This author further brings in the evidence to suggest that 1993 estimates of special development zones within the cities announced by the local governments ranged from 6,000 to 8,700 in number. These being in contravention of the national and provincial government regulations, 1,000 of them were cancelled by 1994 (Huang and Yang 1996 in Gopalakrishnan 2007: 1493). A rough estimate by Cartier (2001) put total area thus committed to be about 15,000 square kilometres, which was more than the built-up area of the existing cities in 1992.

In India an endless list of SEZs coming up on the periphery of all major metros can be put together. As per the data of the Ministry of Commerce, Government of India, as on April 5, 2007[26] total of 234 valid formal approvals for the SEZs have been given of which 63 SEZs have already been notified and 171 notifications of approved SEZs were pending[27]. Since then 132 more have been approved taking the total approved number of SEZs to 362 of which 136 had been notified[28]. Many of these are on the periphery of the metropolitan cities. Besides these, many cities also have High-Tech Zones also on the periphery of metropolitan cities (See Maitra forthcoming, 2008 for Delhi; Mahadevia and Parashar forthcoming 2008 for Pune; Prasad and Ramachandraiah forthcoming 2008 for Hyderabad, Shaw forthcoming 2008 for Kolkata).

Some of the industrial parks or special development zones have airports and seaports. Pudong has both, an airport and a seaport. Binhai new area in Tianjin too has an airport and a Port. In fact Tianjin Port possesses the biggest container dock of the country and is connected to over 300 ports of 170 countries world over[29]. Similar special development zones have not yet developed in India, but, are likely to develop in Mumbai, with the development of Navi Mumbai SEZ (NMSEZ) located in Navi Mumbai (New Mumbai[30]), a public sector planned and developed city outside Mumbai to take off the load from Mumbai city. The NMSEZ has the site of the proposed new international airport and the existing port of Mumbai named Jawaharlal Nehru Port (JNP), the largest Port on the west coast of India. NMSEZ is spread over al area of 50 sq km[31], taking up about 14.5 per cent of the area of Navi Mumbai.

Marcuse and Kempen (2000: 4) state that the new urban form in the cities that have globalised includes: (i) Areas that are considered enclaves of the rich, the representatives of an extremely mobile top operating at the global level and who live in 'exclusionary enclaves' or 'citadels'; (ii) gentrified areas of the professionals along with pockets of the poor; (iii) ethnic enclaves or minority enclaves (for example China towns in large number of North American cities, Vietnam town, Latino town and so on in North American cities, areas occupied by the African Americans in US cities) or Muslim ghettos in Indian cities (see Mahadevia 2007b for Ahmedabad); and (iv) A new type of ghettos inhabited by the urban poor, fully and long-term excluded group at the bottom. Concentration of slums in some segments of city can be seen in most Indian cities. We see concentration of migrants, also called the floating population, on the city periphery in Chinese cities (Peng and Zhu 2007, Chroed 2000).

Pressure of the Real Estate Lobby

Such exclusive developments are part of the development strategy that relies on real estate for economic growth. Haila (2000: 2241) illustrates that rent is important source of revenue and profit for the economies of Singapore and Hong Kong. In Hong Kong, 40 per cent of the bank lendings were in the property sector (in 1997) (Sender 1997: 66 in Haila 2000: 2249). In both the cities property development companies constituted an important sector in the stock market (40% in Hong Kong in 1997 and 11.2% in Singapore in 1994) and taxation of real estate formed important source of public revenue (Haila 2000: 2249). In this context, the real estate firms have pressurised the local governments and continue to do so to change policies in their favour.

Pressure from the real estate firms on the local governments to make policies favourable to them have been observed in many countries. In India, the corporate houses have built pressure on the state governments to acquire land from the farmers on their behalf for the development of SEZs and pass Township Policies that give them tax exemptions. The pressure of real estate on the local governments have led to changes in land legislation at the local level, such as increase allowable built-up area on the plot represented by concept of Floor Space Index (FSI)/Floor Area Ratio (FAR), allowing increasing heights, etc. with the argument that this would increase city's competitiveness. Chapter 3 by Mahadevia and Narayanan discusses at length the legislative changes introduced in Mumbai to make it a World Class city. Mahadevia (2007c) has listed some of these legislative changes in Indian metropolitan cities.

Similar arguments were put forward by the real estate firms in Japan (Sorensen 2003: 528), arguing that if Tokyo had to be a competitive World City in relation to Shanghai, Hong Kong and Singapore, it had to redevelop central parts of Tokyo city. The bonuses that the real estate companies got from the government were deregulation and increase in floor area. Even historically, the Tokyo Metropolitan Government created favourable conditions for the development of high tech towers and high amenity living space on the city's water front. While in the Anglo American literature on World Cities and their spatial restructuring through market forces, Tokyo's restructuring has been 'State-dominated' argues Saito (2003). The pro-real estate changes in the city planning, namely deregulation, privatisation and fiscal retrenchment introduced by the Prime Minister of Japan resulted in explosion of real estate projects in central Tokyo and taking over of the life space of communities by the economic space. Inner city communities were destroyed; in case of small plots where the tenants were unwilling to move or owners were unwilling to sell, 'land sharks' (real estate gangsters) used intimidation, threats and violence to encourage people to leave (Hayakawa and Hirayama, 1991: 156 in Sorenson 2003: 527).

In China, local political leaders have been quite favourable to the demands of the real estate sector. A local leader's career path and chances of promotion are tied closely to the economic performance of his/her place of administration (Ma 2002: 1562). For local economic development, real estate is used in a very major way. The local level development control depends greatly on the administrative discretion of the planning department (Wu and Yeh, 1999). There have been many local level decisions permitting different development controls to attract investments.

Increased Demand for New Commercial Spaces

Globalisation has created new 'new middle classes' in Asia since the mid-1980s (Robinson and Goodman 1996), which has begun to consume in the internationalised way and has consequently changed its culture in cosmopolitan directions (Clammer 2000). This has led to enhanced private consumption. Major cities in Asia, Singapore, Bangkok, Manila, Kuala Lumpur in the decade of 1990s (Clammer 2003), Beijing, Shanghai, and all major cities in China from mid-1990s and Mumbai, Delhi and its surroundings, Ahmedabad, Hyderabad, Banaglore, etc, in India from the beginning of 2000, have seen expansion of consumer culture. This has changed urban landscapes. Mega international retailing outlets such as

Walmart, Carre Four, Vanguard, and local such retailing outlets such as Reliance Mart in India, have sprung up in the newly created spaces called Malls in large numbers in most Asian cities. Many of them have come up on the city periphery as in case of Ahmedabad (Chapter 4 by Mahadevia and Brar) and many other cities in Asia, where the lands are available in large chunks. In Mumbai, the malls are coming up on the closed textile mill lands (Chapter 3 by Mahadevia and Narayanan). In China, they are springing up in all parts of the city, as per the dynamism of the district government within a city, which are using real estate development as a local economic development strategy. Singapore is known for shopping and relentless economic growth since 1970s, has improved the incomes of the citizens resulting in expansion of consumption (Chua 1998). All these have required land allocation for the construction of new commercial spaces. The outcome has been increase in property and land prices across board in the Asian cities.

Local Land Politics

Solomon Benjamin (in Chapter 5) and Benjamin *et al* (Chapter 7) have looked at the transition from traditional land occupancy patterns to modern—'legal' occupancies and the political processes that brought about the traditional occupancies in the first place and conditions that make the transition, what the chapters articulate as 'Closure' possible. Chapter 5 by Benjamin lays the theoretical context for the case studies presented in Chapter 7.

Chapter 7 presents case studies of East and South Bangalore. It illustrates that the marginal and low income groups accessed urban land through occupancy rights claimed as a result of political space afforded by the present electoral democracy. The traditional ownership rights and the informal occupancy rights wove a complex web of land tenure system, denying a possibility of clear and marketable land title. This went to the benefit of the informal sector occupants, who are conversant with negotiating the informal spaces. The corporate sector, on the other hand, requires clear and marketable land titles, which, the new forms of governance structures supported by the middle class organisations desire. In fact, in case of South Bangalore in particular, the process of legalisation of land titles opened up the informal spaces for the take over by the large corporate sector entities. Two case studies within Bangalore are taken up, one in East Bangalore and other in South Bangalore, both in the peri-urban context. These case studies show that growth benefits have trickled down to a section of urban informal sector through the land market. Hence, tenancy laws, giving tenurial rights to the cultivators in the urban periphery has led to prosperity of those who accessed these lands.

The Chapter also points to the fact that the urban marginal and low income groups are better able to negotiate the local political processes. But, when the new form of politics comes in with higher level of governments, in case of Bangalore the state government along with the globalised financial institutions, the corporate sector is better able to deal with it and the marginal groups loose out. In other words, the much maligned 'Clientalist politics' of the Indian electoral democracy—maligned by the 'clean governance requiring' urban middle classes—has opened up spaces and therefore possibilities of trickle down benefits accruing to the lower classes and castes in the urban areas.

The accounts of transformation indicate a strong 'hand of the State'. The example is acquisition of land by a State entity Karnataka Industrial Area Development Board (KIADB) for the industries but then passed on to the IT sector. This attracted larger players in the real estate from all over the country and also abroad with the opening up of the real estate sector for foreign players, to the land market of Bangalore. In contrast, the smaller developers formed partnerships with smaller and medium sized farmers and local politicians—moving local councils to extend basic infrastructure and services in lieu for 'betterment charges'. The chapter argues that the small developers emerged as competitors of the large players. The competition was sought to be won by the large players using Master Plan concept, by which it is easy to brand the small players as 'un-planned, encroachers' that come out of corrupt 'vote bank' politics. The whole process first starts with vilification of 'vote bank' politics. Media plays an important role in creating social sanction for this vilification and then fervour for a new vision, such as 'turning Bangalore into a 'Singapore'. The two chapters therefore illustrate that the land markets are never free of politics or non-market forces.

Increasing Inequality and Exclusions

Market forces act with impersonal ruthlessness, crushing old, inert practices and initiating new dynamic ways of functioning. Hence, globalisation process has also inflicted costs to which there has been strong reaction. Firstly, it has increased economic polarisation. In the first section, increase in global economic inequalities have been shown with the GDP data, where inspite of increase in GDP and per capita GDP in Developing Asia over the last two and a half decades, the gap between the developed world and Developing Asia has increased slightly. The

United Nations Development Programme (UNDP), in the global HDRs has been arguing that the global income inequalities have gone up since 1960s and this has translated into increase in inequalities in human development achievements (UNDP 2005). This of course has not gone unchallenged and some scholars have argued that by P.P.P. income, global inequalities have declined (Dowrick and Akmal, 2003).

Table 1.7: Increase in Consumption/Income in Asian Countries

Country	*Period*	*Percentage increase in income/expenditure*	
		Bottom 20%	*Top 20%*
People's Republic of China	1993-2004	3.40	7.10
India	1993-2004	0.05	2.03
Bangladesh	1991-2005	0.07	1.60
Nepal	1995-2003	1.92	7.23
Malaysia	1993-2004	2.25	2.23
Vietnam	1993-2004	3.37	4.69
Philippines	1994-2003	1.25	2.27

Source: Asian Development Bank (2007), p. 7.

Concerns have been expressed about increasing inequality within the countries of Asia. The Gini coefficient of expenditure/income distribution is the highest for the People's Republic of China (PRC) and Nepal among the Asian countries, the coefficient being 48 for the former in 2004 and for the latter in 2003 (ADB 2007: 3). It is 36 for India in 2004. For most other Asian countries it has been around 40 for the years between 2002 to 2004. In the last 10 to 15 years, in most Asian countries, except Malaysia (Table 1.7), the expenditure increase has been much higher for the top 20 per cent of the population than for the bottom 20 per cent of the population. However, Latin American and Caribbean countries have the highest Gini coefficient of 57.1 (by P.P.P.), Brazil has Gini coefficient of 59.3, whereas East Asia and the Pacific have Gini coefficient of 50 and South Asia of 33.4 (UNDP 2005: 55). Different nature of State in East Asian and Southeast Asian countries (discussed later in the chapter) than in Latin American countries and even in South Asian countries gets the credit for keeping the inequalities low in the process of rapid economic growth.

Within the nations, regional inequalities have increased. China is an example where inequality in income between the coastal and inland China has increased. This is partly the outcome of gradual opening up, from four SEZs to coastal cities, to coastal regions to inland areas (Nolan 2004; UNFPA 2007). But, inequalities have increased within the cities in terms of consumption in metro cities in India as Dubey and Mahadevia (2001) have shown using consumption expenditure data.

The GDP and revenue income data of different districts of Tianjin City at two time points, 2000 and 2005 shows that inequality across the districts have increased (Mahadevia Chapter 8). For those unfamiliar with the urban structure of Chinese cities, the city is divided into districts and districts into sub-districts.

In the urban areas, local officials have become sales force for economic development and job creation (Savitch 2002). They have become proactive when it comes to attracting investments, but, when it comes to addressing the issues of poverty, they remain laggard and inefficient. The creation of "enterprise zones", SEZs, Hi-Tech zones, etc. are pushed with great speed whereas the slum development is very slow or unaddressed.

An important aspect of agenda for equity is housing for the poor. It is here that unless there is a proactive state policy, there are large marginalisaitons. There are five chapters in this book on housing marginalisation. The article by Lalit Batra and Diya Mehra (Chapter 11) discuss at length slum demolitions in Delhi, the purpose of these demolitions, the brutal process through which they take place and post-demolition situation of the slum dwellers in case they have been rehabilitated by the State. They argue that the slum demolitions are for production of neo-liberal space through furthering privatisation and commodification of land. In this, among other instruments, an increased reliance on "accumulation by dispossession" (Harvey 2002) has played a central role. Like Solomon et al (Chapter 7), these authors also argue that the 'socialistic' master planning failed to provide affordable housing to city's poor. Now the custodians of the Plan themselves are arguing for the withdrawal of the State from housing sector and seeking the 'participation' of large corporate real estate players. The moot question is that when the State, which has at least some democratic accountability, failed the poor, can the market, which is accountable to none but profits, be relied upon to provide succour to the poor.

Article by Mahadevia and Narayanan (Chapter 18) is on slum demolitions in Mumbai. The chapter discusses that each new vision for Mumbai is followed by massive slum demolitions. The massive 2004-05 demolitions, the focus of the chapter, showed the complicity of the local as well as state level elected leaders in this action of the local government. The chapter then goes on to discuss the politics that spur such demolitions. The chapter shows that there is no one reason for slum demolitions, but, the prominent ones are the collusion of the state level politicians with the large real estate developers on one hand and accumulation of wealth by a few through dispossession and marginalisation of the poor on the other. Article by Amita Bhide (Chapter 19) is also on the slum demolitions in Mumbai where she argues that displacement of the poor has emerged as an almost inevitable accompaniment to development in Mumbai. She shows that there has been multi-quartered attack on the poor, by the: (i) development planning, (ii) administrative vigour, (iii) 'citizens' voice, (iv) judiciary, (v) media, and (vi) city politics.

Everything is not well with events such as Olympics or Asian Games or Common Wealth Games that the cities attempt to attract for increasing their competitiveness, visibility and announcing that they have arrived on the world scene. In Delhi, social activists, for example have been saying that the 2010 Games would push out the poor from the city through slum demolitions and those lands would be handed over to the real estate players; push the small industrial units out of the city and with them the poor, something that has already happened; adversely impact the livelihoods of the poor through ban on street vending and restriction of cycle rickshaws in the city; cause serious environmental damage to the city, cause demographic imbalances; and creat large slums on the periphery where the migrant labour brought for the construction purposes would finally squat[32]. This is shown in Batra's and Mehra's chapter on Delhi and also by the Chapter by David Westerndoff (Chapter 15) on Chinese urban development experience.

Beijing Olympics, according to a field study by a Geneva based housing rights organisation, Centre on Housing Rights and Evictions (COHRE), has displaced at least, 1.25 million people and unknown number of people forcibly evicted by April 2007. These displacements and evictions are an outcome of urban development linked to the Olympic Games. Another 250,000 people are expected to be displaced in the final year before the Olympic Games, resulting in a total of 1.5 million people being displaced in Beijing by August 2008 due to Olympics related development. The report further states that many of these displacements would have nonetheless happened because of large scale urban development and the model of urban development followed in Beijing (and so in other Chinese cities). The scale of displacements has more than doubled since Beijing was elected as an Olympic Host City. Over the period between 2006 and 2008, an average of 60,000 homes per year were or are being demolished, displacing 156,000 people per year. These figures do not include approximately 400,000 migrants living 'temporarily' in 171 neighbourhoods in situations of extreme insecurity, having come to Beijing due to lack of livelihood opportunities in rural areas[33].

David's chapter on China's urban experience shows that the insecurity of tenure has emerged in Chinese cities since late 1970s, which coincides with the period of economic reforms. This was followed by urbanisation of rural lands since 1985, which further weakened the security of tenure in rural China. Lands were acquired for SEZs, hydropower projects, university cities, villa and golf course complexes and transportation infrastructure. In urban China, housing reforms towards development of housing markets weakened the security of tenure for the urban poor. In the initial period of housing reforms, compensation was a major issue for the households that had to move. Since 1998, when welfare housing was abolished and the occupants of former public housing were asked to purchase the units, a strong sense of ownership developed among the urban households and since then any relocation and displacement has become a contentious issue although the State always gets its way. Eviction and demolition can proceed legally before judgment is rendered. Since large scale urban renovation projects are being undertaken across the cities of China, massive displacements have taken place whose estimates are not available, except the COHRE study mentioned above. The Chapter also discusses the housing problems for the migrants, given the restrictive nature of *hukou* (residential permit) system. The Chapter finally indicates the sensitivity of the government to the exclusions in the housing market and introduction of market and non-market measures to overcome these exclusions.

Many countries have their own internal exclusions. In China, there is a bias against migrants, particularly the poor rural migrants through the *hukou* system. This system discriminates against the migrants in access to housing and basic services such as education and health facilities. In 1996, 51 per cent of developing countries had policies to lower migration to urban agglomerations; this proportion rose to 73 per cent in 2005. (See United Nations 2006 in UNFPA 2007: 81). There is higher incidence of poverty among the migrants than among the permanent residents in Chinese cities (ADB 2001: 93). As a result, the urban-rural and coastal and inland inequalities have increased in China over time (China Development Research Society and United Nations Development Programme, 2005). In India, the migrants are discriminated against through housing policies, through issue of Identity Cards (called ID cards) given to those who have come to the city upto a particular date, called the cut-off date for issuing ID cards. This politics of cut-off date is discussed at length by Mahadevia and Narayanan in Chapter 18. But, it is more than anti-urban bias of the policy makers that is being talked about so often (UNFPA 2007) in India. The urban poor squatting on lands (public and private) was not seen as a problem till the time property markets begun to pick up in urban India since early 1990s (See Mahadevia and Singh 1998 for property market rise in some metro cities in India).

There is one article on capture of water supply by the corporate and elites of the city (Chapter 13 on Hyderabad by Ramachandraiah). The context of the article is water scarcity in the twin city of Hyderabad-Secuderabad and measures taken by the state government to enhance water supply to the city. The decline in traditional sources of water in the city led to the city tapping long-distance water sources, in the process leading to cost increases. Eventually, with the reforms coming in and high-end users exerting pressure on the parastatal, which supplies water in the city, the scare water resource has got diverted to the users such as IT companies, business education institution and so on, increasing intra-city inequality, with the poor left in the lurch to find their own solutions.

Acharya, in his article on Hanoi City (Chapter 14) has an interesting take on the concept of 'inclusions' and 'exclusions' in the context of former socialist economies. He argues that if 'inclusion' and 'exclusion' are commonly understood with reference to 'equity' and are processes that check or enhance marginalisation by providing or restricting opportunities to different sections of the society then the socialist Vietnamese State was both inclusive and exclusive. It was 'inclusive' because it was more responsible to the people and basic needs of citizens were taken care of than now. But this period 'excluded' large majority of the people to participate in gainful urban activities by restricting migration of the rural people. The regime also 'excluded' people from participating in civic organisations other than the ones prescribed or provided by the State. The ability of the citizens to dissent and actively participate in debates and policy matters were severely limited. The contention here is that these concepts will have to be understood in a wider context mainly because the factors that determine 'inclusion'/ 'exclusion' are diverse and are place and time specific. He further argues that the socialist 'inclusive' growth model followed during the pre-reform period was pauperising the entire society and 'sharing of poverty was a common syndrome than sharing of wealth'! But, post-reforms (*doi moi*), new forms of exclusions as in market economies have set in Hanoi city.

Many scholars have argued that the neo-liberal globalisation "proceeds selectively, including and excluding segments of economies and societies in and out of the networks of information, wealth and power that characterize the new dominant system" (Castells 1998: 162). In case of cities, the city segmentation discussed earlier in the chapter, creates this selective linkage with globalisation.

Many articles in this volume are narrating this aspect of marginalisations and exclusions, particularly the cases coming out of the Indian cities. In the literature on social exclusions, the neo-liberals argue that exclusions are inevitable and side effect of restructuring of global production processes, which would be taken care of in the long run through growth. Another framework, which Beall (2002) terms transformational, looks at social exclusions embedded in the formal and informal institutions of a society, that exclude a certain set of people getting evicted from the economic and spatial spaces that they previously occupied (previous to the new economic forces coming into being). Hence, selective globalisation, enmeshed with the local social relations and local history, lead to selective exclusions. In other words, more egalitarian societies would have different outcomes with the onset of economistic globalisation than the inegalitarian societies. In China, which was egalitarian pre-reforms, has therefore different outcomes with the opening up of the economy than opening up of the socially inegalitarian India, and as a matter of fact, all of South Asian countries.

The State Character

Inclusions or exclusions are dependent on the nature of the State and governance. Hence, high economic growth rates in one context may result in exclusions and in a different context may result in inclusions. In other words, inclusions or exclusions are dependent on whether the State has redistributive policies or not, how capable the population is to take advantage of the increase in growth rates and how participatory and transparent the governance is. Participatory and transparent governance is tied to level of decentralisation of governance and citizens' role in deciding development priorities, financial allocations and implementing and managing development activities. Capability of the population is related to education levels, health status, and social equity, the last one a result of political structure and the first two of the public policies. It is with regards to this very important aspect that the Asian countries differ from each other.

Much of the early literature on globalisation has commented on the decline of the sovereign nation State and the increasing influence of the TNCs in the policy making (Vliet 2002). It was realised that this has not always been the case. The Asian ascent globally is often attributed to the 'Developmental State' in many of the countries. Developmental State has emerged in the countries that embarked late on the industrialisation and economic growth path, which in fact is the case with the Asian economies. The first Asian country where the Developmental State emerged was in Japan, after it came out of the Second World War. Instead of following the liberal capitalism path, Japanese Nation-State engaged itself in the industrialisation process, through State regulations and non-market governance mechanisms to restrain competition in order to concentrate resources in strategic industries and maintain orderly economic growth (Hill and Kim 2000: 2174). Further, short term profits were rejected to secure workers' cooperation in promoting productivity. By the end of 1960s, Japanese "State emerged with strong capacity to sustain economic growth in contrast to the more free-wheeling role played by the market in Anglo-American capitalist economies. Japanese managers emphasised co-operative industrial relations in contrast to their conflict-prone Western counterparts" (Hill and Kim 2000: 2175). This pre-eminence of State in all matters of economic growth was extended to even urban policy making, and as discussed in the earlier section, redevelopment of Tokyo and its emergence into a Global City is very much attributed to the direct policy measures and intervention by the Nation- State. It need be mentioned that some scholars do not yet consider Tokyo as a global city (Hill and Kim 2000, Sassen 1999 modifying her earlier argument), which however is not the point here.

It is argued that the Asian State is a Developmental State, which sets all of them apart from the Anglo-American State (Hill and Kim, 2000). In essence, only the East and South-east Asian States have been Developmental States whereas the rest of the Asian countries have followed their own paths, to which we would come later on in the section, at least with regards to India. Developmental State, what Leftwich (2002: 61), calls as a transitional form of modern State that has emerged in late-developing societies, is a State where the political and bureaucratic elites have achieved relative autonomy from the socio-political structures of the society and which they use to promote rapid economic growth, with less or more vigour or ruthlessness. This agenda is typically driven by an urgent need to 'catch up' with the developed world, to industrialise, promote economic growth and by that improve the material and social well-being of its citizens. It is also associated with high degree of both economic and political nationalism. A Developmental State has autonomy to pursue developmental goals with less need to placate sectional interests than in other countries, as in case of India where the State has been responding favourably and strongly to the interests of the powerful landlords or powerful oligopolistic groups in the private sector (Nolan 2004: 65, Frankel 1978).

White (2002), Leftwich (2002) and Robinson and White (2002) have distinguished between democratic and non-democratic Developmental States; China and Singapore being examples of the latter whereas Malaysia an example of the former (but with a dominant political party) (Leftwich 2002: 63). However, it is conceded that the Chinese State is changing and becoming more accommodative of other forces such as private sector and also of bringing in elections for the key positions in the government. Indian State is classified by Leftwich as partly democratic Developmental State and partly democratic non-Developmental State; the former because of the country's increased economic growth rate after mid-1990s and the country being one of the largest electoral democracy. We dispute this classification of Indian State, but, about it later. While not going into the discussion of democratic *vs* non-democratic Developmental State, it is important to understand that even for the well functioning of markets, State is an important player for whatever role it sets itself to play.

For example, poverty reduction because of the sustained high growth has been accompanied by increase in income inequality in South-east Asian countries. In contrast, Japan has done quite well with regards to wealth distribution through various policy measures (Marcotullio, 2003: 231). China has reduced poverty with dominant role of the State in capability enhancement of the population and redistributive mechanisms in place. Many researchers and political observers have given credit to the Chinese Socialist State for drastically improving the health and education status of Chinese people till the period China was a closed economy (see for example Sen 2005). Even, in the recent years, when the inequalities have increased, the Chinese State is making great attempts to redistribute through equity transfers (Nolan, 2004). Nolan states that China has been a successful experiment in development because the "State has continued to play a critical role in maintaining social stability, resolving problems of market failure, regulating the distribution of income, wealth and life opportunities, and regulating the way in which China interacts with the global economy" (Nolan, 2004: 3). In China, the responsibility of the leadership is massive, as the price of failure is huge (Nolan, 2004: 4).

Nolan (2004) also states that Chinese State has been able to effectively do equity transfers to the backward or disadvantaged regions than 'capitalist' developing countries such as India and Brazil. This, the Chinese State could do through taxing the developed regions and transferring the surplus to the less developed regions. In the urban areas, as Mahadevia (Chapter 6 and Chapter 8) shows, there is taxing of the enterprises that is generating revenues for the city. There are also equity transfers to the less developed districts within the cities studied, exemplified in very low inequality in social infrastructure within the cities and between the cities. Also, development of Chongqing is an outcome of equity transfers by the national government.

Restructuring of Chinese cities in the last 15 years, has been 'State-dominated' (Ma 2002); "despite the forces of globalization, liberalization, decentralization of administrative and fiscal power, and the presence of multiple actors in China's economic restructuring, the State that has shaped China's urban transformation is omnipresent. The role of the State, of course, is not a new theme .... But in understanding China's urban transformation it needs to be articulated and foregrounded to a more prominent position." (Ma 2002: 1546-7). Active support by the State to the private sector, including the real estate firms is theoretised by some as "local State Corporatism" (Oi 1992, 1998, 1999). The Chinese local State can also be called 'Entrepreneurial State'.

The chapter by Lim Poim (Chapter 16) on rehabilitation policy in Shanghai illustrates the various rehabilitation policies put in place by the Shanghai Municipal Government overtime to support massive urban renewal efforts. Poim shows that in the early periods, these rehabilitation efforts were largely successful and were meant for purely social objectives of improving the living conditions. But, Shanghai's renewal process now has new strategies and mechanisms developed simultaneously for her new challenges. Through land exchange, whole scale redevelopment and other incentives, the government has managed to stimulate large-scale property development and improved the housing shortages. However, despite these new policies, regulation and financial mechanisms, there are issues with regards to enforcement and monitoring of the relocation/rehabilitation packages, marginalised and displaced communities, issues of affordability due to rising home prices and loss of cultural heritage. The chapter argues that although the city government has taken on new role as "CEO of the city", there is a need to balance out economic and social interests. In short, the article points to the changing character of Chinese State from being a welfare State to neo-liberal one, the latter one pre-concerned with economic growth alone.

David Westerndoff's chapter also indicates the change of Chinese State from a welfare State to more neo-liberal State but in the recent years being increasingly concerned about inequalities and marginalisations in the housing market. China's leaders recognise the seriousness of the problem of assuring adequate housing for all urban residents, which the government is seeking to solve through market and non-market methods such as rein in the explosive increases in housing costs, build or purchase from the market rental housing for the lowest income strata and to offer subsidised housing to help middle income families purchase their first homes. Low-income (rental) housing along with subsidised commercial housing will be located adjacent to the major mass transit arteries, as is being planned for Beijing and has been implemented to some extent in Shanghai. While such accommodations may be at some distance from the central city, the new communities are being designed to offer convenient access to full health, educational, commercial and recreational infrastructure. As a whole, these initiatives have not been implemented effectively. Westerndoff's assessment is that even under the most optimistic scenario for implementing the policy and corrective measures, the near term housing problems of low-income households are likely to grow.

Although, State in Singapore is called authoritarian, it has played an important role in not just the economy but also in welfare distribution and maintaining social stability in multi-ethnic Singapore. Van Grunsven (2000) shows that there has been significant role of the government in the economy extended to the provision of housing in Singapore. Article by Lim Lan Yuan in this book on Singapore (Chapter 15) also indicates this, though this article could have given more evidences of the achievements of the government policies. Van Grunsven (2000: 107) states that there is hardly any housing deprivation in Singapore and a remarkable feature of this achievement is that it is provided, regulated and managed by the government and more than 90 per cent of it is owner-occupied. The city does not have any housing segment, rental or owner-occupied, in irregular settlements. Further, given the ethnic diversity in the city-state and also a situation of a particular ethnic group (Malays) at the bottom of the hierarchy living in informal settlements in early 1960s, the other highlight of the government housing policy was residential integration and dispersal of ethnic minorities in different housing developments through a deliberate policy of intermixing of different ethnic groups. The third important feature was that the housing was made affordable for all and hence the role of private sector in the housing was minimised. The overriding consideration was removing the blight from the city that would not befit 'modern Singapore' (Van Grunsven, 2000).

The case of Indian State is entirely different than that of Chinese. All the articles in this book on Indian State indicate the exclusive nature, one that has been extremely pro rich than pro poor. The tales of brutal displacement (Chapter 11 by Batra and Mehra and Chapter 18 by Mahadevia and Narayanan), selective public investments in Ahmedabad (Chapter 4 by Mahadevia and Brar), State institutions and the large financial firms assisting the corporate builders taking over the informal spaces of the urban poor in Bangalore, something that the informal sector had attained through clientalist politics (Chapters 5 and 7 by Benjamin and Benjamin *et al.* respectively), State supporting unequal water distribution and permitting corporate take-over of scarce water resources in Hyderabad (Chapter 13 by Ramachandraiah), the State along with the civil society and support of the judiciary evicting slums (in Mumbai Chapter 19 by Bhide and in Delhi Chapter 11 by Batra and Mehra) and finally State accepting the corporate sector's vision for Mumbai City (Chapter 3 by Mahadevia and Narayanan) are evidences of exclusive character of Indian State. Benjamin (Chapter 5) alleges that inter-twined are the interests of the corporate sector (in this case an IT Company) and of the incumbent Chief Minister in money-making through real estate, which are behind Bangalore's aspiration to be Singapore.

In India, the State is democratic to an extent, because of regular elections held, but, not necessarily developmental (as only recently, the economic growth rates have increased in India) and not necessarily redistributive. Nolan (2004: 71) says: "A notorious deficiency of the Indian State has been its lack of coherent regional policy and, apart from famine relief, the national government has strikingly failed to mobilise resources to assist backward areas". Kohli and Mullen (2003: 193) call Indian State a soft State, which has not been able to promote socio-economic development. They also argue that Indian State has failed on both the fronts, on radical redistribution as well as ruthless economic growth. "The 'socialist' commitment of India leaders, for example, was rather shallow: although the rhetoric may have helped build short-term political capital, pro-poor policies were seldom pursued vigorously in India" (Kohli and Mullen, 2003: 194). They further state that economic reforms since 1991 has led the Indian State to become more liberal in the sense of business interests and that the Indian politics has drifted right-ward creating more harmonious State-business relations with a positive impact on growth, while the massive problem of poverty continues. Mahadevia (2003a) has shown that the socialist rhetoric in urban policy making was a hoax, and the concern for equity was at best an euphemism for State supported capitalistic growth, State support to a few to amass massive wealth through land deals and middle and elite classes to capture State subsidies in the cities. The demolitions of slums, as and when the landed classes have required, have continued unabated in the Indian cities (Chapter 18 by Mahadevia and Narayanan have shown this for Mumbai, Mahadevia 2002c and Batra and Mehra Chapter 11). Verma (2002) has argued that slumming the cities have been a deliberate State policy. The other side of the story of Indian State is its electoral democracy, which has provided some space to the urban poor to counter the repeated onslaught of the State machinery on their lives and living (Chapter 18 by Mahadevia and Narayanan).

This author's assessment is that Indian State is being pushed by the Indian elites to become 'Developmental State' like China, with the argument that that India cannot achieve high economic growth rates if it remains a soft State as Kohli and Mullen (2003) have described the Indian state to be. The statements of the Indian elites about their visions for urban government and the Indian English language dailies running campaigns on behalf of the urban elites about improving the city conditions, or the Vision of a World Class city emanating from the business houses of Mumbai, are examples of the Indian elites wanting Indian State to be 'Developmental' in one sense. Of course, they also bring in the rhetoric of social development. But, the idea is to push the State to devote resources and bring policies that would bring in transformation of a part of the city. They are also asking the State to change the land legislation to promote high end real estate projects.

The Indian elites have one-sided interest in the notion of Developmental State, one that is coherent enough to push rapid economic growth, but, not one that is welfare distributing as well and building people's capabilities through social development and equality. The classic example of this one-sided understanding of a Developmental State is represented in the new vision of urban governance put forward by the Bangalore Agenda Task Force (BATF), which is a partnership between the Chief Minister of the State, Municipal Commissioner of the City and the CEO of the largest IT firm of the city (Ghosh, 2005). We may go a step forward and argue that Indian State has not been a 'Soft State' as Kohli and Mullen (2003) argue but an 'Instrumental State' (Przeworski 1990), wherein the State is a machine in the hands of the propertied classes to amass wealth. This is atleast what we have seen in urban India. In that case, the survival and welfare of the urban poor comes from resistance against such processes, an aspect that is discussed in the last section.

Decentralisation and Shift from Government to Governance

The new State that is emerging in this globalised phase, even in Asia is one that is getting decentralised. In the process of linking cities with the global economy, decentralisation allows local policy makers to have more effective control over the key processes for successful integration (World Bank, 1999: 2). The World Bank (1999: 3-4) suggests that the sub-national/local governments can improve the urban environment by: (i) financing capital investment in infrastructure directly through partnerships with private investors or by helping municipalities raise capital on financial markets; (ii) efficiently provide basic services through privatisation where appropriate; (iii) creating well-functioning land markets in which ownership rights are clearly established; (iv) creating legal environment conducive to entrepreneurship and growth; (v) protecting property rights; (vi) designing policies that create a critical mass of specific industries; (vii) creating a forum for private and public sectors to communicate and set common goals for the city; and (viii) attracting and building human capital.

Silver (2003) has argued that pervasiveness of decentralisation as a part of the process of globalisation in the developing world has come about because of the consensus within the international donor community that this was a preferred model for the nations struggling to provide basic services in the face of rapid urbanisation (p. 421). Since 1980s, these organisations have pushed decentralisation through direct technical assistance and policy reform with improved fiscal performance. Silver states that the common elements of donor driven decentralisation are: privatisation of urban service delivery, improved tax collection, utility and service pricing based upon willingness to pay, introduction of long range capital planning, enhanced local revenue generation and transfer of responsibilities from the central government to the local governments (p. 422).

The emergence of the 'new middle classes' in Asia has also led to increased political demands from them for greater participation and democratisation. This has implications in China, which has been under single party rule, to bring in elections at the local government level. Clammer (2003: 406), states that the enhanced private consumption goes hand in hand with expansion of the consumption of public goods. Political visibility of the middle classes has been pushing for more public goods to guarantee security of private consumption. For example, pushing for more roads so that the private luxury real estate consumption can be supported. Thus, private goods consumption confers identity and status, the collective resources are directed to class-interest ends. "The pursuit of private consumption both requires a social framework in which such 'freedoms' are protected and the allocation of public resources (such as education, health care or housing) that reduce the burden of provision on individual consumers while simultaneously creating the conditions of effective social reproduction for the classes benefiting most from access to these public resources" (Clammer 2003: 406-7). That is achieved through decentralised governance and the question of emergence of true civil society needs to be looked into critically.

Clammer (2003: 409), also states that the emergence of middle classes, particularly in the South-east Asian states, who have their class-interests at the centre, has led to them supporting soft authoritarian and neo-liberal economics and politics in Singapore, statist 'new order' politics in Indonesia (until they were partially delinked from Suharto's policies. Clammer (2003) also states that fundamentalist religious movements are the expressions of the middle class leadership (Robinson 1998: 61).

In India, the middle classes have begun to assert through increased legal activism. A case in point is the mindless demolitions of 'unauthorised' developments in Delhi—unauthorised as they are in violation of the Delhi Master Plan—which were ordered by the Supreme Court of India after a Public Interest Litigation (PIL)[34] filed by a Resident Welfare Association (RWA) of one middle class locality. A RWA is part of the civil society, through which the Delhi government is attempting to decentralise governance. The outcome has been, demolitions of all the commercial establishments in the residential zones. Slums, which are also clear violation of Delhi Master Plan, were also ordered to be demolished and have been demolished in Delhi (Chapter 11 by Batra and Mohra). Dupont and Ramanathan (2005) have shown that the Delhi High Court took an extremely legal view of slums on public lands as encroachments and asked that they be removed so that the public lands could be restored to owning agency for public facilities, such as landfilling sites, etc. In other words, the Delhi High Court asked for not tolerating any violation of the Master Plan, with regards to the slums. It also dismissed the plea of resettlement as merely encouraging dishonesty and violation, amounting rewarding the pickpockets (Dupont and Ramanathan, 2005), a brutal position that was stayed by the Supreme Court. In Mumbai, 'citizen's' organisations such as AGNI have filed petitions in Mumbai High Court for the demolition of slums and removal hawkers from the city pavements, all in the name of public interest. Such organisations work through RWAs, which have been formed in many cities for managing solid waste, as a part of decentralisation of governance in many cities (See Mahadevia and Wolfe 2008 which has cases of seven cities in India).

Several scholars have observed the emergence of middle classes in the 1990s, after the reforms. They have observed that these classes have ideologically justified the pursuit of individual wealth as never before (Corbridge and Harriss 2000: 121). The reforms have exposed and reinforced what Varma (1998: xii) described as "a crippling ideological barrenness [of the middle and elite classes] which threatens to convert India into a vastly unethical and insensitive aggregation of wants". Such social movements in India, discussed above are natural progression of such self-serving middle classes.

In China, decentralisation from the central government to local governments has a long history, starting from political decentralisation in the Maoist period for political mobilisation to administrative and fiscal decentralisation from 1980 onwards (Qian 2002). The excessive fiscal decentralisation and powers to local governments led to the decline in the national government revenues and decline in the possibility of equity transfers by the national government to the less developed regions. Tax reforms were carried out in 1994 and certain tax revenues were allocated to the national government to boost its revenues (Bahl 1999). At the same time, the decentralised structures created for political mobilisation, such as the Street Offices and Neighbourhood Committees are now used for decentralised governance (rather decentralised administration), such as solid waste collection, welfare functions, displacement management for the urban renewal projects, birth control, etc. (Choate 1998, Wu 2002, Mahadevia 2007b). But, these structures of decentralised administration in Chinese cities are falling apart in the new gated communities and private commercial housing, where the emerging middle classes and the elites live[35]. Further, in many such communities private property management companies have replaced the traditional Street Offices and Neighbourhood Communities.

On the other hand, there has been limited but successful decentralisation in Indonesia. Decentralisation in Indonesia came about as a result of the politics of post-Suharto regime, to do away with the control of the local decisions by the government employees who were on the payroll of the central government (Silver 2003). Suharto exercised control all over the country through the central government employees who were running the local governments. Instead, the local level employees were put on the payroll of the local governments, and for which fiscal devolution was enacted. Hence, central government transfer to the local governments increased and inter-regional inequality in fiscal transfers reduced. But, it also led to increase in overall inequalities, as the provinces that had better natural resources could generate higher revenues than the others. There has been therefore different experiences with decentralisation in different Asian countries. In India, it has led to elite capture of urban governance and policies, in China the middle classes and elites have withdrawn from governance, in Indonesia, it has to do undoing a corrupt regimes politics and in Singapore it has meant containing unsettling of dominant State.

New Social Movements/Resistance to Marginalisations

The New Social Movements (NSMs) have originated from those getting marginalised or displaced by the processes of globalisation. These have also unfolded in the urban areas. At the same time, globalisation has also brought in linkages of different groups resisting their displacements and marginalisation from the urban systems and their demands, that of the squatters, occupational groups and specific sectors of the disadvantages, now formally represented by the World Social Forum and Regional Social Forums such as Asian Social Forum, etc.

The NSMs, states Purcell (2002), have been marked more by optimistic projections than by in-depth analysis of the role that they have played in the urban politics (pp. 23). Purcell also asks important questions about the just how significant the NSMs have been and what role they are likely to play in the future. Nonetheless, now volume of literature exists on the NSMs, which states that these are extraordinarily diverse in nature; they are environmental protection movements, they are of the marginalised populations advancing new political claims and resisting the marginalisation processes that set in because of the global integration of the city. They arise among the immigrants, women, specific ethnic groups, working poor, and homeless to resist the ongoing social and spatial restructuring of the globally integrating cities. They are called new because they are political mobilisations around categories other than 'class' (Purcell 2002: 25). These movements are for getting greater access or maintaining existing levels of access to the local collective goods. Often, these are of the new middle classes, as discussed in a section earlier and in that case they are more for advancing the specific sectional interests in access to local collective goods.

This book has three chapters on the NSMs, but in the Indian context. The Chapter 18 on Mumbai by Mahadevia and Narayanan describe the resistance put up by the evicted slum dwellers in the city in 2004-05 and pushing for their claims on the urban space through playing within the Indian electoral democracy. The resisting slum dwellers' coalition with the support of the human and housing rights activists and certain well known individuals of the city bypassed the state government that had ordered the demolitions and approached the Congress Party leadership in Delhi (the Congress Party being the dominant partner in the state government) to put a stop to the demolitions and also ask for comprehensive resettlement plan. In the context of this demolitions of 2004-05 and also the past one, Bhide (Chapter 19) discusses various responses of the civil society to the question of slum demolitions in Mumbai, that have ranged from resistance by the communities affected, albeit in a fragmented manner, struggles moving along the divided lines as the communities themselves are divided and the NGO led rehabilitation efforts while the slum dwellers living under continuing threat of evictions. She then points out various challenges ahead for the civil society and concludes that the mapping of the contours of the struggle demonstrate that although there are hopes and there are also hurdles in the uphill task of gaining legitimacy for the poor in India cities.

Conflicts have increased in India around issues of globalisation manifesting in the cities. Mahadevia and Parashar (forthcoming 2008) had shown that conflicts have emerged in Pune city in India as a result of such a dual approach to urban development. All over India, there are protests by the farmers against land acquisition processes. These have converted into social movements. Nandigram near Kolkata saw firing by the police on the protestors against acquisition of their farm land. The state government, thereafter, decided to shift the project to another site where the land is barren[36]. The Maha Mumbai SEZ near Mumbai was initially planned on 13,000 hectares (Bunsha 2006), but protests against land acquisition led to the SEZ authorising agency giving permission to develop only 5,000 hectares[37].

Roychowdhury's article (Chapter 20), based on the example of Bangalore, on urban activism states that new forms of urban activism have replaced the traditional struggles of the less privileged, typically waged by trade unions and left-leaning parties because of the shrinking of formal sector workforce. Urban activism has shifted to a broad spectrum of rights of citizens. Adopting the theoretical framework of 'political society' of Chatterjee (2004), which are transitory political mobilisations of the underclass who function in the terrains of illegality in contrast to 'civil society', which represents associational forms within a legal framework but a depoliticised one, Roy Chowdhuri analyses the case of Bangalore Slum Federation, which came up for the land rights of the slum dwellers. She argues that beyond the immediate objective defined by a specific issue there is little to hold such associations together over a period of time or to extend their activities to diverse sources of deprivation that affect people living in slums.

The other more urgent question that she asks with regards to such formations is; defining a collective identity only in terms of this single objective, unanchored in a wider world view or vision, and perhaps most importantly, lacking any substantive links with the structures of political power (via parties, or other established political lobbies), in what sense can one speak of political society as a substantive agent of political action in the struggle for welfare? The article also argues that while activists are engaged at various levels, there is no one single developmental model that drives activism around the multiple issues of urban poverty. The article then gets more political and says that the discourse and activism around livelihood rights and projects on basic amenities such as housing, water, sanitation, and so on, are relatively non contentious issues. On the other hand, any engagement with questions of employment and income would involve activists in larger questions of the structure of the economy and the broad direction of economic policies. The urban activism has been focussing on the former than the latter.

Finally, the article states that given the multiplicity of the many communities as well as the diversity of the issues being addressed, activism is organised around small groups lobbying over specific issues, rather than collective questions. This positioning obviously rules out the question of larger mobilisations for political purposes, and sets its own limits to the impact that such activism can have over broader questions of economic policy.

The article by Benjamin *et al.* (Chapter 7) discusses the political process of inclusions observed within Bangalore and which is true for all cities in India. The article argues that for cities (or their particular parts) to be 'inclusive' of poor groups is hardly a normative issue. Instead it refers to forms of claim making where poor groups act as active agents in conditions of severe contest. In such contested terrain, their support and political access in local government turns out to be a critical factor. When this level of governance is eroded, poor groups run the severe risk, as seen in the case studies of Bangalore, of being ghettoised and moved out of political and economic terrain. Lastly, the article argues that central to the notion of inclusive or exclusive cities or neighbourhoods, is the form of political claim making, and how these are reinforced by economy and institutional structure. Second, the field is hardly neutral. Thus, if we see cities as being inclusive of the poor or particular groups within the poor, they may be closing up political and economic space to other and possibly elite groups. It is hardly surprising that elite groups seek to dilute that part of democracy that they find moving resources away from them.

Organisation of the Book

The articles in this book deal with all the issues discussed in this chapter except those related to urban governance. Large number of them are on the processes of exclusions. The State Policies supporting exclusions are strongly discussed in case of Indian cities. In Chinese cities, and Hanoi, both, inclusions and exclusions can be observed. Singapore's housing policy is inclusive. Thus, we get a mixed picture about the inclusions and exclusions in the Asian cities covered here. In Indian cities, public actions to overcome exclusions have been presented through 3 articles.

After this introduction chapter, there is a chapter on overall employment situation in Indian metropolitan cities. This is followed by chapter on vision for Mumbai city and segmentation of Ahmedabad City. Then there is a chapter on notion of inclusion and exclusion in context of urban India. Then follow the chapters inclusions or exclusions or both in Indian and Chinese cities and Singapore and Hanoi. The last part has three chapters on public actions in Indian Cities.

NOTES

1. Japan is the main foreign financial backer of the $90bn project to build a Delhi-Mumbai Industrial Corridor (DMIC). This corridor is being visualised like the Hi-Tech Corridor between Tokyo and Osaka. Initial work on the 1,483 km-long industrial thoroughfare, which will run through Uttar Pradesh, Delhi, Haryana, Rajasthan, Gujarat, Maharashtra and Madhya Pradesh, is set to begin in January, concluding in 2012. It will boost industrial parks and special economic zones as well as three new ports, six airports, new roads and a 4,000-megawatt power plant to serve it. Indian government is hoping that Japan would invest significant proportion of estimated $320bn required over next five years to improve infrastructure. Of this investments in metro rails, flyovers, etc. are of interest to Japan. (Source: http://news.bbc.co.uk/2/hi/business/6951396.stm of August 20, accessed on August 25, 2007).

2. Data in this entire section from hereon is from United Nations Conference on Trade and Development (2007).
3. Chandrababu Naidu gets defeated in 2004 May elections. His party's rout is complete, in the state assembly elections and national Parliament elections, because of his pre-occupation with IT economy, at the neglect of issues of survival of rest of the population. The rural areas in part of the state were reeling under severe drought. Farmers were in severe distress, that had led to spate of suicides by farmers. While, Naidu had changed the face of Hyderabad-Secunderabad twin Cities, with series of flyovers, wide roads, greens, beautification of important public places in the city, setting up of Cyberabad on the outskirts of Hyderabad, and linking the city with the Cyberabad with expressway, something that global citizens like and something that is appreciated globally as well as by national business class, the rest of the population of the state felt neglected. Naidu's rule is quintessential of the dichotomies expected in the cities at the forefront of globalisation in India.
4. US dollars. Footnote by the author.
5. Source: http://en.wikipedia.org/wiki/Megacity.
6. National Democratic Front, formed of main political party Bharatiya Janata Party (BJP) and its allies. Footnote of the author.
7. United Progressive Alliance, formed of main political party (Indian National) Congress, Parliamentary left parties and other allies.
8. Bracket by the author.
9. Speech titled 'To Implement Scientific Development Concept and Construct Harmonious Cities of Charm' by CHENG Andong, member of the Standing Committee of Chinese People's Political Consultative Committee (CPPCC), Deputy Director of the Economy Subcommittee of CPPCC and the Director of the 5th Council of China Research Society of Urban Development (CRSUD), at the closing ceremony of the 5th Representative Conference of CRSUD held at Hangzhou City, June 11-12, 2005 (China Research Society of Urban Development 2005: 25).
10. Speech by CHENG Andong; op. cit.
11. http://www.chinadaily.com.cn/bizchina/2007-07/14/content_5435040.htm.
12. *Dharna* means demonstration.
13. Indian Institute of Management, Bangalore.
14. Member of Legislative Assembly of the state, who is an elected representative. This MLA is depending on the agitating techies for pushing for a policy than taking it up with the government, which is an irony.
15. News item titled 'Bannerghatta Road drives IIM-B students to streets' in *Times of India*, October 6, 2004, from the website: http://www1.timesofindia.indiatimes.com/articleshow/873568.cms
16. Kumbhakarna is a mythical figure in Epic Ramayana, who is sleeping all the time and was sleeping when his brother's empire was conquered by Lord Rama, the protagonist of Ramayana.

17. News item titled 'IT majors to boycott Bangalore IT.Com' in Times of India, October 9, 2004, from website: http://www1.timesofindia.indiatimes.com/cms.dll/articleshow?msid=879298.
18. March 29, 2002, *People's Daily*. (Source: http://english.peopledaily.com.cn/200203/28/eng20020328_93035.shtml, accessed on September 27, 2007.
19. China Daily August 4, 2006 (Source: http://www.china.org.cn/english/olympic/176915.htm, accessed on September 27, 2007).
20. India e News, September 17, 2007. (Source: http://www.indiaenews.com/sports/20070917/70711.htm, accessed on September 27, 2007).
21. http://www.chinadaily.com.cn/bizchina/2007-07/09/content_5421621.htm.
22. http://www.chinadaily.com.cn/china/2007-07/04/content_910144.htm#.
23. http://www.chinadaily.com.cn/china/2007-07/04/content_910144.htm#.
24. National Urban Transport Policy, Draft, Ministry of Urban Development Government of India May, 2005, from the website.
25. Based on travels of Darshini Mahadevia in Chinese cities.
26. http://commerce.nic.in/PressRelease/pressrelease_detail.asp?id=1990.
27. As per the website of Ministry of External Affairs, developed by Federation of Industry and Commerce India (FICCI) and BISNET, 100 SEZs have been notified so far. (Source: http://www.indiainbusiness.nic.in/industry-infrastructure/infrastructure/sez.htm)
28. The Hindu, August 9, 2007, http://www.hindu.com/2007/08/09/stories/2007080962182100.htm.
29. http://www.teda.gov.cn/englishnew/local/overview.htm, accessed on May 9, 2007.
30. Navi Mumbai is a modern township spread over an area of around 350 sq. km (Source: http://www.navimumbaisez.com/overview.htm, accessed on September 10, 2007).
31. Source: http://www.navimumbaisez.com/overview.htm, accessed on September 10, 2007.
32. India e News, September 17, 2007. (Source: http://www.indiaenews.com/sports/20070917/70711.htm, accessed on September 27, 2007).
33. http://www.cohre.org/store/attachments/COHRE's%20Olympics%20Report.pdf, accessed on September 27, 2007.
34. PIL is an instrument that the citizens of India have been given by the Constitution of India to challenge the acts of omission and commission by any government body in India. This has been introduced in the Constitution to make the Indian State accountable to its citizens and has been very well utilised by human rights activists in the past to challenge gross violations of the fundamental rights of the Indian citizens by the Indian State itself. If the Indian State is not implementing its own laws, such as not implementing say Delhi Master Plan, which is a statutory document, then, any citizen can file a writ in a High Court or Supreme Court to bring to task the authority that is not implementing the law. That is how the Delhi Master non-implementation was brought under the purview of a PIL.

35. Based on Darshini Mahadevia's travel and discussions in Tianjin City in May-June 2007.
36. http://www.expressindia.com/latest-news/No-rollback-on-Singur-project-says-Buddhadeb/216889/.
37. http://www.hindu.com/2007/08/09/stories/2007080962182100.htm.

2[1]

METROPOLITAN EMPLOYMENT IN INDIA

DARSHINI MAHADEVIA

Introduction

Little is known about type and quality of employment in the metropolitan cities and changes in the same since the onset of economic reforms. It is also not know whether all metropolitan cities have responded uniformly to the forces of economic globalisation. Our guess is that each city would have a nested response to the new opportunities provided and constraints imposed by the forces of globalisation, depending on its history, geographic location and policy regimes at the state level. Inspite of the fact that each metro as well as now even non-metro cities are making attempts to attract 'high-tech' or 'new-economy' industries, most of the former in particular are mired in their former traditional economies that are providing gainful employment to a large section of the existing population, while absorbing the new economic activities.

This article presents the employment data of only eight metropolitan cities, seven of which, Mumbai, Kolkata, Delhi, Chennai, Bangalore, Hyderabad and Ahmedabad have been given the status of a megacity by the government of India. Pune is the eight city included in analysis in this article. Using the unit (individual) level data of the National Sample Survey (NSS), it is possible to identify few metropolitan cities[2]. For this article, we have used the data of the three NSS rounds, 1987-88 (43rd round), 1993-94 (50th round) and 1999-00 (55th round). This means, that our analysis spans a period of 13 years, or roughly one and a half decade. The NSS data do pose a problem of sample size in each city. But, since the analysis is confined to large metropolitan cities, the sample size is adequate for city level analysis. Even the NSS publications give metropolitan city-wise data on employment and unemployment. For all metros together, the sample size was 60,167 in 1999-00. Only in Pune, sample size was less than 1,000 individuals in one year (1999-00). In all cities, the sample comes to about 0.10 per cent of the total population. The article presents work participation rates, unemployment rates, nature of employment, sectoral classification of the workers and the occupational classification of the workers in the eight metro cities and all metros together.

Population Growth

In the decade of 1990s, when the overall urbanisation rate was 2.75 per cent per annum (p.a.), population growth rate in Kolkata, Chennai, Hyderabad and Mumbai was lower than 2.75 per cent p.a. (Table 2.1). Further, the population growth rate of Kolkata Urban Agglomeration (KUA) and Chennai Urban Agglomeration (CUA) was even less than the natural growth rate of population in India, indicating that there has been out-migration of population from the whole of KUA and CUA, not just their municipal corporation areas. Mumbai Urban Agglomeration's (MUA's) population growth rate declined to 2.65 per cent p.a. in the decade of 1990s, much lower than 4.34 per cent p.a. in the previous decade. Except the urban agglomeration areas of Hyderabad, Pune and Delhi, all other metropolitan agglomerations witnessed decline in annual population growth rate in the decade of 1990s as compared to the previous decade. This is in sink with overall deceleration of urbanisation rate in the country in the decade of 1990s as compared to 1980s.

Table 2.1: Population Data of Select Metropolises

Metropolis	*Population in million*			*Annual Growth rate (%)*		*Net in-migrants 1991-01 (lakhs)*	*Net in-migrants per day*	*Migrant percentage in population increase*
	1981	*1991*	*2001*	*1981-91*	*1991-01*			
1. Mumbai	8.24	12.60	16.37	4.34	2.65	8.59	235	22.80
2. Kolkata	9.19	11.02	13.22	1.83	1.84	-3.46	-05	-
3. Delhi	6.73	0.42	12.79	3.92	4.27	24.25	664	55.49
4. Chennai	4.29	5.42	6.42	2.37	1.71	-2.52	-69	-
5. Hyderabad	2.55	4.34	5.53	5.46	2.45	1.87	51	15.75
6. Bangalore	2.92	4.13	5.69	3.53	3.26	6.06	166	38.84
7. Ahmedabad	2.55	3.31	4.52	2.64	3.16	4.16	122	36.81
8. Pune	1.60	2.49	3.76	3.95	4.21	6.95	190	54.71
Total*	37.16	51.73	68.30	3.36	2.82	46.20	1266	27.88
All urban	159.50	217.20	285.00	3.14	2.75			

*Total of the eight metropolitan cities.

Note: The population data is of the Urban Agglomeration and not of the municipal corporation limits.

In the decade of 1990s, migration caused population increase in Mumbai was only 0.55 per cent (considering 2.1 per cent as a natural population growth). Thus, of the 37.7 lakh persons added to the urban agglomeration area of Mumbai (MUA) in the decade of 1990s, only 8.59 lakh, that is 235 persons per day or 22.80 per cent of the newly added population was of net in-migrants (Table 2.1). Delhi Urban Agglomeration (DUA) is the only one among the eight large metros that has continued to attract large number of net in-migrants; 24.25 lakhs (55.49%) being added to its population due to in-migration and 19.45 lakhs added due to natural population increase in the 1990s. Pune is another city that had more than half the newly added population comprising of net in-migrants. Thus, while KUA and CUA witnessed absolute population decline in their urban agglomeration areas, in the rest of the metros, the population increase in the urban agglomeration areas is largely because of natural increase in population, with the exception of Delhi and Pune. The problems of the metropolitan cities therefore cannot be attributed to the new migrants.

Work Participation Rates

In this section, Work Participation Rate (WPRs) data disaggregated by gender, for principal status workers[3] (Table 2.2) and principal + subsidiary status workers[4] (Table 2.3) and for three time points are analysed. The difference in values given in Table 2.2 and Table 2.3 indicate the data values for those solely engaged as subsidiary status workers (Table 2.4).

For the males, the WPRs, both for the principal status workers as well as for principal + subsidiary status workers, are higher in the metropolitan cities as compared to all urban areas. For the females, the situation is the opposite; all urban has higher WPRs than all metros. This pattern is observed for all the three NSS round data. Thus, work availability is higher in metropolitan cities than other urban areas for males and more work is available to females or more females want/have to work in other urban areas than the metros. This can be seen in Tables 2.2 and 2.3 when data on only principal status workers and principal + subsidiary status workers is observed. But, presence of subsidiary workers is higher in all urban than all metropolitan cities (Table 2.4), indicating higher incidence of under-employment in other urban areas than in the metro cities for both males and females. This indicates that work is available round the year in the metropolitan cities than in all urban areas. Also, it may be necessary that available work is taken up round the year for survival in metropolitan cities.

Table 2.2: Work Participation Rates, Principal Status Workers (%)

Metro Cities	Male			Female		
	1987-88	1993-94	1999-00	1987-88	1993-94	1999-00
1. Mumbai	52.23	56.12	55.02	10.71	13.75	11.07
2. Kolkata	56.13	61.17	61.03	12.59	12.07	10.70
3. Delhi	53.90	53.82	52.40	8.01	9.16	8.64
4. Chennai	53.24	57.06	55.92	13.29	16.31	18.08
5. Hyderabad	49.47	50.55	46.38	9.89	10.89	10.09
6. Bangalore	47.81	53.69	58.16	10.69	10.09	16.97
7. Ahmedabad	48.66	51.43	54.00	7.39	11.56	13.42
8. Pune	50.45	51.26	51.82	13.36	16.56	14.82
All Metro Cities	51.78	54.12	53.20	10.29	11.49	10.80
All Urban	49.56	51.34	51.28	11.80	12.13	11.71

Table 2.3: Work Participation Rates, Principal + Subsidiary Status Workers (%)

Metro Cities	Male			Female		
	1987-88	1993-94	1999-00	1987-88	1993-94	1999-00
1. Mumbai	52.67	56.49	55.75	12.91	16.13	12.83
2. Kolkata	57.83	62.92	62.01	14.58	14.25	12.50
3. Delhi	54.40	53.82	52.56	9.00	9.56	10.75
4. Chennai	53.58	57.14	56.03	15.20	16.73	18.77
5. Hyderabad	50.38	50.66	46.43	10.86	11.27	10.20
6. Bangalore	48.46	53.94	58.24	12.28	11.29	18.07
7. Ahmedabad	48.96	51.53	54.21	9.56	13.25	15.01
8. Pune	52.16	51.40	51.84	14.10	19.44	15.56
All Metro Cities	52.48	54.45	53.55	11.92	12.93	12.44
All Urban	50.65	52.10	51.76	15.22	15.47	13.91

The WPRs of males are higher and that of females are lower in metropolitan cities than in all urban areas possibly because of: (i) the work available is of the type where male workers get employed, (ii) work available have wage levels that could be sufficient enough for the survival of the whole family not necessitating women members' participation in the labour force; (iii) work available is at long distances, which is not congenial for women and hence, women may drop out of the labour force. Whether, work available is at high wages or at low wages would be explained through data obtained from occupational and industrial classification discussed later in the paper.

In all urban areas and also in the metropolitan cities, the WPRs have increased in 1993-94 as compared to 1987-88, but then declined again in 1999-00, for principal status as well as principal + subsidiary status workers, for the males as well as the females. Thus, on the whole, in the urban areas in general and also in all the metropolitan cities together, work availability has increased in the initial period of reforms. But then, towards the end of the decade of 1990s, marginal decrease in work availability can be observed. This trend may have to do with emergence of 'jobless growth' in the later half of the decade of 1990s. However, as compared to 1987-88, in 1999-2000, the WPRs for male and female and as principal status workers and principal + subsidiary status workers are higher, indicating increase in availability of work in the urban areas as well as metro cities.

Once again, the work availability has increased in the present decade. The 2004-05 NSS (61st round) data indicates that principal + subsidiary status WPR for males have increased to 56.6 per cent in 2004-05 from 53.5 per cent in 1999-00 and for the females have increased to 14.6 per cent from 12.4 per cent in the same period in the metros. For all urban areas too, the figures are 54.9 per cent (2004-05) and 51.8 (1999-00) for the males and 16.6 per cent (2004-05) and 13.9 per cent (1999-00) for the females (Mahadevia and Sarkar forthcoming, 2008).

There is one exception to the above mentioned trend. In case of females, the WPRs by principal status as well as principal + subsidiary status are marginally lower in 1999-00 (11.7% and 13.9% respectively) as compared to 1987-88 (11.8% and 15.2% respectively) for all urban areas. That means that work availability for women in the urban areas other than metros in 1999-00 had deteriorated even below the situation in 1987-88, which was a bad drought year in India. Or is it because of the drought, more females had come out to work in the labour force?

There is significant decline in the proportion of those employed as just subsidiary workers in both metropolitan cities and all urban areas together. Further, there is higher proportion of those employed in just subsidiary capacity in all urban areas than in metropolitan cities. In 1999-00, just 0.35 per cent of male workers were employed as only subsidiary workers in the metropolitan cities whereas this figure for all urban was 0.48 per cent (Table 2.4). Among female workers, 1.64 per cent in the metropolitan cities and 2.20 per cent in all urban areas were employed as sole subsidiary status workers. Higher WPR among females in non-metros is explained partly by availability of part time work.

Over time, among the male workers, proportion of subsidiary status workers has declined in the metropolitan cities if 1999-00 is compared with 1987-88 year. But, if 1999-00 is compared with 1993-94, then, we find that there is slight increase in proportion of males employed as only subsidiary workers, from 0.33 per cent to 0.35 per cent. A matter of concern here is that there is a simultaneous decline in WPR as principal + subsidiary status workers among males, indicating noticeable decline in principal status workers among males in the second half of the decade of 1990s in the metropolitan cities. This means, that for the males, there is decline in availability of work in the end of the decade of 1990s, leading to slight increase in subsidiary status workers. In all urban areas, among the male workers, the situation is different. The decline in principal + subsidiary status WPR in 1999-00 as compared to 1993-94 is because of decline in subsidiary status workers in 1999-00 to 0.48 per cent as compared to 0.76 per cent in 1993-94. Thus, in the decade of 1990s, there is decline in male WPRs towards the end of the decade because of decline in principal workers (accompanied by slight increase in subsidiary workers) in the metropolitan cities and decline in subsidiary workers in all urban areas.

Table 2.4: Work Participation Rates, Only Subsidiary Status Workers (%)

Metro Cities	*Male*			*Female*		
	1987-88	*1993-94*	*1999-00*	*1987-88*	*1993-94*	*1999-00*
1. Mumbai	0.44	0.37	0.73	2.20	2.38	1.76
2. Kolkata	1.71	1.75	0.98	1.99	2.18	1.80
3. Delhi	0.50	0.00	0.16	0.99	0.39	2.11
4. Chennai	0.33	0.08	0.11	1.91	0.42	0.69
5. Hyderabad	0.91	0.11	0.05	0.97	0.38	0.11
6. Bangalore	0.65	0.25	0.08	1.59	1.20	1.10
7. Ahmedabad	0.30	0.10	0.21	2.17	1.69	1.59
8. Pune	1.71	0.14	0.02	0.73	2.89	0.74
All Metro Cities	0.70	0.33	0.35	1.64	1.44	1.64
All Urban	1.09	0.76	0.48	3.42	3.35	2.20

Each of the individual metro cities has very different situation with regards to the WPRs. First we would look at the male WPRs. In the status as principal workers, in 1987-88, the four large metropolitan cities, Mumbai, Kolkata, Chennai and Delhi had higher WPRs than the average for all metropolitan cities. In 1993-94, Delhi drops out of this list and in 1999-00 Bangalore and Ahmedabad enter the list. The highest WPR for the males has been in Kolkata for all three NSS years; 56.13 per cent, 61.17 per cent and 61.03 per cent in 1987-88, 1993-94 and 1999-00 respectively (Table 2.2). In the second position have been Delhi (53.90%) in 1987-88, Chennai (57.06%) in 1993-94 and Bangalore (58.16%) in 1999-00, all for three different reasons with different types of employment. Bangalore in 1987-88 and Hyderabad in 1993-94 and 1999-00 had the lowest WPR for the males as principal status workers.

For principal + subsidiary status workers, Kolkata, Delhi and Chennai in 1987-88, Kolkata, Chennai and Mumbai in 1993-94 and Kolkata,

Bangalore, Chennai, Mumbai and Ahmedabad in 1999-00 had higher WPRs than the average metropolitan WPRs.

Chennai has high WPR as principal + subsidiary status workers in all the three years, mainly because of high principal status workers, indicating round-the-year high work availability in the city. Same is the case with Bangalore and Ahmedabad which have higher WPRs as compared to all metro average in 1999-00.

For female workers, WPRs for principal status workers and principal + subsidiary status workers is not high only in large metros, as was the case for the male workers. In principal status, metropolitan cities that have high WPRs, higher than the average are: Pune, Chennai and Kolkata in 1987-88, the same three cities and Mumbai and Ahmedabad in 1993-94 and Chennai, Pune, Bangalore and Ahmedabad in 1999-00. There is no obvious pattern. In the principal + subsidiary status WPRs, in 1987-88, two other metropolises had higher than all metro average WPR; Mumbai and Bangalore. This means that these two cities also had high proportion of subsidiary workers among women. Mumbai certainly had higher than all metro average percentage of subsidiary workers from 1993-94 onwards. And thus, the city also has higher WPR in principal + subsidiary status workers than metro average.

A point to note is that in Pune, female WPRs as principal status workers and principal + subsidiary status workers have been quite high in all the three years, and also higher than all metro average. That has not been the case with male WPRs, of both the statuses in the city. In Ahmedabad, Bangalore and Chennai, there is consistent increase in female WPRs in principal status. In Bangalore, the percentage of subsidiary female workers is less than all metro average. In Ahmedabad, there is consistent decline in percentage of subsidiary workers among females. In Chennai, there is significant drop in subsidiary status workers in 1993-94 from 1987-88 level and then just a small increase in 1999-00.

Pune has the highest female WPR in 1987-88 and 1993-94 and Chennai in 1999-00 among principal status workers and Chennai, Pune and Chennai registered highest female WPR in principal + subsidiary status workers, in 1987-88, 1993-94 and 1999-00 respectively. Chennai is one of the large four metropolises whereas Pune is among the second rung of metropolises in India. It seems that the female WPRs have to do more with also male wage levels and cultural factors as also with the local economy. Female participation in the labour market is a result as much of availability of employment (pull factors) as with the compulsion of the household to send women member (s) to the labour market (push factors) and also with working and living conditions in the city. Mahadevia (2002a) has argued, based on 1987-88 and 1993-94 NSS data that female members were pushed to take up round-the-year employment in Ahmedabad city because of closure of textile mills and lack of any other employment opportunities for male members.

In Hyderabad, in the three years, male and female WPRs, as principal status and principal + subsidiary status workers, are less than all metro average. Percentage of subsidiary status workers among male and female has declined in the city over time. It is likely that the wages of principal status workers are adequate to support the family, which not necessitating females to work. This is a situation of formal employment and regular work availability in the city. During 1987-88 to 1999-00 period, percentage of principal status workers has declined among males and marginally increased among females, indicating that such formal jobs are declining somewhat.

In Ahmedabad, there has been a consistent increase in WPRs as principal status workers and also as principal + subsidiary status workers over the period, for males as well as females. Further, among the females, there is consistent decline in the percentage of subsidiary workers, indicating that more and more women are coming out in the labour force for round-the-year employment. In 1999-00, the female WPR was 15.01 per cent (principal + subsidiary status). Mahadevia (2002a) has argued that it is because of low wage employment for the men. Thus, women are coming out in the labour force in this city because of push factors. At the same time, work is available to women for the whole of the year in the city.

Bangalore is a city with 10 percentage point increase in male WPR in principal + subsidiary status and more than 10 percentage point increase in male WPR in principal workers status in the whole period. There is about 6 percentage point increase in female WPR in the principal status and principal + subsidiary status. In 1999-00, female WPR was 18.07 per cent (principal + subsidiary status), which is about 6 percentage point higher than all metro average. There is all round increase in work availability in Bangalore. This is a sign of improving employment situation in the city.

Mumbai is a story of declining industrial city and emergence of a service economy. The male WPRs have been higher than all metro average in nearly all the years, in principal status and principal + subsidiary status workers. But, female WPRs in principal status have been lower than all metro average. Male WPRs in principal status and principal + subsidiary status, have increased over the whole period, from 1987-88 to 1999-00, but with a decline in the same in 1999-00 as compared to 1993-94. Female WPR in principal status has similar behaviour. In the principal + subsidiary status, WPR has not registered any change in the whole period, but a slight increase in 1993-94 and then sliding back to 1987-88 figure in 1999-00. Further, in 1987-88 and 1993-94, there was not much engagement of male workers as subsidiary status workers, the figures being 0.44 per cent and 0.37 per cent respectively (Table 2.4). Our guess is that it was not necessary to do so given that a large proportion were formally employed in industries, mainly textile mills. In 1999-00 there is slight increase of males employed as just subsidiary status workers to 0.73 per cent, which is higher than all metros average. While that happened, the overall WPR declined as compared to 1993-94. This is a situation of emerging distress in employment sector. Overall increase in WPRs is also indicating that more males are requiring to work, and, at the same time more work is also available. This work is in manual labour type, as we would see later.

If men have gone into manual labour jobs then, it would be jobs at low incomes, necessitating women to come out and work. Further, given that the cost of living in Mumbai is high, it is quite unlikely that women are not willing to work. It is possible that women may not be taking up work due to long distance required to commute to place of work. It is also unlikely that women are not finding work here. But, it is possible that low skilled jobs where women tend to get into are taken up by recent single male migrants to the city. Also, the per cent women engaged in subsidiary capacity only is higher than all metro average in all the three years. The women may be taking up work whenever that is available near their place of residence and are not going for round the year available jobs if they need to commute for long distances.

Pune, as mentioned earlier, is a peculiar city with relatively high female WPR, in principal status and principal + subsidiary status. In 1993-94, the female WPR (principal + subsidiary status) had gone up to as high as 19.44 per cent, more than 7 percentage point higher than all metro average. In 1999-00, the figure came down to 15.56 per cent, which was just 3 percentage point higher than all metro average for the same. Further, in all the three years, the male WPRs have been lower than all metro average. There is decline in male WPR (principal + subsidiary status) over the period from 52.16 per cent in 1987-88 to 51.84 per cent in 1999-00, whereas there is slight increase in the same for females from 14.10 per cent in 1987-88 to 15.56 per cent in 1999-00. Even there is not much subsidiary status work resorted to, either due to lack of availability of such work or non-requirement for additional work due to possible sufficient incomes from the main income earner of the family. The latter is more likely.

Chennai has consistently high WPRs for males and females, in principal status and principal + subsidiary status. The per cent population solely engaged as subsidiary workers is quite low for both males and females, with an exception of year 1987-88 that had somewhat high subsidiary status workers among females. Since then, females have been working mainly as principal workers. In 1999-00, female WPR (principal + subsidiary status) was the highest in this city.

Kolkata has observed highest male WPR in all the three years and higher than all metro average WPR for the females in two years except 1999-00. This is true for principal workers and principal + subsidiary workers. While there is increase in male WPRs in Kolkata over the period, there is decrease in female WPRs over the period. The male WPR increased from 57.83 per cent in 1987-88 to 62.01 per cent in 1999-00 (among principal + subsidiary status workers) and female WPR declined from 14.58 per cent to 12.50 per cent. Also, the city has the highest principal + subsidiary status WPRs in the three NSS rounds, the WPRs being 57.83 per cent, 62.92 per cent and 62.01 per cent among all the metro cities (Table 2.3). This means that Kolkata not only has high round-the-year availability of work but also has high subsidiary work availability. Like Mumbai, there is high proportion of subsidiary workers (more than 10% of the total workers) among females. Even among males, there is higher than all metro average figures for subsidiary workers. But, since the overall (principal + subsidiary status) WPR is high, the proportion of subsidiary workers to the total workers is low.

The population growth rate of Kolkata has stagnated, and there has been out-migration from the city in the last two decades. It is likely that the employment quality is not so good in the city and working at low wages entails more family members to come out in the labour force. This could also cause high WPRs among females, which however is not the case as we would see later. On the contrary, there is higher incidence of subsidiary workers among females than all India average indicating lack of availability of work for them as well. Presence of higher than average subsidiary status workers among males as well as females indicates that city would do well to generate more employment.

Last metropolis, Delhi, has one of the lowest female WPRs in principal status workers and principal + subsidiary status workers among all the metros. The male WPRs are also not higher than all metro average for principal status as well as principal + subsidiary status workers, except for the year 1987-88. Further, the male WPRs have declined over time. The principal + subsidiary status WPR declined from 54.40 per cent in 1987-88 to 52.56 per cent in 1999-00. The female WPRs in the principal + subsidiary status have increased from 9.00 per cent in 1987-88 to 10.75 per cent in 1999-00, only a marginal increase. A point to note is that the proportion of subsidiary workers among females has increased in 1999-00, 2.11 per cent as compared to just 0.39 per cent in 1993-94. Thus, female WPR increase (principal + subsidiary status) in 1999-00 is because of increase in subsidiary status workers among them. Once again, either economic pressures have pushed out more women to work, but, they are working on part time basis or women are not working round the years as they are not finding jobs near their place of residence. With regards to women, the situation is not very clear. But, with regards to men, it is likely that low income population requiring high labour force participation among males and females is not coming to Delhi because of many restrictive policies in the city. If the low income groups were to come to the city, they would find jobs in low paid, Casual Labour sectors. It would be seen later that in Delhi, proportion of Casual Labour has been low and has declined over time.

Unemployment Rates

We have only looked at usual status Unemployment (UE) rates for principal and subsidiary workers together. First of all, all metros unemployment rates for males and females for all the years, except for males in 1993-94, have been higher than all urban unemployment rates. Thus, for males, unemployment rates in 1987-88, 1993-94 and 1999-00 have been 6.37 per cent, 3.78 per cent and 4.85 per cent respectively for the all metros whereas 5.16 per cent, 4.05 per cent and 4.51 per cent respectively for all urban together. For the females, these rates have been 8.67 per cent, 8.22 per cent and 6.70 per cent respectively for all metros and 5.93 per cent, 6.24 per cent and 5.63 per cent respectively for all urban (Table 2.5).

For males, WPRs and unemployment rates both are higher in metropolitan cities as compared to other urban areas. This could be because of larger proportion of population desiring work and getting work in the metropolitan cities as compared to other urban areas. This also indicates that there is higher availability of work in metropolitan cities than in other urban areas. It also means that large number of males of the working age are willing to remain unemployed till right type of jobs are available. In non metros, the situation is just revere; lesser proportion of males are interested to work and a higher proportion of them find work, leading to low unemployment rates. For the females, it is high unemployment rates in metros as compared to other urban areas but, low WPRs in the metros as compared to the other urban areas. If WPRs and unemployment rates are added together, then, in case of females, the figure is higher in all urban as compared to all metros. That means that higher percentage of women are out in the labour force in other urban areas than in the metros. Thus, lesser women are desiring work in the metropolitan cities due to relative economic prosperity of the household, but a significant proportion of them are not finding work or are unable to access work, probably due to accessibility issues. In other urban areas, higher proportion of women (as compared to all metros) are desiring work and a large proportion of them are able to find work or access work.

Table 2.5: Usual Status Unemployment Rates, Principal + Subsidiary Status Workers (%)

Metro Cities	Male			Female		
	1987-88	*1993-94*	*1999-00*	*1987-88*	*1993-94*	*1999-00*
1. Mumbai	8.30	5.32	7.16	9.83	7.18	12.22
2. Kolkata	6.59	5.00	4.95	11.91	14.57	8.87
3. Delhi	3.98	0.87	2.54	8.80	6.20	3.65
4. Chennai	9.21	5.44	4.97	10.68	11.24	4.40
5. Hyderabad	4.46	1.97	6.31	5.88	0.62	3.78
6. Bangalore	6.05	3.75	2.65	4.56	13.18	7.38
7. Ahmedabad	7.32	4.52	1.07	1.62	13.79	0.77
8. Pune	4.41	4.76	2.53	8.16	5.89	3.27
All Metro Cities	6.37	3.78	4.85	8.67	8.22	6.70
All Urban	5.16	4.05	4.51	5.93	6.24	5.63

In the whole period, in all metropolitan cities together, the usual status unemployment rates have decreased whereas the WPRs have increased. Among males however, in 1993-94, unemployment rate had gone down significantly as compared to 1987-88, and then increased in 1999-00. This coincided with significant increase in WPR in 1993-94 and a slight decline in the same in 1999-00. Among the females, there has been consistent decline in unemployment rates from 8.67 per cent in 1987-88 to 8.22 per cent in 1993-94 to 6.70 per cent in 1999-00. With regards to female WPRs over time, there was a significant increase in 1993-94 as compared to 1987-88 but a marginal decline in 1999-00 as compared to 1993-94. Thus, in the period of economic reforms, there is increased availability of work for women in the metropolitan cities as their unemployment rates have gone down. But, in the first half large number of women came out in the labour force and large number of them got work as compared to 1987-88, but then towards the end of the decade, slightly lesser number came out in the labour force and most of them got the jobs. For the men, however, around the same proportion of them have come out in the labour force in the two periods, but, if the work availability is high then the unemployment rates are low and if the work availability is low, the unemployment rates are high. For other urban areas as well, same is the case with regards to males. But, in other urban areas, for females, lesser number of them have been interested to work towards the end of the decade of 1990s, but larger percentage of them are getting work.

The Figure 2.1 can be interpreted as follows: (i) Blank is best with those coming out in the labour force finding work, probably at high incomes. Hence, the WPRs are also low as not many are coming out in the labour force. It is possible that cost of living in these cities is low hence labour force participation required is low. That can be possible given that the cities in this block are second tier of metropolises except Delhi, whereas Delhi has highly subsidised services and hence low cost of living. (ii) Light grey is situation of high WPR because of high availability of work, but, also because of some having low wages requiring higher work participation. (iii) Medium grey is a situation of lack of availability of work leading to low WPRs. This is a situation of emerging stress in the employment sector. (iv) Dark grey is a situation of highly stressed employment sector where WPRs are high either because of low wages, that is highly informalised or tertiarised sector economy or high cost of living.

Figure 2.1: WPR vs Unemployment, Males and Females

		Males		*Females*	
		High UE	*Low UE*	*High UE*	*Low UE*
1987-88	High WPR	Chennai Kolkata	Delhi	Mumbai Chennai Kolkata	Bangalore Pune
	Low WPR	Ahmedabad Mumbai	Hyderabad Bangalore Pune	Delhi	Hyderabad Ahmedabad
1993-94	High WPR	Chennai Kolkata Mumbai		Ahmedabad Chennai Kolkata	Mumbai Pune
	Low WPR	Ahmedabad Pune	Hyderabad Bangalore Delhi	Bangalore	Hyderabad Delhi
1999-00	High WPR	Mumbai Chennai Kolkata	Ahmedabad Bangalore	Bangalore Mumbai	Ahmedabad Pune Chennai
	Low WPR	Hyderabad	Pune Delhi	Kolkata	Hyderabad Delhi

It is also possible because of high proportion of young population in the city, mainly of single male migrants, all either employed or seeking work. Three of the four large metros are in this category, Kolkata and Chennai in all the three NSS rounds and Mumbai from 1993-94 onwards suggest that high WPR and high unemployment rates are cause of demographic composition of population as also highly stressed employment sector.

Chennai and Kolkata are consistently in category (iv) type of situation with high WPRs and high unemployment rates for males. This is a situation of low wages for many and continuously high unemployment rates. Mumbai enters this category from 1993-94 onwards for males. While the situation remains the same for Chennai and Kolkata with regards to male employment-unemployment, it worsens in Mumbai from 1993-94 onwards. Among females, Chennai and Kolkata remain as high WPR and high unemployment cities till 1993-94. In 1999-00, unemployment reduces and WPR has increased among women in Chennai, that is work availability has improved for women. In Kolkata in the same year, while the work continues to remain of low wage type, the women are getting out of the labour force with reduced WPR and reduced unemployment rates. But, compared to all metros, unemployment rates continue to remain high for the females in Kolkata.

In category (i) type of employment situation have been Hyderabad and Bangalore in 1987-88 and 1993-94 for the males. In 1999-00, employment situation in Hyderabad worsens with increase in unemployment rate and reduction in WPR. It is possible that formally employed have lost employment among the males. In Bangalore, the WPR has increased significantly in 1999-00 as compared to 1993-94, accompanied by decline in unemployment rates. This could be interpreted as positive that more work is now available in the city. It can also be interpreted as more males are now required to work in the city. It is most likely to be the former case, with increase in single male migration to the city, all of whom finding work leading to high WPRs. In Hyderabad, in 1999-00, females remain in the category of low WPR and low unemployment rate, indicating that the loss of employment among males has not yet pushed women to come out in the labour force in the city and they remain in category (i) type of employment situation.

Bangalore remains in the lower shades of grey in 1987-88 and 1993-94 with respect to employment situation of women; in category (ii) type of employment situation in 1987-88 (high WPR and low unemployment rate) and in category (iii) type of employment situation in

1993-94 (low WPR and high unemployment rate). In 1999-00, there is a sudden increase in WPR as well as unemployment rate among females. It is also sudden increase in Casual Labour and increase in manufacturing sector employment among women in the city in 1999-00, as it would be seen later. Meaning, that women's presence in the labour force has increased because some of the male workers are getting into low wage jobs situation and women need to come out and work to supplement incomes. Some may argue that because employment situation has improved so much in the city that even women are pulled to the labour market. But, unemployment rates being high, not all of them are getting work.

Ahmedabad has been in the category of high unemployment and low WPR for the males till 1993-94, that is the city has been in the category (iii) type of employment situation for males. In 1999-00, there is slight improvement with low unemployment and high WPR, that is, shift to category (ii) type of employment. Females move from low unemployment and low WPR situation, indicating adequacy of male employment and wages to support the family to high WPR and high unemployment type of situation, where women have been forced to come out in the labour market to look for work and many more are willing to participate to tide over low incomes of the households as a consequence of decline in quality of employment for males. In 1999-00, when situation for males improve a bit, female move to a situation of high WPR and low unemployment rate. Some women may have withdrawn from the labour market or all those who had entered in 1993-94 found work. But, it is a situation of some improvement in the labour market for men and women both in 1999-00. But, even then, women have moved to Self Employment category in 1999-00, that is all those who entered the labour market in 1993-94 could find Self Employment type of work by 1999-00, as we would see later. Men have now found work in 1999-00, which is in the Casual Labour type of jobs, as we would see later. Hence, it is a situation of low wages in the economy for both males and females.

In Mumbai, in 1987-88, the situation is of high unemployment and low WPR for the males. This is a situation of recent loss of jobs. By 1993-94, the WPRs increase but unemployment rate also increases for men indicating that at low wages of the men, many more are willing to join the labour force. Since, migration rate post 1991 has not been so high, it would not be because of single male migrants having high WPR coming into the city. It is therefore a situation of low wage employment for more making it necessary for more male members of the family to join the labour force. But, such an employment is available regularly, round the year leading to decline in subsidiary workers on one hand and increase in regularly employed on the other. In 1999-00, the situation worsens a bit with increase in subsidiary workers at high WPRs and high unemployment rates. For women in the city, the employment situation was slightly better in 1993-94 with low unemployment rate and high WPR than 1987-88. In 1999-00, women move to high unemployment and high WPR category, but the WPR remaining the same as in 1987-88. There is also an increase in SE like the situation of women in Ahmedabad, which we would see later.

Nature of Employment

For all the urban areas together, in 1999-00, about two in every five male workers were engaged as regular workers (Table 2.6), whereas in all metropolitan cities together, this number was slightly more than 50 per cent. The metropolitan cities therefore offer more RE to male workers than other urban centres. If more work was available, more males would be looking for work and hence unemployment rates are also higher in the metropolitan cities. At the first glance, robustness of the metropolitan economy as compared to non-metropolitan economies can be seen. However, from 1987-88 to 1999-00, there has been a decline in proportion of male workers engaged as regular workers from 55.27 per cent to 51.21 per cent, a decline by 4 percentage points. In 2004-05, however, the decline of Regular Employment among males has halted and there is marginal increase in the same to 51.6 per cent among the metro cities (Mahadevia and Sarkar forthcoming, 2008).

Even in all urban, there is a decline in the proportion of regularly employed workers among males, but, the decline is by only 2 percentage points from 43.7 per cent to 41.7 per cent from 1987-88 to 1999-00. In 2004-05, there is slight decline again in proportion of RE among all urban males, the proportion reaching 40.6 per cent (Mahadevia and Sarkar forthcoming, 2008). In all urban areas, therefore though male WPRs have increased in 2004-05, the new work available is not regular type but in self employed category (44.8% in 2004-05 as compared to 41.4 per cent (Table 2.6).

Proportion of male workers employed as CL has been quite less in all urban areas as well as metropolitan cities; one in every six male workers in all urban and one in every eight male workers in all metropolitan cities are employed as CL. However, there is an increase in proportion of CL among males by two percentage points from 1987-88 to 1999-00, in both all urban areas and also all metros. In all urban areas, for the males, two percentage point decrease in RE has resulted in increase in CL by same percentage points. In metropolitan cities, there is two percentage point increase in CL and two percentage point increase in SE due to four percentage point decrease in RE. While all CL in the urban areas is likely to be low wage kind, all SE is not of the same kind. SE can also be in higher professional services. In 1999-00, 36.5 per cent male workers in all metros cities and 41.4 per cent male workers in all urban were working as self employed.

Table 2.6: Nature of Employment, Principal + Subsidiary Workers (%)

Metro Cities	*Self Employed (SE)*			*Regular Employed (RE)*			*Casual Labour (CL)*		
	1987-88	*1993-94*	*1999-00*	*1987-88*	*1993-94*	*1999-00*	*1987-88*	*1993-94*	*1999-00*
Male									
1. Mumbai	32.46	32.63	28.47	62.83	65.35	67.79	4.71	2.02	3.74
2. Kolkata	36.69	33.78	43.04	54.18	54.27	43.36	9.13	11.95	13.59
3. Delhi	38.33	44.09	43.61	58.04	45.15	53.79	3.63	10.76	2.60
4. Chennai	30.13	28.66	29.73	49.82	46.74	48.68	20.06	24.60	21.59
5. Hyderabad	36.41	31.37	35.03	51.11	55.44	50.17	12.48	13.19	14.80
6. Bangalore	28.63	31.71	26.92	52.42	53.37	58.32	18.95	14.92	14.76
7. Ahmedabad	34.69	35.23	36.92	44.91	51.24	32.95	20.40	13.53	30.13
8. Pune	26.14	33.33	44.77	58.32	61.25	47.95	15.54	5.41	7.27
All Metro Cities	34.07	35.31	36.51	55.27	53.92	51.21	10.66	10.77	12.28
All Urban	41.64	41.62	41.43	43.65	42.16	41.67	14.71	16.22	16.90
Female									
1. Mumbai	30.91	27.61	29.46	62.63	69.10	65.32	6.46	3.29	5.21
2. Kolkata	31.67	28.27	29.31	63.72	62.87	55.89	4.60	8.86	14.80
3. Delhi	30.37	24.90	31.77	66.70	57.21	64.20	2.93	17.89	4.03
4. Chennai	26.03	12.63	26.91	56.14	64.24	61.87	17.83	23.13	11.23
5. Hyderabad	38.08	21.39	21.60	34.77	47.82	39.78	27.14	30.79	38.62
6. Bangalore	31.46	29.31	25.93	32.21	62.44	56.40	36.33	8.25	17.67
7. Ahmedabad	38.18	43.58	64.73	29.50	27.30	19.82	32.32	29.12	15.45
8. Pune	20.14	27.09	44.89	75.65	58.76	48.82	4.21	14.16	6.29
All Metro Cities	31.62	28.25	35.67	55.02	56.60	51.61	13.36	15.15	12.72
All Urban	47.12	44.76	45.16	27.49	29.15	33.07	25.39	26.09	21.77

The situation in 2004-05 is different for all urban as well as metro cities as compared to the trend observed during the 1990s; in all urban the proportion of CL has declined to 14.6 per cent and in all metros has declined to 9.4 per cent (Mahadevia and Sarkar forthcoming, 2008). Since the RE male workers has not increased much in the metro cities and declined in all urban, the decline in casual proportion has been balanced by increase in SE among male workers in both the metro cities and all urban. The proportion of SE in all metros has increased to 39.0 per cent in 2004-05 (Mahadevia and Sarkar forthcoming, 2008) from 36.5 per cent in 1999-00 (Table 2.6) and in all urban to 44.8 per cent (Mahadevia and Sarkar forthcoming, 2008) from 41.4 per cent in the same period.

Among the females, contrary to general understanding, more than 50 per cent are employed as regular workers and just 35.7 per cent were working as self employed in the metro cities. There is not much difference in the nature of employment of males and females in the metropolitan cities. In 1999-00, 35.67 per cent among females and 36.51 per cent among males were working as self employed; 51.61 per cent among females and 51.21 per cent among males were regularly employed; and 12.72 per cent among the females and 12.28 per cent among the males were working as CL. This is not the case with all the urban areas. There is much higher proportion of CL employment among females (21.8%) as compared to males in all urban areas and much higher casual employment among females in all urban areas as compared to metropolitan cities. Thus, females in the non-metros get CL type of employment.

Like males, RE among the females has declined in all metros from 55 per cent in 1987-88 to 51.6 per cent in 1999-00. Like males, there is some increase in RE in the females also in 2004-05 to 52.5 per cent (Mahadevia and Sarkar forthcoming 2008) in the metros. But in all urban, RE among the females has increased from 27.5 per cent in 1987-88 to 33.1 per cent in 1999-00 (Table 2.6), which has further increased to 35.6 per cent in 2004-05 (Mahadevia and Sarkar forthcoming 2008). This has not been the case with regards to males in all urban. Clearly more RE is getting generated for the females in urban centres other than the metros.

Like in case of males, SE among females has also increased in the metros; from 31.6 per cent in 1987-88 to 35.7 per cent in 1999-00 (Table 2.6) to 38.5 per cent in 2004-05 (Mahadevia and Sarkar forthcoming 2008). In all urban areas, during the period from late 1980s to late 1990s, SE among females had declined from 47.1 per cent in 1987-88 to 45.2 per cent in 1999-00. In the present decade, once again SE has increased in all urban among them to 47.7 per cent (Mahadevia and Sarkar forthcoming 2008). This indicates that CL among the females in all metros as well as all urban has significantly reduced; from 12.4 per cent in 1999-00 (Table 2.6) to 9.0 per cent in 2004-05 (Mahadevia and Sarkar forthcoming 2008) in all metros and from 17.9 per cent (Table 2.6) to 16.7 per cent (Mahadevia and Sarkar forthcoming 2008) in all urban during the same period.

In short, in all metros, among the males, the trend of decline in RE of the 1990s has halted in the recent decade, along with increase in SE and decline in CL among them. Among the females in the metros, the same trend can be observed. But, in all urban, among the males, the decline in RE of the 1990s continues in the present decade accompanied by significant increase in SE and decline in CL. Among the females in all urban, the RE increase of the 1990s continues in the present decade and it is only among this group that the RE has continued to improve over the last one and a half decade. This has resulted in significant decline in CL among females in all urban, accompanied by first decline and then increase in SE among them.

Further, in all urban areas, higher proportion of workers were employed as CL as compared to metropolitan cities, whereas in metropolitan cities, per cent SE and per cent RE were higher than the same in all urban areas. It has been shown elsewhere (Dubey and Mahadevia, 2001; Dubey and Gangopadhyay, 1998; Dubey *et al.*, 2000) that CL is associated with high poverty. Hence, extent of poverty in other urban areas is higher than in metropolitan cities. A study by Mahadevia and Sarkar (forthcoming 2008) has also shown that with the increase in size of urban settlement, incidence of poverty (measured by head count ratio) decreases.

Across individual metro cities one can observe wide variation in the nature of male employment. Mumbai has the highest proportion of RE among the males in all the three years; 62.83 per cent, 65.35 per cent and 67.79 per cent in 1987-88, 1993-94 and 1999-00 respectively (Table 2.6). Among the females, the city was at the top in proportion of RE in 1993-94 and 1999-00, 69.10 per cent and 65.32 per cent respectively. The city had very low proportion of CL among both males and females. Over the 1987-88 to 1999-00 period, there has been little decline in both CL and SE among males and females in the city. There has been little difference in the nature of employment of males and females. Given that the WPRs, male and female, are relatively high in the city, the employment situation in the city appears good. But, there continues to be high unemployment rates among the males in the city, also indicating that not adequate work is being generate.

Ahmedabad and Bangalore come in a category where employment situation is quite vulnerable. In 1987-88 and 1993-94, there was low RE (44.91% and 52.42% respectively for the two cities in 1987-88 and 51.24 per cent and 53.37 per cent respectively in 1993-94) and high CL at low WPR among the males. In 1999-00, the situation worsens for the males in Ahmedabad with high WPR and high CL (increase to 30.13%) type of employment, indicating high WPR among males is poverty induced. Males are getting into what ever available CL at low wages. In Bangalore, the situation improves for the males in 1999-00, with high WPR and employment in RE category (Figure 2.2).

Figure 2.2: WPR vs Nature of Employment, Males

		High RE	*Low RE*	*High CL*	*Low CL*
1987-88	High WPR	Delhi	Chennai Kolkata	Chennai	Kolkata Delhi
	Low WPR	Mumbai Pune	Hyderabad Ahmedabad Bangalore	Hyderabad Ahmedabad Bangalore Pune	Mumbai
1993-94	High WPR	Mumbai Kolkata	Chennai	Chennai Kolkata	Mumbai
	Low WPR	Hyderabad Pune	Ahmedabad Bangalore Delhi	Hyderabad Ahmedabad Bangalore	Pune Delhi
1999-00	High WPR	Bangalore Mumbai	Ahmedabad Chennai Kolkata	Ahmedabad Bangalore Chennai Kolkata	Mumbai
	Low WPR	Delhi	Hyderabad Pune	Hyderabad	Pune Delhi

Note: Darker the shade of grey higher is the vulnerability of employment.

Hyderabad is the third city where there is low RE for males as compared to all metro average in two (1987-88 and 1999-00) of the three years. Recall that the city also had low unemployment rates and we concluded that possibly men have high wage employment not necessitating more male members coming out in the labour force to work. That does not appear to be the case. Percentage male workers employed as SE is close to the all metro average in 1987-88 and 1999-00, but percentage male workers employed as CL is higher than all metro average by two percentage points. This means that the situation is low wage type of employment for some and even then not many men are entering the labour force. For others RE is mainly in clerical type of jobs, that is, semi-skilled category of work (as we would see later). May be work is not available and hence males are not coming out in the labour force leading to low WPR and low unemployment rates.

Because of vulnerable employment of men, women's participation in the labour market increases from 1993-94 and there is low RE among them. It is mainly SE for women. In 1999-00, 64.73 per cent working females were SE in Ahmedabad, an increase from 43.58 per cent in 1993-94 and 38.18 per cent in 1987-88. In 1999-00, in Bangalore, there is high WPR among females, more than half of them working in RE category. In Hyderabad, among women, there is very high CL employment.

In fact, there has been increase in CL employment among females from 27.14 per cent in 1987-88 to 30.79 per cent in 1993-94 to 38.62 per cent in 1999-00. While SE has increased among females in all metros, in Hyderabad, CL employment has increased.

In Kolkata, among males, there is high SE, which has increased over time from 36.69 per cent in 1987-88 to 33.78 per cent in 1993-94 to 43.04 per cent in 1999-00 (Table 2.6) and RE has declined over time from 54.18 per cent and 54.27 per cent in 1987-88 and 1993-94 respectively and 43.36 per cent in 1999-00. Among the females in this city, although RE dominates, there is increase in CL and decline in RE. In Chennai, among males, per cent of RE is lower than per cent RE in all metros and CL per cent is higher than the per cent for the same in all metros. Among females, there is very high proportion employed as RE. In the city, there is high vulnerability of employment of males. Possibly, female RE is balancing out the male vulnerability in the employment.

Lastly, in Delhi, there is quite high SE among males and quite high RE among females than the respective percentages for the same for all metros. This is at low WPR. The city does not come into the category of vulnerable employment, for the males and females.

Figure 2.3: WPR vs Nature of Employment, Females

		High RE	*Low RE*	*High CL*	*Low CL*
1987-88	High WPR	Mumbai Pune Chennai Kolkata	Bangalore	Bangalore Chennai	Mumbai Pune Kolkata
	Low WPR	Delhi	Hyderabad Ahmedabad	Hyderabad Ahmedabad	Delhi
1993-94	High WPR	Mumbai Pune Chennai Kolkata	Ahmedabad	Ahmedabad Chennai	Mumbai Pune Kolkata
	Low WPR	Bangalore Delhi	Hyderabad	Hyderabad Delhi	Bangalore
1999-00	High WPR	Bangalore Mumbai Chennai	Ahmedabad Pune	Ahmedabad Bangalore Kolkata	Mumbai Pune Chennai
	Low WPR	Kolkata Delhi	Hyderabad	Hyderabad	Delhi

Note: Darker the shade of grey higher is the vulnerability of employment.

Industrial Classification

The data on industrial classification of workers by metro city given in Tables 2.7 and 2.8 is the reprocessing NIC 5 digit data[5] for 1999-00 and

NIC 3 digit data for 1993-94 and 1987-88[6]. The data on 10 categories of industrial classification has been made comparable for the three years based on the comparability table given in NIC Classification of 1998. Column 3 in the two tables gives data on the primary sector. Columns 4 and 5 represent the secondary sector and the rest of the columns represent tertiary sector. As large number of jobs are in the tertiary sector and there are numerous different activities in the tertiary sector in the urban areas, attempt has been made here to disaggregate this sector to the extent permitted by the sample size. A broad classification into primary, secondary and tertiary sector would not have revealed much, as attempted by Mahadevia and Sarkar (forthcoming 2008) for different size classes of urban centres for major states in India. When, the figures in Tables 2.7 and 2.8 are totalled up for three broad sector classifications, primary, secondary and tertiary, the figures for all metros and all urban areas differ by decimal points from the data given for all metros and all urban for the three sectors by Mahadevia and Sarkar (forthcoming 2008) as here we have used five-digit NIC classification whereas in the former, analysis was based on 1 digit classification. This analysis by individual metropolitan cities and by size class of towns by Mahadevia and Sarkar (forthcoming 2008) assumes importance in light of the fact that 1981 and 2001 population censuses do not give classification of workers by 9 industrial categories and give only for five categories where all urban industrial activities are lumped together under 'all others' category.

Firstly, we will analyse for male workers. On the whole, there is much higher proportion of male workers engaged in primary work in all urban as compared to all metros. As high as 7.54 per cent male workers in all urban areas were employed in primary sector in 1999-00, as compared to 1.22 per cent in all metros (Table 2.7). These figures in 2004-05 are 7.1 per cent and 1.7 per cent respectively (Mahadevia and Sarkar forthcoming 2008), indicating a very slight increase in primary sector employment among males in the metros and a very slight decrease in the same among males in all urban. However, for all urban, there has been a decline in primary sector employment from 10.35 per cent in 1987-88 to present level. There is almost no change in proportion of male workers engaged in primary sector in all metros over time, as the percentage figure is quite low. What is interesting to observe is that in 1999-00, 1.91 per cent male workers were engaged in primary sector in Ahmedabad, and there has been an increase in employment in this sector in Mumbai from 0.97 per cent in 1987-88 to 1.21 per cent in 1999-00. In Bangalore too, there has been an increase in primary sector employment from 1.21 per cent in 1987-88 to 1.43 per cent in 1999-00. As the proportions are quite low, such changes may mean little and could be also because of small sample size. In Mumbai, primary sector employment is expected to be in fishing.

As per our classification of workers by industrial activities, manufacturing sector is the largest employer of male workers in metropolitan cities as well. In 1987-88, 32.23 per cent male workers were employed in manufacturing and production of electricity, gas and water in all metros. In 1993-94, this figure went down to 29.10 per cent and to 27.44 per cent in 1999-00. There is therefore a decline in manufacturing sector employment among males over time in the metropolitan cities. This is not unexpected. What is unexpected is that still, the proportion of workers employed in manufacturing and production of electricity, gas and water is higher in metropolises together as compared to all urban areas. Thus, manufacturing continues to dominate metro economy and manufacturing units continue to be located in and around metropolises than other urban areas. In 1999-00, only 22.99 per cent male workers were employed in this sector in all urban areas. This is a decline from 27.16 per cent in 1987-88 and 24.50 per cent in 1993-94. Wholesale and retail trade dominates the economy of other urban areas where 26.37 per cent male workers were employed in 1999-00. This is an increase from 21.41 per cent in 1987-88 to 22.79 per cent in 1993-94.

Individual cities where manufacturing continue to dominate (in 1999-00) are Ahmedabad (33.24%), Bangalore (30.36%), Mumbai (27.98%) and Kolkata (27.79%). The last two metros have percentage figures which are just above the all metro average. But, inspite of closure of textile mills in Ahmedabad, one in every three male worker in the city is employed in manufacturing.

Bangalore having high proportion of manufacturing sector workers indicates that there has been a hype created with regards to employment in the IT sector in the city while the city's employment is still dominated by the manufacturing sector. This is so much for Bangalore being an IT city! Absurdly, the policy focus and the resource allocations in the city have shifted to the IT sector, as various documents and newspaper reports reveal and the individuals in the IT industry have been making great efforts to influence city development policies to suit their own requirements. It is likely that IT sector is generating indirect employment. And there is some impact of increased employment, a large part of it expected in the IT sector, on other employment sectors. There is a large increase in construction sector employment for males in the city from 7.32 per cent in 1993-94 to 12.44 per cent in 1999-00. In 1987-88, 8.83 per cent male workers in Bangalore were employed in construction. And if one moves around in Bangalore, construction boom is evident. In the IT corridor of glass buildings to house IT companies, or flyovers are being constructed. Many new malls have come up. The IT employees have high purchasing power that has led to retailing boom and increase in space required for retailing outlets[7]. There is thus an important indirect impact of IT sector on Bangalore city's employment structure.

In Mumbai, the manufacturing sector employment among males has come down to 27.98 per cent in 1999-00 from 36.62 per cent in 1987-88 and 32.87 per cent in 1993-94. Male employment in wholesale and retail trade is only 21.53 per cent in the city in 1999-00, some increase from 19.05 per cent in 1987-88. Part of the decline in the manufacturing sector jobs (a decline of about 8 percentage point) has shifted to construction sector, where male employment has increased by 3.5 percentage point in 1987-88 to 1999-00 period. In 1999-00, 7.47 per cent male workers in Mumbai were employed in construction. There is also decline in proportion of males employed in financial and real estate services and computer and other high end services, and increase in social and other services, public administration and transport storage and communication. In per cent terms, employment in financial and real estate services is not so high among males in Mumbai (just 3.85% in 1999-00), contrary to our expectations, given that the city is known as the financial capital of India.

Bangalore, besides being a manufacturing or secondary sector city, also has 22.26 per cent population engaged in wholesale and retail trade, a small decline from 23.78 per cent in 1987-88. Just 4.34 per cent males were employed in computer and other high end services in Bangalore in 1999-00. In 1993-94, this figure was 4.78 per cent and in 1987-88 it was 9.28 per cent. Probably, the sample has not been able to cover the IT and ITES (IT enabled services) sector well. As per a survey by Carol Upadhyay and A. R. Vasavi, between 200,000 and 250,000 were estimated to be directly employed in the IT and the ITES (IT enabled services) in Bangalore city[8]. That meant that between 6.0 per cent and 7.5 per cent of the total workers in the city were directly employed in the IT and ITES sector. Even then, other economic activities provide employment in the city, more than the IT sector. There is increase in RE in Bangalore in 1999-00 as compared to previous two NSS rounds, and at the same time, there is also increase in manual labour type of jobs (where proportion has increased from 41.08% in 1993-94 to 43.58% in 1999-00) and partly in skilled managerial and technical jobs (where proportion has increased from 23.03 per cent to 24.26 per cent in the same period), as we would see later in Table 2.9. Thus, part of the new RE created is also manual labour type, and this would be in the construction activities. It is also likely that there have been low skilled jobs generated in other service sectors, but where it is more as salaried jobs than daily wage jobs. Since, both managerial and technical jobs and manual labour jobs have increased in Bangalore city, inequalities would have increased in the city with high wages in one sector of the economy which is tied to the IT and low wages and unskilled employment in other large sector of the city's economy.

Ahmedabad has declined as a manufacturing sector, but still, 33.24 per cent male workers in 1999-00 were engaged in it. But, still this is a decline from 44.44 per cent in 1987-88. To compensate for manufacturing employment loss has come up wholesale and retail trade where employment has increased from 21.06 per cent in 1987-88 to 29.95 per cent in 1999-00 among the males. Even percentage of construction workers has increased from 3.15 per cent in 1987-88 to 7.67 per cent in 1999-00. While the trade and commerce would increase employment in self-employed category, construction would have increased employment in CL type of work. And in fact, there is an increase by 10 percentage points in CL type of work and 2 percentage point increase in SE type of work among males in the city in the same period. Interestingly about 44 per cent of males were employed in manufacturing in 1987-88 and same per cent were employed as RE in the same year in the city.

Transport, storage and communications have continued to employ about 10 per cent to 11 per cent of male workers in all metropolitan cities and about 9 per cent to 10 per cent workers in all urban areas. Across the cities, we do not find much of a pattern except that Delhi has continued to have least proportion of male workers employed in this sector.

There is an overall increase in per cent of males employed in construction sector in all urban areas as well as in the metro cities. In all metros, the proportion has increased from 6.16 per cent in 1987-88 to 7.40 per cent in 1993-94 to 7.19 per cent in 1999-00. In all urban areas, these figures are: 5.91 per cent, 6.99 per cent and 8.75 per cent respectively. Male workers employed in social and other services has increased in all metros and all urban areas and even individual metro cities with exception of Ahmedabad.

Unlike males, there is drastic reduction in proportion females engaged in primary sector in the metropolitan cities together, from 5.39 per cent in 1987-88 to 2.83 per cent in 1999-00. In 2004-05, there is an increase in primary sector employment among the female workers to 3.8 per cent in the metros (Mahadevia and Sarkar forthcoming 2008). Female WPR increase in metros is possibly a shift to primary sector, indicating some type of distress employment. At the same time, in all urban areas, as high as 18.3 per cent female workers continue to work in primary sector (Mahadevia and Sarkar forthcoming 2008), a marginal decline from 18.63 per cent in 1999-00. In 1987-88, this figure was quite high, 30.06 per cent. Compared to males, per cent females employed in manufacturing and production of electricity gas and water is less in the metropolitan cities. In 1999-00, 27.44 per cent males but 22.55 per cent females were employed in this sector. In all urban areas, the situation is reverse, with proportion of female employed in manufacturing is higher than proportion of males employed in manufacturing.

Construction, wholesale and retail trade, transport, storage and communication, hotels and restaurants are sectors where clearly female presence in terms of percentage figures is less than the male presence. Figures of per cent females employed in these sectors is less than figures of per cent males employed in these sectors. In wholesale and retail trade and in transport, storage and communication, the gap in the per cent values for females and per cent values for males is quite high. While variation across metro cities with regards to per cent employed in wholesale and retail trade is not so high for the males, for the females, one finds a very high variation. For the males, the values of per cent employed in this sector vary between 19 and 32, for the females the values vary between 7 per cent and 32 per cent. In all metro cities individually, with exception of Bangalore and Delhi, in all metros together and in all urban areas, there is an increase in per cent females employed in wholesale and retail trade, from 1987-88 to 1999-00.

In Ahmedabad city, proportion of females employed in wholesale and retail trade is as high as 31.25 per cent in 1999-00, and this is an increase by 22 percentage points from 1987-88 to 1999-00. Increase in female WPR in the city is partly explained by increase in female participation in this sector. Further, it is more likely that females are employed in retail trade and not wholesale trade. Activities of NGOs such as SEWA (Self Employed Women's Association) support women's engagement in retail trade activities such as vending. Retail trade, that is vending and hawking are two very important trades for women in Ahmedabad city and for which space is required and which the current drive of upgrading Ahmedabad to mega-city status are not permitting.

Table 2.7: Industrial Classification of Principal + Subsidiary Workers, Male

Metro Cities	*Primary*	*Manufacturing & Electricity, Gas & Water*	*Construction*	*Wholesale & Retail Trade*	*Hotel & Restaurant*	*Transportation & Communication*	*Financial Services & Real Estate*	*Computer + other high end services*	*Public Administ-ration*	*Social + Other Services*
1987-88										
1. Mumbai	0.97	36.62	3.98	19.05	3.96	11.78	5.77	9.22	3.30	5.35
2. Kolkata	1.09	31.05	6.15	21.33	2.50	9.58	3.96	10.55	4.36	9.43
3. Delhi	0.93	31.60	6.15	21.34	4.46	8.49	5.58	12.59	3.84	5.03
4. Chennai	1.44	26.77	9.94	25.09	2.68	11.04	5.10	9.84	2.47	5.64
5. Hyderabad	3.15	17.92	8.10	29.91	1.34	14.27	3.20	13.93	3.82	4.38
6. Bangalore	1.21	31.79	8.83	23.78	4.32	9.91	3.32	9.28	1.92	5.64
7. Ahmedabad	1.17	44.44	3.15	21.06	2.40	11.55	4.49	7.66	1.28	2.81
8. Pune	2.08	26.05	5.65	13.65	3.71	13.39	2.68	19.30	11.56	1.93
All Metros	1.25	32.23	6.16	21.45	3.22	10.49	4.76	11.21	3.74	5.50
All Urban	10.35	27.16	5.91	21.41	2.90	9.75	3.14	10.75	4.15	4.48
1993-94										
1. Mumbai	0.52	32.87	4.26	22.22	3.44	10.20	5.51	3.01	6.78	11.19
2. Kolkata	1.53	22.91	3.94	25.77	1.66	11.47	2.63	2.81	14.27	13.01
3. Delhi	1.20	26.93	11.20	23.39	3.06	7.53	3.42	1.95	12.07	9.26
4. Chennai	1.06	24.58	14.03	21.19	3.07	11.04	2.46	2.83	12.85	6.90
5. Hyderabad	1.11	23.42	11.42	22.56	2.68	11.61	6.29	2.76	8.99	9.18
6. Bangalore	1.71	33.47	7.32	20.96	2.98	6.08	4.52	4.78	12.03	6.16
7. Ahmedabad	0.44	28.65	6.74	21.18	2.39	15.96	2.34	1.00	9.89	11.40
8. Pune	1.48	27.99	7.62	23.86	0.45	11.91	3.37	5.18	8.27	9.86
All Metros	1.63	29.10	7.40	22.65	2.59	10.25	3.81	2.63	10.53	9.40
All Urban	10.31	24.50	6.99	22.79	2.71	9.75	2.38	1.61	8.73	10.25
1999-00										
1. Mumbai	1.21	27.98	7.47	21.53	4.29	13.35	3.85	5.07	7.19	8.05
2. Kolkata	0.35	27.79	4.45	27.65	3.46	13.36	3.72	4.11	3.59	11.50
3. Delhi	0.47	25.47	4.01	31.97	2.24	6.93	2.75	3.20	13.92	9.04
4. Chennai	1.05	24.95	10.66	21.20	3.62	14.38	4.18	2.63	5.27	12.06
5. Hyderabad	0.58	13.18	12.79	28.73	4.31	14.05	5.24	2.99	11.18	6.95
6. Bangalore	1.43	30.36	12.44	22.26	1.75	9.20	3.34	4.34	7.69	7.19
7. Ahmedabad	1.91	33.24	7.67	29.95	3.91	10.50	1.87	0.79	3.18	6.98
8. Pune	1.43	22.43	6.95	19.95	3.95	14.05	4.51	2.80	10.16	13.77
All Metros	1.22	27.44	7.19	25.69	3.35	11.70	3.25	3.05	7.97	9.14
All Urban	7.54	22.99	8.75	26.37	3.13	10.39	2.43	2.03	7.89	8.49

Table 2.8: Industrial Classification of Principal + Subsidiary Workers, Female

Metro Cities	*Primary*	*Manufacturing & Electricity, Gas & Water*	*Construction*	*Wholesale & Retail Trade*	*Hotel & Restaurant*	*Transportation & Communication*	*Financial Services & Real Estate*	*Computer + other high end services*	*Public Administration*	*Social + Other Services*
1987-88										
1. Mumbai	7.64	23.34	1.40	7.90	3.00	3.30	5.70	12.19	15.44	20.12
2. Kolkata	3.99	20.23	0.60	4.70	1.02	1.88	0.48	7.84	17.08	42.13
3. Delhi	2.39	17.11	3.63	9.88	1.68	2.61	12.03	15.31	25.06	10.29
4. Chennai	3.74	26.30	7.50	10.32	1.78	2.10	0.94	9.66	17.14	20.52
5. Hyderabad	6.36	22.22	11.16	13.84	0.00	1.19	1.39	7.98	7.63	28.23
6. Bangalore	3.52	39.14	16.95	14.94	0.93	0.53	2.66	5.98	7.39	7.90
7. Ahmedabad	14.24	33.84	1.54	9.61	0.00	3.42	1.67	8.95	14.55	12.18
8. Pune	2.45	10.45	0.75	8.68	0.00	0.12	4.94	16.61	31.30	24.68
All Metros	5.39	23.73	4.70	9.74	1.53	2.23	3.97	10.48	16.75	21.48
All Urban	30.06	27.25	3.95	8.36	1.66	0.93	1.19	5.03	10.28	11.31
1993-94										
1. Mumbai	0.37	19.22	1.60	12.61	2.51	3.15	6.60	2.90	5.32	45.70
2. Kolkata	0.18	13.57	0.85	8.51	0.89	0.91	2.16	0.00	21.65	51.28
3. Delhi	2.55	10.05	6.26	12.48	0.55	1.31	3.42	2.87	27.40	33.10
4. Chennai	0.35	21.62	10.92	10.45	1.54	1.38	2.86	1.07	10.24	39.56
5. Hyderabad	1.02	11.12	25.36	4.79	0.94	1.21	3.18	3.96	10.14	38.27
6. Bangalore	8.25	26.32	1.87	10.44	0.99	1.71	7.28	5.39	11.02	26.73
7. Ahmedabad	0.97	23.76	3.32	18.35	0.20	2.74	2.23	0.48	3.28	44.67
8. Pune	6.37	18.57	2.46	13.10	0.00	1.29	3.40	1.34	9.57	43.90
All Metros	4.16	18.40	5.06	11.48	1.10	2.07	4.08	2.09	11.26	40.31
All Urban	25.53	24.52	4.09	8.85	1.40	1.27	1.31	0.65	4.82	27.57
1999-00										
1. Mumbai	1.11	18.39	1.69	16.91	1.46	4.38	5.16	4.69	2.29	43.30
2. Kolkata	0.00	11.22	0.36	13.18	5.85	2.13	1.74	1.23	3.70	60.59
3. Delhi	5.48	21.72	0.00	7.50	0.84	1.70	0.99	3.08	17.20	41.49
4. Chennai	0.62	28.55	3.10	12.10	2.50	2.91	3.96	0.31	2.18	43.78
5. Hyderabad	0.00	8.79	24.24	16.91	1.69	3.50	0.68	1.91	7.99	34.31
6. Bangalore	0.96	42.75	6.34	11.26	0.09	1.17	10.99	1.72	4.30	20.42
7. Ahmedabad	3.60	31.86	0.30	31.25	0.11	5.42	1.88	0.83	3.05	21.68
8. Pune	3.38	18.22	0.00	20.85	3.91	2.67	0.00	0.17	1.71	49.09
All Metros	2.83	22.55	3.35	15.09	1.90	3.12	3.38	2.08	4.67	41.03
All Urban	18.63	23.94	4.91	14.75	2.24	1.78	1.39	1.01	3.92	27.45

In Mumbai, women's participation in this sector has increased from 7.90 per cent in 1987-88 to 16.91 per cent in 1999-00, which is indeed an increase by 9 percentage points but not as much as in Ahmedabad. Declaration of no hawking zones, evictions of hawkers from Mumbai footpaths would have adverse impact on livelihoods of women in the city. In Pune, there is 12 percentage point increase in female employment in wholesale and retail trade sector. In other cities, although the share of this sector in total employment of females has gone up, the increase is not so dramatic as in Ahmedabad, Pune and Mumbai.

There is a high clustering of female workers in social and other services. 41.03 per cent females in 1999-00 in all metros, but just 27.45 per cent females in all urban. The figures for individual cities for the year 1999-00 are: Kolkata as high as 60.59 per cent; Pune 49.09 per cent; Chennai 43.78 per cent and Mumbai 43.30 per cent. Mumbai, Chennai and Kolkata also had high WPR. Thus, high WPR and increase in the same is explained by female employment in social and other services in these cities. But, in Chennai, this is more of a RE. Hence, females here are engaged in social and other services which are regular salaried employment.

In Bangalore, where there is high WPR, as high as 42.75 per cent women workers were engaged in manufacturing sector in 1999-00. Other important sector for female employment in the city is in Financial and Real Estate Services. In Mumbai, the clustering of female employment is in social and other services, followed by manufacturing and then wholesale and retail trade. In Ahmedabad, women workers are concentrated in the manufacturing (possibly in garment making), wholesale and retail trade (about 31% employed in each) and then social and other services.

On the whole, there is quite high fluctuation with regards to type of work women do than what men do. At the same time, it can be seen that women are present in only certain economic activities, unlike men, who are found working in all types of economic activities. If the NSS sample size were to be larger, a much more detailed analysis of employment sectors in urban areas and even individual cities could have been possible.

Occupational Classification

Occupational classification data is based on NCO Classification of 1968. We have only looked at one digit classification and clubbed the one-digit groups to get three basic types of occupational groups: (i) managerial and technical jobs which are skilled jobs, (ii) clerical jobs which are semi skilled jobs and require literacy and some basic level of education; (iii) manual labour jobs which are in the contemporary world considered unskilled or less skilled that can be easily picked up. Some of the jobs put in the last category by us are also artisan activities, which in a way are skilled and carried on through the family. But, as these jobs involve manual labour and get low returns in the labour market, these have been clubbed with manual labour. The day highly skilled artisans are valued in our society their employment would be classified as technical jobs. And we hope that this would happen some day.

First of all, for the males as well as females, per cent workers employed in managerial and technical jobs is higher for all metros than for all urban areas. For example, in 2004-05, 21.7 per cent employed males and 24.7 per cent employed females were in managerial and technical jobs in the metros, when these figures for all urban areas were 18.0 per cent and 20.9 per cent respectively (Mahadevia and Sarkar forthcoming 2008). For the male workers there is slight increase in the proportion in this category of workers from 20.78 per cent in 1999-00, for the female workers there is a significant decline in the proportion employed in such skilled jobs from 30.89 per cent in 1999-00 in the metros (Table 2.9). This means that the female WPR increase in the metros is explained by increase in other types of occupations and that is more clerical type of jobs, as we would see later. These figures for all urban were 16.54 per cent for males and 20.04 per cent for females in the same year, indicating that even in all urban areas, there is slight improvement in the quality of male employment which is not the case with regards to female employment.

This difference between metro cities and all urban is observed for other two NSS rounds as well. Thus, evidently, managerial and technical jobs are more located in the metropolitan cities than in other urban areas. Secondly, the percentages figures are higher for females than males in managerial and technical jobs. The gap between men and women is much wider in the metro cities than in all urban, but, a gap that has declined in 2004-05. This indicates that there is lower gender disparity in managerial and technical jobs in the metropolitan cities.

In the clerical jobs, in metros, there are higher percentage figures for women than men, once again indicating a lower gender disparity in clerical jobs in the metro cities. In 2004-05, the proportion of male and female engaged in clerical jobs are 37.6 per cent and 48.5 per cent respectively in the metros and 36.0 per cent and 37.3 per cent respectively in all urban (Mahadevia and Sarkar forthcoming 2008). In all urban there is lesser incidence of clerical jobs among females than in the males, indicating that in non-metros, in the clerical jobs there is large presence of males as well, whereas in the metros, such jobs are a domain of females.

Male employment in the metropolitan economy is largely in manual labour type of jobs closely followed by clerical type of jobs. That is the case in the whole urban economy. The proportion of males employed in manual labour type of jobs is much higher in the other urban areas than in the metropolitan cities. For example, in 1999-00, 41.72 per cent males in all metros were employed in manual jobs, but, this percentage in all urban was 47.84 per cent (Table 2.9) and in 2004-05, these figures were 40.6 per cent and 46.0 per cent respectively. Similar pattern can be seen for other two years as well.

In contrast, female employment in the metropolitan economy is dominated by clerical type of jobs followed by manual labour jobs. But, in all urban areas, the female employment is clearly dominated by manual labour type of jobs. For example, 48.45 per cent working females in all urban were employed as manual labour whereas this percentage for all metros was 25.98 per cent in 1999-00. In 2004-05, these figures were 41.8 per cent and 26.8 per cent respectively (Mahadevia and Sarkar forthcoming 2008). In the metropolitan cities, while two in every five workers among males were working in manual labour jobs, only one in every four working females were employed in these type of jobs. Thus, in the metropolitan economy, possibly, females do not tend to go for manual jobs or females do not access or are not able to access manual labour jobs. It is possible that some of the manual labour jobs in the cities are in the construction, loading and unloading and such type of jobs where single male migrants are found. Metropolitan cities have highly adverse sex ratios due to the overwhelming presence of single male migrants. The new migrants tend to get into unskilled labour jobs.

Why there is high availability of manual labour jobs to women in other urban centres? Firstly, because that is to a large extent is the availability of such jobs here (as this percentages in this category are higher for males as well as females) and also primary sector employment is found in large proportion in all urban. There is a large difference in the type of work that women do in metropolitan cites and than what they do in other urban areas. This is not the case with men.

There is thus crowding of males in manual labour type of jobs in metros whereas there is high presence of females in manual labour type of jobs in all urban.

Table 2.9: Distribution of Principal + Subsidiary Workers by Occupation Type (%)

	Metro Cities	Managerial/Technical			Clerical			Manual Labour		
		1987-88	1993-94	1999-00	1987-88	1993-94	1999-00	1987-88	1993-94	1999-00
	Male									
1.	Mumbai	18.32	21.02	18.74	39.14	40.47	35.29	42.54	38.51	45.97
2.	Kolkata	20.27	12.71	24.26	44.18	51.84	38.90	35.55	35.45	36.84
3.	Delhi	19.60	23.22	27.67	41.30	37.52	47.07	39.10	39.26	25.25
4.	Chennai	20.28	19.11	22.57	37.68	34.92	30.18	42.04	45.97	47.25
5.	Hyderabad	11.51	19.49	19.70	49.37	41.34	43.68	39.12	39.18	36.62
6.	Bangalore	14.75	23.03	24.26	41.11	35.89	32.17	44.13	41.08	43.58
7.	Ahmedabad	9.14	12.36	19.77	37.75	36.52	30.88	53.11	51.12	49.35
8.	Pune	18.59	29.31	34.23	37.49	37.67	31.18	43.92	33.02	34.59
	All Metro Cities	17.39	18.58	20.78	40.34	39.29	37.51	42.27	42.13	41.72
	All Urban	12.50	13.84	16.54	38.11	36.64	35.62	49.39	49.53	47.84
	Female									
1.	Mumbai	23.66	24.39	31.89	54.58	57.36	48.92	21.77	18.26	19.18
2.	Kolkata	30.49	26.83	28.21	55.81	57.14	60.33	13.70	16.03	11.46
3.	Delhi	34.93	32.82	52.79	44.53	49.41	31.12	20.55	17.77	16.10
4.	Chennai	23.37	17.99	25.72	47.00	48.75	49.40	29.63	33.26	24.87
5.	Hyderabad	7.05	21.42	19.54	56.06	35.72	44.79	36.88	42.86	35.67
6.	Bangalore	9.75	18.34	31.15	45.39	49.06	37.66	44.86	32.60	31.19
7.	Ahmedabad	15.44	11.94	32.47	37.34	40.80	25.44	47.22	47.26	42.09
8.	Pune	27.48	35.72	30.86	59.27	48.09	46.66	13.26	16.18	22.49
	All Metro Cities	23.38	24.20	30.89	50.28	47.57	43.13	26.35	28.23	25.98
	All Urban	13.43	15.32	20.04	28.14	28.71	31.51	58.43	55.97	48.45

In the latter, there is also large proportion of females employed in agriculture leading to such high proportion of women employed as manual labour in all urban. Given that the female WPR is low, their actual employed numbers would be very low and gender disparity is cutting across all employment sectors in the cities.

There is an increase in availability of managerial and technical jobs over time in the metropolitan cities as well as in all urban areas for males as well as females. There is some reduction in clerical jobs available to males and females in metros but an increase among females and reduction among males in the availability of clerical type of jobs in all urban. These increases are accompanied by decline in proportion of male and female workers employed in manual labour type of jobs. There may not be an absolute decline in manual labour type of jobs in the cities in general and metropolitan cities in particular, but, with economic growth, more higher end jobs are getting generated in the urban economy as well as metropolitan economy.

As seen before, the WPR increase in either all urban or all metros is not so high. Thus, high end jobs generated in the metropolitan and urban economy is not adequate enough to increase employment in the two economies. If there was a possibility to increase manual labour type of jobs in the urban and metropolitan economies, there could be improvement in employment availability in the cities in general and metropolises in particular and which could lead to higher urbanisation rate than what we are witnessing today.

Pune, Chennai and Delhi had higher percentage workers employed in managerial and technical jobs than all metro average for the same, for the males in all the three years. Kolkata has higher proportion than all metro average in 1987-88 and 1999-00. In Mumbai, this was the case in 1987-88 and 1993-94 for the males. In Bangalore this has been the case for the males in 1993-94 and 1999-00. In contrast, Ahmedabad in all the three years had higher than all metro average percentage of workers employed in manual labour. Evidently, for vast majority of male workers in Ahmedabad, it is availability of manual labour type of jobs. For all the three years, it is also the case for Bangalore. But, Bangalore also had higher than all urban average of percentage workers employed in managerial and technical jobs for two years, 1993-94 and 1999-00. This indicates that there is high disparity in male employment in Bangalore city. This is also the case with Chennai in 1993-94 and 1999-00.

Hyderabad is a city with dominance of clerical jobs; their proportion being higher in the city than in metros among males. In Kolkata and

Delhi also this is the case. But, in these two cities, there is also higher presence of managerial and technical jobs, indicating that these two cities are middle class and high class cities. Ahmedabad is low class of employment. Chennai and Kolkata have high disparities. Mumbai is moving to become middle and low class city, with predominant employment of males shifting to clerical and manual jobs in 1999-00. Pune is a high class city as far as male employment is concerned.

Ahmedabad and Bangalore (for all the three years), Hyderabad (for two years, 1993-94 and 1999-00) and Chennai for two years, (1987-88 and 1993-94), had higher than all metro average per cent female workers employed as manual labour. Thus, not only there is high disparity among males in the employment sector in Bangalore but there is also high gender disparity in the employment sector in the city in terms of quality of employment.

Conclusions

This analysis shows that there is indeed variation in the employment characteristics of different cities. Further, our understanding of economies of some of the important (or star) metropolises stand challenged from this analysis. We would summarise below the employment structure of each of the eight metropolises analysed here.

First Mumbai. Mumbai is moving to become middle and low class city, with predominant employment of males shifting to clerical and manual jobs in 1999-00. Proportion of managerial and technical and clerical jobs has declined among males and manual labour jobs have increased. Further, for males, there is RE as manual labour. The city has high WPRs than all metro average but, there is slight increase in subsidiary employment among males in 1999-00. At the same time manufacturing has declined and service economy has emerged. This is employment in wholesale and retail trade, construction, social and other services, public administration and transport storage and communication. There is decline in proportion of males employed in financial and real estate services and computer and other high end services. In per cent terms, employment in financial and real estate services is not so high among males in Mumbai contrary to our expectations, given that the city is known as the financial capital of India. Hence, the city's employment has shifted towards low end services towards the end of 1990s. Non-availability of quality employment coupled with social and political factors could have led to lowering of migration rate in the decade of 1990s.

Female WPRs are lower than all metro average and have not changed over the whole period. Given that cost of living in Mumbai is high, it is quite unlikely that women are not willing to work. It is possible that women may not be taking up work due to long distance required to commute to place of work. It is also unlikely that women are not finding work here. But, it is possible that low skilled jobs where women tend to get into are taken up by recent single male migrants to the city. Also, the per cent women engaged in subsidiary capacity only is higher than all metro average. More than 10 per cent women employed are working in this city as only subsidiary workers. In 1999-00, there is shift towards SE among women at low WPRs.

Bangalore is a city where for the males, employment has increased in technical and managerial jobs on one hand and also in manual labour type of jobs on the other in 1999-00, indicating increase in disparity in quality of employment due to globalisation. Further, higher proportion of females have employment in manual labour, just like in Ahmedabad. Thus, there is also high gender disparity in the city in terms of quality of employment, which must be reflecting in disparity in incomes. The WPRs have increased greatly for males as well as females in 1999-00 as compared to 1993-94. This could be impact of two developments: (i) migration of unmarried techies to the city who tend to have high labour force participation rates, and (ii) high employment in low wage manual labour type of employment for others and for females in other than IT economy. IT economy could itself have generated low wage manual labour type of employment in the economy. Surprisingly, 30 per cent of male workers are still employed in manufacturing in the city and just 4.78 per cent male workers were found employed in computer and other high end services. Another research on Bangalore estimates that 6.0 per cent to 7.5 per cent workers in the city were in IT and ITES, which is not commensurate to the city's image as an IT city.

Ahmedabad is a city with economy in distress. Ahmedabad has declined as a manufacturing sector, but still, 33.24 per cent male workers in 1999-00 were engaged in it. But, still this is a decline from 44.44 per cent in 1987-88. To compensate for manufacturing employment loss that in the wholesale and retail trade has increased. Even percentage of construction workers has increased from 1987-88 to 1999-00. While the trade and commerce would increase employment in self-employed category, construction would have increased employment in CL type of work. And that is what has happened. This has brought out more women in the labour force, working in manual labour type of employment as self employed. For males as well as females, there has been a consistent increase in WPRs as principal status workers and also as principal + subsidiary status workers over the period. Further, among the females, there is consistent decline in the percentage of subsidiary workers, indicating that more and more women are coming out in the labour force for round-the-year employment. CL has increased among males. But, at the same time, there is also an increase in technical and managerial jobs, indicating emergence of inequality in the male employment. In fact, in all the eight metros covered by this paper, there has been a very high increase in managerial and technical jobs in the decade of 1990s, the increase being much more than 3 percentage points for all metros and 4 percentage points for all urban. Hence, this change in Ahmedabad is in line with the overall change in the large metropolises in the reforms period.

Pune is a metro with high proportion of employed males in managerial and technical jobs and employed females in clerical jobs. Male employment is less in manufacturing but more in transport and communication, public administration and other services. The city has lower than all metro average WPRs for males and also decline in subsidiary workers. Among females the WPRs are high but there is high decline in the same in 1999-00. The city has low and declining unemployment rates, for males and females, all signs of a robust economy. But, at the same time, it is also increase in SE among males and females. The city is emerging therefore as a high wage service sector economy.

Chennai and Kolkata are cities where there has been increase in disparity in quality of employment in the period of globalisation. In 1999-00, in both the cities, there has been increase in managerial and technical jobs and also increase in manual labour jobs for the males. Among the females, it is increase in clerical jobs. Both cities have high WPRs and high unemployment rates for males and females in most of the years. While, Kolkata has high proportion of males in SE category and in increasing proportion, Chennai has higher proportion of CL. For females it is RE in the two cities. Difference between the two is that Kolkata was a manufacturing economy whereas Chennai has been a service economy. Females in both the cities have been employed in social and other services that are low paid. Thus, Chennai and Kolkata have become service economies with a section of workers getting work in high paid managerial and technical jobs while large portion of male workers remaining in manual labour type of jobs. But, the high end services have expanded in the period of globalisation, which has increased disparities in the city.

Lastly Delhi is also a service economy with declining manufacturing and increasing trade. It being a national capital also has high proportion of male and female workers in public administration. The WPRs are low and so are unemployment rates indicating relatively higher wages or incomes from businesses that does not require more members of the family to come out in the labour market. Further, there is also a decline in manual labour jobs and increase in managerial and technical jobs among males and females, which is also indication of improving wages and incomes in the economy. The city has very little CL. Among males there is very high SE and among females there is very high RE. Thus, in the trade it is high end trade and not petty trading activities like in Ahmedabad. Thus, Delhi's economy is also quite robust and has improved in the period of globalisation.

Globalisation has brought improvement in the jobs in the metropolitan economy, particularly in the large metropolises as seen in this article. But, the situation of the entire metropolitan population has not improved much. In cities such as Ahmedabad, employment situation for the majority has deteriorated. Thus, disparities have increased in the labour market in all the metropolitan cities. At the same time, in most cities, including Bangalore, manufacturing remains the largest employment sector for the males. IT and other new economies do not have much of presence in the employment sector in most metropolises. Nonetheless, it is the representatives from the IT sector who are pushing for changes in the mega city policies. Secondly, to make the mega cities more inclusive, attention should be paid to the low wage activities which are mainly in the tertiary sector. Further, all these activities should find space in the cities and the city development policies should not be driven by just few activities as it is happening now.

NOTES

1. This chapter is based on research undertaken through IDPAD project.
2. NSS's urban data is divided into different stratums. The state data is divided into regions. In 1987-88, stratum 6 & 7 represented the metropolitan cities (million plus); in 1993-94, stratum 6 & 7, and stratum 8 & 9 (in case there was another metropolitan city in the NSS region). From the region where these stratums are in, it is possible to identify the city. In 1999-00, stratum 1 to 6 represent metropolitan cities; 1 & 2 for the first metro city in the region, 3 & 4 for the next metro city in the region and 5 & 6 for the third metro city in the region.

3. Those who get work round the year, that is for more than 183 days a year.
4. Subsidiary status workers are those who get work for less than 183 days a year. As per the population census data, these are called marginal workers.
5. NIC Classification of 1998.
6. NIC Classification of 1987.
7. As per the presentation made by Carol Upadhyay in 'Land, Economy, and Governance in a Globalising Bangalore' Workshop held in Bangalore on February 25, 2005, under the IDPAD project titled "Inclusive Mega Cities in Asia in a Globalising World".
8. As per the presentation made by Carol Upadhyay in 'Land, Economy, and Governance in a Globalising Bangalore' Workshop held in Bangalore on February 25, 2005, under the IDPAD project titled "Inclusive Mega Cities in Asia in a Globalising World".

3[1]

SLUMBAY TO SHANGHAI
Envisioning Renewal or Take Over?

DARSHINI MAHADEVIA and HARINI NARAYANAN

Introduction

In 2004 January, Mumbai hosted the World Social Forum (WSF) event, which had moved out of Brazil for the first time since it was being held. The WSF is a loose collective of grassroots movements resisting takeover of their life spaces by the forces of economic globalisation and the ideologies campaigning/practicing alternative development models to the neo-liberal globalisation—an alternative to globalisation led by the dynamics of capital. As if a rebuttal to the event, but of course independent of it, the business class of Mumbai was busy preparing a new vision for Mumbai, for transforming her into a 'World Class City', a home grown vision for Mumbai, but influenced by the existing notions of a 'global city'. This vision has similarities with what the ADB's urban policies' prescription (Stubbs and Clarke, 1996[2]) or what was to emerge as JNNURM vision of a metro city a year later. The Vision Plan, called Vision Mumbai—Transforming Mumbai into a World Class City', was ready at the time of the WSF event in Mumbai. This Vision Plan sanctified series of evictions in Mumbai. Closely following the preparation of this vision plan came the announcement by the new Prime Minister of India, Dr. Manmohan Singh that Mumbai will be like Shanghai in India. This was followed by a statement from the Deputy Chief Minister of the state of Maharashtra: "Today, Shanghai has become a symbol for Mumbai—that city started from zero and see where it is today. Citizens here will start having confidence in the government when they see Mumbai's transformation in the next five years"[3]. This vision therefore became 'Shanghaing Mumbai'.

Closely on the heals of this document came a massive slum eviction drive towards the end of 2004, which continued through early 2005. The 'Shanghaing Mumbai' operation therefore became synonymous with slum evictions. To this was added another eviction; of all 'unwanted economic activities'—the closure order of the dance bars[4] of the city coming from the state government—and then evictions of the hawkers and then the pavement dwellers beginning in 2006. Of course the closure of the dance bars was not directly linked to the Mumbai Vision Plan, but it was definitely linked to the hypocritical morality of the middle classes of the city, to whose dreams the vision plan panders to. Thus, the mission Shanghaing Mumbai, that is implementation of the vision of Making Mumbai into a World Class City got closely identified with the displacements of the poor and their economic activities from this emerging World City, something quite in contrast to what the WSF campaigns for!

Systematic built-in exclusions in the policy and policy implementation process is quite a change from an era, when the then Bombay, now Mumbai, was a melting pot for all people and all cultures, truly representing Indian nationhood. Immigrants from Pakistan at the time of partition and then the from all corners of the country came and settled in Mumbai, finding employment mainly in the manufacturing industries (predominantly textiles) and the film industry. This went on till 1980s. The city became the main financial centre with the Bombay Stock Exchange (BSE) located in the city. The city housed and houses headquarters of the financial institutions, starting with the Reserve Bank of India (RBI). It also became the headquarters of most of the Corporates of India. The city provided economic space to all. It came to be called a 'city of dreams'. With all this went an image of glamour, emanating from the presence of the film industry, financial sector and the corporate houses.

Over time, this glamorous city of Bombay declined; about 60 per cent of population came to live in slums[5]; proliferation of slums came to dominate the city landscape; pollution and water problems became acute; garbage dumps found everywhere; river Mithi flowing through the city became a narrow black effluent channel; and on July 26, 2005 the entire suburban Mumbai was inundated beginning with unprecedented heavy rains in a short span but water logging caused because of bad waste management and construction on the natural drains. This deluge was followed by an outbreak of dengue and leptospirosis, which resulted in many deaths[6]. Bombay thus became a 'Slumbay', a term used for the declining city.

Officially, Bombay got renamed as Mumbai, the vernacular name of the city. This re-christening was a political act of the Marathi Chauvinist party, at a time when Mumbai began aspiring to be a 'Global City' (Sassen 1991, 2001, Friedmann, 2000, Friedmann and Wolff, 1982). With this, a message was sent across that non-Marathi migrants were not wanted in the city. This paradox is striking; denying citizenship and restricting political space for some in a globalising and liberalising city. This was followed by a campaign of 'Mee Mumbaikar' (I, the resident of Mumbai) in 2003-04, which put forth the idea that the slum dwellers should be disenfranchised. Before the 2004 May elections, some prominent citizens of the city had filed a Public Interest Litigation (PIL)[7] in the Mumbai High Court asking the election commissioner to disenfranchise the slum dwellers arguing that if they were living illegally, they could not be considered legal citizens of the city and therefore could not be eligible to vote. This was a move to label the dwellers of Slumbay as illegal (and hence criminals) and by that question the citizenship rights of a large section of city's population.

The new millennium brings the possibility of forging much closer global ties, opening up of the economies and opening up of the minds, linking of the world through ICTs (Information and Communication Technologies). This time Shanghai becomes Mumbai's metaphor of development. This vision has a strong backing of the Chief Minister of Maharashtra, Mr. Vilasrao Deshmukh[8] and even the Prime Minister of India. Against the background of increasing displacements of the poor and their economic activities, on the moral, legal or economic grounds, it became necessary to analyse the contents of this vision in greater details, against the contemporary history of developments within the city. The central enquiry in this article is how this vision would unfold within the city against the background of her contemporary history, response to globalisation and the aspirations of the elites and the middle classes of the city.

Mumbai in India

Mumbai is the most important megacity of India in terms of economy and hence articulates national economic interests in the global economy. Inspite of Bangalore, Hyderabad and Chennai, the IT cities of India, Mumbai continues to be the most internationally connected city of India, in terms of air passenger and freight traffic and port traffic. The second rung metros, namely, Bangalore, Hyderabad, Ahmedabad and even Pune, have also been connected by the foreign airlines to international destinations since 2005. Nonetheless, Mumbai is way ahead of all the other airports in terms of aircrafts, air passengers and air cargo handled (Table 3.1). In 2002-03, Mumbai handled 145,571 aircrafts in total, whereas Delhi's airport handled 93,463 aircrafts (64% of Mumbai's) in the same year (CMIE 2004). Mumbai airports handled 26 per cent of the total aircrafts, 28 per cent of the total air passengers and 31 per cent of the cargo handled in this year and these figures for Delhi airport were 17 per cent, 21 per cent and 28 per cent respectively (Table 3.1).

Table 3.1: Air Traffic at Major Airports, India

Major cities	*% Share of Total Air Traffic (2002-03)*			*Distribution of international air traffic passengers*		*International passengers to total air passengers*	
	Aircraft fleet	*Passengers handled*	*Cargo handled*	*2001-02*	*2002-03*	*2001-02*	*2002-03*
Mumbai	22.4	27.9	31.3	36.3	34.3	43.1	41.5
Mumbai (Juhu)	3.6	0.6	0.1	—	—	—	—
Total Mumbai	*26.0*	*28.4*	*31.4*	*36.3*	*34.3*	*43.1*	*41.5*
Delhi (IGI)	16.7	20.7	28.1	27.3	25.9	43.7	42.3
Chennai	7.9	9.5	13.9	12.8	13.1	46.0	46.8
Kolkata	5.8	6.4	5.9	4.3	4.0	23.1	20.7
Bangalore	7.2	6.9	8.7	1.5	2.5	8.9	12.2
Hyderabad	4.5	4.3	2.1	2.4	3.1	19.8	24.0
Ahmedabad	2.1	1.9	1.1	1.3	1.2	22.4	22.2
All Airports	100.0	100.0	100.0	100.00	100.0	34.0	33.7

Source: CMIE (2004).

Although New Delhi is a national capital, Mumbai acts as a main entry point for international travellers. In 2001-02, nearly one-third of the international aircraft traffic was handled by Mumbai Airport, followed by Delhi (26.02%) and Chennai (11.51%), which is way behind (Table 3.1). Mumbai's share has reduced in 2002-03 by nearly 3 percentage points, but, mainly because of coming up of some other destinations in the country. With over 30 per cent of international air traffic to India, Mumbai still gives an impression of a major economic hub in the country with the best international linkages. This observation is further strengthened by destination of international passenger traffic (Table 3.1). Once again, Mumbai handled about a third (34.3%) of the international air passenger traffic whereas Delhi handled only one-fourth (25.9%). Further, 41.5 per cent of the air passenger traffic at Mumbai airport was of international travellers whereas at Delhi airport, the international travellers formed 42.3 per cent of all air passenger traffic. Bangalore and Hyderabad has shown an increase in the percentage share in the total international passenger traffic. Of the two airports privatised by the central government in January 2006, one is Mumbai. GVK[9]-South African Airports consortium has won the bid[10] and Rs. 2,400 crores would be invested till 2010 for first phase of Mumbai airport modernisation.

Data of late 1990s (D'Monte 2002) showed that a resident of Mumbai had 16 times higher bank deposits than all India average. Head office of most of the Indian and foreign banks are located in the city. As many as 130 foreign institutional investors are based in the city. It processes half the country's imports and exports, accounts for half the corporate tax and excise duties. Maharashtra attracted 12 per cent (Rs. 15,600 crores) of the total Foreign Direct Investment (FDI) in India during 1991-97. It is the home for 52 of the top 100 Indian companies. Mumbai also has known academic and research institutions such as Indian Institute of Technology, Bhabha Atomic Research Centre, Tata Institute of Fundamental Research, Tata Institute of Social Studies, Bombay University, and so on (D'Monte 2002: 26) In August 1999, the state had lost out to Delhi as the favoured destination for FDI: $ 2.7 billion versus $ 2.3 billion (D'Monte 2002: 22-24). In 2006, Maharashtra has lost its position as the most industrialised state of India[11]. Lastly, Mumbai contributes Rs. 40,000 crores of income tax revenue to the central government (Bombay First-McKinsey 2003 and Government of Maharashtra 2004). This is not because of large incomes being generated in the city but because income tax returns for large many corporates are filed from Mumbai, their headquarters. Nonetheless, this figure indicates Mumbai's importance in the national economy.

Air connection, port facilities and stock exchange are three economic activities through which Indian economy connects with the global economy. Hence, their important presence gives the city a status of 'Global city', however at the third tier of Global city hierarchy (Friedmann, 2000). Increasing global economic linkages puts onus on the city and the state government to improve infrastructure and living conditions in the city, to become global destination of capital and business people. The Mumbai Vision document therefore comes in to fulfil this aspiration of the city. Beginning of the changes within the city to become a globally linked city began some 20 years back, when the expulsion of industrial working class began.

Expelling the Working Class

Deindustrialisation

From a colonial city, Mumbai became a major manufacturing hub of India.

With it, the city became the melting pot of India's population. The city also absorbed and integrated migrants that came to India in wake of partition. In the early twentieth century, cotton textiles dominated Mumbai's economy and then came in other industries such as engineering, chemicals and food processing. In 1961, manufacturing provided 41 per cent of Mumbai's employment with the textiles about half of it (Patel 2003: 1, 6-9). In 1976, 27 per cent of the city's organised work force was employed in the textile industry and by 1991 the figure was down to just 12.5 per cent. In absolute terms, employment in the same declined from 250,000 in 1981 to 75,000 in 1991 and has steadily dwindled further (Patel 2003: 19). A significant part of the manufacturing was contracted out to informalised processes of manufacturing. A vivid description of some of the contracted out jobs can be found in Seabrook (1987) and more recent publication on Dharavi (Sharma 2000). With the decline in the textile industry on one hand and the entire manufacturing on the other, the tertiary sector increased from 39 per cent in 1952 to 60 per cent in 1991 while formal employment in private sector declined (Deshpande and Deshpanade 1991). The manufacturing sector has got more informalised with units with less than 10 workers increasing from 27.5 per cent in 1970 to 46.3 per cent in 1991 (Patel 2003, quoting Deshpande and Deshpande 1991: 19).

Table 3.2: Registered Industrial Units, Mumbai (1971-2002)

	1971	*1981*	*1991*	*2002*
Total no of registered Units	5,411.00	8,583.00	9,066.00	7,262.00
No of working units	5,132.00	7,770.00	7,832.00	6,562.00
Total Workers (in lakhs)	5.93	6.04	4.47	3.17
Compound annual growth rate (CAGR) of registered units	2.59	4.72	0.55	–2.00
CAGR of working units	2.36	4.23	0.08	–1.60
Working units/registered units	0.95	0.91	0.86	0.90
CAGR of employment	1.62	0.18	–2.97	–3.08

Source: From files of Chief inspector of Factories.

It is not just the formal sector industries that have seen closures and hence overall decline. Even small-scale industries (SSIs) have declined. Mumbai accounted for 71.3 per cent of the SSI units of Maharashtra in 1961, employing the same proportion of workers (Dewan 2005). Over past four decades the number has declined drastically to merely 11 per cent of units and about 15 per cent of workers (Dewan 2005). The SSIs are located in Industrial Estates. According to Bombay Small Scale Industries Association (BSSIA) there are 730 industrial estates located in Mumbai and cities of the urban agglomeration, such Thane, Mira Road, Bhayender, Bhiwandi, Ulhasnagar, etc. Economic survey of Maharashtra reveals that number of SSI units in Mumbai have increased from 12,610 in 1990-91 to 17,156 in 2000-01 and employment from 106,413 in 1991 to 150,779 in 2000-01. Number of units thus registered a growth rate of 3.1 per cent p.a. whereas the employment registered a growth rate of 3.5 per cent p.a. The BSSAI gives an entirely different figure of functioning SSI units in Mumbai, 193,000 employing around 10,596,000 workers as of now (2004-05). If this indeed is true then, this big gap between the official figures of workers in SSIs and the figures of BSSIA can be explained by casual nature of their work. Dewan (2005: 27-28, 38) argues that this means only 5.6 per cent of the SSI workers are registered in the company ledgers whereas 94.4 per cent of the rest of the workers are employed on 'daily voucher' basis. According to Dewan 97.5 per cent of these daily workers are men (Dewan 2005: 27-28, 38). The SSI sector that is labour-intensive has also declined like the factory sector and those who remain employed in the sector work in highly vulnerable employment conditions.

The data from the Chief Inspector of Factories (CIF) (Table 3.2), which is for registered industries[12], clearly indicates decline in manufacturing industries in the decade of 1990s in the city. However, employment decline in them and stagnation of their growth rate had started since the decade of 1980s itself. For example, in 1980s, the Compound Annual Growth Rate (CAGR) of number of registered units was 0.55 per cent p.a., of working units was 0.08 per cent p.a. and of employment was –2.97 per cent p.a. (Table 3.2). In the decade of 1990s, all the three CAGRs are negative, –2.00 per cent p.a., –1.60 per cent p.a. and –3.08 per cent p.a. respectively. From Table 3.2 it can also be seen that although the number of units saw high growth rate during 1971-81 period (4.72% p.a.), the employment increased at only 0.18 per cent p.a. in the same period, indicating increasing capital intensity of manufacturing sector. Improvement of manufacturing technology since the gradual opening up of the economy since 1980s and then significant liberalisation since 1991, along with industrial location policies and master plan controls on industrial locations has led to manufacturing sector being displaced from Mumbai city.

Casualisation

Deindustrialisation has resulted in increase in casualisation and vulnerabilities in the employment sector. Chapter 2 by Mahadevia in this book has discussed the employment level and quality in Mumbai city. Accompanying the casualisation of work is declining work opportunities and declining income in the city. This has resulted in outmigration from the municipal corporation area of Mumbai or main city of Mumbai.

A section of population employed in the informal sector is the hawkers. It is estimated that there are 200,000 hawkers in Mumbai (Bhowmik 2000). Taking 36 per cent as the WPR of the whole city (Table 2.3, Chapter 2), about 5 per cent of the total workers of Mumbai are employed as hawkers. Those illiterate or semi-literate and unskilled take to hawking for living. A study of hawkers in Mumbai by TISS and YUVA showed that one fourth of them were illiterate, they sold low valued and often inferior quality goods—the cost of the wares sold varied between Rs. 500 and Rs. 2000[13]. A National Alliance of Street Vendors of India (NASVI) study of hawkers found that 20 per cent of the hawkers sampled in Mumbai were working in the organised manufacturing, mainly textiles, before they joined this profession (Bhowmik 2006).

While, hawking creates employment, hawkers have an economic role. They cater to the poor and the lower middle class for most of the latter's daily necessities. This is a way to keep wages low even in the formal sector. In other words, if wages of workers in the organised and unorganised sectors are to be kept low so that the employers (of capital) can reap large profits, the cost of living of the workers has to be kept low. Hawkers step in to fulfil that role. Thus, industries can employ workers at low wages; households can employ help, get a driver, etc. at low wages, get clothes ironed and get vegetables and fruits at low prices. By this process, the formal sector is able to extract more labour surplus from their employees, as the entire informal sector subsidises the most organised sector. Thus, hawkers and informal economies and informal housing available at relatively low costs have an important economic role in the urban areas of the developing economies. In other words, for the formal economy to appropriate high surpluses, informal economies and informal housing are necessary! The richer class also purchases fruits and vegetables from the hawkers. About 30 per cent of the city's working class were eating atleast one meal from the hawkers, middle class was spending atleast Rs. 1,000 per month per household to buy goods from the hawkers and lower middle class was spending Rs. 500 to Rs. 800 per month per households for the same. The entire urban economy would be dysfunctional without the services of the hawkers (Bhowmik 2006). Those depending on the hawkers would want them at convenient locations, such as railway stations, near work places, and so on, so that they need not spent more energy and time on travel for shopping. However, where the new economy does not need these services, for example in the IT sector, where a part of the wages are in the form of coupons of formal sector food and other consumer goods outlets, the hawkers are not required and hence are not allowed to vend. Thus, nature of urban economy itself has spurred growth of hawking activities.

With the increasing congestion on the streets because of increase in vehicular traffic, there is pressure to widen the roads and create parking spaces. Thus, the hawking spaces are vanishing in the cities, and also in Mumbai. The city has created no-hawking zones. Even slums are evicted if they are on plots reserved for parking (Mahadevia and Narayanan, Chapter 18). Declaration of no hawking zones and evictions of hawkers from Mumbai footpaths would have adverse impact on livelihoods of women in the city, as they continue to be predominantly employed in petty services sector (See Chapter 2). Thus, it was the industrial working class that was expelled first and now a section of the informal sector workers.

Poverty and Income

We do not have city level poverty data for 1999-00[14]. But, we have estimates for the two earlier NSS rounds, 1987-88 and 1993-94. In 1987-88, the per cent population below poverty line in Mumbai (that is the Head Count Ratio—HCR) was 15.64 per cent, which went down to 10.29 per cent in 1993-94[15]. In the same year, the HCR for all metros in Maharashtra went down from 23.96 per cent to 17.00 percent[16]. In 1999-00, the HCR for all metros in Maharashtra has further reduced to 13.99 per cent. In 1999-00, the HCR for Bangalore was 5.74 per cent and for Kolkata was 9.72 per cent. In Bangalore, there has been a drastic decline in incidence of poverty from 17.21 per cent in 1993-94 to 5.74 per cent in 1999-00. In 2004-05, the all metro poverty in Maharashtra has increased to 16.49 per cent and that in metro Karnataka to 7.89 per cent. In Tamil Nadu, all metro HCR has reduced from 31.95 per cent in 1993-94 to 11.36 per cent in 1999-00 to 8.74 per cent in 2004-05 and Chennai would have lot to contribute to this all metro poverty decline in the state (Mahadevia and Sarkar, forthcoming 2008). This indicates that there are absolute poverty related issues remaining in Mumbai and other metropolitan cities of the state. This will be supported by the data on incomes.

Table 3.3: City Income

Year	NSDP (Rs. Lakhs)		PCNSDP (Rs)		NSDP growth (Constant)	PCNSDP growth (Constant)
	Constant	Current	Constant	Current		
1999-00*	3,548,741	5,191,996	30,459	44,563	—	—
2000-01*	3,443,105	5,204,779	29,080	43,959	-2.98	-4.53
2001-02*	3,671,431	5,903,450	30,533	49,095	6.63	5.00
2002-03@	3,964,932	6,708,350	32,402	54,821	7.99	6.12

@ Preliminary
* Provisional
Source: Based on Economic Survey of Maharashtra of different years.

The city's per capita income in 2002-03 was Rs. 54,821 (at current prices) Table 3.3, whereas that of Maharashtra has been Rs. 29,590 (at current prices). This means that city's per capita income was 1.85 times that of state's per capita income in the year. Further, Mumbai's NSDP was 22.72 per cent of state's income when the city had 16.89 per cent of state's population. It is quite evident that the city is important for the state's economy. Mumbai's NSDP is 2.95 per cent of the national GDP and that of Maharashtra state is 13 per cent of the national GDP in 2002-03, indicating that it is important in the national economy. Noticeable is the negative growth of NSDP and per capita NSDP (PCNSDP) of the city in 2000-01 from 1999-00. The city's NSDP and PCNSDP growth rates are not any far higher than the growth rates of national GDP and per capita GDP. In fact, they are lower. The average annual rate of growth of NSDP and PCNSDP of the city from 1999-00 to 2002-03 has been just 3.73 per cent and 2.06 per cent respectively, which are lower than national average GDP and PCGDP growth rates. Stagnation in the city economy can be observed from these statistics. Thus, no matter the city has high global connectivity because of air linkages and harbour facilities on one hand and the financial institutions' location on the other, the city's economy is not doing so well in the last few years.

Spatial Impacts of Deindustrialisation

Mumbai is the largest metropolis of India with 16.37 millions population (of the urban agglomeration—MUA) in 2001 and estimated population of 18.34 millions in 2005, making it the second largest megacity in the world (Mahadevia Chapter 1). The city has however observed deceleration in its population growth rate in the decade of 1990s, the growth rate coming down to 2.65 per cent p.a. in the decade of 1990s from 4.34 per cent p.a. in the previous decade (Table 2.1, Chapter 2). Mumbai's population growth in the decade of 1990s has been lower than all-India urbanisation rate of 2.75 per cent in the 1990s. In the decade of 1980s, the city's population growth rate was higher than all-India urban population growth rate of 3.14 per cent. A deceleration in population growth rate is expected at some point in time and that has begun to happen. Further, population of other urban centres in Maharashtra is growing, leading to decline in Mumbai's share in total urban population of the state from 41.26 per cent in 1991 to just 33.90 per cent in 2001.

Table 3.4: Population and Population Growth Rates of MMR

Unit	*Population*			*Annual growth rate (%)*	
	1981	*1991*	*2001*	*1981-91*	*1991-01*
Municipal Urban Agglomeration (2001)					
1. Greater Mumbai	8,243,405	9925,891	11,914,398	1.87	1.84
2. Thane	474,365	803,389	1,261,517	5.41	4.62
3. Kalyan-Dombivali	578,353	820,089	1,193,266	3.55	3.82
4. Navi Mumbai	-	318,447	703,947	—	8.26
5. Mira Bhayander	-	175,605	520,301	—	11.47
6. Ulhasnagar	273,668	369,077	472,943	3.04	2.51
7. Ambernath		125,801	203,796		4.94
8. Kulgaon-Badlapur		52,154	97,917		6.5
Sub-Total (A)	9,569,791	12,590,453	16,368,085	2.78	2.66
Other Corporations and Municipal Councils					
1. Bhiwandi-Nizampur	115,295	379,070	598,703	12.64	4.68
2. Nallasopara		67,732	184,664		10.55
3. Vasai	34,943	39,781	49,346	1.31	2.18
4. Virar	—	57600	118945	—	7.52
5. Navghar Manikpur	—	59324	116700	—	7
Sub total (B)	150,238	603,507	1,068,358	14.92	5.88
Raigad District					
1. Alibagh	14,081	16,289	19,491	1.49	1.81
2. Karjat	-	19,304	25,544	—	2.53
3. Khopoli	32,102	45,039	58,657	3.44	2.68
4. Matheran	3,920	4,708	5,139	1.85	0.88
5. Panvel	37,073	58,986	104,031	4.75	5.84
6. Pen	14,772	21,588	30,203	3.87	3.42
7. Uran	15,168	17,775	23,254	1.6	2.72
Sub total (C)	117,086	184,289	266,319	4.64	3.75
Urban MMR (A+B+C)	9,837,116	13,376,249	17,854,935	3.12	2.92
Rural MMR	1,254,576	1,156,115	1047,124	-0.81	-0.99

Source: Population and Employment Profile of Mumbai Metropolitan Region.

Within the Mumbai Urban Agglomeration (MUA) area, the population growth has shifted to Navi Mumbai (8.26% p.a. growth) and Mira Bhayander (11.47% p.a. growth) in the 1990s (Table 3.5). Kalyan-Dombivali Municipal Corporation registered a slightly higher population in the decade of 1990s (3.82% p.a.) as compared to the previous decade (3.55% p.a.). Thane Municipal Corporation's growth has also slowed down in the decade of 1990s (4.62% p.a.), though its growth rate is still high. Notice that the urban population growth rate in the whole of Mumbai Metropolitan Region (MMR) has also been just 2.92 per cent p.a. and in the MUA was just 2.66 per cent p.a. in the 1990s, indicating that Mumbai and its surrounding areas have reduced attraction for the new migrants. In Chapter 2, Mahadevia has shown that the net immigration to the MUA has been just 8.59 lakhs during the 1990s.

Table 3.5: Wardwise Population and Growth Rates (% p.a.)

Wards	*Population*			*Annual rate of growth*	
	1981	*1991*	*2001*	*1981-91*	*1991-2001*
A	168,220	194,840	207,510	1.48	0.63
B	147,310	117,730	140,480	-2.22	1.78
C	270,700	197,220	190,670	-3.12	-0.34
D	384,040	344,880	378,610	-1.07	0.94
E	517,070	467,500	439,390	-1.00	-0.62
F	814,700	847,830	922,470	0.40	0.85
G	983,000	1,004,910	1,047,710	0.22	0.42
Mumbai Island	*3,285,040*	*3,174,910*	*3,326,840*	*-0.34*	*0.47*
H	706,840	798,740	915,170	1.23	1.37
K	925,680	1,242,680	1,500,510	2.99	1.90
P	663,730	928,690	1,226,560	3.42	2.82
R	561,920	977,880	1,453,440	5.70	4.04
Western Suburbs	*2,858,170*	*3,947,990*	*5,095,680*	*3.28*	*2.58*
L	434,020	616,600	774,810	3.57	2.31
M	565,770	822,910	1,080,850	3.82	2.76
N	599,420	686,760	614,950	1.37	-1.10
S	278,460	373,500	691,110	2.98	6.35
T	222,550	303,260	330,170	3.14	0.85
Eastern Suburbs	*2,100,220*	*2,803,030*	*3,491,890*	*2.93*	*2.22*
Greater Mumbai	8,243,430	9,925,930	11,914,410	1.87	1.84

Within the Mumbai city alone, that is within MCGM jurisdiction, population growth rate was just 1.84 per cent p.a. in the decade of 1990s, which is lower than 2.1 per cent p.a. natural population growth rate of India, means that some population has already left the city. If we apply 2.1 per cent as natural population growth rate then, about 3 lakh persons (or about 67,000 to 68,000 households) have left the city in this decade. In the previous decade, that of 1980s also, same was the situation with the MCGM population growth rate being 1.87 per cent p.a. Again, in the 1980s, about 3.2 lakh persons left MCGM areas to live in other parts of MMR, but not the Navi Mumbai areas. In 1990s, the other cities of MMR continue to grow along with a few nodes of the Navi Mumbai, mainly Vashi and Panvel. Post 2000, this trend has enhanced, particularly with the improvement in transport connectivity of Navi Mumbai nodes with Mumbai mainland through suburban railway.

It will be useful to see where in Mumbai the population growth deceleration has taken place. Deceleration in population growth in the MCGM has taken place in the western suburbs; where growth rates have declined from 3.28 per cent in 1980s to 2.58 per cent in the decade of 1990s and in the eastern suburbs where the growth rate has declined from 2.93 per cent in 1980s to 2.22 per cent (Table 3.5). In the decade of 1980s, island city had witnessed a negative growth rate of—0.34 per cent p.a. In the decade of 1990s, it has slightly improved to 0.47 per cent p.a. Though outmigration continues from the island city, the rate has decelerated. There is some densification happening in the island city in the decade of 1990s.

One such ward is B, where the p.a. growth rate has become positive, 1.78 per cent p.a in 1991-01 as compared to –2.22 per cent p.a. in 1981-91 (Table 3.5). Is this because of pushing of Muslim population to ward B in wake of 1992 riots? Ward B is where Muslim population is concentrated (based on physical verification) and our discussions with researchers in Mumbai who indicated that there has been internal migration in Mumbai after the communal violence of 1992-93, when Muslims moved into and non-Muslims moved out from Bhendi Bazaar and Teen Dongri area and Muslims also moved out to Mumbra on the mainland towards Navi Mumbai. In wards C and D also, the population decline has slowed down or halted in this decade. This could be due to halt in commercialisation of these wards, as large-scale commercial activities have shifted to Bandra-Kurla complex located in Ward H (east). Wards F and G have also observed increased population growth rates in the decade of 1990s as compared to the previous decade, which could be due to high-density towers coming up under Slum Redevelopment Schemes (SRS) or mill land redevelopment. This trend would accelerate with the recent Supreme Court judgement on Mill lands. This we would discuss later.

In the western suburbs, ward H has observed increase in population growth rate in the decade of 1990s (1.37% p.a.) as compared to the 1980s (1.23% p.a.). This could be because of new developments coming in this ward in the 1990s.There are also a large number of SRS schemes in this ward (Table 3.7). The SRS schemes are largest in number in ward K (26.5%), followed by ward G (18.2%) and ward H (13.0%). Thus, SRS scheme is partial answer to densification of wards G and H. Other reason ofcourse is the Bandra-Kurla complex around which some city revitalisation has taken place. SRS is not the only answer because;

population growth in ward K is lower in 1990s as compared to previous decade inspite of it having the largest number of SRS. In the eastern suburbs, except ward S, all other wards have observed deceleration in population growth in the decade of 1990s.

Table 3.6: Distribution of Slum Rehabilitation Schemes

Ward	*No of SRS scheme*	*% age of SRS projects*
A	0	0.0
B	0	0.0
C	0	0.0
D	0	0.0
E	2	0.8
F	13	5.1
G	46	18.2
H	33	13.0
K	67	26.5
L	13	5.1
M	6	2.4
N	14	5.5
P	26	10.3
R	21	8.3
S	2	0.8
T	10	4.0
	253	*100.0*

Source: Slum Redevelopment Authority (Status as on December, 2004).

Pre-Shanghaing Transformations

Real Estate Projects[17]

Over the past 15 years, the old industrial core of Mumbai has undergone widespread spatial change of a magnitude that has not occurred in the city in 150 years. This current restructuring is part of a larger attempt to transform Mumbai from an 'industrial' to a 'corporate' city. The ongoing changes can be first seen in the morphologically distinct square mile of land around Parel, in south-central Mumbai, where nearly all the city's 60 textile mills and workers' tenements were built between 1854 and 1925, and where new real estate projects have come up. The spatial changes are result of a politico-economic shift that brought with it sweeping changes in economic, industrial and land-use policy and as a result simplified the processes of industrial closure and retrenchment on one hand and effecting the zoning changes that would help to transform the land that was 'freed' from traditional manufacturing uses. In an immediate sense, the attempted restructuring was fuelled by the anticipated spurt in investment (domestic as well as foreign) in the immediate post-liberalisation period that informed a lot of speculative investment behaviour in the real estate sector. In broader terms, the spatial change was motivated by a widely anticipated transformation of the local labour economy, from an overwhelmingly 'industrial' to a 'modern', service-based one, in line with similar patterns of economic change in the industrialised world.

For the first time, the real estate speculation picked up in the early 1990s and then the bubble burst (Mahadevia and Singh 1998). Once again, in the early 2000, at the time when the main ruling party at the national level gave the slogan of 'India Shining' before the 2004 elections, it was based on the revival of the manufacturing sector on one hand with national level growth rate reaching 8 per cent and above. Feeling good factor in turn fed into the real estate boom.

Post-2000, real estate's energies have been focused on—apart from IT parks and business centres—luxury hotels and large, U.S.-style, covered, centrally temperature-controlled malls. The Mumbai Metropolitan Region (MMR), which is to have almost 30 of them over the next few years, is second only to the Delhi National Capital Region (NCR) where financial commitments have been made for 60 malls. A recently published mall-trade publication made the straightforward admission that one important reason for the sudden spurt in mall-building in the latest phase of economic liberalisation was simply that builders needed to look for newer avenues to invest in, after the boom in residential and corporate construction abated by the late 1990s. Where shops were once promoted by individual retailers, either responding directly to local needs or following state-sponsored shopping-district projects, the mall "boom has been fuelled by the attractive returns obtained by... mall developers over the last couple of years" (Retail Real Estate: Malls in India, undated: 8).

Though the physical changes are visible all over the MMR, they are particularly dramatic in some locations. The central Mumbai mill district has been the first to change, with many mill sites redeveloped into multi-storied residential, commercial and modern-sector office complexes. In the first wave of real-estate development, a few patchy developments of seamless conglomeration of steel-and-glass edifices were created amidst the skyline of dilapidated turn-of-the-century workers' chawls. It was then doubtful whether the entire space would be filled up with new developments. In the first phase, the government was also pondering over the land use and development policies. The second phase of real estate boom has started to fill up the voids here, although once again in a patchy manner, with new colourful and stylistic multi-storey buildings sticking out in the skyline.

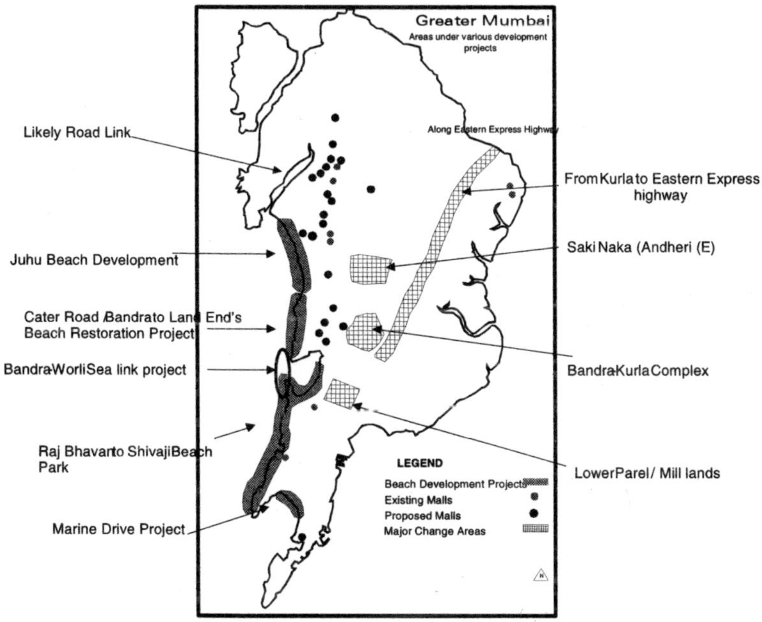

Fig. 3.1: Malls and New Developments

The other major real estate development has been the Bandra-Kurla Complex (BKC), close to the existing domestic and international airport. This complex has been built and the area developed by the MMRDA, on reclaimed land of Mahim creek and Mithi river, just north of the island city several decades ago with the intention that it would eventually replace the southern tip of the island city as the core business district. While the reclamation and development of the area started well in mid 1980s, it finally became the new economic hub of the city by the late 1990s. By early 2000s, it transformed into the national financial hub, with several financial institutions like the Reserve Bank of India, the National Stock Exchange (NSE), the National Bank for Agricultural and Rural Development (NABARD), Infrastructure Leasing and Financial Services (IL&FS) and several public—and private-sector banks, as well as the offices of pharmaceutical companies, the Bharat Diamond Bourse, a couple of very upscale private schools (Dhirubhai Ambani International

School) and a heart institute (Asian Heart Institute)—in short, as a microcosm of new-economy activity centres.

Just across the creek, moving south from Bandra-Kurla complex to the island city, is the Asia's largest slum pocket, Dharavi. The landscape that one would see from the tall buildings of Bandra-Kurla complex is of slums and polluted marshes of the creek, which were once full of mangroves, which were cut and land reclaimed by MMRDA to develop land for this complex. The Andheri-Saki Naka belt around the domestic and international airports is seeing feverish construction activity related to information technology (IT), new export-processing enclaves and business centres.

In the most recent phase, the arterial Eastern Express Highway, which stretches northwards from Kurla to Mulund and further into Thane district, which once had an almost unbroken line-up of engineering and pharmaceutical units—including Burroughs Welcome, Hoechst, Richardson Cruddas, Blowplast and GKW—that were set up soon after the textile mills came up during Mumbai's period of rapid industrialisation, now lie dotted with abandoned buildings, some already metamorphosing into expensive residential and commercial, or 'hospitality' complexes, others still awaiting transformation. The western-line suburbs appear all set to rival the Delhi NCR's 'Mall Mile' in Gurgaon, given that the majority of the proposed malls are along this strip, though the Mumbai city, Navi Mumbai and Thane areas will also have a few of these so-called 'large-format' shopping locations. Navi Mumbai is also in the throes of change—including, possibly, a new international airport.

Infrastructure Projects

The Shiv Sena-BJP government, when in power in the state government, had constructed 50 flyovers through Maharashtra State Road Development Corporation (MSRDC) in Mumbai in the decade of 1990s, purportedly to ease the traffic congestion on the roads. In continuation of this, two major infrastructure projects are under implementation now, Mumbai Urban Transport Project (MUTP) and Mumbai Urban Infrastructure Project (MUIP), the former funded by the World Bank and the latter by the state government. Both are being implemented by the MMRDA. While the MUTP is for the mass transportation within the Mumbai Metropolitan Region (MMR), the MUIP is to supplement MUTP, and is for the Greater Mumbai area, with the main objective of road network improvements and efficient traffic dispersal system in the city.

The MUIP is Rs. 2,648.00 crores project, which would improve 462 km of Development Plan (DP) roads[18]. The MMRDA is the designated nodal agency for implementation of MUIP. The projects identified by the concerned agencies such as MMRDA, MCGM, MSRDC and Public Works Department (PWD) are expected to be completed within three years of its starting. The components of the project are: (i) DP Roads—52 in the eastern suburbs, 60 in the western suburbs and 22 in the island city, (ii) elevated roads—6 in the eastern suburbs and 4 in the island city; (iii) flyovers—10 in the eastern suburbs, 17 in the western suburbs and 14 in the island city; (iv) Railway overbridges—1 in the eastern suburbs, 7 in the western suburbs and 8 in the island city; (v) vehicular subways—8 in the eastern suburbs and 1 each in the western suburbs and the island city and (vi) pedestrian subways—27 in the eastern suburbs, 5 in the western suburbs and 24 in the island city. Along with the objectives such as preparing a traffic dispersal model for efficient mobility and connectivity, developing major north-south road links in suburbs including a Mass Rapid Transit connectivity and strengthening east-west connectivity, is the objective of providing high capacity uninterrupted road connection to both the Airports, one that is existing and one proposed near Navi Mumbai on the mainland. About 35,000 slum families to be affected by the project would be provided rehabilitation, to be located in Mankhurd ward[19]. It is not known how the loans would be repaid and whether there is any revenue model in MUIP.

MUTP is a sequel to Bombay Urban Transport Project (BUTP) completed in 1984 at the cost of Rs. 39 crores[20]. MUTP envisages investment in suburban railway projects, local bus transport, new roads, bridges, pedestrian subways and traffic management activities. Mumbai Rail Vikas Corporation (MRVC), a joint venture of Railways and Government of Maharashtra, is set up for implementation of rail projects under MUTP and other projects of Railways in the MMR. The total estimated cost of the project is to be Rs. 4,526 crores, of which the World Bank has sanctioned a loan of Rs. 2,602 crores, which is 57 per cent of the total cost. The project implementation period is 2002 to 2008. Incidentally, the MUTP proposal is adopted by the Mumbai Vision Plan document, considering it an important component of converting Mumbai into a World Class city. The cost break-up is: (i) Rail transport component—Rs. 3,030 crores; (ii) Road transport—Rs. 829 crores; (iii) Rehabilitation and resettlement (R&R)—Rs. 468 crores, (iv) Taxes, duties and fees —Rs. 199 crores. Inclusive of all costs including R&R costs, the road component will cost Rs. 1,016 crores and rail project would cost Rs. 3,510 crores. If we look at the components of the rail project, there would be improvement but not a drastic make-over in the suburban rail transport, as the main thrust is to increase the present carrying capacity by increasing the tracks and increasing the number of coaches. In the road component, two new link roads have been proposed besides building of some railway overbridges and purchase of new buses for the Bombay Electric Supply and Transport (BEST) Undertaking. 19,128 slum families required to be moved have been provided with a housing of 225 sq ft unit[21]. Society for the Promotion of Area Resource Centres (SPARC) has been appointed as the main NGO partner for the rehabilitation purpose.

Legislative Changes

The real estate lobby has been helped by many legislative changes in the last decade. It is worth discussing them here. In the early 1990s, several changes in the Development Control Regulations (DCR) were carried out. The first one was in 1991, when Section 58 of the DCR was changed by the state government. Under the changed rules, "a [textile-] mill owner was permitted to sell or redevelop his land, provided one-third [of the land] was surrendered to the municipal corporation for public amenities and another third to the Maharashtra Housing and Area Development Authority (MHADA) for low-cost housing. The remaining third was for the use of the mill-owner" (D'Monte 2006)—though he or she could use the buildable capacity of the entire plot on this one-third, so the mill-owner actually lost nothing. An argument was put forward by the labour organisations that the thousands of mill-workers who were put out of jobs through the economic changes—often with very meagre compensation packages—ought to be included in the parcelling out of benefits, and there was a suggestion floated that the 'one-third' rule should be modified to a 'one-fourth' rule that included mill-workers as beneficiaries of the sale or reuse of the land. This suggestion, however, died a quiet, barely debated death.

Ten years later, in 2001, the state of Maharashtra "surreptitiously amended this clause to make it apply only to vacant land—as distinct from the entire footprint of the mill. Since mills, characteristically, occupy a huge footprint—each worker has about 32 sq metres of space in a shed—the amendment fraudulently deprived Mumbai of several hundred acres of space at one stroke." (D'Monte, 2006). Mills lands—including those belonging to the public-sector National Textile Corporation—sold for phenomenal prices, thereby raising the index value of property in the central Mumbai mill district exponentially overnight. A PIL contested the change of 2001 in Clause 58 of the DCR in court. The Mumbai high court supported the petitioners, but the Supreme Court of the nation threw the petition out in a fast-track hearing a few months later. The field is now completely open to mill-owners who would be property developers—whose ranks include members of the political elite as well as big-time developers from Mumbai and Delhi, apart from the mill-owners themselves. The developments that will now clutter the very core of the city will change Mumbai forever, and put paid to any chances of either green spaces or living spaces for the poor.

Another effort was introduction of land management tool such as the Transfer of Development Rights (TDR) and increase in FSI to attract private builders in housing the slum dwellers under the SRS administered by the Slum Rehabilitation Authority (SRA). This scheme was originally introduced by the Shiv Sena (SS)—Bharatiya Janata Party (BJP) government in Maharashtra state in 1997, following the recommendations of a committee set up in 1995 by that government. This committee, headed by then Chief Secretary Dinesh Afzalpurkar, suggested among other things that close to 80 per cent of the slums in the Mumbai area could be resettled in situ.[22]

This scheme, which "attempts to tackle the oft-experienced issue of [the] lack of resources for housing provision by bringing in the market any private initiative" (Bhide et al 2003: 6 & 11) hoped to attract private builders by giving them the benefit of extra FSI on sites where they agreed to rebuild existing slums. Also, they could avail of development rights elsewhere or from elsewhere in these locations. In other words, they could sell a sizeable number of flats in the open market through special benefits, provided they housed all the earlier inhabitants of the site and by this make their profit along with rehabilitating the slum dwellers. This scheme lost steam after the real estate crash of the late 1990s. However, after the SS-BJP government was replaced by a Congress-NCP one, the scheme was continued, with some changes. Various studies have shown, however, that builders are only interested in redeveloping slums on prime locations where the profits may be maximised, and that slum-dwellers in less favourable sites who have tried to form cooperatives of their own to rebuild their homes under the scheme have found the going much harder than have the more powerful builders (Mitra, 2005). Among all the slum development schemes introduced till now the SRS is the most obviously market-oriented scheme of them all. As we would see later, this is what continues as the policy in the Mumbai Vision Plan.

The pre-Shanghaing Phase of Mumbai's transformation has distinct characteristics; the emphasis is on the development of high-end real-estate projects such as malls, tall chrome-and-glass buildings for offices and residences to support the new economy, and showpiece infrastructure projects like flyovers and sea-links.

Critiquing Vision of Global Mumbai

The vision is not for Mumbai to become Shanghai but for Mumbai to achieve the role that Shanghai played in pushing national economic growth on one hand and, in the process, transform itself. Shanghai was the commercial capital of China till the communist takeover in 1949. Then, Shanghai became one of the modern industrial centres of China, contributing surplus to the national economy. Shanghai's renewal was taken up in the first half of 1990s, through development of Pudong Area on the right bank of river Hangpu. Then started the rise of Shanghai as one of the attractive global city of China and also in the world. Real estate followed by infrastructure projects played an important role in this process of Shanghai's transformation. Today, Shanghai is the only city that has a magnetic levitation (meglev) train used as suburban transport in a city, which connects the Pudong international airport[23] to the Pudong city centre. The city also has number of elevated highways, subway, parks, convention centre, city development museum, heritage areas and most noticeable of all tall glass buildings, the Pearl tower in the Pudong area.

This reference of Shanghai has slipped into the policy statements of the politicians of Maharashtra State, in which Mumbai is located. The current Chief Minister of Maharashtra, Mr. Vilasrao Deshmukh had following to say on the vision for Mumbai[24]:

> "Citizens will see many suburban road projects completed on a war footing by next December, although the rehabilitation of as many as 20,000 slum families is an onerous task. The proliferation of slums throughout the city has created obstacles for development and today there are demands that the cut-off date for regularising hutments be extended to 2000. But the existing law clearly stipulates that protection to slums can be given only if they existed prior to January 1, 1995.
>
> I admit that the Congress-NCP[25] manifesto did promise to extend this cut-off date to 2000. However, any amendment to the existing law will only be done after reaching a consensus with all political

parties, including the Shiv Sena and BJP. There is no pressure on me to halt the ongoing demolition drive and I am not going to stop the BMC. Instead, we need to go further and investigate the people behind the growth of slums—for instance, the slumlords and officials who protect them. In the first phase, encroachers coming in the way of public utility projects will be removed. In the second phase, those who have taken over footpaths will be cleared. Those slum dwellers who are eligible will be rehoused. Yes, some of my party members do keep reminding me about our pre-poll promise. So I tell them to let us at least start tackling illegal hutments that came up from 2000 to 2004.

"Today, Shanghai has become a symbol for Mumbai—that city started from zero and see where it is today. Citizens here will start having confidence in the government when they see Mumbai's transformation in the next five years. This is not mere talk. We want citizens' groups to support us. Their advice and suggestions for improving the city will be considered. There are many experienced people among them and we will not deny them this opportunity. For instance, architect Charles Correa's plan for redeveloping closed mill lands while envisaging more open spaces is surely in the city's interest."

Further, in another interview the Chief Minister states that:

"I have a dream to make Mumbai a world class city. The Prime Minister, Dr. Manmohan Singh, has assured us all possible help in this endeavour. We have already started planned work in this regard and within five years you will see transformed Mumbai. This will provide new opportunities and avenues in IT and ITES-related activities. I am confident that global leaders in this sector will give their first preference to Mumbai for their new ventures."[26]

The vision of the Chief Minister of the state knits well into the 'Vision' of turning Mumbai into a 'World Class City' that is being promoted by prominent representatives of corporate sector as well as leaders of the political establishment. Both Prime Minister Manmohan Singh and Maharashtra Chief Minister Vilasrao Deshmukh have said, in public fora, that they hope to turn Mumbai into Shanghai—never mentioning that Shanghai's current new-economy successes have been built on decades of agricultural change and rapid industrialisation in the city's hinterland on one hand and high levels of human development[27], as is the case with the whole of China.

Economy

The beginning of the executive summary of the Mumbai Vision Plan states: "To become a vibrant international metropolis, Mumbai must ensure that its economic growth is comparable to world-class levels while simultaneously upgrading the quality of life it provides to its citizens. At present it is slipping up on both dimensions. If it wants to achieve this status, the Government and the citizens need to undergo a change in mind-set rather than continuing to think incrementally." (Bombay First-McKinsey 2003: 1). There is a lot of emphasis on term citizenship. This would mean that those not having citizenship rights would be directly excluded.

The new vision plan has been presented to the public through a document titled 'Summary and Recommendations' prepared by McKinsey and Company for Bombay First, a 'citizen's group' promoted by the Bombay Chamber of Commerce and Industry, which tells us in its report that it worked closely with the MCGM, the MMRDA and the Government of Maharashtra (GOM). This is the first identifiable document that uses both the terms 'vision' and 'world-class city' in the context of Mumbai. This report, which came out in late September 2003, recognises that to "become a vibrant, world-class city, Mumbai needs to grow at 8-10 per cent per annum: an increase of 4-5 percentage points over what it achieved in the (previous)[28] four or five years." What are the significant elements of the transformation that these vision documents seek? It proposes to increase the income growth by focusing on "four thrust areas: high-end services; low-end services; hinterland-based manufacturing; and its transformation into a consumption centre" (Bombay First—McKinsey 2003: 13).

The "low-end service sector" that will, presumably, provide employment to the bulk of the employable population would include "construction, hotels/tourism/recreation and modern format retail". In other words, the high-skilled, reasonably secure and well-paying factory jobs of the industrial growth phase will be replaced by the contractual, service-based economy, more vulnerable employment situation than before. The new vision is in the direction of the reality, where there has been a shift towards low-wage, insecure, service sector economy, which resembles a pre-rather than a post-industrial economy, and not high wages as envisaged by the vision. The 'high-end' service sector—identified by

Bombay First-McKinsey as including financial services, healthcare, IT and IT-enabled services, and media/entertainment/telecom. Mall-building is singled out as a means of "boost(ing) the construction and retail industries which are the key drivers of economic growth and employment" (Bombay First-McKinsey 2003: 15). All manufacturing activity is to be restricted to the 'hinterland' which is not specified locationally, so it is not clear whether the revenues from the 'hinterland' will be available to Greater Mumbai or not. There is no idea how this drastic economic transformation is to be achieved in very short period of time. Are we dreaming or is it a way to suggest expelling of the existing economic activities under the endorsement of the Vision Plan.

The Chief Minister's Task Force (CMTF), constituted within weeks of the Bombay First-McKinsey report's publication, clearly acknowledges that it is a response to the report. In its own report of early 2004, the CMTF agrees with the McKinsey report that Mumbai needs to boost its economy around "high-end services" but also needs to find "employment for less skilled populations", and recommends that "Mumbai... work to generate low-end, high-volume services like infrastructure development, construction, retail and hotels and tourism". It suggests that the manufacturing 'hinterland' could be a resuscitated Thane-Belapur industrial belt, which will be boosted by being turned into a 'Special Manufacturing Zone', on the lines of a Special Economic Zone (SEZ)—in other words, a place where tax breaks, captive infrastructure facilities and most important of all, 'progressive' labour laws that discourage job tenure and unionising are in place by law. This has happened in fact, with two large SEZs, one, Navi Mumbai SEZ (NMSEZ) located in Navi Mumbai, and two, Maha Mumbai SEZ (MMSEZ) located just outside Navi Mumbai limits but within the MMR. The latter one was initially planned on 13,000 hectares (Bunsha 2006), but has been given a permission to develop only 5,000 hectares[29]. The NMSEZ, has the site of the proposed new international airport and the existing port of Mumbai named Jawaharlal Nehru Port (JNP), the largest Port on the west coast of India. NMSEZ is spread over al area of 50 sq km[30], taking up about 14.5 per cent of the area of Navi Mumbai.

Subsequently, the Indian Merchants' Chamber (IMC) organised a series of seminars on the subject of "Making Mumbai a World Class City", and published a document titled "Development of Mumbai City: Mumbai Past Present and Future", based on a series of presentations made by various political parties and the IMC itself. In its own vision for Mumbai, "The city in 2020 could be free of industry." "I learn", says

Shailesh Haribhakti, President, IMC, "that the very last manufacturing activity in mid—and south Mumbai—(the) Glaxo factory at Prabhadevi—has closed down for good. The place needs to be converted into a centre of population engaged in green, clean activities such as biotechnology, information technology, design, entertainment and all the things that Mumbai is known for. Business process outsourcing, education and trading could become the new activity in this vibrant city" (Haribhakti undated: 165).

Transportation

Obviously, such a vision is impossible to support without adequate infrastructural backing, and once again, the IMC provides the most dramatic picture: "Let's take a journey to 2020 and let's look at what Mumbai can be. Let's imagine that we have landed at Sahar (Chatrapati Shivaji International) Airport and from there an absolutely clean, modern six-lane highway takes us right to the freeway system which connects the... airport to all parts of Mumbai whether it is south Mumbai or north Mumbai or east or west. The slums which greet us today will, by a miracle of science and technology, (be) cleaned up, rehabilitated. An uninterrupted highway takes us to Bandra and from (t)here the sea-link takes us to Worli and onward to downtown South Mumbai, which has miraculously been freed of the polluting cars that today greet us" (Haribhakti undated: 165).

Both, the Bombay First-McKinsey and CMTF reports emphasise the need for the increase and improvement in rail and road transport facilities—both of which are already underway through the Rs. 4,526 crore World Bank supported MUTP, and the Rs. 2,648 crore MUIP, both discussed earlier, and the need to have the Bandra-Worli tollway sealink completed expeditiously, so that the 'high-end' new economy may proceed swiftly and smoothly from the airports and their workplaces around the airports to the island—city's business districts, completely bypassing the older commercial and residential areas along the way. There are plans for increasing train capacity, but not much about the city's bus service. This is surprising, considering that in Mumbai, the BEST, the autonomous unit of the MCGM that runs the city's bus-transport service, has a total fleet of 3,075 buses (the second largest among the metro cities, after Delhi) has only been able to increase its fleet by 6.9 per cent over the last half decade (1995-96 to 2001-02), which is quite insignificant when compared with Delhi (which registered an 185% increase), and Ahmedabad (25%)[31]. The MUTP provides for purchase of 500 buses and nothing more. In that case, improvement from point to point, from 3,075 buses in 2001-02, to 3,575 when the 500 buses get added would only be 16.3 per cent, which is not much of an improvement. This is of course, in part because Mumbai relies more heavily on its train than its bus services for public transport.

These apart, the Bombay First-McKinsey document includes proposals for an "inner ring rail" loop linking Goregaon, Andheri, Bandra, the Bandra-Kurla Complex and the Andheri-Ghatkopar stretch, an "inner ring freeway" link between the under-construction Bandra-Nariman Point sealink and the proposed East Island freeway, and an "outer ring-rail and freeway" link that will connect the island city eastwards and northwards to Nhava Sheva and the Mumbai-Pune expressway, then back to the Vashi-Belapur expressway and Kurla in the eastern suburbs. Then, of course, there will be the Mumbai metro. There is a great emphasis on the road projects and high-end economic activities. It is clear for whom these are to be, if we bring in the grievances of IT and BT professionals and lobby in Bangalore and extend their demands to other cities where such activities would come. In Bangalore, these lobbies have been hollering for only road infrastructure[32].

Financing

The report is hazy about the financing for all these projects, and hopes that three-quarters of an estimated Rs. 200,000 crores needed over the next 10 years for all the additional infrastructural projects will come through private financing. The report points out comfortingly that Shanghai spent the same amount of money over the same period on beefing up its infrastructure. This means that total Rs. 50,000 crores or Rs. 5,000 crores per year would have to come from the public sector. Of this, the government will have to put in only Rs. 1,500 crores upfront, whereas the rest Rs. 3,500 crores per year, would come as long term loans, to be repaid back through user charges and increased tax collections (Bombay First-McKinsey 2003: 24). This puts onus on the MCGM to ensure that the urban poor are not priced out of the public services. However, nothing much is known about the financial implications of this route of development.

Would the city residents, in particular the low income ones be able to bear the increased costs of public services? Answer is only when they would get better jobs at higher pay. Do we wait for the employment situation to improve? No says the report. The employment situation will improve only if investments would come into the city, and that would happen only when the infrastructure starts improving. Hence, the plan has to be immediately put in implementation. What would be the implications of the plan on the existing urban poor in the interim period is not thought of and not discussed. Most likely, as the experience shows, they would end up paying through their nose for the public services or they would be left to fend for themselves, as they have been doing till now.

The government vision document echoes the figures exactly, stating rather expansively: "To become world-class, Mumbai requires Rs. 200,000 in investment over 10 years, mostly from the private sector." It agrees with Bombay First-McKinsey that the financing should be through a public-private partnership, that the city's 'land assets' can be used to boost revenue that will go into a separate Mumbai Development Fund that will be "ring-fenced" by law, and monitored by a special, state-government appointed Secretary for Mumbai and a Citizen's Action Group "made up of eminent citizens and chaired by the Chief Minister".

MMRDA has already been doing this. For example, India's largest corporate house, Reliance Industries has entered the real estate market and clinched a land deal in Bandra-Kurla complex by a winning bid of Rs. 1,104.11 crores for a 7.5 acre plot[33], that is, Rs. 33,800 for 1 sq ft of land. Reliance plans to build a convention centre here. This is also very much a part of the Vision 2013 proposal.

Then the question arises as how the Rs. 1,500 crores government contribution has to come and another Rs. 3,500 crores capital investment has to come from borrowing or capital market then, do the MCGM have a capacity to get such amounts. The MCGM's total budget for year 2004-05 (proposed) was Rs. 7043.7 crores, of which Rs. 1,612.6 crores is for capital investments (MCGM 2005). The similar sized amount has to be raised by the MCGM or MMRDA for these works. In most likely possibility, it will be the MMRDA that would take this job and not the MCGM. The MMRDA may hope for the amount of Rs. 1,500 crores or less from the National Urban Renewal Mission (NURM) introduced in December 2005. A newspaper report stated that Mumbai was to get only Rs. 700 crores under the NURM for the year 2006-07[34], an amount which the Bombay First is not happy about[35].

Governance

As the features of a latter-day 'Bombay Plan' emerge, it also becomes clear that power is sought to be taken away from the elected and administrative arms of the local municipal government, and shared between the state government and 'eminent citizens'—in other words, representatives of the private sector, as is the case with the Bangalore Agenda Task Force (BATF), which famously includes Nandan Nilekeni of Infosys.

One of the prominent corporate leader had following to say about megacities in general and which is pertinent for Mumbai as well:

> "major cities be centrally administered areas reporting to the President so that the state leadership is not divided between the welfare of the rural and the urban regions."... "Maybe the time has come when we need to have serious political leadership which means business. One which would make an all-out effort to solve the problems of the urban areas." ... "In Mumbai or Delhi or Kolkata, you see the cities crumbling—there is no concerted initiative that is looking at the big picture and providing the basic services—good roads, airports and power" ... and there must be appointment of a cadre of officers, "preferably from premier schools of management and with competitive salaries so they can take up the cities' problems on an urgent basis."[36]

The same corportate leader, prominently quoted by local media on a recent visit to Mumbai stated that the office of the Municipal Commissioner (MC) needed to be abolished, and replaced by a one with a municipal 'CEO'.

The Municipal Commissioner of Mumbai also has prepared a Vision Document from the MCGM side. It has remained a low key document. This document only talks of a modest Rs. 300 crores contribution from the Municipal Corporation of Greater Mumbai to the MUIP, and otherwise confines itself to promises to improve existing services like water supply, sewage disposal, education and healthcare.

Housing

One area that all the vision documents expend a lot of energy on is housing and slum management. At the upper end, further relaxation of transaction costs and stamp duties are suggested, as also the doing away with the rent control legislation so as to increase the stock of rental housing in Mumbai, which is now as low as 5-10 per cent (as against international figures of 40-50%). They are also all very concerned about Mumbai's slums—MCGM estimates suggest that 60 per cent of Mumbai's population lives in slums[37] (the 2001 population census puts the figure at 54.1% India, Office of the Registrar General & Census Commission (2005), and it is impossible to get anywhere in Mumbai without driving past a shantytown or pavement settlement—which is rather damaging to the vision of a 'world-class city. The Bombay First-McKinsey plan offers a set of methods by which over a million low-income houses may be constructed over a 10-year period, to rehouse the city's slum-dwellers. For a start, the existing SRS, the document states is "commercially unviable" because of its "generosity" in promising "free housing". Instead, it says, rehoused slum-dwellers should either pay a lump sum for their new property or a "user charge" of Rs. 750-1,500 per month. They would, of course, also pay property taxes as well as charges for maintenance and facilities like water and electricity (which last all slum-dwellers already do, even if within an informal system)—and pay-per-use toilets. The report also suggests that the controversial cut-off date for slum-dwellers eligible for rehousing be retained at January 1, 1995, and that the choice of (re)developer for a particular slum be based on "market-based" auctions (Bombay First—McKinsey 2003).

The Maharashtra government report also favours making slum-dwellers pay for their housing, with the suggestion that this will discourage encroachments—apparently because there will be no free housing to be had. However, unless vacant land is closely guarded, studies have suggested that a policy of making the poor pay for housing only induces them to sell the new homes and move back to somewhere that it is possible to live at a cheaper level—which is by no means an irrational human choice (Government of Maharashtra, 2004). None of the reports address the patterns that are emerging as a result of the SRA projects that have already been completed—for one thing, it is already substantially market-driven: the viability levels are such that only very large, high-value projects situated along major road or rail arteries are truly successful, and given that most of the money has to be committed up-front, the system favours professional developers rather than local community and non-governmental organisations that have also participated in SRA schemes (Mitra 2005). A study by Mukhija (2003) of a SRS in Dharavi pocket implemented by NGO SPARC showed that it took the NGO about 15 years to complete the project. The main problem was getting finance, which the SPARC being a powerful NGO could get. Mitra's (2005) study of a SRS in a slum pocket implemented by another NGO named Slum Rehabilitation Society also indicated that finance was a problem to begin the project, even if all the residents had agreed to participate. Lastly, not all NGO initiated slum rehabilitation can be successful, as Contractor *et al.* (2005) of CEHAT find. The SRS is not a full answer to the housing problems of Mumbai.

From 1995 to 2004, in 9-year period, only 206 slums were taken up under the SRS scheme and 32,625 housing units were constructed, which is covering only about 4 per cent[38] of the total slum population of the city! SRA also states that 704 slums have been approved for SRS, which would construct 177,484 units (as of December 2004). If all of them get completed in the following 5-year period, then only 18 per cent of the total slum population would be covered. Therefore on an average around 1.6 per cent of the slum population is getting rehabilitated annually (Mitra 2005).

Government appointed Tinaikar Committee Report into the success of SRS alleges that SRS is a fraudulent scheme: SRA as "of the builders, by the builders, and for the builders". According to the Committee report, Public land in Mumbai's prime areas was handed over to builders for a pittance; rules were violated while arranging loans for developers; builders abandoned construction mid-way without completing them; and some projects did not even take off after getting commencement certificates. The report further states that the schemes relying on builders to construct houses for slum dwellers are doomed to fail. "The size of the problem," his report said, "is of a magnitude with reference to which the achievement over the last 10 years of the slum rehabilitation scheme is so minuscule; the gains derived by some developers by grabbing premium plots of public authorities for a song, are so high; and excessively liberal development control rules to `facilitate' the developers to make unlimited profit at the cost of integrated development of (this) metro city so brazen; that the continuation of this policy... is bound to be disastrous.". How far is it desirable to depend on only SRS for addressing the slum housing question, which all the vision documents do?

This government document also addresses the problem of Dharavi—commonly referred to as 'Asia's largest slum'—which occupies land that was once a marshy backwater beyond the city limits, but is now right in the epicentre of the new developments, immediately to the south of the Bandra-Kurla Complex, east of the new Bandra-Worli Sealink, west of the Eastern Express Highway—and stretched out bare along the road to the airports. Most promoters of the new economy and of the vision of Mumbai as a "world-class city" would like to wish Dharavi away. Given Dharavi's close location to the Bandra-Kurla Complex, it cannot be wished away; the land here is gold mine. Still, proposals for the "redevelopment" of Dharavi that envisage hiving away at least the most visible parts of it, abound. The Government of Maharashtra document suggests that "at least three sectors of Dharavi" be developed "for commercial or office use", and that the Bandra-Kurla Complex be extended to Dharavi (GOM 2004).

A project proposal called 'Dharam' (for Dharavi Mandal) proposed by developer Mukesh Mehta, suggests that the parts of the sprawling slum that border the Bandra-Kurla complex and Mahim be sold off for private development by outside parties, and that the area immediately behind these sold-off sections be turned into green areas. This is Rs. 5,600-crore plan, wherein Dharavi's 174 hectares will be divided into 10 zones for residential, commercial and industrial development. The builder will also have to construct schools, hospitals, gardens and playgrounds. To cross-subsidise the project, the developer gets a portion of the land for commercial development[39] . Dharavi's original inhabitants are to be rehabilitated behind this buffer green zone, far away from the main arteries of the "world-class city". Presumably, once the areas of Kurla and Sion—which now directly face the portions of Dharavi where the original slum-dwellers are to be clustered together under Mehta's plan—also gentrify, they can be provided screens and buffers of the kind now allotted to Dharavi's western and northern face in this plan. All these could be achieved by increasing the FSI, argues Mehta's Plan. There has also been proposal to shift some of the slum dwellers from Dharavi to the salt-pans in the north, a plan that was approved by the Government of Maharashtra, to be put on hold after the Tsunami disaster of 2004[40] . The proposal to use salt-pan lands for housing is part of the Vision document.

The residents of Dharavi are highly sceptical of this project proposal. Dharavi has godowns and industries, whose owners may resist shifting. It is a tall order to rehabilitate 6 lakh residents, given the success rate of SRS. Once again, how far SRS and builder driven housing policy is the solution for Mumbai's slums? If it is not then what are the motives behind such schemes such as Dharavi redevelopment and SRS being accepted as solution for slum problem of Mumbai? Is this a dream sold to drive away the slum dwellers?

It is in the context of this desire to arrive at a city beautiful by simply wiping away its slums that the unprecedentedly large-scale slum demolitions and evictions that took place in Mumbai in December-February, 2004 need to be studied. As is commonly known, the government periodically issues cut-off dates to decide on whether slums may be legalised or not. The most recent such notified date was January 1, 1995: in other words, all slums that have come up after that date are unprotected and, therefore, may be demolished without any legal requirement to resettle. According to a survey conducted by the MCGM, around 35 lakh (3.5 million) people in Greater Mumbai fall in this unprotected category. However, the pressure on Maharashtra Chief Minister Vilasrao Deshmukh to demonstrate his government's willingness to work to turn Mumbai into a world-class city was clearly so intense that on December 8, 2004, he announced that the state government would demolish all post-1995 "encroachments". The extent, process and politics of slum demolitions is discussed in another paper (Mahadevia and Narayanan, Chapter 18).

Studies have shown that even state-supported housing projects have proved unaffordable for lower middle-class buyers (Narayanan 2003: 202-203). It is doubtful whether the market reforms proposed to bring down the price of real estate in Mumbai will benefit any but the best-off category of buyers, though a rationalisation of rental legislation might indeed bring some relief to a larger number of residents.

A Corporate Take-Over?

The corporate sector has latched on to the term 'World Class City'. The politicians like the metaphor of Shanghai, as by invoking China, they can be more opaque in decision-making than they have been till now. The central government finance ministry has been interested in developing Mumbai as a Regional Financial Centre (RFC)[41] . Whatever name given, the metaphor is the same; make Mumbai suitable to play a global role, through a process that is least transparent as possible. What to do about the low-income groups, the slum dwellers, the hawkers, etc., the legacy of a declined industrial centre or slumbay? Would they be included? The message is clear; with the increased hostility towards the slum dwellers and other poor, they are unwanted in a 'Global City' as Mumbai. The Visions are to convert the informally organised city into a formally organised one. There are two ways of doing it, to either integrate the informal sector within the new dispensation by improving their capabilities or to throw them out to the extent necessary and possible. To go through the first route requires patience and time and massive institutional efforts that currently do not exist in the city.

Today, certainly, Mumbai is not in a position to offer globally competitive quality of life to anyone. The present transformation proposed is on the backdrop of a city that has been already segmented by class (Mahadevia 1998), religion (Punwani 2003) and caste (Vora and Palsikar 2003), where the interests of the real estate lobby have subverted the city planning efforts (Banerjee-Guha 1995), where the housing struggles have continued through its modern history (Das 2003, Bhide Chapter 19, Mahadevia and Narayanan Chapter 18). The transformation is also in the backdrop of deindustrialisation and informalisation. The city has also become hostage to the interests of the real estate, which has pushed 60 per cent of her population to live in the slums.

In the last fifty years of city's development, from being a dream city it has become Slumbay, a city becoming more and more hostile to the migrant population, particularly low income ones and the poor. About net 3 lakh people have left MCGM area in the decade of 1990s and just 8 lakh new migrants have come to the MUA area in the decade, which is not much. Inspite of restrictive migration policy and one child population policy, Beijing city had experienced a growth rate of 3.37 per cent p.a. in 1991-2001, when MUA experienced just 2.65 per cent p.a. population growth rate. The city of Mumbai therefore has not been welcoming to the migrants since last two decades and particularly not welcoming to the low-income rural migrants. The base of formation of a 'Global City' in context of Mumbai has been exclusions. In that case, how would one not expect the new metaphor of a global city to be anything but exclusions!

Inspite of the rhetoric, Mumbai cannot be a World Class City; if the needs of the Mumbai's poor and the slum dwellers are not met. Large many academics, journalists and activists in Mumbai and countrywide have decried slum demolitions and also the Vision Plan. They have argued that slum dwellers are being made scapegoats for all the failures of Mumbai, when they occupy only 8 per cent of land; 60 per cent of the city's population living on 8 per cent of city's lands! The slum dwellers are also not consuming much of the city's resources, nor are they going to utilise the new infrastructure to come. The viability of some of the new infrastructure proposed is also being questioned. In a seminar held in Mumbai on March 2 and 3, 2005, wherein the planners, architects and activists participated, they not just ridiculed the Mumbai makeover, but also criticised the slum demolitions and demanded to evoke the spirit of an older city. They said that grand projects cannot make a great city[42]. There has been unequivocal criticism of slum demolitions under the guise of using Shanghai as a metaphor. The Vision Plan is called 'Mumbai Take Over' (by the builders) plan by some.

Would the Corporate sector not have visualised the difficulty in such a transformation of Mumbai, particularly the financial difficulties? Where would so much of private funds come in when they have not come into the city for the infrastructure projects till now? If the metaphor of Shanghai or any other Chinese city, say Beijing has to be used then, it need be known that these two cities have not raised any capital funds or floated bonds in two years, 2002 and 2004 (Mahadevia 2007a) for capital investments in infrastructure projects; about 30 per cent to 40 per cent of the capital funds come as loans (from Construction Bank of China) and the rest are the funds raised by the city governments themselves from their own enterprises and sale of lands. Even FDI is not a source of capital investments in these two cities (Mahadevia, 2007a). Mumbai may not have such high creditworthiness to rake in more loans. And if lands have to be used for infrastructure use then the lands have to be owned by the city or state government, like in China where all the lands are owned by the city government and hence can do whatever they want to do with these lands. Use of lands for raising resources for infrastructure in Indian cities would mean selling of small parcels of lands that the municipal and state governments have to the private builders, the latter raking in moolah while the public lands would not be available for housing of the poor. This would mean continuing severe evictions to wrench away the lands from the slum dwellers. If the World Bank offers loans then it would also have a rehabilitation component in it, which would raise up the project costs. Thus, neither finance nor the lands are going to be easy to get.

Then, is this project of converting Mumbai into a World Class City unviable in the short run system that India has and has the corporate sector realised it? We think that non-achievability of the vision is clear to every one, including the visionaries. Our suspicion is that such Vision Plans are a ploy to force the state and municipal government to push out as many slum dwellers as possible into those nooks and corners of the city where they cannot be seen. All Global Cities in Asia have their share of poor who are so hidden away from the eyes of the richer sections, tourists and global business class. Further, the elites also want to lay claim to public finance, to the extent they can extract, from the state government and central government to build the infrastructure that would ease their living and give them a quality of life of global standards or better. For Indian Corporate class, what more could be an amiable goal than live a first world quality of life at third world cost of living! "You may also continue to live in Bangalore and enjoy a cost of living one-fiftieth of the cost of living in Japan. You will live like royalty.", said Ohmae (2001: 38), in the plenary address to the Conference on Global City Regions held in 1999 at the School of Public Policy and Social Research, University of California, Los Angeles. That would be possible if the overall labour costs in the economy are kept low. That is only possible through the presence of informal sector in the city, but not in the places where they can be seen. However, not many poor are required to fulfil this role of giving the rich a low cost living. Hence, the rest have to be in any case expelled, directly through demolitions and indirectly by the constant threat of evictions and their criminalisation.

Liberalisation has brought in new demands upon urban space which have to be met given that the business interests are very strong in these cities. Indian business class, the Indian corporates aspiring global role, see globalisation as an opportunity for themselves. Indian bureaucrats have always had good relations with the corporate body, as it was a necessity of the corporate body in the license-raj era. Now, the bureaucrats have begun to join corporate houses after their retirement, due or premature. Hence, in all the urban policy matters, it is the corporate sector representatives that have been called forth to participate and not anyone else, not even academics engaged in teaching of urban planning.

Such a skewed distribution of resources, land and financial, cannot happen without the participation of the State in the process, if the State does not act as an instrument in their favour. Only the State has a legitimate authority to include or exclude. Thus, this Vision Plan is a lobbying tool on one hand and showing the possibility of raking in a moolah for a few politicians, particularly those in the real estate business[43] . The model of a 'Developmental State' is being invoked for this purpose by bringing in the example of China. But, the story of building of Shanghai on a socialist base of Maoist era is conveniently forgotten by the lobbiers of this Vision Plan—in that case lands have to be socialised for building a grand city like Shanghai and not the converse.

The Vision plan that comes has nothing much to do with the reality. The comprehensive master plans have not worked for various reasons. But, these have been invoked only when the poor have to be evicted or threatened. The new Vision plan probably is also not bothered about the reality and hence has not been based on the reality. The corporate sector just wants Mumbai to be of their own taste irrespective of what happens to the entire city. The idea is to convert part of Mumbai into a World Class City and leaving the rest of the city as it is or even worse off given that the latter might be starved of funds if the former gets disproportionate share and with high real estate prices the urban poor thrown out of the city to the extent possible. That is what the World Class City in its totality would be. The idea is to convert Mumbai into a Global City in parts with the help of the Neo-liberal Developmental State, which is ironically in a largest democracy is turning more and more hostile towards the poor[44] .

NOTES

1. This chapter is based on research undertaken through IDPAD project.
2. Details of the ADB policies are in Chapter 1 of the book.
3. Deshmukh, Vilasrao (2004) 'A Shanghai in the making', as told to Nauzer Bharucha of *Times of India*, Source: http://timesofindia.indiatimes.com/articleshow/971208.cms.
4. These are the pubs where young women from low income families danced to entertain the clients.
5. As per MCGM website: http://www.mcgm.gov.in/forms/Masterdisplay.aspx?slmno=Mzg%3d-wXIpbBtWrGI%3d
6. Agrawal, Dipti Tuesday, August 16, 2005 (Mumbai): (http://www.ndtv.com/template/template.asp?template=health&id=77472&callid=1) A number of patients are still battling with leptospirosis in Mumbai. The pressure is growing on the city's municipal hospitals as the local hospitals do not have the requisite equipment to deal with the disease. Mumbai alone has seen over 120 leptospirosis deaths.
7. Public Interest Litigation (PIL) as it is known, is a very special legal tool available to the citizens of India, which can be utilised by them when any State agency, either violates the fundamental rights given to Indian citizen (s) in a gross way or does not fulfil its mandatory functions, by approaching the High Court (as the state level) or Supreme Court (at the national level). PIL started as a legal redressal tool for the citizens in the late 1970s and has gathered importance since then. From the decade of 1990s onwards this tool has been used frequently in case of executive failure and forcing the executive to form necessary policies from time to time.
8. As per interview given by him to a newspaper. Deshmukh, Vilasrao (2004) 'A Shanghai in the making', as told to Nauzer Bharucha of *Times of India*, Source: http://timesofindia.indiatimes.com/articleshow/971208.cms. The cut off date had to be subsequently be extended.
9. GVK is the Indian partner in the consortium.
10. http://www.thehindu.com/2006/02/01/stories/2006020105891200.htm.
11. Value added contribution to manufacturing sector by Maharashtra for 2003-04 is 19.1 per cent as against 19.8 per cent by Gujarat and by that Maharashtra looses its dominant position among Indian states in manufacturing sector (*Times of India*, Ahmedabad, March 22, 2006.)
12. SSI units using less than 7.5 kW of power could apply directly to the Municipal corporation. Hence about 10000 units have not recorded with the directorate of industries.
13. 'Census Survey of Hawkers on Municipal Lands' conducted by the Tata Institute of Social Sciences (TISS) and Youth for Unity and Voluntary Action (YUVA) on behalf of Brihanmumbai Municipal Corporation in March 1998.
14. Estimation of poverty has to be done for the year 1999-00 using the NSS data on consumption.

15. The HCRs are estimated using the Expert Group Poverty Lines. See Dubey and Mahadevia (2001).
16. This and the rest of the poverty estimates in this paragraph are from Mahadevia and Sarkar (forthcoming 2008).
17. This section is largely written based on the research team going around the city.
18. http://www.mmrdamumbai.org/projects_muip.htm.
19. http://www.mmrdamumbai.org/projects_muip.htm.
20. http://www.mmrdamumbai.org/projects_mutp.htm.
21. http://www.mmrdamumbai.org/projects_mutp.htm.
22. From the SRA website, http://www.sra.gov.in/HTMLpages/History.htm.
23. The new international airport in Shanghai, located in Pudong area. The older airport, HangQiao is also functional and is in the main city.
24. Interview of Vilasrao Deshmukh, 2004, by Nauzer Bharucha cited above.
25. Nationalist Congress Party, an alliance partner of Congress in Maharashtra State. Footnote by the author.
26. http://www.frontlineonnet.com/fl2206/stories/20050325001911200.htm.
27. In the recent articles, Amartya Sen (2005), attributes high economic growth in China to high levels of human development, which is a distinguishing factor between China's and India's development paths.
28. Bracket by the authors.
29. http://www.hindu.com/2007/08/09/stories/2007080962182100.htm.
30. Source: http://www.navimumbaisez.com/overview.htm, accessed on September 10, 2007.
31. Data based on CMIE (2004), March.
32. News item titled 'Bannerghatta Road drives IIM-B students to streets' in *Times of India*, October 6, 2004, from the website: http://www1.timesofindia.indiatimes.com/articleshow/873568.cms. It mentioned that the IT professionals and Indian Institute of Management Bangalore students went on a demonstration demanding good roads in Bangalore and that they should be given a priority.
33. *Indian Express*, January 17, 2006. Source: http://www.expressindia.com/fullstory.php?newsid=61564.
34. Report in daily *DNA*, March 1, 2006, Source: http://www.dnaindia.com/report.asp?NewsID=1015521.
35. Report in Hindu, February 28, 2006; Source: http://www.thehindubusinessline.com/2005/03/01/stories/2005030101431900.htm
36. Statement of Infosys Chairman.N.R. Narayanamurthy, who is now on a project called 'City and Infrastructure'. The source is news item titled 'Let Centre command metros: NRN' in *Times of India*, October 13, 2004, from website: http://timesofindia.indiatimes.com/articleshow/883085.cms.
37. http://www.mcgm.gov.in/forms/Masterdisplay.aspx?slmno=Mzg%3d-wXIpbBtWrGI%3d
38. Data of complete units from SRA in Mitra (2005).

39. Bunsha, Dionne (2004): "Developing Doubts", Frontline, Vol. 21 (12), Jun. 5-18; Source: http://www.hinduonnet.com/fline/fl2112/stories/20040618002704400.htm.
40. http://timesofindia.indiatimes.com/articleshow/984432.cms.
41. Editorial in *Economic and Political Weekly*, March 25-31, 2006.
42. http://timesofindia.indiatimes.com/articleshow/1041696.cms.
43. The nexus between the politicians and builders is well known in the city and some of the politicians are also becoming builders themselves (See Mahadevia and Narayanan, Chapter 18).
44. There are innumerable instances of State hostility towards those who either lost out or did not partake in the benefits of post-independence developments in India, which are not couting and narrating here for the want of space.

4[1]

CHANGES AND CONTINUITIES IN DEVELOPMENT PRIORITIES
Ahmedabad

DARSHINI MAHADEVIA and HARPREET SINGH BRAR

Introduction

Ahmedabad was declared a megacity in the Union Budget of 2005-06[2]. The city planners and the media hyped up the event and a year later (on February 14, 2006), the Gujarat State, in which the city is located, extended the boundary of Ahmedabad City overnight and to the surprise of all[3], by merging seven municipalities[4] with the AMC limits. By that, the Ahmedabad Municipal Corporation's (AMC's) population increased to 5 million from 3.64 million and the city area to about 500 sq km[5] from 198 sq km before. Since 2005-06, all development actions in the city have been supported by the new acquired status of a megacity! Ahmedabad is also covered by the JNNURM.

The reasons given for expanding the limits of Ahmedabad is better governance and better provision of facilities in the newly merged areas. While all these small municipalities had experienced high population growth and high density development from 1991 onwards; their local governments could not cope with the operation and maintenance of the new infrastructure it is argued. This would give Ahmedabad a physical prowess of being a large megacity on one hand but also create problems in governance on the other.

Living in the city, one experiences an upbeat mood in the city. The talking points among the elite classes particularly and the city managers and planners have been improvement in the roads, new property development and all other expected changes in the city in the coming half a decade. One has also witnessed rapid changes in the city since the economic reforms began, particularly in last 10 years, namely rapid developments on the western periphery of the city, where many new malls have been and are being constructed, roads have been widened and new public spaces been developed. Also, the residential, recreational, and institutional areas are properly planned with wide roads and newly built open spaces—as parks and gardens. Before 1990, almost all the residential area comprised of row housing and the bungalows. But the increasing economic pressure on land has led to the change in the physical structure in this part, which is now more of high-rise buildings in the western periphery (Mahadevia and Bhatt 2002). The western periphery is bound by a highway called Sarkhej-Gandhinagar (SG) Highway, beyond which is the development zone with restricted FSI. Hence, as of now, the area beyond SG highway on the west, is low rise development comprising of individual bungalow units and some low-rise apartments.

In contrast, the eastern areas, the walled city and the eastern industrial areas of Naroda, Odhav and Vatva, are highly congested, with narrow roads and residential, commercial, industrial, and public and semi-public activities intermixed with each other. The entire part of the city severely lacks in green and open spaces. More than 50 per cent housing in east Ahmedabad is slums and *chawls* (industrial workers' housing) (Mahadevia 2002b). After they were amalgamated in the AMC, underground network of water supply, sewerage and storm water drain lines are being laid but have taken more than 10 years to complete. Large parts of the eastern periphery are therefore dug up at the moment of writing this article. Ironically, the entire eastern periphery is still not fully covered by infrastructure projects even 20 years after its amalgamation in the AMC limits. Because the Town Planning (TP) schemes were prepared in the eastern parts after they were already fully constructed, a large part of this segment is in violation of the development plan and TP schemes.

The two parts, the western globalised part and the marginalised eastern part of the city are divided by Sabarmati River. The latter includes the old walled city and further east the industrial areas. This Ahmedabad has problems of increased suicide rates due to economic distress among young men and employment and marriage concerns among young women; in 2005-06 year, as compared to previous years, rate increased to three suicides per day through the year, according to a vernacular daily[6]. The survival concerns have become acute in the households which have transited from formal to informal sector, such as of the textile mill workers who transited into petty service sector, or of the AMC sweepers whose children are working as casual labour getting one-third the salary of their parent or parents. 'This other Ahmedabad has been repeatedly affected by the communal violence, the most recent and well planned was the 2002 one[7], that led to nearly total division of the city into the Hindu and Muslim areas, a city divided by the border (Mahadevia 2007c). This other Ahmedabad also has the residents of Sabarmati riverfront, who are to face evictions soon because of the Sabarmati Riverfront Development Project (SRFDP), the largest slum displacing project of the city till now.

A little more on the segmentation of the city on the communal lines. The city is the stronghold of Bharatiya Janata Party (BJP), the right-wing Hindu party, which has won all but one election of the AMC in last two and a half decades, with the support of the cadres of Hindu fundamentalist organisation, the Vishwa Hindu Parishad (VHP). The city has experienced numerous communal violence, early one in 1946, then in 1969, and then repeatedly since early 1980s. The violence has been more than riots, and have been largely one-sided attack of the Hindu fundamentalist elements (which are well organised) on the Muslims[8], the largest minority community[9] of the city.

By many counts, Ahmedabad is a unique city. The city had many firsts to her credit in history and has many firsts even in the period of economic reforms and the city also had and has some unique characteristics. Some examples are: it was called 'Manchester of India' in the history because of large number of textile mills in the city, had the first textile mill established with indigenous capital (Gillion 1968), was a city where Gandhiji set up his base (called Sabarmati Ashram) to lead Indian independence movement against British, was the first city to float tax free bonds in the reforms period (and since then has floated two more bond issues), has a successful partnership programme for slum development under implementation in last decade[10], had a welfare oriented and powerful local government till very recently[11], has strong presence of charity and development organisations in the non-governmental sector, and many others. The public body, the AMC has been interestingly inclusive, as far as the interests of the low-income groups and localities where the low-income groups live. Interestingly, it has been a very modest and practical city, not been much into either projecting itself or hyping its image till recently. However, all that is changing, especially in the city's effort to globalise and now to be noticed as a megacity.

Monsoon of 2005 also brought out another stark reality of Ahmedabad City, an outcome of neglect of public services while paying more than necessary attention to city infrastructure projects, or campaigning for bringing Narmada waters to the city, development of malls and so on. Monsoon of 2005 witnessed surfacing of diseases such as dengue, which continued through to the winter of 2005-06 (Mahadevia 2006c). The main reason for this was denudation of water in the monsoon of 2005, a result of drains not being cleaned and maintained and garbage not being picked up and disposed. Though Ahmedabad City, unlike other cities, has paid attention to laying underground sewerage and drainage networks in the whole city, including in urban periphery, the problem of public health persists.

Since 2000, the development projects selected in the city are quite skewed. For example, the city has built a new airport terminal and airport facilities such as runway and buildings have been upgraded and now a few international carriers land in the city. Both the domestic and international terminals of the airport are under further expansion and renewal phase. But, one does not find upgradation of the Ahmedabad Railway Station. The long distance bus terminals are in abysmal conditions, proposed to be upgraded through PPP. This skewed vision of city development emerging in the city and the reflection of the same in the public authority budgets is the central focus of this article.

This article narrates the changes observed in Ahmedabad in last one decade, in terms of new developments that have taken place and changing priorities of public policies. The latter are observed through not pronouncements but through priorities in public resource allocation, particularly the public finance allocation. In this, we would look at the priorities in capital expenditures (capital investments) by the AMC in its jurisdiction and by the Ahmedabad Urban Development Authority (AUDA) in the peri-urban areas, and recurring expenditures by the AMC in its jurisdiction. We have not looked at recurring expenditures in the peri-urban areas, comprising of number of small municipalities[12] and *Gram Panchayats*, as that would have been impossible. In any case, their budgets are small. There is a sequel to this article (Chapter 10), in which we look at the benefit incidence of public expenditures to the slums of the city.

Demography

Ahmedabad is and has been for centuries the largest city of Gujarat. Ahmedabad Urban Agglomeration (AUA), with a population of 4,519,278, (4.52 millions) is the 7th largest UA in the country. The AMC population in 2001 was 3,515,361 (3.52 millions). But, after the latest boundary expansion AUA's population might just have inched closer to that of Hyderabad UA, which was 5.5 millions in 2001. Gujarat is one of the relatively rich states of India and has seen high economic growth rate since the onset of economic reforms. The overall economic growth rate in 1993-94 to 1999-00 period has been 5.53 per cent and per capita domestic product growth rate has been 4 per cent in the same period (Hirway and Mahadevia 2005). Given that the megacity is in a relatively rich state of India, one can see the prosperity spilling out in this largest city of the state.

Table 4.1: Population (in lakhs) and Population Growth Rate (% p.a.), AUDA

Location	*Area (sq.km.)*	*Population size (lakhs)*				*Growth rate (% p.a.)*		
		1971	*1981*	*1991*	*2001*	*1971-81*	*1981-91*	*1991-01*
AMC	190.84	16.12	21.59	28.76	35.20	2.96	2.91	2.04
Total AUDA	1294.65	20.58	28.88	38.81	47.09	3.45	3.00	1.95

Source: Based on Census of India, 2001.

The population of AUDA, spread over 1,294.65 sq. km has increased by 3.45 per cent p.a. during 1971-81, at 3.00 per cent p.a. during the 1980s and at 1.95 per cent p.a. during 1990s (Table 4.1). These rates are higher than the population growth rate of AUA in the respective period (Chapter 2). Except the last decade, 1991-01, in all other decades AUDA's annual population growth rates have been higher than that of the AMC.

Urban Governance

A brief understanding of city governance is essential to understand the financing of infrastructure and assessing development priorities. At present, the local government of Ahmedabad is a Municipal Corporation (the AMC), whose area is divided into 43 wards. The AMC has planning and service delivery responsibilities over only its jurisdiction. That leaves the peri-urban areas out of the reach of the AMC's functioning. For planned development of the city periphery the AUDA was constituted by the Government of Gujarat on 1st February, 1978 under the provision of the Gujarat Town Planning and Urban Development Act, 1976. The AUDA area has been carved out from four districts viz. Ahmedabad, Kheda, Mehsana and Gandhinagar covering a total area of 1,294.65 sq. km. The area includes one Municipal Corporation (AMC), 6 Nagar Panchayats (NPs), converted into municipalities in 2005 and by 2006 government order amalgamated into AMC) and 143 Gram Panchayats (GPs). The total population is estimated in 2001 is 45.19 lakh (city + overgrowth figures). With the latest city boundary expansion, AUDA limits have remained unchanged.

Unlike other states, Urban Local Bodies (ULBs) in Gujarat perform all the service delivery functions, unless it is not in a financial position to do so. The ULBs take care of capital as well as recurring costs for all the services and they are empowered to levy certain taxes, mainly property taxes now and before the abolition of octroi, the octroi. The smaller municipalities are unable to undertake capital projects, particularly after the abolition of octroi tax way back in 1999, and hence in the municipalities around a large city such as Ahmedabad, development authorities such as AUDA have to step in for the purpose. And that has been happening in Ahmedabad. The AUDA has made capital investments whereas the operation and maintenance expenditures are met by the ULBs in the urban periphery. But, AUDA maintains the roads it has constructed as of now. These ULBs not being able to meet even this obligation, it is argued, led to amalgamation of the peri-urban areas into the AMC. The AUDA had delegated the powers to the AMC to prepare and enforce TP Schemes[13], lay physical networks for water supply, sewerage and storm water drains and construct roads, and take up any other development activity in the latter's jurisdiction. In the rest of the AUDA areas, AUDA itself performs these tasks.

Development and Expenditures in AUDA Areas

AUDA, that makes capital investments in the peri-urban areas, has very limited sources of revenue, namely the 'betterment charges' it collects from the users, fees—service and amenities fees—security deposit, incremental contribution under TP scheme and the development charges under the AUDA Act. Thus, it is mainly relying on the sale of land or commercial development of land to generate its own revenues. TP scheme mechanism, allows the AUDA to retain 40 per cent of the original land after plot reconstitution for laying trunk infrastructure and roads. 10 per cent of land of the original plot size, that is 25 per cent of the land retained by the AUDA, is sold to generate the funds. These funds have been inadequate for taking major infrastructure works and hence the AUDA has relied on the grants and loans from the state government as well as loans from the financial institutions like the Life Insurance Corporation (LIC), the Housing and Urban Development Corporation (HUDCO), the World Bank and the Asian Development Bank (ADB) and so on for capital works.

Table 4.2: Development Expenditures Proposed in AUDA (in March 31, 2005)

Sl. No.	Project	(in Rs. crores)
1.	Construction of Ring Road	250
2.	Construction of New area T.P. Scheme	100
3.	Construction of 9 flyovers and ROB	120
4.	Water supply scheme for 19 villages of West AUDA area	45
5.	Water supply scheme for 19 villages of East AUDA area	160
6.	Sewerage scheme for Western AUDA, N-W periphery	104
7.	Sewerage scheme for East AUDA	80
8.	Strom water disposal, interlinking of lakes & development of lakes in West AUDA	45
9.	Strom water disposal, interlinking of lakes & development of lakes in East AUDA	40
10.	Solid waste disposal, developing land fill sites and providing processing plant	15
11.	Environmental Development, Public parks in West & East AUDA in 40 ha. Land	15
12.	Road side plantation & central verge and beautification	5
13.	Construction of 10,000 houses for slum dwellers	100
	Total	1079

Source: From AUDA files.

Note: 1 crore = 10 million or 100 Lakhs

After Ahmedabad was declared a megacity, the AUDA proposed projects worth Rs. 1,079 crores (Table 4.2) to tap central government fund allocation[14]. The break-up of the proposal was: Rs. 370 crores (34%) for the roads, Rs. 489 crores (45%) for water supply, sewerage and storm water networks, Rs. 100 crores (9%) for housing the slum dwellers, part of it to be used for rehabilitating those displaced by various development works. At the same time, the AMC had prepared project proposal worth Rs. 1,500 crores under the megacity scheme. Now, the JNNURM has replaced the megacity scheme.

Important development activities by the AUDA in the recent years have been: (i) construction of Outer Ring Road, (ii) development of water bodies as public places, (iii) development of community parks, (iv) laying of Narmada Pipe line for providing drinking water, (v) preparation of TP Schemes, and (vi) solid waste management as per the Supreme Court ruling.

Construction of Outer Ring Road: This is a major capital investment of the AUDA. This is a ring road to the west of SG Highway mentioned earlier. This road has been named 'Sardar Patel Ring Road' or SP Highway. Because of the westward development in Ahmedabad, the SG Highway, which was the earlier periphery of the AMC, has experienced rapid development of commercial, residential, recreational and religious

Photo: Harpreet Singh Brar

Photo 4.1: A New Mall with MacDonald and Big Bazaar Retail Outfit, Ahmedabad

Photo: Harpreet Singh Brar

Photo 4.2: A Multiplex, Ahmedabad

Photo 4.3: Proposed River Front Development, Ahmedabad

Photo: Darshini Mahadevia

Photo 4.4: Ongoing Work of Riverfront Development, Ahmedabad

activities from 1995 onwards. SG Highway is part of the National Highway no. 8 that connects Ahmedabad and Delhi. This was used by the transport vehicles connecting Saurashtra and Kachchh with Delhi and North India. To avoid the through traffic mingling with the local traffic, AUDA developed SP Highway (ring road) as a bypass for the former. The SP Highway has now become the new boundary of the AMC. The agricultural lands between SG Highway and SP Highway have already been sold out by the farmers and are being developed for high income 'gated community type' developments. Such developments are also coming up beyond the SP ring road. Further, some important public buildings such as the Science City have come up on the SP ring road. The AUDA has constructed this ring road by taking a loan of Rs. 100 crores from the HUDCO. The project was implemented on a war footing. At present, other than couple of Rail Over Bridges (ROB), the rest of the ring road is completed and is functional. The uncompleted parts are towards the east Ahmedabad.

This is a prestigious project of AUDA and the work was completed in a very short time. There were plans afoot to collect toll on this road, which has not yet been put into execution. The property price increase in western Ahmedabad can be fully attributed to the construction of this ring road.

Narmada Pipeline for Water Supply: Water supply in the AUDA areas is either by the local government—municipalities (formerly the *nagar panchayats*) or the *gram panchayats*—or by the housing societies themselves through their own bore-well. In other words, the water supply system in AUDA areas is highly decentralised, unlike centralised water supply system in the AMC. The water quality in the AUDA areas in west Ahmedabad is very poor; the water has high level of dissolved salts and in some places even high (more than permissible) fluoride content. Those who can afford have shifted to bottled drinking water, supplied in containers of 10 or 20 litres. Availability of water is also a problem, that is, water quantity is also insufficient. Housing colonies, whether individual bungalows or high or low rise apartments have to spend on electricity for pumping the ground water and often on purchase of water through water tankers. To permanently resolve the water problems, the AUDA decided to buy Narmada waters, flowing through Narmada canal, located in the west of Ahmedabad City and construct pipeline for distributing this water to the housing colonies in the west.

Lake Revival and Development: The AUDA has plans to undertake development of 10 lakes coming under its jurisdiction. These are located at Makarba, Prahaladnagar, Memnagar, Vastrapur, Ambli, Thaltej, Sola,

Chandlodiya, Gota and Bodakdev. The private parties would be responsible for the development of lakes and they would be given rights to operate there for the specified period. From this list, Vastrapur lake has already been developed.

The project work involves: (i) desilting for restoration of lake storage capacity, (ii) constructing percolation wells in lakebed for ground water recharging, (iii) peripheral area development works including bank protection, landscaping, jogging tracks, and recreation facilities, and (iv) taking up catchment development works. Thus lake revival and development would lead to construction of recreation facilities, amphitheatre, children's park, boating facilities and jogging park.

Table 4.3: Estimated Costs of Lake Revival and Development

Sl. No.	*Lake*	*Storage Capacity (MCM)*	*Total Estimated Cost (In Rs. million)*
1.	Vastrapur	0.109	12.2
2.	Prahladnagar	0.167	11.7
3.	Memnagar	0.220	16.2
4.	Ambli	0.111	11.0
5.	Thaltej	0.322	17.0
6.	Sola	0.246	15.0
7.	Chandlodiya	0.136	12.1
8.	Gota	0.240	16.6
9.	Bodakdev	0.144	10.0
10.	Makarba	0.265	16.3
	Total	1.960	138.1

Source: From the files of AUDA.

There is also a plan to interlink these lakes, which would be laying of interconnecting pipelines from Narmada main canal to the River Sabarmati, with links to all the 7 of the 10 lakes en-route. It is proposed to use Narmada waters to keep these lakes full round the year, particularly when the rainwater collected in the lakes during the monsoon would dip towards the end of the winter. It is being argued that water tables in the city would come up gradually by this and would eventually lead to improvement in water quality in the western AUDA areas. All the lakes listed in Table 4.3 are in west Ahmedabad and that there is no lake development proposal for east Ahmedabad areas.

Solid Waste Management: The latest initiative taken by AUDA is the door-to-door solid waste collection under the directions and guidelines of the Supreme Court. Of the 7 rules stated by the SC for the solid waste collection[15], rules 1 to 5 to be followed by the nagarpalikas/municipalities are: door-to-door solid waste collection, segregation and transportation to the dumping site. The rules 6 and 7 are mandatory for the AUDA, which includes the proper and scientific dumping of the collected solid waste.

In order to improve the efficiency of the Solid Waste Management (SWM) system in the city, AUDA has invited private firms to implement modern SWM practice. The system envisages a door-to-door collection of solid waste (organic/inorganic as well as recycle waste) and its transportation to the big containers by the private firms. These firms would bear the cost of putting up these containers. Transportation of the collected waste to the landfill site and the proper disposal of the wastes would be by the AUDA. The AUDA has identified a proper landfill site after proper studies.

Capital Expenditure by AUDA

The AUDA's total capital budget has increased by more than 7 times during 2001-02 to 2004-05 period, from Rs. 3,152.88 lakhs (Rs. 315.29 million) to 22,674.4 lakhs (Rs. 2267.44 million) (Table 4.4). The capital expenditure budget of the AUDA has moved very close to that of the AMC's, although that of the latter is for much larger population than the former's population. Evidently, the per capita expenditures by AUDA on physical infrastructure would be far higher than the same in the AMC areas. One might argue that the AMC is carrying out incremental capital expenditures in its area. Therefore, it is not surprising that AUDA areas, especially on the west have far better infrastructure than the AMC areas also on the west. This has not gone unnoticed by the people of west Ahmedabad and also by the media. Further, the AUDA has been able to complete the capital works much faster, say, laying of roads, sewerage and storm water drains and water supply lines much faster than the AMC.

Table 4.4: AUDA's Capital Expenditure on Various Infrastructure Projects (Rs. in crores) (current prices)

Item	*1999-00*	*2000-01*	*2001-02*	*2002-03*	*2003-04*	*2004-05*
Water works	0.00	0.00	0.00	26.66	35.60	71.37
Sewerage and Drainage works	3.60	4.93	2.56	11.18	8.84	20.62
Road, railway overbridge, building & others	19.25	21.09	18.93	52.54	87.69	91.86
Recreation and Landscape	0.35	0.58	0.81	1.34	1.57	3.93
Housing Projects	2.40	5.08	6.96	7.45	9.69	11.71
Various loan repayments	0.98	2.06	0.00	0.83	6.06	24.69
Other Miscellaneous	0.91	1.48	1.11	4.51	2.49	0.40
Infrastructure Development Projects	27.48	35.24	30.37	104.52	151.93	224.68
Total Capital Budget	27.99	35.99	31.53	108.89	160.27	226.74

Source: AUDA budgets from AUDA files.

Note : 1 crore = 10 million or 100 lakhs.

Table 4.5: Proportion of Capital Expenditure on Various Infrastructure Projects, AUDA's (%)

Department and accounts head name	*1999-00*	*2000-01*	*2001-02*	*2002-03*	*2003-04*	*2004-05*
Water works	0.00	0.00	0.00	24.48	22.21	31.48
Sewerage and drainage works	12.85	13.70	8.12	10.27	5.51	9.09
Road, R.O.B, building & others	68.79	58.60	60.04	48.25	54.71	40.51
Recreation and landscape	1.23	1.61	2.58	1.23	0.98	1.73
Housing projects	8.57	14.12	22.07	6.85	6.04	5.17
Various loan repayments	3.49	5.73	0.00	0.76	3.78	10.89
Other miscellaneous	3.24	4.12	3.51	4.14	1.55	0.17
Infrastructure development projects	98.18	97.89	96.32	95.99	94.79	99.05
Total Capital Budget	100.00	100.00	100.00	100.00	100.00	100.00

Around 97 per cent of the expenditure made by AUDA over the last 6 years is on various infrastructure development projects. Of this, the highest, nearing 50 per cent is on roads, railway overbridges and buildings. Our judgement is that most of it is on the road projects and not buildings. Then is the expenditure on water works, which comes to 22 per cent of the total expenditures in the same period. However, to note is that water works have started only in the last three years, from 2002-03 onwards (Table 4.4 and 4.5). Otherwise, road projects took up about three-fifths of the funds for the capital projects of AUDA. To make expenditures on the water works, the AUDA increased its capital budget by about 3.5 times in 2002-03 from just Rs. 31.5 crores in 2001-02. In 2002-03, even the funds spent on road projects increased by 2.75 times as compared to the previous year. About three-fourths of the total funds spent by the AUDA in the last three years are on road projects and water works.

In the water works, a large part was spent on the laying of water supply distribution system in 15 Gram Panchayats/Nagar Palikas in 2004-05 and on various aspects of water works such as construction of overhead tanks, constructing sump, drilling of tubewells to source water, development of other sources of water, water treatment and so on. The funds for water supply distribution network have come as loan from the ADB and other sources in 2004-05 and other funds in 2003-04 (Table 4.6). It is however not known what the other sources of funds are for the water works.

AUDA could increase its capital budget through borrowing from the HUDCO, the ADB and other sources as seen above. The HUDCO loan repayment is small amounts (Table 4.7); Rs. 43.75 lakhs in 1999-00, Rs. 206.25 lakhs in 2000-01 and Rs. 99.02 lakhs in 2003-04 (about 35 crores). But, it is large amounts borrowed from the ADB for the water supply project that comprises large proportion of debt repayment in the last year of our analysis (2004-05); about 59 per cent (Rs. 1454.56 lakhs) of the total repayment. While the road projects have been taken with the HUDCO loans, water supply projects have been through the ADB loans[16]. Along with other loan repayments (principal + interest), loan charges in 2004-05 was about 11 per cent of the total capital expenditures of AUDA (Table 4.4). The amount has increased 25 times since 1999-00 to 2004-05. In the year 2004-05, nearly Rs. 2,469.08 lakhs (Rs. 24.70 crores) were made as loan repayments.

Table 4.6: AUDA's Capital Expenditure on Water Works (Rs. Lakhs)

Expenditure head	*2002-03*	*2003-04*	*2004-05*
Water project work	2459.29	2186.02	2610.00
Water treatment plant	206.71	904.05	0.00
Water supply distribution system under ADB	0.00	160.50	0.00
Water supply distribution system for 15 GP/NP—Non ADB	0.00	309.26	0.00
Water supply distribution system for 15 Others & ADB	0.00	0.00	4480.04
Land Acquisition for water works	0.00	0.00	47.35
Grand Total on Water works	2666.00	3559.83	7137.39

Source: AUDA budgets from AUDA files.

AUDA is also paying loan for construction of Economically Weaker Section (EWS) housing under VAMBAY (Valmiki Ambedkar Awas Yojana). But, housing component is just 7 per cent of the total expenditures over the six years. Housing expenditures have been incurred in all the six years, but, its share appeared significant only when the AUDA's expenditures were small, which was the case till 2001-02. Housing expenditures have been made largely to rehabilitate those displaced by AUDA's other infrastructure projects; one of the large rehabilitation is for the slum dwellers displaced because of Vastrapur lake development. Loan repayment for VAMBAY was Rs. 369.28 lakhs in 2004-05.

Table 4.7: AUDA's Loan Repayment (Rs. Lakhs)

Expenditure head	*1999-00*	*2000-01*	*2001-02*	*2002-03*	*2003-04*	*2004-05*
Repayment of IDSMT Loan, Seed money loan	54.00	0.00	0.00	0.00	0.00	43.00
Repayment of HUDCO loan	43.75	206.25	0.00	0.00	99.02	0.00
Interest on loan (Housing)	0.00	0.00	0.00	20.89	46.37	0.00
Interest on loan (General)	0.00	0.00	0.00	0.63	0.00	0.00
Loan repayment & interest-EWS/VAMBAY	0.00	0.00	0.00	0.00	0.00	369.28
Repayment of loan & interest SP ring road	0.00	0.00	0.00	0.00	0.00	602.24
Interest on loan (water supply main)	0.00	0.00	0.00	0.00	169.00	0.00
Repayment loan	0.00	0.00	0.00	61.26	0.00	0.00
Repayment of loan-Main & ADB	0.00	0.00	0.00	0.00	291.87	1454.56
Grand total of various loan repayments	97.75	206.25	0.00	82.78	606.06	2469.08

Source: AUDA budgets from AUDA files.

It is not yet known as to whether AUDA would service the loans for the expenditures on projects that have gone to the AMC area after the very recent expansion of the AMC boundaries or would pass the loan to the AMC.

AUDA has resorted to selling its lands for loan repayment. In April 2006, AUDA auctioned 20 plots[17], some of them sold at unusually high rates and purchased by large realty firms, such as Reliance Industries Limited, which has entered the realty market of Ahmedabad in only 2006. AUDA collected Rs. 172 crores through the sale of these 20 plots[18]. In fact, AUDA has been time and again selling its lands for raising finance, which is then invested in infrastructure such as roads, water supply, sanitation and storm water drains.

Developers however feel that the pace of infrastructure development in the AUDA area is not at par with the realty development. They think that the future of the city is in western suburbs, which are rapidly expanding and are currently under the AUDA control. They think that to develop a 'brand Ahmedabad', there is still a need to beautify the city's landscape, develop well paved roads with footpaths, develop many more green spaces than at present, and have an efficient and modern public transport system. This they think the AUDA is unable to do because of its limited resources. But, then would the AMC be able to do so, given that it has to spent on maintenance of the infrastructure as well.

AMC—Budgets

The municipal budgets are divided into two broad headings, the recurrent budget or the revenue budget, which has incomes and expenditures in the short-term, mainly within the year and the capital budget, which are incomes and expenditures on long term projects, whose duration is more than one year. Before we go into analysing development priorities of the AMC, we would look at the entire budget of the AMC. A clarification; the AMC budgets analysed here are for the old limits of the AMC of 198 sq km.

Overall Budget[19]

The size of the AMC budget was around Rs. 1,000 crores till 2005-06, precisely Rs. 1167.17 crores in 2005-06. The budget size of AMC has increased to Rs. 1,600 crores in 2006-07's proposed budget. This is on account of increase in capital budget because of the funds to be made available under the JNNURM.

Table 4.3: Overall Budget, AMC (Rs. Crores) (at current prices)

Item	1997-98	1998-99	1999-00	2000-01	2001-02	2002-03	2003-04	2004-05	2005-06
	AE	AE	AE	AE	AE	AE	AE	RE	BE
Revenue Income	420.73	475	566.12	562.58	561.85	615.64	690.68	793.36	938.28
Capital Income	190.89	91.71	117.42	155.96	241.70	75.91	320.71	294.84	411.97
Capital Income—Revenue transfer	131.89	35.21	69.42	155.96	241.70	38.91	192.68	181.75	228.89
Total Income	552.62	510.21	635.54	718.54	803.55	654.55	883.36	975.11	1167.17
Revenue Expenditure	313.9	360.24	441.78	489.28	481.78	489.42	482.78	568.15	691.68
Capital Expenditure	65.33	81.10	191.06	137.27	169.96	137.62	243.39	294.74	301.89
Total Expenditure	379.23	441.34	632.84	626.55	651.74	627.04	726.17	862.89	993.57
Budget Surplus	173.39	68.87	2.70	93.11	251.81	99.76	204.30	112.22	173.60
Revenue transfer to capital account	59.00	56.50	48.00	0.00	0.00	37.00	128.03	113.09	183.08
% growth over previous year (constant prices)	—	-17.39	31.63	14.43	12.04	-17.89	35.94	9.81	18.00

Note: The total income figure here counts revenue income transfer to the capital account only once.

AE = Actual Expenditure, RE = Revised Expenditure Estimates, BE = Budgeted Expenditure Estimates

Source: Based on AMC Budget Documents (Some downloaded from net and availed in soft copy from the AMC).

The AMC budgets have generally been revenue surplus, with total income exceeding the total expenditure. For example, Rs. 173.60 crores was budget surplus in the year 2005-06 (Table 4.8). Budget surplus is not a very good sign of the municipal corporation's efficiency and indicates its inability to undertake development works, inspite of availability of finances. This indeed raises questions about the AMC's ability to undertake development works under the proposed JNNURM, which has increased the budget size by 37 per cent in 2006-07 from the previous year. Another feature of AMC budgets is transfers of surplus from the revenue account to the capital account. In 2005-06, as per the budget estimates, Rs. 183.08 crores was transferred from the revenue account to the capital account.

Tax income, which comprised about 80 per cent of the total revenue income of the AMC till 1998-99, has declined over time and has reached about 74 per cent in 2004-05. In 2005-06, its share remains the same as in 2004-05. Of concern is the decline in the share of property tax in the total revenue income, its share coming down from about a quarter in 1997-98 and 1998-99 to about 16 per cent in 2004-05 and 18 per cent in 2005-06. The share of octroi tax has varied between 54 per cent and 59 per cent. The concern is on two counts. The property tax is a progressive tax, in which the property owners pay the tax and as per the new formula of tax, they pay for the appreciation of property rates due to infrastructure investments by the municipal corporation and because of the land market appreciation. The other aspect of concern is such high contribution to revenue income by the octroi tax which is expected to be withdrawn.

Proportion of non-tax income in the total revenue income has increased from 4.3 per cent in 1997-98 to 9.3 per cent in 2005-06, this source's share in total revenue income is still less. Non-tax revenue is mainly income from municipal properties and different cesses and fees. The other source is grants and contribution, which include state government grants—lumpsum and programme/project grant—and contribution from the development funds given to the elected members of municipal corporation, state legislative assembly and parliament. Its share has fluctuated in the period studied here and has only marginally increased (by one percentage point) from 1997-98 to 2005-06. This source's share has remained at about one-eighth of the total revenue income.

Special water and sewerage charges were introduced for the first time from 2003-04, its proportion is still miniscule to the total revenue. Share of other sources of income, not specified, has increase by two percentage points over the period. But, its share is also low in the total revenue income.

Table 4.9: Composition of Revenue Income, AMC

	1997-98	1998-99	1999-00	2000-01	2001-02	2002-03	2003-04	2004-05	2005-06
	AE	AE	AE	AE	AE	AE	AE	RE	BE
Revenue income (Rs. Crores)	420.73	475.00	566.12	562.58	561.85	615.64	690.68	793.36	938.28
Octroi (%)	57.65	55.64	54.62	57.68	54.66	58.69	58.05	57.73	55.57
Property tax (%)	24.00	25.05	20.61	17.39	21.64	19.69	17.36	16.28	18.12
Total tax (%)	81.65	80.69	75.22	75.07	76.30	78.38	75.41	74.00	73.69
Income under special act (%)	0.10	0.06	0.04	0.02	0.03	0.03	0.00	0.00	0.00
Non tax income (%)	4.32	3.73	3.61	4.36	5.57	4.80	7.38	7.39	9.31
Income under special act & non tax income (%)	4.42	3.79	3.65	4.39	5.60	4.82	7.38	7.39	9.31
Grants & contribution (%)	11.20	11.76	17.49	18.14	15.91	14.49	11.92	13.50	12.32
Other income (%)	2.73	3.77	3.64	2.40	2.20	2.31	2.84	2.84	2.76
Water & sewerage charges (%)	0.00	0.00	0.00	0.00	0.00	0.00	2.44	2.27	1.92
Others (%)	2.73	3.77	3.64	2.40	2.20	2.31	5.29	5.11	4.68
Total	100.00	100.00	100.00	100.00	100.00	100.00	100.00	100.00	100.00

Source: Based on AMC Budget Documents (some downloaded from net and availed in soft copy from the AMC).

Table 4.10: Composition of Capital Income, AMC

Sources of Capital Income	*1997-98*	*1998-99*	*1999-00*	*2000-01*	*2001-02*	*2002-03*	*2003-04*	*2004-05*	*2005-06*
	AE	*AE*	*AE*	*AE*	*AE*	*AE*	*AE*	*RE*	*BE*
Total Capital Income (Rs. Crores)	131.89	35.21	69.42	155.96	241.70	38.91	192.68	181.75	228.89
Income from Bond (%)	75.82	0.00	0.00	0.00	41.37	0.00	30.10	0.00	43.69
Income from loans (%)	3.55	47.43	56.69	81.99	41.54	15.82	44.63	62.00	28.40
Income from contribution (%)	2.82	14.56	9.35	4.20	2.11	26.23	4.31	4.73	3.71
Income from grants (%)	17.53	35.88	32.48	12.71	14.80	53.02	20.19	28.03	7.41
Other Income (%)	0.28	2.13	1.48	1.10	0.18	4.93	0.77	5.24	16.80
Total (%)	100.00	100.00	100.00	100.00	100.00	100.00	100.00	100.00	100.00
Revenue transfer to capital account (Rs. Crores)	59.00	56.50	48.00	0.00	0.00	37.00	128.03	113.09	183.08
Total income available for capital investments (Rs. Crores)	190.89	91.71	117.42	155.96	241.70	75.91	320.71	294.84	411.97
Revenue transfer as % of total income available for capital investments	30.91	61.61	40.88	0.00	0.00	48.74	39.92	38.36	44.44

Source: Based on AMC Budget Documents (Some downloaded from net and availed in soft copy from the AMC).

Decrease in share of tax income has been compensated by increase in the share of non-tax incomes, water and sanitation charges and other incomes. In value terms, the tax income has increased by about Rs. 350 crores, that from non-tax, water and sanitation charges and other income has increased by about Rs. 100 crores. Thus, if the octroi would go, other sources of revenue income are not buoyant enough to support the present level of expenditures. In such an eventuality, the revenue transfers to the capital account as well as budget surplus would go. Also, the city would have to depend on the transfer of funds from the state government, increasing its dependence on the latter.

In value terms, capital income has been highly fluctuating, as it always is the case. Also have fluctuated the shares of different sources of the capital income. Whenever the AMC has issued capital bonds, the amount of capital income has gone up. In absence of bonds, the AMC depends on loans. Together, these two debt sources have contributed the largest to the total capital income, contributing from 60 per cent to 80 per cent of the total capital income in all but three years in the period under study. If the revenue transfer amount is added to total capital income, which gives us the total capital income available for investments then, the revenue transfer's share to total capital income has been about 40 per cent or more in all but two years in the period studied. Thus, revenue transfers also play an important role in capital investments by the AMC. These would be affected when the octroi would be withdrawn.

Lastly, the AMC's capital budget has only doubled (at current prices) from 1997-98 to 2005-06 and in 2005-06, it was nearly the same amount as the AUDA's budget in 2004-05. Even the JNNURM support would not augment the AMC budget as much as the AUDA was able to do through the use of land readjustment (TP scheme) method. Plainly, the AUDA was able to do so because its TP schemes are implemented on largely undeveloped lands whereas the AMC is constrained by implementing TP schemes on the developed parts and thus not being able to get its land share to be used for infrastructure projects and raising resources for the same.

A brief discussion on revenue expenditure pattern has been taken up to see the impact of increased borrowings of the AMC for infrastructure projects. Proportion of revenue expenditure on administration, which includes general administration, tax collection, and property and land acquisition, has increased somewhat over the period, from 14.8 per cent in 1997-98 to 16.6 per cent in 2005-06 (Table 4.11). The fifth pay commission was implemented prior to this period of analysis and its impact could be seen in the previous analyses of AMC finances[20].

Table 4.11: Composition of Revenue Expenditure, AMC

Expenditure heads (%)	*1997-98*	*1998-99*	*1999-00*	*2000-01*	*2001-02*	*2002-03*	*2003-04*	*2004-05*	*2005-06*
	AE	*AE*	*AE*	*AE*	*AE*	*AE*	*AE*	*RE*	*BE*
Total revenue expenditure (Rs. Crores)	354.94	410.56	488.44	557.57	548.65	605.21	575.62	766.12	736.32
General admin. & tax recovery	12.32	13.51	14.96	13.29	13.33	13.65	14.73	13.08	14.57
Property, land acquisition & mgmt	2.50	2.32	2.39	2.21	2.08	2.01	2.02	1.83	2.04
Public safety	3.48	3.38	3.16	3.05	4.18	3.12	3.56	2.96	5.96
Conservancy	6.08	6.02	5.70	5.99	5.20	4.78	4.88	4.32	4.67
Road cleaning & refuse removal	9.43	10.62	11.68	10.38	9.89	9.13	10.04	9.26	11.95
Public health	2.47	2.36	2.23	2.14	1.85	1.55	1.77	1.56	2.26
Medical aid	11.31	10.54	10.57	9.53	9.25	8.06	8.21	7.00	11.19
Water supply	11.12	10.68	9.97	10.38	11.00	10.91	10.71	9.18	10.36
Public works	3.04	3.22	0.00	3.28	3.29	2.76	3.06	2.71	3.02
Road, bridges, footpaths & storm water drains	2.96	3.17	3.08	2.89	2.40	2.43	2.31	2.00	2.15
Public education	18.74	17.18	19.61	20.68	20.68	18.19	19.37	17.35	22.37
Garden, museum, playgrounds	1.33	1.37	1.55	1.47	1.29	1.00	1.00	1.00	1.20
Market & slaughter house	0.05	0.05	0.06	0.06	0.05	0.03	0.05	0.04	0.05
Registration of births & deaths	0.23	0.20	0.21	0.14	0.18	0.21	0.20	0.23	0.28
Publicity & information	0.11	0.06	0.05	0.09	0.05	0.31	0.30	0.17	0.18
Licensing, removal of encroachment & administration of shops	0.44	0.45	0.48	0.48	0.42	0.23	0.36	0.33	0.40
Loan charges	11.56	12.26	12.07	12.25	12.19	19.13	16.13	25.84	6.06
Miscellaneous	2.83	2.62	2.22	1.69	2.66	2.51	1.29	1.15	1.28
Total	100.00	100.00	100.00	100.00	100.00	100.00	100.00	100.00	100.00
On public health	17.98	19.01	19.62	18.51	16.95	15.45	16.68	15.14	18.88
On water supply	14.16	13.89	9.97	13.66	14.30	13.67	13.77	11.89	13.39
On administration	14.82	15.82	17.35	15.50	15.41	15.66	16.75	14.91	16.61

Source: Based on AMC Budget Documents (Some downloaded from net and availed in soft copy from the AMC).

Table 4.12: Composition of Capital Expenditure, AMC

	1997-98	1998-99	1999-00	2000-01	2001-02	2002-03	2003-04	2004-05	2005-06
Total Capital Expenditure (Rs. Crores)	65.33	81.10	191.06	137.27	169.96	137.62	243.39	294.74	301.89
Zonal Priority works	0.00	0.00	0.00	0.00	0.00	0.00	0.00	0.00	16.86
Grants works	9.99	16.10	8.58	11.08	12.01	21.98	15.13	20.18	7.00
Works from GSDMA-ADE Grant	0.00	0.00	0.00	0.00	0.00	4.47	5.60	7.08	1.97
Medical college and equipments	0.00	0.00	0.00	0.00	0.00	0.00	0.00	0.00	2.98
Road, footpath & pavement	25.43	18.69	8.09	7.48	2.96	2.18	5.52	11.08	11.17
Bridges	11.71	13.84	7.50	7.04	1.48	0.08	1.33	2.68	2.70
Storm water drain	0.63	0.38	0.31	0.64	0.30	0.55	0.63	4.43	4.45
Drainage project	3.99	3.37	5.43	5.61	2.26	0.98	4.73	5.60	4.85
Water project	25.24	23.89	60.01	39.04	6.35	9.66	16.92	15.47	13.38
Public latrines & urinals	0.92	0.58	0.56	0.73	0.27	0.21	0.25	0.00	0.33
GIDC effluent disposal scheme	0.00	5.19	0.43	8.76	1.37	0.21	0.27	0.00	0.00
Riverfront development board	0.77	0.25	0.18	0.22	0.06	0.07	1.06	5.90	1.99
Solid waste management	0.00	0.00	0.00	0.00	0.00	0.00	0.00	0.00	6.71
Lighting	3.21	0.89	0.42	0.39	0.90	0.00	0.66	0.43	0.66
Public places	2.63	2.03	0.88	1.76	0.31	0.43	0.46	0.96	1.66
Slum networking project	0.25	1.58	0.69	0.53	0.26	0.17	0.03	0.75	1.00
Housing & other projects for E.W.S.	2.62	1.66	2.60	11.44	2.78	0.46	0.65	0.63	1.32
Slum & health quarter repairing works	0.00	0.00	0.00	0.00	4.19	1.85	0.00	0.00	0.00
School repairing works	0.00	0.00	0.00	0.00	4.10	0.00	0.80	0.00	0.00
Works for new TP scheme	0.00	0.00	0.00	0.00	0.00	0.00	0.00	0.00	1.32
Works of TCIDS	0.00	0.00	0.00	0.00	0.00	0.00	0.00	4.08	5.39
E-governance	0.00	0.00	0.00	0.00	0.00	1.91	0.67	1.37	0.66
Office buildings and other works & equipment purchase	12.61	11.55	4.31	4.48	1.58	1.79	1.84	3.53	0.99
Miscellaneous works	0.00	0.00	0.01	0.82	0.00	0.50	0.00	1.58	2.67
Loan to AMTS	0.00	0.00	0.00	0.00	0.00	0.00	24.09	14.25	9.94
Repayment of HUDCO loan (Pre-Repayment)	0.00	0.00	0.00	0.00	58.84	27.07	0.00	0.00	0.00
Repayment of ICICI loan (Pre-Repayment)	0.00	0.00	0.00	0.00	0.00	25.43	19.36	0.00	0.00
Total	100.00	100.00	100.00	100.00	100.00	100.00	100.00	100.00	100.00

Note: GIDC = Gujarat Industrial Development Corporation; GHB = Gujarat Housing Board.
Source: Based on AMC Budget Documents (Some downloaded from net and availed in soft copy from the AMC).

Another important head is public health, which includes within it expenditures on conservancy, road cleaning and refuse removal and public health (Table 4.11). Proportion expenditure on this head has gone down from 18.0 per cent in 1997-98, 19.6 per cent in 1999-00 to 15.1 per cent in 2004-05. In 2005-06's proposed budget, its share has gone up to 18.9 per cent. A part of the public health expenditure, which includes costs of solid waste management is now being passed on to the households through new partnership models wherein the households are expected to pay the waste collector engaged in door-to-door waste collection[21]. It is likely that the costs of waste management and hence expenditure on public health has been reduced somewhat by outsourcing the waste collection system to a contractor who engages labour at much lower wages than what AMC would pay their regular workers.

Except for two years, revenue expenditure on water supply has remained between 12 per cent and 14 per cent. There is a steady decline in the share of medical aid in the total revenue expenditure, if we do not take 2005-06's BE into account. Share of public education went up till 2000-01, after which it has declined. This pattern is accompanied by increase in the share of loan charges in the total revenue expenditure. In fact, as per the RE for 2004-05, the proportion of loan charges in the total revenue expenditure has gone up above 25 per cent, the cut-off point for acceptable debt service ratio[22].

Yadav (2005) has shown that the debt service ratio has been kept below the acceptable limit of 0.25 by the AMC by holding back on the principal amount payment of certain government loans taken by the AMC. If this is taken into account then the financial health of the AMC is getting strained in the recent years because of multiple borrowings to accelerate capital works, necessary to convert Ahmedabad into a megacity. The JNNURM being implemented would accelerate this indebtedness of the city. Increased share of loan charges has crowded out shares of public health, public education and water supply on the revenue account. It has also led to reduction in the expenditure share of administrative works.

Yadav (2005) also shows that the size of capital expenditures (Table 4.12) has been large for certain years, 2001-02, 2002-03 and 2003-04, because high coupon rate loans have been paid back through low coupon rate borrowings. In effect, the capital works done is worth less than the total amount of capital expenditure shown in the budget. Thus, in Table 4.11, one finds two headings, prepayment of HUDCO loan and ICICI loan, having significant proportion of capital expenditure share; 58.8 per cent in 2001-02 and 27.1 per cent in 2002-03 of the capital expenditure were spent on prepayment of HUDCO loan and 25.4 per cent in 2002-03 and 19.4 per cent in 2003-04 of the total capital expenditure were spent on prepayment of ICICI loans. This means that the actual total expenditure in 2001-02 and 2002-03 was half and in 2003-04 was 80 per cent of the total stated capital expenditure in the budget. Though this is a good financial management, presenting capital expenditure budget in this manner is misleading.

For most of the years, the important items of expenditure on the capital budgets have been various grants' works taken up, including the grants spent by the elected representatives for small construction works; roads, footpaths and bridges (including flyovers), water project and storm water drains and sewerage networks (mentioned as drainage project in Table 4.12).

After the 2001 earthquake, Gujarat State Disaster Management Authority's (GSDMA)'s grant to the AMC, with the funds from the Asian Development Bank (ADB) have been used for repairs of government buildings, such as schools, etc. damaged due to the earthquake. Another new expenditure head in the recent years is the Riverfront development company, which received 5.9 per cent (Rs. 17.40 crores) of the capital expenditure budget in 2004-05 (as per revised estimates) and about 2 per cent (Rs. 6 crores) of the same in 2005-06. The riverfront project's cost is Rs. 1,200 crores[23], which is far higher than the contribution of the AMC to the company (Special Purpose Vehicle—SPV), set up for the purpose. In the recent years, the AMC has also given significant amount as loan to the Ahmedabad Municipal Transport Services (AMTS); Rs. 58.3 crores (24.1%) in 2003-04, Rs. 42 crores (14.3%) in 2004-05 and Rs. 30 crores (9.9%) in 2005-06.

It seems that the capital expenditure allocations vary from year to year as per the priorities of the AMC. They are also prone to be influenced by the pulls and pushes of the different interests lobbies. Although, the AMC had developed a capital investment plan for a five year period in late 1990s[3], no systematic capital expenditure pattern indicating specific priority of the AMC can be observed from the overall capital budget. Lastly, as we would see later, the capital investments are project based and depend on the funds available from different sources and can be based on somewhat adhoc decisions.

Capital Budget Details

The capital budget has been analysed only for four major heads: (i) water works, (ii) drainage and sanitation works, (iii) roads and street lights and

(iv) solid waste management. First of all, the share of infrastructure projects in the total capital budget has decreased from 86 per cent in 1999-00 to less than 50 per cent in 2003-04 (Table 4.13). This is the outcome of capital income being used for prepayment of ICICI and HUDCO loans since 2001-02, as already discussed above. Reduction in the size of capital budget has therefore affected the infrastructure projects.

Table 4.13: Budget Allocation under Infrastructure Projects, AMC

Expenditure Head	*1998-99*	*1999-00*	*2000-01*	*2001-02*	*2002-03*	*2003-04*
			In Rs. lakhs			
Water works	1937.99	11473.78	5363.48	1079.69	1445.84	4326.17
Drainage & sanitation	2491.25	2736.83	2658.21	2283.48	2816.80	5289.24
Roads & street lights	2687.75	3052.66	2041.36	914.15	301.27	1789.57
Solid waste	2.84	133.81	49.49	1.07	1.14	28.53
% Share of infrastructure	77.32	86.73	72.59	24.03	32.81	46.59
Total capital budget	8109.74	19106.16	13614.78	16996.22	13761.57	24339.19
			% to total infrastructure expenditure			
Water works	27.22	65.95	53.04	25.24	31.67	37.84
Drainage & sanitation	34.99	15.73	26.29	53.37	61.70	46.26
Roads & street lights	37.75	17.55	20.19	21.37	6.60	15.65
Solid waste	0.04	0.77	0.49	0.03	0.02	0.25

Source: Based on AMC Budget Documents (Some downloaded from net and availed in soft copy from the AMC).

Among the infrastructure projects, water works have received the highest attention of the AMC in two (1999-00 and 2000-01) of the six years of this analysis. In three years, 2001-02, 2002-03 and 2003-04, drainage and sewerage projects have received the highest attention. Only in 1998-99, roads and street lights had received the highest attention. As Table 4.12 shows, the AMC has increased its share of capital expenditure on the roads in the last two years, 2004-05 and 2005-06. Solid waste management gets miniscule amount of attention in the capital budget allocation.

Capital Expenditure on Water Works

The main water works have been (i) water project taken up through the HUDCO and USAID loans, which is mainly east Ahmedabad project on which Rs. 1,401.34 lakhs were spent in 1998-99, Rs. 3,606.12 lakhs in 1999-00, Rs. 2,893.06 lakhs in 2000-01 and Rs. 874.20 lakhs in 2001-02; (ii) Raska Weir project on which Rs. 7,364.16 lakhs were spent in 1999-00, Rs. 2,174.02 lakhs in 2000-01, Rs. 69.21 lakhs in 2001-02 and Rs. 453.27 lakhs in 2002-03; (iii) water project taken up through capital bonds, once again in east Ahmedabad, on which Rs. 436.10 lakhs were spent in 2002-03 and Rs. 2,937.96 lakhs in 2003-04; (iv) water works under the disaster management loan of the ADB on which Rs. 174.08 lakhs in 2002-03 and Rs. 220.37 lakhs in 2003-04 were spent; (v) zonal water works on which Rs. 10.84 lakhs were spent in 2002-03 and Rs. 742.35 lakhs in 2003-04. All other heads such as water works in Gujarat Housing Board (GHB) projects, water source augmentation and provision of water supply to the slums received very small amounts. In fact the last item received Rs. 0.65 lakhs in 1998-99, Rs. 7.53 lakhs in 1999-00, Rs. 5.02 lakhs in 2000-01, Rs. 1.03 lakhs in 2001-02 and Rs. 0.87 lakhs in 2002-03. A sudden increase in capital expenditure in water supply in 1999-00 has been because of the Raska Weir project. In 2006-07 budget, Rs. 118.29 crores, that is 13.9 per cent of the total capital budget would be spent on the water supply related works[24]. In short, the periphery of east Ahmedabad has received attention from the AMC for the water supply provision in the recent years.

Capital Expenditure on Drainage and Sewerage Works

From 2002-03, expenditure on sewerage and storm water drain works have exceeded that on the water supply. In the drainage and sewerage works, Sabarmati river cleaning project has received the largest amount (Rs. 2,768.99 lakhs in 2003-04, which was more than half the amount expended on drainage and sewerage) (Table 4.13). This head is followed by items such as Gujarat Industrial Development Corporation (GIDC) effluent disposal scheme and the drainage and sewerage works after the earthquake from the GSDMA-ADB grants. The former is to take care of chemical wastes following the directions from the Gujarat High Court, and has received Rs. 1,851 lakhs over this six year period.[25] Rs. 1,322 lakhs have been spent from GSDMA-ADB loan. Further, whenever a specific funding is attached to a project then more expenditure is made on that item, as with regards to HUDCO and USAID loans and even bond funds. This is in sink with the system of project funding, which can be spent on that specific head only. Thus, like with the water works, the sewerage and drainage works are dependent on project funding.

At the city level there are few public urinals. To improve the situation 'Pay and use toilets' are being constructed at various locations in the city limits and for which amount of Rs. 60.72 lakhs was allocated in the year 2003-04. Along with these Rs. 45.68 lakhs were also released for subsidised toilet construction scheme. Although, water inundation is a very frequent event every monsoon, just Rs. 437.5 lakhs were spent on storm water drains in this six year period. In 2003-04, Rs. 154.22 lakhs were spent on this head.

Table 4.14: Capital Expenditure on Drainage and Sewerage Works, AMC (Rs. lakhs)

Item	*1998-99*	*1999-00*	*2000-01*	*2001-02*	*2002-03*	*2003-04*
Storm water drains general, TP scheme and zonal	30.76	59.25	87.60	50.62	55.01	154.22
Drainage pipeline T.P. Scheme	6.55	7.33	4.38	1.61	8.05	0.00
Drainage pumping station	9.54	0.00	0.00	0.00	0.00	0.00
Drainage general	46.04	55.73	56.51	25.30	25.27	108.36
Drainage pipeline chlorination	0.00	0.00	20.71	5.90	2.30	0.00
Drainage project	73.24	31.33	12.48	63.89	17.01	0.00
Drainage cleaning	0.00	100.00	0.73	100.00	0.00	0.00
Drainage project (HUDCO bond USAID project)	126.15	839.93	665.56	177.83	0.00	0.00
Drainage project (Tax free bond)	0.00	0.00	0.00	0.00	43.92	800.23
Naroda, Vatwa, Odhav, & GIDC drainage	1.97	0.43	1.20	0.30	0.00	0.00
Drainage general (Zonal works)	0.00	0.00	0.00	0.00	35.62	224.36
Drainage Total	263.49	1034.75	761.57	374.83	132.17	1132.95
GHB drainage	1.14	2.75	4.82	8.44	2.14	0.00
Drainage facility in slum areas	0.00	0.31	0.36	0.00	0.60	0.00
Sabarmati river cleaning grant works	784.30	564.64	383.15	1346.61	1993.75	2768.99
GIDC effluent disposal scheme	420.72	82.18	1021.87	232.04	28.44	65.65
GSDMA/ADB grants	0.00	0.00	0.00	0.00	441.47	890.60
Pay and use toilet	0.00	1.92	6.19	0.00	9.64	60.72
Toilet	117.93	150.65	129.12	65.88	47.23	45.68
Others (modern equipment for drainage cleaning, etc.	23.40	14.59	33.39	11.11	55.82	76.74
Grand total drainage and sanitation works	1641.74	1911.04	2428.07	2089.53	2766.27	5195.55

Note: GIDC = Gujarat Industrial Development Corporation.

Source: Based on AMC Budget Documents (Some downloaded from net and availed in soft copy from the AMC).

The emphasis on water supply, sewerage and storm water drainage continues in AMC's budget for the year 2006-07. Rs. 274.73 crores, that is, 32.3 per cent of the capital budget, has been proposed to be spent on these heads[26] (Table 4.14).

Capital Expenditure on Roads and Flyovers

The third major area of expenditure in infrastructure development is on improving the roads, constructing flyovers, widening bridges over river Sabarmati, laying footpaths and putting street lights and other road furniture (Table 4.15). The highest expenditure in this has been on construction of new roads asnd resurfacing of existing roads. Total of Rs. 5,527.54 lakhs have been spent on this item over this six year period, taking up more than half the total capital expenditure on this main head.

Expenditures on other items are: widening of bridges on the river (Rs. 36.6 crores); flyover construction (Rs. 4.2 crores) and footpath construction (Rs. 4.7 crores).

In 2006-07 budget, there has been a significant increase in allocation for road and bridge projects. Rs. 120 crores (14.1%) of the proposed capital budget, would be on integrated road development and city beautification projects; Rs. 24.73 crores (2.9%) would be on a flyover at Maninagar; Rs. 33 crores (3.9%) would be on a new bridge over river Sabarmati. In all 36.9 per cent of the total capital budget would be on the road, flyovers, bridges and footpaths[27].

Table 4.15: Capital Expenditure on Roads and Street Lights Works, AMC (Rs. lakhs)

Department and accounts head name	*1998-99*	*1999-00*	*2000-01*	*2001-02*	*2002-03*	*2003-04*
Street lights	51.76	74.19	49.57	152.88	0.00	122.33
New roads and resurfacing	1385.65	1434.90	910.72	458.91	276.32	1052.04
Footpath	87.07	81.18	69.47	22.79	7.47	205.05
Flyover	0.00	0.25	85.47	0.00	10.55	324.81
Ellis bridge	455.67	534.32	398.06	2.09	0.00	0.00
Other bridge	666.13	874.19	482.90	249.47	0.12	0.00
Parking centre	0.00	0.00	0.00	8.13	0.00	0.00
Traffic control box	41.47	53.63	36.17	19.88	6.81	85.34
Grand total	2687.75	3052.66	2041.36	914.15	301.27	1789.57

Source: Based on AMC Budget Documents (Some downloaded from net and availed in soft copy from the AMC).

Zonal Expenditures

In each of the main head of the capital works discussed above, there is a sub-head of zonal works. Some amount is allocated for zonal works for all capital expenditure heads (Table 4.16). Zonal estimates are available only for one year, 2005-06. East and north zone received about 49 per cent (about 24.5 per cent each) of the total capital expenditure in the proposed budget of 2005-06. But, both these zones have only 22.2 per cent of the total population of the AMC in this year, indicating that these two zones are priority for the AMC. And this is rightly so, as these two zones lack in infrastructure, given that the peripheral areas of these two zones were amalgamated within the AMC in 1986. Southern zone also received higher proportion of allocation as compared to its share of population. The reason is the same for zones eastern and northern zones.

Table 4.16: Zonewise Population and Expenditure, AMC

Zone	*Population*	*% of Population*	*Amount (in lakhs)*	*% of total amount*
East Zone	784,234	22.28	367.35	24.49
North Zone	779,742	22.15	365.81	24.39
West Zone	675,362	19.19	230.23	15.35
South Zone	702,950	19.97	339.64	22.64
Central Zone	577,797	16.41	196.97	13.13
Total Population	3,520,085	100.00	1500.00	100.00

Source: AMC's proposed budget for the year 2005-06.

Some New Developments

Most of the new developments after 2000 have been in west Ahmedabad, by the AUDA, where new roads have been laid, new parks developed and also a few lakes have been developed. While the public authority has focused on infrastructure, the private developments have been organised retailing outlet such as Piramyds of the Piramal group, Pantaloons, Big Bazaar, Star Bazaar of the Tata's, Lifestyle stores, etc.; restaurants and for sure MacDonald's and Pizza Huts; high end multi-storey residential buildings and large many gated communities. All but one mall have come in western Ahmedabad, and big ones have come up along the SG Highway. Every large retailer has an outlet in west Ahmedabad. Three of the four MacDonald's are in west Ahmedabad. Also, three large multiplexes are on the SG highway. Two multiplexes, one in south Ahmedabad and one in east Ahmedabad are an exception to the general trend.

Riverfront Development

"Its like a dream that one lives. Waking up by the river; driving down the riverside, a board meeting with the vast blue vista in the background and then a cruise across the water for a power lunch on the other bank. And then, a dinner on a gloating restaurant with family to chill out." "... In the midst of concrete and steel, that's the dream thes city planners are conjuring up for apnu Amdavad." " On two stretches of 11.5 km each on both sides of the river, the future of a decaying city takes shape. It will create a central business district on the water front, that would rub shoulders with the world's best—Melbourne that's only 800 m and Singapore, 1.2 km. The highpoint are the concrete walkways along the river on both sides, where people can stroll, while the second level, will have public roads, footpaths and gardens. This level will house the tall buildings including the tallest in Gujarat. The buildings will include offices, hotels, a few malls and residential complexes."[28] This is the romantic picture of the proposed riverfront development.

Besides these new real estate projects, three new bridges would be constructed over the river. Not forgetting the tradition, there would be bank development (*ghats*) for the worshippers and washermen. River will continue to have important institutions on the bank such as Gandhi Ashram and a cultural place Natrani. Also planned is a parking lot at a distance from offices, with buses ferrying people from these lots to their offices and back at regular intervals.

The total cost of SRFDP is Rs. 1,200 crores[29]. The source of funds for the project would be HUDCO loan; Rs. 200 crores have been sanctioned; loans from consortium of banks (Indian Bank, Union Bank, Corporation Bank, State Bank and LIC) worth Rs. 50 crores have been sanctioned; and Delamore & Owl Group of UK is expected to invest Rs. 400 crores in the company, MoU for which has been signed. The project would be implemented by the SPV named Sabarmati Riverfront Development Corporation Limited (SRFDCL), which has been registered as a company. The SRFDCL has been given authority to amend the Gujarat Development Control Regulations (GDCR) Act to ensure harmonious development of the riverfront[30]. The reclaimed land will be given to the developers from 2007 for development. It is hoped that the project cost will be met through this and loans will also be repaid through this. FSI permitted would be 3 instead of 1.8. 35 hectares of land will be made available for commercial and residential development of 168 hectares to be reclaimed for the project between Subhash bridge on the north and Vasna on the south. First phase development will be between Nehru bridge and Gandhi bridge, wherein Rs. 500 crores are expected through the sale of land.

According to a writ petition filed in the Gujarat High Court for ensuring rehabilitation of all those to be displaced by the project, 30,000 households are living on Sabarmati river bank[31]. Reclamation of 162 hectares of land of river Sabarmati has already begun and so has embankment construction. The work is progressing inspite of High Court order stating that the project cannot progress without adequate rehabilitation policy in place. On paper, rehabilitation is offered for 4,000 households, to be rehabilitated in 20 sq yards apartment unit, for which loan of Rs. 60,000 would be made available. However, no firm site (s) for rehabilitation purpose has/have been identified, creating tremendous anxiety among to be affected people, to say the least. The project has strong backing of the city and state government, politicians, city planners and above all the developers. It is expected that the riverbed lands being reclaimed would be sold soon. The Chief Minister of the state of Gujarat has held festivals on the reclaimed part of the river bank to indicate that the project is a priority for the state government.[32]

After the announcement of riverfront project, new hotel properties are in the pipeline. A 242 room facility is to be set up on the banks of Sabarmati, near the airport by Luxembourg based venture capital company, 'Capital Tree Group (CTG) Ltd.' in joint venture with an unidentified local real estate developer. The company has already acquired 30,000 sq yards of land and would acquire another 10,000 sq yards. The construction would begin in February 2006. This company would also acquire a Swedish airline that has existing rights for Ahmedabad and Amritsar. The CTG would pump in US$ 150 million (around Rs. 690 crores) and hold 55 per cent stake, local developer will hold 30 per cent stake in form of land acquisition and another 15 per cent would be held by Ahmedabad-based Opal Travels Pvt. Ltd, in which CTG has invested US$ 10 million.[32]. Lalit Suri, the hotelier of India, of Bharat Hotels Ltd. is also slated to have acquired 23,000 sq meteres of land near Indira bridge to build a 200 room hotel, that would get completed by 2007[33].

Other Projects

Ahmedabad city is laying a Bus Rapid Transit (BRT) Corridor. Budget of 2006-07 has allocated Rs. 100 crores for this project, which is 11.8 per cent of the total capital budget of Rs. 850 crores[34]. City beautification projects such as Gandhi Ashram area development, Kankaria Lake development, etc. have been proposed. In 2006-07 budget Rs. 120 crores (14.1 per cent of the total capital budget), has been proposed to be used for road development and city beautification projects[35].

New Marginalisations

Lack of Attention to Eastern Ahmedabad

Nikol area, in eastern periphery of Ahmedabad, which is an industrial area, has been facing problems of water logging. It is chemically polluted water, released by the industries of the area. The Gujarat Pollution Control Board gave clear instructions to AUDA to construct a pipe line to ensure disposal of chemical water so that Nikol area residents do not bear the brunt of the chemical pollution. But, AUDA did not bother. When residents of Nikol, under the aegis of Nagrik Hitrakshak Samiti (Citizens' Interest-

Protection Committee), went and met the AUDA officials about this and asked them why the Gujarat Pollution Control Board (GPCB) order was not heeded to, the concerned official of AUDA said: "What is our income from eastern Ahmedabad? Get whatever you want through an agitation". The message was clear; since the AUDA does not get any income from eastern Ahmedabad, it was not interested in making any investments there. Thus, if the residents wanted the implementation of laws there, they should pursue the path of agitation. According to the convener of the committee, Mr. Mahendra Patel, the state's CM had stated, after the win of BJP in Ahmedabad Corporation, that the difference in level of development between east and west Ahmedabad would be eradicated. Were AUDA officials hearing to what the CM had promised?[36]

Increase in Cesses and Taxes

In 2006-07 budget, water cess rates have been increased and so have the property tax rates been increased. Water and sewerage cess have also been increased by Rs. 50 to Rs. 500. It starts with residential units larger than 50 sq m (Table 4.17). There is increase in property tax rates, from Rs. 10 to Rs. 14 per sq m for residential properties and Rs. 22 to Rs. 26 per sq m for non-residential properties.

Table 4.17: Water and Sewerage Charges

Residential unit size	*Current rate (Rs.)*	*Proposed rate (Rs.)*	*Increase (%)*
< 25 sq m	0.00	0.00	
50 sq m	100.00	150.00	50
50-100 sq.m	200.00	300.00	50
> 100 sq m	300.00	450.00	50
> 200 sq m	1500.00	2000.00	25
Industrial units, factories (only those processing and production units)	400.00	600.00	50
Other non-residential properties	600.00	800.00	33
> 150 sq m other properties	1500.00	2000.00	25

Source: *Gujarat Samachar*, February 4, 2006, and http://www.egovamc.com/amc_budget/Budget_0607.PDF.

Increase in Property Prices and Realty Businesses' Interests

Big realty firms' interest in Ahmedabad City has increased in last three years. This has resulted in increase in property rates in the city. Table 4.18 shows that the residential and commercial property prices have doubled in the city in the last three years, from 2003 to 2006, on an average. This is because many large realty firms have begun to invest in Ahmedabad. The city, at the moment has lower land prices than other metros of India, and hence the realty firms would reap higher profits by investing in Ahmedabad than in other metros. Some large national level realty firms, such as the DLF, the Rahejas, the Hiranandani Constructions, Shapoorji Pallonji, etc. have begun purchasing lands in the city in the recent years[37].

Table 4.18: Property Prices, Ahmedabad (Rs. per sq. yard)

	2003	2004	2005	2006
Residential—Satellite Road	8,000-12,500	9,500-15,500	15,000-20,000	20,000-23,000
Commercial—SG Highway	12,000-15,000	15,000-17,500	18,000-21,000	23,000-30,000

Source: *The Times of India*, Ahmedabad, May 13, 2006.

Conclusions

Ahmedabad has emerged as a split metro, especially in the last decade and a half with increasing pressure on the city to become a global city. This is a marked change from being an inclusive city before this. Her elevation to a megacity status has been taken advantage of to bring in new infrastructure projects, especially road, water supply and sanitation projects, albeit in the western periphery, which is fast emerging as a global city. Ahmedabad was one of the first cities in India to construct a multiplex. Since then, multiplexes and malls have multiplied in numbers on the western periphery. The city's urban development authority, the AUDA, has been proactive in rapidly developing the western periphery thus and that too in a very short period. This has assisted the property developers immensely; the western periphery has now developments such as high end gated communities, proposed new townships, well laid and wide roads, and in some parts also water supply network to reach Narmada waters to the residential colonies. This first round of new developments in the city has been on the western periphery, where the AUDA's infrastructure investments have immensely benefited the real estate developers. In the private conversations it is commonly mentioned that one of the former Chairman of AUDA, who has become powerful within the ruling political party of the state, is a builder and was personally interested that such infrastructure investments are made by the AUDA. Not just him, but, many real estate developers have benefited from the AUDA's proactive role.

The AUDA's proactive role on the western periphery has enhanced the split within the city, between the east and the west, between the local and the global, between those eking out their survival somehow and those rolling in wades of money displayed by increase in consumerism in the western areas, expensive cars on the road, spiralling property prices and increased international air traffic to and from the city. Now that these developed areas have been transferred to the AMC and most likely the loan repayment liability as well, the AMC might service the loans through either its general revenues or through sale of its properties. In both cases, the poor would loose out, as one sustainable way of increasing general revenues is through increase in user charges for the services that the ULB provides and which may adversely affect the poorest and sale of public lands for raising funds would make land availability for the housing of the urban poor impossible. It is however too early as of now to state what would happen.

Will this situation change with part of AUDA areas being merged with AMC? The first impact this move is likely to have is with regards to revenue generation. Being an ULB, the AMC has taxation powers, which the AUDA does not have. The AMC would therefore be able to collect more revenues and probably spent more on the maintenance of the infrastructures created by the AUDA. If the AMC adopts AUDA's practice of using lands as a resource for raising resources for infrastructure, the pace of infrastructure development may not reduce for the paucity of funds. But, AUDA had focused attention on west Ahmedabad and it delivered. While the AMC's attention would be distributed over the entire area of 500 sq km and over number of development concerns. Infrastructure development pace may reduce due to lack of organisational capability than lack of funds. Further, the AMC being an elected body, cannot neglect some parts and pay attention to just a few portion of the city, as the AUDA did.

The real estate lobby (the developers' lobby) is being considered as a key suspect in the expansion of city limits. The developers' lobby is normally a key suspect when the land related policy decisions are taken. The suspicion becomes stronger when it is public knowledge that the former Chairman of AUDA is a builder, as already mentioned. It is being alleged that the developers close to the ruling political party, who have purchased lands from the farmers (in their own names or fictitious names[38]) in Ahmedabad's peripheral areas, were interested in expanding the city boundary so that they could reap stupendous profits by manifold increase in land and property prices as also increase in the

FSI that would come with becoming urban. When in non-urban areas, land prices are low, and the developers purchase such lands and then build pressure on the city government to expand the city limits. Thus, by expansion of city limits, developers' and builders' profits increase multi-fold. Hence, builders' lobby is always interested in pushing for FSI increase. Expansion of city limits is a legitimate way of doing so. This is what has happened. On the other hands, the new areas included in AMC limits were already developed and had fragmented system of service provision, which gets unified with the decision to expand AMC limits.

The AMC is not in a position to generate large amounts for capital investments as AUDA had done. This means that now the investments in merged parts of the AMC would slow down. But, it would also mean that the AUDA would invest in areas much beyond the SP ring road, which would open up virgin areas for land speculation by the developers. Through this, the real estate market of Ahmedabad city would move once again beyond what are the presently developed areas.

With the promise of withdrawal of thse octroi, the AMC's finances are going to come under tremendous stress. This has come at a time when its jurisdiction has been increased 2.5 times! Unlike the AUDA, the AMC has not been able to use land for raising capital funds and has been depending on either raising bonds in the capital market or taking loans for capital investments, as our analysis shows. This would constraint the AMC's capability to make capital investments. The AMC has kept its debt service ratio under the acceptable limit by postponing repayment of principal amount for the loans taken from the government agencies. This shows that it is not in a position to take any further financial liability. It has been able to reduce some of its revenue expenditure by outsourcing certain tasks, such as solid waste management to the private contractors or getting on board the community partnerships that would take care some of the collection costs. Increase in debt services has been accommodated by the AMC by cutting down expenditures on public health, medical aid and education and not increasing the expenditures on water supply. With the new areas being brought within its jurisdiction and limited tax sources, particularly after the removal of octroi tax as announced, would highly stress the AMC's capability to manage and develop the city further. It will also push the AMC for further reliance on cost recovery models for the infrastructure projects.

The capital works in the AMC have been progressing through project mode, depending on the funding available. The infrastructure development therefore is project by project, which firstly slows down the progress, as we can see for the east Ahmedabad infrastructure works ongoing for now more than 10 years and makes the process ad hoc. But, upto 2003-04, the AMC's priority in capital investments were water supply and sewerage and drainage works. From 2004-05, road projects are gaining ascendancy in financial allocations, as the need of the hour in a globalising megacity is. Also, a positive dimension of AMC's capital works was that it was spending on east and north Ahmedabad, where it was necessary to do so. With the amalgamation of west Ahmedabad periphery, some pressure from here would build up, given that all the new high end real estate developments are here. One has to wait and see whether the AMC shifts its geographic priorities now.

Ahmedabad's response to forces of globalisation has been however a bit slow than that observed in other cities of India, such as Delhi, Mumbai, Bangalore and Hyderabad, as other articles in this book indicate. The city has seen relatively equity oriented development investments. This is the first city to go for a BRTS and has not yet planned a metro rail project though the idea keeps floating around. That has been the case with regards to the main ULB, the AMC. However, the parastatal land development authority, which is the AUDA, has displayed a clear bias towards the high end real estate developments and has made investments to benefit this group. It is this bias of the AUDA that has converted the western periphery of Ahmedabad into developments suitable for a globalising megacity. With the pronouncement of megacity status for the city, the AMC has also tilted the balance in favour of projects that would benefit the real estate developers; a good example of that is the riverfront development project. This project would clean up the river but will also displace the riverbank dwellers. It will rehabilitate some and leave in lurch the rest. Realty development requires improvement in road networks, and that is where the attention of the AMC has shifted after 2003-04. It seems that this would continue. But, being an elected body and because of its inclusive history, the AMC is not able to totally exclude certain regions and certain activities. Hence, the Ahmedabad's response to globalisation has been a vacillating one, between inclusions and exclusions. This some consider is slowing down the march towards a 'World Class Megacity' and some consider a process of 'Inclusive Growth' within a democratic polity.

NOTES

1. This chapter is based on research undertaken through IDPAD project.
2. See, http://timesofindia.indiatimes.com/articleshow/1036510.cms.
3. It is not clear why this sudden decision was taken and that too after the passing of the 2006-07 year budget of the AMC.
4. The seven municipalities amalgamated with the AMC are: Bodakdev, Vastrapur, Thaltej, and Makarba on the west and Nava Odhav, Nikol and Nava Naroda on the east of the AMC.
5. *The Times of India*, Ahmedabad, February 15, 2006.
6. *Gujarat Samachar*, Ahmedabad, April 19, 2006.
7. See Concerned Citizens Tribunal—Gujarat 2002 (2002a and 2002b); National Human Rights Commission (2002) whose members were: Justice J.S. Verma, Chairperson; Justice K. Ramaswamy, Member; Justice Sujata V. Manohar, Member; and Virendra Dayal, Member (This is a statutory body set up by the Government of India); Amnesty Internationals' 2003 report, from its website http://web.amnesty.org/report2003/ind-summary-eng; Balagopal (2002), Breman (2002); and various other fact finding missions.
8. See Breman 2002, Shah 2002, Mahadevia 2002, Patel 2002; Varshney 2002.
9. Comprising 15 per cent of city's population, as per population census of 1991.
10. This is the Slum Networking Programme (SNP), on which a lot has been written in literature. See Dutta (2002), Joshi (2002), which talk about the positive achievements of the programme; and Acharya (2002), which discuss about the limitations of the programme. This is not an exhaustive list of studies on the SNP.
11. See Mahadevia (2002a and 2002b) and Mahadevia (2005), for the development of this argument.
12. This is pre-amalgamation situation. From now on, our analysis is of the pre-amalgamated AMC boundary of 198 sq km entity, since all the data pertains to this entity.
13. Development through TP scheme is through land readjustment method, in which the developing authority takes a share of the adjusted plot, for its own use, such as laying infrastructure and for selling in the market for raising financial resources.
14. Megacity funding was: 35 per cent grant from the central government, 15 per cent grant from the state government both to be used for setting up a revolving fund of which only 25 per cent would go to the city government or the development authority as grant, and 50 per cent is the agency's, ULB's or development authority's own contribution. In essence, the development agency had to raise 87.5 per cent for the project.
15. For the details of these rules see Mahadevia, Wolfe and Parashar (2000).
16. It is likely that India is not taking loans from the ADB for the road projects and is continuing to borrow for projects dealing with poverty, education, health and other immediate development concerns.

17. *The Times of India,* Ahmedabad, April 6, 2006.
18. *The Times of India*, Ahmedabad, April 6, 2006.
19. Data is from the AMC budgets and from a master's dissertation of School of Planning by Yadav (2005).
20. See Kundu 2001, Mahadevia 2001 and Mahadevia and Mukherjee 2003.
21. See Acharya and Parashar (2008), for case of Vejalpur municipality in AUDA.
22. Debt service ratio is loan charges (principal repayment + interest payment) divided by total revenue expenditure.
23. *The Times of India*, Ahmedabad, December, 2, 2005.
24. See Mahadevia and Mukherjee 2003 and Mukherjee 2002.
25. *Gujarat Samachar*, February 5, 2006 and http://www.egovamc.com/amc_budget/Budget_0607.PDF.
26. *Gujarat Samachar*, February 5, 2006 and http://www.egovamc.com/amc_budget/Budget_0607.PDF.
27. *Gujarat Samachar*, February 5, 2006 and http://www.egovamc.com/amc_budget/Budget_0607.PDF.
28. *Times of India*, Ahmedabad, December, 2, 2005.
29. *Times of India*, Ahmedabad, December, 2, 2005.
30. According to Anil Mukim, the Commissioner of AMC. Dec. 2, 2005.
31. Special Civil Application No. 6280 of 2005, filed in The High Court of Gujarat.
32. *Times of India*, Ahmedabad, December 1, 2005.
33. *Times of India*, Ahmedabad, December 2, 2005.
34. *Gujarat Samachar*, February 5, 2006 and http://www.egovamc.com/amc_budget/Budget_0607.PDF.
35. *Gujarat Samachar*, February 5, 2006 and http://www.egovamc.com/amc_budget/Budget_0607.PDF.
36. *Gujarat Samachar*, Ahmedabad, December 4, 2005.
37. *The Times of India*, Ahmedabad, April 18, 2006.
38. For details of types of land transactions in Ahmedabad periphery, see Mahadevia (2003a). A Tehelka (a weekly newspaper) reporter following this story was questioned by the anti-terrorist squad of Gujarat government on some fictitious charge. This indicates culpability of the ruling party in the matter of land transactions in the city's periphery.

5[1]

INCLUSIVE OR CONTESTED
Conceptualising a Globalised Bangalore[2]

SOLOMON BENJAMIN

What does being globally connected mean for the local in cities of the South? What is the form of contested urban terrain between big business and other economies? This paper looks centrally at the relevance of the issue of 'inclusion and exclusion', in the context of globalised cities. At one level, Bangalore as India's IT capital provides some useful insights into some of the detailed institutional changes that facilitate big business take over of productive locations and terrains. It also, by way of rooted ethnographic research, point to the need to develop new conceptual categories. In the introductory section, I discuss conceptual frames by which we might read contested city terrain. In doing so, I aim to the way to appreciate the nuanced discussions in paper 2 of this set, Chapter 7 of this volume.

Conceptualising 'Inclusion and Exclusion' and 'Globalised Cities'

'Inclusive cities' can be closely linked to the notion of 'Inclusive Globalisation'. The latter could mean several things. But perhaps one could be the free flow of migrants across borders initiating trade`, their settlement, and social and cultural transformations into new and complex imaginaries of citizenship. Translated into a city concept, the issue would relate to its formative process: Cities as a location for migrants to come, settle, and in doing so, re-shaping that city's culture, economy, and politics. The issue is topical, where cities increasingly become tied to particular identities that explicitly or implicitly get tied to particular ethnic identities that are assumed to be the 'pure' stock which over time have been laid by 'outsiders'. In Bombay being termed as Mumbai, is paralleled by xenophobic call of '*amchi Mumbai*', while Delhi was sought to be cleaned of its migrant 'Bangladeshis' (read Muslims), or Bangalore being termed as 'Bangaluru' to reflect the Kannadiga aspirations. Thus, the politics of being 'inclusive' is critically important—reflective of globalisations, increasingly multi-ethnic groups sharing and contesting over economy and space, and of course pressing public offices to move the system in their favour.

Some Discomforting Conceptual Questions

In this set of two inter-related papers, I suggest that while the issue of being inclusive is important, it is essential to consider an 'urbanist' perspective to pose the issue of cities being 'inclusive' in a more radical way:

- Does the concept of cities being 'exclusive—inclusive' actually de-politicises the issue of power?
- Do these concepts portray a futuristic destiny, where cities, under corporate led globalisation, with the assistance of benevolent managers and planners and the Nation State, achieve a 'balance'.
- Poorer groups, in this position, are portrayed to be disconnected from the benefits of globalisation and a neo liberal market. If so, do these concepts allow the 'balance' via a situation assumed in the 'short run' for the poor to survive via a Welfare State, but ultimately, be accommodated within overarching 'economic development'.
- Does this view of cities, while keeping alive the position of planners and those who administer the State with benevolence, in effect ways of conceptualisation that open up space for a neutered "planning" to remove the possibility of the radical?

This research attempts to raise conceptual issues of how does one 'read' contestation. It does so, since rooted evidence from a globalising city like Bangalore and from its Hi Tech areas suggests, conceptual problems. A possible future agenda could look at more such settings in other metros. But given the extensive currency in both academic and also the development industry, there are other equally political questions that implicate power. This is not the relationship of power that is 'out there in the field', but rather closer home to the domain of the researchers and the research process. Thus, for a start, I pose some possibly useful questions to ask:

- How did such a concept come into being?
- What are it's connections to large donor funding to 'third world cities'? I refer to not just funding for large development and infrastructure projects, but also via think tanks and research institutes, into 'policy research'.
- If cities are seen setting for global investments and much higher rate of returns via emerging markets, need to be safe guarded against 'political risks'? If so, what exactly are being seen as 'political risks' and concepts like urban inclusion/exclusion?
- Finally, do these concepts in effect justify the smooth flow of capital?

These questions on the location and process of the research lead to other more self reflexive in nature:

- Is the concept of exclusion and inclusion acceptable to progressive researchers since the possibility for radical/ revolutionary change as envisaged in the 1960s is lost? If so, is there an assumption that transformation can happen only *outside* the commodity process—rather than imagining the possibility that in could otherwise?
- Is there a fear of 12th century European 'Millinariaumistic anarchy' or as Linebaug and Rediker point to the Many Headed Hydra[3] ? Is this complimented by an implicit (and perhaps tired) acceptance of the inevitability of the 'smooth flow of corporate globally connected capital'? If so, does this in effect acceptance of the setting of a mega as a pre-requisite? Is this 'acceptance' implicated in the abundance of policy research that now dominates the intellectual field and funding?
- Is the tiredness of radical imagination posed in the view of space being 'secondary' as a political terrain (as Massey argues, relative to Time) and thus reduced to a functional setting?

One of the main elements of exploring the politics of the way we conceive city contestation is not just that of demographic or economic data in isolation, but rather how this is centrally implicated in the politics of space. In this set of two papers (this chapter and the next) and especially the second, space will be discussed particularly in the form of land settings and markets—in their deeply material being. The important point will be that this materiality is fluid and contested—shaped not just by 'private initiative' but also by public actions of government at various levels.

This spatiality of materiality seems critically important to consider. When the issue of inclusiveness is framed in abstraction without the spatio-cultural—political setting of cities, this misses out essential form of political claim making. Thus, considering space and locality is not just a mere illustration from 'case studies' but rather to help build a theory of urban politics. Here, I differentiate between 'locality' and local. The latter refers to a binary—with perhaps 'global' and in doing so, undervalues one (local) against the other (global). Locality on the other hand, emphasises the open fluidity of particular types of economies. These, while having significant 'local' connections, can also have complex 'global ones'. What makes for locality is the emphasis on forms of control. In breaking across a binary of a 'local' and 'global' it reinforces the importance of local in its value of a politics of space, which I shall argue are embedded in the materiality of land, and location.

A related argument that I shall focus on is that when cities are seen as being 'inclusive' or 'exclusive' lends a binary that suggest actions that result in that situation *outside* the structure of the city itself, where contests locate outside inhabitants and their own capabilities. In doing so, one could argue that such dualistic frameworks conceptualise contests to be in dirigisme of a Nation State or then, part of a globalised homogenous market. It is also set in a framework that is inherently positivist. Poor group would be assumed to be marginalised and voice less. In this situation, the development project would at first glance seem to contrast across ideological extremes: For those who see a role of the Market via its un-stoppable greater penetration, poor groups would increasingly be induced and enthused with entrepreneurship that moves them out of poverty and thus, exclusion. The role of the State here would vary from providing them with basic skills to play and become 'stakeholders' in the global market, to moving out completely from this economic drama and let the un-evenness of the stage be levelled out by the market process[4].

In contrast are those who see varying roles of the Nation State, with public policy more interventionist. It can intervene to ensure access to basic food, education, health, full employment, housing for those groups who are left out of an economy, and especially when it is increasingly globally centered. A variation would be; get the State to focus on health, education, and basic nutrition, but keep employment and housing out of the State purview. A significant aspect of this would be a 'rights based' legal and administrative environment. This would ensure that demands made by the 'excluded' are met, with the help of 'Civil Society' (both NGOs, and academic think tanks). In this developmentalist paradigm, such social and political pressures are essential to ensure that the State internalises a 'pro-poor' agenda and sets in place a legislative framework paralleled by an administrative structure for appropriate implementation. If contest is recognised in how elite groups also attempt to 'capture the system', more reactionary NGOs work towards increasing the 'voice' of the poor as a way to pressure the system to work in their favour. For both of the latter 'progressive' and left of centre groups, globalisation is a creator of great divides and accentuates social tension by the exclusions created. If so, this view justifies a response and direction to social movements via the intellectual assistance of progressive groups as a way to initiate a truly participative process to develop alternative visions.

Interestingly, rather than 'social movements' by the oppressed led by progressive left leaning NGOs, the last five years has witnessed a rapid rise of elite based NGOs and 'Civil Society' seeking more extensive market based 'reforms' from government. These groups view the heavy influence of government and bureaucracy as main impediments in a path towards being globalised. For this group, when cities are better managed and competitive, they attract global investments. The alternative visions here come from vision documents prepared by International Consulting groups. Their powerpoint presentations point to place in global markets and a supposed road map for 'reform based' economic development. Media attention, rather than on the extensive evictions of poorer groups, has been more on publicising the lack of progress along an obviously elite development path. Thus, if there is indeed a social uprising, it has been in the form of vocal and increasingly networked groups of elite Resident Welfare Associations (RWAs). These groups, in Delhi, Bombay, and Bangalore have sought to organise themselves to pressure the government. Such pressure comes not from internal to the political domain, but from the use of the 'Right to Information'—which arguably is on several grounds:

- First, to shape investments in already 'developed' part of the city;
- Second, to resist 'vote bank' politics where they find a severe counter in the poor mostly voting;
- Third, to undermine and dilute the power of municipal bodies where poor groups have easiest access.

A measure of the 'success' of such elite mobilisation, while still to be tested fully, is in the JNNURM. This programme that centralises all central government funds has its allocation procedures driven by a very conservative 'good governance' measure in the form of '*area sabhas*'. The core idea is to get the elite sections of a ward, almost always residing in the Master Planned areas, play a key role to decide on investments over those that are in the relatively un-planned and usually 'illegal' areas.

Locating The 'Urban' in Binaries

I now return to the argument that a binary is most likely to suggest an analysis of actions and processes *outside* the structure of the city itself. I have argued in the preceding text, that the poor are assumed to be relatively voiceless and incapable of autonomous action. Economic growth and social empowerment 'comes/happens to them' from an external agency: An increasingly globalised market, or then, a strongly re-distributive role of the Nation State. In this perspective, cities are reduced to demographic entities, or formed from the grouping of various ethnic groups. Space and location, or land, is assumed to be either a homogenous and largely functional entity. Rather than possessing any distinctive aspect, these become settings for markets to operate from, or then, within a centralised planning frame, to be Master Plan to ensure 'equitable distribution' of 'public' goods.

There seem to be two fundamental assumptions at the core of the above way of thinking. First, is a conception of the poor including within the progressive position, that set them within a largely "Income" situation that in turn is underpinned by the notion of a benevolent Nation State. Second, and related to this, poor groups exist mostly as 'passive' economic and political agents, who are mainly 'beneficiaries'.

What is interesting is the strong similarity in viewpoints to the globally enabled Neo liberal right. These groups, organised at one level via business and trade organisations like the Federation of Indian Chamber of Commerce and Industry (FICCI) and Confederation of Indian Industries (CII). Their 'voice' is heard directly at the policy level with the more senior of bureaucrats in attendance. Consistently, in several of their conferences, the call to modernise cities as locations for global investments centre around the following policy prescriptions: The call to the 'Nation State' to ensure 'well functioning and organised' markets! A summary of their policy prescriptions include:

- More and better housing (though location de-emphasised),

- Access to economy viewed as 'travel to work' time, and thus forming the basis of resettlement and rehabilitation, but also large scale transportation infrastructure in terms of flyovers,
- More and more effective normative driven Master Planning, as a way to re-place local politics and 'vote bank' politics,
- Clean land titles as a way to 'equity',
- De-emphasis on municipal councils to empower Mayors and senior administrators under the authority of a reformed "Nation State".

Some quotes from actual presentations and discussions during big business international forums reinforce these points:

> "*....Need more Master Planning and organised cities, Clear titles and GIS, good housing for all and no slum conditions,*" (One of Delhi's biggest Real estate developer and also made famous after a fire in a cinema).
>
> "*...We need Good Governance, re-develop slum areas. Better land titles. Planned development...Good housing...get rid of the bureaucrat—politician nexus and Vested interests—line up those local politicians on the roadside and shoot them...*" (Bombay's most famous Real estate developer).
>
> "No WB consultant could have managed the elected Council to ensure the reforms... need to reign in local politicians and bureaucrats to bring them in line. The BATF as a Trojan Horse amongst the councillors..." (Core member of the Bangalore Agenda Task Force—BATF).
>
> "*...Place metro cities under "President's rule" to ensure Planned development ...*" (India's most famous IT honcho and also on several anti-piracy forums.)
>
> "*...the Bhoomi (digitised land records) brings transparency and accountability by snatching power away from local politicians...*" (The Project Designer, a senior Bureaucrat of what is now a World Bank made famous "E-Governance initiative).

The main argument is that a narrow concern with the macro allows for a blurring of the conceptual sharpness, and in turn, an effective capture of terminology. There is a limited literature that looks at the importance of land market in its economic and political aspects. But even here, the politics is set with a binary of the Nation State or then, a global homogenised market. The issue of the politics of space as being complex, dynamic, and possibly autonomous entity as effectively argued by Massey (2005) remains un-attended:

> *'...(The) crucial characteristic of 'the spatial' which constitutes it as one of the vital moments in the production of those dislocations which are necessary to the existence of the political..."* (Massey 2005:39) & *'...dislocation is the source of freedom'* (Laclau 1990:60 in Massey 2005)[5].

In fact, the concern with global cities, as I shall argue later, is over shadowed by an emphasis on 'infrastructure' as a pre-requisite to locate cities on the global stage[6]. This in turn moves analysis away from the city, and reduces it to passive settings to be bestowed upon (via enlightened public policy) with infrastructure that sets it in a new league[7].

To illustrate this critique, I present a way in which our own researched territories in Bangalore could suggest a binary conception: The Nation State and also the Global Market, and as part of this, suggest a linearity of development where modernity builds and plans over the more indigenous settlements. East Bangalore, beyond the Airport and on towards Whitefield in the south, and ITPL towards it's north is characterised by large IT companies, SEZ, large high-end housing projects. Interspersed between these are zones of Small Scale Industries (SSI) factories—generally in a state of disuse. Finally, more hidden from view, but certainly extensive on inner roads, are village settlements and small developer 'revenue' layouts located on tops of three 'hills'. These are slum like settlements. Our point of revealing this diversity, even if not bound in a common linear thread of story-line, is to move arguments of contest and context beyond ideological assumptions towards a more careful consideration of the locality of history. By locality of history, we specifically move beyond viewing the 'subalterns' as 'marginals'—even when particular groups 'loose out' in contest with richer groups or those closely connected with State 'policy making'. In the Whitefield area of East Bangalore, the Nation State would be associated with the SSI factories, and large tracts of Master Planned housing. A more contemporary role would be public interventions to provide the SEZ, large infrastructure in the form of the dedicated expressways, and large-scale land acquisition for dedicated plots for the hi-tech. This includes the showcase ITPL. The global market is equally if not even more visible. Some of the biggest global names are listed on the boards of the shiny granite and steel towers. The rows of SUV vehicles carting BPO employees are another indication, along with rows of shops selling global brand names. Within this perspective, the contrast between the shiny reflective glass faced hi-tech towers, and the more subdued slum settlements could be interpreted in terms of a linear progressive developmental history. Here, the latter being remnants of a pre-IT past and would over time face erasure as 'development' or as 'modernisation' proceeds. A visit to the settlements on the low hills around Whitefield reveals signboards of the Dalit Sangarsh Samiti (DSS[8]) and its three affiliates. This too could at first glance, signify another marker of space set within the binary. This is in the ability of poor groups to claim via 'social movements' pressure the Nation State as a way to occupy space. The assumption would be that if the DSS were not available, the poor would find no place in what are some of the most expensive real estate markets in Bangalore.

Thus, a first visit and drive through this part of Bangalore would almost visually confirm what would be a narrative of 'modernisation and economic development'. For those of a contrasting ideological perspective, travels through this landscape would suggest the inevitability of displacement—although where resistance via organised progressive movements gain some success for at least for one section of the poor. Such a view may suggest the fragility and limited possibility for any success in confronting openly globally inclined policy when public interventions happen in favour of big business. But, if this argument is taken to its logical conclusion, it paves the way for erasure of very place it is seen to provide for: remaining 'unplanned' slums would necessarily give way to the 'planned' service economy. In effect, this analytical position accepts the death of localised contest, to shift appeal and advocacy at a higher level. This could be an appeal to higher level of normative centralised planning and perhaps even the judiciary. Recent events would then suggest a serious crisis. For one, the very forces promoting capitalistic globalisation call for renewed and strengthened normative planning. Second, the highest judicial authority has over the last decade in particular not been famous for progressive judgements. If at all, they have led a significantly powerful pressure to cleanse cities of their poor.

From Ideological Divides to 'Locality Histories'

Our research in adopting a more ethnographic methodology and a closer look at the complex of histories raises the issue that above mentioned assumptions of developmental linearity, the singular actions of the Nation State or the global market are misplaced. Our histories around the occupation of space as detailed in Chapter 6 show that territory—space, economy, and social grouping evolve around complex jigsaw of occupations. Although we adopt a 'historical' approach, this is hardly linear and show how at particular point in time, different communities/ castes, including those of the IT and big business, occupy and control land.

For instance, unlike first impressions, the occupation by poorer groups of areas on top of the hill in Whitefield have increased and not decreased. And most important, this vast bulk of the increased occupation has happened not all by the 'social movements' led by the DSS but rather by claims to land and locations established via a municipal and village council centred politics. For instance, in one key location in *Pattun Agaraha*, the DSS among other groups were directly instrumental for only 100 families in being re-settled there. Today, there are more than 1,200 families (and occupation keeps growing) assisted by local government action. An important issue here is that it's not just the settlement of land, but paralleled by improvements of infrastructure, services, that are mainstreamed into local administration. All this is at a time when land values in this larger region of Bangalore are one of the highest in the city, and very contested locations. If one went by the Nation-State conceptualisation, the reality on the ground provides a sharp contradiction. Locations where poorer groups have lost out claims are those where the State and the Central government have intervened in direct ways. They have used policy to shape and institute monopoly access to centralised information on land titles as a way to initiate acquisition. There is little evidence that these are levels of the State where in a positivist sense, can help ensure 'rights' of the poor.

These are two very quick illustrations that suggest the need for more nuanced conceptualisation. Drawing on the cases presented in Chapter 6, from the perspective of 'Locality Histories' we could hypothesise several conceptual points:

First, locality histories are hardly linear. These are constituted by various events, accidents. Just because we use the term 'locality' it does not imply an obsession with the 'local'. On the contrary, we attempt to move beyond the binary of 'local' and 'global' to look at the complex links between these in the way they find root in locality. A 'locality' view allows us to concretely analyse relatively global processes[9].

Second, in focusing on forms of contestation, we do not intend to portray poorer groups as 'victorious' or then, their binary, as passive victims. Instead we propose that understanding ways of contestations that are rooted in locality. These refer to processes of claiming by particular groups to land, location and the use of particular institutional mechanisms. Thus, in doing so, we reject positivism, the attempt to be predictive, and also suggest concepts such as 'inclusiveness' are irrelevant or need to be re-worked considerably.

Third, in following Dharmakumar (2001)[10] and Habib (1995), we see land to be settled as a process of 'occupancy'. This allows us to witness the dynamic, and within this, competing claims within a complex settlement process, and in effect, competing occupancy underpinned by political aspects. Such an approach to land and space opens up a realm of politics that more developmentalist approaches miss. For instance, in a study on Karnataka's land digitisation programme, the *Bhoomi*, Benjamin et al (2005) have argued how land title digitisation to reduce 1,500 forms of recording land tenure to 256 allowed large players to take over territory. These contrasted offieial claims that this would make land administration more efficient and spur 'economic development' (Benjamin *et al.* 2005). It also however, co-related to what big business sees as significant policy paths to 'facilitate the market'[11]. In this conceptual frame, it allows us to treat 'ownership' not as an absolute, but one that is socially and institutionally determined. In doing so, it is useful to categorise various types of land as they get opened up for occupation through claims for both housing and economy.

In the text below, I will first review some key features of Bangalore's economics to locate the IT in a wider economy, then follow up with a discussion of its institutional—'governance' politics. This will be then followed by looking at the way this situation is viewed by particular literature that delineate particular views on the city. To sharpen analysis, I purposely exclude the more glossy almost PR category of work[12]. Instead, I have purposely selected more serious writings on the city. Finally, I return to ways in which a progressive globally connected city is conceived. This discussion will then set a useful base for our own detailed field investigations in East Bangalore.

'Reading' Bangalore

Bangalore, now at the centre of a growing infrastructure debate, has gained the reputation of being India's 'Silicon Valley'. However, as with other Indian metros, it confronts increasing divides. In 1991, the difference between the lowest 20 per cent and the highest 20 per cent was 1:5. In 2001, this had increased to 1:50. A review of the spatial distribution of infrastructure and services showed that Master Planned areas support corporate economies, but the small firm economies are located in non-Master Planned areas. In 2004, a group of French consultants hired by the Bangalore Development Authority (BDA) to develop the new Master Plan, based on their satellite photographs, came up with a startling conclusion that only 16 per cent of the city's roads were tarred and that Master planned neighbourhoods ranged between 25 per cent and 10 per cent of the residential area. If one included the 7 surrounding smaller city councils, the planned part of the city could reduce to 4 per cent or less. It was likely than the 16 per cent of the tarred roads are focused mainly on 10 per cent of the city area to 4 per cent of the metro area. The link to economy shows the 'Silicon City' tag as being a particular imaginary. The NSS data of 1999-00 shows IT to be slightly above 4 per cent of the labour force[13]. Studies conducted in 2004-2005 comparing the hi-tech IT and ITES with Silk Processing and Manufacturing, and Garments, showed these to be in labour force (both direct and second level linkages) in numbers: 180,000-220,000, 220,000-240,000 and 280,000 respectively.

These figures even if we add for some degree of error, show that the Master Plan process has been elitist. It is obvious that cities like Bangalore are not 'equitable' or 'inclusive' and represent an urban terrain where power is not 'equitably' distributed. This conclusion could be arrived at, without significant surprises, via a developmentalist/demographic approach. But as cities go, this is hardly surprising. The more substantive issue is whether the quest and anxiety for 'equality' were a useful way to understand cities? Is this approach not already implicated in a larger narrative of the binary of the Nation State-Market? A related issue would be the relationship between a positivist position and forms of governance.

One could argue that a Nation State or Market would be reflected in a progressive pro-poor agenda at higher levels, and relatively 'incomplete' responsive action at local level. Similarly, from a market perspective, one would find if a developmentalist argument would follow its trajectory, there would be greater openings for poor groups via national level actions, and serious constrains at the local level. The text below shows both of these to be problematic but in effect, possibly conceptualisations that have little bearing on how cities work, and especially for the poor. To understand this more clearly, I shall lay out the main elements of key institutional shifts and structures. These essentially show the complexities and politics of what becomes known as 'policy' but three other issues:

- First, that the 'Nation State' and its counter in 'Civil Society' is nothing other than particular groups occupying particular economic and political space;
- The second point refers to space, and particularly land. These boxes show how rather than playing a neutral functional role, space is deeply implicated in the way land and location find valorisation to fuel this process. Moreover, rather than diminishing over time, these form an essential element in the play and unfolding of power in the city arena.
- Finally, city trajectories are driven by complex materiality of locality to be one if not a critically important factor in shaping it's process in complex, un-predictable, and un-even ways.

I have dealt with this in detail elsewhere and shall in this paper, outline key themes by way of an illustrative excerpt below[14]. The Bangalore case is a particularly useful one, as it has been posed as a nation wide 'best practice'. This is particularly around the creation of the Bangalore Agenda Task Force (BATF) in 1998—which as the excerpt below suggests has both a complicated history, and also in turn, complicates future events.

Excerpt: Powers of 'Good Governance'

Contestation over land settings cannot be divorced from the politics of governance. Bangalore acquired the reputation in the late eighties and early nineties as being one of the fastest growing cities in India. It was another issue that this came out of a faulty reading of data not adjusting for changes in territories. Apart from growth rates, the issue was certain that land markets fuelled particular development euphoria and became the main stay of politics at various levels. This was paralleled, in the euphoria of the Y2K expansion of the elite and aspiring elite to go the IT way, and if possible locate in Bangalore another Silicon Valley. The share markets shot up, and this elite public imaginary reinforced the public image of most famous Indian IT Company. Significantly, from much earlier in the late eighties early nineties, the connections between

Deve Gowda and re-shaped land markets to gain personal profit have been common knowledge. As prime minister for a short time, his partner politicians at the state level introduced the possibility of vast parcels of land being acquired publicly via the Karnataka Industrial Area Development Authority (KIADB) by way of its special committee set up for special economic zones. Not surprisingly, the mid nineties saw a very volatile land market in the Whitefield area with one of the highest growth rates in the country. Significantly, property agents in this area point to NRI investments, and especially those made by the city-State of Singapore. The focus was the Singapore Technology Park or ITPL in the Whitefield area of East Bangalore. Significantly, equity from the Government came in the form of land via the KIADB. Thus, a key connection between land and its speculative potential, the players at a variety of levels—those of the state government institutions, politicians and administrators, international finance from east Asia. Thus, Bangalore's globalisation is set in an earlier history of the early to mid-nineties, when a number of important interventions were made in the land markets. These interventions were aimed to bring in bigger (and later, IT connected) land developers as players and also to empower the land acquisition process. The former, were land developers that were backed by political interests at the highest level. The latter, happened by a range of new policy initiatives around 'single window clearance' to promote industrial growth, to empower the KIADB. The KIADB modelled on its Maharashtra counterpart, in this new avatar was a cornerstone for promoting mega projects of mega size[15]. Thus, the most famous one was the declaration of the new Airport in the north of the city. It was local knowledge; of land being speculated and bought over by the then Prime Minister's closest confidants.

The mid to late nineties saw a change of regime and a Chief Minister guided by a particularly 'reform' oriented municipal commissioner who was later to join the World Bank. With the pre-Y2K IT euphoria, in 1998, the SM Krishna government found it useful in promoting IT. While there were other symbolic imaginaries promoted to push start Bangalore into being a Singapore, common knowledge again pointed to profits from land, this time reinforced via connections with international finance. Thus, building on Dev Gowda's land based incentives, IT and other companies with international connections were padded with huge tax breaks. Outlook, a weekly news magazine soon caught on to the Infosys—Bangalore—CM connection to bring out a sharply written text[16]. Significantly, this was also the time when an investment arm of the Singaporean government invested in Infosys[17]. Another interesting financial connection to this company is claimed by an ex-International banker, who mentions investments at an earlier date to shore up it's globally driven hi-tech stock, by it's CEO's nephew. The nephew was made famous in what is known as the Harshad Mehta share market scam of the early nineties, and later the Life Insurance Company (LIC) scam of 2001[18]. There was another player—the World Bank which in the words of the CM inaugurating the Banks first in the south conference, was till then unable to 'enter' urban Karnataka. Thus, it was in these circumstances that the BATF was created.

Others have written about the BATF and its immediate politics, and its promotion of an agenda of globalised best practice of management that especially targeted municipal government on grounds of increasing Transparency and Accountability *via* Fund Based Accounting Systems (FBAS). It is important to note the linkages with 'civil society' that formed a parallel. While the BATF that was seen as the 'supply side', some of the BATF members also set up the Jannaagraha that was to be the 'demand' side of the governance equation. It was quite another issue that major corruption from the mid-nineties onwards, was located at the level of state government and linked to mega projects and empowering of parastatal agencies linked to real estate. Such a governance regime, coupled by international funding for large infrastructure formed an essential pre-requisite for an imaginary of the mega.

The public imaginary—especially the media, was at two levels. First, the aim of being Singapore, and second, the main constrain being that of corruption, that in turn, was also seen as a manifestation of the lack of planning. The target here was the land mafia to take over the city, promoted by vested interests within the municipal body and spearheaded by corrupt councillors and the lower level bureaucracy. At this time, the Appeals committee of the BMP was also sought to be dissolved, and to further strengthen administrative control, a special advisor was created to 'vet' large infrastructure proposals by the Town Planning Committee to the corporations Standing Committee. To further address this, the PROOF was set up in partnership with a NGO, and a private research agency to bring to dock the municipal body's accounts as an effort to instil greater accountability. Thus, it is hardly surprising that there was an emphasis on 'planned' development that also provided a key role for the Bangalore Development Authority (BDA). Empowerment of BDA was to lead to extensive demolitions of 'un-authorised construction' and buildings violating approved plans that earned the commissioner of the BDA the title of 'demolition man'. Thus, two major foci in the BATF and its civil society avatar, the Jannaagraha, was to reign in the political autonomy of the BMP, and as part of this, empower what was termed as 'citizen power'. The stress on 'citizenry' had a earlier history in the Swabhimana initiative in middle and high income South Bangalore's Jaya Nager and BTM layout, as well other locations in Central Bangalore as in Malleshwaram. The Swabhimana, supported by a senior administrator saw essentially elite groups seeking out to 'clean and green' Bangalore, and protecting their master planned designated parks and open spaces from squatters and hawkers. Thus, in many ways, the Jannaagraha was a further consolidation of these essentially middle class and anti poor attitudes by providing them an institutional platform for this to happen. The BDA's other task was the redevelopment, of supporting infrastructures for mega projects: Flyovers, large infrastructure schemes, and the hiring of French consultants to use GIS as a way to systemise planning.

Most illustrative of this trend was the IT corridor—a Rs. 1000 crore project notifying 13,700 hectares of prime development land[19]. This was set in motion by a special project vehicle (SPV) the IT Corridor Development Corporation (ITCDC) publicised by the corporate led Bangalore Agenda Task Force (BATF). The ITCDC emerged from a dedicated Master Plan by a Singapore based company, which included township development[20]. Ending November 2002, major national dailies in India placed as front page news an accusation at the Davos, World Economic Summit by the president of the Bellandur panchayat (village council) in Bangalore's southern periphery against India's best known IT company Infosys of "land grabbing" 118 acres[21]. The president claimed that the land included highly productive wetland and threatened the livelihood of numerous small farmers and workers. Located in Bangalore's proposed "IT Corridor" the Karnataka Industrial Area Development Board (KIADB) who acquired the land on behalf of the IT company, offered the farmers only Rs. 800,000 an acre when it's market value ranged between 4,000,000 to 6,000,000, and in the case of wetland, upto Rs. 14,000,000 an acre[22]. The president also said that such developments had opened the area to land speculators who coerced locals into selling out, often using muscle power. A couple of weeks earlier, a news item in the Times of India North Indian edition reported on Infosys's negotiating down the city administration of Chandigarh to provide them 20 acres of land with significant concessions in price-made possible by a "single window clearance system"[23]. About a year earlier, the KIADB was accused of blocking a public road in handing over land to Infosys near the city of Mysore leading to villagers protesting to the ministers during a visit[24]. In July 2003, local groups in Mangalore protested against the KIADB's allocation of 45 acres of their land to Infosys. Earlier in 2002, villagers and other local groups had protested when highly productive wet land were notified for compulsory acquisition and allocated for Infosys to build their campus. In January 2003, there were other "land scams". This time panchayats in Bangalore's northern periphery, also declared as a IT and Bio-tech corridor, accused the KIADB of favouring large developers including a five star hotel, amusement parks at the cost of small farmers and farm workers[25]. Here too, the village council claimed that the land forcibly acquired was under-valued when allocated to the developers. This included land under the "green belt" and also land belonging to the University of Agricultural sciences[26].

In the narrative above, I have not just aimed to highlight an institutional description, but rather to show how various interests moved towards a particular institutional architecture. The reader will note that land issues play a central role. In 'reading' this narrative, I intend to show the complexity of policy that hardly comes from 'neutral' normative sources, and is deeply implicated in the way lobbies work—including those funded and supported by the World Bank. If so, one is struck by the irrelevance of binaries, of assumptions of a particular trajectory towards 'modernity'—elements of a framework that constructs urban relationships around a trilogy of the Nation State, Civil Society, and Market. One is also struck by the irrelevance of a view that lays emphasis on 'Planning' to achieve 'balanced' growth, and to make cities 'inclusive'. It also returns to the more political question (s) that preface these two papers: Does the concept of cities being 'exclusive-inclusive' actually de-politicise?

The narrative also raises another issue: Can one expect such a "resurgent" civic society to effectively counter a corporate takeover? And more important perhaps, is it in fact useful to think of society in such generailisable terms devoid of politics? One may argue that even a 'progressive' position of 'the capture of the State', assumes the State as a distinctive entity. That argument would follow the logic that through the actions of corporate lobbies, the State looses it's 'autonomy' and ability to act along pre-defined norms of social justice. Thus, the advocacy agenda by activist groups and by intellectuals is to act as safeguards to ensure progressive policy. To understand this more clearly, we look at some recent works on Bangalore, its economy, history and planning.

Planning and Modernising Dis-order

One of the most exhaustive and recent works on Bangalore is 'The Promise of the Metropolis: Bangalore's Twentieth Century' is by Janaki Nair (Nair 2005). What is particularly relevant here is her descriptions of the complex and diverse ethnic groups, their associated cultural and political life, and the cities diverse economies. But central in the argument, as the title highlights, is the anxiety over the fractures in the planning process, and the serious difficulties in becoming, what is stated as 'the metropolis'[27]. One of the core elements of the conceptual frame is that of processes of incomplete citizenship (to be able to 'pressure the State'), an overarching notion of the lack of an 'inclusive' planning process, and an assumption of a trajectory towards modernity. In adequacies here are not just the issue of illegal transgression, but also rapid growth, and the existence of diverse localities. The conceptual issue in this book is not the lack of recognition of diversity, but rather, its' assumption of the need to locate this in an overarching structure.

While there are useful inserts of locality, what is not clear if this anxiety emerges from the way power gets played out at that level, or is one omnipresent? The next issue is the representation of the city. One key issue here, as Peattie points out, is the ideologies and conceptions of urbanity that underpin ways in which city data is presented. One issue here is on the way census or other forms of economic data is collated and its politics of who gets 'included or excluded'[28]. There is another issue pertinent to the argument made here. Data, economic or those describing social groups, are collected and organised by particular government/ private departments or organisation and thus are shaped by particular models of how the groups surveyed need to be 'planned for' or rather, to fit into categories set externally.

Much of 'planning and economic data' from this perspective is heavily implicated in the binaries that I have critiqued. If so, than a key question would be can one use such data beyond a very simplistic sketch? Would then 'narratives' from more rooted sources turn out to be imposed illustrations, rather than un-packing analytical categories from more extended narratives? A third criticism is that of stealth and quiet politics. Earlier work has shown how in contested settings, poor among other relatively less poor, resort to quiet strategies rather than a politics of explicit protest[29]. If so, then this makes the dependence on data to reveal new conceptual frames even more unlikely. While Nair's work on Bangalore due to its richness of description does allow some alternative analysis to be teased out. However, other studies on Bangalore make this task impossible. The problem here is not just the data, but, rather of the larger narrative within which this city is placed. The work by Heitzman (2004) attempts to chronicle the emergence of Bangalore's IT and global connectedness. But here too, the un-ease comes from not just the lack of planning but rather, the fractures in being 'modern' and connected. Heitzman shows (much like Nair) the progression from earlier city forms to the chaotic today—where the IT tag is fractured among other interests and constrained by money, and rivalries. What is important in reviewing these works is that the conceptualisation of the city is placed in a larger trajectory whose thematic categories homogenise locality into a confused mass of diversity. It is as if the mess of the local gets rarefied as one moves into a higher domain of national level economic aggregates, and the world of global flows. Perhaps such a move is useful. The main issue explored in this set of two chapters (this and Chapter 7) is if understanding the constituent elements of cities, and the conceptual categories that are used for this, need to be rooted in a locality. If so, is the reading of such localities 'dense' enough to point to conceptual categories especially if one questions the conventional frame.

Here however, the issue is not the value of a normative approach but rather its limited use in understanding how cities really work and how power is defined. Thus, what are of interest are the processes that underpin the condition, that from a normative perspective is seen to be 'exclusive', inequity. It is in this background that we promote an approach that lays emphasis to take a closer look at local histories. These are necessarily multiple, perhaps contradictory, shaped by accidents at both micro and macro and set within a dynamics of space. Thus, such an approach is almost bound to reveal 'incomplete' spaces in its narrative. If so, than the elements that Nair, Heitzman, Aranya among others point to, as fractures and dis-junctures are expected elements—rather than being exceptions or then, and indication of the 'failure' of planning or the Market. The central value of such a more rooted conceptualisation that focuses on forms of 'occupancy' is that it brings forth the politics of a part of a city at that particular time, being exclusive or inclusive for a particular group. Even if incomplete, it moves towards an approach of posing the question, whose inclusivity and at the cost of whom?

Localising the Conceptual Frame

In the above text, we have questioned the conceptual structure that underpin terms like 'inclusive-exclusive' by showing the contradictions in the trilogy of the Nation State-Market-Civil Society. Were one to accept the idea of a city being 'inclusive', than central to this imaginary would be a trilogy of:

(a) "Inclusiveness" assisted by the Nation State to ensure 'planned development as way to ensure social justice'. In particular, progressive groups within the formal party systems—both left and special groups with interests of Dalits and other downtrodden are assumed to exert pressure via the Nation State to take progressive stands and safeguard against the evils of Globalisation. Such progressive political space is opened up by constitutional and legal provisions along a 'rights framework';
(b) From a contrasting ideological perspective, inclusiveness resulting from 'Modernisation' when cities assimilated in the global market place and uplifting in the process, the 'marginals' who till then are trapped in 'pre-modernist' patron client relationships and a low productive informal sector underpinned by traditional land practices and governance systems. In this view, the poor are transformed from being passive into 'entrepreneurial citizens'.
(c) Inclusiveness ensued by an active 'Civil Society' that tempers the 'market' and regressive actions by the Nation State, by ensuring 'transparency, good governance, and setting in place instruments of 'participatory governance and planning'. Such social movements assisted by constitutional and legal provisions that ensure all, including the poor, to enjoy the rights and privileges of 'full citizenship'. As enlightened citizens, they are able to temper the market but also force the State to make globalisation work in their favour.

This paper suggests all three elements to be both conceptually flawed to understand contested institutional, economic terrain. In all three positions, locality based politics is either assumed to be a counter to the proposition or of little consequence. In parallel, and seen to be an outcome to locality of politics, is a view of city spaces being spatially ill planned and 'fractured' territories. Within the view of the Nation State, local politics—municipal or panchayats (village councils) are assumed to be captured by the local elite to enslave the poor within feudal relationships to restrict city territory to be 'inclusive'. Furthermore it is their sanction and proactive regularisation and land occupation that results in 'unplanned' development and fractures that disrupt the possibility of 'planned development' towards equity and social justice.

Interesting, but also expectedly, the neo-liberal position is also not very different in faulting both local government and also 'un-planned' development. In this view, the actions of local government and their promotion of 'un-planned' development draw public investments away from ways to make cities globally competitive via mega project investments and infrastructure. These mega territory intensive investments find urban space already occupied and the necessary planning process too 'politicised' rather than being shaped by techno-managerial ideals. In addition, the in-ability to provide better services at 'financially sustainable' terms is located centrally in local government's corruption and the lack of 'political will' accentuated by 'vote bank' politics. This is seen to constrain the modernisation process towards economic development and thus cities to make their citizens entrepreneurial and globally responsive. Within this, the poor, set in the quagmire of locality based politics and feudal outlooks miss out on valuable opportunities in a possible service sector.

In the view that sees Civil Society as a panacea to city inclusiveness; local politics is hardly the epitome of transparency. Nor is it, given the complexity and seemingly messiness of politics and its patron clientilistic nature, an appropriate location for popular mobilisation for transformative social movements. One could argue that it is this agenda that attempts for 'participatory' planning and 'public accountability' seeks to address. There is a tension—ideological, of the particular actions promoted under the rhetoric of 'Civil Society', as we have seen in the initial report, has shifted towards the neo-liberal ideal in opening up space for the privatisation of basic services and the new Urban Reforms Agenda or new governance systems like that of the BATF. It can also, move towards the 'progressive' end emphasising the 'rights' agenda. In both these positions however, there is unanimity over the issue of local politics, local government, and a view of city space as a problematic of fractures and un-planned development that in-turn reflect less or incomplete citisenship.

In the next article (Chapter 7), we root our critique of the above-discussed trilogy by focusing on contested terrains in East Bangalore. This view shows 'fractured terrains' and the locality of politics to have very complex histories in the way they are spaces of active engagement by a variety of poor groups for whom land, economy and local politics is essential for survival and to move on in life. As with all local histories, our slice will be incomplete. However, there is enough to question normative visions of the trilogy.

NOTES

1. This chapter is based on research undertaken through IDPAD project.
2. The author and his colleagues Bhuvaneswari R., Manjunath, Chitra, Valli, and Rajan would like to thank the IDPAD who provided funding for this work under the aegis of a larger project "Inclusive Mega-Cities in Asia in a Globalising World" co-ordinated by Dr. Darshini Mahadevia of the Centre for Development Alternatives, Ahmedabad and Dr. Erhard Berner, of the Institute of Social Studies, The Hague. While the usual disclaimers apply, Dr. Mahadevia and the CFDA provided material resources and also valuable comments and suggestions, as well as access to background material. Given the complex circumstances here in Bangalore that affected the schedule of the research, Dr. Mahadevia was accommodating in this process. We would also like to acknowledge the valuable opportunity for our research group to attend conferences in the project and share our experience and gain from others. The research was undertaken in very difficult field conditions when the research sites have been under severe transition. We thus gratefully acknowledge the co-operation extended by the numerous residents, local politicians, small developers and property agents, village officials in both East and South Bangalore.
3. Linebaugh and Rediker (2000). Drawing from this work, I have visualised the 'Hydra' in the context of actions of a systemic nature that occupy various kind of spaces. These are spaces in municipal government, in economy dominated by small interconnected firms, in the incremental settlement and occupation of land, and in shaping multiple legalities in what Santos terms as 'porous legalities'. The Hydra processes are anarchic. These contest 'urban designed' or master planning. In occupying space, institutional, economic terrain this has deeply political implications. It is hardly surprising that for the mainstream media, policy groups, the Hydra poses a particular fear, and referred to as: Pandoras's box, vote bank politics, land mafia, slum *goondas*, pirates. This is despite the fact that perhaps 80 per cent of metro populations use and evolve, and feed and benefit from practices in daily life that centre around the Hydra. While my article in the Sarai reader 05 Bare act illustrates this, to pose a counter, you can't really have a Gandhi or a Nehru as a 'Hydra'. However, one could conceptualise a situation where 'popular' appropriation, forms of Gandhianism can turn out to be hydraish if they subvert competing forms of capital (See Benjamin 2005).
4. This position is reflected in the policy efforts of groups like the 'Centre for Civil Society', a group professing a neo-liberal ideal as part of their efforts to promote a reform agenda and economic development.
5. See Chapter 3 of Massey (2005).
6. See chapter 7 'Glocal Infrastructure and the Splintering of Urban Economies' in Marvin and Graham (2003).
7. For an extensive description and also critique of the World City theory, see, Knox and Taylor (2000).

8. Dalit or the Scheduled Castes (SCs) refer to the lower castes groups. Many of these form the poorest groups but not always—as subsequently seen in one of the case studies.
9. For instance, if were to conceptualize and analyze global financial flows within this approach, we would focus on tracing in great detail the institutional arrangements, the internal administrative conventions and actual procedures used (as distinct from 'policy') and most critical, the power relationships that underpin these.
10. Dharmakumar (2001), see especially Chapters 5 and 6.
11. For instance, the presenter on land laws that impact real estate development in peripheral areas suggested that developers and financial institutions address complex counter claims by small farmers and developers by lobbying the state government to acquire land on their behalf with instruments such as the KIDBI Act, and using the Karnataka Industrial Area Development Board. Presentation by Umakanth in 'Suminfra 2004: Summit on Sustainable "PPP's in Infrastructure," CII—Government of Karnataka Conference, Bangalore, 2-3 September, 2004.
12. An example of this in seen in Friedman (2005).
13. See Chapter 2 by Mahadevia in this book.
14. A detailed discussion of this is given in Benjamin (2007).
15. See the documents on the KIADB by the Alternative Law Forum at their website (www.alforum.net).
16. *"Does Infosys run Bangalore?"*, from Outlook, *Bangalore Diary Magazine* 17 Dec., 2001.
17. Information provided by a talk by Narendra Pani at the Arrupe Forum Research Meet, November 2004.
18. Samit Ghosh September 2005, and see Sucheta Dalal's book: "The Scam, and those who got away" Manohar Press Delhi.
19. Gowda Arvind "Private sector to develop IT corridor", *Times of India* 10th March, 2003.
20. As I discuss later in this text, this is facilitated by the State legislature amending the Town Planning act to allow private builders to undertake "town ship" development—but on land acquired via State powers
21. "*Infosys accused of land-grab*" Times of India National News Nov. 26th. 2002; "*Bellandur farmers want CBI probe into land deal*" Times of India Dec.3. 2002; "*Govt. acquiring land to help builders*" Deccan Herald News Service. Dec.3. 2002. The press reported that the villagers were willing to talk to Infosys if they bought only dry and not wet land: "*Villagers seek talks with Infosys*" in The Hindu, Bangalore City edition Dec. 2 2002.
22. A letter to the Deccan Herald: "Land grab row: Did Infosys get a favour?" http://www.deccanherald.com/deccanherald/dec03/mailbag.asp provides some useful insights on the issue.
23. Raj Machhan "*How Infosys deal was clinched?*" Times News Network Monday, November 18, 2002.

24. See: "Lift block on road, orders minister" The Times of India News Service February 24, 2001. See: http://timesofindia.indiatimes.com/cms.dll/html/uncomp/articleshow?artid=22463419&sType=1
25. DH News "*Land scam unearthed in Hebbal*" Deccan Herald February 13th, 2003 See: http://www.deccanherald.com/deccanherald/feb13/state.asp
26. Interestingly, in October 2001, a serious political issue was the allocation of a valuable plot of 100 acres in the Bangalore University of Agricultural Sciences to a Bio-Tech company. This resulted in a protest by professors and students both of whom were beaten up by the police enforcing the government order. Significantly, the university's board of governors ruled against the allocation and are now threatened with removal by the state government. Later, due to the extensive pressure by the student, the faculty, and a supportive press, the government was forced to seek land in locations with arguably less real estate potentials when the investors that included private, the State Government, and financial institutions were not interested. See: "*IT mafia running Krishna govt, alleges Srinivas*" BANGALORE, Oct 1, 2001; Arun B S, "Bio-tech park in Bangalore to be inaugurated soon" Deccan Herald News Service New Delhi, Nov. 11, 2001; "*Pvt investors not in favour of change; Govt scouts for new bio-tech park site*" Deccan Herald, BANGALORE, Oct 2, 2001; Thus, while that movement was successful in protecting land in these locations, the present one instrumented by the KIADB is relatively more effective.
27. See for instance, 'BDA and the Traffic in Illegalities' Page 177, section in Chapter 4, The map is not the territory: Law and the Production of Space.
28. This is pointed out by Indu Prakash Singh when pressing the Census authorities to include street dwellers in Delhi as part of a drive to enlist them to vote.
29. See: (1) Benjamin S. 2003 *From Income to urban contest in global settings: Chronic Poverty in Bangalore* in a book on Chronic Poverty published by the Chronic Poverty Research Centre, University of Manchester and the Indian Institute of Public Administration. (Also working paper #4 in the same series) Forthcoming in Environment and Urbanization; Also see *"Women in the Informal Economy in Bangalore"* Paper presented in a seminar by the ISST, ILO on 'Decent Employment for Women in India' held in Bangalore April 2004; (2) Benjamin and Bhuvaneswari (2001); (3) Van Der Linden and School (1983); and (4) Singerman (1995).

6

GLOBALISATION AND INFRASTRUCTURE DEVELOPMENT IN CITIES OF CHINA

Comparing Beijing and Dongguan[1]

DARSHINI MAHADEVIA

China's Global Economic Integration

People's Republic of China (PRC) is the fastest growing economy in the world today and has maintained a very high annual growth rate, of about 9 per cent, for now more than two decades. During the two decades, 1978–98, the per capita GDP growth rate has more than quadrupled and living standard of the ordinary Chinese has improved greatly in the period (Qian 2002: 1). This trend continues even in the new millennium. Inspite of the Asian financial crises of 1997, the PRC maintained high economic growth rate. During this period China provided much needed stability to the regional and even the world economy. In the process of rapid economic growth, PRC has witnessed very rapid decline in the number of absolute poor. According to National Bureau of Statistics (NBS 2003), 14.2 million, that is 5.8 per cent of the urban population was below poverty line in 1991. In 2000, the number of poor declined to 10.5 million and poverty rate declined to 3.4 per cent (ADB 2004a: 89). Athar Hussain (2001 in ADB 2004a), an independent scholar finds that there was reduction of urban poverty from 6.25 per cent in 1995 to 4.73 per cent in 1998.

Investments in manufacturing and fixed assets has been the main driver of the economy. For example, in 2003, the ADB's Report on 2004 outlook mentions that investment contributed 6.3 percentage points to growth, when consumption contributed 3.9 percentage points and net exports subtracted 1.1 percentage points from the total growth figure. In this year, fixed asset investment soared by 26.7 per cent, 9.8 percentage points higher than the previous year. Public sector investment, which accounted for 72.1 per cent of total investment, surged by 28.2 per cent, driven largely by local government investment decisions. A rapid expansion of bank lending, continual FDI inflows, and a property market boom were major factors contributing to the investment surge (ADB 2004b: 41). Since 1998, ratio of investments to total GDP has remained higher than 37 per cent (ADB 2004b), crossing 40 per cent since 2002.

Gradual Integration

China's economic growth story is the country's gradual integration with the global economy, based on human development that led to benefits of rapid economic growth spreading more evenly than the experience of most countries. Cook (2000: 3) argues that "reduction of poverty and maintenance of social stability in the process of economic reforms, has been an outcome of institutional mechanisms that China has developed that has led to wider sharing of benefits of growth and at the same time providing basic level of social protection to some of the vulnerable sections of the society". This is very important to understand when the issues around equity would be discussed later on in the article.

The economic reforms in China, unlike the shock therapy induced through external pressures coming from the International Monetary Fund (IMF) and the World Bank in other socialist economies such as former United Soviet Socialist Republic (USSR), and eastern block countries, have been gradual and internally initiated. The economic reforms have been an outcome of the internal political struggle within Chinese Communist Party (CCP). The market economy path, with Chinese characteristics, was introduced by Deng Xiaoping, after the demise of Mao Zedong. They were first introduced in 1980 in four SEZs, Shenzhen, Zhuhai, Shantou (all in Guangdong province), and Xiamen (in Fujian province), close to Hong Kong and Macao and also Taiwan. This was strategic as that led to investments coming into these zones from these three places. While these four cities experienced market reforms, the rest of the country continued with the socialist economy. Many successful practices were tested inside these zones, such as new accounting methods, employment practices, new technologies, and marketing techniques, and were later adopted elsewhere (Qian 2002: 6). The SEZs had the initial objective of producing goods for export to earn foreign exchange. They offered a range of inducements to foreign investors, including tax holidays, early remittance of profits, and good infrastructure.

The reforms were first introduced in cities located in Pearl River Delta. Then, they were extended to cities in Yangtze River Delta. The reforms came to Shanghai only in 1993, after Deng Xiaoping's famous visit to South, mainly Guangdong and Fujian province. In 1988, three "open economic regions" were designated—the Yangtze River (Changjiang) Delta Economic Region (around Shanghai), the Pearl River (Zhujiang) Delta Economic Region (around Guangzhou), and the Minnan Delta Economic Region (around Xiamen) (Yeh and Xueqiang 1996). From 1999, the government of PRC has carried on with the western (region) development strategy and simulated measures to attract foreign investments coming from Hong Kong, Macao, Taiwan and other countries to these provinces.

In 1984, eastern region attracted 96.73 per cent of the total FDI and other investments (mainly in the manufacturing), when the central region attracted only 1.19 per cent and western region only 2.08 per cent of the investments (Table 6.1). Guangdong province alone had attracted 73.42 per cent of the total investments in that year. In 2001, the share of eastern region in the total investments has gone down to 87.84 per cent and that of central provinces has increased to 9.20 per cent and of western region to 2.96 per cent. Even, the infusion of investments on the eastern coast has not been at one time. The process has been "going north and advancing west". Investments were first diffused in the southern coast, then to central coast and then to central region. The northern coastal region, in which Beijing and Tianjin are located, continued to maintain a stable share through out the major periods.

Table 6.1: Distribution of Foreign Direct and Other Investments, PRC, by Regions

Region	*Periods*			
	1983-90	*1991-99*	*2000*	*2001*
Total (US$ million)	16330.21	289743.8	42043.86	48313.53
Total	100.00	100.00	100.00	100.00
Eastern (coastal) region	90.09	87.73	88.07	87.84
— Northern coast	20.76	20.81	20.47	21.97
— Central coast	13.28	24.17	26.63	27.77
— South coast	56.06	42.74	40.97	38.09
Central region	5.30	9.15	9.02	9.20
Western region	4.60	3.13	2.91	2.96

Source: Wei (2002).

The definition of urban in China is such that it is useful in attracting foreign and other investments (Yixing and Ma 2003). Hence, it is the cities that have benefited out of economic reforms. FDI in the cities were first permitted in manufacturing, then in real estate and then in select services (Yeh and Xueqiang 1996). With China's accession to WTO foreign investments would be permitted in all services.

Table 6.2: Top 20 Cities in FDI Receipt in 2002

City	*Province*	*Population (million)*	*City size*	*FDI received in year (US$ '0,000)*	*as % of total FDI*
All cities		32,9.24	—	4,847,274	100.00
Beijing		10.67	Super-city	507,334	10.47
Shanghai		12.70	Super-city	500,888	10.33
Tianjin		7.52	Super-city	378,941	7.82
Shenzhen	Guangdong	1.39	Mega-city	319,100	6.58
Suzhou	Jiangsu	2.12	Super-city	207,176	4.27
Guangzhou	Guangdong	5.84	Super-city	202,999	4.19
Wuhan	Hubei	7.68	Super-city	157,602	3.25
Nanjing	Jiangsu	4.80	Super-city	146,017	3.01
Dongguan	Guangdong	1.56	Mega-city	145,868	3.01
Dalian	Liaoning	2.73	Super-city	142,642	2.94
Shenyang	Liaoning	4.89	Super-city	138,915	2.87
Wuxi	Jiangsu	2.16	Super-city	123,169	2.54
Qingdao	Shandong	2.42	Super-city	117,699	2.43
Foshan	Guangdong	3.39	Super-city	98,355	2.03
Ningbo	Zhejiang	2.03	Super-city	75,842	1.56
Zhuhai	Guangdong	0.79	Big-city	69,800	1.44
Zhongshan	Guangdong	1.36	Mega-city	63,900	1.32
Xiamen	Fujian	1.37	Mega-city	62,093	1.28
Fuzhou	Fujian	1.58	Mega-city	56,100	1.16
Changchun	Jilin	3.04	Super-city	56,079	1.16
Chongqing		9.99	Super-city	25,122	0.52

* Calculated over permanent population.

Source: Based on China Statistical Press (2003).

Note: City classification: (i) super-city, population more than 2 million; (ii) mega city—population between 1 million to 2 million; (iii) big city—population between 500,000 to 1 million; and so on. (*Source*: Ministry of Construction (2003).

Top 20 cities have received 73.66 per cent of the total FDI received in the year 2002. In 1990, the top 20 cities had received 78.32 per cent of the total FDI received in that year, with Shenzhen (14.14 per cent of total investment) at the top (Yeh and Xueqiang 1996). In 2002, it is Beijing which is at the top with 10.47 per cent of the total FDI received by the cities in that year, closely followed by Shanghai. Both Beijing and Dongguan, cities presented in this article have remained in top-20 cities in both the years. Hence, this study looks at the issues of equity in two cities that have been recipients of large amounts of FDI for more than one and a half decade now. In 1990, cities of Guangdong Province were in the lead in receiving the FDI (Yeh and Xueqiang 1996). In 2002, the three national level cities move up in the top three position in this regards (Table 6.2). There are 15 cities common to both the lists; besides the large three national cities, Shenzhen and Dongguan are Dalian, Guangzhou, Foshan, Xiamen, Fuzhou, Zhuhai, Nanjing, Zhongshan, Qingdao and Shenyang. This indicates that although the macro policies permit FDI investments all over the country, there is not much diffusion of FDI in other cities than the ones that have been traditionally attracting the FDI. Further, although Chongqing, which has been declared as national level city in mid-1990s, has not yet attracted much FDI.

Comparing Beijing and Dongguan—Economy and Development

The total population of Beijing in 2003 is 14.56 millions an increase from 13.64 millions in 2000 (Table 6.3). As per population census, Beijing's total population in 2000 was 13.57 million, an increase from 10.82 millions in 1990. Yixing and Ma (2003) have explained why there is difference between population census and statistical yearbooks' population figures. We need not go into it, but state that the population figures in the yearbooks are estimated figures whereas the population census figures are actual headcounts. Dongguan's population in 2002 was 5.90 million as per the statistical yearbook. There are more than 700,000 compatriots from Hong Kong and Macao (Dongguan Municipal Land Resource Administration Bureau, 2003). Beijing's population size is therefore 2.4 times that of Dongguan. Beijing comes in the category of super-city whereas Dongguan comes in the category of mega-city. In 2002, Beijing topped the list of cities in terms of total FDI received, whereas Dongguan was at 9th position as discussed earlier in the article. In 1990, Dongguan was at 7th position and Beijing in 6th position in receiving total FDI.

The total population growth rate of Beijing was 2.30 per cent per annum (p.a.) in 1990-2000 decade, which was less than the population growth rate of the entire urban population in China (4.28 per cent p.a.). The total population growth of Dongguan in this decade was quite high; 7.51 per cent p.a. Of the total population of 5.90 million in 2002, only 1.56 million or 26 per cent were permanent population in Dongguan. The temporary residents were 4.34 million or 74 per cent of the total population. These are registered migrants. The unregistered floating population in both the cities are not reported in these figures. In Beijing, just 25 per cent population were temporary migrants in 2002. In 1995, while Dongguan had 50 per cent of the population as temporary residents,

Beijing had 40 per cent population as temporary residents. Thus, Dongguan's population growth is in the category of migrant population whereas that in Beijing is because of increase in category of permanent population. Population control policy has kept natural increase in population low. This means that Beijing's population growth is because of granting of permanent residency to the migrant population as well as new migrants.

Table 6.3: Total Population in Millions, over Time and Annual Growth Rate (%)

	1990	*1995*	*2000*	*2002*	*1990—2000*
Beijing—Total	10.86	12.51	13.64	14.23	2.30
Dongguan—Total	1.97	2.86	4.07	5.90	7.51
Beijing—permanent population	—	7.34	9.74	10.67	—
Dongguan—permanent population	—	1.44	1.53	1.56	—
Migrant as % of total pop.—Beijing	—	41.33	28.59	25.02	—
Migrant as % of total pop.—Dongguan	—	49.65	62.41	73.56	—
All China Urban*	296	—	456	—	4.41
All China Urban**	301.83	351.25	458.80		4.28

Note:The data for the city is for the administrative city.

Source: (i) For Beijing, Beijing Statistical Yearbooks of different years.

(ii) For Dongguan, Dongguan Municipal Bureau of Statistics (2003).

(iii) For all China, China Statistical Yearbooks of respective years.

* As per Population Census.

** As per China Statistical Press (2003, 2001, 1996, 1991).

It is possible that Beijing is denying temporary residential permit to many migrants whereas Dongguan is not. There could be large number of unregistered migrants in Beijing; those not having temporary residency permits. Sociological studies have shown that permanent residents of Beijing display strong dislike for the rural population[2], whom the local government (district government) may not be giving even temporary residency. Registering as temporary residents gives migrants a partial right to work and live in the cities, it does not grant them full citizens' rights such as access to state-sponsored food, housing, education, and health services (Li 2001). There are thus not many benefits of getting temporary residency permits. On the contrary, migrants have to pay fees for temporary residency cards, which the district governments are eager to collect and migrants are not too keen to pay. Further, time spent on getting these cards also dissuades the migrants from applying for them. Local authorities in several areas whom Li (2001) interviewed stated that less than half of the migrant population in their areas were un-registered. Thus, population of Beijing could be much more and proportion of migrant population could be much more than 25 per cent in 2002.

In contrast, Dongguan's economic growth is because of migrants and the economy cannot shun them. It might be easier for the migrants to register in Dongguan. Some of the newspaper reports state that the whole province of Guangdong is having severe labour shortage[3], which means that cities such as Dongguan cannot discriminate against migrants if the city has to maintain its economic growth rate. Thus, registration of temporary migrants would be prompt in Dongguan than in Beijing. The first issue of equity between the two cities is that in Beijing there is discrimination against the migrants whereas Dongguan welcomes migrants.

Detailed break-up of workers across 15 sectors (Table 6.4) indicates that still, manufacturing remains the single largest employment sector in Beijing, employing 23.28 per cent of workers in 2002. This is a decline from 26.92 per cent in 1997. In Dongguan, there are no other sectors as important as manufacturing, which employs 55.14 per cent of the total workers in 2002, an increase from 42.90 per cent in 1997. Beijing is a service economy with 55.85 per cent workers employed in the sector, an increase from 52.13 per cent in 1997. In Beijing, in 2002, social services engage the second large proportion of workers, 17.28 per cent followed by construction (14.43%).

High proportion of workers engaged in construction in Beijing indicated high investments going into real estate development and in infrastructure projects in the city. In 1997 also, this sector engaged the third largest proportion of workers, 13.12 per cent. In contrast, just 5.20 per cent workers in Dongguan are employed in construction sector. As seen in the earlier section on FDI, Beijing is receiving the highest amount of FDI, a significant proportion of it going to the real estate projects. On moving around the city, it can be observed that these are all real estate projects on the high end, that is creating high valued private housing projects and commercial complexes including large malls. This sector is contributed 7.6 per cent to the city's GDP against employment of 13.12 per cent in 2002 (Table 6.6), which means that it is a labour intensive sector, and that per capita income in this sector is less than the average incomes in other sectors and also for the whole economy as a whole. Same is the case with social services sector, which is a labour-intensive sector employing 17.28 per cent of the total workers but only contributing 10.0 per cent of Beijing's GDP in 2002.

Table 6.4: Workers in Different Occupations and their Growth Rates (1997 and 2002)

	Beijing		Dongguan		Growth rate (1997—02) p.a.	
	2002	*1997*	*2002*	*1997*	*Beijing*	*Dongguan*
Population (permanent population)	—	—	—	—	3.01	1.20
Total workers	100.00	100.00	100.00	100.00	0.41	3.51
Agriculture	0.68	1.11	0.06	25.25	–9.12	–70.08
Mining and quarrying	0.55	0.84	0.01	0.02	–8.03	–12.94
Manufacturing	23.28	26.92	55.14	42.90	–2.82	5.32
Electricity, gas and water production and supply	0.82	0.88	0.60	0.71	–1.55	–3.10
Construction	14.43	13.12	5.20	4.21	1.98	4.49
Geological prospecting and water conservancy	0.24	0.24	0.08	0.11	0.00	–5.23
Transport, storage, postal and telecommunication services	4.15	4.76	5.17	5.82	–2.65	–2.18
Wholesale and retail trade and catering services	10.57	15.28	16.16	10.42	–7.07	9.36
Banking and insurance	1.81	1.66	3.11	1.67	1.80	13.42
Real estate trade	3.55	1.57	0.52	0.48	17.79	1.73
Social services	17.28	11.57	4.63	1.55	8.41	24.69
Health care, sports and social welfare	3.00	2.65	2.88	1.84	2.53	9.57
Education, culture and arts, radio film and television	9.14	8.18	4.23	2.93	2.27	7.84
Scientific research and polytechnical services	5.80	6.66	0.19	0.07	—2.66	21.35
Government agencies, party agencies and social organisation	4.70	4.56	2.02	2.02	0.67	0.12

Note: Data is for the administrative towns of the city.

Source: China Statistical Press (2003, 1993).

In the five years, 1997-02, Beijing city has observed a decline in employment in the secondary sector occupations except construction, which has grown at 1.98 per cent p.a. (Table 6.4). Of particular importance is to observe decline in the employment in manufacturing sector that declined at 2.82 per cent p.a. In wake of Beijing Olympics, the employment in construction sector would go up. New jobs have been generated in the tertiary sector; real estate trade registering 17.79 per cent p.a. growth rate and social services 8.41 per cent p.a. growth rate. The social services consist of community services and computer applications. High growth rate in employment in the real estate trade supports the argument made earlier about investments coming to this sector on one hand and creation of employment in construction sector on the other. However, on the whole, the growth of employment (0.41 per cent p.a.) is slower than the growth in population (3.10 per cent p.a.), and which is a matter of concern. These data would be excluding the unregistered migrants, who would be overwhelmingly in the services sector, many of them being in informal petty services that offer low incomes.

In Beijing, the workers that have gone out of manufacturing sector have got employed in social services, as there is a significant increase in the proportion of workers in social services. As observed above, this occupation has observed very high annual growth rate in workers in the period. This is substantiated by the newspaper clipping that suggests that the displaced workers of State Owned Enterprises (SOEs) are retrained to get absorbed in social services sector, which includes community services as well computer applications.

In Dongguan, the second-highest employment is in wholesale and retail trade and catering services (16.16 per cent in 2002 and 10.42 per cent in 1997). Employment in all other sectors is less than 5 per cent in both the years. Only interesting change from 1997 to 2002 in Dongguan is decline in agriculture sector workers from 25.25 per cent in 1997 to 0.06 per cent in 2002. Further, percentage workers in manufacturing and percentage GDP from manufacturing are nearly the same figures, 55.14 per cent and 51.50 per cent respectively in 2002. Services sector employed 38.91 per cent workers and contributed 40.55 per cent to GDP. Thus, even services sector has similar share in GDP and employment. Agriculture sector contributes 4.5 per cent of the GDP in 2002, when it share in the employment is only 0.07 per cent. Dongguan is a fruit growing region and exports fruits to other parts of China. An article that describes Comrade Deng Xiaoping's visit to Shenzhen in

1992 mentions that Dongguan was one of the towns in Guangdong that produced best litchis in the country[4].

In contrast to Beijing, in Dongguan, there is a high growth rate of employment in manufacturing units, at the rate of 5.32 per cent p.a. in this 5-year period. Same is the case with employment in construction sector, which has increased at the rate of 4.49 per cent p.a. in 1997-02 period. The overall employment has increased at 3.51 per cent, which is higher than the growth rate of permanent population. Manufacturing and construction sector both have registered higher growth rate in employment as compared to total employment growth rate. In Dongguan however, the employment in real estate trade has not picked up, although one sees many new real estate projects underway in the city. There is significant increase in employment in social services in Dongguan (24.69 per cent p.a.), a sector that has low share in total employment. In Dongguan, there is also high growth rate in employment in other tertiary sector activities that contribute to the social development, such as health, education, etc.

Beijing had 4.70 per cent workers employed in government agencies, party agencies and social organisations (including NGOs) in 2002. This percentage in Dongguan was just 2.02 per cent. Further, employment in this has increased at only 0.12 per cent p.a. in Dongguan and at 0.67 per cent p.a. in Beijing. In both the cities, government and political party employment has not increased, but, Beijing still has higher proportion of workers in this than Dongguan.

The above analysis shows that Dongguan is a manufacturing economy, with less inequalities in incomes within it across different sectors. Therefore income disparities across the population is less. In contrast, Beijing has very high inequalities in incomes across different sectors of the economy, indicating very high inequality in general in the city. Also, enough employment for the entire population is not there. It seems that after the restructuring of the SOEs, which started around 1997, has led to stagnation in employment growth. While, Beijing may have high FDI as compared to Dongguan, and also higher incomes as compared to Dongguan, as we shall analyse next, there are sections of population that are either not having employment or are having employment with lower levels of income. Dongguan's economy therefore is more equitous than Beijing's economy.

The total GDP of Beijing is almost five times that of Dongguan. In 2002, the total GDP of Beijing was RMB 312 billion (Table 6.5). In 1991, the total GDP of Beijing was about RMB 44 billion (China

Statistical Press 1992). In real terms, in the decade of 1991-2001, the city's GDP has grown at 9.53 per cent p.a. In 1992-2002 decade, Beijing's GDP has increased at 11.12 per cent p.a. That is, in 2002, Beijing has seen quite high growth of GDP. While the city's GDP increased at a very high growth rate, employment has not grown at this rate, nor has the population increased at such high rate. This indicates that per capita incomes are increasing rapidly in Beijing.

Table 6.5: Total and Per Capita GDP at Current Prices

	2002	*2000*	*1995*
Total GDP (in billion RMB)			
Beijing	312.45	233.23	123.88
Dongguan	67.29	48.97	20.56
*Per capita GDP**			
Beijing administrative town	22,574	18,178	11,149
Dongguan administrative town	11,408	12,023	7,194

* Calculated over total residents.

Note: Data is for the administrative towns.

Source: Based on China Statistical Press (2003, 2001, 1996).

Dongguan's GDP has become RMB 67 billion in 2002 from mere RMB 6 billion in 1991 (China Statistical Press 1992). The city observed tripling of its GDP between 1991 and 1995 and then doubling of its GDP in the next half of the decade. The city saw its GDP increase at about 20 per cent p.a. from 1992-02 and at 19 per cent p.a. between 1991-01. This is quite high GDP growth rate as compared to whole of China. Dongguan has seen higher GDP growth rate than Beijing, during the decade of 1990s.

The total Gross Domestic Product (GDP of Beijing was RMB 366.31 billion in 2003, with per capita GDP of RMB 32,061 (Beijing Municipal Bureau of Statistics 2004). In 2002, Beijing's GDP was RMB 321.27 billion, which was 3.07 per cent of the total national GDP, when Beijing's population formed only 1.11 per cent of the national population[5]. The total GDP of 321.27 does not tally with the figures in Table 6.5, as the GDP figure in the latter is for only administrative town whereas that given here is for the whole city.

In 2002, Beijing's per capita GDP was RMB 28,449, when the national level per capita GDP was RMB 8,184. That is, per capita GDP in Beijing was 3.5 times that of national per capita GDP. In US dollars terms, Beijing's Per Capita GDP was US$ 3,444 or in purchasing power parity (P.P.P.) terms it was US$ 13,628[6]. This would put Beijing in the category of medium income countries.

Photos: Darshini Mahadevia

Photo 6.1: Highways within Beijing

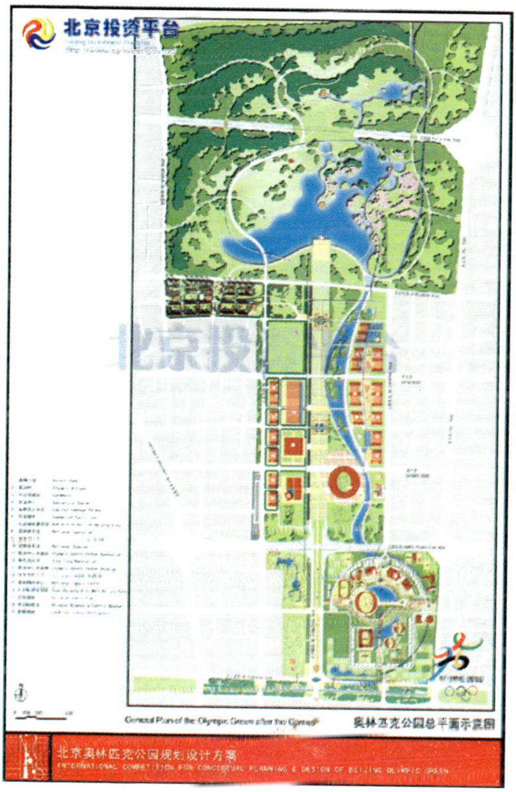

Photo 6.2: Olympics Green, Beijing

Photo 6.3: Metro System, Beijing

Photos: Darshini Mahadevia

Photo 6.4: Olympics 2008 Stadiums, Beijing

Photo: Darshini Mahadevia

Photo 6.5: Central Plaza, Dongguan

Photo: Darshini Mahadevia

Photo 6.6: New Real Estate, Dongguan

Photo: Darshini Mahadevia

Photo 6.7: High-tech Park, Dongguan

Photo: Darshini Mahadevia

Photo 6.8: Migrants' Housing, Dongguan

Per worker, average GDP of Beijing is quite high, RMB 47,301 in year 2002. The inequality in the distribution of per worker GDP is quite high in the city (Table 6.6). Construction sector that has 14 per cent of the total workers has per worker GDP contribution of RMB 29,123, which is quite less than the average per worker GDP contribution. The social services sector has 17 per cent of the workers and contributes RMB 35,185 per worker to the GDP. Wholesale and retail trade and catering also has quite low per worker GDP. Wages in these three sectors would therefore also be less. And together, 42 per cent of the total workers in Beijing are engaged in these three sectors alone. In contrast, per worker contribution to GDP in banking and insurance sector, that is in the high end financial services is quite high, RMB 570,443, indicating this sector pay high wages to their employees. The co-efficient of variation of per capita GDP contribution across sectors is 57.34 per cent, which is quite high.

Table 6.6: Break-up of Beijing's and Dongguan's GDP, 2002

	Beijing		*Dongguan*
	GDP (%)	*Per capita GDP (RMB)*	*GDP (%)*
Primary Sector	*3.1*	*14,501*	*4.51*
Secondary Sector	*34.7*	*48,061*	*54.94*
Manufacturing	27.1	60,193	51.50
Construction	7.6	29,123	3.44
Tertiary Sector	*62.2*	*53,117*	*40.55*
Transportation, storage, posts and telecommunications	7.3	66,996	12.86
Wholesale, retail and catering	8.0	25,420	5.31
Banking and insurance	14.6	570,443	5.77
Real estate	5.1	97,665	4.38
Social services	10.0	35,185	8.19
Health, sports and social welfare	1.7	38,934	0.75
Education, culture, art, radio, film and television	6.6	49,506	1.80
Scientific research and poly-technical services	5.3	64,701	0.08
Government organs, party organs and social bodies	2.6	36,639	1.27
Others	0.9	12,919	0.14
Total	*100.0*	*47,301*	*100.00*

Note: These statistics are for the whole city.

Source: Beijing Municipal Bureau of Statistics (2004) and *Dongguanshi Tongjiju Bian* (2003).

Evidently, finance sector is very important for Beijing's economy. An article that appeared in Business Weekly on March 22, 2004, argued that Beijing should be converted into a global financial hub and certainly a regional financial centre in Asia Pacific Region. The article argues:

"When foreign banks are allowed to do Renminbi business in China, they will seek to merge or acquire Chinese banks or outlets with their huge capital. In the reshuffling process of its financial sector, Beijing has been positioned in an advantageous way."

"Headquarters or Beijing branches of 15 nationwide banks, 23 listed firms, and 66 central government-owned enterprises are located on what is known as Financial Street (to the west of the old royal City near Fuxingmen and north of it) with total assets surpassing 15 trillion yuan (US$ 1.8 trillion). Their annual turnover is more than 2 trillion yuan (US$ 241 billion) in 2002, while at the same time China's gross domestic product (GDP) was about 10 trillion yuan (US$ 1.08 trillion)."

"So far Financial Street has attracted 17 national banks and nine national insurance firms, and the financial assets they control surpass 11 trillion yuan (US$ 1.325 trillion), or 80 per cent of the nation's total monetary volumes. They created a total turnover of nearly 600 billion yuan (US$ 72.3 billion) and profits of nearly 40 billion yuan (US$ 4.82 billion) in 2002. Given the fast-paced development of Chinese economy and its huge growth potential, if Beijing can grasp the chance, it will be able to grow into a regional financial centre in the Asia-Pacific region."[7]

One article by Chen Gang that appeared in China Daily, June 30, 2004, argues that Beijing should aim to reach a situation like the Global business centres such as New York, London and Tokyo, which have nearly 80 per cent of their GDP from tertiary sector, mainly high-end service sector economy (Chen 2004). Whether Beijing would become the Asian or global financial hub or not, it is slated to be a Global City, by hosting 2008 Olympics.

Dongguan is one of the 21 cities of Guangdong province, a province that has been receiving the highest foreign investments for long and which was one of the first provinces to be taken up for economic reforms. Dongguan is one of Guangdong's recent success story. The city is also called a 'Boom Town'[8]. It is located between Guangzhou (the provincial capital) and Shenzhen (one of the first SEZs of China), on Guangshen highway that connects Guangzhou to Shenzhen, 50 kms east of Guangzhou, 90 kms north of Shenzhen. Hong Kong is 47 nautical miles and Macao is 48 nautical miles from Dongguan. Twenty years back, Dongguan was an unknown agricultural county, and a fishing town. An article that describes Comrade Deng Xiaoping's visit to Shenzhen in 1992 mentions that Dongguan was one of the towns in Guangdong that produced best litchis in the country[9].

The total GDP of Dongguan in 2002 was RMB 67,289.10 million (Guangdong Provincial Bureau of Statistics 2003) (same figure as in Table 6.5) and the per capita GDP in that year was RMB 11,408 (at current prices), calculated over all the residents of the city and not the permanent population, as is often done in China. This is however a decline from per capita GDP of RMB 12,096 in 2000 (at current prices)[10]. The officially reported per capita GDP is RMB 43,401 in 2002[11] and RMB 37,777 in 2001 as these are calculated taking into account only permanent resident population (Guangdong Provincial Bureau of Statistics 2003).

Dongguan has developed a foreign-oriented economy. It has become an industrial city. Its comprehensive economic strength has put it among the top 30 cities in China. In the five years of the Ninth Plan period, the city's total GDP came to RMB 174.62 billion, with an annual growth rate of 17.89 per cent. The foreign exports volume surpassed RMB 200 billion (Dongguan Municipal Land Resource Administration Bureau 2003).

Unlike Beijing, more than half of Dongguan's GDP comes from manufacturing activity (Table 6.6). Hence, it is an industrial city in true sense. Tertiary sector contributes only two-fifths of its total GDP. In the tertiary sector, transport, storage and communications is the most important (12.86 per cent of GDP), followed by social services (8.19 per cent of the GDP). Unlike Beijing, health etc. and education etc, contribute very little to its GDP. Share or financial services, banking and insurance, in the total GDP is far lower than the share of the same in Beijing.

The article by French very vividly describes what Dongguan is today:

> "Dongguan has exploded from a mere town to a city of 7 million in a little over 20 years. But the city officials are not content with a 23 per cent annual economic growth rate. They are putting the finishing touches on a vast, entirely new annex city that they hope will draw 300,000 engineers and researchers, the vanguard of a new China."
> "Dongguan is one of a score of Chinese megacities whose extraordinary growth reflects China's boom and its challenge. The country's rapid urbanisation is helping to lift hundreds of millions of rural Chinese out of poverty. But at the same time, these new second-tier cities are locked in a ferocious competition, spawning ambitious development plans that escape the control of the central government in Beijing."

> "In fact, Beijing has found its powers to slow runaway growth to be surprisingly limited, in part because provinces and cities resist efforts to rein in their investments. Although the central government allots money to pet development projects, provinces raise money for their own projects by selling rights to develop real estate. In many cases, local officials are judged in part by economic measures—how many jobs they create, how many big buildings spring up. That means that many provincial officials are trying the same formula: manufacturing and export zones, research parks and self-styled Silicon Valleys like Pioneer Park in Dongguan." "The unchecked development means there is little ability to consider China's needs as a whole, or to prevent duplication and waste."

In the year 2002, Beijing received US$ 1,792.57 million (Beijing Municipal Bureau of Statistics 2003) of foreign investment (3.29 per cent[12] of the foreign investments of US$ 52,471.26 million received by China). These figures are for the whole city and do not therefore tally with the figures given in Table 6.2. In comparison to Beijing, Shanghai had received 8.14 per cent and Guangdong Province had received 21.60 per of the foreign investment received in 2002[13]. In whole of China, about 70 per cent of the foreign investment was in manufacturing sector, whereas in Beijing only 36 per cent of the foreign investment was in this sector. About 18 per cent of this investment was in real estate services in Beijing, whereas this figure for whole of China was around 11 per cent in 2002. Evidently, in Beijing, the foreign investment is in tertiary sector, computer applications, information services, other consultancy services and other services (not specified in the data source), and real estate services.

As mentioned before, Guangdong province gets the highest foreign investments in China even today. Dongguan is one of the beneficiaries of this. In 2002, total foreign capital used in Dongguan was US$ 1458.68 million (Table 6.2), which was lower than in Beijing in the year. Also, Dongguan received about 13 per cent of the total foreign investments received by Guangdong in the year. In the previous year, the city received foreign investment of US$ 1,147.21 million. The total exports in 2002 from the city were US$ 23,733 million (20 percrnt of the exports from Guangdong) and imports were US$ 20,508 million (20% of the imports into Guangdong). That is, exports were to the tune of 291 per cent of the total GDP of the city[14]. These high figures of exports and imports get reflected in the fact that Dongguan has around 14,000 overseas invested enterprises, of which 12 are in Fortune 11 list and 33 are in Fortune 500 list (Dongguan Municipal Land Resource Administration Bureau 2003).

Status of Municipal Facilities

Beijing and Dongguan have higher level of municipal facilities than all cities average with respect to water supply coverage and per capita use, gas coverage, per capita road space area and road density. For example, water supply coverage and gas coverage rates for both the cities are far higher than all cities average. Other indicators such as road surface area per capita and overall density of road network are doing better in Beijing and Dongguan than all cities average. In both the cities, there is 100 per cent coverage rate for water supply, whereas for all cities in China, it is only 78 per cent (Table 6.7). Gas coverage rate in both the cities is nearly 100 per cent whereas in all cities it is 67 per cent.

Table 6.7: Level of Municipal Facilities, 2002

	Item	*Unit*	*Beijing*	*Dongguan*	*All Cities*
1.	Daily water consumption per capita	Litre	236.58	371.93	213.02
2.	Water coverage rate (% population covered by water supply)	%	100.00	100.00	77.85
3.	Gas coverage rate (% population covered by gas supply)	%	99.57	100.00	67.17
4.	Motor vehicles for public transport per 10,000 persons	Number	21.63	4.77	6.73
5.	Road surface area per capita	Sq m.	8.05	11.69	7.87
6.	Overall density of road network	Km per sq km of area	1.20	3.26	0.41
7.	Density of sewers	Km per sq km of area	5.91	7.65	6.66
8.	Proportion wastewater treated	%	45.04	14.70	39.97
9.	Proportion of wastewater treated in centralised treatment plants	%	45.04	14.70	24.28
10.	Public green space per capita	Sq m.	10.08	3.04	5.36
11.	Green space as proportion of total built area*	%	40.82	10.19	25.80
12.	Harmless disposal of domestic garbage	%	86.35	15.22	54.31
13.	Night soil disposal rate	%	30.64	93.53	67.60
14.	Flush latrines as proportion of total latrines	%	65.15	100.00	51.70
15.	Proportion of solid waste collected	%	87	100	—

Note: * Refers to ratio of area of parks and green land of built districts to the surface area of the built districts at the end of the reporting period.

Source: China, Ministry of Construction (2003) for all items.

Dongguan has better level of facilities as compared to Beijing in percentage of households having flush latrines, density of sewers and night soil disposal rate. This could be because Dongguan is a new city where it was possible to provide individual latrines in the residential areas and also put in sewerage networks in them. Beijing is a historic city, with traditional core, where the housing, called *hutongs*, do not have either individual latrines nor pour flush latrines. These are not there in 35 per cent of the housing units in Beijing, not because of lack of funds but because of the structure of the city. Even percentage solid waste collected is higher in Dongguan (100%) than Beijing. This could be because of small size of Dongguan city. Also, Dongguan has higher per capita availability of water than Dongguan, mainly because Beijing is in a dry region that is drought-prone whereas Dongguan is in Pearl River Delta, with abundance of water resources.

With respect to remaining facilities, Beijing has better level than Dongguan and all cities. These facilities are; public transport vehicles, proportion of wastewater treated and wastewater treated in centralised treatment plant, per capita green space, green space as proportion of total built area, and harmless disposal of domestic garbage. In these facilities, Dongguan has worse position than even all Cities. Thus, the large city of Beijing has better funds and better level of municipal facilities than Dongguan with exception of a few facilities.

Infrastructure Investments

The infrastructure investments is through the Urban Construction and Maintenance Fund (UCMF). Data for only one time point, 2002, is presented here. The sources of income for the UCMF are:

(i) *State budgetary appropriations*—Includes appropriation from the budget of the central government for capital construction, special expenditure, re-credit loan, discount funds, arranged expenditure for innovation projects and test of new products, urban construction, construction of simple commercial buildings; appropriation from development funds in underdeveloped areas; and appropriation in the budget of local (provincial) governments earmarked by the central government for urban construction.

(ii) *Domestic loans*—Refers to various funds borrowed by the city from banks and non-bank financial institutions for investment in fixed assets, including loans appropriated by higher responsible authorities, special loans by the central government and loans arranged by the local governments from different domestic sources for the city.

(iii) *Foreign investments*—Refers to foreign funds for the purpose of construction and purchase of fixed assets (including equipment, materials, technology, etc.) and includes FDI, foreign funds borrowed and managed by the central government (loan by foreign governments and international financial institutions, export credit, commercial loans by foreign banks, issue of bonds and stocks at the international financial markets) and other foreign investments (including equipment payment provided by foreign businessmen). It excludes self-owned foreign exchange reserves such as state foreign exchange, local foreign exchange, retained foreign exchange, adjusted foreign exchange and foreign loan issued by the Bank of China from self owned funds, etc. Foreign funds are calculated based on the foreign exchange rate with the RMB.

(iv) *Self raised funds*—Refer to funds beyond the budget, which are raised by various regions, enterprises and institutions for the purpose of investment in fixed assets during the reporting period, including self-owned funds by departments of the central government, local governments, enterprises and institutions.

(v) *Others*—Refer to funds received during the reporting period, which are not included in the above-mentioned sources, including funds raised through the society, individual funds, donations, and funds appropriated by other organisations.

The UCMF in Beijing had received funds worth RMB 27,589.33 million in 2002 (Table 6.8), which formed 15.57 per cent of the total fixed assets investment in the city and 8.83 per cent of the city's total GDP in the year. Beijing's receipt in this fund was 16.5 times that of Dongguan in this year. Thus, in Dongguan, the revenue in this fund came to just 8.73 per cent of the total fixed assets investment and 2.49 per cent of the city's GDP in the year 2002. Thus, revenue and therefore expenditures on infrastructure are much less as a proportion of the total GDP in Dongguan than in Beijing. Beijing's population is 2.5 times that of Dongguan, its GDP is 4.6 times that of Dongguan and size of UCMF is 16.5 times that of Dongguan in year 2002. With investments coming in for the Olympics, this gap between the two cities would widen. There is therefore very high inequality between the two cities in terms of infrastructure investments, an inequality that would increase.

Table 6.8: UCMF, Sources and Amount, 2002

	Item	*Beijing*	*Dongguan*	*All Cities*
	Total revenue of UCMF in (RMB million)	27,589.33	1,673.36	315,617.58
	UCMF per capita (RMB)	2,905	665	896
	Total revenue as % of GDP	8.83	2.49	5.81
	Total revenue as % of total fixed assets investments	15.57	8.73	13.68
1.	Urban maintenance and construction tax	9.03	2.46	10.01
2.	Additional fees imposed for use of public utilities	3.68	0.36	1.58
3.	Central financial allocation	3.05	0.00	2.41
4.	Local (provincial) financial allocation	5.66	40.01	12.44
5.	Domestic loan	40.48	0.00	27.69
	(a) National debt financed with local budget	2.58	0.00	2.10
6.	Foreign Investment	1.22	24.70	1.93
	(a) Foreign direct investment	0.20	0.21	0.26
7.	Bonds	0.00	0.00	0.09
8.	Stock financing	2.46	0.00	0.22
9.	Water resource fee	1.95	1.75	0.39
10.	Self-raised funds by enterprises and institutions	15.79	13.73	19.03
11.	Fees for expansion of municipal utilities capacity	0.88	2.30	2.74
12.	Fees for use of municipal utilities	2.56	6.21	2.83
	(a) Toll on roads and bridges	0.17	4.58	0.71
	(b) Wastewater treatment fees	1.93	0.84	1.13
	(c) Garbage treatment fees	0.02	0.76	0.17
13.	Land transfer fee	3.64	5.26	8.97
14.	Other revenue	9.59	3.23	9.65
	Total revenue	*100.00*	*100.00*	*100.00*

Source: Data from China, Ministry of Construction (2003).

For the reasons of difference in the volume of revenues accrued to UCMF in the two cities, it would be useful to look at different sources of revenue of these two funds. Beijing is able to collect nearly 9 per cent of its revenue from Urban Maintenance and Construction Tax (UCMT) whereas Dongguan is only able to collect 2.5 per cent from this tax (Table 6.8). Dongguan gets no central financial allocation whereas Beijing gets 3.05 per cent of the UCMF contribution from this source, which is higher than the national average of central assistance to cities. This may have gone up because of Olympics. Beijing borrowed a lot in 2002 from different sources for the UCMF. Domestic loan as a proportion of total revenue was 40 per cent for Beijing whereas it was 28 per cent for all cities and none what so ever for Dongguan. Beijing is able to borrow for urban infrastructure. However, Dongguan has been able to get foreign investment contribution to its UCMF receipts to the extent of 25 per cent in this year, whereas Beijing got only 1.2 per cent and all cities together got only 1.9 per cent. It is the investments coming from Taiwan, Hong Kong and Overseas Chinese in the city. For Dongguan, local financial allocation, that is, allocations from Guangdong Provincial Government, is very important, and in 2002, this source contributed 40 per cent of the total UCMF receipts of the city.

Self-raised funds by enterprises and institutions, important source of revenue for the cities in the highly decentralised financial system of the country, has contributed 19 per cent of the total revenue to all cities in China. Its contribution in Beijing is 15 per cent and in Dongguan is just 13 per cent. Selfraised funds refer to funds beyond the budget, which are raised by various regions, enterprises and institutions for the purpose of investment in fixed assets during the reporting period, including self-owned funds by departments of the central government, local governments, enterprises and institutions. It also includes funds that come through lease of lands. Though some figures are given here, it is likely that the figures could be higher than reported and would be in the category of off-budget funds (See Bahl 1999 for definition). Other revenue, which is contributions through donations, beneficiary contributions, etc. was 9.6 per cent in Beijing whereas only 3.2 per cent in Dongguan and 9.7 per cent for all cities in China.

Land transfer fees are important source of revenue for all cities together, about 9 per cent of the revenue, but, this is not the case with regards to the two cities studied here. Dongguan is getting higher share of its revenue from collection of fees for use of utilities as compared to Beijing. Dongguan is especially collecting quite some funds from the toll-tax on roads.

To sum up, Beijing is able to borrow more than Dongguan for urban infrastructure. The debt repayment on this may be passed on to Beijing residents in the future. How the debt repayment would be is not known. City's debt would go up in light of the new investments coming in for Olympics. Would the city pass on this debt to those population having low incomes given that Beijing has very high income-inequality? Beijing is receiving central assistance whereas Dongguan is receiving provincial assistance to the tune of 40 per cent of its receipts in UCMF. Central assistance to Beijing is not as high as provincial assistance to Dongguan. Beijing's collection from UCMT is higher than Dongguan in terms of its share. Recollect that this tax is levied on the industries and enterprises. It is also collecting higher proportion of additional fees, which are again levied on the enterprises. Thus, enterprises in Beijing are contributing upto 13 per cent of the UCMF for the city's infrastructure development. In Dongguan, this percentage is only 3. This is also because, Dongguan being a small city, depending on rapid growth of manufacturing, may be giving concessions to the enterprises to locate in the city, which Beijing does not have to do. On the contrary, Beijing government is charging all types of fees to the enterprises, foreign (e.g. McDonald's) or national (Wong 1998 in Bahl 1999: 143), which is leading to high share of self-raised funds in Beijing. Thus, Dongguan is not able to bring in cross-subsidies in the city. As a result, the city has to charge for the use of municipal utilities, the share of these charges is much higher in Dongguan than in Beijing. It has also to depend on provincial support. What has saved Dongguan is its ability to get FDI in the infrastructure sector. If that was not the case, the city would not have been able to develop its infrastructure to the level it has done. If a non-coastal city or a city that is not in Guangdong was taken for comparison, the FDI not being there, the size of UCMF would have been smaller.

Expenditures incurred from the UCMF indicate the development priorities of each of the cities. Beijing is spending lesser proportion of its funds on new fixed asset investments as compared to Dongguan and is spending slightly higher than Dongguan on maintenance of the existing assets (Table 6.9). This is obvious as Dongguan is a newly developing city whereas Beijing has fixed assets created over long period in history. Beijing is just spending 1.23 per cent of its funds on payment of domestic and international loans in 2002. This seems to be quite low. May be, in the future, this figure will go up, as the city has a very high proportion of its revenues from loans, which will have to be serviced in the future. Or, the city is accounting debt services on some other account, which is not part of the UCMF. Investment in fixed assets is the main purpose for which the resources of UCMF are utilised in both the cities.

Roads and bridges take up the largest proportion of resources of this fund in both the cities and in all cities in China. Beijing spends 44 per cent of UCMF resources on this head whereas Dongguan spends 31 per cent and all cities spend 35 per cent on this head. In Beijing, the next largest share is taken up by public traffic (16%), that is, creation of infrastructure for public transport. This means that 60 per cent of the resources of the UCMF in 2002 were utilised for transportation infrastructure, including infrastructure for public transport. In Dongguan, public transport's share was only 3 per cent and for all cities in China, the share of this head was 9 per cent.

Table 6.9: Composition of Expenditure from UCMF, 2002

	Beijing	*Dongguan*	*All China*
Total expenditure (RMB million)	27,331.05	1,450.25	317,802.53
Expenditure to income (%)	99.06	86.67	100.69
By Purpose—Total	*100.00*	*100.00*	*100.00*
1. Expenditure on investments in fixed assets	79.72	83.73	77.01
2. Maintenance expenditure	11.96	9.64	10.02
3. Payment for domestic and international Loans	1.23	0.00	8.93
4. Tax	0.00	1.10	0.34
5. Other expenditures	7.09	5.53	3.69
By Industry (Activity)—Total	*100.00*	*100.00*	*100.00*
1. Water supply	2.19	8.25	4.97
2. Gas supply	5.76	1.08	2.66
3. Central heating	0.55	0.00	3.58
4. Public traffic	16.36	3.38	8.54
5. Road and bridge	44.48	30.74	34.87
6. Sewerage	6.85	2.16	8.40
7. Flood control	3.34	1.94	2.89
8. Landscaping	4.56	5.66	8.27
9. Environmental sanitation	9.34	3.71	4.39
10. Other expenditures	6.57	43.09	21.43

Source: Data from China, Ministry of Construction (2003).

Roads and bridges head covers cost of freeways and highways constructed in Beijing city. There have been many demolitions of small buildings along the major roads, something that comes through informal discussions with those knowledgeable about the city. There are no estimates of these as yet. Along with these, small (informal) enterprises too have been demolished. These small trade and business establishments employ sizeable population (10% of the total workers in the category of wholesale and retail trade) and these would have been affected. It was mentioned earlier that the per capita GDP from these activities is quite low and hence it is these low income groups that would have faced displacements for modernising the city highway system. While such a development would benefit those with private cars the whole city would pay the loans, which are one of the important sources of funds for urban infrastructure. Not just Beijing, but, this is the story of most cities of China and also most cities of India (See Chapter 4 for municipal budget priorities of Ahmedabad).

Water supply attracts higher share in Dongguan than in Beijing. About 43 per cent of the resources are expended in Dongguan on other expenditures. It seems that these would be on the development of public plaza in the city on Dongcheng *Dadao* (Grand Avenue) and other city beautification projects. In Beijing, other expenditures attract only

6.6 per cent of the revenues in 2002. Much higher proportion of revenues is spent on environmental sanitation and sewerage in Beijing, in comparison to Dongguạn. This could be possibly because of large size of the city and the need to internationally show case the city. The expenditures made on Olympics facilities in Beijing are not reflected in these figures as these expenditures are not out of the UCMF.

Although, expenditures on investment in fixed assets is higher in Dongguan than in Beijing as a proportion, in per capita terms, that in Beijing is more than 4 times that in Dongguan and more than 3 times that in all cities together (Table 6.10). Overall expenditures made from this fund are five times than that made by Dongguan on per capita basis and 3 times that of all cities. Thus, Beijing is far ahead of all cities in China and Dongguan in terms of per capita investments from this fund. On roads and bridges, Beijing is making 10 times per capita investments than Dongguan. Part of the reason for this could be scale of Beijing city as compared to Dongguan. For all activities, investments made by Beijing are far higher than that made by Dongguan on per capita basis. Exception is the head of other expenditures. In water supply, Beijing is making just 1.3 times the per capita expenditures made by Dongguan. Hence, the gap here is not much. What is heartening is that even medium sized cities in China, in especially economically fast growing provinces are primarily making investments in water supply.

Table 6.10: Per Capita* Expenditure on Different Heads UCMF, 2002 (RMB)

	Beijing	*Dongguan*	*All China*
Total expenditure	2877.86	575.95	902.35
By Purpose			
1. Expenditure on investments in fixed assets	2,294.20	482.25	694.94
2. Maintenance expenditure	344.28	55.52	90.42
3. Payment for domestic and international Loans	35.32	0.00	80.59
4. Tax	0.00	6.31	3.10
5. Other expenditures	204.07	31.88	33.30
By Industry (Activity)			
1. Water supply	63.09	47.50	44.83
2. Gas supply	165.65	6.22	23.97
3. Central heating	15.76	0.00	32.31
4. Public traffic	470.94	19.44	77.07
5. Road and bridge	1,279.97	177.06	314.65
6. Sewerage	197.21	12.43	75.84
7. Flood control	96.20	11.16	26.07
8. Landscaping	131.29	32.58	74.64
9. Environmental sanitation	268.68	21.38	39.60
10. Other expenditures	189.06	248.18	193.37

Note: * Per capita expenditures are calculated taking the population figures given in China, Ministry of Construction (2003).

Beijing's Olympics Investments

The Olympics 2008 facilities will be mainly located in Chaoyang District, in the north of the district and outside the fourth ring road and also north of the facilities created for 1990 Asian Games held in Beijing. Beijing will be developing new sports facilities for the purpose, which is the most important aspect of Olympic economy. But, besides these facilities, Beijing is expanding public transit system with the construction of new subway lines; expanding highway system; building six new towns that would ease the pressure on the central city of Beijing; improving environmental services such as solid waste management; renewing the historic districts of the city and of all, laying stress on new economy within city in place of old (manufacturing) economy. The new economic activities are those in the electronics, bio-technology, and financial services.

Table 6.11: Investments in Olympic Economy

Item	*Beijing Municipal Development and Reform Commission (a)*		*Alternate estimatesi*[15]	
	Billion RMB	*Billion US$*	*Billion RMB*	*Billion US$*
(i)	*(ii)*	*(iii)*	*(iv)*	*(v)*
Total	*1500*	*181.4*		
Stadiums	22	2.7		
Expressways	31	3.7		
Subway	55	6.7	63 (b)	7.6 (b)
Environmental protection	36	4.4		
Hi-tech industries	150	18.2		
Finance, trade, logistics, exhibition and tourism sectors	300	36.3	200 (a)	24.2 (a)
New towns	800	96.8	134 (b)	16.2 (b)
Education, culture, healthcare, community services and public security	100	12.1	80 (a)	9.7 (a)

* Located in the districts of Daxing, Fangshan, Tongzhou, Pinggu, Huairou and Shunyi.

Source: Based on articles from *China Daily*[16].

The creation of new sport facilities would require an investment of RMB 22 billion (Table 6.11). In all, RMB 1,500 billion, that is RMB 375 billion per year, would be spent over the four years from 2004 to create infrastructure for Beijing Olympics. Of this, RMB 800 billion is only for the construction of new towns in outer suburbs of Beijing to take care of population moving out of the city to decongest the main city. To get a sense, in 2002, Beijing had invested RMB 177.2 billion in fixed assets investments (Beijing Municipal Bureau of Statistics 2004). Over the period 2004-08, an amount 2.1 times the current investment level will be required only for the Olympic infrastructure. Then, the ratio of fixed assets investments to GDP would further increase.

The physical infrastructure expansion, that is, construction of expressways and subways and environmental protection would require an investment of RMB 86 billion. These items would fall under UCMF purview. In 2002, the size of UCMF was RMB 27.6 billion, of which RMB 16.6 were spent on transport infrastructure. RMC 86 billion has to be spent over a period of four years, that is RMB 21.5 billion a year would be required for transport infrastructure, which is more than Beijing's current capacity to fund. It is 1.3 times the current investments in transport infrastructure. Beijing is looking for new sources of finance for creating transport infrastructure for the Olympics.

Beijing Municipal Development and Reform Commission announced that the Beijing would open its doors to overseas or domestic private-owned companies to invest in the city infrastructure. For the purpose, the Beijing government has opened a website inviting investments in Beijing. Infrastructure includes supply of water, gas and heat, treatment of waste and public transport. By this, government will be able to save large sum of money.

The local government of Beijing also announced in early 2003 that it would issue bonds worth Yuan 2 billion (US$ 240 million) in 2004, to finance its subway lines 4 and 10, whose total cost is expected to be 30.1 billion yuan (US$ 3.6 billion). The principle adopted will be of BOT (Built Operate Transfer) or TOT (Transfer Operate Transfer)[17]. It looks that the city government would issue bonds; funds thus raised would be transferred to the subway company. In addition, the subway company would also get foreign investments with the efforts of the municipal government.

Budget Analysis

Budget is a financial statement of the local government's annual income and expenditure. In Chinese cities, these budgets are for recurring expenditures as well as for social sector expenditures. The capital investment in infrastructure is through special funds, such as UCMF for urban construction activities. Special funds have also been created in the recent years for specific activities, discussed at length in Chapter 17.

The total budget size of Beijing in 2002 was RMB 52,433.1 million or RMB 52.43 billion (Table 6.12). Beijing's budget size increased at 15.4 per cent in 2001-02 and at 188.3 per cent (both at current prices) in 2000-01. In 1994-95, the budget size showed an increase of 189 per cent (calculated from raw data). From 2000 to 2001, Beijing budget size tripled. It seems that Beijing has improved its financial position to create facilities that would let it bid for Olympics. In the coming years we would see further improvement in the budget size and investments made in Beijing.

Table 6.12: Total Budgetary Revenue (Income) in Million RMB (Current Prices)

	2002	*2001*	*2000*	*1995*	*1991*
Beijing	52,433.1	45,416.8	15,755.1	10,744.5	6,596.5
Dongguan	5,529.3	4,501.6	3,022.3	1,156.2	351.4
All Cities	520,621.1	445,861.7	343,788.8	222,644.1	123,051.3

Note: Data is for the administrative city.

Source: Data from China Statistical Press (2003, 2002, 2001, 1996, 1992).

The budget size of Dongguan is one-tenth that of Beijing in 2001 and 2002 years. In 2000, this ratio was one-fifth. In 1995, a year that saw very rapid increase in Beijing's budget size, once again, Dongguan's budget size was one-tenth that of Beijing. If the temporary population is included in the population figures then Dongguan's population has remained at about one-third that in Beijing. This indicates a high disparity in per capita budget size between Beijing and Dongguan. Dongguan's budget size increased by 22.8 per cent in 2001-02 and at 48.9 per cent in 2000-01. The effect of 1994 fiscal reforms saw increase in Dongguan's budget size by 50 per cent (in 1994-95) (calculated from raw data).

The budget to GDP ratio has improved in the recent years in Beijing. That is because of better collection of taxes in the recent years. The ratio has reached 0.17, which is far higher than the budget to income ratio for all the cities together (0.10) (Table 6.13). Dongguan has very low budget to GDP ratio (0.08). This could be because of the fiscal incentives given to enterprises with foreign investments or collaboration. There is much higher possibility of extra-budgetary means of raising revenue in Dongguan than in Beijing. This might well be the case and hence, the city might not be showing the budgetary income that would be liable to be shared with the provincial government.

Table 6.13: Budget to GDP Ratio

	2002	2001	2000	1995	1991
Beijing	0.17	0.17	0.07	0.09	0.15
Dongguan	0.08	0.08	0.06	0.06	0.05
All Cities	0.10	0.08	0.07	0.06	0.14

The total budgetary expenditure in Beijing in 2002 was RMB 60.7 billion (Table 6.14), an increase of 8.6 per cent over the previous year. In comparison, Dongguan's budgetary expenditures were just RMB 6.5 billion, about one-tenth of that in Beijing. The budgetary revenues of Dongguan were also one-tenth that of Beijing in 2002.

Table 6.14: Total Budgetary Expenditure (in Million RMB) (Current Prices)

	2002	2001	2000	1995	1991
Beijing	60,727.8	55,910.6	18,828.8	13,349.3	5,805.7
Dongguan	6,496.1	4,786.5	3,361.0	1,321.7	222.0
All Cities	700,800.8	555,479.2	438,933.1	253,566.2	84,636.2

Note: Data is for the administrative city.

Source: Data from China Statistical Press (2003, 2002, 2001, 1996, 1992).

Most years since 1994, the cities have shown deficit budgets (Figure 7.1). That may be partly because of transfer of part of their revenues to the national government and partly to be in a bargaining position with respect to provincial governments. In case of Beijing, since it is a national level city, showing of deficit budgetary position would be to bargain for more funds from the national government.

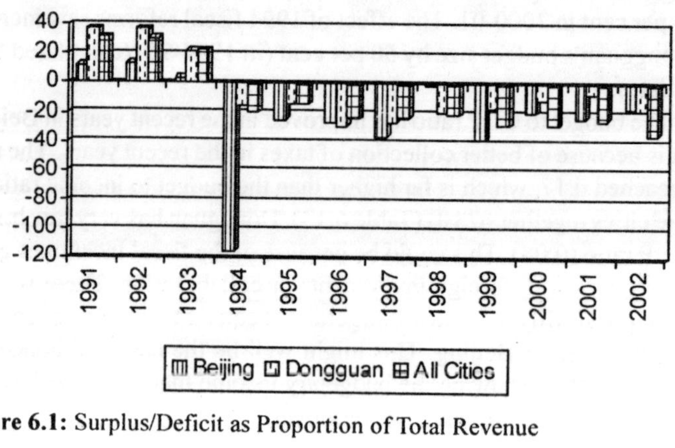

Figure 6.1: Surplus/Deficit as Proportion of Total Revenue

In Beijing, health, education, sports, culture and broadcasting, together, reach 1995 proportion in 1997 and 1998 (Table 6.15). But, after that they remain at about 22 per cent, except the year 2001, when the percentage goes down to 20 per cent. From 1997 onwards, percentage expenditure on health has gone down steadily. Other expenses have fluctuated between 20 per cent and 30 per cent. Other expenditures form a large proportion in the total expenditure. In public security and legal services, expenditures have gone up marginally. The expenditure on capital construction has gone up. It went upto 17 per cent in 2001, but, then declined to 10 per cent in 2002. In 2001, when the total budgetary income and thus the expenditure went up all of a sudden, allocation to capital construction increased significantly in absolute as well as proportionate terms.

Table 6.15: Budgetary Expenditure Details, Beijing City

Item	*2002*	*2001*	*2000*	*1999*	*1998*	*1997*	*1996*	*1995*
1. Capital construction	10.2	16.6	13.0	12.8	11.6	10.6	11.6	8.8
2. Enterprise innovation	6.6	6.3	7.4	8.8	6.9	6.4	7.1	5.6
3. Geological prospecting	0.1	0.1	0.1	0.0	0.0	0.0	0.0	0.0
4. Science and technology	2.4	2.2	2.3	2.5	2.2	2.4	2.4	2.4
5. Agriculture, forestry, water conservancy and meteorology	3.7	3.5	3.7	3.7	3.8	4.2	4.0	3.8
6. Industry and transport	0.5	0.5	0.5	0.4	0.4	1.4	1.3	1.1
7. Commerce	0.0	0.0	0.0	0.0	0.1	0.2	0.2	0.3
8. Health	6.0	5.9	6.4	6.4	7.3	7.3	18.7	24.8
9. Education	13.7	12.9	13.6	13.9	14.7	18.1		
10. Sports, culture, broadcasting, etc.	2.3	2.1	2.1	2.1	2.5			
11. Pension, funds for retired people and relief funds	7.6	6.7	6.6	6.1	6.3	5.0	2.4	3.2
12. Social security subsidy	1.5	1.1	1.0	0.9	0.6	0.0	0.0	0.0
13. Government administration	5.6	4.9	4.7	4.5	4.7	4.8	5.3	4.6
14. Public security & legal services	8.0	7.0	7.6	7.4	7.8	7.1	7.5	7.1
15. Price subsidies	0.7	1.2	2.1	2.8	5.0	5.9	7.0	6.5
16. City maintenance	5.3	4.9	5.4	4.8	4.6	4.4	3.5	5.4
17. Circulation funds	0.0	0.2	0.1	0.4	0.4	0.6	0.3	0.0
18. Other expenses	25.8	23.8	23.5	22.4	21.1	21.6	28.7	26.5
Total expenditure	100.0	100.0	100.0	100.0	100.0	100.0	100.0	100.0
Total expenditure (RMB billion)	62.83	55.91	44.30	35.52	28.07	23.64	18.74	15.44

Note: The total expenditure given here do not tally with the total budgetary expenditures taken from China City Statistical Yearbooks, data given in Table 22 because, this table data is for the whole city whereas in Table 22 is for the administrative city.

Source: China, National Bureau of Statistics (2002, 2001, 2000, 1999, 1998, 1997, 1996, 1995).

Other expenses category formed the largest proportion of total expenditures. These include expenditures on other departments and debt servicing. The UCMF does not display much amounts for debt-servicing though it shows quite high loan amount, at least in case of Beijing.

In Dongguan, in 2002, half the local budget expenditures were on two heads, capital construction and departments of health, education, culture and sports (Table 6.16). In this year, higher proportion of the total local expenditures was incurred on these two heads in Dongguan than in Beijing. This was because, firstly, Dongguan was not spending anything (was spending less than 1 per cent of total expenditure) on social security. Also, Dongguan does not have tradition of having large SOEs. SOEs employees have protected employment and in eventuality of their restructuring, the local government is required to set up a social security fund. Since, Dongguan does not have strong presence of SOEs, the local government may not have been required to contribute to such a fund. Secondly, employment in Dongguan is in private sector, and of mainly migrant population, which does not have social security coverage.

Table 6.16: Composition of Local Budgetary Expenditures, Dongguan

Local expenditure for	*2002*	*2001*	*2000*
Capital construction	25.44	25.01	8.16
Enterprises innovation	0.22	0.34	0.47
Science and technology promotion	4.31	0.86	2.96
Supporting rural production	3.18	4.19	6.91
Operating expenses of department of farming, forestry, water conservancy and meteorology	2.57	1.86	5.02
Fees of industrial and transportation departments	0.74	0.75	0.06
City maintenance	9.93	9.13	12.28
Operating expenses of departments of science, education, public health and sports	22.69	22.14	25.81
—Science	0.24	0.32	0.28
—Education	18.50	17.87	20.29
—Public health	2.30	2.37	3.60
—Sports	0.49	0.61	0.45
Pension and relief funds for social welfare	0.72	0.79	0.86
Government administration	6.72	6.05	8.87
Public security agency, procuratorial agency and court justice	10.66	12.46	13.82
Other expenses	12.81	16.42	14.78
Total local expenditure	*100.00*	*100.00*	*100.00*
Total expenditure (RMB billion)	*6.50*	*4.79*	*3.36*

Note: The total expenditure given here do tally with the total budgetary expenditures taken from China City Statistical Yearbooks data given in Table 22.

Source: Dongguanshi Tongjiju Bian (2003).

Expenditure on Social Security head is miniscule. It is also possible that smaller cities like Dongguan, in race to create a 'global city', that is in race to create infrastructure that enhances the city's stature, may be compromising on social security provision.

Another difference between Dongguan and Beijing is that the former has not taken much of loans for development activities as it has been able to attract foreign investments. Hence, the percentage of total expenditure made on other expenses category is less in Dongguan than in Beijing. Dongguan has slightly higher proportion of total expenditure made on health, education, culture and sports than Beijing, but only in 2001. In 2002, in both the cities, about 22 per cent have been spent on these activities. Lastly, in Dongguan, when expenditure on capital construction has increased in terms of percentage share, the share of all other expenditure heads, including on health, education, etc. has gone down. In fact, the share of health, education has gone down from 25 per cent in 2000 to 22 per cent in 2001 and 2002. Thus, one can argue that indeed the projects to enhance the image of the city have led to decline in city's expenditures on social sectors in Dongguan. Further, such expenses are made by also ignoring the social security responsibility.

About 74 per cent of the revenue in 2002 and 73 per cent in 2001, in Beijing came from enterprise tax, operation tax and value-added tax. Dongguan was getting 88 per cent of its revenue from total taxes and 84 per cent from the enterprise taxes. While Beijing still has SOEs, the enterprises in Dongguan are largely private sector. With further privatisation of SOEs in Beijing, this source of revenue will go down. Dongguan shared 67 per cent of its revenues with the higher levels of government. Lastly, there are no heads that give information about charges to the people for the use of public utilities and so on, that would have bearing on equity issues.

Concluding Observations and Comments

This research indicates that the two cities of China, Beijing and Dongguan, have invested heavily in urban infrastructure. However, Beijing has made many times more investment than Dongguan, firstly because the former is a capital city and secondly because it will host 2008 summer Olympic games. In contrast, the latter is a provincial city and has to share significant proportion of its income with the provincial government. Besides the Olympics facilities, Beijing now has new subway lines coming up, sixth ring road completed, new highways, road widening in the historic district conservation and renovation, green spaces, McDonalds and Pizza Huts, and international level arts and culture facilities. Beijing has attractive living environment to provide to the international business and administrative class. The economy is robust and growing. Since some of the new infrastructures is with the latest technology, these are better than even the cities of the developed world. For example, the subway trains are with better technology than one finds in say Paris or New York.

Dongguan being a smaller city, and a city that has provincial level importance, does not have such large infrastructure projects like Beijing. But, the city has elevated highways, connecting major cities in the region. Many more are to come as per the reports in the newspapers[18]. The city has wide roads, big malls, and now a new 'cultural centre' coming up. The cultural centre is a large well developed open space in the centre of new part of the city, on Dongcheng *Dadao*, having an opera house and a concert hall, a library, convention hall, musical fountain in the open space and many such attractive hard landscapes. There is a walking street with interesting street furniture and statues, something like Wangfujing street in Beijing, but at a scale suitable to the size of the city. The city has strong links with Taiwan, Hong Kong and Macao, with sizeable compatriots from there, mainly Taiwanese living in the city and many more owning properties in the city. Taiwanese are to set up major hospital for the Taiwanese in the city[19]. CEPA (Closer Economic Partnership Arrangement)'s implementation would further integrate the economy of the region, Hong Kong, Macau and Guangdong province. The city is called a hi-tech city because of the location of hi-tech industries. Thus, Dongguan is also projecting itself as a 'global city' with strong regional linkages.

For those not attracted to such 'glam and glitter', of the cities, and more concerned with quality of life for the poor, then; these two cities have 100 per cent coverage of water supply. Dongguan has 100 per cent coverage of sanitation, which Beijing does not have. It is not because of the lack of resources or political will that Beijing does not have full coverage of sanitation, but, it is because of the city structure. Old city, that is the historic core, has traditional courtyard houses, called the *hutongs*, which are now densely packed with built spaces and most of them do not have individual baths and latrines. Possibly, large parts of the area does not have underground sewerage network as yet. Through demolitions of parts of the area for road widening and redevelopment projects, underground sewerage lines are being laid in some parts. Neither of the two cities have slums so characteristic of developing country cities. Wide roads have footpaths for pedestrians and bicycle lanes for bicyclists. Closer to the character of slums are the *hutongs* in Beijing and old city area in Dongguan. But, still, the living environment is not so bad as in slums. In some pockets in south, and south-east and even central city, there are small dilapidated housing, once again not as bad as slum housing. The unregistered migrants live in over-crowded *siheyuans* (houses with a courtyard at the centre and built rooms on four sides) on the city periphery (Li, 2001), in sub-divided houses or in illegally rented public housing in the city.

Absolute deprivation found in many developing country cities cannot be found in the two cities. As discussed in this paper, the urban poverty defined by income is very low. But, there is high inequality in the cities, as it has been illustrated well for Beijing in this article. Since the two cities studied here have large and globally integrated economies and have been attracting FDIs for quite some time now, they have high per capita GDPs and hence a population with higher income levels than other cities. Hence also, one does not find absolute deprivation in the two cities to any great extent. According to an ADB report (ADB 2001: 93), just 4.6 per cent among local population, but, 10.3 per cent among the migrant population were below poverty line in Beijing in 1999. For Dongguan, we do not have this data. Possibly, migration control prevents 'slum ghetto' like situation in cities in China and thus also in the two cities studied here. Thus, the two cities have many achievements with regards to development and well-being of the citizens.

Amidst these, new equity concerns are emerging because of the two cities, excessive obsession with making a statement about themselves as 'global cities'. In fact, all cities in China now want to be such, as the city profile of these cities shows. All want broad, six to ten lane roads, six lanes in the centre, and two lanes each on the sides for bicycles and slow traffic and parking, tall glass buildings, convention centres and exhibition halls, malls, new public buildings of modern architecture, a golf-course, and so on. Information of all these is showcased in a city exhibition and a website announcing new investment projects. The equity concerns do not emerge along the basic deprivation issues, as in other developing countries. The equity issues are related to consumption levels, access to social security, access to good quality education and access to primary health care, whose prices are increasing in wake of the privatisation process. The last point is acknowledged by United Nation Development Programme's (UNDP's), concept note for 2004 Human Development Report (HDR).

In fact, Chinese cities have gone far ahead with diverting resources to large infrastructure that would make them globally competitive cities, much more than other developing countries' cities have done. In other developing countries, literature shows, only the mega-cities have been in race to make and project themselves as globally competitive. In China, the idea of creating globally competitive cities pervades down to the small cities. An exorbitantly priced publication, "The Yearbook of China's Cities, 2002", brought out by China Research Society of Urban Development (2003), 162 cities have showcased themselves as prospective destination of investments in the coming future. In this, large cities have done better than smaller ones, who are following the steps of the large cities through diverting their priorities away from social services and welfare. This limited study of two cities, Beijing and Dongguan, suggests this to be happening. Study of many more cities should be able to tell us more about this phenomenon.

Comparing Beijing and Dongguan

Chinese urban system is highly unequal. This comes out by comparing Beijing and Dongguan, the former a national level city and national capital whereas the latter a prefectural level city, but in a province that has received very high investments.

Beijing is a service economy whereas Dongguan is a manufacturing economy (more than half the workers engaged in this sector). The lack of data on the distribution of employment among temporary population hinders our analysis as the proportion of temporary population is about 75 per cent in Dongguan. Beijing is a service economy with more than half the workers employed in this. This means that the former has less income inequalities across different sectors. In contrast, Beijing has very high inequalities in incomes across different sectors of the economy, indicating very high inequality in general in the city. Dongguan's economy therefore is more equitous than Beijing's economy. Beijing has seen continuous spree of construction, with 1 in 7 workers in the city engaged in construction. This is remarkably high proportion. Growth rate in this sector has been however less 1.98 per cent in 1997-02 period. Nonetheless, it is higher than overall employment growth rate. Concern in Beijing is that enough employment is not getting created.

Both cities have observed much higher growth rates of their GDP during the decade of 1990s as compared to growth rates in all cities together and also growth rate of the whole economy. The GDP growth rate of Dongguan is spectacular. At high GDP growth rate, Beijing is not generating adequate employment for her population whereas Dongguan is. And as per the recent newspaper reports, Dongguan is not getting workers as the economy can still absorb more workers than it is getting. Dongguan's economy is therefore employment generating whereas Beijing's economy is not. Further, both cities are in the top 20 with regards to FDI. But, in comparison to their GDP, the FDI received is low in percentage terms.

The UCMF size was 15.5 per cent that of the total fixed investments in Beijing and 8.7 per cent of the same in Dongguan. About 55 per cent of the fixed assets investments in Beijing in 2002 was in real estate (China, Ministry of Construction, 2003). If that amount is deduced from the fixed assets investments total amount then, in Beijing 34 per cent of the other than real estate investments is on infrastructure through UCMF. In Dongguan, this figure is just 10 per cent. In Beijing therefore infrastructure investments accounts a significant proportion of total fixed investments. Thus, any changes in the budgetary spending from 2001 onwards has to be analysed for impact of increased investments by the two cities on infrastructure development.

Beijing's population is 2.5 times that of Dongguan, its GDP is 4.6 times that of Dongguan, its fixed assets investments is 9 times that of Dongguan and size of UCMF is 16.5 times that of Dongguan in year 2002. With investments coming in for the Olympics, this gap between the two cities would widen except with regards to population.

Beijing is able to borrow more than Dongguan for urban infrastructure. The debt repayment on this may be passed on to Beijing residents in the future. How the debt repayment would be is not known. City's debt would go up in light of the new investments coming in for Olympics. Would the city pass on this debt to those population having low incomes given that Beijing has very high income-inequality? Beijing is receiving central assistance whereas Dongguan is receiving provincial assistance to the tune of 40 per cent of its receipts in UCMF. Central assistance to Beijing is not as high as provincial assistance to Dongguan. Beijing's collection from UCMT is higher than Dongguan. Recollect that this tax is levied on the industries and enterprises. It is also collecting higher proportion of additional fees, which are again levied on the enterprises. Thus, enterprises in Beijing are contributing upto 13 per cent of the UCMF for the city's infrastructure development. In Dongguan, this percentage is only 3. This is also because, Dongguan being a small city, depending on rapid growth of manufacturing, may be giving concessions to the enterprises to locate in the city, which Beijing does not have to do. On the contrary, recall that Beijing government is charging all types of fees to the enterprises, foreign (e.g. McDonald's) or national, which is leading to high share of self-raised funds in Beijing. Thus, Dongguan is not able to bring in cross-subsidies in the city. As a result, the city has to charge for the use of municipal utilities; the share of these charges is much higher in Dongguan than in Beijing. It has also to depend on provincial support. What has saved Dongguan is the city's ability to get FDI in the infrastructure sector because of its location. If that was not the case, the city would not have been able to develop its infrastructure to the level it has done. If a non-coastal city or a city that is not in Guangdong was taken for comparison, the FDI not being there, the size of UCMF would have been smaller.

All cities are spending between 30 to 60 per cent of their UCMF resources on transportation, a large proportion being spent on creation of road infrastructure than on public transport facilities such as subway, which are equally expensive. Beijing will have to increase its investments in transport infrastructure by 1.3 times than the current level to meet the needs for the Olympics. For this, Beijing is looking to new sources of funds such as Bonds and foreign investments. While the subway company would get the foreign investments, Beijing government would issue the bonds in the market on behalf of the company to get additional funds. Till 2002, the UCMF of the city had not issued any bonds.

About 74 per cent of the revenue in 2002 and 73 per cent in 2001, in Beijing came from enterprise tax, operation tax and value-added tax. Dongguan was getting 88 per cent of its revenue from taxes and 84 per cent from enterprise taxes. While Beijing still has SOEs, the enterprises in Dongguan are largely private sector. Dongguan shared 67 per cent of its revenues with the higher levels of government, while Beijing does not seem to have done so.

Dongguan was spending less than 1 per cent of total expenditure on social security. Beijing was spending much more share. Hence, citizens of Beijing are rather well protected with regards to social security provisions than citizens of Dongguan. In Dongguan, when expenditure on capital construction has increased in terms of percentage share, the share of all other expenditure heads, including on health, education, etc. has gone down. In fact, the share of health, education has gone down from 25 per cent in 2000 to 22 per cent in 2001 and 2002. Thus, one can argue that indeed the projects to enhance the Dongguan's image city has led to decline in city's expenditures on social sectors.

Equity Issues

Between the two cities, Beijing is more discriminatory against the migrants whereas Dongguan is welcoming to the migrants, particularly because of its manufacturing economy. Ofcourse, in both the cities, and in all cities across China, the system of *hukou* is discriminatory against the migrants, as rural *hukou* denies access to certain basic services such as health and education and welfare services to the temporary migrants.

In China's urban system, larger cities get preference over the smaller cities and designated cities by the national government get preference over the other cities in terms of powers and availability of finances. Thus, there are such large differences in investments and incomes between Beijing and Dongguan.

Beijing has become a service economy. This has brought in many low paying service jobs in the city on one hand and high paying service jobs on the other, increasing income inequalities within the city. Further, inspite of high economic growth rate of the city, the nature of growth is such that it is not able to generate adequate employment for her population. Dongguan does not have these concerns.

There is vast difference in level of health facilities between Beijing and Dongguan, the former having three to four times the facilities than the latter. This is the reflection of the inequality in the whole urban system that gives preference to the larger cities than the smaller cities, the former being picked up to link globally and showcase China or the province in the international economy whereas the latter being left to itself. Though Dongguan is a city receiving large volume of FDI and in that sense is also globally linked city, there is vast difference in facilities availability between Dongguan and Beijing, the latter having better facilities than the former.

There is vast difference between the two cities in terms of sources of UCMF. Smaller city such as Dongguan is forced to depend a lot on the provincial transfers, self raised funds, land transfer fees, and fees for the use of municipal utilities (user charges). Beijing is getting the enterprises to contribute a part of infrastructure fund, which Dongguan, in competition to attract manufacturing industries, is unable to do so. It is likely that there are many cross-subsidies built into the financing of public utilities in Beijing than in Dongguan. But, this may not continue in Beijing, given that city will have to service the debt due to borrowings for Olympics.

In city such as Beijing, emphasis is on creation of new roads than on public transport facilities. That is, investments and borrowing is for infrastructure from which the city would not be able to charge user fees. Road construction is creating increasing debt for the city residents. It is also leading to displacements of residences and small economic activities. Something that this auther has seen and has been told.

Beijing Olympics would require large funding from private and capital market sources. For subway system, it is stated that the city government would issue bonds and would also seek foreign investments. The subway system is owned and operated by a company, and it has a revenue model. Current subway ticket price is fixed rate of 3 RMB on any line for all distance. There are three subway lines, 1, 2 and 13. The first two are interconnected and have a ticket price of 3 RMB. Line 13 goes to suburbs and riding on it alone costs only 3 RMB. But, most people coming from suburbs to city centre would need to use subway line 13 along with line 2 or with line 2 and 3. In that case, the one-way ticket price would be 5 RMB per person. A person going to the city centre and coming back from the suburbs would therefore spend 10 RMB per round trip. If a person is working in the city centre and living in the suburbs would be spending 250 RMB per month on commuting if only subway system is used. In combination with public bus, as many people may have to do given that the coverage of subway line 13 is very limited, the cost would go up to 300 RMB per month. For an average Beijing worker, the average annual wage per capita was RMB 25,312 in 2003 (Beijing Municipal Statistical Bureau 2004), or RMB 2,109 per month. Use of subway line 13 in combination with line 2 or line 2 and 3 would mean spending about 12 per cent of their monthly income on just commuting! There is already a section of population in Beijing that is priced out of the use of subways and is using the buses, which are cheaper but more time taking.

The new issues of inequity in Chinese cities have to be paid attention to and researched in further details. Till now, much of research on cities, available in English language, is on investments, regional inequalities, urbanisation trends and patterns, city revitalisation projects, restructuring of SOEs, social security, urban governance with emphasis on functioning of street offices and neighbourhood committees, and infrastructure investments. There has been articles/papers arguing for increasing privatisation of infrastructure or inviting private infrastructure investments in the cities. There is very little work on what is happening within the Chinese cities, issues of city fragmentation and segmentation, migrant population and in particular unregistered migrants (very difficult to research), financial position of city governments, gender concerns, and other issues of equity emerging within the cities. Research on these areas would help correct the policies in place and reallocate financial and other resources in the cities.

NOTES

1. This research has been carried out with the support of Asian Scholarship Foundation (ASF) Fellowship. Author is thankful to David Westendorff for comments on the first draft, to Centre for the Study of Contemporary China, Tsinghua University, Beijing for hosting the researcher during the fellowship period and to Prof. Shen Yuan for Facilities extended from the Centre during my Stay in Beijing.
2. See Li (2001). Baranovitch (2003).
3. http://www.chinadaily.com.cn/english/doc/2004-08/25/content_368592.htm. *China Daily*, August 25, 2004. This report states: "He Zhi, an employee with a toy factory in Dongguan, Guangdong Province, left for the Spring Festival for his hometown in Southwest China's Sichuan Province earlier this year. He was told by the factory to try to bring back with him some more migrant workers. 'We were told that a reward of 50 to 100 yuan (US$6-12) will be granted for each person we bring in,' he recalled. However, not many succeeded, including He."
4. http://www.chinadaily.com.cn/english/doc/2004-07/01/content_344604.htm. An article in *People's Daily*, "Records of Deng Xiaoping's Shenzhen Tour", July 1, 2004.
5. National level data from; China, National Bureau of Statistics (2003).
6. Considering exchange rate being 1US$ = 8.26 RMB and using PPP$ to RMB ratio given in China, Human Development Report, pp. A2 as 1US$ = 2.0875 RMB for year 1999. (Source: Stockholm Environment Institute with United Nations Development Programme 2002).
7. Business Weekly, March 22, 2004, from website: http://www.chinadaily.com.cn/chinagate/doc/2004-03/22/content_317013.htm
8. Term used by Howard W. French (2004) in an article in New York Times.
9. http://www.chinadaily.com.cn/english/doc/2004-07/01/content_344604.htm. An article in *People's Daily*, "Records of Deng Xiaoping's Shenzhen Tour", July 1, 2004
10. GDP and population data from *Dongguanshi Tongjiju Bian (2003)*. In the tables later in the article, data is taken from China Statistical Press, 2001, the per capita GDP in 2000 comes to RMB 12,023.
11. If this figure is taken as the per capita GDP then, adjusted to PPP, the city's per capita GDP would be US$ 20,000, very close to per capita GDP of USA!
12. The China Statistical Yearbook, 2003, gives a figure of US$ 1,724.64 million foreign investment received by Beijing. This is 3.29 per cent of the total foreign investment received by China.

13. Based on China, National Bureau of Statistics (2003).
14. Data in this paragraph are from Guangdong Provincial Bureau of Statistics (2003).
15. The figures are quite fluid. It almost looks like the figures are thrown around. Each time a figure appears, it does not tally with the previously given figures. Even if the figure appears in a newspaper article on any day, it does not tally with the figures given in another article on the same day. Alternate estimates are from another article in *China Daily* that appeared on April 19, 2004. The total investment estimates also had appeared in the same paper on the same day but under different article. One could therefore take these figures as approximates.
16. (a) "Beijing Maps Out Olympic Economy", *China Daily*, April 19, 2004. Source: http://www.chinadaily.com.cn/english/doc/2004-04/19/content_324434.htm. and (b) Li (2004).
17. *China Daily*, Beijing, November 26, 2003, pp. 3.
18. For example, the report titled, "30,000 km highways to create economic hub", in Hong Kong edition of *China Daily*, June 2, 2004. http://www.chinadaily.com.cn/english/doc/2004-06/02/content_335770.htm
19. "A hospital exclusively for the use of people from Taiwan will be built in Dongguan, reports Guangzhou Daily". http://www.chinadaily.com.cn/english/doc/2004-08/20/content_367356.htm. *China Daily*, August, 20, 2004.

INCLUSIONS AND EXCLUSIONS IN STATE POLICY

7[1]

'FRACTURED' TERRAIN, SPACES LEFT OVER, OR CONTESTED

A Closer Look at the IT-Dominated Territories in East and South Bangalore

SOLOMON BENJAMIN, R. BHUVANESWARI, P. RAJAN and MANJUNATH

Occupation, Occupying, and 'Locality Histories'

In this chapter, we show how land is settled and occupied by various groups and a useful way to conceptualise this process is via what we term as 'Locality Histories'. We start with cases from the IT dominated parts of East Bangalore, followed by those in South Bangalore that adjoin Banergetta road.

Mainstream Interpretations

The heterogeneous territory in these parts of Bangalore at first glance can suggest both the 'hand' of the Nation State, and also the Global Market that builds and plans over the more indigenous settlements. The former could be easily associated with the SSI units and large tracts of Master Planned housing. In East Bangalore, this is followed by a more contemporary role in providing for the SEZ and large infrastructure in the form of the expressway and large dedicated plots for the Hi-Tech. This includes the showcase ITPL. The global market is equally if not even more visible. Some of the biggest global names are listed on the boards of the shiny granite and steel towers. The rows of Sport Utility Vehicles (SUVs as they are called) carting BPO employees are another indication, along with rows of shops selling global brand names.

Within this perspective, the contrast between the shiny reflective glass coated hi-tech towers and the more subdued slum settlements could be interpreted as the latter being remnants of a pre-IT period that would face erasure over time as 'development' or 'modernisation' proceeds. A visit to the settlements on the low hills around Whitefield reveals signboards of the *Dalit Sangarsh Samiti* (DSS[2]) and its three affiliates. This too could at first glance, signify another marker of space: The ability of some types of poor groups to claim and hold on and occupy space in what is obviously getting to be very expensive real estate. Finally, the spatial consequences of the 'good governance' agenda are also evident. Anti-corruption raids against some of the local municipal offices with their high visibility leave the main provider to be the state level agency to focus on high-grade infrastructure and services—yet another marker of territory here. Thus, a first visit and drive through this part of Bangalore would almost visually confirm what would be a narrative of modernisation and economic development. In this perspective, the erasure of the remaining 'unplanned', the slums, the fractures is almost complete—to open space with those of the planned service economy.

For those of a contrasting ideological perspective, travels through this landscape would suggest the inevitability of displacement—although where resistance via organised progressive movements some success for at least one section of the poor may appear. In such a view, a drive through most of the landscape may suggest it's fragility in confronting openly globally inclined policy with heavy State interventions in favour of big business. The fractures are evident—in the spatial divides in access to infrastructure and services driven deep by the imaginary of the global city; in effect, the death of localised contest, and thus perhaps an appeal to a much higher normative level of centralised planning, government, and perhaps even the judiciary.

From Ideological Divides to Locality Histories

We take a closer look and one that is more historical to discover how the above assumptions are misplaced. Our histories around the occupation of space as detailed below show how it is around complex jigsaw of occupation where at a particular point in time, different communities/ castes, including those of the IT and big business occupy and control land. For instance, and points we will return to, is that unlike first impressions, the occupation by poorer groups of space in what are now central high value and contested locations have *increased* and not decreased. As significant, although assisted at some point by organised Dalit movements, this has happened via municipal and village council centred politics that is often viewed as being messy. For instance, in one key location, the DSS among other groups were directly instrumental for only 100 families in being re-settled there. Today, there are more than 1,200 families and settlement keeps growing—assisted by local government action. As significant, locations where poorer groups have lost out claims, are those where the state and high levels of government used its monopoly access to centralised information on land titles to initiate acquisition—rather than use this to ensure 'rights' of the poor. These are two very quick illustrations to suggest the problems with first impressions, and especially those formulated along pre-conceived ideological assumptions.

From the perspective of 'Locality Histories' we arrive at several conceptual points:

First, that Locality Histories are hardly linear and constituted by various events, accidents. Just because we use the term 'locality' it does not imply an obsession with the 'local'. On the contrary, we attempt to move beyond the binary of 'local' and 'global' to look at the complex links between these in the way they find root in locality. A 'locality' view allows us to concretely analyse relatively global processes[3].

Second, in discussing contestation, we do not intend to portray poorer groups as 'victorious' or then, as passive victims. Instead we propose that understanding ways of claiming by a particular group to land, location and the use of particular institutional mechanisms helps to reveal the complex ways of power that underpin contestation. This approach helps to shift the conceptual frame outside the trilogy previously outlined. Thus, in doing so, we reject the positivism and attempt to be predictive, and also suggest concepts such as 'inclusiveness' are irrelevant in describing situations of contestation;

Third, in following Dharmakumar and Habib[4], we see land to be settled as a process of 'occupancy'. This allows us to witness the dynamic and within this, competing claims within a complex settlement process. This also helps us to develop conceptual frames to understand modes of competing occupancy underpinned by their political economies. For instance, in our earlier study on Karnataka's land digitisation programme, the *Bhoomi*, we argued how land title digitisation to reduce 1500 forms of recording land tenure to 256 allowed large players to take over territory (Benjamin et al 2005). These contrasted official claims that this would make land administration more efficient and spur 'economic development' (Benjamin et al 2005). It also however, co-related to what big business sees as significant policy paths to 'facilitate the market'[5]. Also, this conceptual frame allows us to treat 'ownership' not as absolute but one that is socially and institutionally determined. In doing so, it is useful to categorise various types of land as they open up claims for occupation as both housing and also economy (Benjamin 2004). East Bangalore, beyond the Airport and on towards Whitefield in the south, and ITPL towards it's north, is on first sight, characterised by large IT companies, a Special Economic Zone (SEZ), large high-end housing projects. Interspaced between these are zones of SSI factories—generally in a state of disuse. Finally, more hidden from view but certainly extending on inner roads, village settlements and on tops of three 'hills' or settlements on higher ground. These are slum like settlements. Our point of revealing this diversity, even if not bound in a common linear thread of storyline, is to move arguments of contest and context beyond ideological assumptions towards a more careful consideration of the locality of history. By locality of history, we specifically move beyond viewing the 'subalterns' as 'marginals'—even when particular groups 'loose out' in contest with richer groups or those closely connected with State 'policy making'.

Occupation Territories Around Whitefield

Keeping the centrality of land in its political rather than narrow functional aspects, we list in the text below, the main types of land tenure in the Pattandur Agrahara. Some of these, like those of *Inam* land detailed below, relate to the issue of how the state government's planning and industrial development institutions re-categorise a range of customary land tenure (or forms of claiming) to be 'government land' which in turn makes possible large mega projects. Thus, what makes for contested terrain is the complexity of land related politics between several types of local agents and agencies of Government like the KIADB. The contest here centre around customary land practices as part of one part of economy, and those who cater to big business, redefining land tenures as a way to 'play the global market'.

On the nature of information: In listing the complexities of claiming around customary land, our intention here is not specifically 'historical accuracy.' Rather it is to suggest the complexity of claiming and counter claims around customary tenures in very contemporary and now globally connected contestations.

Our key informant in these narratives is a young man of 30. He has worked with several NGOs, but also as his 'side business' deals in local land markets in the Whitefield area. Thus, it is significant to note that the information provided below has come not from archival records. Instead, it is from an actor and informant who 'plays the local land market especially '*Gomala*' or village common land. For such agents, information on customary tenures and the way they fit into contemporary regulations, and how this competes with acquisition under the new industrial promotion norms, is a matter of livelihood and survival. For instance, in our detailed sessions with him, his accounts of the way ITPL (the hi-tech IT Park showcased by the Government of Karnataka) was set up, was interspaced in discussion with narratives of customary tenure forms. One of the key tenure forms that kept repeating was that of various forms of *Inam* and *Gomala* land, suggesting that we explore this in greater detail as a way to understand the politics of occupancy. There are obviously several gaps and issues of consistencies in the narratives that follow. These are not those of memory but rather reflect the selective appropriation, persistence, and transformation and how in-grained systems of customary land claims are in a very contemporary politics shaped by global forces. Luckily for us, our informant is not burdened with the guilt of 'modernity' or 'traditionalism', or then, trapped in the world of binaries. He explains:

> "... *Inam* land includes *Thoti* or 'Village cultivated' land; *Inam* '*Neergante'* (land surrounding village tanks to protect the water body); *Poojari Inam* or Village religious land; *Kaji Inam* or Muslim individual or group as in Masjid; *Jodhidar Inam* or village accountant land assessor bestowed by Mysore Maharaja; Some of these lands also relate to a particular lineage that allow descendents to claim particular rights. For example in the case of *Thoti* land, a *thoti* is a person who is responsible for guarding the village."

During the king's time, he was also the person who made public announcements including for new births and deaths in the families inhabiting a particular village. For this function, the king usually allotted a certain portion of land, which would be passed on an inter-generational basis. If in a particular village, no such person is available, the king would have appointed a person from another village. This involves not just the use of land but also, as those belonging to the *Thoti* families, to receive a stipend from the government. There are additional details which define obligations between the State and particular groups. For instance, there are two types of land tenure within *Thoti* land. The first is *thoti manya* land and the second is *Naye manya*. The *Naye manya* land given to a person who has duties to bury animal carcasses in the village. His remuneration is given partly in salary and partly as cultivable land a mix of dry and wet land. Such lands have been allotted by the *Jodhidhar* and cannot be sold in the open market. Such conventions are not 'traditional' and at present, the *Thasildar* and the Assistant Commissioner can re-allot the land to the same person under "*re-grant*" scheme. Land 'regularised' under this *re-grant* scheme has a particular designated value but different from its market value. In the re-grant scheme, the Deputy Commissioner could stipulate the potential use of such land accompanied by 'time restrictions' as to when such land can be sold. This process involves the permission of the Assistant Commissioner and Deputy Commissioner.

At present, the owners of *Thoti* land had sold their land without any permission and such sales are not recognised by the court of law. In the instance of a civil case concerning such land, there is thus a strong possibility of the verdict being in favour of the original owners. There are numerous conflicts in both the villages over sale of such land resulting in people going to the court[6]. Another important land tenure category is that of '*Pujarimania*'. This refers to land allotted to the priests and as with *Inam* land, cannot be directly sold in the market, and requires an administrative process and the permission of Deputy Commissioner. As with the *Inam* land, there are cases where allottees have sold the land and their next generation have gone to court and got the land back. Another land tenure form is that of *Neerukanti mania*. As the name suggests (*neeru* = water), this land is given to those persons who were appointed to maintain tanks. His job was to ensure that other villagers do not encroach or use the tank wetlands for settlements, and also to regulate the water supply. Under the Mysore maharaja period, it was planned that each village should have a tank and a well for irrigation. The land owners, individual agriculturists would pay part of their produce for looking after the land[7]. There are other forms of special 'granted land' such as '*Dhobi mania*'—for those who wash clothes, and '*Akkasalya mania*' used for threshing, drying and storing the grains.

Our informant dwelled at length on the issue of '*Gomala*' land. He said that there are several types of land which include use as: (i) Burial ground; (ii) Tanks and wells for community water supply; (iii) *Gunduthoppu*—used by the villagers for resting—an equivalent of park and also used for grazing. Most categories of *Gomala* land have been taken up by farmer for cultivation—made possible by a state government order *'Begar Hukum'* via the *Thasildar* office Form No 22. Form 22 provides occupiers authority to cultivate land. Following the application under Form 22, the *Thasildar* can, via Form No 56 or 9 collect revenue from the *'Begar Hukum'* land. This system of regularisation of occupancy is similar to land used for urban settlement even before it is officially declared to be 'converted' to urban use. This is carried out via the sub-registrar's office, which then allows the local council—municipal, or *panchayat* to collect 'development charges' in lieu of infrastructure and services. If the occupant intends, this can be followed by a 'DC conversion'. This allows access to financial institutions and greater security of tenure. There are other land categories: *Kandaya* land or revenue land that is also used by farmers for settlement purposes. When transferred between generations these are termed as 'inherited' or *Swayajitha* (ancestral) or then *Pithajitha* (Father's land). In addition to occupancy based situations, *Gomala* land can be under particular 'grant' schemes be allocated to the SC/ST groups, or then for community amenities.

The main issue that emerges from such complexity of tenure is that various groups stake claims drawing on a variety of historical and contemporary processes. While many of these are centred around local conventions and institutions; the efforts to promote large mega complexes take support from competing rules and procedures of appropriation set within a rhetoric of modernisation. With this frame in mind, we now return to a closer look at this territory of East Bangalore. Given the complexity of the range of settlements, for the sake of simplicity, we categorise them as two sets of settlements: Those on the three hills and those of the valley. While the former generally include a range that house poorer and middle income groups, the latter include occupation of land for the Hi-Tech IT, high end housing and commercial complexes, and also the SSI designated areas.

East Bangalore—Hillside Occupation Around Pattandur Agrahara

The hillside, in East Banaglore, refers to three rock outcrops or '*guddes*'. The *gudde* originally was considered a sacred rock and used as a place of worship by people from 30 villages around, including Pattandur-Agrahara. At present, it has developed as a settlement and has various groups occupying the '*Gomala*' (village common/grazing) land claiming their places through a variety of ways. As the accounts below reveal, these are themselves inter-linked rather than being distinct events. The original settlement since 1895, was located in the land parcel survey no 54. This was part of five villages and had a large wooded area. Adjacent to this was the village common land (*Gomala* land) on survey numbers 52 and 53 that was occupied by an Anglo-Indian Dr. Brake (whose brother-in-law's daughter presently resides here). However, a rumour that this wooded area was occupied by sacred groves and also haunted, drove the families living there to shift to Agrahara in the Valley area. When these families shifted, the SC families re-occupied the *gramthana* land and named it as *Atti*. Another part of the *gramthana* land was occupied by other groups: Kurubas and Reddy's.

In the early to mid-1970s, the KIADB initiated a resettlement in several stages after that organisation began to acquire land in various locations in the larger district to set up the SSI industries. The resettlement colony was proposed on one of the three *guddes*. The other two *guddes* were occupied by private parties—one by the *'Sai-Baba'* ashram (a self professed 'Godman' and his followers with national and international influence), and the second by a private entrepreneur manufacturing and locally famous brand of ice-cream. The resettlement colony was proposed on a portion of the '*Gudde*' land allotted for cultivation purposes by the Deputy Commissioner in the 1960s. As a result, the formal title of the bulk of the area vested with the government as agriculture use (rather than as village settlement) and thus opening the land for acquisition under eminent domain for the proposed resettlement purposes. The lower slopes of the *Gudde* housed a few Anglo Indian families settled here since the time when Whitefield was developed by the British—dating back a hundred years.

In 1972-73, Rajgopal Reddy was the chairman of Whitefield *Panchayat*, with P. Krishnappa, the village *panchayat* member—both of the Janata Dal. In this period, Krishnappa subdivided the land into 600 sites and allocated them to devotees of Sai-Baba ashram, employees of the BHEL (Bharat Heavy Electrical Limited—a public sector undertaking), employees of a factory Alembic Glass, and also villagers in the surrounding area. To keep control on the land as well as the occupants, the allottees were not shown the actual sites that defined plot boundaries and road access thereby, the allottees had land titles but they did not know its exact location creating a great confusion. Some land was left open (unoccupied) as a result, and in this confusion, two *pourakarmikas* (lower level sanitation workers) employed in the Whitefield *Panchayat* erected thatch huts on the empty land. Until 1980, none of the plot owners settled in that place. In 1985, the allottees used to come and check their sites but did not construct any houses there as the site resembled a forest and no one took any initiative to clear it.

Part of these 450-500 plots was *Kharab* (degraded) land. In 1980, the *Ambedkar Sangha* (an association/field unit of the DSS) visited the area and saw this as an opportunity to develop a political presence in the area. The DSS group promoted, perhaps sold at a very nominal rate, and supported construction of additional huts—helping to settle in this way, most of the land allocated in 1972-73. Most of these groups came from other localities of Bangalore as well as other cities and towns. They formed the local unit of DSS. Also, by this time, some of the allottees had sold their land titles for throwaway prices ranging from Rs. 500-1000. By 1996, the settlement grew as people from the surrounding villages and factory workers erected huts.

While in 1990, there were only 90 huts on the rock outcrop whose occupation was supported by the DSS, by 1995, this had increased to 250 with tacit support of both the *panchayat* and town municipal council. Much of this increase was due to an inflow of migrant construction workers from Andhra Pradesh and Tamil Nadu, who first constructed huts for temporary stay but then never moved out.

By the late 1990s the settlement increased to 500 huts, some of which were quite well established belonging to lower middle-income groups. At present, there are 3,000 houses in the settlement. The streets today in contrast to the settlement of the late 1990s have streetlights, and there are also several 'mini-water schemes' that help service the area. All this civic improvement has come about from the consolidation of this area as a vote base. At present there are 4,000 voters within the settled area of the *Gudde*. This politics and occupation is significant given the overall area's real estate markets. Since 1995, they have been booming and highly contested. As we discuss subsequently, the *panchayat* and city councils are also under pressure from various parastatal agencies on issues of both finance and infrastructure. Despite this, the settlement has grown even when the DSS's own influence in the settlement process declined fairly early on in the process. The DSS over time split into several forms. There is a fracture in the party affiliation of DSS leaders—some belong to Congress, others to Janata Dal, and BJP. As a result of this the original DSS has split into PVC (Praja Vimochana Cheluvali—who supports Mavalli Shankar—the Congress state leader); KJS (Karnataka Janandolana Sanghathane—headed by Mariappa—state leader Janata Dal); and Muslim support Bahujan Samaj Party (BSP). Some of these, the KJS as we shall see below, played a key role in partnership with local municipal and village politics.

At present, the three *Guddes* have a mixed population. This is in terms of incomes and employment and also ethnic groups. For instance, the poor here include both older settlers but also recent renter occupants. There are also better off people who live in small plot dominated private subdivisions of the Revenue Layouts. There is now also a greater diversity of ethnic groups: many north Indians skilled and semi—skilled workers in various construction companies, employees renting space here who work in nearby software units. Presently, only half of the households are *Kannadigas*[8], almost a third being Telugu speaking, 10 per cent Tamils, and the rest include the Muslims, Malayalis, Gujarathis and Marathis[9]. This diversity is complimented by the Anglo Indians further down hill.

Looking even closer at particular parts of the *Gudde* reveals several sub-plots of occupation suggesting complex layers of occupation and contest. For instance, in 1980-81, part of the *Gudde* that was adjoining the land designated for resettlement, was occupied by members of *Thigala* caste (vegetable growers from Tamil Nadu) led by their leader. Their leaders also started to sell land to outsiders who were severely contested by leaders of *Dalit* group leading to a caste riots between *Thigalas* and the *Dalits*. Following this, an *Ambedkar Sangha* from a neighbouring village motivated other *Dalit* households there to occupy the *Gudde* in 1990. In parallel local leaders continued to sell land to people from various castes. To counter this, Dalit leaders mobilised people from their caste to settle in the *Gudde*. Simultaneously they attempted to mobilise 50 families of about 300 people to settle on the *Gudde*. In 1993 the then District Collector (DC) intervened. Accompanied by the *Thashildar* (village land officer appointed by the Revenue Department of the State Government) they visited the area and surveyed it. This was followed by an attempt to demolish the huts on Thigala and also the Dalit side. The DSS obtained stay order against the demolition. By 1993, following the stay order on demolition various ethnic groups had settled on particular locations facilitated by their particular '*sanghas*' (or associations) and in the case of the Dalits, the local wing of the DSS: Members of a *Kuruba* sangha occupied land to the left of the *Gudde* and also just below on the foot hills, with the Thigalas community on the right, the Dalits on the centre, and Kurubas on the left and on the lower slopes. Post 1995, the form of land supply shifted to more 'commercial' forms in the form of '*gramthana*' and revenue site layouts. Some locals claim that it was not until 1997 that their settlement begun on the slope. Till then, *Gudde* being considered a sacred site, yearly *Jatra* (ritual procession) by local villagers to it took place on the slopes every year.

Interview with Mr. Venkatesh, District President KJS

Venkatesh, aged 33 lives in Kadugodi near Belathur colony. Originally from Tamil Nadu, he became a political activist after witnessing conflicts between higher castes and the SC group. In 1996, he moved to Bangalore after an agitation against Deve Gowda, then a minister in the Karnataka government. He is the district president of the organisation since 2001.

The KJS's main agenda is to identify vacant land belonging to the government in the surrounding villages (Jigni, Arugatte, Adụr, Sidi Hosakote, Chittanayakanhalli Samandur, and Guddathi Yeranahalli) and then assist SC groups to squat on these lands. For this purpose, they have formed local *shakhas* (units). The general approach is, the KJS first visits a village, forms a *shakha* and then carries out a survey of homeless people. This is paralleled with stock taking of *Gomala* (common) and *Gramthana* (Village common) land. With this information, the SC groups in that village are motivated to occupy the government land. While they usually target government land, this can also include land plots owned by the higher castes that are under legal conflicts. In the case of latter, they also take to legal recourse by filing a petition in the court. Their other focus area is to help SC groups get basic services and infrastructure, and for slum dwellers to get ration cards. At present, members of KJS have got membership in the local gram *panchayat* and in the City Municipal Council (CMC). In the election held in 2006, their state office had asked the Dalits to support Janata Dal (S) candidate.

Venkatesh provided a vivid illustration of the type of actions they are involved in and how deep is their interaction with the local government to support their activism. In his own village, he found a particular land parcel controlled by the government that was acquired by Hosakote Taluk Board. While on some of the land, a college was constructed, part of the land still remained vacant. From the latter, part of the land was also allocated for temple and school. The vacant land was however occupied by a group of dominant SC caste members. Venkatesh then mobilised the poorer SC groups to come and occupy this land by erecting 27 thatch huts. They then upgraded these huts to Asbestos Sheet or tiled roofed houses, and then filed a case under the *'Akrama—Sakrama'* clause to regularise land as a way to access electricity and other services. In the meantime, Venkatesh, via his contacts in the *panchayat* made sure that infrastructure facilities were extended to these huts. While this happened, the state government passed an order to provide free electricity to the residents in non-notified settlements. With this order in hand, Venkatesh motivated the residents to submit a memorandum to the executive engineer at the Taluk level to implement the order. However, at the instigation of the person who was originally controlling the land, the higher level *gram-panchayat* (federation of village councils) wanted to demolish these huts for which it obtained DC order to the effect. The higher level *gram-panchayat* came twice and demolished some of the huts that were re-built. Following this in 1998, Venkatesh along with 27 residents and KJS staged a '*dhrana*' (or 'sit in') in the Tahsildar's (*panchayat* officer) office. Further attempts of demolition were stopped after that action. Following that the residents used their own finances and connections with *panchayat* elected persons to get ration cards, electricity, and further upgraded their houses. Such actions and experience helped Venkatesh get into politics and specifically with the KJS whose help he had sought in this matter.

The KJS went into the *Gudde* in 1997. The main agenda of the KJS was to regularise the portion occupied by 97 huts. To do this, they reorganised the huts, allotted plots and laid the roads so that this would confirm to the routine regularisation procedures after the registering of this layout as 'non-agricultural' land. At that time, they re-allotted the *Pattas* (titles) to those occupying the sites. Some of the original allottees, who did not come into this area, lost out in this process. In 1999 to 2000, the government issued the *Akrama-Sakrama* orders to also avoid the illegal tapping of public utilities including electricity. The KJS motivated residents to obtain legal connection to install electric meters and 150 houses obtained regularisation and connections. Another of their actions here related to dealing with water crises. Prior to 1996-97, the area had a severe water problem. Residents needed to pay ½ a rupee per pot. The *panchayat* attempted to supply water via tractors but this too was uneven. Following this, the KJS staged a *dhrana* in front of DC's office and after negotiation, the DC sanctioned one bore well. The KJS ensured that the order stipulated that it's construction be near the *Gudde*, against other politicians with a constituency of villagers in the valley who wanted the bore well placed near the Pattandur tank. Following such actions, the entire area was added to the City Municipal Corporation of KR Puram. This act would help 'settled' area now to be declared as 'urban' and thus with easier access to basic civic amenities. The KJS with their close links to the CMC helped in this process. At present there are 3 major voting blocks with each block having between 1,500-3,500 votes.

While the above mentioned actions with the KJS helped settle the area, other informants note that it was only after 2000 that the bulk of the area settled. This was paralleled by local politicians becoming part of a growing market of real estate aimed at the lower and lower-middle income groups. Today, poorer people occupy sites on the lower slope, while on the plateau where plots are of regular size, there are richer groups. The total population is in the range of 9,000, with a voter's list of about 3,500 to 4,000. As a further illustration, this informant gave prices for a plot of 20 feet by 30 feet over the years as follows:

2000: Rs. 15,000 (lower slope) and Rs. 70,000 (upslope)
2001: Rs. 30,000 (lower slope) and Rs. 90,000 (upslope)
2002: Rs. 50000 (lower slope) and Rs. 1 lakh (upslope)
2003: Rs. 1 lakh (lower slope) and Rs. 3 lakhs (upslope)
2004: Rs. 3-4 lakhs (upper slope and slightly less on lower slope)

Rents for houses located on top of the hill range between Rs. 500-2,000 and this demand started from 2001. In 2001-02 a building with a Asbestos Sheet roof with access to water facility would rent out at Rs. 500 to Rs. 1,500 per month while one with two bedrooms and a more permanent cement roof would cost between Rs. 1,000 to Rs. 1,500; Owners do not prefer rent on formal rental agreement due to the fact that the ownership records are unclear and hence the tenants might permanently stake claim to the house. There have been four such incidents in the area. Thus, the system adopted, as most parts of Bangalore, is to have an 'advance' based '*bhogee*' which is a 2 ½ to 3 year lease system. This system carries an 'advance' that ranges between Rs. 25,000 to Rs. 30,000 for one with a permanent cement roof, and Rs. 2,500 to Rs. 10,000 for houses with an asbestos cement roof.

A highly commercialised process dominates the major part of the settlement process even if exact property titles are not clear or established. This paradox is in part related to the politics of occupation where 'vote bank' politics is closely related to interventions to improve physical infrastructure and to stabilise de-facto claims. These areas have contributed to the political fortunes of people who are today significant political leaders-building their careers on a political economy of local land markets. For instance, the *Gudde* settlements presently with a voting list of 4000, was till 1996, under the Whitefield *Gram-panchayat* and under Varathur MLA constituency. After 1996, it was placed as part of the more powerful Mahadevpura city council and recently it has been formed as Bangalore East Taluk MLA constituency during the Minister A. Krishanappa's period. The MLA and now Minister Krishnappa has been elected as village *panchayat* member since 1960. It is significant that in the more recent 2003 state elections this MLA is said to have suffered a serious political setback since the real estate funding moved towards a mega project circuit to cut-off local political claimants.

In all the narrative around the *Guddes* shows that its politics of development, even if seemingly messy is a complex process that goes beyond an 'organised social movement'. Even in the case of the Dalit groups, key role played by the KJS was very much like a '*sangha*' whose leadership played a complex lobbying and strategic role. In this contested terrain, *sanghas* strategise their politics in consultation with local politicians from the *panchayats*, town council and also higher level ones. At first glance, such contests seem highly localised and mostly related to ethnic groupings in their claims over the *Gudde* land. It is portent to keep in mind the type of occupation. More than 90 per cent and increasingly, settlement is getting closely linked to the tacit support of the town council (and earlier the *panchayat*). The settlement process, further on, gets closely linked to financial arrangements related to the extension of basic services and infrastructure and the complexities of both de-facto and officially announced regularisation processes: 'Regularisation' also includes at times more official announcement of 'opening of registration' of converted and non-converted agricultural land, and extension of civic amenities like that of electricity. At most other time, it is a day to day action in procedures of local government to extend services.

The politics of occupation then points to a much wider political process of local government. At an institutional level, these politics contests with that of much higher level agencies that have the backing of the state government and now increasingly globalised financial institutions. If so, such a consolidation of 'regularisation' based politics does not end with the sanction of occupation, but rather, it opens a window to funding of infrastructure and services. These are claims being made in a political context where funds are allocated to high-end infrastructure and services. If for instance, the political space in the larger region were declining, one would hardly have witnessed the expansion of the settlements around the *Gudde* given especially, their dependence on public water supply and electricity. Instead, one would have seen stagnation in the settlement process. If the DSS connected groups had remained along the path assumed to be a 'social movement' than their actions could hardly be sustainable when the immediate needs were highly materialistic; of land, of the need to operate via local municipal and village politics rather than opposition to these. Thus, in many ways, a closer look at the occupation of the *Guddes* suggest the consolidation of a type of politics that is normally dismissed as being non-transparent, un-democratic, and the one dominated by 'Clientalism Politics'. This issue of conception becomes clearer when we look at occupation processes in the 'Valley' as described below.

East Bangalore—Settling the Valley

Accounts of settling the valley reveal a more explicit 'hand of the State'. This is in the way it makes way for the globally connected IT via the institution of the KIADB. We focus on the settlement of Pattandur Agrahara that originated in the 1950s. The older settlement is the Agrahara about 100 years old. In 1950, before the formation of the Karnataka state, when this area was still within the jurisdiction of the Mysore Presidency, the settlement started with 10 families being allotted '*Jodidhar*' land (or land from the 'royalty'). In addition, some SCs families occupied land upslope away from the main village, naming their settlement as *Atti*. By 1965, this had increased to 65 families of which 10 were SC while the rest were of the Kurubas and Gowdas. In 1970, the SC houses increased to 30, and by 1975, another 15. The Gowdas increased by 20 families. These increases were not really new settlers but a result of marriages and family growth. Most houses in the village were thatched huts while that of the landed castes like the Gowdas were mostly with Mangalore tile roofs. Much of this growth was by way of occupying land within the village settled area or just beyond on 'revenue' land.

In the late 1970s however, the settlement's growth was influenced by specific interventions by the state government. While these did not form the bulk of growth in any way, they did bring specific interventions not just on housing but also civic amenities. It also reflected the entry of state level politics in addition to those that were focused at the *panchayat* level. In 1978, 28 houses were constructed for SC under *Ashraya* scheme. In 1980, the Congress government in power allocated 25 SC families sites that measured 30′ by 40′. These were occupied by extended and growing families from the original settlers living as joint families. For example, if there are three brothers in a house, two of them moved out and got these houses under the scheme. Similarly, houses and free sites were distributed to Gowdas as well. By 1990, people began upgrading their Mangalore and thatch roof houses to those with Asbestos Cement sheet under a scheme promoted by the Vijaya Bank in 1991. The Bank 'adopted' this Agrahara to provide loans for petty shops, bullock loans, and to also obtain electric connections. They also gave loans for smokeless *chula* (cooking stove) for 15 houses, and motivated villagers to send their children to school. Even till this time, development in the settlement was slight with some increases mainly due to family extension and growth rather than new comers. The Gowda families increased to 135.

One could argue that such 'targeted' programmes from a 'social' perspective and from a administrative driven planning process served to 'clear' local territory of competing claims over economy, over space and location, and in effect the political and institutional structures by which these were established. Thus, it was with the advent of large master planning in the area, after the KIADB had effectively re-organised tenure forms, that the development occurred. This allowed, as we discuss below, the Singapore Technology Park, (or the ITPL), and as a spur, to demand for residential and other IT commercial space that eventually paved the entry for large-scale developers. With them, about five years later by 2000, territory opened for high-end finance circuits connected to global institutions. These in turn, a decade later, saw increased funding by major international institutions like the World Bank's IFC, US Aid, the ADB, and JBIC. These institutional players emerged as part of an effort of corporate led privatisation of basic amenities like water, and other infrastructure projects. A closer look at the ITPL is particularly rewarding from this perspective.

Settling the IT

The land on which ITPL is located was initially "Agrahara *Inam*" land. In 1954, 5 acres of this land was granted by the then Diwan of Mysore Presidency as free land for agriculture to the SC and ST residents of the surrounding villages. These groups had paid taxes since 1954. As the land was granted by the then Diwan, the state government formed a few years later, refused to extend or reinforce their title with specific deeds. At present ITPL covers 33 acres of land, of which 18 acres are the government lands and 13 acres are the private lands that belonged to a single owner—an Anglo Indian named Major Shitijh Benjamin. The major sold a portion of the land to another private manufacturer who constructed a factory manufacturing honey. In the remaining land the major had a plant to recycle water. After 1991, the valley area saw the entrance of large scale developers that catered to NRIs. This started with 'Ajit Mansion'—the first real estate operator to come to Whitefield and the first to negotiate with local farmers. The KIADB who had first started to acquire land for SSIs in the area in the 1970s, intensified their acquisitions from 1984-86. This was initially for the SSIs but later on, some of this land was converted to an 'Export Promotion Zone' (EPIP). In the early 1990s, part of the EPIP was allocated as an IT park to form the ITPL. In

1993, the KIADB had initially fixed the compensation at Rs. 300,000 per acre. This was eventually increased to Rs. 1,200,000 when conflicts over compensation started in the area. The then MLA—Ashwath Narayana Reddy bargained on behalf of the farmers and increased it to Rs. 12 lakhs. This decision immediately impacted land markets and soon NRIs and foreigners from Singapore, Malaysia invested in the area around the existing settlements like Pattandur Agrahara. Plans for locating IT industry here was initiated in 1993-94 when Veerappa Moily was Chief Minister and P.V. Narashima Rao the Prime Minister. This was soon after the 'liberalisation' of the economy in 1991. At that time, there was an official delegation from Singapore who negotiated with the Prime Minister and following it, with the Chief Minister of Karnataka. Once an account of these discussions was published in the newspapers, real estate agents started to visit this area. This pushed the land market price upwards and also the demand for high end development. In 1990-1991, an acre of land was priced at Rs. 150,000. By 1992-93, it had increased to Rs. 250,000 and by 1994 jumped to Rs. 2,500,000 and by 1995 to between Rs. 5,000,000 to Rs. 8,000,000 and even Rs. 10,000,000 an acre! Here this spectacular increase in values was paralleled by an attempt of establishing strict control of the type of players in the 'market' to be mainly larger private corporate and institutional players. This was via the planning process, regulations, and institutional procedures to move out smaller land developers who till then aligned with local councils to settle and develop land.

The ITPL, with Ratan Tata as its president was constructed with a unique partnership: 40 per cent Government of Singapore; 35 per cent Government of India; 25 per cent—Government of Karnataka (GoK) with profits shared proportionately. The GoK's contribution came from the KIADB who offered the land as share capital. The national and state elections saw the Congress government loosing power and in Karnataka Deve Gowda became Chief Minister. One story is that as a way to re-align the arrangement of interests between the real estate and political circuits he increased the registration value of property transactions. This act dissuaded foreign investors to route money into real estate. This was paralleled by problems in getting stamp papers for registration of the land transactions. Overtime, it emerged that Karnataka state was amidst one of the largest scams in the country, the stamp-paper scam, the main accused in the case who is in jail, accusing all the major political party leaders to be in league with him in the heydays of the scam. And, this scam had to do with the land transactions in the eastern and northern peripheral areas of Bangalore city, which was dominated by big business of Bangalore.

There were still more acquisitions by the KIADB, this time focusing on more interior plots. A branch office of KIADB was started there in 1995 as part of the emphasis on 'single window clearances' and special incentives for investments into mega projects. This was paralleled by the construction of the expressway that linked the complex to Bangalore city and the airport. Thus, by 1995, the MNC General Electric (labs), the Sai Baba hospital and also the Vaidehi hospital had around 400 acres allotted to them. Two persons, one a former Indian Revenue Services (IRS) officer with the GoK and another within the KIADB recollect that the KIADB provided huge subsidies to GE, the Sai Baba hospital, among other large ventures like the Toyota Kiloskar in Bidadi (in the city's western periphery). This included 300 acres of what were originally '*Jodidhar*' land, and the rest of the 100 acres being *Gomala*. However, there was not much infrastructure development and the EPIP zone was not occupied till 2000. Prior to acquisition, both types of land '*Jodidhar* and *Gomala*' were claimed by it's occupants who were mainly small farmers. These groups were not clear of the tenure and assumed that all land was *Gomala* to assume that eviction by the State using the land acquisition law would be difficult. However, three factors went against them. First, rather than the land acquisition act, the Government used the KIADB act—far more powerful and efficient. Second, much of the land was *Jodidhar* and thus appropriated to be under state control as it technically had it's single claimant in the '*Jodidhar*' (as the protector of the land) as missing. This allowed for even easier acquisition. Third, the mega projects had huge state backing with high visibility international funding and in the case of the ITPL, the state government was a 'partner' and it's contribution being via the land acquisition agency the KIADB! Also, this was a time when the IT elite and their partnership in large developers seeing a possible market in returnees NRIs, had consolidated their political clout. The government since 1995 had instituted 'single window clearances' and in parallel, the central government had offered significant fiscal incentives to the IT. Paralleled with this, were the growing regulations against small developers and stalling of revenue land development by banning registration of its sale.

Whitefield thus emerged as a location for high-end services. This emerging real estate market along with public attention to the ITPL led to the rapid development of Pattandur Agrahara in 1995. The KIADB was also active in promoting extensive land acquisitions for larger garment and SSI factories. Many garment industries had re-located to Bangalore from Bombay as a result of the riots there following the bomb blasts of 1992. The setting up of garment units in this and other areas of Bangalore especially in its west, spurred real estate markets. In Pattandur Agrahara, much of this was in terms of rental markets for the incoming industrial workers within the SSI and Garment factories. An interview with a *panchayat* member and senior politician is revealing of the political circumstances of the development in this area and the kind of contests.

An Account of Pattandur Agrahara by Krishnappa-Ashraya Committee Member of the Panchayat

Krishnappa, 42 years old, entered politics at the time of Indira Gandhi's prime-ministership. He still remains with the Congress party and professes his aim is to work for the upliftment of the SC/ST community. His main effort is to get them infrastructure facilities as well as to help them access education. His other main objective is to ensure that SC/ST people access the 18 per cent grant scheme of the government where by funds are allocated for pro-poor public works. His area of assistance to SC/ST groups includes two city municipal councils Mahadevpura with its 31 wards, and the KR Puram CMC with 35 Wards. During his tenure as *panchayat* member, between 2001-2003, he constructed 300 houses for the SC/STs that were allotted to widows, handicapped, and orphans in addition to those SC/ST families below poverty line. While he keeps a focus on SC/STs, he also helps other families belonging to any caste below poverty line. In 2003, he had issued ration cards, got bus facilities—2 buses from Agrahara to majestic and Shivaji Nagar. Since, 2004, all developmental works in both the CMCs have come to a standstill. His activities go on, but, in a constrained way. He then formed a *sangha* called '*Ambedkar Sasharatha Samithi*' and also started a library for the youth in the village. Krishnappa's future plans are to upgrade open drain to an underground drainage, from the ITPL site to Nellurhalli. At present, this open drain breeds mosquitoes leading to large-scale health problems in the settlement. This is also important as presently the wastewater from the ITPL and large and famous hospitals such as the Satya Sai Baba and Vaidehi, dump their wastewater into the Nellurhalli tank. Another plan, being a member of *Ashraya* committee, is to obtain Cauvery water and to distribute '*hakkupatra*' or land title deeds for the residents of the Gutte. He views water issues as being critical. In the beginning, the population was less and people did not feel the adverse impact of the wastewater. But now that the population has increased and the settlement has extended up to the tank bed, water problems have emerged. The *panchayat*'s approach is also to evolve an internal governance system for conflict resolution rather than the present situation where residents have to turn to the courts.

A view of the wider territory in this area shows a variety of land uses that include the ITPL, but also other large industrial plots. As mentioned earlier, in 1992, the land was selling at Rs. 15,000 an acre. With the above mentioned institutional changes, the land prices increased to between Rs. 500,000 to Rs. 10,000,000 an acre by 1994-95. One example here is that a high-end layout on a 15-acre plot of land. The land developer purchased the first parcel of land for Rs. 35 lakhs per acre and then within three months the second parcel's price rose up to Rs. 40 lakhs; and then finally increased to Rs. 50 lakhs to Rs. 70 lakhs. Thus, every three months saw a jump of Rs. 20 lakhs per acre! There were also substantial increases in small plot prices. In 2000, a plot of land measuring 30 feet x 40 feet was priced at Rs. 300,000 or Rs. 250 per sq ft. By 2004, this had increased to a square foot rate of Rs. 450 per sq. ft in the same locality.

It is important to note that land markets are heterogeneous and shaped by a variety of non-economic factors. Thus, they need to be seen in the context of their institutional dynamics and also the type of actors these promote or demote. Stories of such increases attracted developers and financiers from other parts of Bangalore and also, much larger ones from all over India, and especially Bombay and Delhi. Real estate emerged as being severely contested—where smaller developers as is the norm, formed partnerships with smaller and medium sized farmers and local politicians—moving local councils to extend basic infrastructure and services in lieu for 'betterment charges'. In contrast, larger developers including those from Bangalore catered to more global markets in alliance with larger financial institutions (also invested in by international capital). For these groups, the actions of smaller developers, farmers, and local councils, who by extending services increased de-facto tenure, were competitors. Given the stress on Master Planning as a way to make Whitefield a global location, it was relatively easy to portray such competition as 'un-planned, encroachers' that came out of corrupt 'vote bank' politics. The access of larger developers and financiers to policy circuits in senior administrators and state level politicians opened up significant lobbying power, where the rhetoric of turning Bangalore into a 'Singapore' fed such a fervour. Thus, it is hardly surprising that significant changes in policy shifted real estate terrain in favour of larger players. Witnessing such price increases, the largest 4 developers, catering to the IT and with excellent business relationships with higher levels of government sought two strategies: first, as an argument for the speedy development of mega projects, they sought the KIADB with its modified land acquisition procedures, to acquire large parcels of land on their behalf. The issue here is not just a discounted price available via State acquisition (undertaken in public purpose) but, rather, seeking a way to avoid being involved in complex rounds of negotiation with farmers (who could form a consortium to hike prices). Second, to access, via a modified use under the new policy thinking, pre-existing large plots that were earlier designated as the SSI units. Thus, the fact that this part of Bangalore had the Mahadevpura industrial area housing SSI and older industrial units (now facing a crisis given the increased real estate markets) proved to be a substantial boon to larger developers and their internationally connected financial institutions.

The economic and political clout of the large developers within policy circles, and the substantial profits to be made, would at first glance suggest a rapidly declining presence of smaller real estate developers, and with it fewer locational and spatial openings for relatively poorer groups. To an extent, this is apparent in Whitefield. Even so, what makes for a contested terrain, despite such power, is the issue of the persistence of a relatively quiet politics of occupation in and around the settlements. This is not to say that real estate prices have not increased. In fact the severe threat to large corporate capital has come from within a core element of the commodity process: land development. What is also significant is that such a process has been severely un-settling of 'property' that from a perspective of corporate control, would like to be framed as being homogenous, and given the way large developers are financed, to be 'digitally tradable'. Instead this commodity process is located in the occupation of territory within and surrounding existing settlements like Pattandur Agrahara and *Gudde*. These are territories that exist in a 'grey zone' of mixed land use, semi-rural and most important perhaps, characterised by diverse tenure regimes. This greyness of tenure related to forms of occupancy are in turn, reinforced by diverse forms of 'regularisation'[10]. Together, they strengthen 'de-facto' tenures to underpin the process of 'un-settling property regimes'. It is not easy to 'measure' the extent of such un-settling territory due to its subtle nature and difficulty visually to distinguish between 'older' and more contemporary forms of occupation. To understand this more clearly, it is useful to return to the type of economic expansion that happened in this area in the early to late nineties.

In, 1990 there were 15 large SSI factories here. By the late 1990s, almost 50 large companies had moved into this area spurring high demand in the construction industry. By 2002 there were almost 200 SSI and larger firms and numerous smaller ones. One needs to understand the entry of large firm and globally connected firms also by their complex localities of what is a numerous but relatively hidden work force. In doing so, the argument is not what economists of either ideological extreme focus on: the extent of employment within the IT and high end, versus the 'lower end' service class. Such economic rationalities feed into, among other ways of conception, into that of the binary of inclusiveness and exclusiveness. Instead we suggest a more politicised approach aimed to lay out the framework of contest more clearly. Thus, what is of central concern is commodity centred 'occupation'. Here, as a response to both 'urbanisation' and also the global process, territorial occupation in-effect, signifies a hydra like cancer to eat the very territory sought out by the global capital. As in the case of the *Gudde* mentioned earlier, one indication comes from the operation of real estate markets that forms a key marker—rather than a 'marker' being a social movement that is visible as public demonstration, or then, public events of 'participatory budgeting' as witnessed in Brazilian towns and cities.

For instance, in response to the growing multi-nationals invested IT and high-end residence complexes, a German company 'Group 4' located itself in the Whitefield area. The company employed mostly migrants from other parts of Karnataka and India. Some of these were more skilled, being ex-army employees and thus by 1997-98, monthly rents jumped from Rs. 1,000 to even touch Rs. 5,000. This was in part, since companies had a policy to provide/reimburse housing expenses of senior management. However there was such a high demand for rental housing in locations accessible to the IT complexes in the area that it did lead to a point of saturation. However there were wider impacts. Our informant, who actively plays such real estate, provides vivid descriptions of the increasing types of occupation from the type of uses, the types of real estate markets, and entry of a variety of ethnic groups. Pattandur Agrahara like other settlements in this area, developed diverse rental markets that includes some that went 'up-market'. Others, soon after 1990, catered to migrants from other states—Tamil Nadu, other regions of Karnataka, Andhra Pradesh, Kerala, Bihar, Orissa, U.P., Manipur, Meghalaya who settled in this area. These in-coming groups sought employment predominantly in construction industry (contract for tiling, carpentry, plumbing, masonry), in security agencies, as '*ayahs*' (house maids), as garment workers, and also vehicle drivers. Most of these groups stayed in rental houses in the small plot dominated 'revenue' and '*gramthana* layouts'. For instance, in 1993-94, at the height of the property boom, our informant points to many houses that had 'country' tiles being upgraded to have Asbestos Cement sheet ones. Rents moved up from Rs. 150-250 per month to Rs. 350—Rs. 400 per month. As elsewhere, these were also characterised by complex forms of leasing—a '*bhogee*' that is a 2 ½ to 3 year lease initiated with a fixed lump sum amount given to the 'land lord' that takes the place of monthly rent. This helps to free up capital for other investment and especially to buy land.

We now present local 'stories' that show the intensity and diversity of economic activity. While the better off obviously make huge surpluses, what are of interest is the connections to land and economy across groups. Such accounts compliment other cases that we have detailed in previous cases—those in the 'slum' settings of West and South Bangalore, and also studies of Chronic Poverty in central city areas. In Pattandur Agrahara there are presently three broad income groups. The high-income groups are farmers with more than 10-20 acres that have constructed between 20-30 houses for renting. Here, each person would earn at least Rs. 120,000 per month from renting alone. The common 'trajectory' would be for such large farmers to sell land for Rs. 80 lakhs an acre, to then invest in richer agricultural land locations further away. Another variation for this group would be to sell their agricultural land and invest partly in rental housing in the extra land available near their residential settlement. Other purchases in consumption items would include cars worth Rs. 5-10 lakhs. These farmers, with such large parcels however, would be relatively very few—usually not more than 10 per cent of all the land owning classes.

The Case of Kemppaiah below Provides a Useful Illustration. Kemppaiah Aged 80

Before Whitefield developed into an IT node, Kemppaiah was involved in both dairy and agriculture. Between 1950-1970 he sold 200 litres of milk a day to various traders in Shivaji Nager, Ulsoor, Cox town, and Cantonment (*Dandu*). He also had business links with Mumbai and stayed in that city for 5 years trading gold and silver. After that he returned back to Agrahara, and began to sell garlic and onions in *santes* (local farmers' markets) in the surrounding areas on various days of the week: in KR Puram on Tuesday, in Kadigiodi on Thursday, in Varthur on Sunday, and in Hoskete on Friday. In these *santhe,* he used to have a turnover of 25-30 bags each of 60-80 kgs. Due to his trading and business activities he knows Bangalore city very well. In 1970, he was the first to construct a bore well in his fields of 7 acres in the village. Kemppaiah grew mulberry plants for sericulture in 3 acres. This allowed him to sell silk cocoons that have a cycle of 40 days, and in 1970, got a very high profit of Rs. 25,000 every 40 days. This was apart from a good income from agriculture and his other trading activities. In 1980, he invested these profits into five houses given out on rent for Rs. 350 month giving him an income of Rs. 1,500 month. In 1994, he was upgrading these rental units to increase his income. His land being along the main road found many buyers in 1994. In 1995, at the age of 70, Kemppaiah stopped both the mulberry and *sante* trading and sold his 3 of the 7 acres to private developers. The first acre was sold for Rs. 55 lakhs, the second for Rs. 65, and the third, for Rs. 80 lakhs. During this time, there were weekly fluctuations in land prices. Part of the proceeds he has invested in buying 40 acres of land in Old Madras road in Kolar—a smaller town about 40 km from Nelluralli in the Whitefield area. For this, he paid Rs. 35,000 per acre. In that land of 40 acres, he has dug a bore well and is presently cultivating it. In Pattandur Agrahara, he has invested in 8 buildings—all given out for renting. Of these two large building were built for Rs. 25-30 lakhs, in one of which, the ground floor is occupied by his family. The first floor is giving him a rent of Rs. 18,000. The rest of the three are built for about Rs. 5 lakhs each and are rented out to 5-6 families. From these 18 families he is getting an income of Rs. 25,000. From the remaining building of Rs. 25 lakhs, Kemppaiah gets a rental income of Rs. 25,000-30,000. He recalls that when he constructed his first rental unit of 5 rooms, these had an asbestos cement sheet roof. He has not made many changes in these buildings. Earlier he was getting Rs. 1,500 from those rooms, now he is getting Rs. 4,000. Most of the money he has is invested in new buildings.

Kemppaiah has four children. The first is the local labour contractor taking up civil works from the CMC and Gram panchayat. He employees about 40 local people, and get an income of Rs. 5,000-6,000 net per month after expenses. The second son supplies water to the factories in the areas surrounding the ITPL, drawing from the bore well in Nelluralli. He also owns a tractor for this purpose. He has employed two families, and after expenses, he earns Rs. 8.000 to Rs. 10,000 per month. Kemppaiah's third son died but his wife is given the responsibility of the financial and management of the entire joint household's finances. Kemppaiah however, controls the overall finance. His fourth son a B-Com graduate has joined as a supervisor in a MNC and earns Rs. 15,000 to Rs. 20,000 per month. Kemppaiah has also donated money to the local ashram and also the temples. During the festival time, he donates food and clothes to the temples. For these social functions he spends Rs. 50,000-75,000 per year. He says that none of the sons have any 'bad habits' or are 'alcoholic'. He himself is very frugal and does not waste any money. He belongs to the SC caste and has a lorry, two Maruthi 800 cars, and 3 two wheelers that are given on rent.

From Kemppaiah story, we can see the intensive involvement with real estate and how this inter-mixes with a variety of trade and business links. These are not restricted to just Whitefield, but extend into Bangalore. Looking at other cases, we find similar engagement with a variety of economic circuits but centrally land and land markets, although of a smaller scale. The middle range of farmers owning between 5-10 acres have also purchased sites in other places and invested in rental properties. They earn between Rs. 30,000-50,000 per month. As Whitefield developed manufacturing and commerce, this groups have also invested in small passenger and transport vehicles like 'metadors' (vehicles with carrying capacity of 10-15 people), invested into local finance and well as in some cases, into funding workshops and petty business.

Krishanappa Age 65 Years

Krishanappa, a resident of Pattandur Agrahara completed 'SSLC' between 1950/60. He joined Alembic glass factory after that and was given permanent employment in the factory where he worked for 5 years. At that time he also got an opportunity to join HAL, in its helicopter division, and took Voluntary Retirement from the previous job. He owned 3 acres of rain-fed land and also did some agriculture. In 1994-95, after ITPL announcement, outsiders came wanting to purchase his land. In 1994-95, two Reddy developers from Richmond town offered to buy his land. He sold one acre for Rs. 30-40 lakhs, of which, a part he invested in constructing an Reinforced Cement Concrete (RCC) house—a Ground and 2 floors. With the remaining, he upgraded his own house to build three floors of which two were given for renting at Rs. 6,000 and Rs. 5,000 per month rental. He also constructed another RCC house also for rent. His original house, build on a plot measuring 30′×60′ has his third son living there. Krishnappa has 6 children and all have finished school. The first son is a bank manager, lives in Malleswaram, while the second son works with Karnataka Electricity Board (KEB) and resides in their quarters. The third son, Suresh owns a printing press and lives in Agrahara. The fourth one is an engineer-contractor and now takes up construction contracts in Agrahara. The fifth and sixth sons live with him. The fifth son works in a private pharmaceuticals company and the sixth son has a provision store in Nelluralli. Krishanappa is one of the leading financiers in Pattandur Agrahara and is joined in this business with his fifth and sixth son and wife. They mainly lend to small workshops, owners of provision stores, and also for construction of houses. Besides they also give loans for purchase of automobiles (two and four wheelers). According to his close relative, Krishnappa lends annually atleast Rs. 25 lakhs in finance business at rates of 3-5 per cent per month. His first son, the bank manager, whose monthly income is estimated between Rs. 15,000 to Rs. 20,000 has a four wheeler and two wheeler. His second son, with a motor cycle earns Rs. 18,000 per month, while his third son also with a motorbike earns an average of Rs. 10,000 per month, but his income fluctuates. His fourth son earns around Rs. 8,000 per month. His son, owning a provision store along with his finance partners earn roughly Rs. 50,000-80,000 per month in interest alone and the sixth son has a motorbike. Krishnappa, himself, despite all his wealth, owns a rather simple 100 cc two wheeler. In this account, as the earlier one, much emphasis was laid on both the material connections of business and land.

In contrast to the above cases, the vast bulk of small farmers (mostly SCs and few Kurubas) own between less than an acre to about 1 ½ acres of land—most of which would be dry and rain fed land. With the increasing real estate prices, this group used their surpluses to upgrade their old houses. Some sold their existing houses to move into rental properties with a monthly income of Rs. 10,000-15,000. A few bought gold. There are also serious problems. Our informant says that almost 20 per cent of the small land-owning families have lost their profits from land sales due to their alcoholism and initial lavish life style. This is partly due to the state government strictures on 'unplanned developments' and demolition of small firms designated as 'land use violations'. Such a situation cut down employment and also left fewer local investment opportunities especially in rental opportunities. Even so, 80 per cent of the original landowners live in their own houses constructed of AC sheet roofs. Presently these groups of people work as domestic helps and as employees in manufacturing factories, garment units, as security personal, and within smaller fabricator workshops, and in petty business. There are few accounts of landless labourers and many of these are likely to be in coolie work both here and in more central parts of Bangalore.

M.P. Krishanppa, 45 Years and Worker in the Alembic Glass Factory

He looks old and worked as a casual labour in Alembic glass factory where he was a gardener for 15 years. His monthly earning used to range from between Rs. 150 to Rs. 180, with little variation in his salary scale over the years. He has studied upto 8th standard, and has recently formed a *saṅgha* of all the casual labourers to be linked with trade unions. With these links, they started to negotiate with the factory and after a lot of fights and deliberations his salary was increased to Rs. 300. Once the casual workers started their fight with the management, the permanent workers also started to increase their demand. Consequently, the factory provided settlement to permanent workers and closed the factory. The land values have also increased in the area leading to lots of closures.

Closure in the Valley

This last case points to an emerging difficulty in local contestation especially after 2002. This period saw tighter control over real estate markets in favour of large developers, a Chief Minister directly backing the Bangalore 'demolition' (rather than Development Authority) headed by its iron fisted administrator, and the promotion of mega IT industries. All these combined to reduce the economic and political territory of local municipal and village councils in their ability to extend basic infrastructure for territories occupied by 'revenue' and '*gramthana*' layouts. The SSI units began to close down as their owners confronted a 'carrot' in very high real estate prices, and to sell out. Such options were made more attractive when it was also increasingly difficult to access workers who now had to travel great distances to work with fewer options of residence in local areas. In addition, industrial activity had shifted further south east towards Bomasandra and towards Hosur. Thus, the entry of the IT and its related 'gated' apartments and services was paralleled by de-industrialisation. Apart from the service related jobs that directly connected to the IT, other employment and residence for middle income and poorer groups moved into areas like the *Gudde,* or than settlements on the major roads leading into Bangalore like Marathahalli along the extensions of Airport Road. Thus, vast areas of this part of Bangalore have been zoned and priced out of the type of economic activities, which could absorb either these financial surpluses, or then form avenues for labour processes in small businesses and manufacturing. 'Closure' in this area for smaller investing and worker groups emerged from a combination of very high real estate but also one that is shaped by strong institutional activity by higher levels of government[11]. 'Closure' of occupancy, economic and political space comes with shifts in claiming processes to land.

One significant question is whether the emphasis on 'scheme' based supply systems generates an anti-politics. The history of this is from a much earlier time, but one that lent itself to the new politics in this part of Bangalore. This started with the 'formal' issuance, in 1970, *hakkupatras* (land titles) by the state government to 50 houses. In 1980, during the Chief Ministership of Gundu Rao, investments were made to develop main roads and 'houses constructed' for allottees of the recognised poorer groups. This got extended in 1993 when *Ashraya* houses were built. Similarly in these periods, Ration cards and *bhagya jothy* schemes (single point electricity) were implemented. In 2003 *Ashraya* schemes were implemented[12].

Loans were also provided to SC/ST. The state government has constructed a government school and BTS buses were provided. Also electricity, library, fair price shop, sodium lights were provided. All of these interventions, which may be seen as the 'social face of public policy' happen in what is a very narrow operational space of economic, spatial, and institutional territory. This becomes evident in the type of *sanghas* (Chart 7.1), which just as in the case of the *Gudde* history mentioned before, operate within specific territory.

An illustration of the narrowing of contest is given in the instance of the *Ambedkar Prachara Sangha.* In 1990, they took on a particular land issue related to the vacant land behind ITPL. They came to know that this land belonged to government because of a survey undertaken to allot land for ITPL. This particular parcel however was left out. Once ITPL was not getting this land, the *Ambedkar Prachar Samithi* targeted for that portion. This land however was occupied by a group of Sikh migrants. The *sangha* identified this, and filed a case with the DC office to have the land allocated to them and formed 46 plots on this site measuring one and a half acre. Thus, what is significant here is the inability of this and other *sanghas* to contest the overall decision of the ITPL land allotment. In fact, a relatively narrow political space opens up via the process that makes for the ITPL and the contest here is with relatively dis-empowered 'outsider' migrants.

Chart 7.1: *Sanghas*, their Activities and Leaders

Name of sangha	*Activities*	*Leaders*
Ambedkar prachara sangha (branch office-head office in Binnypet)	• To resolve conflicts amongst SC/ST residents in the area. • To address social issues like problems affecting SC/ST people due to city policies. • To motivate SC/ST children to attend schools and provide them free books. • To help people in getting caste certificates, when they could not get them on their own. • The main functionaries have a music group. They contribute a percentage of their earnings to the sangha. • To collect donations from political leaders during election that goes to the fund. • Formation of self help groups in the area. • To conduct yearly meeting at the head office level—at this meeting issues related to employment, land problems as well as other difficulties faced by SC/ST are discussed. This sangha provides a forum for demanding facilities and loans from the government. • They have formed only 46 sites measuring—15' × 20'; 25' x 22' and at present 25 families have occupied these sites. In September 2003, they have named this place as *Ambedkar Prachara Samithi nagara*	30 members—who are the main functionaries. Of this 6 are very active.
Ambekar Sashatratha Sangha	• This has been formed as part of a literacy programme by the office of Development Commissioner. • Legal awareness on issues related to sale deeds, youth rights, women rights. • Non formal education programme. Under this scheme each area gets a grant of Rs. 40-50000. This is to be used in a year for equipments. It is spent usually on TV, furniture. They have also collected library books and newspapers. The library opens from 6.30-9.30 in the morning and from 5-7 in the evening.	*Sangha* activities managed by two people—appointed by the government.
Ecumenical Christian Centre (ECC)	• Education, child health, awareness on mother's health. Free meal for children. Also provide play aid for children. As a Church based NGO it runs an *anganvadi* and provides awareness on health and nutrition to women and children.	
Mahila samaja	• Runs savings and credit programme • Also concentrates on women's issues	Vijayamma, Vijayalakshmi & Saraswathy
Navagraha prathishthana sangha	• Registered—they mainly focus on performing *pujas* (religious ceremonies) once a year. • Their aim is to focus on temple development in the locality	
Vinayaka yuvakar sangha	• Youth association Active only during *vinayaka chathruthi.*	

Much of the politics of contest refers to land in the Whitefield—Mahadevpura being developed as 'revenue layouts' and also 'DC converted' revenue sites and how these processes confront those of 'planned development'. Apart from that there are other types of contests—that of *Gomala* land. At one level, this contest is at the mega scale, where the state government appropriates *Gomala* and Inam land to re-allocate these to the IT or as SEZs. At another level, are elite private entities from Bangalore, who use the route of 'trusts' to influence higher levels of government machinery to access land for 'public service'. These include the Srinivasa trust with 40 acres, the Satya Sai (of the famous 'Godman') charitable trust that has around 26-30 acres, a much larger land allocated to another 'spiritual leader' the Sri Sri Ravi Shankar, and also NGOs in the area. Finally, at the level of actors like our informers, are those that play the local land market catering to groups of both land owning Gowdas and Reddys and also SC/ST groups. It is the last that dominates, but also seen to be the most 'messy' and steeped in local politics.

Our point in this discussion is not to suggest that there are clear 'victors' or that the 'local' is faced with a complete erasure in the face of powerful and well connected global capital. Instead, to suggest that the nature of contested terrain is necessarily complex, messy, and steeped in complex localities that defies assumptions of modernity and tradition.

'Closure and Occupancy' in South Bangalore

'Closure' that contests with 'Occupancy' is perhaps more stark in South Bangalore, in the ward no. 60. Here we see that within pockets, there are valuable opportunities but in the larger neighbourhood district, it is a combination of real estate and also class/ethnic politics that pushes low-income groups to pockets rather than broader occupation. The excerpt from our fieldwork (though not as detailed as in East Bangalore) is valuable to conceptualise this argument about forms of occupancy and contest. In the text below, we emphasise the variety of overlapping histories even if these face dis-junctures, from the point of view of both the complex events shaping development, but also from the perspective of the persons who told us these. This includes residents, local leaders and senior politicians of the area and also from the perspectives of the persons who carried out the interviews since they themselves worked in this area. The last is important as the interviewers are not just 'field staff' but are also informants on a lifestyle that they have come to observe over the years. Our idea in these narratives is to bring out the complex of occupancy and conflict. In many ways, these narratives compliment those we undertook in a previous research in the relatively more 'planned' areas of the BTM layout and Jaya Nagar. In that research, (available online and thus not extracted here), we focused on how higher income groups and the elite acted via their Resident Welfare Associations (RWAs) to close territory for the poorer sections. Their partner in this closure was an initiative called the '*Swabhimanya*'—a form of participatory civil society management supported by the then chief administrator of the Bangalore city municipality. The accounts provided here compliment two other works (one of which is available online). The first is a working paper that looks at later development of *Swabhimanya* in the 'new civil society' arrangements in Bangalore, and how these fit into a wider global agenda Benjamin and Bhuvaneswari (2001). The second, is a detailed study, including sites in South Bangalore (and not far from the research sites mentioned here) of Chronic Poverty (Benjamin 2004b). Our intention here, in the background of the above cited works, is to draw on the detailed narratives below, to add to our argument: Contestation is a complex non-linear historical process that is intensely material around the concept of occupancy. At the core of this materiality and its politics is land and location as these shape economies. Here it is important to note that claims on land are shaped not in the positivist thinking around absolute 'de-jure' titles, but rather in a grey and fluid situation of de-facto tenure. Even so, the intensive engagement with real estate markets shows this to be an intensive material process. Linked to this is a political materiality. Here, the issue is of extension of services, processes of regularisation and eviction, gradual upgrading of civic amenities—and all of these as we have discussed in earlier work, driven by a politics of stealth. Although these circuits are moved at times into higher levels of government, these are bounded by a locality of everyday life. Thus, as seen in the case of the settlements in East Bangalore, even when 'scheme' based interventions of the 'Nation State' are mentioned, these are drawn on from the perspective of how these impact de-facto tenure, and are driven and shaped by a politics of locality.

If so, our emerging conceptual frame further distances the binary of 'inclusive or exclusive' and its underpinning in notions of 'modernity'. What we seek instead, are more rooted understanding of contestation around occupancy and their multiple materiality.

Localities

The ward of Jaya Nagar (No. 58) was split into two wards in 1995-96. Ward No. 64 as Gurupanpalya and Ward No. 60 as Patabiramnagara. In many ways, although physically constrained by the intense master planning in the area, neighbourhoods here still maintain useful opportunities for their residents. They can enjoy, given their long established claims to land, low rents and leases and thus cheap real estate, but also access markets for hawking and other support such as domestic help from surrounding richer neighbourhoods. Perhaps most important, it is the relatively richer groups renting in adjoining and parts of their own 'revenue' layouts that provide this opportunity rather than the master planned elite areas. Those, in fact place strictures against hawkers to enter and are also relatively low density. The larger Gurupanpalya ward has some low income areas, namely, Gurupanpalya Arasu Colony, Corporation Colony, Indira Colony, DK Nayakar Slum, Puttenpalya, Karipalya slum, Drive in theater slum, etc. that are both 'revenue and *gramthana* layouts' on private 'revenue' or village settlement land.

Part of this ward is planned by the Bangalore Development Authority (BDA). These areas form part of Jaya Nagar 9th block that lies east of the 8th. The main Banergetta road adjoins the revenue pocket of Gurupanpalya Arasu colony. This is a 40 years old slum of which 50 per cent are Tamil population, and 15 per cent Telugu with 20 per cent Kannadiga and 15 per cent Muslim. In looking at these local histories, just as in the Whitefield cases mentioned earlier, we see various forms of contests. Later in this text we also provide an account of the local politicians attempt to address these various contesting groups.

The Gurupanpalya Arasu colony, when started in the 1960s, was a very sparsely developed one, when pig rearers and pork sellers called *Andijogi* purchased land here. This group was seen to be 'innocent and illiterate' and not that many—only 20-25 families. This was followed by Tamilians who as construction workers came and squatted on land belonging to the municipal corporation. While they built huts the main problem they faced was that of basic amenities. To address this, they formed a sangha called the *Ambedkar Shema Abruti Sangha* in the 1980s under a local leader *Swami Velu Shankar*. Shankar helped them to organise to ensure basic development of the areas through Diwakar. He was responsible for the formation of one of the associations (of the many 'sanghas' that operate in this area): Karnataka Sanjay Slum Development Social Welfare Association. This association was formed in 1979. There are seven office bearers in this association and one representative from each of the 125 houses. One of the achievements of this association is obtaining the right to occupy the burial adjoining Arasu colony. The plot adjoining the colony was a burial ground and thus, there was no water facility. The early settlers also did not have any ration card. The association fought through the courts for occupying the burial ground and both these lands fell under the jurisdiction of BDA. With the political and lower level bureaucratic pressure and also the courts, the BDA transferred the land to KSCB for notification. This was initially 3P, 3F, 11P, 11F, 17F, and 17P that are sections of the Karnataka slum act that allowed them access to identity cards in 1991 and also basic services. In 1991, the association obtained ration cards for the residents. The KSCB did not get involved in house construction. Unfortunately for the renters here, reaching the notification of 17 P has meant that there was now a plan for construction of houses for the 'recognised' residents. Under the pressure of the more established group's association, the BDA transferred the slum to housing board for the construction of houses, and the housing board has organised for a loan from HUDCO. In order to get this plan sanctioned the association worked through the MLA Ramesh. Now around one and a half crores of rupees has been sanctioned for the house construction. This amount was allotted for construction of flats; each unit measures 22′×10′.

The public housing built here also had a complex history. Initially, the Karnataka Housing Board (KHB) constructed quarters but these were of very poor quality and were transferred to Karnataka Slum Clearance Board (KSCB). Total 216 houses were constructed. Each house costed Rs. 40,000 and the allotted persons had to pay each month Rs. 540. After 10 years of occupation, the residents get a *patta* (titles) allowing them to sell the house for approx. Rs. 90,000 to Rs. 160,000.

Near the built quarters, there are also about 750 huts. Although 377 houses were sanctioned, at present there are 216 units (roughly 2 units per block—ground and first). The remaining households are still staying in temporary thatch huts. In addition, another 100 new huts have sprung up. There is still a conflict between the residents and housing board over this house construction. The KHB stated that the cost of each unit is Rs. 33,000. Each resident has to give Rs. 5,000 as advance. The remaining principal along with an interest of 14 per cent is to be repaid over a period of 20 years. After the houses were constructed, they were not allotted. So the association representing the relatively higher income residents fought with the housing board. This conflict reached a flash point and then to violence leading to the arrest of association members. The association members obtained a stay order and the arrested member was also released.

The association leaders then asked the residents to occupy the houses according to the original allotment list. A year later, the housing board told the residents that they have to repay a loan of Rs. 45,000.

Subsequently, the KHB increased the amount to Rs. 65,000 and presently they have quoted Rs. 80,000 to Rs. 100,000 as the cost of each unit. Until now, the cost of the house and hence the loan to be repaid by the residents has not been finalised. The association leaders are putting forth the argument that the residents cannot repay a loan whose amount is increased every year and when the *hakkupatra* (titles) has not been given. In the meantime, the association has obtained electricity connection for individual households through Ashraya scheme. The KHB did not provide any water or sanitation connection. Through the Ashraya, water and sanitary connection was given in 1995. The same year, they have constructed a community centre under the MP's grant. The MLA was highly supportive in getting these funds.

Of the 7 members, who form the core of this association two have died. The NGOs Women's voice, KKNSS and AWAS came to Arasu colony, and conducted meetings, but the association members stated that they did not do any work. According to the association members, the above mentioned three NGOs used to hold meetings for predominantly women, but did not do any other work. While these organisations helped individual members, they did not provide any support for community work. At the time of house construction, the three organisations did not support them. World Vision and Maya are currently active in this settlement. Their layout residents have organised a *sangha* called *Varamahalakshmi* SHG run by the NGO APSA. Most of these people are as carpenters, painters, barbers; none have any government jobs. The NGOs sponsored education for children, gave individual loan of Rs. 1,000 for electricity connection and also loans for business and for house repair. They have also organised self-help groups (savings and credit *sangha*) and have linked these groups to Canara bank. The bank has provided loans to the members of self help group. However, NGO promoted SHG and micro-credit form only a third of their money circulation—most is via trade based finance and loans from money lenders as that gives them more flexibility and dynamism. St. Johns Medical College is now running a free clinic for children and women.

The neighbourhood has a *Mariamya* temple and a church. Part of the Gurupanpalya area has a group of 35 houses with one owner with the rest being on a renting and lease basis. Normally, the rent is between Rs. 700 to Rs. 1,000, and advance between Rs. 10,000 to Rs. 15,000 and lease is Rs. 55,000 to Rs. 100,000 for 1-2 years. The same families have been living here since the last 20 years and despite the area is 'DC converted', the land rent and lease in that area is very less. Women are mostly domestic workers and vendors. The children go to a low-end private school. They have chosen not to move out and stay as renters since all facilities are available nearby—corporation water, medical school, and common toilets located nearby. This is shared in terms of two—three families for one toilet. They have one place for washing clothes, which is shared. The rented houses are normally in the form of single room 10′×10′ and 10′×15′, and also some houses having additional rooms (with a kitchen). Most slum dwellers find employment nearby as stone workers, construction, kerosene sellers, carpenters, painters, *agarbatti* (incense stick) making, garment manufacturing, small business hawkers and domestic servants.

Another slum here is called Puttayanapalaya located next to the Arasu colony. This settlement is now dominated by Kannadigas, but was formed about 30 years ago. This group faced problems from other residents in Puttayanapalaya over issues of civic amenities as well as on ethnic grounds. This conflict was so strong that their leader Samuel was physically attacked. Their first councillor was Nagiah of Janata Dal, who helped in the regularisation of the squatter settlement during the time of Someshshekar, who was then the BDA chairman. During the Chief Minister Ramakrishna Hedge's time, in 1992, they were allotted a plot of 22′ × 10′. In 1995, the Ashraya committee pegged the value of each site with one room at Rs. 77,000 and the loan was to be paid back over in 20 years. In 1995-96, sanitary connections, roads and a community hall (for marriage and death functions) were built under MP's grant. By 1995, the Deputy Mayor Sampath Kumar (JD) helped residents access electricity and resolve difficult water problem by putting in a bore well and revive an old well. By this time, NGOs also began to work in this area. The NGO *World Vision* gave each family a loan of Rs. 1,000 to be paid back in 10 instalments. From the St. Johns hospital outreach service mentioned earlier, they got a school and a *balwadi* and begun getting free treatment.

What is locally termed as the 'Corporation colony', started with 370 households set out as single storied row-houses. The houses and its street are neat and clean and in many ways, has much better environs than many middle income residential areas of Bangalore. The number has now increased to 1,800 households, all of whom have also been allocated ration cards. From a situation of no water or electricity in 1991-93 period, when the settlement started, ten years later, most civic amenities, including street lights are available on regular basis. Much of these changes came about via an intensive politics that had to contest with not just allocations to other poorer slums, but more specifically with Bangalore's well connected elite living in Jay Nagar. What worked for these residents is that they were able to mobilise their association 'Gandhi *Sangha*' in very effective way with such a large consolidated vote bank to get all the civic amenities in one go. For this, they organised and approached all the party candidates with the claim that they will have a block vote if they got civic amenities. What also helped them was that although they are located in the heart of South Bangalore and it being so heavily Master Planned, the land they occupied has now been designated as 'corporation' land—an outcome of earlier politics. Knowing all this, and the importance of political timing, the four organisers constructed the *sangha* room and then directly approached the MLA who was from Congress I for support. Being South Bangalore, and dominated by Master Planning, MLAs are more important players here. Thus, their *sangha* came to be perceived as a 'Congress group' when their councillor was from Janata Dal. With all these, they decided to move to a higher level of government. It need be stated that the *sangha* has been negotiating with the government since 1970, giving a memorandum to the then Chief Minister Devaraj Urs. In 1985, during the period of the Chief Minister Gundu Rao they took the support of Ramalinga Reddy, now a MLA but then a councillor, to demand via a petition for 'Possession Certificates' to get security of tenure of the land. We provide accounts of part of this process through interviews with several prominent locals who took on a leadership role.

Karpana is an old man of about 65 years and recalls that originally, their settlement was located in the City Market in 1955. He is president of the corporation slum development association. At that time, there were about 1,200 families. The then newly established state government shifted these squatters to Magadi road, Sanjay Talkies, and JP Nagar, and this location called Corporation colony. They were of the last 370 houses shifted here and he describes this area as being 'wild'. For each family, a plot of 25′ × 40′ was given free and mostly allotted to SC/ST groups. Karpana recollects that unlike today when the houses are of asbestos sheet roofs, the government then built only tile roofed houses, but with no road, electricity and water. When the evicted families were allotted the sites here, not all came. Only 50 to 75 of the 370 accepted due to the lack of facilities. He recollects that at that time (in 1973-74), Ramalinga Reddy was a councillor and helped them access Possession Certificates, Ration Cards, ID card, sale agreement, voter list and betterment charges. Over time, from the initial 75, more came in and now there were more than 1,800 families, and all have got ration card. Together they amount to 6,000 voters. They have also established a *'Mahatma Gandhi Harijana*

Sewa Sangha', registered in 1957. The association also organises their 'native' village festival within the settlement every year. There is also a youth *sangha* (*Ambedakar youth sangha*)—involved in sports during *Ganesha* festival and adult education. The neighbourhood demanded and got 5 government fair price shops. The associations have also facilitated the distribution of the Ration and BPL cards. Karpana has his own cycle shop. The residents here also had serious problems with Puttanapalaya youth gangs. However, as their area got settled, this became less of a threat as they too formed several *sanghas* to counter this threat.

Karpana mentions that prior to Diwakar, at the times of Ramiah councillor (of JD), Chandrashekara was the MLA. He got into politics due to his involvement in the local development activities. Karpana stood twice for elections and spent Rs. 30,000 in 1980 and Rs. 35,000 in 1985 but lost to Diwakar both the times. According to him, he lost out due to the corruption in the voting process. He says that because he is poor and un-educated, he has no support from higher level residents or the party. He acknowledges that during Diwakar's time, the area got developed. Among the 6,000 voters, 4000 are Tamils, 1,000 Telegus, 1000 Kannada and 15 Muslim houses amounting to about 100 voters. He has also built a *Muthmariama* temple and also a *Munishewara* temple. For the first temple, Rs. 25,000 was sanctioned under MP development fund. Electricity was introduced during Gundu Rao's period and in 1981, they got *Swadina Patra*—or possession certificates.

Muniswamy is another local leader and at 30 year old. He is educated, a first-year commerce from Vijaya evening college. After the college, he tried out various jobs as a painter, an autodriver, and then social worker. At 21, he married his classmate a Kannadiga (although being a Tamilian) and they have two children. Muniswamy worked with the Superintendent of Police for 3 years, and also works with the MLA Diwakar in the morning. In the afternoon, he is a wholesale fruit vendor in the city market, where his mother has a shop allocated to her since the last 30 years. His sister, a widow, with 4 children, also helps in the shop. He goes to the city market at 4 am and returns at 10 am, after which he comes to Diwakar. Diwakar allocates the BMP Congress party's contract work such as road repairs, painting, small civil works etc. through Muniswamy. Muniswamy says that residents here mainly seek proper *khata* and sale deeds. With his help and political connections, under the 18 per cent scheme they can register titles at a far less amount than the regular rate of Rs. 20,000. The residents also pressed that such property registration on the first party basis as part of the original 370 allotted, which can then be sold to them.

Their land is surrounded on three sides by many IT buildings, and with such titles, their land values move up more than three times every quarter. Thus they want to also capitalise on this. At present, with the possession certificates, they cannot play this market.

Such narratives of Muniswamy and also Karpana are usefully viewed in the context of complex forms of land occupation. The case of Nanjapa layout here helps to understand the importance of political connections that operate at various levels.

Nanjapa Layout is about 2 acres and 10 '*guntas*' (1 gunta = .025 acres or 101.25 sq.m.) all of that is revenue layout. Of this, 6 *guntas* is "*kharab*"(degraded or left-over) land. Earlier, the revenue layout came under the Bommanahalli *gram panchayat* and adjoins the Madiwala lake. The lake belonged to the Jairaj "jodidar" or landlord. Between 1984 to 1994, the area was under the Notified CMC. In 1995, it came under the BMP. In 1985, the state governor inaugurated a bus stop as part of the re-development of the lake. Before its settlement, all of this land was 'dry land' and farmers grew only *ragi* and *jowla*. About 20 years ago, the land owned by the wife of Nanjapa was sold to small developers and cut into 34 plots aimed at the poorer groups. Thus, most of these were 30′ x 40′. In 1978-79, Mico layout not far away was formed that gave a spur to the larger district. Thus, between 1975 to 1980, one acre of land here was priced at Rs. 10,000. In 1980-85, mud roads were developed, and the price of one acre moved up to Rs. 25,000 to Rs. 50,000. In 1995-2000, when the entire neighbourhood district has witnessed huge changes in property, one square feet was sold at between Rs. 600 to Rs. 750. With the development of the adjoining Gundu Rao layout, values again increased and also attracted more settlers. Thus, from the previous 34, there are now 400 plots and houses. A water pipeline has been built since the last five months and connections are now available. However, no water is available via these pipes and residents are forced to use bore well and well water. Even so, the rents in this area, given the proximity to the IT buildings, are still quite high—between Rs. 500 to Rs. 3,000 per square foot. The adjoining Someshwara colony has had a relatively difficult history. One of the problems was that this settlement came up on "*gundu thopu*" or *gomala* land which the State government re-categorised as 'government' land. In 1987, the BDA notified the land for acquisition, but by 1992, the BDA passed a resolution and distributed ID cards. But this was for only 6 people belonging to the Congress I. 70 per cent of the people got an eviction notice. This led Haridas (whose profile is discussed below) and

Muniswamy (discussed above) led the local group to contest this notice. They prepared a memorandum that was routed through the ruling party to the Revenue officer, the Deputy Secretary. At the time of the election in 1991, for the purposes of votes, they were able to obtain '*hakku patras*' Possession Certificates and electricity connections though the 'bhyaga joti' scheme for all houses. In 1998, they gave a notice for the registration of sites, which however, were given to only 4 people.

Haridas, 50 years old, is a diploma engineer and runs the Vidya Joyti School catering to students from pre nursery to 'SSLC'. He started this school in 1983 and also worked as a secretary in the Railway trade union. He comes from Kerala and has been in Bangalore since 1968, and is also a voluntary worker with several NGOs, KKNSS and AWAS, Women's Voice, and other slum organisations. In 1984-85, he built an '*Anganwadi kendra*' (tailoring and children's crèche) and handed this over to Karnataka Women & Child Development Department to manage it. The centre operated for 15 years but closed down 2 years back. Along with the community, Haridas also built two temples. One is *Karmiamma* temple, and the other *Sanimahatma* temple. In 1970, they faced problems of local toughs setting fire to huts in the area, running an extortion racket, and residents could not do any thing without the permission of these '*goondas*'. At the festival time, the toughs would demand money. He became famous, when with the help of both the elderly and the youth in the neighbourhood, he solved the problem. Since then, he has been doing a lot of social work and the community people call him '*Swamy*' (loosely translated as 'respected one'). Haridas had land in Kerala, which he sold to purchase one acre land in Vonasandra and built the school there with his own money. In 1987, he purchased 1 acre and 10 *guntas* at Rs. 142,000 and distributed this to 110 very poor families like handicapped, deserted, widow for their housing. Each family got a plot of 15′ × 20′, and this settlement was called 'Jothi Nagar. Haridas's school caters to very poor children and gives them free admission. The students who have studied there ended up as "rank" students and entered into professions as doctors, engineers etc. He proudly mentions that one of his students Kavita, won a gold medal in Mathematics with 97 per cent in 1992. Another, Ravethi also secured 98 per cent in Mathematics. Both these children were from the slums. In 1995, Haridas's wife Radha stood for local councillor elections from the BJP party but lost by only 123 votes. He spent Rs. 35,000 for that election. At this time, Haridas witnessed how some of his own people put fake votes and got disillusioned with 'politics'. However, he maintains good relationship with politicians of all parties. Whenever the slum requires any basic needs, he helps them through his connections. As he is involved in such social work, his wife manages the school. Radha was initially working in a government school, but resigned to join politics, and now manages their school. Presently, their slum settlement has got it's piped water network completed, but mainline supply of water still needs to be extended along with sanitation.

Haridas, very familiar with the area, recollects that the posh BTM layout was earlier *gramthana* and grazing land belonging to the Madiwala and Bommanahalli *Gram-panchayat.* Prior to 1980, the land was cultivated with *Ragi, Jowla.* In 1978, the BDA notified the area as a development area to form the colony. Adjacent, the MICO layout for the factory workers was started by the MICO Layout Association Co-operative Development Society. During the time of the Chief Minister of Devraj Urs and Gundu Rao, the Mico association decided to develop the land. Around 1990, builders visited the land to sub-divide the land and by 1995, a major from the army built the first house there. He vividly recollects the land prices. In 1975 an acre sold for Rs. 10,000, and in 1978 the BDA awarded just Rs. 60,000 for 3 acres 16 guntas. By 1980 a revenue site of 30' x 40' was priced between Rs. 5000 to Rs. 12,000. By 2004, a square foot on the main road sold at Rs. 1600-2000. While in 1985, much of the land was empty with few buildings, by 1995, a colonel and his colleagues from the Army built 4 to 5 houses. After this initial development, other areas were developed: Yacooba Nagar, Dollars Colony, Pushpa Layout, Ayaippa Layout, KAS Officers Colony, Central Silk Board quarters, etc.

To fully appreciate these locations as complex political terrain, it is useful to visit the narrative of an important local politician of the predominantly Master Planned South Bangalore. The point here is not just the vast range of works but rather, their seeming contradictions. These lie not in 'fabrication' but rather, in complex demands made from local contestation over resources and the way higher income groups and more centralised 'party politics' and its' funding push for the mega.

An account of the local politician Diwakar's and also his father's life history reveals the complex politics that is shaped by local demands but also their gradual moving into the city and state Party system that facilitates it's own re-working of city terrain. Diwakar's father, Dr. Chandrashekar Rao was a prominent doctor. In 1964, when the locally famous BT Somanna headed the City Improvement Trust Board, his father was the joint director health secretary in the area and had built up a lot of social base. His constituency was the slum dwellers of Ragigudda and Ashok Colony and others, who got free treatment from him through health camps. The senior Diwakar moved into politics with this social service background. His son came into politics from the union background, but also tapping into his father's locally established vote base. He earlier worked in HMT and was part of part of the AITUC union leader, then the city youth congress leader, and later the Congress Sewa Dal and the National Student's Union of India (NSUI[13]) of the Bangalore City's president. His work in the area attracted the attention of the then CM Gundu Rao and also the MLA Ramalinga Reddy. In 1990, he was elected in ward no. 60 as the corporator, and chairman of the Taxation and Finance committee and also head of the opposition. During his tenure of 5 years several development works were carried out. Diwakar, in his interview, sees his main achievements as the following:

- Built corporation quarters
- *Bhayaga Jothi* scheme for street and single bulb point lights
- Water point for local areas (common tanks)
- Community toilets
- Community halls.
- Ration card
- ID Card
- Possession Certificate
- *Hakku Patra* (land titles)
- *Pucca* Roads

One can see from the above, these cater to a variety of local constituencies that over time are of diverse income and ethnic groups, and also from a variety of employment categories. Thus, what is significant here is the range of political interventions as they respond to complex and often contradictory demands made by a variety of income groups. In his interview, he further elaborated how he was responsible to collect money from people to build the temple and the gate and also a contribution of Rs. 2 lakhs from the Mayor's fund. In 1994-95, Diwakar prepared the budget for Rs. 9 crores for Bangalore city development. This was for the various departments like: health, revenue, works in progress, horticulture department and 18 per cent SC/ST scheme. In the ward, he got funded community centres and tailoring centres. He also got two playgrounds in his ward, Jaya nagar 3rd block and Shalini Play ground. Diwakar also got roads widened and also the installation of Sodium vapour lights in Jaya Nagar 4th. Central circles were built at the prominent junctions. He got roads extended in Muniswamy layout. In two places he built two BMP higher primary schools and at Marenahalli a Corporation primary school. He also built mini over head tanks in Tilak Nager No. 32 cross, East End main road Rama mandira, Puttanyapalya 9th Block at Jaya Nagar. He also got built several bus stops in Jaya Nagar area. Diwakar also initiated several tailoring centres like in Corporation Colony Jaya Nagar and Arsu Colony at the east end of Jaya Nagar, organised training courses and got the trainees stitching machines from the corporation. He also got chain link fences done at Shalini Playground and also corporation ground and other places. Diwakar also introduced parks along most of the important streets. In the slums, he built 370 houses and for the SC/ST under the 18 per cent scheme, got 225 houses in the low income slum of Arsu Colony, 375 households in Corporation Colony, 180 houses in Marenhalli and for 54 *pourya karmikas* (class IV municipal employees—mostly street sweepers) housing free electricity under *Bhayagaya Jothi* scheme. For the very poor, he conducted mass marriages through the *Jaya Nagar Sewa Samiti* via his own funds. Diwakar also ensured that 400 houses got *Hakku patra* (Possession Certificate) and ID card for 1,500 EWS people. He says that he has strived to treat the SC/ST as mainstream and as upper class people. He also attended to issues like KEB voltage fluctuation, betterment charges, arranged for ward meetings with the revenue officer. The Jaya Nagar MLA constituency has 8 councillors. He has maintained good relationships with other party councillors.

In what seems like a contradiction to the above, Diwakar says that he also presented the Mega City fund project for the city in the council. At the end of the interview, and perhaps seeing the authors of the report as being an 'undercover' journalist for an English newspaper like *Times of India*, he was also full of praise of SM Krishna, and helped move Bangalore to be more important than Hyderabad. But this would also be in line with complex local demands and also an increasingly aggressive party system whose funding and political mobility is centred around mega engineering works and making Bangalore a global workplace. If so, the narratives above reflect complex forms of occupancy based politics, and where efforts to cater to one group forms both 'exclusion' to others, but also perhaps 'openings' when funds allocated for mega engineering projects find a 'seepage' into other more local demands via municipal politics.

From Positivist 'Inclusion' To Contests around De-Facto Materiality

Our main findings are that the declining claims of poorer groups happen in different ways:

- In South Bangalore, this is associated with land systems closing access, which is also reinforced by "middle class activism". Here, earlier terrains of Revenue/*Gramthana* Layouts were taken over via Master Planning, by housing Co-ops and the relatively large industrial plots. Later, these opened up territory to the MNCs and IT companies, and their associated large private corporate housing complexes. This also included "participatory planning" where claim making via high level Bureaucratic and "civil society" circuits paved the way for "middle class activism". This raises important questions of both the assumptions about social capital and notions of civil society.
- In East Bangalore, poverty and exclusion is associated with closing of economic and political territory due the shifting of 'levels' of contest from p*anchayat* and municipal councils to state level. Again, like in the South Bangalore case, this is paralleled by closure of land systems—but more as a result of state interventions to develop mega projects in favour of the IT, as well as real estate induced 'sickness' in what was older industrial territory. An earlier terrain of Revenue/*Gramthana* Layouts taken over by first *avatar* (pre IT) of KIADB actions, boom of the mid-1990s prompts large land developers in partnership with *panchayat* elite. This also paved the way for the Post IT *avata*r of KIADB and the "ITPL" type partnerships for MNCs. The new 'Gated Communities' evolved in response to these. In addition, the *Bhoomi* programme reinforced this situation. Poorer groups were left with tinkoring the system via '*gomala land*' type politics and economics. However, the high level politics promoted under the rhetoric of "Good-Governance and Best Practice" of the BATF opens up land market as a sort of revival of the mid-1990s boom. This allowed a monopoly of four to five large developers and their political affiliates, to transform large parcels of Public Sector Unit (PSU)/earlier KIADB allocations into new large players. Poorer clusters seek supports in limited pockets by DSS and its 'sister' organisation

in a Party based political terrain. These have limited success because the wider contest over territory are effectively ghettoised on a hill top overlooking the new terrain of fractured *panchayats* made even more fractured by the new urban reforms programmes, actions of Bangalore Water Supply and Sewerage Board (BWSSB), Karnataka Urban Infrastructure Development Finance Company (KUIDFC).

- In both cases, we also find a reinforcement of party systems of politics that take over more complex local political terrain. As a result, this leaves the smaller but accessible political circuits to only the most vocal of the poor and those are not necessarily the poorest. In this situation, political claim making for the poorer groups and their connected alliances in other groups has very limited space. This contrasts with our analysis of West Bangalore's Azad Nagar/Valmiki Nagar, where politics is centred on local leaders and councillors pushing higher level 'party' systems. Significantly, those areas were also characterised by a lack urban planning and its base of 'surveying/enumeration'.

Our main conclusion from considering these two locations in Bangalore is that for cities (or their particular parts) to be 'inclusive' of poor groups is hardly a normative issue. Instead it refers to forms of claim making where poor groups act as active agents in conditions of severe contest. In such contested terrain, their support and political access in local government turns out to be a critical factor. When this level of governance is eroded, poor groups run the severe risk, as was seen in our case studies, being ghettoised and moved out of political and economic terrain. Our wider research suggests that such erosion of local political space is closely connected to the promotion of mega hi-tech projects and also Master Planning. Thus, when these are major interventions, to expect that a terrain can be made inclusive seems naïve at the best.

Our cases of South Bangalore suggest that one cannot depend on 'civil' society to take the stress off from poorer groups, or to open up political and economic territory that works in their favour. On the contrary, new alliances between civil society and various privatisation programmes promote elite NGOs to play a well-funded role of "structured civil society participation". These as part of new donor accounting ease, also facilitate other fund routing like that of micro-credit which may constrain the operational sphere of smaller more progressive NGOs. If so, the assumption of civil society to negotiate with the 'State' on behalf of the poor is just as naïve as expecting mega projects which sap away public investments into high grade infrastructure and services. Finally, considering the centrality of land shows us the way this is set in a terrain of large and powerful players. Moreover, these are now backed by the power of a State that is distinctly pro-big business at the national level policy making. Other factors are increasingly authoritarian party politics spurred by insecurity of party indiscipline to tolerate little space for local autonomy. All this is compounded by substantial funding from international capital seeking fresh grounds for investments, pushing for a pro-big business dominated market reforms agenda. If so, land issues when clarified and made transparent are likely to be captured by the elite, or be acquired for large mega projects facilitated by the state on grounds of 'public purpose'. All these factors make securing land via quiet occupancy—seeking the support of political and lower bureaucracy to stake claims rather than explicit social actions, more tenable. Where occupancy has indeed come out of progressive party systems and actions, these are relegated to very specific locations. If so, the ability of the poor to depend on explicit mobilisation via 'social movements' seems highly un-realistic and the space most accessible is that of local government control of settlements in urbanised villages or specific outlying areas of smaller municipal corporations.

This analysis suggests that central to the notion of inclusive or exclusive cities or neighbourhoods, is the form of political claim making, and how these are reinforced by economy and institutional structure. Second, the field is hardly neutral. Thus, if we see cities as being inclusive of the poor or particular groups within the poor, they may be closing up political and economic space to other and possibly elite groups. It is hardly surprising that elite groups seek to dilute that part of democracy that they find moving resources away from them.

NOTES

1. This chapter is based on research undertaken through IDPAD project.
2. Dalit or the Scheduled Castes (SCs) refer to the lower castes groups. Many of these form the poorest groups but not always—as subsequently seen in one of the case studies.
3. For instance, if were to conceptualise and analyse global financial flows within this approach, we would focus on tracing in great detail the institutional arrangements, the internal administrative conventions and actual procedures used (as distinct from 'policy') and most critical, the power relationships that underpin these.

4. Dharmakumar (2001), Chapters 5 and 6 Habib (1995).
5. For instance, the presenter on land laws that impact real estate development in peripheral areas suggested that developers and financial institutions address complex counter claims by small farmers and developers by lobbying the state government to acquire land on their behalf with instruments such as the KIDBI Act, and using the Karnataka Industrial Area Development Board. Presentation by Umakanth in 'Suminfra 2004: Summit on Sustainable 'PPP's in Infrastructure," CII—Government of Karnataka Conference, Bangalore, 2-3 September, 2004).
6. Author: One of the problems, (as seen in our case descriptions later in this text) is of the state government being able to easily acquire such lands for 'public purposes' since local records are no longer easily available and as in our analysis of the Bhoomi programme referenced earlier, these are centralised and a range of customary tenure forms amalgamated into 'sarkari land'
7. *Author*: Such land tenures become significant when we consider how in the Whitefield area the KIADB appropriated vast lands to homogenise tenures and in effect erased such claims on water bodies that surround the hi-tech IT buildings (ITPL, GE), high end 'gated' housing complexes, and also hospitals such as the Sai Baba Hospital. Thus when sewage from these were left un-treated into the lakes, there was little possibility for the villagers living immediate around these to appeal, and had to consolidate their political clout to address this issue.
8. Kannada speaking population; Kannada being the language of Karnataka state in which Bangalore is.
9. Malayalis are from Kerala, Gujarathis from Gujarat and Marathis from Maharashtra.
10. *See* Benjamin (2004a) for more details on this.
11. Thus, in an alternative situation, a larger group of ethnic and class groups could occupy physical space, consolidate an economy in small manufacturing and service related to locations and real estate, and extend a Municipalized—Panchayat council politics. Such territories would form a severe contest for larger players who would have to deal with territory for both residence and economy being occupied by large clusters of small firms. All this would pose a severe contest to a variety of groups and specific political circuits: High end real estate players catering to the IT and IT related housing and commercial services; their partnerships with higher levels of political circuits; and, Party politics at the state and national level.
12. There are attempts to extend 'claims'. For instance, apart from the relatively few houses built, or electricity extended under schemes such as the *Ashraya or bhagya jothy*, their mere listing of a large number of intended beneficiaries acts as a 'de-facto' tenure claim for them.
13. Congress I's student wing.

ANNEXURE A
BASIC LAND TYPES AND RELATED TERMINOLOGY

Pani or RTC	:	Documents the history of claims on various aspects connected to a plot of land. This includes the claims of various institutions and people on that land
Khata	:	Right to title as listed in the revenue registry
Pada	:	Default of land tax on a particular land
Inam land	:	Land that was previously 'gifted' by the royalty or their representatives
Gomala land	:	Village common land, or any land whose ownership cannot be established.
Grant land	:	Land allotted by the state free of land
Gramthana land	:	Village land
Kharab land	:	Officially uncultivable land
Sarakari land	:	Government land

8

INTER-CITY AND INTRA-CITY INEQUITY IN CHINA

Case of Tianjin and Chongqing[1]

DARSHINI MAHADEVIA

Context

When I had proposed to study the infrastructure financing in China in 2003, I did not know that it would give me an opportunity to explore many dimensions of China's economy, polity and society. I have maintained for a long time that study of urban areas gives an opportunity to understand a society very well as the cities are concentrated expression of a society. Urban infrastructure financing in any country is related to her administrative system (who is in charge of a city); institutions for development and finance; her governance (who takes decisions, how decisions are taken and what is the local politics that influences local decisions and differentiates one city from the other); national financial system including that of taxation, finance mobilisation, and lending; national level goals and distributive policies; country's integration with global economy and role international development organisations; and local (city level) incomes and their distribution.

When I first landed in Beijing in 2004 April, I was surprised by the organised airport, metered taxis outside, policemen managing the traffic, a huge multi-storeyed parking lot outside the airport, airport bus to the city, and then when on the road neon light advertisements on the roads, traffic moving at a high speed in the freeway, maze of flyovers at some points, large glass buildings, mega stores, many MacDonald's on the way, and so on, everything that represents globalisation, while I was prepared for a developing country situation and also a more austere Communist China. And then, the first few weeks were full of many surprises. No doubt, the city was preparing for 2008 Olympics. I was awestruck with the first image of Beijing city. And then over time I realised that entire Beijing city had become a construction site.

And then in 2007 in Tianjin. I reached the University of my Affiliation, Tianjin *Cai Jing Da Xue*, (Tianjin University of Finance Economics—TUFE), from Beijing airport in a car (that came to pick me up) gliding on one freeway after another, without touching the regular road till we almost reached the university. The next morning, and then every morning, I was woken up early by a loud thunderous sound, like that of an airplane, of a passing metro. It is an elevated metro, at almost the level of my room on the third floor in a building of TUFE. The structure was completed in 2005 November when I had visited a friend at TUFE, who had told me then that this would be operational soon and that it would be very convenient and also cheap to reach TUFE from the station. In the first week of arrival in Tianjin, I took a joy ride in it. In the course of my early days here in April 2007, I discovered that now the entire central station area of the city was dug up and under construction to integrate new subway lines under-construction with the central station area. Thus, I could not find any of the sites that I had visited in May 2004! Two new metro lines are under construction and one of them would be linked to the main railway station. Tianjin is to host earlier rounds of football matches for the Olympics 2008. In the three months at Tianjin I realised that this city was also entirely under construction. All the old housing areas of the central district of Heiping had been demolished for new real estate projects. Not this district alone, but even the adjoining districts of Nankai and Hexi were under massive construction boom, with new real estate projects coming up. Many expressways are under construction in the city. A fast Light Rail Transit (LRT) is expected to come up by the end of 2007 connecting Tianjin and Beijing to cover the distance in 30 minutes time from 1 hour by the bullet train now and 2 hours by regular train. Tianjin has already been connected with Binhai New Area with a LRT.

Such large-scale infrastructure projects, roads and sub-ways and large real projects are not restricted to the mega cities alone, Beijing, Tianjin, Shanghai and so on. The fourth national level city, Chongqing, that is expected to be the gateway to central China and is also called the new economic frontier[2], is also observing massive construction boom. Construction boom and large infrastructure projects can also be found in smaller cities. I went to Dongguan in 2004 and was shocked to see the scale of development. And then went to Yichang in 2007, a small town where the Three Gorges Project is located, and once again was surprised at the scale of development, particularly the wide roads, bus lanes, bicycle lanes and large real estate projects.

Any one with experience of researching other developing country cities would wonder where the funds for such massive capital investments in urban infrastructure are coming from and are the local government priorities getting skewed in this race for making of 'competitive' cities? This author's research on Indian cities indicates that when the local government's priorities shift to such economic infrastructure, their attention and hence their funding to social infrastructure such as water supply, sanitation, health care, etc. reduces, which gets passed on to the citizens themselves. Thus, first the pricing of these services increase and then the subsidies begin reducing. At the same time move to privatise these services begin. In India, some efforts at water privatisation have shown undue advantage to the private water companies at the disadvantage of the citizens[3]. And in most such moves of the city governments, the citizens have objected and refused to accept the new arrangements. It has also been found that much as the local governments are more than eager to undertake massive road projects, construction of flyovers, and expressways to reduce the travel time on the roads, they are not so eager to improve the water supply and sanitation systems, resulting in frequent outbreaks of epidemics, now pre and post monsoon and inundation during the monsoons (See Mahadevia and Wolfe 2008). While the city governments are more than eager to spend public funds on road construction and flyover construction, they are as eager to privatise water supply and sanitation!

For PRC too, Mahadevia (2006a, 2007a) has pointed out that the administrative and responsibility allocation system in urban system is such that the city's municipal governments, with larger revenue powers and base have functions such as construction of city level infrastructure, namely expressway construction, etc. whereas the district level governments are in charge of local level infrastructure such as local roads, water supply and sanitation, garbage removal, etc. Further down, the Residents' Committees are responsible for social welfare functions. This has created a situation of institutionalised inequity in urban infrastructure provision. The high level of fiscal decentralisation and passing down the expenditure functions to the local governments has a potential of creating intra-city and inter-city inequalities. On top of this is the *hukou* system that discriminates between the permanent and temporary residents on one hand and both and the floating population on the other in the provision of various services, particularly water supply, sanitation and social welfare activities.

This would mean that the large cities have advantage over the other cities. Also, in the PRC's fiscal system, specific funds are allocated to the cities if they raise their own resources and place their demand to the higher order government for matching support. In case of Tianjin, Beijing Shanghai and Chongqing, the national level government would use its discretion to grant special funds. Beijing has the clear advantage over the rest three national level cities goes without saying, as it is the capital and now the host of the forthcoming 2008 Olympics—when Olympics moves out to the developing world for the first time. Tianjin does not have any clear advantage in that sense, as illustrated by Mahadevia (2007a).

After some days, when I moved around in Tianjin city, away from the central districts to other districts, I observed a very different situation. The housing areas in districts such as Hongqiao were very much run down. The roads were not in very good condition. Even in parts of Hexi district where I lived, the condition of roads was not so good. There were no or broken footpaths. Water supply had nearly universal coverage but toilets were shared in low income communities and localities. This was also observed in Beijing in my 2004 stay and even in 2007 when I went around. But, road conditions are uniformly good or acceptable in most parts of Beijing, even Hutong areas where the toilets and water supply are shared. In national level cities, including Shanghai, and Tianjin, except some districts and parts of some other districts, the situation of infrastructure such as roads, sanitation and housing require much improvement. While many freeways are being constructed even in Chongqing city, on the whole the city has narrow roads because of its topography, housing is old, narrow lanes are dingy and the entire city requires great attention while the outer districts have new real estate development.

What is common across all the national level cities and even smaller cities, is good airport, well connected through a series of freeways, wide boulevards in central city areas, massive ongoing real estate projects which are high end commercial buildings and high end residential developments in pockets, a pedestrian shopping district, subway(s) wherever the city size is large, wide roads with bicycle lanes and wide footpaths in the main areas. But, the rest of the areas require great attention and investments, something that is not likely to come by in the near future given the fiscal situation of the local governments.

This is the story of Urban China, increasing disparities between the national level cities, between large cities and small cities, between coastal cities and non-coastal cities and among the urban districts in a large city. This is the context of this research. This paper provides statistical evidences for the increasing inequalities in Urban China. The statistical evidences are provided within the limitations posed by the Chinese statistical system.

This paper is on Tianjin city and her comparison with Chongqing, the fourth National level city. It is also about intra-city inequalities in Tianjin city. It introduces Tianjin city and then constructs the situation of intra-city inequalities in the city. Then, it analyses the out of the budget expenditures on urban infrastructure in Tianjin city to explain that the out of budget expenditures can be made only in cities with vibrant land market and high economic growth rate. In such a situation, the less developed districts and the less developed cities are at distinct disadvantage. Lastly, the paper looks at inter-city inequalities between Tianjin and Chongqing, both national level cities, the latter receiving large national government transfers as a part of the national western development strategy.

Tianjin—An Introduction

This National level city, Tianjin, has two big advantages; (i) it is strategically located on Bohai Bay[4]—where large reserves of oil have been found in 2007 and which would give economic push to the city—and has the largest port in northern China and (ii) it is a major manufacturing city of PRC. It was the second largest manufacturing city in the country at the beginning of the 20th century[5]. Tianjin Port possesses the biggest container dock of the country and is connected to more than 300 ports of 170 countries world over. The city has 156 of the 164 categories of industry defined by the government[6]. Besides the traditional industries such as machinery, metallurgy, electronics, textiles and chemicals that have been contributing to the city's economic growth, four key industries of automobile, electronics, petrochemical products and metallurgy have been added in the last decade. The latest news is that Airbus is to locate its manufacturing unit in Tianjin Economic Development Area (TEDA)[7], first of the Airbus's manufacturing facility outside the Europe.

Tianjin is the fourth largest city of PRC, with the year-end permanent population of 769.60 *yi wan* (10,000) (7.70 millions) in 2005 and 764.37

yi wan in 2004 (Table, 2-3, Tianjin Municipal Bureau of Statistics 2006). In the latter year, the population of the largest city of China, Shanghai was 1289.13 *yi wan*, of Beijing was 1092.85 *yi wan* and of Chongqing was 1017.57 *yi wan*. But, the permanent population of administrative city of Tianjin is 1043.00 *yi wan* in 2005 (Table 1, China Research Society of Urban Development 2005). But, this is not the urban population, which is defined as the one that lives in the area that is under the administration of City Municipal Government[8]. Of this (of 769.60 *yi wan*), 532.42 *yi wan* (69.2%) were classified as non-agricultural population. This means that remaining 30.8 per cent in Tianjin urban area were agricultural households. In the entire administrative city of 1043.00 *yi wan* population, 73.8 per cent is classified as urban living in the districts under the city administration (Table, 2-3, Tianjin Municipal Bureau of Statistics 2006).

Table 8.1 shows the importance of Tianjin in the national economy. While, the total city's population has been just 0.8 per cent of the total national population (Table 8.1), the city's share in economic development is far higher than its population share. Its GDP of 3,697.62 million yuan in 2005 was 2.0 per cent of the total national GDP. In 2000, the city's share in the total national GDP was less, at 1.7 per cent. The city therefore has seen improvement in its economic fortunes in the current decade. Growth rate of total permanent population has been 0.8 per cent p.a. from 2000 to 2005 and that of its GDP has been 16.8 per cent p.a (in real terms at 15.5 per cent p.a.). Evidently, the city's real GDP growth rate has remained far higher than the average of China. That however, does not reflect in employment situation. City's share in total national employment is just 0.7 per cent, slightly less than its share in the total national population. But, the total employment has increased at 2.2 per cent p.a. from 2000 to 2005, at a higher pace than population growth rate but at much lower pace than the GDP growth rate. This is an encouraging sign.

The lower share in national employment and higher share in national GDP than its population share indicates very high labour productivity in the city. And that is possible only through manufacturing sector. This observation gets corroborated by the fact that manufacturing sector GDP of the city is 2.4 per cent of the national manufacturing sector GDP, which has increased at 18.9 per cent p.a. rate from 2000 to 2005 (Table 8.1). The city's manufacturing sector has much higher share in national manufacturing sector than the city's total GDP in total national GDP. The converse is true for the tertiary sector.

Table 8.1: Tianjin in the Nation

	Indicator	2000		2005		G.R. pa. (%)*
		Tianjin	% to nation	Tianjin	% to nation	
1.	Permanent population (year end) (10,000 persons)	1001.14	0.8	1043.00	0.8	0.8
2.	Total persons employed (10,000 persons)	486.89	0.7	542.52	0.7	2.2
3.	GDP (100 million yuan)	1701.88	1.7	3697.62	2.0	16.8
4.	GDP in secondary sector (100 million yuan)	863.83	1.8	2050.3	2.4	18.9
5.	GDP in tertiary sector (100 million yuan)	764.36	2.0	1504.1	2.0	14.5
6.	Gross output of light industry (100 million yuan)	190.61	2.0	346.45	1.7	12.7
7.	Gross output of heavy industry (100 million yuan)	439.49	2.8	1489.84	3.3	27.7
8.	Total investment in fixed assets (100 million yuan)	608.80	1.9	1516.84	1.7	20.0
9.	Freight handled at ports (10,000 tons)	9582	7.6	24,069	8.2	20.2
10.	Total value of exports (US$ 100 million)	86.29	3.5	274.15	3.6	26.0
11.	Foreign capital utilised (US$ 100 million)	28.25	4.8	36.46	5.7	5.2
12.	Local general budgetary financial revenue (100 million yuan)**	133.61	1.0	331.9	2.2	20.0
13.	General budgetary financial expenditure (100 million yuan)	187.05	1.2	442.1	1.8	18.8
14.	No. of hospitals (unit)	488	0.7	461	0.8	-1.1
15.	No. of hospital beds (10,000 units)	3.88	1.3	3.95	1.3	0.4
16.	No. of students at colleges and universities (10,000 persons)	11.77	2.1	33.16	2.1	23.0
17.	Urban Construction and Maintenance Fund (UCMF) (10,000 RMB)	804,145@	2.6	1,855,892	3.4+	31.8

* The growth rates for monetary values are in current prices.

** Does not include transfers from the central government

@ In 2002 and not in 2000.

\+ The national total of UCMF does not include that of Beijing. Thus, in 2005, Tianjin's share in nation has gone up

Source: (i) All except row no. 25 from Table 1-17, Tianjin Municipal Bureau of Statistics (2006). (ii) Row 25, from China Research Society of Urban Development (2003, 2006).

These figures indicate that Tianjin's main economic base is manufacturing and not service sector, as is the case with Shanghai and Beijing (Chapter 6). This is inspite the fact that the industries, particularly the polluting ones, were shifted out of the six major urban districts of Tianjin, to the periphery and eastwards, in the 1990s. Further on, the high labour productivity is because of predominance of heavy industry in the city's economy, gross output in which increased at 27.7 per cent p.a. in 2000-05 period, and city's share in the gross output from heavy industry in the nation being 3.3 per cent, higher than its share in the GDP in the secondary sector.

The growth of heavy industries can be attributed to foreign capital investments, particularly in the TEDA area. Further, the heavy industries are export oriented, the city taking advantage of the port facility. The foreign capital utilised in the city is 5.7 per cent of the same in the country in 2005, which is an increase of 5.2 per cent p.a in 2000-05 period. But, in this period, the exports from the city increased at 26.0 per cent p.a. increasing the city's share in the national exports to 3.6 per cent (Table 8.1). The city's share in national exports is higher than the city's share in the national GDP and city's share in national GDP of the secondary sector. The city's economy therefore is dominated by and upswing in its economic fortunes have been because of export-oriented heavy industries, located in the TEDA area, after 2000.

While Tianjin city has much higher performance in economic indicators of development, it does not have such high performance in social indicators of development as compared to national achievements. For example, it has only 0.8 per cent of the national hospitals (not far from its population share) and 1.3 per cent of the total hospital beds in the nation (Table 8.1). However, it has slightly higher share of students in colleges and universities (2.1 per cent of the nation), and this could be because it is a national level city. This means that there is some equalisation policy in place with regards to social development. It also means that inspite of high GDP growth rates, the incomes are not getting translated into investments in social infrastructure.

Another evidence of some equalisation measures in place is that even if the large cities in general may be contributing much higher to the national economic growth than their population share, their local governments do not have disproportionately high share of income and expenditure. For example, Tianjin city had only 2.2 per cent of the national local government income and spent only 1.8 per cent of the national local government expenditures (Table 8.1). But, because of high GDP growth rate in 2000-05 as compared to national GDP growth rate, the city's local government's share in national local government income and expenditure have increased in 2005 as compared to 2000 and both these indicators have registered a growth rate of 20.0 per cent p.a and 18.8 per cent p.a. respectively in 2000-05 period, far higher than the total GDP growth rate p.a. Inequity is building up. Even with regards to investments in Urban Construction and Maintenance Fund (UCMF), the city's share in the total was just 2.6 per cent in 2002 and which increased to 3.4 in 2005. This increase in its share in the UCMF is because of non-reporting of investments in Beijing's UCMF in 2005.

If the following facts are put together: (i) increase in local government income and expenditure does not mean that there is marked improvement in health facilities; (ii) increase in GDP does not mean increase in local government expenditures (iii) increase in GDP means increase in UCMF; one can deduce that increase in income is getting translated into improvement in physical infrastructure such as roads and public spaces rather than improvement in social infrastructure.

Regionalisation in Tianjin City

Post-2000, the economic growth in Tianjin city has shifted to the coastal districts and a few districts of the main city (Nankai and Hexi See Map 17.1) (Table 8.2). The GDP growth rates have accelerated in Tanggu (where TEDA is located) and Nankai and improved in Dagang (also a coastal district). The growth rate of Hexi district, which was higher than the city growth rate in 1995-2000 at 18.9 per cent p.a., remains nearly the same (18.1%) in the latter period. Even in Hedong district, decline in the GDP growth rate in the latter period is low as compared to the previous period. But, the rest of the districts of the main city, namely Heiping, Hebei and Hongqiao and the suburban districts of Dongli, Xiqing, Jinnan, Beichen, Wuqing and Baodi have registered drastic reduction in real GDP growth rates in the 2000-05 period. All these nine districts had lower rates than the city's real GDP growth rates. Baodi and Wuqing have registered very low overall GDP growth rate in 2000-05 period. Tanggu has registered the highest overall real GDP growth rate in 2000-05 period of 26.6 per cent p.a., followed by Nankai (24.7 per cent p.a.) and Hexi (18.1 per cent p.a.). On the whole, in the last 10 years, Nankai district has registered the highest real GDP growth rate, followed by Tanggu and Hexi.

Tanggu, Nankai, Hexi and Dagang districts have also registered high real per capita GDP growth rates of 25.4 per cent, 23.9 per cent, 16.9 per cent and 15.3 per cent p.a. respectively in 2000-05 period (Table 8.3). Even Hedong district is not far behind them in terms of real total and per capita GDP growth rate. But, all the central districts and the coastal districts start with far lower per capita GDP base than the six suburban districts of Dongli, Xiqing, Jinnan, Beichen, Wuqing and Baodi. Also, these six suburban districts have far larger total GDP and lower population than the six central and three coastal districts. But, these districts had witnessed high growth rates in the 1995-2000 period whereas the central city districts and coastal districts have witnessed economic growth in the post-2000 period.

Map 8.1: Map of Tianjin City

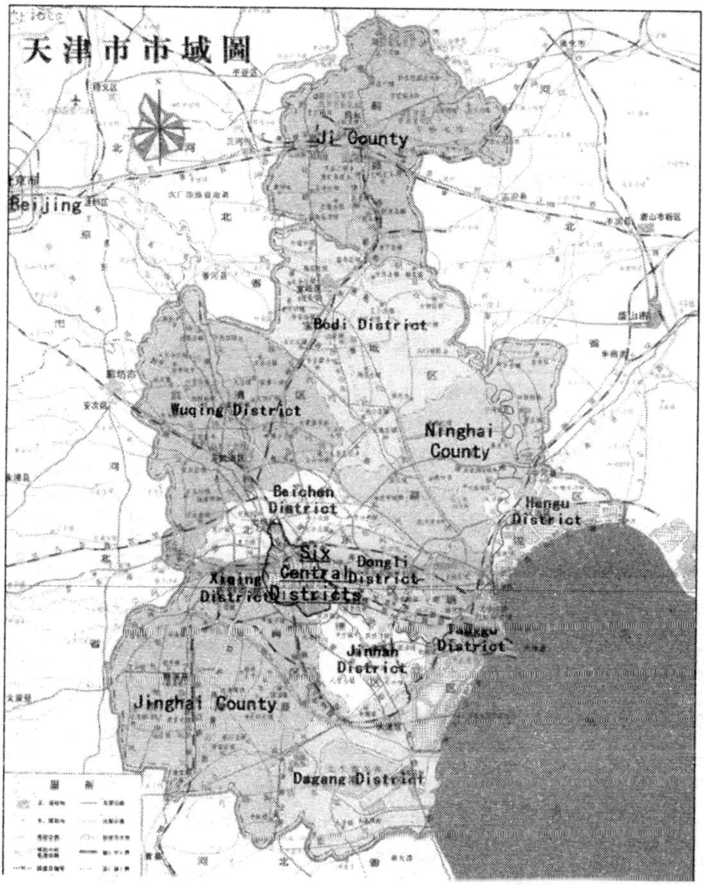

Table 8.2: Main Urban Districts' Total GDP and Real Growth Rates, Tianjin

Urban District	Total GDP (10,000 Yuan)			Real GDP growth rate		
	1995	2000	2005	1995-2000	2000-2005	1995-2005
Heping	111,394	308,242	593,900	20.2	12.8	16.4
Hedong	86,317	221,229	507,400	18.4	16.8.	17.6
Hexi	96,168	251,558	609,900	18.9	18.1	18.5
Nankai	82,001	194,499	620,400	16.6	24.7	20.6
Hebei	87,543	217,651	413,000	17.7	12.4	15.0
Hongqiao	78,361	215,837	391,100	20.1	11.4	15.7
Tanggu	120,468	260,889	897,900	14.5	26.6	20.4
Hangu	67,236	141,929	240,800	13.9	9.9	11.9
Dagang	136,384	304,109	701,800	15.2	16.9	16.0
Dongli	266,035	640,043	1,022,100	16.9	8.6	12.7
Xiqing	298,998	730,135	1,236,800	17.3	9.9	13.5
Jinnan	242,854	547,840	857,000	15.4	8.2	11.7
Beichen	258,092	715,768	1,351,800	20.3	12.3	16.2
Wuqing	500,501	812,295	1,145,400	8.1	5.9	7.0
Baodi	430,009	699,000	742,600	8.1	0.1	4.0
Total Tianjin				10.6	15.5	13.0

sNote:(a) Per capita is calculated using registered population figure.

(b) District GDP figures are from the Tables called Basic Statistics on Districts and Counties. The GDP stated here do not total upto the stated GDP of the whole city[9].

Source: Based on Data from Tianjin Municipal Bureau of Statistics (2002, 2006).

Table 8.3: Main Urban Districts', Registered Population (10,000 persons), Per Capita GDP and Real Growth Rates, Tianjin

Urban District	Population		Population growth rate 2000-05 (% p.a.)	Per Capita GDP		Real per capita GDP growth rate 2000-05 (% p.a)
	2000	2005		2000	2005	
Heping	44.91	43.84	-0.48	6,864	13,547	13.3
Hedong	64.35	69.23	1.47	3,438	7,329	15.1
Hexi	70.37	73.96	1.00	3,575	8,246	16.9
Nankai	77.29	79.73	0.62	2,516	7,781	23.9
Hebei	61.11	62.65	0.50	3,562	6,592	11.9
Hongqiao	56.15	55.16	-0.36	3,844	7,090	11.8
Tanggu	46.54	48.85	0.97	5,606	18,381	25.4
Hangu	16.79	16.91	0.14	8,453	14,240	9.8
Dagang	33.07	35.46	1.41	9,196	19,791	15.3
Dongli	30.41	31.82	0.91	21,047	32,121	7.6
Xiqing	30.64	31.48	0.54	23,829	39,288	9.3
Jinnan	36.65	38.07	0.76	14,948	22,511	7.3
Beichen	31.64	33.02	0.86	22,622	40,939	11.3
Wuqing	79.87	81.72	0.46	10,170	14,016	5.4
Baodi	64.88	65.28	0.12	10,774	11,376	0.0
Total Tianjin	1001.14	1043.00	0.82			12.4
CV (%)	39	39		73	66	

Source: Based on Data from Tianjin Municipal Bureau of Statistics (2002, 2006).

Does the per capita GDP levels and growth rates get translated into total and per capita district government's per capita budgetary incomes and expenditures? That is the point of investigation in the next section.

Municipal Finances of Tianjin

Income

At the aggregate level, the total financial revenue of the Tianjin Municipal Government, whose jurisdiction is over the six central city districts, three Binhai New Area districts and six outer districts, was 725.81 100 million Yuan in 2005 (Table 8.4). This was an increase of 42.4 per cent in real terms over the previous year. But, in 2004, its real growth rate over the previous year was only 8.6 per cent. From 2000 onwards, the total financial revenue of the city has begun to rise rapidly, in real terms (Figure 8.1). Hence, while the overall real compound annual growth rate (CAGR) in 1995-2005 period has been 18.20 per cent, that in 1995-2000 period was 13.63 per cent and in 2000-2005 period was 22.90 per cent.

Table 8.4: Total Financial Revenue, Its Composition and CAGR, Tianjin City

Year	*Total financial revenue (100 million Yuan)*	*Total general budgetary revenue (%)*	*Fund revenue (%)*
1995	117.34	100.0	0.0
1996	137.45	100.0	0.0
1997	169.12	89.5	10.5
1998	186.55	91.2	8.8
1999	206.89	90.5	9.5
2000	244.81	91.0	9.0
2001	304.52	91.8	8.2
2002	375.92	90.4	9.6
2003	451.74	91.0	9.0
2004	502.17	88.6	11.4
2005	725.81	88.9	11.1
Real Compound Annual Growth Rates (%)			
1995-2005	18.20	16.80	20.40
1995-2000	13.63	11.50	8.35
2000-2005	22.90	22.33	28.13

Source: Based on Data from Tianjin Municipal Bureau of Statistics (2002, 2006).

From 1997 onwards, a special revenue item called Fund Revenue comes into picture. Fund revenue is for specific targeted expenditure, for which a fund is created and to which the revenues are transferred to. It is not stated what consists of the fund except that these are specific expenditures for which funds are kept aside. Share of Fund Revenue in the total financial revenue has increased slightly over time, from remaining between 8-9.5 per cent in 1998-03 period to above 11 per cent from 2004 onwards (Table 8.4). This means that targeted expenditures are increasing and hence fund revenues are also increasing.

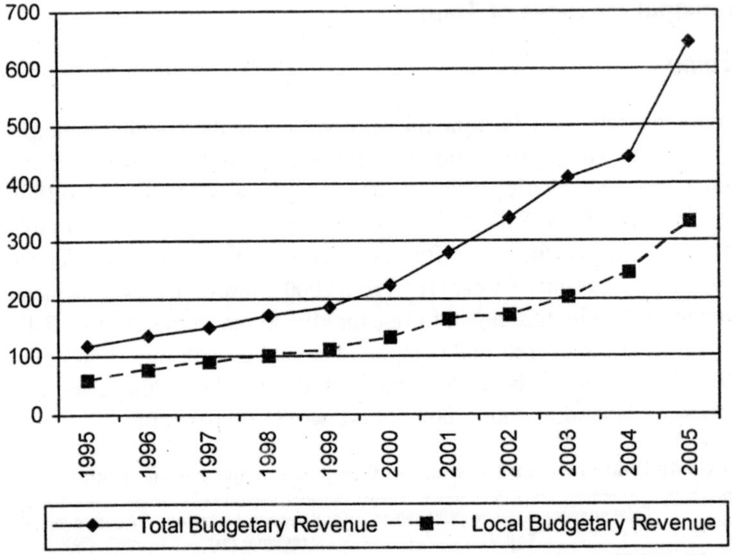

Figure 8.1: Total Financial and Local Budgetary Revenue, 1995-2005, Tianjin Municipal Government.

Of the total revenue collected in Tianjin city, more than two-fifths to half (48.6 per cent in 2005, 44.7 per cent in 2004, 40.0 per cent in 2000 and so on) is passed on to the central government (Table 8.5). From 2002 onwards, half of the income tax collected is being passed on to the central government (Tianjin Municipal Bureau of Statistics 2006: 186) and hence the proportion of income generated in the city passed on to the central government has increased from this year (Table 8.5). Thus, in 2000-05 period, the CAGR of contribution to central government is 27.17 per cent in real terms whereas the general budgetary revenue has registered a CAGR of 22.33 per cent and local budgetary revenue of 18.63 per cent only. This can be seen clearly in Figure 8.1. In the immediate period of taxation reform, that is 1994, when central government allocated certain revenue sources to itself (Bahl 1999), the contribution to central government witnessed CAGR of only 6.73 per cent when the total general budgetary revenue had CAGR of 11.50 per cent CAGR. Since we have not looked at pre-1994 data, we do not know the impact of the 1994 taxation reforms on Tianjin's contribution to the central government. But, these figures indicate that the central government has benefited from increased economic growth rates in Tianjin after 2000, which was not the case in the immediate period after 1994 taxation reforms.

Table 8.5: Revenue Share between Tianjin Municipal Government and Central Government

Year	*General budgetary revenue (%)*	*Local budgetary revenue (%)*	*Contribution to central government (%)*	*Per capita local financial revenue (Yuan)*
1995	100.0	50.2	49.8	659
1996	100.0	55.3	44.7	846
1997	100.0	59.4	40.6	1,196
1998	100.0	59.6	40.4	1,302
1999	100.0	60.3	39.7	1,456
2000	100.0	60.0	40.0	1,707
2001	100.0	58.6	41.4	2,065
2002	100.0	50.6	49.4	2,263
2003	100.0	49.8	50.2	2,649
2004	100.0	55.3	44.7	3,251
2005	100.0	51.4	48.6	4,392
Real Compound Annual Growth Rates (%)				
1995-2005	16.80	17.10	16.50	19.10
1995-2000	11.50	15.53	6.73	18.67
2000-2005	22.33	18.63	27.17	19.46

Source: Based on Data from Tianjin Municipal Bureau of Statistics (2002, 2006).

Table 8.6: Revenue Share Between City and District & County Levels, Tianjin City

	Total revenue at city level	*Budgetary revenue at city level*	*Fund revenue at city level*	*Financial revenue at district & county level*	*Budgetary revenue at district & county level*	*Fund revenue at district & county level*
	a	*a.1*	*a.2*	*b*	*b.1*	*b.2*
2000	—	43.3	—	—	56.7	—
2001	47.9	42.4	83.7	52.1	57.0	16.3
2002	51.9	45.8	81.0	48.1	54.2	19.0
2003	51.2	49.0	62.2	48.8	51.0	37.8
2004	40.7	46.5	57.8	51.3	53.5	42.2
2005	50.2	44.7	72.9	49.8	55.3	27.1

Notes:

1. a + b = 100 %; a.1 + b.1 = 100 %; a.2 + b.2 = 100 %
2. Fund revenue break-up between city and district & county level governments not available for 2000.

Source: Based on Data from Tianjin Municipal Bureau of Statistics (2002, 2006).

Within the city, the revenues are shared between the Tianjin Municipal Government and the District Governments within the Tianjin Urban Area, for making expenditures to fulfil their responsibilities[10]. While the total revenue is shared in nearly equal proportion by the city level and the district and county governments, the fund revenue goes more to the city level government and budgetary revenues are more to the district and county level governments. Only in the recent years, from 2003 onwards, it appears that the city government is passing on increasingly more revenues to the district and county level governments.

Table 8.7: Local Government Income by Urban Districts, Tianjin

Urban district	*2000 (10,000 Yuan)*		*2005 (10,000 Yuan)*		*Real growth rate (2000-2005)*	
	Total	*Per capita*	*Total*	*Per capita*	*Total*	*Per capita*
Heping	38,271	852.17	102,253	2,332.41	20.4	21.0
Hedong	22,015	342.11	77,253	1,115.89	27.1	25.3
Hexi	22,445	318.96	113,046	1,528.47	36.6	35.3
Nankai	21,976	284.33	102,657	1,287.56	34.6	33.8
Hebei	21,442	350.88	49,676	792.91	17.0	16.4
Hongqiao	14,679	261.42	30,382	550.80	14.4	14.8
Tanggu	39,718	853.42	108,465	2,220.37	20.9	19.7
Hangu	9,472	564.15	17,930	1,060.32	12.4	12.2
Dagang	28,815	871.33	50,838	1,433.67	10.8	9.3
Dongli	28,246	928.84	97,988	3,079.45	26.8	25.7
Xiqing	30,957	1,010.35	112,110	3,561.31	27.9	27.2
Jinnan	21,615	589.77	63,602	1,670.66	22.7	21.8
Beichen	32,299	1,020.83	92,430	2,799.21	22.0	21.0
Wuqing	28,769	360.20	77,473	948.03	20.6	20.0
Baodi	15,050	231.97	35,326	541.15	17.3	17.2
CV (%)	34	51	43	56	—	—
City minus districts & counties	578,605	634.44	1,483,171	1,579.00	—	—
Total Tianjin	1,336,069	1,464.99	3,318,507	3,532.92	—	—

Source: Based on Data from Tianjin Municipal Bureau of Statistics (2002, 2006).

More important for this article is the Table 8.7, which gives the total and per capita income of different urban districts. There is significant inequality among the 15 urban districts in terms of total and per capita local (district) government revenue collected. The highest local government revenue collected in 2005 is in Hexi district (113,046 *yi wan* Yuan or 1130.46 million Yuan). In 2000 it was in Tanggu district (39,718 *yi wan* Yuan or 397 million Yuan). Hexi and Nankai districts of the central city have registered the highest real total revenue growth in 2000-05 period. That is also true for the per capita revenue collected. But, the highest per capita local (district) government revenue in 2005 is in Xiqing (3,561.31 Yuan), followed by Dongli (3079.45 Yuan), Beichen (2799.21 Yuan) and then Tanggu (2220.37 Yuan) and other central city and Binhai area districts. The first three districts have high per capita revenues because of their low population. The inequality among the districts in total and per capita revenues generated has increased in 2005 as compared to 2000. The coefficient of variation (CV) was 0.34 for the total revenue and 0.51 for per capita revenue in 2000, which increased to 0.43 and 0.56 respectively in 2005. Thus, inequality among the districts with regards to their local revenue generating capability has increased over time.

Expenditure

The expenditure responsibilities are with the Tianjin Municipal Government on the whole and part of it is being passed down to the district and county governments through sharing of some revenues and letting district governments and county governments to raise their own resources. The overall budgetary expenditure at the city level (city level and the district & county levels together), is higher than the local budgetary income (city level and district & county levels together). For example, the total local budgetary expenditure in 2005 was 44,212 million Yuan and the fund expenditure was 7,816 million Yuan, the local budgetary income was 33,185 million Yuan and the fund revenue was 8,017 million Yuan. While the fund income and expenditure mostly tally over most of the years, the budgetary expenditures are higher than budgetary incomes for nearly all the years of our analysis. This means that the Tianjin city government budgets are running in deficit. This is also the case at the district level and county level observed later on[11].

Share of fund expenditure has increased in the total financial expenditure at the city level over time, from 10-12 per cent upto 2003 to 13-15 per cent later on (Table 8.8). And the real growth rate of fund expenditure is much more (20.10 per cent CAGR) than the real growth rate of total financial expenditure (18.60 per cent CAGR) in the period 1995-05. Also, the CAGRs are higher for 2000-05 period than for 1995-2000 period, in consonance with the pattern of revenue increase. The per capita financial expenditure in Tianjin City is 5,539 Yuan for the year 2005, which includes the fund expenditure also. The per capita expenditure has witnessed a CAGR of 18.00 per cent in 1995-05 period, little less than the overall revenue expenditure growth rate.

Table 8.8: Total Financial Expenditure, Tianjin City

	Total financial expenditure (100 million Yuan)	*Local budgetary financial expenditure*	*Fund expenditure*	*Per capita general budgetary financial expenditure (Yuan)*
1995	90.37	100.0	0.0	1,010.00
1996	110.19	100.0	0.0	1,226.00
1997	140.08	87.6	12.4	1,557.00
1998	155.15	88.9	11.1	1,714.00
1999	177.62	88.6	11.4	1,952.00
2000	209.57	89.3	10.7	2,298.00
2001	259.78	90.3	9.7	2,842.00
2002	300.07	88.4	11.6	3,265.00
2003	350.63	89.0	11.0	3,787.00
2004	431.49	86.9	13.1	4,627.00
2005	520.28	85.0	15.0	5,539.00
Real Compound Annual Growth Rates (%)				
1995-2005	18.60	16.60	20.10	18.00
1995-2000	17.87	15.22	8.61	17.42
2000-2005	19.24	18.07	27.50	18.54

Source: Based on Data from Tianjin Municipal Bureau of Statistics (2002, 2006).

More than half the total expenditure for 2003, 2004 and 2005 and budgetary expenditures for all the years but 2000 are at the district and county level (Table 8.9). So was the case with budgetary revenue for these years. But, that is not the case with regards to fund expenditures. This means that special expenditures from specially set up funds are being made at the city level than the district level. These funds can be, for newly allocated responsibilities of the city government such as social security funds etc. The district and county governments have less possibilities of setting up special funds than the city level government.

Table 8.9: Expenditure Responsibilities at City and District Levels, Tianjin City

	Financial expenditure at city level	*Budgetary expenditure at city level*	*Fund expenditure at city level*	*Financial expenditure at district & county level*	*Budgetary expenditure at district & county level*	*Fund expenditure at district & county level*
	a	*a.1*	*a.2*	*b*	*b.1*	*b.2*
2000	—	51.1	—	—	48.9	—
2001	53.9	49.9	91.7	46.1	50.1	8.3
2002	51.1	46.6	85.4	48.9	53.4	14.6
2003	50.0	48.0	66.4	50.0	52.0	33.6
2004	47.6	45.8	59.4	52.4	54.2	40.6
2005	49.2	45.3	71.6	50.8	54.7	28.4

1. a.1+b.1 = 100 %; a+b = 100 %; a.2+b.2 = 100 %
2. Fund revenue break-up between city and district & county level governments not available for 2000

Source: Based on Data from Tianjin Municipal Bureau of Statistics (2002, 2006).

The highest total public expenditure by any district government in 2000 was by that of the Heping district (48,892 *yi wan* Yuan), followed by Tanggu district (45,634 *yi wan* Yuan) and Nankai district (44,879 *yi wan* Yuan) (Table 8.10). But, the highest per capita expenditure by a district government in 2000 was in Xiqing district (1,223 Yuan), followed by Heping (1,089 Yuan) and Dagang (1,076 Yuan). The lowest total and per capita district government expenditure was in Baodi district. Wuqing district is next to Baodi with per capita expenditure of 462 Yuan. The five remaining districts of the central city (other than Heping), had nearly the same per capita expenditures by their district governments, the value falling between 500 and 600 Yuan. The two other districts of Binhai new area and the remaining suburban districts fall in between, with per capita revenue expenditures falling between the 600-1000 Yuan range.

Table 8.10: Local Government Expenditure by Urban Districts, Tianjin

Urban District	*2000 (10,000 Yuan)*		*2005 (10,000 Yuan)*		*Real CAGR (2000-2005)*	
	Total	*Per capita*	*Total*	*Per capita*	*Total*	*Per capita*
Heping	48,892	1088.67	110,159	2,512.75	16.3	16.9
Hedong	34,743	539.91	89,493	1,292.69	19.5	17.8
Hexi	39,809	565.71	98,196	1,327.69	18.5	17.3
Nankai	44,879	580.66	103,337	1,296.09	16.8	16.1
Hebei	32,773	536.30	80,487	1,284.71	18.4	17.8
Hongqiao	29,073	517.77	60,566	1,098.01	14.5	14.9
Tanggu	45,634	980.53	147,046	3,010.15	25.0	23.8
Hangu	14,184	844.79	37,350	2,208.75	20.0	19.9
Dagang	35,596	1,076.38	96,104	2,710.21	20.6	19.0
Dongli	29,377	966.03	104,696	3,290.26	27.5	26.4
Xiqing	37,486	1,223.43	154,484	4,907.37	31.3	30.6
Jinnan	23,745	647.89	100,953	2,651.77	32.1	31.1
Beichen	32,173	1,016.85	113,068	3,424.23	27.2	26.1
Wuqing	36,927	462.34	145,158	1,776.28	30.0	29.4
Baodi	27,779	428.16	74,173	1,136.23	20.4	20.2
CV (%)	26	35	31	49		
City minus districts a counties	956,450	1,048.74	2,000,867	2,130.15		
Total Tianjin	1,870,521	2,051.01	4,421,207	4,706.87		

Source: Based on Data from Tianjin Municipal Bureau of Statistics (2002, 2006).

The situation changes in 2005. Xiqing district comes at the top to lead in total district level expenditure (1,544.84 million Yuan). Tanggu remain at the second position with expenditure of 1,470.46 million Yuan and in the third position comes-up Wuqing with total expenditure of 1,451.58 million Yuan. In Xiqing district is located Huayuan Hi-tech Economic Development Zone, bringing in high revenues and requiring high investments. Wuqing district falls on the highway connecting Tianjin and Beijing and has, in the recent years, received investments to improve rail and road connectivity with Beijing. But, this district is third from the bottom in terms of per capita local government expenditure of 1,776 Yuan. In per capita terms, Xiqing district leads with government expenditure of 4,907 Yuan. It is followed by Beichen (3,424 Yuan) and Dongli (3,290 Yuan). Hongqiao district is at the bottom with per capita local government expenditure of 1,098 Yuan and above it is Baodi district with the same of 1,136 Yuan.

Table 8.11: Revenue and Expenditure Differentials, Tianjin Districts

Districts	2000		2005	
	Revenue-Expenditure	Expenditure/Revenue	Revenue-Expenditure	Expenditure/Revenue
Heping	-10,621	1.28	-7,906	1.08
Hedong	-12,728	1.58	-12,240	1.16
Hexi	-17,364	1.77	14,850	0.87
Nankai	-22,903	2.04	-680	1.01
Hebei	-11,331	1.53	-30,811	1.62
Hongqiao	-14,394	1.98	-30,184	1.99
Tanggu	-5,916	1.15	-38,581	1.36
Hangu	-4,712	1.50	-19,420	2.08
Dagang	-6,781	1.24	-45,266	1.89
Dongli	-1,131	1.04	-6,708	1.07
Xiqing	-6,529	1.21	-42,374	1.38
Jinnan	-2,130	1.10	-37,351	1.59
Beichen	126	1.00	-20,638	1.22
Wuqing	-8,158	1.28	-67,685	1.87
Baodi	-12,729	1.85	-38,847	2.10

The total revenue income of Wuqing district is just 774.73 million Yuan, almost half of the total expenditures made by the district, indicating that investments are being supported by debt. While it is the case with most districts (Table 8.11), wherein the district government expenditures are higher than district government incomes, the difference between income and expenditures are far higher for some districts with low per capita GDP such as Hongqiao and Hebei, or low per capita revenue income such as Wuqing and Baodi or special development areas such as Binhai (wherein are Hangu and Dagang). It appears that the city governments in the peripheral districts are making large public expenditures even when their revenues are far less than their expenditures to induce economic growth. According to an expert on Tianjin Construction, all district governments and the city government are under heavy debt. They have borrowed from the banks for infrastructure development. Hence, in this

Photos: Darshini Mahadevia

Photo 8.1: TEDA, Tianjin

Photos: Darshini Mahadevia

Photo 8.2: TEDA, City Centre, Tianjin

Photo: Darshini Mahadevia

Photo 8.3: Peripheral Development, Tianjin

Photo: Darshini Mahadevia

Photo 8.4: Tianjin Metro

Photo: Darshini Mahadevia

Photo 8.5: Street Cleaning, Chongqing

Photo: Darshini Mahadevia

Photo 8.6: Downtown Chongqing

Photos: Darshini Mahadevia

Photo 8.7: Informal Market, Downtown Chongqing

Photo: Darshini Mahadevia

Photo 8.8: Infrastructure on Periphery, Chongqing

Photo: Darshini Mahadevia

Photo 8.9: New Real Estate, Chongqing

current phase of rapid infrastructure development, all the governments are in debt. This indicates that large infrastructure developments are being funded by debt financing. This would be corroborated later on when we look at UCMF revenues. Also, the peripheral districts and those in Binhai new area are going for large scale infrastructural investments for their future growth. The fact that the districts with low per capita GDP are able to borrow is bringing in a situation of some equity in expenditure distribution.

This gets reflected in the CV values. The CV values of total and per capita expenditure over the districts are lower than the total and per capita revenue incomes over the districts. For example, the CV of per capita income is 0.56; that for per capita expenditure is 0.49, in 2005. This shows that there is some system of transfer built in to take care of the equity concerns. However, CV values have increased in 2005 as compared to 2000, for both revenue income and expenditure across the districts, indicating that inequalities are emerging with regards local revenue income generation as well as local expenditures. This observation supports what Mahadevia (2006a, 2007a) has argued in the earlier papers.

Jinnan (31.1%), Xiqing (30.6%), Wuqing (29.4%), Dongli (26.4%), Beichen (26.1%) and Tanggu (23.8%) are the top six in terms of real per capita district expenditure growth rate during 2000-05 period. Parts of Jinnan and Dongli are now included in the Binhai new area and hence here too expenditures have increased in 2005 though they do not exceed much than their respective incomes.

Table 8.10 also shows that the much of public expenditures (that is investments) have taken place in the districts outside the central city in Tianjin. The Binhai new area and suburban districts have an advantage of vacant lands, which have been brought under large real estate projects and also special economic development areas. This itself provides large funds for the district government. Once these developments take place, in anticipation of the future incomes from the real estate as well SEZs, the district governments borrow to make investments in large local infrastructure. The central city districts do not have such large land resources, though, here too large-scale redevelopment projects are underway. For example, barring the old European quarters and some monuments/buildings of historic importance, all other old buildings have been demolished in Heping district and new real estate projects are on the way. This can be seen even in Hexi and Nankai districts. But, the magnitude is not as large as in the peripheral districts of Xiqing that this author has visited. The district governments in general contribute land as equity in infrastructure as well as real estate projects. It also auctions the use of land in the market to raise resources. Hence, lands are used in a very large way to leverage private funds and institutional funds for infrastructure and real estate projects. Thus, the districts on the periphery have greater advantage than those in the central city.

In short, there are some districts in Tianjin that have higher incomes than the other districts and hence also have higher revenues and expenditures than the other districts. But, some districts on the periphery, that have land as a resource, are utilising it to increase firstly their public expenditures and through that attract new investments to boost their economic growth. Even then, some of the districts, the old industrial districts such Hongqiao, Hebei and Hedong are being left out. When these districts would be developed, and the accepted model of development is infusing investments in real estate development, there would be significant displacements[12].

Non-Budgetary Income in Urban Construction Fund, Tianjin

This fund is called Urban Construction and Maintenance Fund (UCMF), from which expenditures on urban construction activities such as water supply, sewerage networks, roads, bridges and flyovers, garden development, etc. are made. The total expenditure made from this fund is available. The budget gives a figure of expenditure on capital construction. But, only part of the capital expenditure from the budget is on the urban infrastructure. The rest of the funds for the UCMF are mobilised from other sources and hence are non-budgetary funds. We have three time point data of the UCMF fund.

The UCMF's resources include contribution of the local government to begin with. One part is the Urban Construction and Maintenance Tax (UCMT) that the local government collects and contributes to this fund. Mahadevia (2006a, 2007a) had shown that the contribution of this source in the total UCMF resources have declined significantly overtime at the national level. So is the case at the local level. Mahadevia (2006a, 2007a) had also shown that for each of the public utility or infrastructure, a separate company is set up. It can be a public sector company, as in case of a water supply company or can be a private company, such as for the metro. Both would get a certain proportion of public funds as a start-up capital. These companies are also allotted public lands, which they can use to raise their capital. Part of the equity invested in the company by the city government is also raised through land lease.

This is normally the case with metro (subway) companies. For example, Annual Report, 2004 of MTR Corporation Limited, is the company that is building Metro Line no 4 in Beijing. The Annual Report states that[13]:

> "In April, MTR signed a Memorandum of Understanding with Beijing Infrastructure Investment Co. Ltd. (BIIC) and Beijing Capital Group (BCG), both subsidiaries of the Beijing Municipal People's Government, with the intention of forming a public-private-partnership for the Beijing Metro Line 4 project. After indepth discussions, in December we entered into an Agreement in Principle with BIIC and BCG to form a PPP company for the investment, construction and operation of the Beijing Metro Line 4. This line will form one of the core transport infrastructure projects for China's capital.
>
> The Agreement in Principle sets out the framework of the partnership for the investment, construction and operation of the line subject to a Concession Agreement with the Beijing Municipal People's Government, for a term of 30 years. In February 2005, together with our partners, we initialled the Concession Agreement with the Beijing Municipal People's Government and now await approval from the National Development and Reform Commission.
>
> The total investment for the project is approximately RMB 15.3 billion (HK$ 14.4 billion), 70 per cent of which, comprising mainly land acquisition and civil construction works, will be funded by the Beijing Municipal People's Government. The partnership project company will invest approximately RMB 5 billion (HK$ 4.7 billion) to finance the provision of trains and related electrical and mechanical systems, and will be responsible for the operation and management of the new line for a period of 30 years. MTR and BCG will each own 49 per cent of the joint venture company, with BIIC owning the remaining 2 per cent. The joint venture company will seek non-recourse bank loans to finance over 60 per cent of the project with the remainder to be funded by equity capital."

Cumulatively, for all the urban construction projects, the UCMF size in 2002 was 804,145 *yi wan* (8,041.45 million) Yuan, which increased to 1,855,892 *yi wan* (18,558.92 million) Yuan in 2005, an increase of 130.8 per cent on the whole (Table 8.12).

Table 8.12: Leveraging Funds for Urban Construction, 2002, 2004, 2005, Tianjin

Item	*2002*	*2004*	*2005*	*GR. 2002-05*	*GR 2004-05*
Tax (UCMT)	8.0	4.7	5.1	46.6	15.3
Budgetary Allocation	18.5	12.7	16.3	103.9	37.8
Central Government Contribution	2.9	0.1	3.6	180.5	5416.7
Debt Borrowing	25.0	62.9	60.1	455.0	2.2
Capital Market	0.0	0.0	0.0		
Foreign Investment	0.3	4.4	1.4	1179.7	-65.2
Self Raised Funds	27.2	7.4	4.7	-59.9	-31.2
User Charges & Fees	1.0	4.2	4.0	852.3	1.8
Use of Land	0.0	0.0	0.9	15216.8	10650.3
Others	17.2	3.7	3.9	-47.6	11.6
Total	100.0	100.0	100.0	—	—
UCMF Size (10,000 RMB)	804,145	1,734,229	1,855,892	130.8	7.0
Tianjin Budget (10,000 RMB)	3,759,200	5,021,700	7,258,100	93.1	44.5
Expenditure on Capital Construction in Budget (10,000 RMB)	393,600	693,900	732,300	86.1	5.5
UCMF:Budget	0.21	0.35	0.26	—	—
Budgetary Allocation* in UCMF/Capital Construction Exp in Budget	0.54	0.43	0.54	—	—
Government Allocations**: Others	29.4:61.6	17.5:82.5	25:75	—	—

* Includes UCMT

** Includes both local and central government

Source: China, Ministry of Construction (2003, 2005, 2006).

The UCMF has witnessed much higher growth than the total budgetary resources growth (93.1%) in this period. Given that the 2004-05 growth in UCMF and total budget is low, the increase in both has begun from 2004 onwards. The size of UCMF is quite large as compared to the budget. The former was 21 per cent of the latter in 2002, but then increased to 35 per cent in 2004 and went down to 26 per cent in 2005. Nonetheless, there is increase in the size of UCMF in proportion to the total budget in this short period looked at here.

Budget makes allocation to head called capital construction, which has varied from 10 per cent to 14 per cent in the period. Of this, about 54 per cent in 2002, 43 per cent in 2004 and once again 54 per cent in 2005 was the contribution to the UCMF. In addition, the UCMT being collected since 1985 (Wu 1999) is also directly transferred to the UCMF account. Like at the national level (Mahadevia 2006a, 2007a), its share in the total UCMF has come down even in this short period of study, from 8.0 per cent in 2002 to 5.1 per cent in 2005. Evidently, tax collections are not adequate enough source of fund for large infrastructure investments required for converting Tianjin and also any developing country city into a 'World Class' City.

Nor are budgetary resources adequate to do so. For example, in Tianjin City, the government resources' contribution, which includes local government contribution, UCMT and central government contribution, are less than 30 per cent, coming down from about 30 per cent in 2002 to 25 per cent in 2005. The period we have captured in our study is the phase of rapid transformation of Tianjin City. However, the central government's interest in Tianjin City has increased from 2005 onwards. This seems to be because of its proximity to Beijing as there is a thinking going on to consider Beijing-Tianjin as one region.

Main source of non-budgetary resources for infrastructure development in Tianjin is debt borrowing. It is the single largest source of UCMF funds, which contributed 62.9 per cent of the UCMF in 2004 and 60.1 per cent in 2005. Its share in 2002 was just 25 per cent. The domestic loans is likely to include loans given by the multilateral agencies, such as the World Bank and the Asian Development Bank, and bilateral agencies (if any) to the national government, passed on to the local government[14]. Also, in 2002, the largest contribution was self raised funds (27.2%), which could be non-systematic ways of raising funds. From 2002, there is streamlining of funds raised, and there is more transparent ways of fund raising for UCMF. This can also be seen in reduction in the share of other sources from 17.2 per cent in 2002 to 3.9 per cent in 2005.

This also indicates that for large investments more transparent and robust approach to resource raising is necessary than leaving it to the local governments to device indigenous ways of doing so. The latter might work if small expenditures, such as one road here and one road there, or improving water supply system in one place or repair sewerage network in other, as one can see in Indian cities, has to be done.

From 2004 onwards, land has become an important component of raising funds for urban infrastructure purposes. This source has registered 15,216.8 per cent growth during 2002-05 period. But, its total share in UCMF was less than 1 per cent in 2005. Possibly, as the mentioned above, the value of land contributed as equity in the joint ventures set up by the municipal government with a private sector company for say metro project (or even road project) is not being added to the UCMF.

Lastly, given that the investments in the infrastructure projects in Tianjin city are through debt borrowings, their servicing requires cost recovery mechanism introduced in the pricing of the services. It can be seen that cumulatively, the share of user charges and fees have increased from 1.0 per cent in 2002 to 4.0 per cent in 2005, an increase of 852.3 per cent over the period. Water prices have increased by 17 per cent for example in Tianjin from December 1, 2005[15]. In nominal terms however, the increase is very small. Our field work also showed that households are not paying more than 10 Yuan per month on water and which is affordable. With the increase in per capita incomes, Tianjin is moving towards a model of cost recovery from infrastructure projects.

This strategy of moving to borrowings and use of lands for infrastructure projects would help only certain districts of the city as already seen in the previous section. It would also help only certain cities where either there is rapid economic growth or where the central government is trying to infuse investments for regional economic growth. While, Tianjin is trying to bring these investments through process of economic growth, wherein some districts have been left out, Chongqing, the fourth national level city is trying to do so through central government fund infusion. This is what we would see in the next section.

Non-Budgetary Income in Urban Construction Fund, Chongqing

Chongqing was declared as the fourth national level city in 1997, as a part of the western development strategy of the Government of China. In administrative area, Chongqing is the largest national level city in area and population. But, its urban population is not the largest, it was the third largest city in terms of urban population in 2005, which was 1017.57

yi wan and followed Shanghai 1289.13 *yi wan* and Beijing 1092.85 *yi wan* in total population. Tianjin, the fourth national level city was way behind with urban population of 764.37 *yi wan* (China Statistical Press, 2006).

Chongqing's economy is 3070.49 million Yuan lârge in 2005 (Chongqing Municipal Bureau of Statistics 2006), which is slightly less than Tianjin's economy of 3,697.62 million Yuan. Since Chongqing's population is larger than that of Tianjin, its per capita income of 9,727 Yuan is about 27 per cent that of Tianjin's per capita income of 35,783 Yuan in 2005. While Tianjin is largely a manufacturing economy with the secondary sector's contribution to the GDP being 55.5 per cent, tertiary sector's 40.7 per cent and primary sector only 3.9 per cent, Chongqing's economic base is dominated by tertiary sector (43.9%), followed by secondary sector (41.0%) and then primary sector (15.1%) which is still very large. In 1995, while the secondary sector had the same share in Chongqing's total GDP (40.6%) as in 2005, the tertiary sector's importance was far less (33.4%) and primary sector contributed 26 per cent to the GDP. Emphasis and investments by the national government in the city has led to its transition to a tertiary economy. It is becoming gateway to the western region, with it emerging as transportation hub (7.1 per cent contribution to the GDP by transport, storage and postal services), trade centre (9.0 per cent share in the GDP) and tourism centre in 2005. Tourism has got a boost in Chongqing in wake of three Gorges Dam project and beginning of cruise on Yangtze river down from the city.

Chongqing was an old industrial base, when, in the early years of Communist rule in China, many heavy industries were shifted inland. Cement and coal were two important industries and then came motorcycle making and car making industries. In recent years, hi-tech industries such as IT, biotech and environmental protection are being promoted in the city, which are ecologically sound economic activities in the fragile ecosystem that Chongqing is. The city also has more than 1000 institutions of scientific research, 29 universities and colleges, and more than 600,000 workers employed in these fields[16].

The focus of central government on Chongqing can be seen from the fact that the UCMF of Chongqing of 22,978.05 million Yuan in 2005 (Table 8.13) was 1.23 times the UCMF of Tianjin, although the latter's budget in the same year was 1.84 times that of the former. Chongqing has been receiving much higher actual contribution from the central government of 1,066.94 million Yuan as compared to Tianjin's receipt of 662.00 million Yuan in 2005.

Table 8.13: Leveraging Funds for Urban Construction, 2002, 2004, 2005, Chongqing

Item	*2002*	*2004*	*2005*	*GR. 2002-05*	*GR 2004-05*
Tax	16.1	7.8	16.7	517.7	153.5
Budgetary Allocation	10.9	7.7	16.0	774.9	146.8
Central Government Contribution	17.1	3.8	4.7	62.4	44.3
Debt Borrowing	20.3	40.2	29.7	773.0	-12.1
Capital Market	0.0	0.0	1.5		
Foreign Investment	1.1	3.9	5.1	2792.1	57.2
Self Raised Funds	5.5	5.9	12.1	1221.0	144.1
User Charges & Fees	15.7	9.8	6.6	150.8	-19.8
Use of Land	8.3	10.8	5.7	312.2	-37.4
Others	5.1	10.0	2.0	141.2	-75.8
Total	100.0	100.0	100.0	—	—
UCMF Size (10,000 RMB)	383,989	1,927,444	2,297,805	497.2	19.0
Chongqing Budget (10,000 RMB)	—	3,024,439	3,949,624	—	30.6
Expenditure on Capital Construction in Budget (10,000 RMB)	—	529,594	733,446	—	38.5
UCMF:Budget	—	0.64	0.58	—	—
Budgetary Allocation* in UCMF/Capital Construction Exp in Budget	—	0.57	1.02	—	—
Government Allocations**: Others	44.1:55.9	19.4:80.6	37.3:62.7	—	—

* Includes UCMT

** Includes both local and central government

Source: China, Ministry of Construction (2003, 2005, 2006).

Also, central government's contribution to the UCMF was 4.7 per cent of the total in 2005 and was 17.1 per cent of the total in 2002. The local government's budgetary allocations have been fluctuating in both the cities. But, there is far higher share of UCMT in the UCMF in Chongqing than in Tianjin. Also, there is much higher share of government contribution to the UCMF in Chongqing than in Tianjin. The latter has been left to raise its own resources.

Being a manufacturing centre, Tianjin is able to raise its own resources, whereas, Chongqing is getting support so that it may be able to generate its own resources in the future. It is possible that given the relatively lower GDP of Chongqing, as compared to Tianjin, the former's ability to borrow from the debt market is low at the moment and the city would wait for increase in economic base to do so. In other words, cities with good economic base only would be able to borrow for its development and others may have to continue to depend on government funding and other sources for the funds for urban construction and maintenance. While Tianjin is depending on debt borrowings for UCMF, the sources of UCMF in Chongqing are varied. While 60 per cent of the UCMF in Tianjin was through borrowings in 2005, in Chongqing, in this year, share of this source was only 29.7 per cent. In fact, in 2005, as compared to in 2004, the actual contribution of debt borrowing to the UCMF has gone down in Chongqing, registering a negative growth rate.

The other important source of UCMF in Chongqing is use of land; 5.7 per cent in 2005, 10.8 per cent in 2004 and 8.3 per cent in 2002 of the total UCMF came this way. In Tianjin, use of land for UCMF is very low and contributes less than 1 per cent in the total UCMF in 2005. The other important source for Chongqing is self raised funds. Contribution of this source to UCMF has gone down in Tianjin, as already discussed. With economic growth, Chinese cities have been able to move to debt funds for infrastructure development and sources of funds have become more transparent. Compared to Tianjin, Chongqing has also been able to attract much higher amount of foreign investment. In 2005, the value of foreign investment in Chongqing in urban construction and maintenance was 4.46 times that in Tianjin and in 2002, this ratio was 1.97 times. This source has registered the highest growth (2,792.1%) in 2002-05 period[17].

Other important difference between the two's UCMF composition is that Chongqing has far higher share of user charges than in Tianjin. In 2002, this source's share was 15.7 per cent, that went down to 9.8 per cent in 2004 and then to 6.6 per cent in 2005. In Tianjin, these three figures were 1.0 per cent, 4.2 per cent and 4.0 per cent respectively for the same three years respectively. Although, the share of this source has gone down since 2002, in actual amount, Chongqing's total user charges were 2.05 times that in Tianjin in 2005, 2.61 times in 2004 and 7.82 times in 2002. Thus, at lower per capita income, residents of Chongqing are paying more user charges than that paid by the residents of Tianjin. Thus, although Chongqing is getting central government attention as a western China growth centre, the city, because of still low per capita income, has to recover the cost of investment through partly charging the users of these utilities. Further study on pricing of different public utilities in the two cities is required.

The comparison of these two cities' UCMF and its composition shows the difference between the two based on their different economic base and their trajectory of growth. While development is being induced in Chongqing through infusion of funds by the central government and the commitment of the local government, in Tianjin, it is through market route, mainly through borrowing from the debt market. The central government is also looking for foreign investments for Chongqing. Tianjin, being a city with higher total and per capita income and manufacturing base, is left to its own to devices to raise UCMF funds. The exception has come since 2005 and most likely is because of Olympics of 2008. To be able to get use the central government investments and international funds, Chongqing is using land, given that its economic base is still small. This comparison therefore shows that if the city's economic base is small but the central government declares (or may be provincial government), the city as a growth centre, then it is likely to get transfers from the higher order governments. If not, then, it would not be able to get many investments in UCMF and would have to depend on land and its other innovative mechanisms to raise funds while going for cost recovery model. It is therefore likely that residents of the smaller cities are paying much more than the large cities as a proportion of their income to access public utilities.

Quality of Life Differences

Difference in the expenditure patterns of the UCMF is likely to impact the level of infrastructure in both the cities and also the quality of life offered to their residents. This section looks at this data and differences between the two cities. Undoubtedly, Tianjin, which has a much longer history of industrialisation and global integration through the port, has far better indicators of life quality than Chongqing, except one (Table 8.14); per capita daily water consumption. Chongqing has higher per capita daily water consumption as it is located on the junction of two large rivers, Changjiang and Jialing whereas Tianjin is in the dry northern belt and is awaiting South-north water transfer project to improve its water situation. Chongqing being an undulating city, has more difficulties in providing water networks, sewerage networks and wide roads and hence unless major efforts are made, would have difficulties in reaching a situation of full coverage of water supply and sewerage systems. Further, both cities have to still go a long way in reaching flush latrines to all the population as 14 per cent population in Tianjin and 22 per cent population in Chongqing do not have access to latrines. Thus, although, the UCMF size of Chongqing is larger than that of Tianjin in the recent years, it is not enough. The central government will have to support the city for many more years to improve the city infrastructure. Lastly, the gap between the two cities is less with regards to basic infrastructure, water supply, availability of flush latrines, sewerage disposal rate, public transport vehicles and doctors per 10,000 population. This is what India needs to learn from Chinese cities.

Table 8.14: Quality of Life, Tianjin and Chongqing, 2005

Indicator	*Tianjin*	*Chongqing*
1. Daily water consumption per capita (litre)	123.56	163.49
2. Water coverage ratio (%)	100.00	79.38
3. Gas coverage rate (%)	98.50	68.84
4. Motor vehicle for public traffic per 10,000 persons	11.23	8.70
5. Road surface area per capita (m2)	10.41	6.64
6. Density of road network (km/square km)	0.74	0.47
7. Density of Sewers (km/square km)	20.55	7.05
8. % wastewater treated	57.96	34.65
9. % wastewater treated in central facility	67.06	22.20
10. Public green per capita (m2)	8.38	5.04
11. % of green space to total built-up district	36.40	22.21
12. Sanitary disposal of garbage (%)	80.52	54.78
13. Sewerage disposal rate (%)	100.00	79.85
14. Percentage of households with flush latrine (%)	86.17	78.07
15. Number of doctors per 10,000 population	25.50	18.50
16. Number of theaters and movie houses per million population*	3.25	1.55
17. Per capita space used (sq.m)	25.80	18.00

Source: (i) China Research Society of Urban Development (2006) for all except those marked in asterix. (ii) Those marked in asterix are from Department of Urban Society and Economic Statistics, National Bureau of Statistics (2006).

Conclusions

This study shows that decentralisation of financial system has led to increase in inter-city and intra-city inequalities in China. As this study illustrates, there is unequal development across the urban districts in Tianjin, the third largest urban economy and the fourth largest national city of China. Three formerly industrialised districts of Hongqiao, Hebei and Hedong have been left quite behind. All the districts of the city are using real estate development as a growth inducing strategy. This is possible because lands belong to the government in China. This study also illustrates the unequal development between two national level cities, Tianjin and Chongqing, primarily because the Chongqing has been opened up for investments and is receiving attention from the central government only since the last decade whereas Tianjin's locational advantage and declaration of Binhai New Area as the third growth region in China has put Tianjin far ahead of Chongqing in terms of economic development. Through central transfers, reflecting in higher amount in UCMF, efforts are being made to improve infrastructure conditions in Chongqing. The city not having as good economic base as Tianjin, has to recover part of the investments through user charges and hence Chongqing's UCMF has far higher share of user charges than Tianjin. Like the peripheral districts of Tianjin, Chongqing is also using land resources for infrastructure investments. This is pricing out a section of population from the housing market and is expected to lead to gentrification[18].

The downside of increasing inequality has been acknowledged in China's highest policy making and government spheres. The current president of the country has therefore put forward a slogan of 'Harmonious Growth'. First of all, use of land for urban infrastructure and banking on real estate development as engines of growth of urban economies, has pushed up housing prices in the cities and made new housing unaffordable to a very large section of population[19].

In the process of rapid economic growth and economic and financial decentralisation, China has, however, not paid attention to mechanisms of control at the local level with regards to financial matters and government waste. Premier's speech to the National People's Congress (NPC) as the head of the State Council also acknowledged the some of the drawbacks of the development process[20]:

(i) "…. there are still serious structural problems in the economy. There is a lack of proper balance among primary, secondary and tertiary industry, urban and rural development and development among different regions are not balanced, and the pattern of investment does not reflect consumer demand."

(ii) "The overall scale of investment in fixed assets is still too large, the problem of excess liquidity in the banking system is serious, and the factors causing overheated investment and excess credit still remain."

(iii) "...the pattern of economic growth is inefficient. This can be seen most clearly in excessive energy consumption and serious environmental pollution."

(iv) "... a number of serious problems affecting the people's interests have not been properly addressed. Problems in food and drug safety, medical services, education charges, housing, income distribution, public security and production safety remain a source of public concern."

(v) "Problems arising in land expropriation and requisition, housing demolition, transformation of enterprises into stock companies and environmental protection that harm the interests of the people have not been fundamentally solved. Life remains difficult for many low-income people."

(vi) "... the government's efforts to improve its performance still (has more) room ... Expenses related to carrying out official duties have not been standardised, and extravagance and waste are inflating administrative costs. In some local governments and government offices and among a small number of their employees, there are problems of bureaucratism, formalism, isolation from the people, neglect or dereliction of duty and even abuse of power and corruption."

NOTES

1. This research was carried out as Asia Scholarship Foundation (ASF) Fellow, during 2004 and 2007. The first ASF fellowship was availed in 2004 for six months (affiliation with Tsinghua University, Beijing) and follow-up availed for three months in 2007 (affiliation Tianjin University of Finance Economics—TUFE, Tianjin). For the follow-up support, wish to acknowledge support of Prof. Zhang Liyan of TUFE and students at the university, in particularly Zhan Runping for logistical support. The author is grateful to Asian Scholarship Foundation, Bangkok for the financial support for the research.

2. By Nils Blythe, see http://news.bbc.co.uk/2/hi/business/6325223.stm.
3. As per presentation by Darshini Mahadevia 'Drinking Water Privatisation in Cities—The Concerns' at the Workshop on *Right to Shelter and Basic Services in Globalising Mega Cities of India*, held on February 10, 2006 at Ahmedabad, organised by Centre for Development Alternatives, Ahmedabad and Institute of Social Studies, The Hague under the IDPAD project.
4. Called Huan-Bohai Region, which has been designated as the third economic growth region after Pearl River Delta and Yangtze River Delta. Binhai New Area in Tianjin is expected to be a growth engine like Pudong in Shanghai as per The National Development and Reform Commission's (NDRC's) Report to the Fifth Session of the Tenth National People's Congress March 5, 2007 on The Implementation Of The 2006 Plan For National Economic And Social Development And On The 2007 Draft Plan For National Economic And Social Development (http://www.chinadaily.com.cn/china/2007-03/19/content_830762.htm)
5. As per the Tianjin Economic Development Area (TEDA) website. TEDA is located in Binhai New Area. http://www.teda.gov.cn/englishnew/local/overview.htm, accessed on May 9, 2007.
6. http://www.teda.gov.cn/englishnew/local/overview.htm, accessed on May 9, 2007.
7. http://www.chinadaily.com.cn/bizchina/2007-05/16/content_873450.htm.
8. For definition of city boundary and urban boundary in China see Mahadevia (2007a).
9. The district totals do not add upto the city total because of methodological problem in calculating GDP at micro level. The GDP calculated at larger geographical units are more accurate than at the smaller geographical units. Hence, the city GDP calculated by the city government is more accurate that the district GDP calculated by the district government. The district GDP data is discussed here only for the purpose of comparison of their economic development.
10. For distribution of functional responsibilities between the city and district governments see Mahadevia (2006a, 2007a).
11. The deficits are met through borrowings, as per some experts in Tianjin City.
12. We visited a community named Qiao Bei Community, Xi Gu Street, Hongqiao District and talked with the representatives of the community in the office of the Resident Committee. The committee represents about 2,000 households or 5,000 population. It is a low income community, with residents formerly employed in State Owned Enterprises (SOEs), which have closed down. They have shifted to tertiary sector employment such as driving taxis (we saw many taxis parked in the lanes), selling fruits and vegetables and other food stuffs, casual labour such in construction, etc. It was a quite afternoon, people possibly in the houses. The streets were nearly clean, garbage collection containers put outside the houses. A large part of

the community is to be displaced as a new real estate housing project is expected to come up soon. The displacement would begin within a period of one year. It is not know how long the process would last. It is expected that the resident community would disperse to various locations, depending on their affordability of new houses. The resident committee members stated that the new house would cost about RMB 3,000 to 4,000 per sq meter. A small subsidy would come from the government of RMB 200 to RMB 300 per month. It is expected that for some this would go towards renting a new place. Possibly, for some this could be used for loan instalment. We however did not discuss about the willingness of the people to shift out of the locality. The locality has water supply provided by a water company owned by the Tianjin Municipal Government. There are local level branches of this company that is providing the water. There are common public toilets. Each household is paying RMB 10 per month for water supply and RMB 2 per month for street cleaning and garbage collection. That seems to be the only expenditure towards public services. These expenses would also go up when they would shift to the new housing, whether developed by the public sector or the private sector.

13. http://www.mtr.com.hk/eng/investrelation/2004frpt_e/F112.pdf (accessed on July 11, 2007).
14. References of individual project funding from multilateral agencies is available. But, there is no systematic information available at the moment on their total funding in different cities of China.
15. The price per cubic meter water used by residents will be raised to 3.4 yuan (about US$0.4) from the current 2.9 yuan, and the price per cubic meter water used by government institutions, industrial, commercial, financing and construction firms will go up to 5.6 yuan from the current 4.4 yuan and 4.6 yuan. (Source: http://www.china.org.cn/english/government/150089.htm accessed on July 12, 2007).
16. http://www.cq.gov.cn/english/Survey/200508311002.HTM.
17. The 13.5 km long monorail of Chongqing has been partly financed by The Japanese Bank for International Cooperation (JBIC) (Source: http://www.monorails.org/tMspages/Chongqing.html.) Possibly, this is the foreign investment component in UCMF.
18. A Report titled "A Fair Play for Housing Rights' by COHRE, a Geneva based housing rights organisation, after studying impact of Olympics in number of Olympic cities finds a process of Gentrification. In Beijing along, 1.5 million people have been displaced in the process of preparing the city for Olympics. This is true for all other Olympics cities. (Source: http://www.cohre.org/store/attachments/COHRE%27s%20Olympics%20Report.pdf
19. The NDRC's Report to the Fifth Session of the Tenth National People's Congress March 5, 2007 on The Implementation Of The 2006 Plan For National Economic and Social Development And On The 2007 Draft Plan

For National Economic And Social Development (http://www.chinadaily.com.cn/china/2007-03/19/content_830762.htm) states: (i) "We will accelerate the construction of low-rent housing and low- and medium-priced condominiums of modest size for ordinary people, and improve and standardize the system of affordable housing to improve the housing conditions of low-income families. We must (bring) regulations .... to curb overheating in housing prices. (ii) We will implement the overall strategy for regional development and promote balanced economic development among regions. (iii) We need to safeguard and promote social stability. We will attach a great deal of importance to solving problems arising from land expropriation and requisition, housing demolition and resident relocation, enterprise restructuring and petitions concerning interpretation and enforcement of the law."

20. Wen Jiabao, Premier of the State Council Delivered Report on 'The Work of the Government' at the Fifth Session of the Tenth National People's Congress on March 5, 2007. (http://www.chinadaily.com.cn/china/2007-03/17/content_830171.htm).

9

FINANCING URBAN DEVELOPMENT IN DELHI
Towards Inclusive Globalisation?

SHIPRA MAITRA

Introduction

Delhi is increasingly becoming a global city. Being a national capital, it is a facing two simultaneous and contradictory crucial challenges; fulfilling the aspiration of a globalising city—of high quality infrastructure for investment-friendly environment, namely state of the art airports, telecommunication, etc.—and need to spend on basic infrastructure such as electricity, gas and water supply, public transport, education and health care and providing these at subsidised rate to make it accessible to low income groups to increase their productivity and break vicious cycle of poverty. The latter public interventions are extremely important for tackling exclusions. Lessons learnt from this globalising megacity's approach in tackling exclusion will indicate future course of financing urban development in India.

This paper tries to focus on the financing urban infrastructure in Delhi. Section 1 describes the economic strengths of Delhi and growth of infrastructure. Section 2 describes the major agencies in charge of city management, their financial conditions and major thrust of expenditure. Section 3 deals with finances of the different public agencies of Delhi. Section 4 gives details on projects proposed under the JNNURM and the Section 5 is the conclusion.

Economic Strength and Infrastructure Growth

Delhi has the highest per capita income, electricity consumption and per capita capital investment in the country. Close to 50 per cent of the total MNCs to India since 1990's have chosen Delhi as their base. The city-state has more private vehicles than the other three metros combined and enjoys the highest per capita ownership of consumer goods. The wide roads, green landscapes, access to some quality schools and hospitals add to its charm. As a result, migrants add roughly 2.5 lakh to its population every year (Table 9.1). During the last decade, growth rate of population has declined in Delhi but that of migrants has increased (Table 9.1). Migration accounts for more than half of Delhi's population increase. Increase in IT activities in the towns around Delhi, namely Gurgaon, NOIDA[1] and Greater NOIDA, because non-availability of as well as expensive land in Delhi, and whose workforce live in Delhi has put tremendous pressure on the city's infrastructure. As in the earlier two Master Plans, the city is endlessly attempting to bridge the gap between the supply and demand of the physical infrastructure through the Third Master Plan (2001-2021) as well (TCPO 2007).

Table 9.1: Composition of Population Growth in Delhi (1991-2001)

Year	*Population (in lakh)*	*Annual growth rate (%)*	*Annual growth rate of migration (%)*	*Migrants as a proportion of annual increase*
1991	95.50	—	—	—
1992	99.37	4.05	1.75	45.6
1993	103.38	4.04	1.95	48.6
1994	107.50	3.99	2.18	52.9
1995	111.74	3.94	2.18	51.4
1996	116.10	3.90	2.29	52.5
1997	120.57	3.85	2.29	51.2
1998	125.14	3.79	2.52	55.1
1999	129.82	3.74	2.59	55.3
2000	134.60	3.68	2.41	50.4

Note: 1 lakh = 100,000.

Source: Planning Department, Delhi Government, source: www.delhigovt.nic.in.

Delhi has been able to capitalise effectively on the new growth opportunities opened up by the economic reforms initiated in 1991. Currently, 78 per cent of Delhi's State Domestic Product (SDP) comes from a strong and growing service (or tertiary) sector comprising of trade, hotels and restaurants, transport, communications, financial and insurance service, real estate, public administration and other business services. Banking and finance, real estate and insurance account for almost 30 per cent of Delhi's SDP (Planning, Department, Delhi Government, 2006).

As a result, Delhi's per capita income today is more than two-and a-half times greater than the national average. Over the past ten years, Delhi along with West Bengal, Karnataka and Tamil Nadu, have recorded the maximum growth rates in per capita income. Delhi's real per capita income grew by 32 per cent during 1981-90. It went up by 60 per cent during the next decade (Planning, Department, Delhi Government, 2006).

Delhi remains an attractive city for jobs. Close to 74 per cent of those working in the organised sector are employed by the government. Of these, however, barely 10 per cent are women. Private sector also is contributing significantly in this growth process, providing employment to nearly 26 per cent of them in the organised sector. Private sector employment has been growing in recent years especially with new employment opportunities opening up in multinational companies, information technology within and on the outskirts of Delhi. However, 85 per cent workers however are still employed in the unorganised sector (Planning, Department, Delhi Government, 2006).

Incidence of Poverty

Delhi's record in reducing levels of income poverty has been quite impressive. In 1999-2000, an estimated 1.14 million people i.e. 9.42 per cent of urban Delhi's population lived below the income poverty line—considerably lower than the national urban average of 23.6 per cent (Table 9.2). The 2004-05 estimates on poverty give much higher incidence of poverty in urban Delhi, 15.20 per cent and 2.23 million of the city's resident's living below the poverty line. From 1993-94 to 2004-05 period, the urban poverty has declined in Delhi by just 0.83 percentage points and the total number of poor have increased by 45.6 per cent. These figures for urban India are 6.66 percentage points and 6 per cent respectively. The slowing down of urban poverty reduction in Delhi could be because it is already at a very low level of poverty. The Table 9.2 shows that the incidence of urban poverty in Delhi is far lower than the same in India.

Delhi's Consumption Expenditure per capita (Rs. 1,538.60) is more than double the average All-India level (Rs. 648.54) and the city occupies the second rank, next only to that of Chandigarh (Rs. 1538.60) in the same. The structural characteristics of consumption expenditure also reflect Delhi's affluence. The proportion of expenditure on non-food items is much higher than the national average, compared to that on food items (Planning, Department, Delhi Government, 2005b).

Table 9.2: Incidence of Poverty: Delhi and India

	Population below poverty line (in lakhs)			*Percentage population below poverty line*		
	Rural	*Urban*	*Total*	*Rural*	*Urban*	*Total*
Delhi						
1983	0.44	17.95	18.39	7.66	27.89	26.22
1993-94	0.19	15.32	15.51	1.90	16.03	14.69
1999-2000	0.07	11.42	11.49	0.40	9.42	8.23
2004-05	0.63	22.30	22.93	6.90	15.20	14.70
India						
1983	2520.00	709.00	3229.00	45.70	40.80	44.50
1993-94	2440.31	762.37	3202.68	37.27	32.36	35.97
1999-2000	1932.43	670.07	2602.50	27.09	23.62	26.10
2004-05	2209.24	807.96	3017.20	28.30	25.70	27.50

Source: From the NSS Round data.

On the other hand, the number of persons living in slums and squatter settlements are increasing continuously. The national capital is attracting migration too rapidly than the supply. The Delhi Master Plan—2021 has estimated a daily inflow of 645 migrants i.e., 235,000 migrants per year in the national capital. This is a little less than the projection (250,000 per year) of the Second Master Plan (1981-2001). A large number of migrants from relatively economically weaker section take shelter in squatter settlements. Many of them are above income poverty line (Rs. 500.00 per person per month in Delhi) but suffer extreme poverty of living environment.

Table 9.3: Status of JJ Clusters in Delhi

Year	*JJ Clusters (No.)*	*Jhuggi HHs (No.)*	*Area in Ha.*	*Population (No.)*
1951	199	12,749	21.1	63,745
1973	1,373	98,483	164.1	492,415
1983	534	113,000	188.3	565,000
1990	929	259,000	431.7	1,295,000
1997	1,100	600,000	902.1	3,000,000
2001	728	429,662	650.2	2,148,310

Note: JJ Clusters are synonymous to squatter settlements in Delhi.

Source: IL&FS Ecosmart Limited (2006).

Increase in the number of the Jhugghi Jhumpri (JJ) dwellers over time show the extent of poverty in living environment in urban Delhi. This assumes strategic importance so far as issues of unorganised settlements are concerned. JJ Clusters are spread all over Delhi, ranging from plots of 0.4 acres with 8 JJs to as large as 50 acres with 10,000 households. The resettlement scheme of the Delhi Development Authority (DDA), pursued during 1962-77, with a concentrated effort in 1975-77 resulted in the resettlement of about 250,000 JJ dwellers in different parts of Delhi. In 1977, the number of JJ households to be resettled was reduced to 20,000. However, it again went up to 113,000 in 1983 (Table 9.3). The number of JJ Clusters declined from 1100 to 728 in 2001 as about 300 clusters were relocated. This number keeps fluctuating from time to time depending on the implementation of the relocation scheme.

These relocation sites have grown up as unplanned settlements owing to increasing population pressure and inadequate supply of services. Among the 728 JJ clusters (2001), only 158 (21.7%) have piped water supply and only 72 (9.8%) have sewer facilities (IL&FS Ecosmart Limited 2006). Deteriorating quality of life intensifies poverty in these settlements where the number of inhabitants has grown from 63 thousand to 2.1 million in 50 years.

Next to squatter settlements, slums also represent poor state of living conditions. The DDA has taken up several slum relocation activities as well as in-situ development programmes for providing shelter and infrastructure to the slum dwellers. Annexure A shows the living conditions in Delhi slums in comparison to the average at all India level in the slums. It shows that 70 per cent of notified slums in the national capital are on public land. If they violate the land use guidelines as provided in the Master Plan, they need relocation, otherwise they are to be provided basic facilities. Non-notified slums are occupying 100 per cent pubic land in the capital, waiting to be regularised in future. All notified slums have been provided with tap water, whereas 71 per cent of non-notified slums also are enjoying this facility. Electricity connections happen to be more in non-notified slums, indicating their capacity to draw power from unofficial sources. No notified slums are connected with underground sewerage services in Delhi, while in the national level, 30 per cent enjoy this facility. In spite of all kinds of contracting out services by MCD, slums are still very much dependent on public system of garbage removal (Ministry of Environment and Forests, Government of India and Planning Department, Government of National Capital Territory of Delhi, 2001). Besides, there are estimated 50,000 to 60,000 shelterless persons in the capital, forming less than one per cent of total population, but significant in terms of absolute number.

Growth of Infrastructure under the Master Plans

Delhi initiated first integrated planned development in the country through its Master Plan in 1961. The National Capital Region (NCR) was conceived at that time to build counter magnets around the capital for dispersal of population and economic activities. (DDA 1990). But the high power National Capital Region Planning Board (NCRPB) could be constituted only in 1985. It involves participation by four states, i.e. Delhi, Uttar Pradesh, Haryana and Rajasthan. One primary reason for the delay in implementing the NCR regional plans has been the political compulsions of individual states. Hence, instead of attracting migrants away from Delhi, the towns in the NCR became more and more dependent on Delhi. Towns like Faridabad, NOIDA and Gurgaon experienced rapid increase in population because of their close proximity to Delhi.

During the initial phase of comprehensive planning for Delhi, the achievements in the provisions of water supply and power were largely satisfactory, though there was miserable failure in the sanitation sector (Table 9.4), where the achievement was only 35 per cent of the target set. In addition, the actual population of Delhi in 1981 overshot the projected population of the first Master Plan of Delhi by more than a million. The sewerage coverage shortage therefore further aggravated.

Table 9.4: Achievements during First Master Plan of Delhi (1961-81)

Category	*Water (MGD*)*	*Sewerage (MGD)*	*Electricity (MW**)*
Target	160	142	457
Actual Provision	193	50	458
Achievement (%)	121	35	100

* Million Gallon Daily
** Million Watt

Source: DDA (1990).

The experience of the First Master Plan formed the basis for the Second Master Plan of Delhi (1981-2001) (DDA 1999). In this Master Plan, the intra and inter-state issues, as well as the need for advance action in key infrastructure provisions were highlighted for the first time. The infrastructure was categorised into physical and social infrastructure. The need for inter agency co-ordination, necessity of long-range city level plans for physical infrastructure as well as identification of zonal priorities to minimize the geographical imbalances in service delivery were some of the major recommendations in this plan. The concept of facility centres to group similar lower order facilities and repair shops were suggested.

Strong recommendations were for monitoring, periodic review and follow-up actions. During this phase, the overall addition to physical infrastructure was more than two times than that of the first phase; still achievements were nowhere near satisfactory level (Table 9.5). Only 38 per cent of the water supply target 21 per cent of sewerage coverage target, 47.4 per cent of the target of power supply and 73 per cent target of solid waste disposal were met.

Table 9.5: Achievements during Second Master Plan of Delhi (1981-2001)

Category	*Water (MGD)*	*Sewerage (MGD)*	*Power (MW)*	*Solid waste disposal (Tons/day)*
Target	874	784	3400	4777
Actual Provision	330	162	1612	3482
Achievement (%)	38	21	47.4	73

Source: Delhi Development Authority (2005).

The Third Master Plan of Delhi (2001-21) (DDA 2005) has projected requirements in core physical infrastructure that need more than doubling of the present capacity. Opening of the economy has added to this burden as MNCs and the large corporate sector would demand from the Delhi government not only increase in quantity but also improvement in quality of services to meet the international standards for creating an investment-friendly environment.

Table 9.6: Availability of Basic Services to Households in Delhi

Facilities within Premises	*1991*		*2001*	
	No. in Million	*%*	*No. in Million*	*%*
Electricity	1.4	79.48	2.3	92.86
Toilet	1.1	63.37	1.9	77.96
Electricity & Toilet	1.1	59.86	1.8	73.77
No Electricity & Toilet	0.3	17.01	0.65	2.55
Piped Water Supply	1.4	75.72	1.9	75.33

Source: Housing Census, Census of India.

Census data also brings out the fact that there has been marked improvement in quality of life in Delhi. During the last decade, availability of electricity within premises has increased to more than 90 per cent of households and almost 78 per cent have been covered by toilet facilities (Table 9.6). There has been marked decline of proportion of households without these two facilities within premises. There has been a little decline in the percentage of households with piped water supply within the premises. However, considering the increase in absolute number of population during the last decade, that it was possible to maintain almost the same level in water supply is no mean achievement. One has to remember that per-capita water supply in Delhi is much higher than the national average.

Social Infrastructure

Table 9.7 shows the comparative achievements of Delhi in education and health. The city has one of the most extensive healthcare systems in the country. It stands next to Kerala in Infant Mortality Ratio (IMR), which was 10 in Kerala and 30 in Delhi among the states (Table 9.7). The state also has an extensive network of educational institutions offering some of the finest education within the country. However, basic education is not widespread in the capital. Nearly 50 per cent of people above poverty line have completed secondary education or above and another 27 per cent have studied till class VIII[2]. In contrast, a third of Delhi's population below poverty line had not finished primary schooling. The state has established one of the largest school systems in the world. Even then, the student/teacher ratio remains high. The private sector also plays an important role in this sector. Almost 75 per cent of the children in the primary school age attend government schools. But at the high school age, it is estimated that more than half of all enrolled children are in the private schools. Close to 53 per cent of households in Delhi avail private medical facilities. The state government has allocated 10.35 per cent of its plan outlay for health in 10th Plan—the highest by any state government in the country.

Table 9.7: Comparative Social Indicators

Item	*Delhi*	*India*
Per-capita Expenditure on Health (2003-04)—Rs.	492.20	159.46
Per-Capita Expenditure on Education (2001-02)—Rs.	1115.76	617.78
Bed/Population Ratio per 1000	2.20	0.70
Life Expectancy at Birth (years)	69.60	62.90
Infant Mortality Ratio (IMR)	10.00	62.00
Literacy Rate (Per cent)	82.00	65.00

Source: Planning Department, Delhi Government (2005a).

Institutional Structure

Delhi became a Union Territory (UT) from 1st November 1956 in accordance with the provision of the State Reorganisation Act, 1956. It continued to be so till the Government of National Capital Territory of Delhi Act, 1991 was passed. This Act provides for a 70 members Legislative Assembly and Council of Ministers to aid and advise the Lieutenant Governor and also powers to make laws on matters contained in the state and concurrent lists applicable to the UT, except for those related to public order, police and land. The full statehood Bill is still pending before the Parliament. The major public institutions responsible for urban development in Delhi are discussed in brief here.

The State Government

The state government in Delhi is known as the Government of National Capital Territory of Delhi (GNCTD). It is headed by the Lt. Governor, who is also the administrator of the UT of Delhi. The Chief Minister, the head of the government, discharges the duties and responsibilities with the assistance of the Council of Ministers.

The governance of Delhi in the present set-up is divided among various constitutional authorities. The Constitutional Amendment (69th Amendment) changed the name of the UT of Delhi to the NCT of Delhi and mandated the creation of a Legislative Assembly. The experience of NCT of Delhi over the last decade has however, shown that while there was one intended devolution of authority, other existing acts and rules effectively curtailed the government from fulfilling its assigned role. Central government continues to enjoy several exclusive powers in matters related to the state thus creating overlapping jurisdictions.

Institutional set-up in Delhi is as varied as its evolution as a city throughout history. It is the national capital; hence there are central government institutions responsible for areas and activities of national importance. It has not still obtained full statehood, but preparations are underway. Nine revenue districts have been formed; state assembly is functional though many state-level functions are not under its jurisdiction. It has three local bodies which are different in character. Only one local body has representative character. The city also has only local body in India which looks after rural areas as well. Thus, the 73rd and 74th Constitutional Amendment, most important legal framework for decentralisation of local governance, is not fully applicable in Delhi. These unique characteristics of Delhi have made governing the first city of India both difficult and complicated.

Local Bodies

The NCT of Delhi consists of three local bodies: Municipal Corporation of Delhi (MCD), New Delhi Municipal Council (NDMC), and Delhi Cantonment Board (DCB). The MCD covers almost whole of Delhi (about 94 per cent of its area and population) leaving very small areas to the other two civic bodies. It has the highest population density and (other two local bodies operate under controlled density) takes the full blast of expanding urbanisation in the capital.

Municipal Corporation of Delhi (MCD)

MCD, established under an Act of Parliament, Delhi Municipal Corporation (DMC) Act, 1957, is responsible for the functions normally assigned to a local government institution in charge of the municipal administration of a city. It also has complete jurisdiction over the entire rural Delhi, thereby being the only urban local body in the country looking after rural areas as well. It is also the only fully elected local body of the capital with 134 wards that has recently been increased to 254. The councillors are elected for five years while the mayor is elected every year by the councillors from among themselves. The executive powers of MCD vest in the Municipal Commissioner, who is appointed by the central government for a period of five years. The Lt. Governor of Delhi forms the link between the MCD and the central government.

The obligatory functions of MCD include normal municipal functions of clearing the city, supplying the basic services like water, electricity, health and primary education. It is empowered to levy taxes on property, duty on transfer of property, tax on advertisements other than newspaper advertisements, fees on buildings sanction plans, education cess, betterment levy and has other usual sources of municipal revenue like the shared taxes.

The MCD was set up at the time when there was no popular government in Delhi and was expected to perform some agency functions as well. Hence, it not only supplied municipal services, but also took up some state government services like transport, power supply, management of hospitals etc. At the same time, it did not have any role over slum development, which remained under central government control. Recently, the National Capital Territory (NCT) of Delhi has taken over transport, electricity and water supply while slum development has been the responsibility of MCD under the direction of central government.

New Delhi Municipal Council (NDMC)

An exclusive committee, known as Imperial Delhi Committee was constituted for the management and construction of the capital city of Delhi in 1913. It was notified as Raisina Municipal Committee under the Punjab Municipal Act, 1911. In 1927, it was renamed as New Delhi Municipal Committee and upgraded as a first graded municipality in 1932 and was entrusted with the responsibility of providing civic services, along with the construction of buildings. In 1994, the NDMC Act, passed by the Parliament, changed its status from municipal committee to municipal council. This Act is structured more or less on the lines of the MCD Act, excepting for its non-representative character. The central government has retained most of the controlling powers over the NDMC, while the state government can also prescribe discretionary functions for the council through general or specific orders. It also can get NDMC's account audited.

There are 12 members of the Council, who are nominated by the Lt. Governor. The only representative character in the Council is the inclusion of local MP and MLA in it. However, the local MP is a special invitee without any voting power. The state government's participation is limited to consultation with the Chief Minister in appointing the chairperson and two others members. The NDMC Act, 1994, is not in conformity with the 74th Amendment.

Delhi Cantonment Board (DCB)

Administration of the cantonment area is entrusted to the Delhi Cantonment Board, under the Ministry of Defence. The Deputy General Officer Commanding (G.O.C.) is the ex-officio President of DCB. The DCB consists of seven members nominated from the army and seven elected members from seven wards. It has a five year term after which fresh elections are held. Its functions are similar to other cantonment boards i.e. maintenance of civic administration within its jurisdiction.

Major State Government Agencies

Transport, electricity and water are three major services provided by the special agencies of the NCTD. The responsibility of these services varied between the central government and the local body from time to time and finally the GNCTD has been entrusted with all the three services. These are the three major sources of absorption of indirect subsidy. They are also to a large extent responsible for deficit in revenue account of the state government budgets as we shall see later.

The Delhi Transport Corporation (DTC)

The first one of the state government agency is the Delhi Transport Corporation (DTC). Prior to independence, bus transportation in Delhi, New Delhi and suburban areas was provided by the private operator, i.e. the Gwalior and Northern India Transport Company Pvt. Ltd. Severe public criticism regarding its inadequacy of services forced the central government to acquire the company. Consequently, the city bus service started as a departmental effort of the Ministry of Transport of the central government. But, later on, a separate the Delhi Road Transport Authority was set up through a legislation. With the enactment of Delhi Municipal Corporation (DMC) Act, 1958, the earlier act was repealed and road transport became a unit of MCD with the name of Delhi Transport Undertaking (DTU). However, the change of guard could not improve its efficiency and loans were rising cumulatively owing to low operational efficiency, leakage in revenue, and increase in operational cost. The Planning Commission's Working Group on Metropolitan Transport Services brought out these inefficiencies and on their recommendations, the central government once again took over DTU. It became Delhi Transport Corporation (DTC) in 1971. With the establishment of GNCTD, it has come under the state government since, 1996.

The Delhi Vidyut (Electricity) Board

Along with the transport, the supply of electricity in Delhi also was under private management before independence. The Delhi State Electricity Board was created in 1952 under the Electricity (Supply) Act, 1948, for generation and supply of electricity throughout the UT of Delhi. The Board was succeeded by the Delhi Electric Supply Undertaking (DESU), which became a constituent of the MCD under the DMC Act, 1957 with electricity included as an obligatory function of the MCD. The DESU was replaced by an autonomous board, called the Delhi Vidyut Board since 1997 under the control of the state government. It was responsible for the provision of electricity to areas falling within the jurisdiction of MCD and supplying electricity in bulk to the NDMC and the DCB, who, in turn, distributed it in their own areas. Very recently, DVB is unbundled into several companies under the Electricity Act, 2000 which has repealed the earlier Act of 1948. Under the new Act, power generation and purchase has remained with the state government, while distribution and collection of bills has been passed to the private sector (Annexure B).

Delhi Jal (Water) Board

According to the DMC Act, 1957 water supply like power was also an obligatory function of the MCD. The Delhi Water Supply and Sewage Disposal Undertaking (DWSSDU) was established under this Act with the responsibility of providing water to the people within the MCD area and supply it in bulk to the NDMC and Cantonment Board and receive the bulk sewage from these local bodies for appropriate treatment and disposal. The Delhi Jal Board (DJB) has replaced DWSSDU under Delhi Water Board Act, 1998. It has become an autonomous board under the government of NCTD.

Central Control on Local Matters

Entry 5 of the state List in the Constitution provides that the government of NCT of Delhi has full authority and powers over local bodies. But, the DMC Act, 1957 gives overriding authority to the central government over matters in the list of transferred subjects. After establishment of the GNCTD, the DMC Act was amended subsequently in 1993 to accommodate new dispensation of power to the local bodies in the spirit of Constitutional Amendments. However, the central government still retains significant control over the local body. There are as many as 46 sections/sub sections of the amended DMC Act in which the central government continues to exercise powers—directly in 29 areas, and through the Lt. Governor in 17 areas. The power to make regulations and bye-laws except the building bye-laws is with the MCD but these are to be laid in each house of the Parliament.

The central government has the power to determine the number of municipal wards while the Lt. Governor is vested with the power of determining the size of wards. The central government makes rules regarding electoral rolls while the State Election Commission in Delhi prepares electoral rolls and supervises local body elections.

The power and functions of the Ward Committees are also decided by the central government though Article 243S (2) clearly assigns this task to the state government.

The MCD's jurisdiction is encroached by several agencies. The DDA is responsible for providing services in the areas being developed. However, once the development works are complete, they are to be transferred to the MCD for provision of services. The delay in this process causes hardship for people but no agency is responsible for providing services till the process of transfer is complete. The central government controls both the agencies, but there is hardly any co-ordination between the two important service providers. The DDA is not answerable to local electorate, but its actions have important bearing on the quality of life of local residents.

Inadequate Power of the State Government

A major function of the local body is regulation of building construction towards organised growth of colonies and provision of required infrastructure. In the DMC (Amendment) Act, 1993, the entire provision related to building regulations including the building bye-laws are to be exercised by the Municipal Commissioner under the control of the central government. The state government is not even consulted in this matter.

Similarly, the state government does not have the power to give directions in matters related to important civic amenities like construction and maintenance of roads, removal of congested buildings, prevention of dangerous diseases, provision of sanitation facilities etc. The state government cannot augment or introduce new requirements in case of taxes on vehicles and animals, advertisements, issuance of license or increase in penalty.

The situation is worse in financial management and control. The GNCTD provides financial support to all plan schemes of the corporation. But the financial authority vests with the Corporation without any role of the state government. It has to provide the MCD with ways and means loan and advances when the MCD fails to meet its statutory obligations but it has no say in disbursement of funds. The state has to support the MCD whenever salaries cannot be paid, but approval from the state is not needed before creating new posts.

Land and local self-government are included in the state list, as per the Constitution. In Delhi, both these items are with the central government. Land use and land development are vitally important for any capital city and so also is public participation in land management. The state government has no say in improvement, effectiveness and efficiency in land management. The DDA exercises wide-ranging power of city management without any scope of people's representatives to participate in the process. The state government has no role in the preparation of Master Plans or Zonal Development

Plans. Hence the linkage and trunk services for water, power, drainage, sewerage, transports that are under the state government are not coordinated. This situation is a direct consequence of the fragmentation between spatial planning and development planning. The Constitution has provided for the creation of Metropolitan Planning Committee (MPC) in order to bridge the gap. That has not been created in the NCTD as the state government has no jurisdiction over land. An MPC will be meaningful only if land use planning is brought within its preview. This lack of control over land restricts the state government from using land as a resource, as at every stage, central government's permission is required.

In the Master Plan 2001, a provision was made that the redevelopment plan of walled city of Delhi would be finalised by the DDA within two years. This has not been done till now. The state government cannot take any action in this regard for lack of authority. Regularisation of unauthorised colonies is another burning issue where the state government is a helpless spectator. The MCD is the authority to do so at the behest of the central government.

Finances of Major Service Providers

The State Government

Delhi government finances three-fourth of its budgets from its own sources, as the central government takes care of some major expenditure. Tax revenues account for over 95 per cent of its total own revenue. The non-tax component of own revenue is insignificant, generally below 3 per cent of the total revenue from own sources. This pattern has not changed over last two decades at least, despite several changes in the administrative structure and fiscal policy of the city-state. This creates a perpetual problem as increase in tax rates is always politically unsound. If new sources of revenue cannot be explored from non-tax sources, the dependence on central grants or market loans will continue, which is not indicative of fiscal sustainability. The state government has generally enjoyed overall surplus budget.

Revenue Base

Sales tax is the principal source of tax revenue, accounting for more than sixty per cent of tax receipts. It is followed by state excise duties (15% to 20%) and stamp duty and negotiation fees (5% to 6%). Motor vehicle taxes, taxes on entertainment, luxury and betting account for remaining 4 per cent to 5 per cent of total tax revenue. This pattern has not shown much variation in the state budgets during last two decades.

The lower share of motor vehicle taxes and land and property related taxes reveal weak tax administration efforts. Delhi has experienced continuous boom in land and property markets for many years. Construction industry accounts for significant increase in employment and value added in the state economy. Yet taxes on capital and property transactions are not sufficiently buoyant. Similarly, despite the number of motor vehicles registered in Delhi being more than the combined figures of other three metros, motor vehicle taxes do not form a significant proportion of tax revenue.

Non-tax revenue generally consists of charges from the sale of general, economic and social services, interest receipts, dividends and profits, most of which are not very significant revenue generators. Dividends are generally on government investments in co-operative institutions and corporation, which is also very low, indicating weak financial management in the co-operative sector. Grants received by the state government in lieu of its share in central taxes form 5 per cent to 10 per cent of its total revenue.

Expenditure

Revenue expenditure of the government of NCT is divided into three main heads: developmental, non-developmental and compensations to the local bodies. Expenditure on development heads accounts for 70 per cent of the total expenditure while the share of non-developmental expenditure is nearly 24 per cent. Compensation to local bodies accounts for approximately 6 per cent.

Economic and functional classification of the budget gives insight into various components of expenditure indicating the priority areas. The available data indicates that wages and salaries constitute more than 50 per cent of revenue expenditure. Economic services constitute less than 10 per cent of revenue expenditure and two important economic services i.e. power and transport are managed by separate organisations. On the other hand, social services are a priority budget head, accounting for nearly 60 per cent of total revenue expenditure and about 50 per cent of total capital expenditure. Major social services of the NCT include education, health and urban development. A very important economic service, i.e. road falls under the priority head.

However, the state Public Works Department (PWD) takes care of state highways only leaving the rest of road construction to the local bodies. Education, comprising general education, technical education, sports, arts and culture, constitutes the single largest head of expenditure in the NCT budget, leaving a relatively small proportion for primary education, which is again the major responsibility of the local bodies.

There has been a phenomenal increase in the number of motorised vehicles in Delhi during the last decade. The total number of such vehicles increased at an annual growth rate of 6-7 per cent while increment in road infrastructure is inadequate (Planning Department, Delhi Government 2005a). Capital expenditure on roads formed less than 5 per cent of total capital expenditure during this period, resulting in shortage of road length availability both compared to population and vehicular growth.

With opening up of the economy, special organisations like the Delhi Metro Railway Corporation (DMRC) have been formed to take care of the transport sector in a significant way. While DTC's budget is shrinking and number of buses reduced, the rapid progress of DMRC is brightening the face of the global city (TCPO 2007).

Urban development is a very important component of expenditure in the national capital which is nearly 94 per cent urban. It consists of a host of programmes related to slum development, basic services and land acquisition. The key component of this sector is slum and squatter settlement which is looked after by the MCD. The state government's expenditure in this area has increased from nearly 2 per cent to 13 per cent of total expenditure during the last decade. Yet, the increasing number of slums and squatter settlers along with the deteriorating living conditions indicate that supply side approach is not adequate to deal with the problems of slums (Maitra 2006).

A number of institutional changes, having direct bearing on the finances of the NCT, have taken place since the constitution of Delhi as the NCT with an elected legislature in 1993. The DTC was transferred to the state government from central government in 1996. The DESU and the DWSSDU were delinked from the MCD and brought under direct control of the state government in 1997 and 1998 respectively and are called DVB and DJB respectively with jurisdiction over the whole of the capital territory excluding the areas under the jurisdiction of the NDMC and the DCB. The process of institutional change is still continuing.

Figure 9.1: Revenue Surplus (+)/Deficit (-) as per cent of GDP

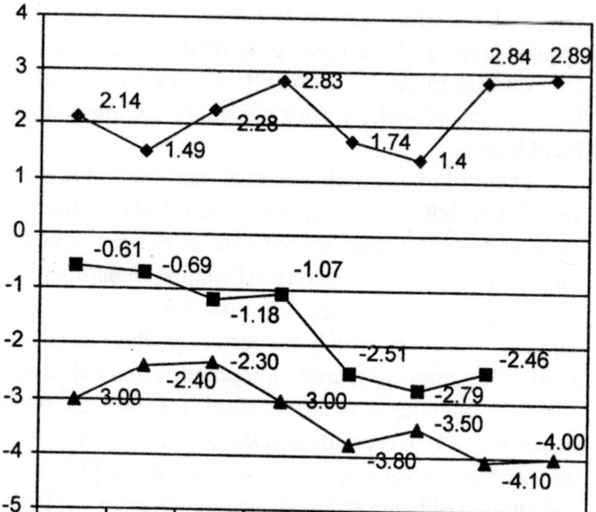

	1994-95	1995-96	1996-97	1997-98	1998-99	1999-2000	2000-01	2001-02
Delhi	2.14	1.49	2.28	2.83	1.74	1.4	2.84	2.89
All States	-0.61	-0.69	-1.18	-1.07	-2.51	-2.79	-2.46	
Govt of India	-3.00	-2.40	-2.30	-3.00	-3.80	-3.50	-4.10	-4.00

Source: Govt. of India, Budget at a Glance—2001-02

Delhi, still being an union territory with a legislative structure, the central government takes up the responsibility of law and order and land. However, the state enjoys more or less the same tax jurisdiction as is available to other states under the constitutional division of tax powers and grants in lieu of share in central taxes. It has been able to maintain a surplus on revenue account because of this special financial arrangement as it does not incur any major expenditure on land development.

Debt and Subsidy

The government of National Capital Territory (NCT) is empowered to borrow only from the central government and has no access to market borrowing or institutional finance. Its total outstanding loan has been approximately 8 per cent to 10 per cent of the Gross State Domestic Product (GSDP) during the last decade. Interest burden has formed a relatively small proportion of GSDP as both sources and loan amounts are limited for the state government.

The government of NCT provides explicit subsidy in interest to the SSIs, fertiliser subsidy to small and marginal farmers, free supply of books and uniforms to primary schools and promotion of non-conventional energy.

Delhi is being projected by the state government as an international city to attract global investment. It is imperative for the agencies managing Delhi's affairs to gear up to the challenge in order to translate the investment opportunities into economic realities. However, the fiscal health of these agencies do not show any sign of change, as reflected in their budgets. Occasionally, some changes in financial management are observed, but they are not sufficient to inject the required professionalism to meet the demands of growing urbanisation process in the capital. An analysis of the state government budget as well as the major agencies operating under it establishes the sorry state of financial management of the city-state whose per-capita income is more than double the national average.

The extent of indirect subsidy has been much more than the direct subsidy. Indirect subsidy is provided through supply of free capital assets like land, waiver of loans, (both principal and interest) lower user charges compared to the cost of production etc. These hidden subsidies are to be calculated from the state budgets and budgets of the receiving agencies. In per-capita terms, these subsidies worked out to be Rs. 850 in the 1970s. This has become more than double in the 1990s, making the capital more attractive for the migrants (IL & FS Ecosmart Limited, 2006).

Revenue Crunch

The state government experiences shortfall in revenue when tax collection targets are not being achieved. A major fall-out of the increasing deficit is the reduction of budgets for social sector.

Social sector expenditure include expenditure on a variety of social services like education, medical and public health, family welfare, water supply, welfare of socially disadvantaged groups, social securities etc. These services are meant for economically deprived in general. Table 9.8 shows a decline in the per cent of social sector expenditure in total expenditure, which is indicative of its activities becoming increasingly exclusionary.

Table 9.8: Pattern of Social Expenditure in State

Year	*Social Sector Expenditure as % to Total*
1994-95	47.02
1995-96	44.84
1996-97	47.09
1997-98	47.11
1998-99	44.56
1999-2000	26.62
2000-01	40.61
2001-02	31.00
2002-03	27.76
2003-04 (RE)	23.74
2004-05 (BE)	26.91

Source: Delhi Government Budgets.

Finances of the Local Bodies

Budget is generally divided into revenue and capital accounts, each of them having a plan and non-plan component. Plan finance accounts for expenditure on new items in the five-year plans while non-plan finance account for continuing expenditure.

The MCD does not have a plan budget. It prepares the non-plan budgets while the whole of plan funds come from the Delhi state government. The MCD accounts for more than one-third of the total plan fund of the state government, thus being the largest recipient of state fund. But share of state fund in public health is very low compared to the fact that the MCD runs 13 hospitals and provides mid-day meals to the primary school children.

Sectoral allocation of the Tenth Plan shows the prominence of urban development (45%) followed by education (19.4%); keeping the expenditure trends unchanged (Table 9.9). Medical and public health received very low share of fund. A new scheme, i.e. Survey and Statistics is added to the Plan Scheme in the 10th Plan for modernisation of the MCD. This is a welcome step towards record keeping and data management—an essential requirement for obtaining credit rating. However, allocation to this head is very low, just 0.14 per cent.

Plan expenditure gets converted into non-plan expenditure after the end of the five-year plan. It can be safely assumed that after the creation of new assets the operational expenditure that was coming from the plan funds earlier would be part of non-plan expenditure, which can be funded from the MCD's own resources. So long as this conversion does not take place, share of developmental expenditure declines in comparison to establishment and maintenance cost. For the MCD, this conversion is never automatic. It is not possible to determine to what extent this conversion has not taken place as this information is hardly made available. This non-conversion, however, has an impact on the city infrastructure as the scope for new assets creation is restricted and the city infrastructure lags behind the growth of population.

Table 9.9: Plan Fund for State 10th Five Year Plan (2002-07)

Sl. No	Name of Sector	Plan Fund (Rs. Lakh)	%
1.	Agricultural & allied Services	5,525	1.53
2.	Rural Development	26,000	7.19
3.	Transport	60,000	16.60
4.	Education	70,000	19.37
5.	Sports &Youth Services	1,550	0.43
6.	Nutrition (Mid-day Meal)	10,000	2.77
7.	Medical	15,000	4.15
8.	Public Health	10,000	2.77
9.	Welfare of SC/ST	300	0.08
10.	Urban Development	162,500	44.97
11.	Survey & Statistics (Computerisation of MCD)	500	0.14
	Total	3,61,375	100.00

Source: Planning Department, Government of National Capital Territory of Delhi (2002).

Major components of plan expenditure are classified into education, medical sector, urban development, rural development, garden and open space, conservancy and sanitation. Expenditure on education has shown the highest growth rate during recent years (1998-2002) (Table 9.10), while conservancy and sanitation expenses showed negative growth; rate, a matter of great concern for the city, which generates 6,500 to 7,000 metric tonnes (MT) of solid waste per day. The annual increase in per capita solid waste generation is around 4 per cent. Plan funds for urban development are growing at less than one per cent. Share of urban development in plan fund is the highest but it is also declining gradually. Over all growth-rate in plan expenditure is slightly higher than the growth in population.

Provision of housing for slum dwellers is a discretionary function for the MCD. But when the slum activities are transferred to the MCD from the DDA, (it has been so for a couple of times previously) the housing programmes launched by the DDA becomes obligatory function for the MCD. The Delhi government releases plan funds for slum development, budget being prepared in its slum wing. The MCD does not have any active role in slum related issues excepting operating as state government agency.

Table 9.10: Plan Expenditure on Major Components of Municipal Functions, MCD

(Rs. Lakhs)

Year →	1998-99	1999-00	2000-01	2001-02	AGR (%)
Education	4304.11	5911.53	11292.94	11103.35	26.73
%	8.46	11.71	18.06	18.40	
Medical Sector	1770.15	2129.44	1748.86	2549.85	9.55
%	3.48	4.22	2.80	4.22	
Urban Development	32296.27	27723.99	33073.77	32782.82	0.37
%	63.45	54.91	52.89	54.32	
Rural Development	2045.75	2821.08	4484.84	3721.62	16.14
%	4.02	5.59	7.17	6.17	
Garden And Open Spaces	525.29	461.34	643.92	699.60	7.43
%	1.03	0.91	1.03	1.16	
Conservancy And Sanitation	9956.26	11438.59	11287.35	9499.25	-1.17
%	19.56	22.66	18.05	15.74	
Total	50897.83	50485.97	62531.68	60356.49	4.35

AGR = Annual Growth Rate
Source: Budget Papers of MCD.

Property tax is the single most important source of income for the MCD, comprising of more than 70 per cent of its total tax revenue, and almost 50 per cent of its total revenue. However, the rate of growth of income from property tax barely reflects the phenomenal growth of property value in the city. Property tax rate, based on the annual rental value, has been the cause of its low yield. Inefficiency in assessment and collection also leads to low revenue generation. According to the MCD sources, there are eight lakh assessed properties in the city, of which only three lakh owners are regularly paying the taxes.

Several studies have brought out that Delhi's property tax system is beset with an extremely narrow base; only around 30 per cent of the total number of properties are assessed for taxation. Many properties are below the exemption limit (Rs. 1,000) in the slum areas and unauthorised colonies. But when they get regularised, the MCD is obliged to provide service in these areas, but revenue generation is negligible.

Revenue expenditure in MCD grew at the rate of 17.9 per cent per annum during last decade while revenue income grew at a lower rate (16%). The major component on expenditure side of the MCD is education, for which it receives state grants. However, during the last decade, expenditure on education has grown at nearly 17 per cent per annum, but education grants grew only at the rate of 10 per cent approximately, resulting in an increasing burden on MCD's own sources.

Table 9.11: Scheme wise Availability of Plan Fund and Financial Achievement

Sl. No.	Scheme	1999-2000		2000-2001		2001-2002		2002-2003		2003-2004	
		Plan Fund (Rs. Lakh)	Fund not Utilised (%)	Plan Fund (Rs. Lakh)	Fund not Utilised (%)	Plan Fund (Rs. Lakh)	Fund not Utilised (%)	Plan Fund (Rs. Lakh)	Fund not Utilised (%)	Plan Fund (Rs. Lakh)	Fund not Utilised (%)
1.	Agriculture & Allied Activity	53.12	25.11	433.91	5.56	252.02	34.31	610.82	56.60	437.50	42.40
2.	Rural Development	3052.00	8.36	4150.00	0.72	3750.00	5.13	5192.56	6.62	5000.00	0.51
3.	Transport (Roads & Bridges)	9750.00	28.21	10350.00	33.99	9217.87	13.82	9823.99	1.56	9500.00	5.83
4.	Education	10008.22	49.04	12523.57	14.46	10542.36	11.79	11499.76	27.57	10161.67	18.55
5.	Sports & Youth Services	25.00	0.00	67.50	1.91	75.00	0.04	50.00	0.36	50.00	0.00
6.	Nutrition	900.00	14.03	1400.00	17.63	1800.00	3.89	2009.90	1.64	1937.00	0.24
7.	Medical Sector	1325.00	6.97	1220.00	12.27	1635.00	0.01	2300.00	3.61	2200.00	21.00
8.	Public Health	946.00	5.19	837.50	32.24	825.00	0.01	1000.00	2.44	1470.00	2.77
9.	Welfare of SC/ST/OBC	117.03	16.76	145.00	72.74	105.00	37.98	0.00	0.00	0.00	0.00
10.	Urban Development	21988.00	12.48	26423.00	9.27	26931.00	11.12	31895.00	6.79	32078.00	4.30
	Total	48164.37	166.15	57550.48	200.78	55133.25	118.11	64382.03	107.20	62834.17	95.60

Source: Annual Action Plan—MCD.

Plan funds are released for twenty-nine scheme under ten sectors. These schemes cover obligatory and discretionary services. This possibly accounts for increase in expenditure for discretionary services if even obligatory services are held up for money. If funds remain unspent, it is added to the next instalment of available funds. Table 9.11 shows that in the agricultural sector, the MCD's unspent fund has increased in proportion during last five years. In education and medical sector, two major areas of obligatory services, the proportion of funds not spent is also significant. Yearly variation in fund utilisation is also very high. Plan funds are allocated subject to budget availability. These are fixed at the beginning of the five-year plan period and are allocated annually. Expenditure efficiency is not a criterion for fund disbursement.

Decadal analysis of revenue expenditure of the MCD shows that the percentage of expenditure on major core services has declined but that on debt has increased by more than double. Expenditure to beautify the city has remained the same in proportion while that on education has declined marginally. In Delhi, there is increasing number of private schools at all levels, so decline in municipal expenditure on education does not imply decline in per-capita availability. But increase in the number of students in municipal school indicates the need for this municipal service even if the private schools are available.

Medical services show three per cent drop in expenditure over the decade, indicating significant pressure on supply. Similar threat is observed in scavenging and roads; the deficiency in these two sectors is quite obvious. Recurring expenditure on all these services declined to signify low maintenance. Meanwhile, increase in the proportion of debt service implies that a sizeable proportion of revenue income is used for loan payment, thereby increasing fiscal stress (Table 9.12).

Table 9.12: Components of Revenue Expenditure, MCD

Items	*1990-91*		*2000-01*	
	Amount (Rs. Lakh)	*%*	*Amount (Rs. Lakh)*	*%*
Education	8,054	28.97	33,894	26.43
Public Health	985	3.54	3,742	2.92
Medical Relief	3,800	13.67	12,445	9.70
Conservancy, Street cleaning	6,163	22.17	26,340	20.54
Scavenging, Drains and Sewers	784	2.82	1,113	0.87
Roads and Public lighting	3,307	11.90	10,765	8.39
Gardens and open Space	1,453	5.23	6,187	4.82
Debt Service	3,252	11.70	33,755	26.32
Total	27,799	100.00	128,243	100.00

Source: Budget Papers and Finance Commission Reports.

Loans and Grants

Plan funds, consisting of loans and grants, forms very important source of external revenue as discussed earlier. Generally, loans accounts for 9 per cent to 15 per cent of the total plan assistance. Bulk of plan loan is for non-remunerative projects, which force the government to write it off sometimes. The MCD has accumulated outstanding loan amount from time to time so that its loan repayment forms 18 per cent to 20 per cent of its revenue expenditure and reached 26.3 per cent in 2000-01 (Table 9.12).

Table 9.13: Plan Assistance for MCD

(*Rs. Lakh*)

Year	1998-99	1999-00	2000-01	2001-02
Plan Grants	34270.38	41166.21	41240.65	42540.08
Loans for Remunerative Projects	0.00	500.00	0.00	0.00
Loans for Non remunerative Projects	3554.37	3254.68	6762.50	7520.00
Total Plan	3554.37	3754.68	6762.50	7520.00
Total Plan Assistance (Loans +Grants)	37824.75	44920.89	48003.15	50060.08
Plan Loans as % of Total Plan Assistance	9.40	8.36	14.09	15.02

Source: Comprehensive Annual Financial Report, 2002-2003, MCD.

Non-plan loans constitute a significant proportion of total loans. It is taken on ways and means account to provide for salaries of the employees. The MCD pays back this loan regularly, so interest component of loans is not much, whereas interest component of plan loans keeps accumulating. A ways and means loan has to be repaid from the corporation's own sources. So interest payment forms a significant proportion of revenue expenditure. Any surplus on revenue account has to meet outstanding ways and means loans, thereby reducing the surplus for capital formation.

Table 9.14: Debt Position of MCD

Year	Outstanding Debt (Rs. In Crores)					Increase over previous year (%)
	Principal		Interest		Total	
	Plan	Non Plan	Plan	Non Plan		
As on 31/03/96	373.37	—	143.07	—	516.44	—
As on 31/03/97	421.55	—	172.28	—	593.83	14.99
As on 31/03/98	481.24	90	207.51	—	778.75	31.14
As on 31/03/99	175.26	110	193.02	—	778.28	-0.06
As on 31/03/00	469.47	235	170.46	7.70	888.63	14.18
As on 31/03/01	492.30	250	158.16	39.74	940.20	5.80

Source: Second Finance Commission of NCT of Delhi, 2004.

Table 9.14 indicates the outstanding debt of MCD during 1996-2001. It has accumulated a total of Rs. 940.20 crores. Against it, arrears in property tax during the same period is to the tune of Rs. 2,569.42 crores. It is clear that improvement in tax administration only, even without other reforms could make MCD one of the revenue surplus corporations, after clearing all its dues.

Property Tax Administration

The most important source of revenue in the MCD, i.e. property tax suffers from serious administrative drawbacks. Number of assessed properties have increased during the last decade but collection rate has ranged between 4 per cent to 21 per cent only. Many properties are outside the tax limit because of very low rent values and did not have much scope for upgradation because of the Rent Control Act. The amended Rent Bill has still not been enacted. But the MCD Act has been amended to delink the new properties from rental valuation and the new Unit Area Method of taxation is in place. The MCD has taken the help of the postal department for new assessment of properties, which is around 12 lakh, according to the MCD estimates. But even without these initiatives, there is a big scope of increasing revenue through improved tax collection as revealed in Table 9.15.

Table 9.15: Property Tax Demanded and Collected in MCD Area

Year	*Number of Properties Assessed for Taxation*	*Demanded (Rs. Crores)*	*Collected (Rs. Crores)*	*Amount collected as % of amount assessed*
1990-91	488,452	1,396.83	127.21	9.11
1991-92	521,786	1,623.95	137.17	8.45
1992-93	524,991	1,850.66	137.22	7.41
1993-94	591,368	2,107.37	205.71	9.76
1994-95	643,555	2,316.09	234.25	10.11
1995-96	704,400	2,553.23	267.14	10.59
1996-97	735,924	2,704.26	331.86	12.27
1997-98	761,568	2,871.62	424.80	14.79
1998-99	792,779	3,007.33	508.09	16.90
1999-00	808,572	3,167.59	596.38	18.83
2000-01	836,951	3,246.64	677.22	20.86

Source: Property Tax Department, MCD.

The DVB and the DJB have stopped paying the MCD any dues since the time they have been taken over by the state government. The largest outstanding property tax arrears are of the DDA colonies. They alone accounts for nearly one third of the total arrears. This happens because the DDA hands over the colonies that it develops to the MCD without authorising the latter to collect property taxes from them. The unclear relationship between the parastatals and the MCD comes in the way of local bodies to move towards self-sufficiency in revenue generation (Table 9.16).

Table 9.16: Property Tax Arrears in MCD Outstanding Against Government Departments (As on March 31)

(*Rs. Crore*)

Department	*1993-94*	*1994-95*	*1995-96*	*1996-97*	*1997-98*	*1998-99*	*1999-00*	*2000-01*
DVB						18.40	23.61	24.15
DJB						10.51	9.75	48.25
DTC						2.13	1.85	
Railways	0.00	3.00	3.24	4.29	5.15	5.57	6.17	6.64
CPWD					10.10	5.77	11.42	14.20
PWD					9.60	6.79	2.88	2.38
AGVC					9.04	8.85	10.57	
DDA	53.00	252.49	240.92	293.11	296.00	307.43	333.11	342.66
ISBT					9.33	9.69	10.55	12.66
Slum department					20.94	22.10	23.85	26.70
Autonomous body-I					185.56	245.85	237.14	237.94
Autonomous body-II					61.56	82.82	82.34	78.86
Government miscellaneous	98.00	71.76	175.28	254.70	41.42	32.99		20.30
Total	151.00	327.25	419.44	552.70	648.52	785.90	753.24	814.71

Source: Property Tax Reforms—Report of the Expert Committee, MCD, 2003.

New Delhi Municipal Council (NDMC)

The NDMC looks after the core administrative areas of the central government as well as the diplomatic enclaves. It is one of the richest municipalities operating over the areas that have controlled density. It incurs highest per-capita expenditure on services with high quality infrastructure. It is probably the only local body whose non-tax revenue is more than the tax revenue. It derives income from four main sources in order of importance, i.e. charges from sale of electricity (65% to 67%), income from municipal works (13% to 15%), property taxes (11% to 13%) and charges from water (3% to 5%).

One major components of revenue expenditure includes purchase of electricity from erstwhile DVB. It accounts for nearly half of NDMC's total expenditure. Next major head is social and economic services consisting of 18 per cent to 20 per cent of revenue expenditure. The NDMC is able to price electricity and water in such a manner that it is able to cover the operation and maintenance costs and maintain a surplus on revenue account. Its tax base is not extensive given that it has either the properties of the national government or that of the governments of other countries (the diplomatic enclave). The railways, state and the central government together own around 80 per cent to 85 per cent of the taxable properties. Both, the national government organisations and the diplomatic enclaves are exempt from property tax payments. But collection efficiency is quite high and properties are well recorded thus making tax administration relatively easier job. Its tax collection increased from Rs. 38 crore in 1998-99 to Rs. 123 crore during 2002-03.

The Delhi Cantonment Board (DCB)

Tax revenue forms the highest share (nearly 90%) in the DCBs revenue income, making share of non-tax revenue quite insignificant. The rest of the revenue deficit is funded by the central grants. The share of development expenditure in the DCB budget is more than 50 per cent of total expenditure. Electricity, water and roads are major heads of development expenses in the cantonment.

The DCB is also a controlled area like the NDMC. Its expenditure responsibility is not flexible. The civilians constitute almost one-third of the total population of the DCB, where some flexible resource generation instruments may be used, but with limited scope. The Ministry of Defence is largely responsible for maintaining quality of life here. Hence, even if the rate of growth of income in the DCB is lower than the rate of growth of expenditure as in case of other two local bodies, the level of services do not deteriorate in the DCB areas.

Overall Observations

Table 9.17 compares the Annual Growth Rate (AGR) of different budgetary parameters of the three local governments in Delhi. It indicates the prominence of the NDMC among the three local bodies. The NDMC is prominent because it caters to the central government, diplomatic enclaves and other VIP areas out of bound of the common residents. Strict land use restrictions in the NDMC help in maintaining the planned developments within its jurisdiction in contrast to the MCD areas where implementation of planned provisions is exception rather than a rule.

Table 9.17: AGR of Revenue, Expenditure and Population in the Local Bodies, Delhi, (1980-81 to 2000-01)

(Per cent)

Item	*MCD*	*NDMC*	*DCB*
Total Expenditure	13.15	17.11	8.01
Total Revenue	12.73	14.23	6.89
Population	4.06	1.26	3.95
Per-Capita Revenue	8.33	12.81	2.83
Per-Capita Expenditure	8.73	15.65	3.91

Source: Budgets of different local bodies and census data.

Analysis of the budgets of Delhi's public service providers indicates trends that are not inclusive in nature. The social sector expenditure is declining both in the state government and the MCD budgets. The private sector expenditure in education and health is increasing making both these facilities more expensive. Delhi has been able to maintain its supremacy over the national average because of huge national and state government expenditures so far. It is only natural that with the increase in per capita income, paying capacity of people will increase and they will try to avail more expensive facilities that are qualitatively better. But there is no prioritisation of government budgets towards meeting the needs of the deprived sections and sectors. Table 9.18 shows the gap in service delivery in state government's Tenth Plan. The primary schools, primarily used by the children from the low income households, have not been constructed in adequate numbers. Construction of new night shelters has not even started. It is unlikely that any of the targets will be fulfilled in the remaining years of the Tenth Plan period. The welfare schemes, primarily for the benefits of the deprived sector, are taking a back seat because of inefficiency and inadequate finance, while remunerative programmes are increasingly being given to the private service providers for speedy implementations.

Globalised city will require high speed roads and flyovers, the construction of which is increasingly being taken over by the private sector. Private sector is coming in a big way for waste management but there is no way of monitoring small contractors and directing them to take up sanitation activities in deprived areas. In the middle-income and high-income colonies, the RWAs are becoming active in the city beautification and water management activities. But in the deprived areas, slow pace of activities are causing concern. Lastly, the loans are accumulating for both the state government and the MCD with increasing share of revenue expenditure going towards loan repayment rather than maintenance.

Table 9.18: The Tenth Plan Targets and Achievements

Category	*Target (No.)*	*Achievements upto 2004-2005 (No.)*
A. Education		
1. Free supply of text books	675000	325000 (48.14%)
2. New school started	70	33 (47.14%)
3. Construction of school buildings	20	3 (15.00%)
4. Constructions of new college buildings	10	2 (20.00%)
5. New MCD schools	150	70 (46.66%)
B. Medical		
1. Opening of health services	60	20 (33.33%)
2. MCD dispensaries	30	7 (23.33%)
3. Beds in state hospitals	3773	495 (13.11%)
C. Urban Villages		
1. Covered with sewerage system	135	99 (73.33%)
2. With drainage system (km)	120	103.96 (86.63%)
3. Street light points	100	
D. Unauthorised Colonies		
1. Water supply facilities	1071	398 (37.16%)
2. Drainage system (km)	446	347.4 (77.89%)
3. Street light points	160	
E. Constructions of Night Shelter	5	0 (0.00%)

Note: Figures in bracket refer to percentage to previous column.

Source: Planning Department, Delhi Government (2005b).

Finances of the Public Agencies

Delhi Transport Corporation (DTC) is the largest metropolitan bus transport system in India. It is still the main public transit option as the metro rail is yet to cover the full city. Consequently, less than 10 per cent of the daily commuters avail the rail transport for entering and travelling within the city. The DTC runs two sets of services; one city service and other intercity service. It also manages a bus service provided by the private operator. The change of guards however has not improved the financial health of the corporation. The mounting losses of the erstwhile DTU continued when it became a corporation. Its gross recovery rate (Revenue/cost) declined from 65.22 per cent to 39.34 per cent during the 1980s and to 23.88 per cent in the 1990s. A major reason for this low recovery is several welfare services such as concessional rate passes offered to the students, the residents of resettlement colonies and the senior citizens; general all route passes; passes to police and press; and free passes to the disabled, freedom fighters, sportsmen, national award winners and war widows with their dependents. The total subsidy in these services was estimated to be 15 per cent to 16 per cent of DTC's total revenue income in 1996-97 (Mathur 2000). In 1996, when the state government took over its control, the central government wrote-off all its loan liabilities and the interest accrued thereon, amounting to Rs. 2,123.21 crores. Even then, its losses were Rs. 283.7 crores the very next year, depicting poor financial management.

As in case of the DTC, the DVB was also continuously facing operating losses during the last two decades. While the central government waived-off all the loans of DTC when it was taken over by the state government, this has not happened in case of the DVB. Consequently, its accumulated deficit has amounted to more than Rs. 5,000 crores during 1999-2000.

The revenue receipts of the DVB consist of income from the sale of electricity, rental of metres, commission on collection of taxes on behalf of the MCD and other miscellaneous recoveries. As discussed earlier, the DVB has been unbundled into six companies, two of them owned by the public sector. The budget analysis of the erstwhile DVB is still relevant to explain the vulnerable state of affairs in the its finances for the period concerned. Major heads of revenue expenditure were general administration, expenditure of generation, distribution, operation and maintenance of power supply and purchase of power, debt and interest payments etc. The DVB's long history of losses has not changed with the changes in organisational and managerial set up changes. The growth in revenue receipts has been consistently behind that of revenue expenditure, accounting for continuous dismal performance.

The DJB purchases bulk of raw input from outside. The major sources of revenue are water tax, user charges, scavenging tax, bulk sale of water and payment received for bulk sewage treatment and disposal. The major heads of expenditure consist of the cost of raw water, debt charges, general administration, operation and maintenance. The DJB maintains four separate accounts of income and expenditure relating to the supply of water and disposal of sewage, i.e. (i) bulk water supply, (ii) bulk sewage disposal, (iii) internal water supply and (iv) internal sewerage and drains. The first two accounts are maintained on commercial lines while the last two are maintained on a cash basis. The expenditures on bulk water and sewage disposal are distributed among the various local bodies on the basis of consumption of water and the cost of bulk receipts of sewage and its disposal after deducting the receipts, if any, from the sale of effluent sludge, sludge gas, etc. Cost of water is the major expenditure head, accounting for 60 per cent to 67 per cent of total expenditure. Debt charges are also an important head constituting another 15 per cent. Total expenditure including debt charges has increased by 88 per cent during the last two decades while revenue has increased by 4 per cent. The accumulated deficits of the DJB have been more than Rs. 1,500 crores during 2000-04 (DJB Budget, 2005-06).

The major contributors to the financial losses of the DVB are unaccounted water use (pilferage of water) and low water rate that do not even cover the average cost of production. In order to meet the recurrent expenditure, the DJB is continuing its old practice of (i) not paying its dues to public and government agencies, especially the DVB, (ii) taking grants and loans from the central government, (iii) deferring interest payments and (iv) diverting capital loans. After privatisation of the DVB, the DJB cannot continue the first practice any longer.

The JNNURM Initiatives in Delhi

As of December 2007, Delhi had not yet submitted any DPR and hence no JNNURM project has yet been sanctioned in the city. A glance at the CDP of the national capital will help to understand the shape of things to come in future. The CDP of Delhi outlines basic infrastructural requirements under sub-mission (i) that will cover all unserviced areas as well as improve the existing conditions. Under sub-mission (ii) it proposes in-situ redevelopment at existing slum and JJ cluster sites, development of serviced plots, development of night shelters, infrastructure upgradation at the slum relocation sites and provision of housing for the poor (Table 9.19).

Table 9.19: Projects for Appraisal under JNNURM

Projects	*Total Cost*	*CG (35%)*	*SG (15%)*	*ULB/FI (50%)*
Sub-mission-1: Urban Infrastructure and Governance				
Water Supply	1632	571	245	816
Sewerage	2755	964	413	1378
Road Network and Transport	13487	4720	2023	6743
Storm Water Drainage	231	81	35	116
Solid Waste Management	593	208	89	297
Heritage and Conservation	582	204	87	291
City Environment	431	151	65	215
Urban Governance	9	3	1	5
Street Lighting	25	9	4	13
Other Projects	20	7	3	10
Sub Total	19740 (81.03)	6909	2961	9870
Sub-Mission-2: Basic Services and Poor				
Urban Poor, Slum and Housing	4400	2200	—	2200
Sub Total	*4400 (18.97)*	*2200*	*0*	*2200*
Grand Total	*24140 (100)*	*9109*	*2961*	*12070*

Source: IL&FS Ecosmart Limited (2006).

Conclusion

Delhi's record in poverty alleviation seems to be quite impressive compared to all-India standard. The volume of migration in the national capital has remained substantial even after development of several areas in NCR. The developed areas like Gurgaon and NOIDA have mostly accounted for the out-migration of the comparatively well-off, while economically weaker sections have taken shelter in the slums, the squatter settlements and the pavements of the city. Slum relocation programmes have been slow in implementation, compared to growth of population. The budget allocation of the state and the local bodies show it is not the shortage of finance but slow pace of implementation, among other issues, that have accounted for exiting and growing poverty in the city. Delhi suffers not so much from income poverty as from poverty of living environment. Land prices are very high in the city. This threatens the availability of land for the urban poor, although most lands in the city are under public control. The funds for poverty alleviation remain unutilised while other remunerative construction projects are completed on or before time with public-private partnership.

The CDP of Delhi also shows continuation of this trend. Road network and transport account for more than 55 per cent of the projects submitted for consideration under the JNNURM. Road and transport facilities may be income neutral but consequent results may not be. Better road network may increase employment opportunities but at the same time will increase property values. The global city needs better motorable roads, better water supply and better entertainment centres which are coming in a big way in the capital. However, unless the government addresses the slum and squatter settlement issues more aggressively, the living poverty is bound to increase in the city. Continuously increasing per capita income has kept the percentage of persons below poverty line quite low in the capital. The state should take advantage of this situation in improving the living environment of the poor. Instead, the CDP projects show that the state has not even specified its share in provision of slum housing under Sub-mission 2. The journey towards global city raises serious doubts about inclusive city management where increasing land price not only threatens affordability but encourages land use for different purposes other than slum housing. The CDP shows lowest priority to urban governance which is the major deciding factor for inclusive policies. The state has initiated many important financial reforms for better financial management of urban infrastructure but the emphasis on inclusive city management is seriously missing.

ANNEXURE A
FACILITIES AVAILABLE IN SLUMS—DELHI AND ALL INDIA (PERCENTAGE)

Category	Delhi	All India
Notified Slum on Private land	0	36
Notified Slum on Public land	70	64
Non-notified Slum on Public land	100	63
Pucca Housing on Notified Slum	100	65
Pucca Housing on Non-notified Slums	27	30
Taps as Major Source of Drinking Water in Notified Slum	100	84
Taps as Major Source of Drinking Water in Non-notified Slums	71	71
Electricity Connections in Notified Slum Households	31	11
Electricity Connections In Non-notified Slums Households	61	25
Underground Sewerage Connections in Notified Slums	0	30
Public Agency Responsibility in Notified slums	70	79

ANNEXURE B
SUCCESSOR ENTITIES TO DVB

The entities operating in the power sector in Delhi, following the restructuring of the sector that came into effect from July 1, 2002, are as follows:

- *Delhi Power Supply Company Limited (DPCL):* This company, the 'Holding Company' of the Transfer Scheme, is 100 per cent owned by the Government of the NCT of Delhi and, in turn, holds 100 per cent of the equity of the Indraprastha Power Generation Company Ltd (IPGCL) and Delhi Transco Ltd (DTL). It holds 49 per cent of the equity of the three distribution companies and is represented on their Boards. It should be noted that DPCL is not a licensee under the Delhi Electricity Reforms Act, 2000 or the Electricity Act, 2003, and is not subject to any direct regulation by the Delhi Electricity Regulatory Commission (DERC)
- *Generating Companies:* These are not licensed and regulated entities under the Electricity Act, 2003, which has freed the thermal generating sector entirely from licensing. However

Transco's power purchases are subject to regulatory approval and, therefore, DERC does examine their performance and their revenue requirements in the course of its annual exercise of approving the price at which Transco purchases power from these companies.

- *Indraprastha Power Generation Company Ltd (IPGCL)*: This is formed out of the generating wing of DVB. It operates three power stations, viz. the old and outdated Indraprastha Power Station and the Rajghat Power House (both coal-based thermal stations), and the Gas Turbine Power Station (GTPS).
- *Pragati Power Corporation Ltd (PPCL)*: The Pragati Power Project was kept formally distinct from the DVB, and registered as a separate company; primarily in order make its financing viable. The Delhi Government wholly owns the equity.
- *Delhi Transco Ltd (Transco)*: This is the company created to take over the transmission business of the erstwhile DVB. As such it is also responsible for grid management, being the State Transmission Utility (STU) under the Electricity Act, 2003. The State Load Dispatch Centre (SLDC) functions within Transco. Further, Transco has taken over DVB's power procurement functions and sells power to the distribution companies (Discoms). The Government's transitional support is funnelled to the consumer by means of reducing the Bulk Supply Tariff at which Transco sells to the Discoms. There is no bar in principle on the Discoms' directly purchasing power from sources they identify and paying wheeling charges to Transco for the use of its system, but this is unlikely as long as Transco's Bulk Supply Tariff remains cheaper than the possible alternatives.
- *Distribution Licensees:* Most of Delhi is served by the three discoms carved out of DVB's distribution business. In addition, the NDMC and the DCB are statutory licensees under their own laws. With the enactment of the Electricity Act, 2003 they have been brought under the regulatory jurisdiction of DERC. The three discoms are:

    (i) BSES Rajdhani Power Ltd (BRPL): This comprises what were earlier the South and West circles of DVB. It has about 8.69 lakh registered consumers. While the BSES label has been retained for the time being, Reliance Energy Limited holds the controlling interest in this discom.

(ii) BSES Yamuna Power Ltd (BYPL): This is the second discom controlled by Reliance Energy Limited; comprises what were earlier the East and Central circles of DVB. These are among the most challenging areas to serve, and this was the discom with the highest opening transmission loss level (57% according to DERC). East Delhi includes disproportionately large (even for Delhi) unauthorised developments. The Central circle includes the most congested areas in Delhi, where capacity augmentation has to be made within the context of severe space constraints and right-of-way difficulties. This discom has about 89.49 lakh registered consumers.

(iii) North Delhi Power Limited (NDPL): This discom, comprising the former North and Northwest circles of DVB and is controlled by the Tata Power Company and, thus, provides benchmarking competition. It serves about 8.54 lakh registered consumers.

- *Statutory licensees:* The NDMC within its area and the Military Engineering Services (MES) within the Cantonment are statutory licensees under their own constitutive laws and are subject to DERC regulation as deemed licensees. The NDMC's annual consumption is about 1100 MU to over a lakh consumers; MES's annual consumption is about 160 MU. These are both small, efficient utilities which have not hitherto been regarded as problematic in any way, but which will now have to modernise some of their operations to comply with DERC-imposed norms, including the Billing and Metering Regulations.

NOTES

1. New Okhla Industrial Development Authority.
2. The data in this paragraph are from Planning Department, Delhi Government (2005).

10[1]

BASIC INFRASTRUCTURE, PUBLIC FINANCE AND SLUM DWELLERS
Ahmedabad[2]

DARSHINI MAHADEVIA and HARPREET SINGH BRAR

Introduction

Ahmedabad has been declared as a megacity, and the city is also covered under the JNNURM. This means that the city would receive grants from the central government for capital expenditure on certain infrastructure identified as key for city's development. Ahmedabad City has also gone to the capital market to raise funds through bonds. The city has issued four bond issues by now. The city has also borrowed from many financial institutions including HUDCO (Housing and Development Corporation), ICICI, etc (See Chapter 4 by Mahadevia and Brar). Both these are because the city has received good credit rating. Like all megacities of India, this city also has aspirations to transform itself into a World Class City, which would offer a globally competitive lifestyle through infrastructure and built and open spaces. The city has taken debt financing route to raise resources for development works. The JNNURM will add to the city's debts.

We have shown in Chapter 4, in the last two years, since 2004, the city has changed its priorities of especially capital investments. The debt financing route taken by the city has also resulted in high debt service ratios on the revenue account. In 2004-05, debt services as a proportion of total revenue expenditure had reached 25 per cent, after which the financial situation of the municipal body would be considered vulnerable. It was also seen that the city had postponed repayment of principal amount of the government loans taken. If the AMC had also repaid the principal amount of the government loans then city's debt services situation would have worsened. But, the debt financing route has led to a situation that the AMC had to introduce new cesses and increase their rates within two years of their introduction and also increase property rate tax. This had to be resorted to because the capital projects taken up through the debt financing route do not have any revenue model. That is, all the new capital projects, which have been taken through debt financing, do not have any cost recovery mechanism. The projects taken up have been water supply works, sewerage networks and storm water drains construction on one hand that would benefit all the urban population and road widening, road resurfacing, flyover construction and widening of bridges over river Sabarmati, that would largely benefit private vehicle owners more than those who use public transport, with the exception of bridge widening project. Hence, in a sense, the financing priorities of the AMC are moving towards projects that would unequally benefit the higher income groups than the poor, as observed in other metro cities as well.

We wanted to test these postulates by us through evolving a methodology and then testing it for analysing public expenditure benefit incidence analysis from the lens of the slum dwellers of Ahmedabad. In short, the questions that we would address in this article are what should be the expenditure priorities of the AMC from the perspective of the slum dwellers of the city and what proportion of public expenditure by the AMC reach the slum dwellers of the city. For the purpose, we have taken four basic facilities; water supply, sewerage that also includes storm water drains, solid waste and internal roads within the slum settlement. This analysis is important because about 40 per cent of Ahmedabad's population lives in slums and *chawls* (one room units laid in a row where quality of life has degraded to the level of slum).

The article first looks at the socio-economic conditions of the slum dwellers and then their housing conditions and access to basic services. Thereafter, the satisfaction level with regards to each of the basic services is measured followed by stated priorities of the slum dwellers, disaggregated by gender, with regards to six basic facilities, which include besides the four mentioned above, education and health. Lastly, we have calculated what proportion of public expenditure on each of the four facilities, reach the slum dwellers.

Primary Survey Methodology

Although the basic services like water, sanitation and road are necessary for everybody, it is important to understand that the priorities for usage of services vary in various economic sections of the society. To get an idea about gender-disaggregated priorities and use of services, we have asked questions separately to men and women in the surveyed households.

Because of the limited resources of time and money, it was not possible to cover many slum areas so as to get the overall picture of the slums in Ahmedabad. Care was however taken to select the slum areas from different parts of the city, coming under the jurisdiction of different local bodies. Total of 5 slums pockets were selected from different parts of the city: east, west, north, and south. Two slums in the south were in the peri-urban area at at the time of the survey. The selected slum areas are marked on Map 10.1.

To get an equal and reasonable size of sample, it was decided to take a sample of 200 households from each slum pocket, i.e. a total of around 1,000 households have been covered in the survey. A detailed questioner was prepared, that solicited information on social status of the household, employment-unemployment status, activity status, house ownership, condition of housing, availability of infrastructure services such as water, sanitation, road etc, use of these services and use of other major infrastructure projects of the city. One male and one female member from each family were also asked to rank the facilities and services requirement according to their needs. Pilot surveys were carried out to test the questionnaire.

The site selection for survey was done in consultation with Saath, the NGO, which is working in the field of slum upgradation and capacity building of slum dwellers in the city for the past some time now. The sites were so selected that the data could be used by Saath for their future community development activities. However, slums were so selected, as mentioned earlier, that all the areas having large slum pockets were covered. While Danilimda and Maninagar lie on the eastern side of the river, Sabarmati, Vasna and Juhapura are on the western side. All these slum pockets selected have more than 2,000 households each. The areas like Sabarmati, Danilimda and Maninagar are further divided into small-small *vas* (groups of hutments) known by different names. According to the need of the study it was decided to do a random sample of around 1,000 households from these selected sites with approximate 200 households from each slum pocket. For this a team of 8 persons was formed to conduct the household survey work in a scheduled time. A one-day training programme was organised to train the surveyors. The survey was carried out during October 2005 to February 2006.

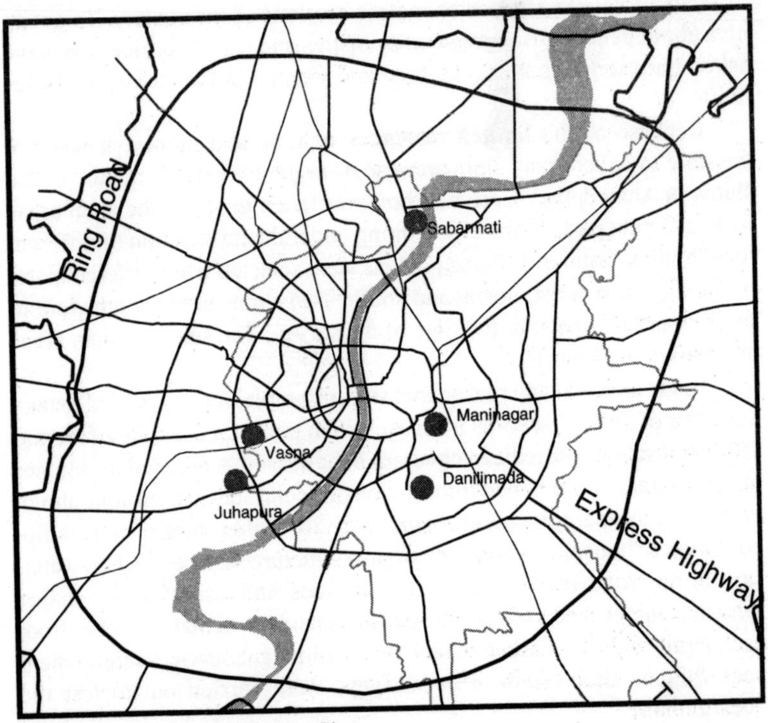

Map 10.1: Location of Survey Sites

Table 10.1 gives the brief of the survey pockets and the survey sites with the number of households surveyed. The first site selected for the survey work was Sabarmati. The area lies north of the city. Most of the slums of this area come under the Sabarmati riverbed land. With the coming of the 'Sabarmati River Front Development Plan', these slums are now to be relocated on the new site. The whole area has households belonging to Hindu religion[3]; with most of the population belonging to the SCs and Other Backward Castes (OBC) category. Four different slum pockets were selected to conduct the primary survey in the Sabarmati area. The next two sites selected were Danilimda and Maninagar on the eastern side of the city. Though Maninagar is purely a Hindu area, Danilimda does have Muslim families. Here the areas are divided according to the caste structure and the region from where the households have migrated. In the west Ahmedabad, very few slum pockets exist, of these the two prominent areas Vasna (Rajiv Nagar), and Juhapura (Sankalit Nagar) have been selected. These two sites though physically close to each other, are quite dissimilar. Rajiv Nagar in Vasna is purely a Hindu locality and Sankalit Nagar in Juhapura is completely a Muslim one. The slums for survey have been selected from five wards of the city.

Table 10.1: Brief of Survey Areas

S. No.	*Survey wards*	*Survey areas*	*Households Surveyed*
1.	Sabarmati	Gandhivas, Haridasnagar, Thakorevas Kailashnagar	204
2.	Danilimda	Babanu Nagar, Aketa Nagar	207
3.	Maninagar	Haripura, Rabari vas, Punjabi ni challi, Prem ni challi	214
4.	Vasna	Rajiv Nagar	211
5.	Juhapura	Sankalit Nagar	198
	Total		1034

It is important to note that the first four areas come under the AMC jurisdiction, whereas Sankalit Nagar of Juhapura is located outside the corporation limits[4]. Presently it is like an orphan as it is under no planning agency, neither the municipal corporation, nor the Development Authority (that is AUDA). In fact, technically, it is part of the AUDA, which has not shown any interest in its development. The municipality in which Sankalit Nagar is located is called Vejalpur, which does not have adequate resources to invest in Sankalit Nagar. Further, this local body is controlled by the Bharatiya Janta Party (BJP), the Hindu right wing party responsible for perpetuating communal mayhem of 2002 as per the Concerned Citizen's Committee report, National Human Rights Commission Report and other independent enquiry commissions as mentioned in our previous article (Chapter 4). It is therefore alleged that the Vejalpur municipality does not have any interests in carrying out development works in Sankalit Nagar. At one point in time, AUDA's chairman, a BJP person, but of a less strident type, had shown interest in development of Sankalit Nagar and had suggested to the residents to form ward committees (as Sankalit Nagar is divided into wards), and then work with AUDA towards its development. This chairman moved out of AUDA and the discussions of development of the area have fallen apart. Residents here relate this fate to the larger political game of the city administration.

Socio Economic Conditions

The household size in the surveyed slums is 5 (Table 10.2), which is close to the average household size of the city of 5.08 as per 2001 census. While 40 per cent of the households had small size (upto 4 members), majority of the households (57%) had a size between 5 to 8 members and just 4 per cent households had size more than 8 members. The largest household size was in Sankalit Nagar (5.4). Slums in Maninagar had the smallest average household size of 4.7. Large families are in negligible number.

Table 10.2: Household Size

Zone	Average Household size	% of HH having household size		
		Small (1-4)	Medium (5-8)	Large (9-12)
Sabarmati	4.9	40	57	2
Danilimda	5.0	38	60	2
Maninagar	4.7	49	49	2
Vasna	5.1	35	62	3
Juhapura	5.4	36	56	8
Total	5.0	40	57	4

The reason for small and medium size families is directly related to the employment opportunities. The moment a person gets job in some far place in city, he moves (along with his spouse and children) to the new place. Moreover, small house-area forces grown up children to move to a new dwelling unit either built close by in the same slum or in a slum close to the place of work of the head of the household who is generally the male. There is therefore a process of nuclearisation of family observed among the slum households of the city.

Table 10.3: Sex Ratio

Zone	Juvenile sex ratio (0-6)	Sex ratio (7-14)	Sex ratio youth (15-25)	Sex ratio (> 26 years)	Overall
Sabarmati	952	874	828	971	907
Danilimda	1196	863	1066	873	953
Maninagar	1048	730	890	951	904
Vasna	850	875	876	893	880
Juhapura	710	774	859	911	849
Total	938	824	898	918	897

Sex ratio or female to male ratio is an important indicator of women's status in any society. But, in the urban areas of India, and more so in slums, it is likely that the sex ratios are quite low because of the presence of large number of single male migrants, who come to live in the city with their kith and kin for a while before getting their spouse and family. Migrants from some states in India do not bring their wife at all. Hence, it is common to find low sex ratios in the urban areas and particularly in the slums. Sex ratio also indicates the stability of the household and also stage of migration of the household.

The overall sex ratio is quite low in the slum settlements surveyed. There are 897 females per 1000 males in all the slums surveyed (Table 10.3). Highest sex ratio among the five slum areas surveyed is in Danilimda slums (953), followed by Sabarmati slums (907) and then by Maninagar slums (904). The least sex ratio is among Juhapura slums (849). Sex ratio in the whole of Ahmedabad Urban Agglomeration (AUA) was 885 in 2001. Thus, except Vasna slums and Juhapura slums, in all other slum areas, sex ratios are higher than the overall city's sex ratio, quite contrary to what we expected.

Since the overall sex ratio is influenced by migration, it would be better to observe juvenile sex ratio, which is 938. This is far better than the overall city's juvenile sex ratio of 792 in 2001. Thus, discrimination against female foetus and female child is higher in the non-slum areas than in the slum areas of Ahmedabad. In Danilimda slums, which has the highest sex ratio, juvenile sex ratio is also highest and above 1000 (1196). Maninagar slums also have higher than 1000 juvenile sex ratio (1048). The overall juvenile sex ratio would have been higher than 938 if Juhapura slums did not have such a low juvenile sex ratio of 710. Even Vasna slums have low juvenile sex ratio of 850.

Sex ratio in age 7-14 and age 15-25 is lower than juvenile sex ratio, indicating that it is this section of population which has presence of single male migrants. In the former age groups, sex ratio is 824 and in the latter age group, the sex ratio is 898, for all the settlements together. It is likely that these have large presence of unmarried young men migrated to the city for work. In age above 25 years, the sex ratio is 918, which is higher than sex ratio of all the age groups for all the settlements and also far higher than Ahmedabad city's overall sex ratio. In this age group the person settles down with a family.

Slums are predominantly inhabited by the lower castes. Our survey also finds that. On the whole, 36.7 per cent of the surveyed households belonged to SC category, 10.2 per cent belonged to ST category and 41.3 per cent belonged to OBC category.

In all individual slums and all the slums together, main employment category is daily wage labour. About 54.6 per cent of the employed in all the slums together are working as daily wagers (Table 10.4). In Vasna slums, 69 per cent are employed as daily wagers, which is the highest proportion among all the slums and in Danilimda 34 per cent are employed as daily wagers, which is the lowest proportion among all the slums. In Danilimda, as high as 33 per cent are employed in government service, which among all the slums together is only 9.5 per cent. In Juhapura slums, no one is employed in government service. Those in the government service are mainly in lower level of jobs, such as vehicle drivers, etc with an exception of Danilimda, which had noticeable proportion (3.4%) of retired persons getting pensions. Danilimda has a high SC population, who are in or have been in government service.

Table 10.4: Zone wise Main Occupation of the Employed (Per cent)

Zone	Government service	Private service	Business	Pension	Daily wage	Driver	House work
Sabarmati	8.0	8.5	17.9	0.5	64.7	0.0	0.0
Danilimda	32.8	19.1	8.3	3.4	34.3	0.5	1.5
Maninagar	2.3	28.0	10.7	0.0	58.9	0.0	0.0
Vasna	2.8	21.3	6.2	0.5	69.2	0.0	0.0
Juhapura	0.0	20.7	16.5	3.7	43.3	6.7	9.1
Total	9.5	19.6	11.7	1.5	54.6	1.2	1.8

A special category of driver was added later seeing the significant numbers employed as drivers, especially in Juhapura slum area, where 6.7 per cent employed thus. Nearing 20 per cent in Juhapura and 28 per cent in Maninagar were employed in private services. This private service mainly comprises of the courier boy, marketing person or job at some local shop. Thus, even in private sector, the slum dwellers have petty jobs which are not well paying. On the whole about 12 per cent were having their own business (mainly petty businesses), in Juhapura, this figure was 16.5 per cent and in Sabarmati it was 17.9 per cent.

Table 10.5: Activity Pattern of Population (Per cent)

Zone	Employed or Pensioner	Non-workers		House Work	Unemployed
		student	children < 7 years		
Sabarmati	41.8	18.3	1.1	21.2	17.6
Danilimda	54.8	19.4	0.7	23.9	1.4
Maninagar	49.9	20.6	0.0	25.0	4.4
Vasna	46.1	26.5	2.1	23.8	1.6
Juhapura	60.2	11.1	2.5	24.8	1.5
Total	49.6	19.8	1.3	23.6	5.7

On the whole, 49.6 per cent of the slum population is employed (Table 10.5). Just 5.7 per cent of them are unemployed. 19.8 per cent are not working because they are students, another 1.3 per cent are non workers as these are children below age 7 years or the elderly and 23.6 per cent are engaged in housework in their own homes or in nearby areas and which would be mainly women. In Juhapura area, 60.2 per cent of the population worked, that is because just 13.6 per cent population was non workers.

Proportion of students in the population is very low here, just 11.1 per cent, indicating that the children drop out of school much early than all other areas and they join the workforce. This is an indication of relatively high level of poverty among the population in Juhapura and also lack of job opportunities for this population demotivating the children and their families to continue with education. In Sabarmati slums, there is low proportion of employed/pensioners because of high level of unemployment. Here, the proportion of students is lower than the average proportion of students in all the five localities. Lastly, Danilimda area, which had the highest proportion of those in government services, the proportion of students is close to average. Thus, among the five localities, Danilimda slums has the best economic status and Juhapura the worst economic status.

Nearly 80 per cent of the children of 7-14 age are going to school (Table 10.6), which indicates good enrolment ratio. But, in Sabarmati slums, just 66.3 per cent of them are going to school. In Juhapura also, proportion of children in this age group going to school is higher than 80 per cent. In Sabarmati slums just 30 per cent of the children in age less than 7 years and in Juhapura, just half of them go to school whereas in other areas, their proportion is above 75 per cent. This indicates that in Sabarmati slums and Juhapura, children start their school later than in other three localities. Further, about 5 per cent of children, mainly girls, in this age group are engaged in housework. But, in Maninagar and Vasna, this figure is about 7 per cent. An alarming fact that came out was that 25 per cent children in this age group stated that they were unemployed, that is they were looking for work but did not get the work in Sabarmati slums. In Juhapura too, 8.3 per cent of children age 7-14 stated that they were unemployed and looking for work and another 4.2 per cent children in this age group were working. Highest proportion of child labour was observed in Danilimda, which was 7 per cent and another 3 per cent were looking for work. Thus, here children out of school are potential child labour, even if they are not getting the jobs.

Proportion of students in age group 15-25 has decreased to 13 per cent from 82 per cent in the age group 7-14, which means that very few children continue their education after class seven or eight. In Juhapura, 61.5 per cent of the youth work and only 8.9 per cent have remained as students after the age of 14. In Vasna, 17.9 per cent youth continue with their studies after age 14. In Sabarmati, Danilimda and Maninagar slums, the proportion of youth continuing studies is low, between 10 to 13 per cent. These youth then opt for private service (13.5%), daily wage labour (27.4%) and house work (31%), whichever is available and suitable to them. The overall unemployment among youth is 7.5 per cent. Highest unemployment among the youth is in Sabarmati slums.

Table 10.6: Age Group Wise Activity Pattern of Surveyed Population (Per cent)

	Zone	Employed/pensioner							Non workers		House Work	Unemployed
		Govt. service	Pvt. service	Business	Retired	Daily wage labourer	Driver	Total	Student	Non-student		
Juvenile (0-6)	Sabarmati								29.9	70.1		
	Danilimda								93.3	6.7		
	Maninagar								96.0	4.0		
	Vasna								75.3	24.7		
	Juhapura								50.0	50.0		
	Total								62.0	38.0		
Age 7-14	Sabarmati		1.1	1.1		2.9	0.0	5.1	66.3		3.4	25.1
	Danilimda		1.0	1.0		5.0	0.0	7.0	88.1		2.0	3.0
	Maninagar		0.0	0.0		3.5	0.0	3.5	88.6		7.0	0.9
	Vasna		0.6	0.0		1.8	0.6	3.0	88.8		7.1	1.2
	Juhapura		4.2	0.0		0.0	0.0	4.2	83.3		4.2	8.3
	Total		1.0	0.5		2.8	0.2	4.5	81.7		4.9	8.9
Youth (15-25)	Sabarmati	0.4	7.0	8.5		28.1	0.0	44.0	10.7		27.0	18.1
	Danilimda	0.0	18.8	4.2		25.4	0.5	48.9	12.7		35.2	3.3
	Maninagar	0.9	13.0	6.0		24.2	0.0	44.1	13.5		33.5	8.8
	Vasna	0.6	8.6	2.5		34.3	0.0	46.0	17.9		33.0	3.1
	Juhapura	0.0	24.8	10.9		20.8	5.0	61.5	8.9		26.2	3.5
	Total	0.4	13.5	6.1		27.4	0.9	48.3	13.2		31.0	7.5
26 and above	Sabarmati	3.8	5.8	13.2	3.5	37.7	0.8	64.8	0.0		28.9	6.3
	Danilimda	0.8	18.6	7.6	5.9	38.2	3.1	74.2	0.0		25.2	0.8
	Maninagar	4.3	12.7	6.3	4.1	42.4	0.0	69.8	0.0		26.9	3.3
	Vasna	2.5	10.6	3.5	7.6	46.5	0.0	70.7	0.2		27.4	1.6
	Juhapura	0.5	13.1	16.3	4.0	28.8	7.5	70.2	0.8		28.3	0.8
	Total	2.4	12.1	9.2	5.1	39.0	2.2	70.0	0.2		27.3	2.6

Table 10.7: Literacy Rate (Per cent)* of the Surveyed Areas

Zone	*Literate*	*Illiterate*
Sabarmati	69.2	30.8
Danilimda	79.1	20.9
Maninagar	56.8	43.2
Vasna	73.3	26.7
Juhapura	77.0	23.0
Total	71.4	28.6

* Literacy rate been calculated after excluding the child below 6 years category.

The average literacy rate (age 7 plus) is 71.4 per cent (Table 10.7), which is lower than the literacy rate (of age 7 plus) of 84.2 per cent in AUA. Thus, slum population has far lower literacy levels than the entire urban population. Juhapura had the highest literacy rate of 77 per cent (age 7 plus) and Maninagar slums has the least literacy rate of 56.8 per cent among the five localities. Juhapura has high literacy rate inspite of early school drop outs here. Danilimda slums have the highest literacy rate but far below that of the entire city.

In all the slums together, just 2.2 per cent of the literate have reached graduate level and 0.5 per cent post-graduate level (Table 10.8). Just 2.4 per cent have reached higher secondary level. As high as 85 per cent literate drop out by class 10 and 35 per cent drop out by class 5. In Sabarmati, where there is highest unemployment, about half the literate have dropped out by class 5. This is the population that is going to get displaced by the Sabarmati riverfront project. With such low literacy levels, they would find it difficult to get resettled in the new place. Only in Danilimda slums, literate people have gone upto graduate level (4.0%) and another 0.9 per cent upto post-graduate category. It is generally observed that when there is a hope that government jobs are going to be available, as would be the case in the families where the household head is in government jobs that the children continue tertiary education. Otherwise, they drop out, males entering the labour market and women staying in the house and engaging in household work. Further, those who have to get into their own business, tend to drop out early from the education system, as we see with respect to Juhapura slums. Where work availability is low, there is a tendency to drop out early from the education system and that is what we find in Sabarmati area.

Table 10.8: Level of Education of the Literates (Per cent)

Zone	*Post Graduate*	*Graduate*	*Diploma*	*Higher Sec.*	*Std. V-X*	*Below Std. V*
Sabarmati	0.0	0.9	0.2	3.6	44.6	50.7
Danilimda	0.9	4.0	0.0	1.6	55.9	37.7
Maninagar	0.8	2.1	0.0	4.0	60.6	32.6
Vasna	0.0	2.1	0.0	2.9	72.0	23.0
Juhapura	0.7	1.6	0.1	0.6	62.1	34.9
Total	0.5	2.2	0.1	2.4	59.9	35.0

Housing and Basic Services Situation

As high as 86.5 per cent of households stated that they lived in self owned housing (Table 10.9). Ownership housing in slums is basically housing with uncertain tenure as a consequence of squatting. Slum settlements first begin as squatter settlements and then consolidate their condition and become regular slum housing. Renting is an expensive option in slums as any one wanting housing would squat if possible than rent a place. Thus, only 13.5 per cent households are renting a house. Renting is high in the slums in Maninagar and least in Juhapura. Atleast, we know that the Juhapura slum has come up informally over a period of time, from the original settlement that was meant to resettle riverfront dwellers. Wherever there is self ownership, there is more unwillingness to relocate. Also, self occupied houses are incremental housing wherein the households have gradually invested in their houses. Thus, the quality and size of housing enjoyed is far more than that enjoyed in case of rental housing at the same price. This data also indicates that the urban poor find their own solutions to housing in absence of any government initiative to reach out to them. Forcible displacements therefore appear morally as well as economically undesirable.

Table 10.9: House Ownership and Type (Per cent)

Zone	*Ownership*		*House type*	
	Self occupied	*Rented*	*Kutcha*	*Pucca*
Sabarmati	88.2	11.8	75.5	24.5
Danilimda	87.4	12.6	53.6	46.4
Maninagar	79.0	21.0	62.1	37.9
Vasna	86.3	13.7	46.4	53.6
Juhapura	91.9	8.1	61.6	38.4
Total	86.5	13.5	59.8	40.2

About 60 per cent of the housing is *katcha* housing, and 40 per cent is *pucca*. But, the *katcha* houses are not like shanties, although constructed using temporary housing materials. Sabarmati riverbank slums are the worst in terms of housing quality; 75.5 per cent of them being *katcha* in quality. This indicates that the household do not invest in incremental housing if there is no perceived security of tenure. More than half the households in Vasna slums are *pucca* in quality. Maninagar and Juhapura have about 60 per cent of the housing as *katcha*, although in the former, there is higher renting and in latter higher self-ownership. The contrast between Maninagar and Juhapura in tenure status can be explained only by their individual history than anything.

Table 10.10: Water Supply Source (Per cent)

Zone	*Tap*	*Stand post*	*Hand pump*	*Private*	*Water tanker*
Sabarmati	54.7	25.4	6.0	13.4	0.5
Danilimda	77.0	0.0	4.8	13.5	4.8
Maninagar	62.9	13.9	23.3	0.0	0.0
Vasna	7.1	0.0	92.9	0.0	0.0
Juhapura	53.8	0.0	25.6	0.0	20.5
Total	48.6	8.4	33.3	4.7	5.0

The various water supply sources for domestic use are tap connection to the individual house, a nearby standpost for group of households, handpump, private borewell, and water tanker. On the whole 48.6 per cent households have individual tap connection, which means that more than half the households do not have individual tap connection (Table 10.10). But across the slums, there is very high variation with regards to water supply source. For example, 93 per cent households in Vasna slums do not have individual tap connection. In Danilimda slums 77 per cent households, highest among all the five slum localities have individual tap connection. Pipe line water connection, either at individual house level or shared through standpost served 57 per cent of all the slum households. In Sabarmati slums this proportion is 80 per cent, Danilimda slums is 77 per cent (as no households use shared water connection) and Maninagar slums is 76.8 per cent. The second worst situation is in Juhapura slums, where only 53.8 per cent had any pipeline connection, which was individual house connection. Thus, the survey revealed that contrary to the perception, northern and eastern slum pockets are better served by the municipal corporation than the western areas. But, that may be because of the location of Vasna and Juhapura slums, which at the time of the survey were outside the AMC limits and their local authority did not provide water supply. This situation would change now that these areas have been amalgamated within the AMC

As high as 43 per cent of households in the slums surveyed had to depend on the other sources of water such as handpumps (33.3%), private borewells (4.7%) and *tanki* (small water tanks at household level) (5%). Vasna slums depended on handpumps (93% of them) and Juhapura slum households not having pipe connection depend on handpumps (25.6%) and water tanker (20.5%). Dependency on private borewells is found in Sabarmati and Danilimda slums, which means that the households are buying water from some private borewell or depending on the charity of the private borewell owner. Those depending on handpumps for drinking water are using the groundwater from shallow depths, which is unfit for consumption because of high levels of salt and other impurities. Even water supply source of those who depend on water tankers is not known and hence the water quality of these two sources is a suspect.

Just 46 per cent of all the slum households received water from a public authority, either the AMC or the Nagar Panchayat (Vejalpur Nagar Panchayat in case of Juhapura slums) (Table 10.11). 75 per cent in Sabarmati slums, 61.8 per cent in Danilimda slums and 63.6 per cent in Maninagar slums get water supply from the AMC. Just 28.8 per cent slum households in Juhapura get water from Vejalpur Nagar Panchayat, indicating some discrimination in water supply to a Muslim locality by the BJP dominated local body. Those not getting water supply from a public authority then depend on private or self source for water supply. Hence, all households in Vasna slums depend on private or their own source of water, 70.2 per cent households in Juhapura and more than 25 per cent in all other slum areas depend on their own sources of water. As observed above both these sources of water would have poor potability and hence the residents of Vasna and Juhapura slums are highly vulnerable to water borne diseases.

Table 10.11: Authority Providing Water Supply (Per cent)

Zone	*AMC/AUDA*	*Nagar Panchayat*	*Private/Self*
Sabarmati	75.0	0.0	25.0
Danilimda	61.8	0.0	38.2
Maninagar	63.6	0.0	36.4
Vasna	0.0	0.0	100.0
Juhapura	1.0	28.8	70.2
Total	40.5	5.5	54.0

From those who depend on common drinking water source, that is the standpost, 70 per cent have the standpost within close proximity (30 meters) of the house (Table 10.12) and take less than 5 minutes to fill water (Table 10.13). Just 13 per cent of households had the common standpost at a distance of more than 100 meters and just 11 per cent of the households took more than 10 minutes to fill water from the common water source. In Juhapura, although there is discrimination by the local body in water supply, water source for 89 per cent was within 30 meters of their house. In Sabarmati, 25 per cent of households had a water source at a distance of 100 meters or more from their house. This could be because the private borewell used by these residents would be far away from their house. In Maninagar slums, 57.5 per cent households were spending more than 10 minutes to fill water.

Table 10.12: Distance of Common Water Source from House (Per cent)

Zone	Less than 10 mt.	10 to 30 mt.	30 to 50 mt.	50-100 mt.	above 100 mt.
Sabarmati	48.4	14.1	10.9	1.6	25.0
Danilimda	17.5	54.0	12.7	4.8	11.1
Maninagar	2.1	74.5	19.1	0.0	4.3
Vasna	21.4	42.9	16.1	7.1	12.5
Juhapura	84.1	4.8	0.0	1.6	9.5
Total	36.9	35.8	11.3	3.1	13.0

Table 10.13: Time taken to Fill Water from Common Source (Per cent)

Zone	Less than 5 minutes	5-10 minutes	10 to 30 minutes	Over 30 minutes
Sabarmati	87.5	12.5	0.0	0.0
Danilimda	66.7	25.4	6.4	1.6
Maninagar	27.7	14.9	57.5	0.0
Vasna	94.6	5.4	0.0	0.0
Juhapura	95.2	4.8	0.0	0.0
Total	76.5	12.6	10.6	0.3

Table 10.14: Water Usage in Liters Per Capita Per Day (LPCD)

Zone	Upto 100 lpcd	101-200 lpcd	Over 200 lpcd	Average lpcd
Sabarmati	40.7	58.1	1.2	97.7
Danilimda	35.7	60.8	3.5	91.8
Maninagar	30.1	66.5	3.4	99.9
Vasna	36.2	62.6	1.1	91.6
Juhapura	46.9	49.4	3.7	83.4
Total	37.8	59.6	2.6	92.8

Because the water is conveniently accessible, water usage in litres per capita per day (lpcd) is also reasonable. Average water consumption is 92.8 lpcd, which is quite satisfactory (Table 10.14). More than 60 per cent of the households used over 100 lpcd of water. Juhapura had the least water consumption of 83.4 lpcd among the five slum localities and best was in Maninagar slums (99.9 LPCD). Thus, even if there is dependency on private sources of water, the water availability is sufficient. This indicates that the households must be paying quite some amount for water supply.

Following the question of access is that of water quality. It is known that the ground water of Ahmedabad and surrounding districts are 15,000 to 20,000 years old and are thus high in salinity and fluoride content. The survey also reported that, the people of Vasna who are totally dependent on ground water stated that their water quality is bad (47.4%) (Table 10.15). Again in Maninagar, where the significant population uses handpump for drinking water, have also reported (11.3 per cent of them) bad quality of ground water. But, on the whole only 13 per cent have reported bad water quality.

Table 10.15: Quality of Water Supplied/Available in the Area (Per cent)

Zone	*Good*	*Average*	*Bad*
Sabarmati	85.6	13.8	0.5
Danilimda	83.9	15.1	1.1
Maninagar	81.2	7.5	11.3
Vasna	32.7	19.9	47.4
Juhapura	90.7	8.3	1.0
Total	74.1	12.9	13.0

It has often been found that slum areas are generally neglected when it comes to laying drains. However, the situation in the surveyed slums is not so bad; 71 per cent of the households stated that there was drainage network in their locality (Table 10.16). Worst are slums in Vasna where less than 20 per cent stated that there availability of drains in their area. In Sabarmati area too, 46.6 per cent households reported that there was no drainage available in their area. At Vasna, the work was on for laying drainage network, while at Sabarmati, the slum portion not having any drainage network is on the riverbed to face demolition as and when the riverfront project would take off.

Table 10.16: Availability of Drainage (Per cent)

Zone	*Availability of drains*		*Situation of rain water drainage during monsoons*		
	Yes	*No*	*Good*	*Medium*	*Bad*
Sabarmati	53.4	46.6	46.1	48.9	5.1
Danilimda	91.8	8.2	24.6	21.4	54.0
Maninagar	93.9	6.1	42.2	34.7	23.1
Vasna	18.0	82.0	21.2	0.0	78.8
Juhapura	99.0	1.0	0.0	1.0	99.0
Total	71.0	29.0	26.0	20.0	54.0

The drains in local parlance means sewerage lines as well as storm water drains. But, these drains are for carrying sewerage. These are not for carrying rain water. Thus, in all the localities together, 54 per cent stated that the situation becomes bad in monsoons due to water logging. In Juhapura, 99 per cent, that is nearly all, stated that the water clogging was a serious problem in monsoons (Table 10.16) and in Vasna 79 per cent stated that was the case. In general, many slums tend to be in low-lying areas or have roads around them laid and resurfaced many times over that tend to be higher than the level of the slums. Thus, every rains, there is water logging. In case of the former, even small amounts of rain flood the area. The rain water has to be then flushed out by hiring the services of private contractor. Only Sabarmati slums reported that there was no water logging in monsoons, that is rain water drainage was good and in Maninagar slums too a large proportion, 42 per cent, stated that rainwater drainage was good. There is therefore a mixed picture; the two areas outside the AMC at the time of the survey stated severe problem of rainwater logging, Sabarmati slums were saved from water logging as the rainwater drained in river Sabarmati and two slums in the AMC had relatively better situation, but not cent per cent coverage.

About 19 per cent of the households stated that they did not have access to any latrine facility (Table 10.17). Sabarmati (31.4%), followed by Danilimda (21.7%) and Vasna (21.3%) were quite bad with regards to availability of latrine facility. 63.3 per cent of the surveyed households stated that they had individual latrine facility. Highest proportion of households with access to individual latrines was in Juhapura (88.4%) followed by Maninagar (78.5%) and then Vasna (76.3%). This means that in Sabarmati and Danilimida high proportion of households, nearly one-third in Sabarmati and two-fifths in Danilimda used shared latrines, mostly constructed by the municipal authorities

Table 10.17: Availability of Latrine (Per cent)

Zone	*No latrine facility*	*Individual*	*Shared*
Sabarmati	31.4	34.8	33.8
Danilimda	21.7	38.6	39.6
Maninagar	15.0	78.5	6.5
Vasna	21.3	76.3	2.4
Juhapura	5.1	88.4	6.6
Total	19.0	63.3	17.7

Table 10.18: Percentage of Distribution of Households by Provider of Sanitation System

Zone	AMC/AUDA	Nagar Panchayat	Private
Sabarmati	84.9	0.0	15.1
Danilimda	90.2	0.0	9.8
Maninagar	66.5	0.0	33.5
Vasna	1.1	1.1	97.8
Juhapura	31.8	9.1	59.1
Total	50.5	2.4	47.1

Provision of sanitation system is one of the essential functions of the public authorities, whether the Municipal corporation or municipality. Even then, as high as 47 per cent households in the surveyed slums stated that they constructed their own sanitation facilities, mainly septic tanks, in absence of any sewerage network. Vasna has no sewerage network and nearly 98 per cent of households stated that they had done their own arrangements. In Juhapura, although 88.4 per cent households had individual access to latrines, only 32 per cent had plugged them into the AUDA's network and 9 per cent had plugged into Vejalpur municipality's network. 90 per cent households in Danilimda, 85 per cent in Sabarmati and 66.5 per cent in Maninagar had AMC provided sanitation network. It is surprising that one-third of the households in Maninagar area were privately taking care of the sewerage.

Table 10.19: Solid Waste Collection Agency (Per cent)

Zone	AMC	Nagar Panchayat	NGO	Private/Self
Sabarmati	45.1	0.0	9.2	45.7
Danilimda	61.7	0.0	29.7	8.6
Maninagar	67.5	0.0	0.0	32.5
Vasna	71.1	7.6	10.0	11.4
Juhapura	1.5	19.7	66.7	12.1
Total	47.9	6.3	23.7	22.1

Other than water supply and sanitation, solid waste collection is also a responsibility of the local authority. Data shows that the concerned public authority, the AMC was collecting solid waste in the four slums under its jurisdiction, but not fully. In Vasna slums, 71.1 per cent, in Maninagar slums 67.5 per cent, in Danilimda slums 61.7 per cent and in Sabarmati slums 45.1 per cent households reported that the AMC was collecting solid waste from their slum (Table 10.19). This means that the rest of the households stated that the AMC was not collecting solid waste from their localities. In Sabarmati slums 45.7 per cent of the slums were collecting and disposing the solid waste themselves and they were dumping it into the bed of river Sabarmati. In Danilimda, 29.7 per cent households stated that an NGO was involved in solid waste collection. In Juhapura slums, just 21.2 per cent households stated that the local authority collected solid waste. Here, two thirds of households reported that an NGO collected the solid waste. It is known that Vejalpur Nagar Panchayat has engaged the services of Self Employed Women's Association (SEWA) for the door to door collection of solid waste (Acharya and Parashar 2008).

Table 10.20: Status of Internal Roads (Per cent)

Zone	*Katcha*	*Pucca*
Sabarmati	79.0	21.0
Danilimda	67.5	32.5
Maninagar	62.6	37.4
Vasna	38.2	61.8
Juhapura	35.0	65.0
Total	55.4	44.6

The last aspect covered under the infrastructure head was the status of internal roads in these slum areas. In the recent times, lot of efforts have gone in re-carpeting the roads in the city. The concentration is primarily on the main roads. To know whether the internal roads of the slums were also re-carpeted, question was asked regarding the status of roads that were in front of their house. The situation of internal roads is not so good. 55.4 per cent households stated that their internal roads were *katcha* (Table 10.20). The situation was bad in Sabarmati, Danilimda, and Maninagar slums, wherein 79 per cent, 67.5 per cent and 62.6 per cent households respectively reported *katcha* internal roads. These are the slums in the north and the east. If the roads were *pucca* the dwellers themselves could have done them up. In Vasna and Juhapura slums, more than 60 per cent households stated that the internal roads were *pucca*. It is indeed a concern that the slums which did not have basic services such as water supply and drainage, had good roads.

Table 10.21: Per cent Households Having Basic Infrastructure Provided by AMC/AUDA

Zone	*Water Supply*	*Sewerage*	*Solid waste collection*	*Pucca roads*
Sabarmati	75.0	84.9	45.1	21.0
Danilimda	61.8	90.2	61.7	32.5
Maninagar	63.6	66.5	67.5	37.4
Vasna	0.0	2.2	78.7	61.8
Juhapura	29.8	40.9	21.2	65.0
Total	46.0	52.9	54.2	44.6

Table 10.21 gives the overall status of AMC/Nagar·Panchayat or AUDA in providing the four basic infrastructure facilities i.e. water supply, sanitation, solid waste collection and road condition. On the whole, for each of the basic infrastructures, less that 55 per cent of all the slum households reported that they received it from the concerned public authority. In the slums in east Ahmedabad, more than 60 per cent households have received water supply and sanitation from the public authority and more than 60 per cent of the west Ahmedabad slums have received *pucca* roads from the public authority.

During the study it was also felt that it is not only the availability of the infrastructure but how much these infrastructures are able to satisfy the needs of the users was important. Thus, we also asked the respondents whether they were fully or partially satisfied with the available infrastructure. To this, 55.2 per cent households stated that they were satisfied with water supply, 43.4 per cent stated that they were satisfied with sanitation, 40 per cent stated that they were satisfied with solid waste collection and 38.5 per cent were satisfied with roads (Table 10.22). We also asked about their satisfaction regarding available education and health facility. 40.8 per cent stated that they were satisfied with education facility and 43.1 per cent were satisfied with health facility. Households in Danilimda were the most satisfied with all the infrastructures. Slums in Vasna were the least satisfied with all infrastructures and then came slums in Sabarmati where also low proportion of households stated that they were satisfied with the available infrastructure. In Juhapura, the situation was mixed, quite high, 71 per cent stated that they were satisfied with water supply, nearly none were satisfied with solid waste collection, and one in eight were satisfied with sewerage, given that they were privately organising all three facilities.

Table 10.22: Per cent Households Satisfied with Available Infrastructure

Zone	*Per cent of households satisfied*					
	Water supply	*Sewerage*	*Solid waste collection*	*Roads*	*Education facility*	*Health facility*
Sabarmati	42.2	38.7	44.1	36.8	25.5	22.1
Danilimda	80.7	83.6	74.4	51.4	65.7	70.0
Maninagar	52.3	64.0	44.9	44.4	37.4	37.4
Vasna	30.7	15.6	32.7	28.3	34.6	37.6
Juhapura	70.6	12.7	2.0	35.5	40.6	43.1
Total	55.2	43.4	40.0	38.5	40.8	42.1

This does not mean that the rest of the households were not satisfied with the available infrastructures. Some were partially satisfied with the available infrastructure. 9.9 per cent households on the whole stated that they were partially satisfied with water supply facility (Table 10.23). For sanitation, this figure was 8.7 per cent, for solid waste 19.4 per cent, for roads 23.6 per cent, for education facility 34.5 per cent and for health 35.4 per cent households stated that they were partially satisfied with the available infrastructure. The rest of the households were dissatisfied with the availability of the basic infrastructure. Except with regards to education and health facility, more than one third were dissatisfied with all infrastructures provided by the local authority (Table 10.24). Highest dissatisfaction was in Vasna slums, followed by Sabarmati slums and then followed by Juhapur slums.

Table 10.23: Per cent Households Partially Satisfied with Available Infrastructure

Zone	*Per cent of households partially satisfied*					
	Water supply	*Sewerage*	*Solid waste collection*	*Roads*	*Education facility*	*Health facility*
Sabarmati	16.7	4.4	19.6	23.0	43.1	44.1
Danilimda	8.7	10.1	19.3	29.7	22.2	23.7
Maninagar	2.3	2.3	19.2	13.6	30.4	31.3
Vasna	12.7	1.0	19.0	29.3	46.8	48.3
Juhapura	9.6	26.4	19.8	24.9	29.9	29.9
Total	9.9	8.7	19.4	23.6	34.5	35.4

Table 10.24: Per cent Households Not Satisfied with Available Infrastructure

Zone	*Per cent of households not satisfied*					
	Water supply	*Sewerage*	*Solid waste collection*	*Roads*	*Education facility*	*Health facility*
Sabarmati	41.2	56.9	36.3	40.2	31.4	33.8
Danilimda	10.6	6.3	6.3	18.8	12.1	6.3
Maninagar	45.3	33.2	35.5	41.6	31.8	30.8
Vasna	56.6	83.4	48.3	42.4	18.5	14.1
Juhapura	19.8	59.4	74.1	37.6	27.9	24.9
Total	34.9	47.5	39.7	37.4	24.3	22.0

Along with the basic infrastructure, survey was also done to find out how many proportion of respondents used different other infrastructures provided by the local authority in whose jurisdiction the slum was. The infrastructure included here were; ring road, flyover/bridge for transportation, garden or park and lake for recreation purpose, government supported slum housing, public toilets, community hall and public transport (AMTS—Ahmedabad Municipal Transport Services). Responses from male and female respondents were separately recorded.

In all slums together, interestingly, 82.2 per cent men and 80.3 per cent women stated that they used public transport AMTS (Table 10.25). Flyover or bridge and ring roads were more used by men than women. 70.1 per cent men and 58.8 per cent women used the ring road and 76.3 per cent men and 70.2 per cent women used the flyover. Less than 25 per cent men used garden or lake and less than 15 per cent women used garden or lake. Thus, the slum dwellers were not using city beautification projects somehow. The respondents were also not using public toilets, most likely the ones being referred here are in the slum settlement itself. This reiterates the fact that the slum dwellers prefer to have individual toilets than use public toilets.

Table 10.25: Usage of Various Facilities by Male and Female Respondents (Per cent)

Facility	*Male*	*Female*
Ring road	70.1	58.8
Fly over/Bridge	76.3	70.2
Garden	24.3	15.2
Lake	20.1	13.8
Public toilet	11.3	6.7
Public transport (AMTS)	82.2	80.3
Community Hall	1.0	0.3

The respondents were also asked to rank the basic services according to their priority. Here again a separate response was solicited from one male and one female member of the household. The survey result shows that, water is the first priority for the residents irrespective of their sex; 45 per cent male and 50 per cent female ranked water as the first priority (Tables 10.26 and 9.27). Similarly sanitation and solid waste collection came as second and third priorities respectively for both the males and females. The gender difference however is there in terms of proportion stating these three as their priorities; higher proportion of women than men stated that these three were their first, second and third priorities. Further gender difference comes in with regards to the ranking of priorities for rest of the three facilities, education, health and road linkage. Males considered road linkage as their fourth priority, followed by health and education. For females, the ranking was just the opposite; education was their fourth priority, followed by health and lastly the roads.

Table 10.26: Ranking of Priority of Basic Infrastructure, by Male

Facility	*Rank 1*	*Rank 2*	*Rank 3*	*Rank 4*	*Rank 5*	*Rank 6*
Education	9.9	10.0	12.2	21.6	11.4	34.9
Health	5.4	14.4	20.3	14.5	39.1	6.3
Water	45.1	30.6	13.3	5.5	3.4	1.9
Sewerage	34.0	37.3	7.5	12.1	6.7	2.4
Solid waste collection	3.5	6.2	32.1	17.7	31.5	8.9
Road linkage	2.0	1.7	14.9	28.2	8.2	45.0

Table 10.27: Ranking of Priority of Basic Infrastructure, by Female

Facility	*Rank 1*	*Rank 2*	*Rank 3*	*Rank 4*	*Rank 5*	*Rank 6*
Education	9.9	4.6	14.7	23.4	13.3	34.1
Health	5.2	17.7	20.0	11.7	36.1	9.3
Water	50.5	27.1	11.4	5.8	2.8	2.4
Sewerage	29.5	41.0	7.6	15.1	3.6	3.2
Solid waste collection	3.4	7.1	33.8	13.8	33.4	8.5
Road	1.6	2.4	12.9	30.1	10.9	42.1

Benefit Incidence Analysis of Municipal Expenditures for Slum Dwellers

Here we have computed the per capita municipal finance reaching the slum households in different parts of city. In our earlier paper (Chapter 4 by Mahadevia and Brar) we have analysed the AMC's and AUDA's budgets. In our survey, three slum localities came under the AMC jurisdiction. For them, we have taken the budget figures of the AMC. Vasna and Juhapura locality come under AUDA for capital investments and under Vejalpur Nagarpalika (municipality) for revenue expenditures. For computing per capita municipal finance reaching the slum households surveyed, we have taken one-year figures, for the year 2005-06, for computing per capita revenue expenditures. For computing per capita capital expenditure, we have taken average annual expenditure over the last five years, given that capital investments are for long term and are invested in parts spatially. Other way of computing capital investments would have been to carry out valuation of the existing infrastructure at current prices and then getting per capita valuation figures for the present level of infrastructure, which we have not done.

The per capita revenue and capital figures are then multiplied by the proportion of households that stated they had access to the infrastructure provided by the public authority, in our case, the AMC or the Vejalpur Nagarpalika[5] for revenue expenditures and AMC or AUDA for the capital expenditures, computed from this primary survey. Then, these figures were multiplied by the proportion of households that stated they were satisfied with the infrastructure. We assume that the households who stated they were not satisfied with the infrastructure facility was because of various reasons; poor quality of infrastructure, its poor maintenance, infrastructure totally dysfunctional. Hence, even if expenditure is made by the local government, that means nothing for those who are dissatisfied. We will thus get a final figure of in Rs. per capita for each of the infrastructure facility. In this study, we have focused on four basic infrastructures, water supply, drainage and sewerage together termed as sanitation, solid waste management and *pucca* (internal) roads.

$$\text{Per Capita Budget Expenditure to Slum} = \text{PCE} \times \text{A} \times \text{S}$$

Where

PCE = Per Capita Expenditure by the public authority
A = Per cent households having access through Public Authority
S = Satisfaction Index

We would first look at the revenue expenditure of the concerned local authority reaching each of the five slum communities. AMC is the authority that takes care of revenue expenditure for the three slum localities studied here; Sabarmati, Danilimda and Maninagar. While the per capita revenue expenditure by the AMC on water supply in its entire jurisdiction is Rs. 253.09 in the year 2005-06, this figure for the three slum localities was Rs. 106.30, Rs. 131.38 and Rs. 93.38 respectively after applying the formula stated above, which is about 42 per cent, 52 per cent and 37 per cent respectively of the average per capita expenditure of the AMC on water supply (Table 10.28). Vasna and Juhapura slums are in Vejalpur Nagarpalika. Here, the per capita expenditure on water supply is slightly less than in the AMC. But, this local body has not been able to reach the slums located within its jurisdiction. Vasna slums do not have any access to public body provided water supply. Hence, benefits of public expenditure on water supply reaching them are 0 and amount of revenue expenditure reaching them is Rs. 0. Juhapura slum reaps 25.9 per cent benefit of the average per capita expenditure on water supply.

Benefit incidence of public expenditure on sanitation to the slums in Danilimda and Maninagar is as high as 80 per cent and 72 per cent respectively. Once again, slums in Vejalpur have been able to get the least benefits. On the whole, for all slums surveyed, benefits of public expenditure (on revenue account) reaching the slum household is 37.6 per cent of the average at the city level.

Table 10.28: Average Annual Per Capita Revenue Expenditure by the Public Authority and Per Capita Revenue Expenditure Reaching the Slums, 2005-06, Current Prices.

Zone	Water Supply			Sewerage			Solid waste			Pucca roads		
	Av. to all hhs (Rs.)	To slum hhs (Rs.)	Slum to av. (%)	Av. to all hhs (Rs.)	To slum hhs (Rs.)	Slum to av. (%)	Av. to all hhs (Rs.)	To slum hhs (Rs.)	Slum to av. (%)	Av. to all hhs (Rs.)	To slum hhs (Rs.)	Slum to av. (%)
Sabarmati	253.09	106.30	42.0	88.39	63.79	72.2	225.95	86.62	38.3	40.68	5.21	12.8
Danilimda	253.09	131.38	51.9	88.39	70.96	80.3	225.95	104.56	46.3	40.68	10.05	24.7
Maninagar	253.09	93.36	36.9	88.39	41.73	47.2	225.95	96.09	42.5	40.68	9.13	22.4
Vasna	250.70	0.00	0.0	24.41	0.00	0.0	5.20	1.30	26.7	26.91	6.15	22.9
Juhapura	250.70	65.00	25.9	24.41	2.50	10.2	5.20	0.11	2.1	26.91	8.57	31.8
Total	252.61	79.02	31.3	75.59	28.39	37.6	181.8	53.21	29.3	37.93	9.30	24.5

The proportion of per capita expenditure in the slums to the average at the city level is 29.3 per cent with regards to solid waste and 24.5 per cent with regards to *pucca* road (or roads *per se*). Benefit incidence to slums for expenditures made on solid waste management is so low because the garbage pick up in the slums is very poor. In the emerging innovative practices of waste management through community involvement, the community associations are generally formed in middle class localities and not in the slum colonies. In one earlier study (Mahadevia and Pharate, 2008) the researchers have observed for Mumbai that the new system of solid waste management through Advance Locality Management (ALMs) by the Resident Welfare Associations (RWAs) exist only in the middle and higher income group housing colonies and not in the slums. The existing system reaches the slums skimpily. The innovative mechanisms of outsourcing would further create hygiene and health problems for the slum dwellers, given that solid waste management is a very important component of public health and hygiene.

An important issue that comes out of this analysis is that benefit incidence of revenue expenditure on roads to the slum dwellers is only 24.5 per cent. If the local bodies and the development authorities keep making expenditures on the roads, the slum dwellers do not benefit much. But, if the expenditures are made on water supply and sanitation, there are higher chances that the slum dwellers would benefit than the expenditures made on roads. The AMC had been making quite high per cent expenditures on water supply and sanitation services till very recently, till 2003-04 (See our paper, Chapter 4). But, since then, higher attention has been going to roads and flyovers projects, whose benefits do not reach the slum dwellers in any great proportion.

Vasna and Juhapura areas have very low public expenditure benefits incidence ratios because they are in a smaller urban local body (ULB), which is a nagarpalika, whose resource base is poorer as compared to a large municipal corporation. Hence, this ULB is unable to make investments in capital projects. Instead, a development authority, here AUDA, makes capital investments in infrastructure projects. AUDA is a parastatal; it is not an elected body, and is therefore not dependent on vote-bank politics. AUDA, as per our visual survey in the city, discussed in our previous paper (Chapter 4), is investing more in the western periphery, as far as all the infrastructures are concerned, than in the south, east and the north. Hence, the two slums in AUDA, which are located in the south of the AMC, have not benefited much from AUDA's capital investments in infrastructure. Since, there are no capital investments; the ULB is not making any revenue expenditures.

Table 10.29: Average Annual Per Capita Capital Expenditure by the Public Authority and Per Capita Capital Expenditure Reaching the Slums, 2005-06, Current Prices

Zone	Water Supply			Sewerage			Solid waste			Pucca roads		
	Av. to all hhs (Rs.)	To slum hhs (Rs.)	Slum to av. (%)	Av. to all hhs (Rs.)	To slum hhs (Rs.)	Slum to av. (%)	Av. to all hhs (Rs.)	To slum hhs (Rs.)	Slum to av. (%)	Av. to all hhs (Rs.)	To slum hhs (Rs.)	Slum to av. (%)
Sabarmati	78.54	32.99	42.0	41.20	29.73	72.2	10.40	3.99	38.4	45.51	5.83	12.8
Danilimda	78.54	40.77	51.9	41.20	33.08	80.3	10.40	4.81	46.3	45.51	11.24	24.7
Maninagar	78.54	28.97	36.9	41.20	19.45	47.2	10.40	4.42	42.5	45.51	10.21	22.4
Vasna	476.56	0.00	0.0	133.44	0.00	0.0	NA	NA	NA	769.06	175.85	22.9
Juhapura	476.56	123.55	25.9	133.44	13.64	10.2	NA	NA	NA	769.06	244.95	31.9
Total			31.3			37.6			29.3			24.5

For the capital expenditures, we have looked at AMC expenditures in first three slums and AUDA expenditures in the next two slums. The proportion of per capita capital expenditure reaching the slum dwellers is the same as that for the revenue expenditures because the method adopted in the computation of per capita revenue and per capita capital expenditures reaching the slum dwellers is the same. But, the per capita amounts are different. For per capita capital expenditures in general for each of the four heads of infrastructure see Table 10.28. In this we can see that per capita expenditure on water supply, sanitation and roads is far higher in AUDA areas than in the AMC areas. And that is quite obvious when we move around in the city. Part of this gap between the AMC and the AUDA in terms of per capita expenditures is the fact that the capital investments in the AMC areas have been made over time whereas, the AUDA has developed the peripheral areas from being farm lands to services urban development only in the last decade. Hence, much more of funds per capita have been invested here than in the AMC areas in the same period. For our computation, for capital investments, we have taken average annual expenditure over last five years only. Hence, we would find more per capita expenditures in the AUDA areas than in the AMC areas.

We wish to make another point as well. AUDA, a parastatal has made selective investments. Its focus has been mainly the western periphery. It is here that the organisation has been able to auction off lands at extremely high prices in 2006, to raise resources to pay off loans taken for western region infrastructure projects, as already discussed by us in Chapter 4. The organisation has not yet shown interests in eastern Ahmedabad, although, it's proposed plan does cover eastern Ahmedabad. We think that the AUDA would not be interested much in developing the periphery of east Ahmedabad and would continue with its focus on west Ahmedabad. This is because; the AUDA is able to get very high auction prices of lands in west Ahmedabad. For example, Reliance Industries have purchased a plot of land from AUDA at a phenomenal price of Rs. 61,000 per sq meter, something unheard in Ahmedabad ever[6]. AUDA would be justified in offering lands at such high auction prices only if it is able to provide infrastructure in the areas around such land parcels. The spiral of high investments in land development and then high prices of lands in specific regions and then once again investments in such regions where there are high potential lands would continue. In western Ahmedabad, therefore, AUDA has not put in investments in pockets where there are slum colonies, but have put in investments in pockets where there are mall and multiplexes and where new commercial and high end housing developments are coming up.

In the end, we wish to state that such an exercise can be done for all other public expenditures as well. Together with a survey of what publicly funded infrastructure the slum dwellers use and what are their priorities, we can comment about the expenditures made by the ULBs and also by the parastatals. We can also carry out benefit incidence analysis for specific schemes or programmes. We can carry out benefit incidence analysis for the women in urban slums or for some specific caste or religious groups. This study is to illustrate that simple increase in municipal budgets or investments in infrastructure is no cause of celebration for the urban poor groups unless allocations and expenditures have been increased on items that benefit them. Gross investment figures do not say much; on the contrary they are highly misguiding.

This study also shows that inspite of the AMC allocating significant proportion of its revenue and capital investments on basic infrastructure such as water supply and sanitation, the proportion that reaches the slum dwellers on per capita basis is less than 40 per cent. This means that if the AMC spends Re. 1 per capita on water supply, then on per capita basis only 31 paise reaches the slum dwellers and if it spends Re. 1 per capita on sanitation, then on per capita basis only 38 paise reaches the slum dweller. This is because either the slum is not plugged into the infrastructure network or if it is then the quality of service is very poor. This calls for improved governance and also improved willingness of the local authorities to reach the slum localities. This requires special efforts. These are now missing in the AMC and hence increased allocations to the city under the JNNURM may not be a cause of celebration, if the willingness to reach out to the slum dwellers is not improved.

NOTES

1. This chapter is based on research undertaken through IDPAD project.
2. Survey carried out in partnership with SAATH in Ahmedabad.
3. The city has been segmented totally by religion; the Muslims living in specific locations whereas the rest of the population with majority domination of the Hindus living in the rest of the city. Even the mixed slum localities in eastern Ahmedabad have observed outmigration of the Muslim households to the Muslim localities of the city (See Mahadevia 2007b).
4. After the expansion of the AMC limits in May 2006 (See Chapter 4), Sankalit Nagar has come under the jurisdiction of the AMC. But, our survey was prior to this change.

5. In Vejalpur Nagarpalika, the expenditure on roads is not mentioned, but that on street lights, etc. is given and which has been taken as revenue expenditure on roads. For solid waste, there is no separate head, but, the information is given under Health expenditure with sub heads as *Safai, Swachchh Nagar Abhiyan* etc. which have been taken for solid waste expenditure computation. The latest available finance data for Vejalpur is for the year 2003-04. We have extrapolated the figures, taking last three years trend to the 2005-06 year.
6. *The Times of India*, Ahmedabad, April 6, 2006.

11

SLUM DEMOLITIONS AND PRODUCTION OF NEO-LIBERAL SPACE
Delhi

LALIT BATRA and DIYA MEHRA

Background

In the past eight years, over five lakh people living in squatter settlements in urban Delhi have been evicted. While the scale of these demolitions is staggering, it is not the first time that such large scale evictions have taken place in the city. Indeed, they are demonstrative of the inherent instability of the slum settlements of the city, no matter how old and how consolidated they are and whatever may be the political regime holding power in Delhi. Such a tendency is primarily rooted in the elite's and now emerging middle class's imaginary of a city that considers existence of slums as lack of 'adequate' progress and development and the slum dwellers persistently representing backwardness, to be removed and their spaces cleared for 'development'.

The current instability, we argue, is created by:

(i) Visions of building a consumptive city for, by and of the middle class and big private capital. This city is orderly, 'clean and green', technologically driven, cosmopolitan in as much as it harbours global/western urban forms while highlighting the city's historical imperial heritage. This is a city, which spatially provides for a leisurely yet disciplined consumerist lifestyle, as well as for hi-tech, high-value industry and enterprises.

(ii) Massive upgradation efforts in the city by its government to

> match the changing contours of the city's political economy and to fulfil this vision. This includes not only new and massive investment in roads and transport facilities, public utilities, green areas, heritage buildings and new grandiose public architectures, but also new forms of governance seeking to streamline, standardise, and privatise processes of urbanisation to be governed by the free-market rules. While the language of such governance includes a commitment to transparent, accountable and thus rational processes, the modes through which such procedures and policies emerge and are implemented, suggest a centralisation of decision making on major issues of urban governance.

The main players in putting such an agenda together are: (i) Those involved with "high politics" (Fuller and Benei, 2000) irrespective of political party (distinguished from the everyday politics of local residents), (ii) private capital, whether in the form of consumers (residential and commercial), producers (builders) or sellers (media, land and real estate companies), (iii) middle class groups and associations such as Resident Welfare Associations (RWAs) and Market Traders Associations in so far as their demands match government agendas, which in the case of slum removal they do, and (iv) the courts, who through legal interpretation, have legitimised the enabling discourse for such agendas and actions, what Baviskar (2003) has calls a "bourgeois environmentalism".

Undergirding these factors, as we have mentioned earlier, is the persistence of a marginalising imaginary that can be traced to the 19th century. This is a lens, a gaze, through which the slum appears as a sign of disease, decay, danger, and indiscipline, all of which are to be replaced by a modern, rational, and orderly 'other'. In what follows, we will provide a brief historical account of the emergence, and persistence, of such a perspective, delineate how slums have come to be formed and managed in the city, and finally turn to the question of the recent demolitions, which are one of the largest displacements of the poor people in the city's history. While our arguments are universal, we have drawn examples for the same from the experiences of the vast slum settlements along the banks of the river Yamuna.

Slums through the Colonial Gaze

Historically, the problematic of the slum can be traced back to the 19th century and to the Mutiny of 1857 in Delhi. Records of the medieval period show that poor quality housing was always in existent in Shajahanabad, Delhi's name in the Mughul times. When the East India Company first took over the city, its officers were, in the most part, content to live in the Mughul capital as they had found it, with many adopting the luxuriant lifestyle of the native elite.

It was the Mutiny of 1857—a large-scale rebellion against the Company's domination—which produced a dramatic shift in colonial attitude. Aware of their small numbers and recent narrow escape, the new administration of the British crown became overwhelmingly concerned with policing the geography of urban centres like Delhi, which had participated in the revolt. Not readily comprehensible to the European eyes, the twists and turns of old city lanes and *mohullas* came to be seen as a source of consistent and potential danger, dissention and disease, which particularly and adversely affected British interests in India (Kenny and Chatterjee, 1999).

'Native' culture was now admonished for its inferiority, its propensity for dirt, filth, dampness and congestion, and an effort was made to introduce contemporary European ideas of city order and planning to ameliorate the poor condition of the city and its inhabitants. In the period that followed, a series of measures were introduced to intervene, perhaps for the first time, into issues of urban form—of how the city's citizenry lived, and in what type of housing. This change in emphasis provided the government a pretext to intervene in many aspects of the local life.

Vast areas of the Old City were demolished to allow for better surveillance; technologies such as sewage were introduced to reduce disease; building by-laws and municipal codes were drafted and expansion plans made to extend a 'modern' Delhi for which land was acquired from many sources (Goodfriend, 1989). Concurrently, as the price of land in Delhi increased with its growing political and economic importance, municipal measures also allowed for growing State determination of the land market, including policies to enforce private title and to prevent illegal 'encroachments' on land. This was part of a larger effort to strengthen private property laws and to bring lands under government and market control.

By 1936, the entire Old Delhi area had been designated a slum under the city's planning codes, the colonial government controlled vast acreage under the aegis of the Delhi Improvement Trust and the colonials themselves had founded a new and separate city—New Delhi—to further remove themselves from their native counterparts. Nationalist leaders complained that revenues garnered from the entire city were used only to improve English areas, ignoring the needs of 'native' citizens. The British, it seemed, justified their rule on their civilizational superiority incorporating it in law, while spending revenues in a manner that ensured that the gap between 'native' and English' would remain, even as they gained further legislative powers to control the city's growth.

Slums in the Master Planning Era

Despite their negative assessment of colonial urban planning and colonial attitudes, the administrative processes of the era were carried forward in the post-1947 period when Indian nationalists took over the reigns of government. Concerned about the problem of unregulated growth in the city, the State in the late 50s sought to systematically intervene in the growth process of the city in order "to check the haphazard and unplanned growth of Delhi...with its sprawling residential colonies, without proper layouts and without the conveniences of life, and to promote and secure the development of Delhi according to the plan" (DDA Act, 1957, in Roy 2004). In the late 1950s, under the guidance of Ford Foundation experts, the Town Planning Organisation (TPO) prepared the first Master Plan of Delhi (MPD-62), which was notified in 1962, for the next twenty years. The inclusion of American experts meant that the new Master Plan envisioned a new kind of modernist city in the global sense in the post-War period, wherein the city was transformed into: "a single State-sponsored homogenous zone, creating a universally rational city divided into functional sectors" (Caldeira 1996 : 317).

The Old City, in this view was seen as "slum, congested, filthy, obsolete, functionally lacking in exclusive land use zones, without any green spaces and socially and culturally stagnant". The plan thus proposed shifting out about 45 per cent of its population in order to decongest and redevelop the old city (MPD-62, Jain 1990 : 79).

However, conceived entirely within the Nehruvian imagination of a planned, modernised, socialist economy, there were some ways in which the Master Plan extended beyond the British City. Befitting the new Nehruvian values of the State, it had equitable population densities, housing and provision of civic infrastructure. And thus more importantly, it had no *new* slums. For in a larger attempt to orchestrate the equable development of the city[1], the Delhi Development Authority (DDA), established in 1957, was mandated with the acquisition, development and disposal of massive tracts of agricultural land that lay within the planned boundaries of the city (Birdi 1982). For the new planners, such a scheme would be effective in preventing any future growth of slums, because unlike its colonial counterparts, the DDA controlled the entire land market, and could thus control land speculation and the volatility of land prices[2]. Consequently, such was the faith in new planning, that the Master Plan, which provides the legal framework for land use in Delhi, does not account for the growth of new slum settlements in the city—an absence that deems them illegal by the virtue of being inappropriate and unrecognised land use. This was because it was premised on the assumption that the governmental agencies providing housing to all low-income residents would also be able to do so for the urban poor coming to the city in the future, upto 1981, the first Master Plan period.

The first Master Plan, with an emphasis on "quality in architecture and civic design consonant with Delhi as a national capital page" (Kenny and Chatterjee, 1999 : 90), expanded the visual and structural character of British Delhi; the hexagonal layout and multi-nodal and polycentric design, planned in extraordinary detail, to ensure rational and orderly growth. Land was segmented, and marked out for different uses. The new zoning laws were overlaid on many other by-laws and codes for physical structure and land-use adopted from the colonial State, and like the colonial inheritances belied the reality of land use in the Old City, which was and remained heavily 'mixed' and undifferentiated.

The new Plan envisioned the city largely as a centre of governance and residence. Indeed, a great deal of emphasis was placed on limiting the population of the city in 1981 to a maximum of 53 lakhs, later revised to 56 lakhs. A set of strategies were adopted in the plan to achieve this purpose; building a 1.6 km wide green belt around Delhi, diverting the surplus population to seven ring towns in Uttar Pradesh and Haryana, decongestion of the Walled City by relocating the population in New Delhi and Civil Lines, prohibiting a number of heavy and polluting industries etc. Further, improvements in agriculture and heavy industrialisation, outside the metropolis and its economic area, were also envisioned, as necessary trajectory for more spread out urbanisation to ensure that unemployment did not create megacities, through the flows of migrants and wealth from the countryside (Suri 1994 and Ramachandran 1989). In this, the Delhi Master Plan set the policy for urbanisation in entire nation which included emphasis on 'decentralisation' of population and 'decongestion' of the city's existing areas by developing new cities and new areas around existing cities, through expansive planning.

The Unintended City

What came of the master plan? Mostly the number of squatters grew exponentially in the post-independence era. Risbud (1999) notes that by 1956, there were already about 22,000 squatter families in Delhi. The growth of squatter settlements continued unabated and, by 1973, there were 98,438 squatter families. Between 1959 and 1973, the overall annual rate of growth of squatter households was found to be 11.8 per cent as compared to 4.5 per cent population growth of the whole city. The number of squatter families has increased unabatedly because of growth of Delhi's economy that acted as pull factor for the migrants and lack of low-income housing in the city. The two issues are briefly detailed out below.

Delhi has been one of the most economically dynamic cities in the country. The city was always a centre of trade and distribution in North India (T&PO 1973). The number of registered wholesale dealers has increased from 69,469 in 1971 to 263,259 in 1997 and the number of workforce employed in the sector has increased from 1.17 lakhs in 1951 to 6.73 lakhs in 1997 (National Capital Region Planning Board—NCPRB 1999). The city today has wholesale market for nine types of goods. Public sector came to be located in a big way in the city after it became administrative capital of independent India. Industries, construction, communications, transport, and financial services being located in the city led to expansion of the city economy and a great attraction for the migrant population.

The wholesale trade originated from the Old City. Although the Master Plans had explicitly banned large, or heavy industry, there was large growth in small or informal manufacturing, particularly in the Old City with such a legacy and also superior transport, electric and other civic infrastructure bestowed on the city, as national capital. The number of manufacturing units jumped by 16 times, investment 140 times and production 180 times between 1951 to 2001, a span of just 50 years in Delhi (Government of National Capital Territory of Delhi—GNCTD 2001 and 2002)! Indeed, close look at Delhi's economy in the post-independence period reveals that the small-scale, informal economies continued to produce more and more wealth, than formal organisations (T &PO 1973). Many goods and commodities consumed in the city were the product of small-scale, low technology, labour-intensive manufacturing, that employed the urban poor. The effective rates of tax and tariff have been substantially lower in Delhi as compared to the neighbouring states. These differences in tax rates with added advantages of better social and physical infrastructure in Delhi have attracted industries and trade and then other services sector, all together attracting migrants and also low-income migrants in large numbers. The low income migrants got absorbed in the informal services sector that displayed definite ethnic and caste boundaries (Prashad 1999). Lastly, the Asiad games of 1982 brought fresh influx of labour into the city, brought in for the purpose of constructing facilities. They stayed back in the city.

As for low income housing, the DDA was to acquire, develop and dispose 27,487 hectares of land in the twenty years period of the first master plan. Of this only 15,540 was acquired. In other words instead of an annual target of 1,372 hectares, only 777 hectares was acquired every year. Similarly, in 1962, the total existing urban residential land was 4,694 hectares. The Plan proposed to add another 14,479 hectares by 1981. But the land actually developed was only 7,316 hectares by 1984. Roughly half the Plan-projected residential land was not developed. The developed lands were distributed in a skewed way. The high-income (HIG) group received more (29%) than their share of 20 per cent of DDA developed housing while Low Income Group (LIG) and Middle Income Group (MIG) received 44.44 per cent and 17.63 per cent, less than their share of 50 per cent and 30 per cent respectively (Association of Metropolitan Development Authorities 2003 : 1-15). Slums have been an outcome of imbalance between the quantum of low-cost housing created and required.

Policies for the Slums[3]

The government responded to the problematic of slums through ad-hoc schemes from time to time and demolitions. During the 1960s, these schemes attempted to 'resettle' slum dwellers according to a planned matrix. In the 1970's, especially during the 'Emergency' period, the first massive slum demolitions were witnesses, when 57,368 squatter families were evicted and resettled on lands far out of the city. By early 1980s, following the popular backlash against the demolitions during the Emergency period, the government decided against eviction and resettlement as a blanket solution for the slums and decided to adopt the policy of in-situ upgradation of slum clusters by providing them civic services on a 'as is where is basis'. After a hiatus of some time on slum demolitions, and with increase in slum population after the Asiad games, in 1990, the Delhi government came up with a new three pronged policy for the slums: (i) relocation, (ii) in-situ upgradation, and (iii) Environmental Improvement of Urban Slums (EIUS). Of this, in-situ upgradation was carried out in only 4 sites in the early 90s; that reinstated resettlement as the only option for managing slum populations in the city.

With the partial exception of the V.P Singh government (1989-90), no government has tried to give any legal identity or tenure to slum dwellers in Delhi. Instead, the illegality of slums and the threat of demolition have been used to strengthen political patronage networks on one hand and provided a steady source of income for the low level officials in the city's planning bureaucracy the police on the other. While the presence of slum dwellers have been necessary for the city's economy, they have never been fully acceptable by the mainstream planning processes and the planning machinery. The rhetoric of 'cleaning up' the city through massive demolitions therefore has cropped up repeatedly, exemplified during the Emergency and the recent demolitions.

The Coming-up of Yamuna Pushta Slums

The urban poor have found housing in either rental units of dilapidated *katras* of the Walled City or in *jhuggie jhopris* (JJ)/*bastis*, that sprawled on the outskirts of the city and in the bed of River Yamuna. Traditionally, the peasant communities held leasehold rights to the riverbed. The first Master Plan had described this area as 'floodable' and except for a few parks, playgrounds and open spaces on the Western Pushta (bank), no development was planned for it. The *bastis* were not the only new structures—the government constructed three power plants, a fly-ash pond, a police training camp, an oil bottling plant, a crematorium and other structures; people who could not afford housing in the formal land market built unauthorised colonies on the Eastern side, and slums on the riverbed.

In 1967, a large number of slums were removed from Jamna Bazaar area near the Nigam Bodh Ghat. The evictees were resettled in Welcome colony in the then Eastern periphery of the city (Tarlo 2000). But the stream of migrants settling on the riverbed continued apace. The rapid development of the area on both sides of the river and proximity of this area to Walled City gave a boost to growth of *jhuggies* on the riverbed, especially between Yamuna Bridge and Nizammudin Bridge as ample job opportunities were available in the vicinity. The slum settlements on Yamuna riverbed expanded as many of the workers that come for constructing Delhi Asiad facilities settled here. Close to a million workers were brought into the city to build infrastructure for the games (People's Union of Democratic Rights—PUDR 1982).

The residents of Yamuna Pushta *jhuggies* accessed lands through variety of ways; the first settlers bought land from farmers cultivating the flood plain (around Salimgarh area) or cleared forest areas (as in Nangla Maachi) filled up swampy lands and subsequently they encroached on surrounding lands as much as they could paying off city officials. They then subdivided the plots to construct rental units for the other poor city residents who came to know about the new development. Over time, slum settlements grew in size, became cosmopolitan in demographic and ethnic composition, got basic facilities such as water, electricity, and other public utilities, and then attracted a number of social service organisations working for the urban poor. While this process did not guarantee constitutional rights or legal title for the Pushta residents, they did come to occupy a grey zone where there was some possibility of collective bargaining in a city and an economy where grey zones abounded.

In an article on the Yamuna Pushta written in 1997, N Rohinkanta Singh describes what he saw of the 144,612 people living in the area:

> "The Yamuna Pushta area comprises (of) the Sanjay Amar and Indira colonies and these are subdivided into 11 smaller colonies. The slum has a Bangladeshi section, a Rajasthani section, and similar sections for people from Uttar Pradesh, Bihar and Nepal. About 70 per cent of the population is Muslim; about 26 per cent is Hindu whereas a handful is Christians and even fewer Sikhs. There are little *pucca* and *kutcha* shacks all over. Some of them are two or three room…others much smaller. Others live in shacks built on rickshaws. There is very little drinking water. There are very few hand pumps. And some aren't so lucky, they have no houses; they live on the pavement. The area has no proper drainage system and the smell of refuse is everywhere."
>
> "Most slumdwellers are rickshaw-pullers, coolies, daily wage earners, rag-pickers, hawkers and domestic help. The women make zips, gift boxes and artifacts of bamboo. Workers have organised themselves in committees like the All-India Drum-makers Welfare Association, and the Akhil Bhartiya Rickshaw-Puillers Association. According to one NGO, there are over 100 committees in the area. 13 NGOs working in the area, there are non-formal educational centres, adult education centres as well as remedial and vocational training classes. The MCD dispensary, funded by the World Bank, provides free medical service. Immunisation and health awareness are the tasks of the 25 *Basti Sevikas* appointed by the community. There is a police booth—a sub inspector, and 25 police man."

The canvas painted by Singh suggests a vibrant and functional habitat and economy which, despite its problems, provided a modicum of security to a large number of people bypassed by the formal planning and policy. If Yamuna Pushta slums were not 'slums of hope' they were also certainly not 'slums of despair'. All this was to change however, by the late 1990s, when the process of eviction was restarted on a massive scale.

Legal Contests En Route to a 'World Class' City

Following the market liberalisation and privatisation policies in the early 1990s, Delhi like other mega cities began to see a number of changes in its physical, economic and cultural landscape. The city became entrepôt for increased flows of finance, goods, services and people across national boundaries. Like other cities, it also saw expansion of consumptive middle class due to increase in prosperity among a section of population, and also expansion of new economic activities such as IT, ITES, financial services, personal care and entertainment services, among others, leading to space demands for new leisure activities, commercial areas, high-end residential spaces, and so on. The city in general and the middle classes and their organisations in particular came forward to seek redressal on what they perceived as a degraded environment—water, air and noise pollution—caused by the new developments. They went to the Courts for the purpose.

The cases filed by 'environmental' activists in the Supreme Court—MC Mehta, HD Shourie, BL Wadehra etc.—would reflect a concern with the ecology of the city 'as a whole'; thus MC Mehta raised questions on air and water pollution, the Delhi ridge, the state of the Capital's parks, and the state of the river Yamuna. Smaller, more localised concerns from middle class Resident and Traders Welfare Associations focused on the problems in their own areas, with cases filed mostly in the Delhi High Court, all with the same vision.

Thus, the petitioners from the Okhla Factory Owners Association stated in their writ petition:

> "… this is a writ petition under Article 226 of the Constitution of India for the enforcement of fundamental rights of the Petitioners as due to failure of supply of constant electric energy, the Petitioners are compelled to close down their units….That further the Petitioners submit that the respondents have failed to maintain civic amenities as there is a acute shortage of power, lack of drinking water, inhuman conditions in which lakhs of people are working…further the respondents failed to provide sanitation facilities as there is blockage of major sewer pipe and sewer water spreads on the roads which has become the play ground for pigs

> and stray dogs and the roads are being used as open toilets and stench is over-powering. Further the Petitioners submit that the roads are completely damaged. Foreigners have refused to come to visit this industrial area which earns foreign exchange worth Rs. 1200 crores and provides employment to 2.5 lakh people."[4]

These petitioners were taking advantage of a new avenue of legal redressal that had opened up from the excesses of the Emergency, when the Supreme Court was seen as having placidly supported Mrs Indira Gandhi's suspension of democratic rights. As many commentators (Sudarshan 1990) have noted that in an attempt to "refurbish" and "assert" its role, the Supreme Court: (i) positioned itself as the saviour of the disadvantaged, who did not usually have access to legal redress and thus to social justice, and (ii) loosened the rules of loci standing for petitioners, both allowing any form of plea, famously even if on a postcard, to be registered as a "public interest litigation", even in cases where the petitioner was not directly affected by the issue petitioned about. PIL would instead be open to "any public spirited individual or social action group to bring an action for vindication" on their behalf. (*MC Mehta* verses *Union of India and Ors, CWP 12739/1985)*.

The residents of the Yamuna Pustha slums got entrapped in this new concern about the river and local ecologies, their degradation emerging as primary problem of the city. The river, itself, first came into focus in the mid-1980s when PILs by environmentalists, and concerned citizens such as MC Mehta, BL Wadhera, brought its degradation to the attention of the Supreme Court. In 1995, in a case called the *Mailee* (dirty) Yamuna case, the Supreme Court took *suo moto* cognizance of a *Hindustan Times* article, bringing in effect the clean up efforts of the river under its purview. The 62,000 *jhuggi jhopris* on the banks of the river, of which the Pushta, and Nangla Maachi were a part, were called into question by a series of cases filed in the Delhi High Court by the Resident Welfare Associations (RWAs), Merchants and Traders Associations (MTAs), and Industrial associations, where the language used by the petitioners was picked up from the language used by the Supreme Court in the larger cases the latter was hearing.

The petition by Pritampura Sudhar Samiti and Okhla Factory Owners Association put forward the plea that slums should be removed from their neighbourhood because:

> "the JJ dwellers defecate in neighbourhood parks causing 'untold miseries to the residents' ...(are) a health hazard to the locality and

> has (sic) transgressed their right to decent living. Besides young girls do not come to their own balconies throughout the day as obnoxious smell pollute the atmosphere and the entire environment.[5]
>
> due to illegal encroachment there is a blockage on the roads and the areas have become very accident prone and traffic jams have become common"[6].

Accepting all these pleas, the Delhi High Court quoting the Supreme Court noted that:

> "Establishment or creation of slums, it seems, appears to be good business and is well organised. The number of slums has multiplied in the last few years by geometrical proportion. Large areas of public land, in this way, are usurped for private use free of cost. It is difficult to believe that this can happen in the capital of the country without passive or active connivance of the land owning agencies and/or the municipal authorities.
>
> Delhi being the capital city of the country is a show window to the world of our culture, heritage, traditions and way of life. A city like Delhi must act as a catalyst for building of modern India. It cannot be allowed to degenerate and decay. The slums that have been created...which is the cause of nuisance and breeding ground of so many ills. The welfare, health, maintenance of law and order, safety and sanitation of these residents cannot be sacrificed and their rights under Article 21 are violated in the name of social justice to the slum dwellers."[7]

In their rulings which successively ordered the removal of all slums on the riverbed, and then in the city as a whole, the courts not only redefined the middle class's right to the Environment as one superseding the right to housing and livelihood, but also came to affirm that slums were the causes of a number of different pollution problems responsible for the deterioration of the quality of life of the citizens. The overwhelming metaphor used by all these PILs is considering the slum dwellers as environmental, moral and technological depredation.

Not only has the court reinvigorated the language of colonial rulers, and the Master Plan in defining 'adequate' city, in contradistinction to the slum, the use of the PILs as a mechanism has put in place parallel governance structure to the democratic structure enshrined in the Constitution. This parallel governance structure has greatly destroyed the systems of the unintended city, by which slum dwellers originally found a place in the city. Irritated and frustrated by the response of the political and administrative wing of the government, the Supreme Court and Delhi High Court have effectively used their powers of contempt, and the space provided by the PIL, to intervene on a plethora of urban issues.

The process that the Higher Courts have followed has been thus. Taking the example of the Yamuna Pushta case; the High Court and the Supreme Court first pulled all the PILs filed by the various middle class associations together to establish 'public interest'. Then the Courts placed on records these cases and passed successive interim orders on different aspects represented by the petitions in such a way that they fell outside the purview of the original case but with far-ranging implications (Vandenhole 2000). For example, the PIL of the Okhla factory owners association to improve their neighbourhood eventually led to an order nullifying the Delhi government's relocation policy and ordering all slums on the Yamuna banks to be removed. In the case of Nangla Maachi, a plea by residents around the Chhattarpur area to regulate traffic translated into orders to examine traffic patterns across Delhi's main arterial roads resulting in demolitions of the slum settlements that were felt as impediments to this smooth functioning of traffic. PIL is a special type of litigation process in which the Court can take pro-active role in investigating the facts put before it, constitute committees to conduct fact finding missions, and present evidence that is not "tested by cross-examination" (Vandenhole 2000) and by that brings together city officials, court commissions and amicus curiae on a democratically non-accountable platform to administratively and logistically work out solutions to the urban 'problems' within the framework given by the Court. At the same time, there is no institutional mechanism in this process to grant the affected party, slum dwellers in this case, a right to be heard. The Court also monitors the implementation of its orders. Thus in the Wazirpur case, after it's ruling of removal of all slum settlements in the Okhla case, it set up a coordinating committee under retired Justice Usha Mehta to oversee the day to day administration and logistics of its order that all "encroachments" be removed from the riverbed.

The court has thus emerged as a significant player directing urban policy in Delhi. While it is true that despite the PIL structure which provides the court vast executive powers, the court is not always successful in having its orders implemented. But, in the case of slum dwellers and slum settlements they have been put into force with remarkable alacrity, largely because of the consensus across all wings of the government and all political parties on relocating slum dwellers far away from the city.

From Labour to Leisure: Transformation of Yamuna Riverbed

In the case of the 2004 Yamuna Pushta demolitions, as the court was ordering the demolition of over 27,000 jhuggis, Mr. Jagmohan, the Union Minister of Culture and Tourism unveiled a grandiose plan for the area once the 'encroachments' were removed. He proposed a 220-acre national tourist and cultural complex on the riverbanks that "would become one of the greatest hubs of cultural tourism and attract hundreds of thousands of domestic and foreign tourists"[8]. He suggested that the area was a breeding ground of *jhuggi dadas* (slumlords), *kabaris* (waste recyclers), owners of polluting factories and large dairy farms who are "strangulating all our constitutional, environmental, cultural and civic values ... destroying our sacred heritage of the past and making the living conditions of the present chaotic and even polluting and corrupting our future,"[9]. The language used by Mr Jagmohan was picked up by all to delegitimise the presence of the urban poor in Delhi.

Mr. Jagmohan's efforts come in a long string of other efforts on the part of the public authorities to 'reclaim' the prime riverbed area for urban development by 'channelising' the river. These efforts were "initiated in 1977 when the Chief Engineer (I&F), Delhi Administration wrote to the Director, Central Water & Power Research Station, Pune, to conduct model studies for channelisation of River Yamuna" (Gupta 1995). In 1989, the DDA declared 3,500 hectares of land in the riverbed as development area. Putting its stamp of approval on the channelisation initiatives, the second Master Plan of Delhi-2001, notified in 1999, stated:

> "Rivers in the major metropolitan cities of the world like Thames in London and Seine in Paris have been channelised providing unlimited opportunities to develop the river fronts. The possibilities in respect of river Yamuna have been studied in depth and indications are that it could be channelised within 550 mt. width and an area of about 3000-4000 hectares could become available for riverfront development" (DDA 1999).

The CWPRS, Pune submitted its draft final report on 'Hydraulics Model Studies for Channelisation of River Yamuna at Delhi' in May 1991, on the basis of which the DDA prepared a Rs. 18 billion (at March, 1992 prices) development scheme for Yamuna riverfront (Gupta 1995). The scheme envisaged development of 8,000 hectares of riverbed area for recreational, residential, commercial, institutional and public purposes with private sector funding to the extent of over 60 per cent of the total project cost.

Nothing much happened to the riverfront development plans for about a decade. But, in the early 2000s, with increased demand of land for public and private sector 'development' projects, the pressure on land in Delhi increased tremendously. Furthermore, land was now required also for 'showcase' projects which would serve to project an attractive image of the city to various forms of international finance looking for welcoming investment destinations to park their surpluses. Thus reached a wide-ranging consensus across all political parties and actors in decision-making positions to take up such large-scale 'luxury' projects without feeling the need to justify them in the name of the poor or for redistributive justice—an hallmark of development activities in the heydays of 'socialistic' planning.

This new climate has created a renewed interest in riverbed area. Many independent plans for the development of the riverbed have been floated. No single one has been fully approved. But, the colonisation of the riverbed has begun with continuous, independent large structures being constructed on the flood planes in last half a decade. Delhi Metro Rail Corporation (DMRC) has built its sprawling headquarters on 65 hectares of riverbed area near Wazirabad. Part of this land is now being used by the DMRC to develop an IT park in collaboration with the government of Delhi[10]. On another 24 hectares near Nizamuddin is used by Swaminarayan Akshardham Trust to build a massive temple. Similarly, 63 hectares of riverbed land has been given to the Yamuna Bio-Diversity Park, situated between Wazirabad and Jharoda Majra village in north Delhi[11].

In 2006, the Delhi government parcelled out 63.5 hectares of riverbed land for constructing the games village for Commonwealth games to be held in Delhi in 2010. Located next to the Akshardham Temple, the 'village' will host 7,500 competitors and officials and will be equipped with "an international zone (with a press room, conference halls, accreditation centre, travel bureau, shopping centres, restaurant, cinema etc.) and a practice area for participants..."[12]. This project is part of a larger project to comprehensively develop the river front as a part of renewing the city for the Commonwealth Games.

The HUDCO has floated a proposal in partnership with a foreign consortium Fairwood, to channelise the river from ITO barrage to Kalindi Kunj Barrage covering an area of 7,000 acres. This Rs. 80,000 crore project would be funded by commercially exploiting ten per cent 700 acres) of the total land reclaimed. The project includes constructing 280 hectares of commercial space, 80,000 residential flats, mega reservoirs to tap rainwater, stadia for Commonwealth, Asian and Olympic games, promenades, fitness centre, leisure clubs and golf course. The promoters claim it to be the largest 'urban renewal' project in India fully funded with private investment with a central business district and light rail transit system[13].

As the transformation of the Yamuna riverbed shows, the demolition of slums from the central parts of the city entails a major transfer of resources from the poorer sections of the society to those well off. If we accept what the DDA has claimed in its Annual Report of 2003-04: "from April 2003 to 31.3.2004 DDA has carried out 354 demolition operations and about 259.44 acres land was made free of encroachments. In this process 13,077 structures of *kucha, pucca* and semi *pucca* nature were removed." And further, it claims that in the three years 2001-02 (DDA, 2004: 50)[14]. Then, at the rate of Rs. 20,000 per sq meter, which is the current land price in these prime localities, *basti* evictions has led to transfer of at the least Rs. 4,000 crores from the slum dwellers to the DDA in just three years.

While the Yamuna Pushta case is one example, the scale and spread of demolitions in Delhi post late 1990s is too vast to accurately quantify. The agencies that carry out slum demolitions and resettlement in Delhi are the DDA and the MCD. The estimate arrived at by authors based on the incomplete information provided by the DDA and the MCD and the data collated by Hazards Centre (2006) suggests that not less than one lakh shanties have been demolished in the eight years since 1999. The demolitions have been carried out in the entire urban area. Though the stated rationale of demolitions is the requirement of land for public projects, in most of the cases, the land thus 'freed' has been used for purposes which have little to do with the needs of the majority of the public. Thus a *basti* of 5,000 families was evicted in 2001 from the commercial district of Nehru Place to make way for a 'spiritual park'. Bannuwal Nagar, a *basti* of 1,600 residents, in North-West Delhi was demolished in April 2006 because it happened to be uncomfortably close to a proposed five star hotel. The owner of the proposed hotel went to the court saying he would not build the hotel till the *basti* is removed. The Court accepted the argument and ordered the removal of the *basti*. Some local people said that the hotel got the land at a price much below the market value because of the Bannuwal Nagar slum in the vicinity! Similarly, thirty years old Sant Ravidas Camp in the West Delhi colony of Vikas Puri was evicted in 2004 to make way for a neighbourhood park for middle class residents of the colony.

Process of Slum Demolitions

Demolition of slums is a fairly complicated process. Typically a notice is given, anywhere between two days or two weeks preceding the actual demolition. The notice is either given to select *pradhans* (*basti* head or strong men), or pasted on a wall in the settlement. In some cases, the *pradhans* are called to the local MCD or DDA office or even the police station and told about the date of the demolition. They are usually 'warned' of the 'consequences' of creating any 'mischief'. Some *pradhans* may want to tell the truth to the local residents, but, people may not believe him given the misgivings about local politicians in general. It is very unusual to find an effective common response of slum dwellers to demolition as the interest of various actors living in slums tend to clash.

The demolitions are managed in such a way that it creates divisions among the residents along several lines. The first division among the dwellers is created through the cut off dates; 1990 and 1998. In general, slum lords, *pradhans* and relatively better-off residents who usually have more then one *jhuggie* in their name overtly or covertly support demolition drive in the hope of getting more than one plot in the resettlement colony. But those having *jhuggies* on main roads that have being used as shops, vehemently oppose demolitions and moving to resettlement colonies because they may not get the plot/unit on the main road. Despite such contradictions in most *bastis*, residents with or without the help of local NGOs/CBOs, try to either stall/delay demolitions or make relocation less painful and more inclusive by filing a court case, launching public protests, or appealing to politicians and city officials.

Before 1990s, slum dwellers received support from most political parties. The local elected representatives wanted to be seen as leading the residents' protests against the evictions. But since 1990s, a major change has occurred; the local elected representatives either remain aloof or vanish from the public gaze before the demolition date approaches. Some of them actively connive with the authorities and middle class citizens to get the slums removed.

There is a palpable tension in the *basti* two or three days prior to the demolition. Police may take *pradhans* and other important residents in preventive detention before the demolition day arrives to prevent any expected 'trouble'. They are released after the *basti* is demolished. Even otherwise, police usually patrol the *basti* during the nights prior to demolition and threaten people to 'cooperate' or 'face the consequences.'

On the day of demolition, the *basti* is usually cordoned off and barring one, all the other approach roads are sealed. The number of police personnel deployed depends upon the 'threat perception' or potential use of violence by the slum residents. The use of violence of any kind, even stone-pelting or an attempt to forcibly stop the bulldozer by slum dwellers has been an extremely rare phenomenon in Delhi, especially post 1990s. Successful militant opposition to stall demolition is even rarer, seen only in a handful of cases in the past one decade. The most prominent among these has been the case of a *basti* in Govindpuri area of South Delhi that succeeded in sending the bulldozer back twice after militant protest. The more common sight though is that once the bulldozer arrives early in the morning people begin dismantling their homes to salvage as much material as possible so as to be able to rebuild their houses in the new locations. And, usually, the authorities give them some time to salvage their belongings. But in some instances, as in the case of a Vikas Puri slum cluster, bulldozer is used straightaway and the hard earned and much loved belongings of people are reduced to rubble. In the case of this particular slum cluster in Vikas Puri when the activists of a local CBO named *Dilli Shramik Sangathan* tried to negotiate with the authorities and police to get some time for people to remove their belongings, they were picked up and made to sit in the local police station till the *basti* was completely demolished.

The officials of the agency carrying out the demolition sit in a vacant place to hand over 'demand notices' to the families 'eligible' for rehabilitation after verifying the documents. To get a plot allocation in the resettlement colony, the household has to present this 'demand notice' and receipt of the deposit of Rs. 7000. This process takes place in the office of the agency concerned within one or two weeks of demolition. There after, free transport has to be provided to the residents to cart their belongings to the rehabilitation site. But, generally everyone except few, have to arrange private transport to shift to the rehabilitation site.

Resettlement

Resettlement is undertaken when implementation of EIUS or in-situ upgradation is not possible. For EIUS option, the land owning agency has to give an undertaking that it does not require its land immediately. In-situ upgradation, taken up along with tenure security, is undertaken when the Land Owning Agency (LoA) forfeits its right over the land. Resettlement is on either 12.5 sq. meters or 18 sq. meters plots. The cut-off date for eligibility was 1990, which was raised to 1998 in 2000. Relocation is carried out when the LoA demands its land back on an immediate basis and also contributes its share for the relocation of families living there. It is worth noting that despite Draft National Slum Policy, 1999, clearly mentioning in-situ upgradation as the preferred strategy, the last time the Delhi government had done in-situ upgradation was in 1994. Thus for the past 12 years not a single slum cluster has been rehabilitated on an in-situ basis. The preferred strategy of Delhi government has been relocation of slums.

The resettlement site is almost always on the outskirts of the city on the undeveloped rural lands, 'yet-to-be-developed' industrial areas and wastelands. Many of the settlements are established on inhospitable patches of land. Bhalsawa, for instance is right next to an overflowing landfill resulting in round the clock stench and contaminated ground water. Madanpur Khadar is built on a fly ash dumping ground. The distance of these sites from the original place of work of slum dwellers is between twenty to forty kms. Because of their marginal location, there is little work at the settlements sites. There are people, especially women workers, who earn less money than they would spend commuting from the resettlement colony to their place of work. So they opt out of the labour market. Those who continue with their earlier jobs see their earnings go down drastically as commuting eats up anything between a quarter to a half of the earnings. The first and most important casualty of 'resettlement', thus, is loss of livelihood and income.

It is now a widely acknowledged fact that laying and demarcation of plots and infrastructure and provision of basic services is done much after people have been moved to these settlements. In fact, contrary to the practice adopted by the MCD, the DDA does not even allot plots prior to relocation. Almost always when people reach or are brought to these sites by the public agency carrying out demolition; they are welcomed by a barren piece of wasteland in the middle of nowhere. They have to spend months pleading or struggling to get plots allotted and demarcated and basic amenities provided. Meanwhile they continue living under makeshift shelters made of plastic or thatch. The allotment of plots entails paying a bribe to local municipal officials. Even then corner plots and those on the main roads are never allotted to slum residents.

Once the allotment is done slum dwellers are hounded by local MCD and DDA officials and land dealers to sell their plots to them at a nominal payment. Indeed hunger, joblessness and lack of services force many people to sell off their plots and get instant cash of Rs. 20,000 to Rs. 30,000. Those who manage to ward off the pressure have to live in *kutcha* houses for a long period of time, as in the case of Bawana, as authorities are reluctant to give permission to build *pucca* houses on one pretext or the other.

The plot allotted is on a five year lease in the case of MCD and ten years license in the case of the DDA. Thus the so-called resettlement ensures tenurial security for only five to ten years. The accounts of earlier 'beneficiaries' of resettlement schemes illustrate the fact that after evictions it takes at least five to ten years for the evictees to re-build their lives (Housing and Land Rights Network—Habitat International Coalition 2002). Ten years down the line when these colonies become part of the extended urban area and land prices shoot up the spectre of evictions would loom again. It takes years, if not decades, of sweat, toil and incremental investment to build spaces like the Yamuna Pushta or Nangla Maachi—delicate linkages between security of work and security of residence, which ensures a general improvement in the life chances of a family. Eviction and resettlement brutally destroys this linkage.

The less said about the services the better. The operation and maintenance of public toilets or *Jan Suvidha* Complexes, as they are called, has been given to private contractors who charge one or two rupees for using the toilet, two rupees for bathing and five rupees for washing clothes. "The average family thus spends Rs. 10 to Rs. 15 a day on visits to the toilet" and also lose their privacy as the contractor has removed door latches (Menon-Sen, 2006). None of these have medical services at the secondary and tertiary level. People are thus forced to visit 'quacks' and Registered Medical Practitioners (RMPs) in cases of ill health and spend a substantial part of their earnings on healthcare.

Education, especially of the girls, is another major casualty of resettlement. The evictions are carried out without any regard to the school calendar. A large number of children thus end up losing at least one year. Furthermore, though most of the resettlement colonies acquire primary schools over some period of time they have to struggle for it. Meanwhile, the economic downfall of the family forces many children to quit schooling altogether. This is especially true for girl students who have to sit at home and take care of household chores and younger siblings while the mothers try to eke out a living by doing home-based work, which pays a meagre Rs. 360 per month, barely 11 per cent of the statutory minimum wage in Delhi! (Majumdar 2005).

Relocation also fragments and destroys community networks established through kinship based migration and years of living together in slums. In times of distress these networks provide invaluable support and succour. These networks get destroyed as allotment of plots is based on lottery system and one doesn't know who one's neighbour would be in the resettlement colony.

Finally, the eviction of working class from the city serves to ensure their ideological marginalisation and reduces their bargaining capacity vis-à-vis the government and the ruling elite. Discontents and protest in the margins of the city are rarely heard by those in the position of power be it media, city elite or higher echelons of the government. 'Out of sight out of mind' principle works towards marginalisation the poor in Delhi city.

Emerging Trends in Low Income Housing

While the policy of eviction continues unabated, there seems to be some thinking going on exploring other ways of reaching housing to the urban poor, such as the Public-Private-Partnership (PPP). In fact, the Draft Master Plan of Delhi-2021 (DDA 2005) proposes to do away with the current resettlement policy and instead construct multi-storeyed resettlement buildings in the urban area itself. While the Draft Plan is yet to be notified, the DDA has already gone ahead in implementing the PPP for housing of the low-income groups. Following the Mumbai SRS model, the DDA sold 35.8 hectares plot in the South Delhi area of Tehkhand to Keneth Builders and developers, which is a 50:50 venture between Indiabulls Infrastructure and DLF Universal (Guha 2006) at Rs. 4,500 crores, the biggest ever single land deal in Delhi. According to the deal, the developer would construct 3,500 EWS flats and 750 HIG flats. This is not just one off project. The Union Minister of Urban Development, Mr. Jaipal Reddy, has been repeatedly announcing similar solutions to the slum problem. In April, 2006, for instance, assuring the poor that their needs will be taken care of while beautifying Delhi he proposed to construct 100,000 dwelling units for rehabilitating slum dwellers over the next two year: "multi-storeyed housing units … constructed through public-private partnership on the land occupied by slum dwellers"[15].

But will the poor be in a position to afford these flats? While the price tag of EWS flats in the Tehkhand deal has not yet been determined, other schemes announced recently by the DDA provide a glimpse of the future scenario of low income housing in the city. In its latest budget, the DDA, reiterating its resolve to remove slums on a priority basis in 2006-07, has proposed to rehabilitate them by building:

> "17,950 EWS flats in 2006-07 while another 3,500 such flats are expected to be constructed under the public-private participation scheme at Tehkhand. Stating that this scheme would help in taking up of development works on a large scale, DDA Vice-Chairman

Dinesh Rai said alternative accommodation would be provided to those displaced. It was also pointed out that all *EWS flats would have an area of 25 square metres and cost around Rs. 2 lakhs each*"[16] (emphasis is ours).

Flats for slum dwellers at Rs. 2 lakhs each! The new housing policy for slum dwellers is thus very clear. The eviction of slum dwellers from their current locations is certainly going to continue. But instead of plots now they would be resettled in multi-storeyed flats. Those who can't afford to pay Rs 2 lakhs for these flats are free to either become homeless or go back to their natives places! Our assessment is that these attempts would amount to squeezing out the land entitlements of the poor.

Conclusion

We have argued that following the ascendancy of policies of economic liberalisation in early 1990s, Delhi is going through a process of rapid transformation, witnessing massive changes in its political economy, socio-spatial configurations, developmental priorities and in the relationships between the middle class and the poor. Megacities like Delhi are today increasingly sought to be modelled on the image of the global cities such as New York, London or Tokyo to function as regional nodes in the global finance mobility, information flows and hi-tech productive activities. The realisation of this vision is seen to depend crucially on correcting the distortions in the functioning of capitalist land market by freeing the land occupied by the poor and employing it for purposes seen to be in consonant with the creation of a world-class city. Consequently, the evictions of urban poor from inner city slum settlements have increased manifold in the past decade. The result is the expansion and deepening of commodity relations in land. The neo-liberalisation of Delhi's space thus entails furthering privatisation and commodification of land through, among other instruments, an increased reliance on "accumulation by dispossession" (Harvey 2002).

We have argued that the pressures to clear the city of slums has come from the middle class, private capital, environmental and citizens' rights groups and, increasingly, the courts. The presence of slums in the city is seen, in this view, as a function of the corrupt, vote bank based politics of the welfare State apparatus, much to the detriment of the rights of the legitimate citizens of the city to a good quality of life (Chatterjee 2004). So the idea of the reclamation of the rights of the citizenry gets translated into the demand for the dispossession of the poor. An ideology of pollution, disease and crime is advanced by 'bourgeois environmentalists' to justify eviction of the poor from inner city areas (Baviskar 2003). It is no surprise then that a large chunk of PILs filed in various courts for the removal of slums are by RWAs of affluent colonies. The courts have also been instrumental in reproducing this ideology as their judgements over the past few years—castigating the poor for many of the ills plaguing the city and castigating the administration for extending its welfare provisions to include 'encroachers'—show (Ramanathan 2004).

We have also shown that internal contradictions and engineered divisions coupled with the survival exigencies of slum dwellers contribute to the lack of a spontaneous unified response to the demolition. Resettlement as an option is available to constantly reducing proportion of slum dwellers. Those who do get resettled find to their horror the debilitating impact it has on all aspect of their life—from employment to health to sanitation to education.

The 'socialistic' master planning failed to provide affordable housing to city's poor. Now the custodians of the Plan themselves are arguing for the withdrawal of the State from housing sector and seeking the 'participation' of large corporate real estate players. The moot question is that when the State, which has at least some democratic accountability, failed the poor, can the market, which is accountable to none but profits, be relied upon to provide succour to the poor. The trends so far seem to suggest that the market led and profit-maximising land and housing development processes would only sharpen the exclusionary and marginalising tendencies inherent in urban development paradigm of contemporary India.

NOTES

1. And in an attempt 'unofficially,' to stop the spread of DLF Ltd., a land developing company that by this time had acquired and developed large areas of land in the quickly spreading city, given the huge inflow of migrants following Partition. DLF Ltd. is now one of the prime developers of land/suburbs on the outskirts of the city having been evicted by the DDA.
2. Indeed a whole slew of legislation was passed to equalize the land market, these included the Urban Land Ceilings Act, the Delhi Rent Act.
3. For more details on policies on slum development, see Batra (2007).
4. Okhla Factory Owners Association vs Govt. of National Capital Territory of Delhi and Others, CWP 4441/1994.
5. Pritampura Sudhar Samiti *vs* Govt. of National Capital Territory of Delhi and ors, CWP 4215/1995.

6. Okhla Factory Owners Association *vs* Govt. of National Capital Territory of Delhi and Others, CWP 4441/1994.
7. Okhla Factory Owners Association *versus* Govt. of National Capital Territory of Delhi and Others, CWP 4441/1994.
8. *The Hindu*, 10 January 2004.
9. *The Hindu*, January 23, 2004.
10. http://plan.architexturez.org/site/mpisg/riverbed/041226.
11. *Tehelka*, August 19, 2006.
12. *Hindustan Times*, July 7, 2006.
13. *Hindustan Times*, July 28, 2006.
14. The same report also states that: "*Land Management Deptt. carried out some major demolition operations during the year which has drawn praise from all sections of society as well as press except the land mafia*". The italics are to emphasis the fact that the authors were also part of the 'mafia' who protested against these demolitions.
15. *The Hindu*, April 26, 2006.
16. *The Hindu*, March 25, 2006.

12[1]

DEMOLITION OF LIVES AND LIVELIHOODS
Mumbai

HARINI NARAYANAN, DARSHINI MAHADEVIA
and RIBY RACHEL MATHEW

Research Methodology

This article looks at the lives and livelihoods of the slum dwellers post demolition. We decided to study this given that many reports about the short term and long term negative fallouts of such demolitions were written in the immediate wake of demolitions. It also became necessary for us to look into this aspect as slum demolitions have become a way of urban development, particularly in the last decade when India has been on high growth path. The slum demolitions in Mumbai came in wake of the Mumbai Vision Plan (Chapter 3). This article is a sequel to the two other articles in this book, one on critical view of the Mumbai Vision Plan (Chapter 3) and politics and process of slum demolitions in Mumbai (Chapter 18).

For studying the impacts on lives and livelihoods of the slum dwellers affected by demolitions, we conducted a survey of residents in some of the recently demolished slums, through focussed group discussions with the affected slum dwellers, interviews of the representatives of NGOs and activists working in the area, other urban researchers and with the authorities responsible for the demolition and household questionnaire surveys. Group discussions held before the main survey helped us to arrive at surmises about the impacts of demolition. The discussions were conducted in Hindi and Marathi, the two predominantly spoken languages in the community. At least four such sessions, each approximately 2 hours long, were held with each community. Based on insights from the baseline study and informal group discussions, the systematic quantitative survey questionnaire was designed to address the issues of housing and demolition. The questionnaire was pre-tested before launching a full-fledged survey. Household questionnaire survey solicited information on: (i) household level socio-economic details, (ii) intra-city migration, (iii) demolition process, (iv) damages caused by demolitions with regards to housing and asset loss, and (v) current and pre-demolition status of housing, basic infrastructure, such as roads, water supply, bathrooms, latrines, solid waste management and electricity. The survey was carried out during June to December 2005[2].

From around 25 demolished slums, we chose seven, based on various criteria including location, the total number of households and access to the communities. We selected 7 slum communities that had faced demolition during December 2004-February 2005; 3 slums from the distant western suburbs, 3 from the distant eastern suburbs, and Bharat Nagar, as an example of a more settled slum in Bandra (E), which was targeted because it is on the banks of Mithi river. We also surveyed Jai Ambe Nagar in the eastern suburbs, because it is populated almost entirely by the notified Pardhi tribe which, because of its additional caste handicap (i.e., being marked as a so-called 'criminal tribe', in addition to the handicaps of poverty and overall lack of opportunity), can find no employment in Mumbai except that of begging.

Eventually, 818 people were interviewed, the bulk of them male, since they were generally the 'heads of households', the only ones who could provide—or were authorised by the rest of the family to provide—us with the required information. Large number of women and children participated in the more informal discussions. Out of these 818 respondents, 36 of the Jai Ambe Nagar were finally not used for statistical analysis. This left us with total of 782 completed questionnaires for quantitative data analysis.

A survey team of 10 individuals from within the demolished community was put together—this worked very well because they really understood the issues involved. Given the complex and sensitive nature of the demolition and its potentially distressing nature, one research associate from the main team was present in the field during the entire period of the survey. The survey team members were trained by us. The training include perspective building, developing a basic understanding of the research process, biases in research and the way to minimise them, inherent ethical issues, the objectives and importance of the each question, strategies for recoding data and field experiences. The field surveyors were also guided in terms of, interview skills, crisis handling skills and rapport-building techniques—though we found that since they were themselves part of the affected community, the last skill came automatically to them in a way that it could never have for the outside investigators.

While the study intends to add to the existing discourse, it has certain limitations. Though we had structured questionnaires, some of the data regarding the situations before demolitions have been underreported.

An interesting experience while carrying out the field survey need to be stated. At Mandala[3], after the first day of household survey, we encountered unexpected difficulties. One individual created ruckus by first not allowing our surveyors to proceed with the questionnaire survey and then insisting that 'forms be filled' of households that he wanted to include in the survey. He threatened our surveyors, because of which a couple of our surveyors did not surface on the next day. No amount of explanation and cajoling by the research team and even the community leaders engaged with organising the slum dwellers for rehabilitation work under the National Alliance of Peoples Movement (NAPM)[4] leadership, helped. We did not know why he was insistent on that. Because of his incoherent behaviour, we first thought that it was an outcome of his inebriated state. But, that was not so. To move further, we asked him to get 'his people' for the primary survey. He brought one lady, who quite apparently did not belong to the slum settlement, as she appeared well to do. We filled up her form; from that we realised that she and her husband with their two children were living in some housing nearby. They were staking claim to a plot of land in Mandala, claiming that they were originally from the settlement prior to even demolitions. This they were not. But, as plotting for the rehabilitation of the slum dwellers was going on, the local middlemen, the *dalals* in local language, were getting their own people's name included in the list of displaced people after taking some amount (Rs. 20,000) from them. This was going on inspite of community leadership and involvement of NAPM. We also witnessed a verbal show down between the local leader of NAPM, a lady and the individual in inebriated state, indicating that the community leaders were aware of these ongoings and were resisting such local corruption emerging in the process of resettlement on Mandala site.

Basic Information about Study Sites

We will start with some basic background information about the study sites and an estimation of how much the victims of demolition knew about what was going and why (Table 12.1). Everybody had some idea about what the city wanted to do with their land, though they had not found this out through official sources; their knowledge or apparent knowledge was based on rumours, the sources of which generally cannot be ascertained. Evictees from Ambujwadi were keenly aware that they were just across the steadily narrowing creek from the big western coastal developments like the Lokhandwala Complex and the emerging new-economy enclave, and informally said they believed that prominent Mumbai-area builders were powering the clearing out of their land.

Table 12.1: Community-wise Overview of Demolitions

Sl. No.	*Community*	*Estimated hhs*	*Sample hhs*	*Month of Demolition*	*Time period*	*Reason for demolition as understood by the affected community*
1.	Annabhau Sathe Nagar, Mankhurd	5000	77	December-2004 January-2005	10am to 5 pm	Illegal settlers
2.	Mandala, Mankhurd	10000	261	December-2004 January-2005	10 am to 5pm	Illegal settlers
3.	Rafi Nagar, Govandi	600	70	December 2004; November-2005	11 am to 6 pm	Land reserved for cemetery
5.	Bharat Nagar, Bandra (E)	300	53	December 2004	12 am to 7 pm	Flood-control & beautification along Mithi river
6.	Ambujwadi, Malwani	14000	220	December 2004; January 2005	10am to 7pm (religious places were destroyed during night)	Illegal settlers
7.	Ali Talao and Rathodi Gaon, Malwani	2000	50	January 2005; April 2005	2 pm to 5 pm	Public nuisance
8.	Azmi Nagar, Malwani	400	51	January 2005	10 am to 1 pm	Illegal settlers

Mandala, in Mankhurd is the one of the biggest slum in the eastern suburbs of Mumbai that faced demolition in 2004-05. There are around 10,000 households (hhs) here (according to the district collector only 8,000 hhs) covering an area of 55 acres land part of which is marshy and gets waterlogged in times of high tide. It is about 15 minutes walk from the Mankhurd suburban railway station. When the east-west connectivity is established in Mumbai, this land would become of prime location. The settlement is mainly spread into two neighbourhoods, Indira Nagar and New Mandala. This was the first time that the entire houses were being

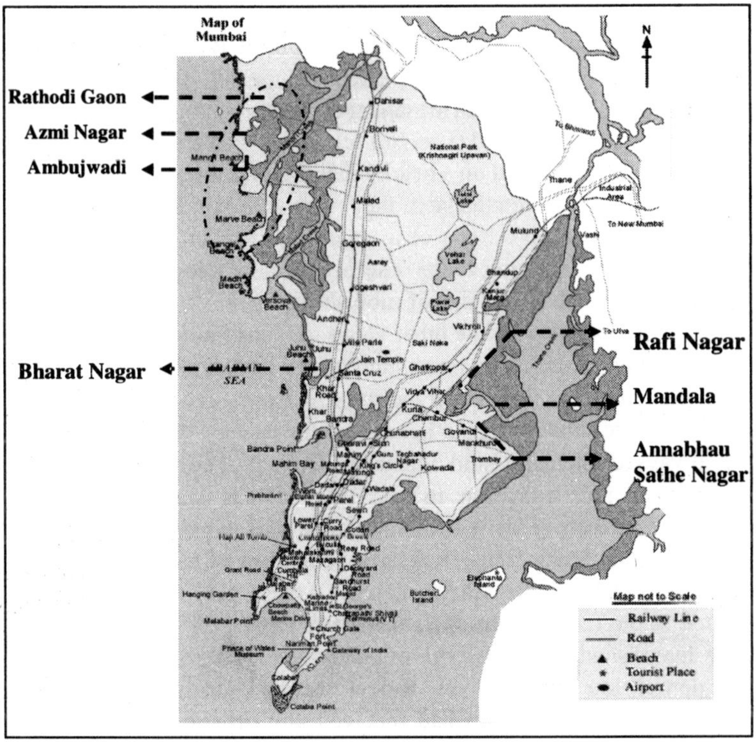

Map 12.1: Location of Demolismhed Slums Surveyed

demolished in one single drive, unlike some houses being spared in the past after taking bribes. Mandala site has also been identified by the authorities as a rehabilitation site for the evicted slum dwellers from the other parts of eastern suburbs. Though no final order has come on this regard, the people from Sanjay Nagar, Rafi Nagar and Chedha Nagar of Mankhurd area have already occupied vacant houses in the area. This created tensions among the dwellers of Mandala. The slum dwellers here had invested thousands in this land and have nowhere else to go. Besides the Rs. 30,000-Rs. 40,000 paid for their hovels, they had invested in truck full of mud and dirt just to firm up their floors. The local Councillor is from the Nationalist Congress Party (NCP), the legislator and Member of Parliament are both Congressmen. The slum dwellers here did not receive any help from their elected representatives.

Rafi Nagar is a slum community where around 5,000 households live directly above garbage dumping site located by the side of a creek. A particularly bizarre tragedy was playing out at Rafi Nagar, which is populated mainly by Muslim rag-pickers and garbage-sorters. They were thrown out on the excuse that the land they were squatting on was required for a Muslim burial ground (*kabristhan*). The evictees, who had nowhere to go, thereafter squatted on a nearby plot that was already being used as a *kabristhan*. A few months later, they were violently thrown out of this second location on the basis of a vague reason: that they would hurt 'sentiments' by squatting there. The people now had no option but to squat on top of the mountains of rubbish that they sorted through every day. It is obvious that unlike other slums, this land is neither productive nor in a prime location. "Even animals have a better life than us. When it rains, the water rises from under the garbage, worms and rats crawl around and the plastic sheets over our heads are blown away. We can't sleep and are always drenched," said Shehanaz Begum. The entire area, like Ambujwadi and, from time to time, Mandala, is heavily guarded by policemen, private security staff and police staff in plainclothes.

Ananbhau Sathe Nagar is a large settlement of around 10,000 hhs adjacent to MHADA flats in Mankhurd. Of these, 5,000 houses that were located in the far-east part of Sathenagar covering 23 acres of flat-land were demolished by the MCGM officials with the help of Mumbai police. The demolition was relatively a new phenomenon for most of these households. None of them had received any official notice from the concerned authorities before demolition. Though the ownership of the land is claimed by the MCGM, a private owner has taken the area on lease and he is paying tax on this land to the MCGM. However the private owner had approached the collector and other concerned officials to stop the demolition drive but they did not considered his request. In the previous demolitions the police had come and destroyed temporary structures and locked up houses in this area, but had not destroyed *pucca*[5] houses, which they demolished in 2004-05.

Bharat Nagar is a single row settlement from Bharath Nagar bridge to Bandra Kurla Complex (BKC) road along the distributary of Mithi river. The residents here knew that their land was on the edge of the valuable BKC, the centre of the new-economy. After the heavy monsoon flooding of 2005, the planners of the BKC were severely criticised for tampering with the course of the Mithi river that flowed through the area and had earlier acted as an important drainage route to the sea near by. The easiest way in which the city could now show that it was taking corrective measures was by clearing out the poor who lived along one small strip of the river. Most of the residents have been residing here since 1995 and demolitions have not been a new phenomenon for them. In 2004 December they had received a notice from the authority for demolition but since the demolition had become part of their life, they did not take it seriously. However the authorities did; and they came well equipped with bulldozers, police and security personnel. Those evicted are living around the demolished site. Razathi (40), who now lives on the road opposite this new wall, says, "We have no work and nowhere to go. They should at least give us some place if they don't want us here". A Samajwadi Party worker is keen to get them resettlement by any means.

Rathodi is village located in Malwani and it constitutes about 8 small settlements. For our study we have selected settlement along the Ali talao (pond). The houses were constructed on narrow plain plot at the foothill of *Rathodi Devi Mandir* (Temple of Goddess Rathodi). The settlement is about 5 minutes walk from the Malwani bus-stop. New constructions and commercial activities can be observed outside the settlement. At the time of the study, most of the houses were made of plastic sheets. This settlement had very few NAPM activists to be of any effect. "*Yahan se kahaan jayenge*," (where will we go from here) says Nazma Hanif Khan (25) who has been staying in Rathodi village for the last 15 years. She was staying in her partly demolished house in the hope that soon everything would be sorted out.

Another site, Azimnagar selected for the survey is about one km from Malwani bus-stop. On December 14th, 2004, the MCGM officials claiming that these people were encroachers of the public land razed around 1,200 houses down. The people in Azmi Nagar returned back to the site in March 2005 and the MCGM officials came again to evict them. However, the residents at Azmi Nagar managed to obtain a stay order from the High Court against eviction. The community did not get help from any NGOs but the local Congress party supported them.

The last site selected for study is Ambujwadi, located in the western suburbs, in swampy areas. The site comes under the Coastal Regulatory Zone (CRZ), where no development work is permitted. Slum dwellers had gradually filled up the marshy land and had made it habitable, which was silently supported by the authorities and the police till then. But, once the land was made habitable, through the sweat of the people, the authorities and the builders lobby were eyeing it for 'development purposes' as if housing of the poor people is not a development activity. This is the largest of all the slums to be demolished in the western suburbs of Mumbai and had 10,000 household living when it was demolished on December 28, 2004. On the other side of the creek is the posh real estate development of Lokhandwala complex and Malad suburbs where largest number of malls are coming up and where even some IT and ITES firms are locating. The residents of the site allege that a bridge across the creek was to be built, that would provide direct connectivity to the site of Ambujwadi and hence the real estate developers had an interest here that led to demolitions.

The site is 23 acres in size. However the officials have stated that it is 83 acres of land in Ambujwadi. It is about half hour's brisk walk from Ambujwadi bus station and almost 3.5 km away from the nearest suburban railway station Malad. Just adjacent to this site are the houses built by MHADA for the low income groups.

According to the dwellers there were around 10,000 hhs (7000 by collector's estimate) before the demolition. After this being identified as rehabilitation site for evicted slum dwellers in western suburbs, residents from other parts of western suburbs, namely Indira Nagar (Kurla), Mora Gaon, Ambedkar Nagar (Juhu), Karbala, Ektha Nagar (Kandivali), Bhabrekar Nagar (Malwani Road) and Suman Nagar (Jogeswari) have shifted to Ambujwadi. As per NAPM survey, there are 13,794 households in the slum at the time of our survey.

Here, the homes were demolished without warning and explanation. The homes were repeatedly demolished. Prior to demolition, Congress party workers had spread rumours that their local Member of Parliament (MP), Govinda, the popular actor of Bollywood, had convinced the officials to stop the demolition and had also obtained a stay order from the court against the demolition drive. But, when the bulldozers arrived with the police, those living near the entrance of the site were shocked. They had little or no time to save their possessions and thus had to bear huge damage. Police arrested the people who tried to protest. Around 32 bulldozers took almost a month to clear up the entire site. All the residences were destroyed during the daytime while all the religious places were razed down around midnight. Municipal workers tore down the temple and then set fire to the debris. Watchmen and MCGM helpers prevented the people from collecting bamboo, roof tiles, plastic sheets and other building materials they had used for constructing their houses.

On our first visit to this site on February 8, 2005, we too had to face the police wrath. This was a day after Medha Patkar of NAPM had conducted meeting of the people telling them that it was their right to fight back and that women should come forward for re-establishing themselves on the site. There was a large posse of policemen on the site.

There were policemen in plain clothes, who refused us entry to the site. The Deputy Collector was on the site, directing and overseeing re-demolitions of makeshift huts. They thought we were journalists as we had cameras. But, finally we managed to witness the demolition going on; the private guards were demolishing, the police were protecting the private guards, the deputy collector was overseeing the demolition and the women were resisting while the men had taken cover fearing their arrests and violence.

All these communities had suffered repeated demolitions. They had not received notices immediately prior to the demolition (Table 12.2). All of them had experienced demolitions in the past.

Table 12.2: Community-wise Demolition Details

Sl. No	*Name of the slum*	*Owner of the land*	*Received notice before demolition*	*No of times faced demolition during the last five years*	*Authorities involved in Demolitions*
1.	Annabhau Sathe Nagar, Mankhurd	MCGM	No	Once in 2005	Collector, MCGM and Mumbai Police
2.	Mandala, Mankhurd	MCGM/ Private owner	No	At least once every year (only locked up houses were demolished earlier)	Collector, MCGM and Mumbai Police
3.	Rafi Nagar, Govandi	Collector & MCGM	No	At least once every year	Collector, MCGM and Mumbai Police
5.	Bharat Nagar, Bandra (E)	DA	Yes	Every year since 1998	DA and Mumbai Police
6.	Ambujwadi, Malwani	Collector	No	Twice	Collector, MCGM and Mumbai Police
7.	Ali Talao and Rathodi Gaon, Malwani	Collector	No	At least thrice in a year	MCGM and Mumbai Police
8.	Azmi Nagar, Malwani	Collector	No	At least thrice in a year	MCGM and Mumbai Police

Socio Economic Background

Of the total respondents surveyed, 42 per cent identified themselves as Hindu and 51 per cent as Muslim. Further, 33.5 per cent identified themselves as being from the SCs and 57 per cent as the OBCs (Table 12.3). This means that the Muslims have identified themselves as the OBCs. The largest numbers of those surveyed were from Uttar Pradesh (47%) followed by Maharashtra (33%). All of them were migrants to the city. But, these were not single male migrants and hence were not recent migrants (who are generally expected to be single males). Almost 92 per cent of the respondents were married and had their families living with them. But, many of them reported that their children had been temporarily sent off to relatives back home after the first brutal wave of demolitions. Like other studies on demolitions, large number of people who faced the brutal demolitions were from the economically most vulnerable section and which explains why they had willed to leave their native homes in favour of extremely harsh and unpredictable living conditions in the distant Mumbai suburbs.

Table 12.3: Social Composition of Slums Surveyed

Sl. No.	Slum name	SC	ST	OBC	General	Total
1.	Annabhau Sathe Nagar	46.48	5.63	38.03	9.86	100.00
2.	Mandala	34.13	0.79	64.68	0.40	100.00
3.	Rafi Nagar	14.71	0.00	85.29	0.00	100.00
4.	Bharat Nagar	31.25	0.00	66.67	2.08	100.00
5.	Ambujwadi	35.98	0.93	56.54	6.54	100.00
6.	Rathodi Gaon	48.89	2.22	48.89	0.00	100.00
7.	Azmi Nagar	43.18	2.27	54.55	0.00	100.00
	Total	35.31	1.35	60.24	3.10	100.00

Table 12.4: Household Details

Sl. No	Name of the Slum	Population	Total hhs	Avg. hh size	Sex ratio	
					Total	0-5
1.	A Sathe Nagar	25,844	5,000	5.17	869	844
2.	Mandala	50,307	10,000	5.03	920	1,439
3.	Rafi Nagar	3,223	600	5.37	861	465
4.	Bharat Nagar	1,313	300	4.38	706	529
5.	Ambujwadi	65,000	13,000	5.00	821	1,094
6.	Rathodi Gaon	10,240	2,000	5.12	1,098	1,643
7.	Azmi Nagar	4,306	1,200	3.59	812	833
	Total	160,233	32,100	4.99	871	1,084

The average size of each household was found to be around five persons, which is close to the average, but this figure does not really reflect an accurate picture of family size. Several families were extremely large, up to 10 individuals in a nuclear unit—again a feature of families facing extreme poverty and low life expectancy—while some were single-member households, which resulted in the average of 5 (Table 12.4). Also, some families had send away their children back home after the demolitions and hence, at the time of the survey, the family size was smaller than usual.

Notably, however, the sex ratios were actually better than that of Mumbai as a whole; in some slums well over the national average, though some of the surveyed communities were found to have abysmally low ratios, too. One cannot really make any strong pronouncements on either finding without studying them both more closely. Given that the figure for marital status was high, though, one cannot say that the number of females overall is low because there is a large number of men here who are single or have left their families back home (Table 12.4).

Table 12.5: Distribution of Above Age 6 Six by Activity Pattern

Sl No	Name of the slum	6 to 14		15 to 25		26 to 59		>59		Total	
		M	F	M	F	M	F	M	F	M	F
1.	Studying	70.1	59.7	17.3	5.9	0.0	0.0	0.0	0.0	26.3	22.4
2.	Working	3.0	0.8	8.3	2.0	73.5	46.2	59.6	17.6	36.1	18.9
3.	Unemployed/ not studying	17.1	28.6	9.0	57.3	18.9	37.4	12.3	35.3	15.9	39.1
4.	No Response	9.8	10.9	65.4	34.7	7.6	16.4	28.1	47.1	21.7	19.6
5.	Total Population	100.0	100.0	100.0	100.0	100.0	100.0	100.0	100.0	100.0	100.0

M = Male and F = Female

The activity pattern emerging from the survey presents a picture of great concern to the employment planners (Table 12.5). Just 36 per cent of males and 19 per cent of females above the age of 6 were working. In the age group of 26 to 59, 73.5 per cent males and 46.2 per cent females were working. This means that the labourforce participation rates, which are above 80 per cent in most slum surveys, are quite low in the surveyed slums of Mumbai, indicating a high level of unemployment among the dwellers of these slums. Our survey also showed that 18.9 per cent males and 37.4 per cent females in the age group 26 to 59 were unemployed. This could be because either they chose to remain unemployed in wake of demolitions or in any case the slum dwellers living in a situation of insecure tenure have high level of unemployment in Mumbai. Both are likely to be the case with regards to the surveyed population. Further, while the average size of a family in a slum is five, in nearly three-fourths of them, there is only one earning member.

In the age group 6 to 14, just 70 per cent of males and 60 per cent of the females were going to school; the remaining were either working or stated themselves to be unemployed, choosing to remain unemployed or not finding work. Since, this is not a working age and the population are outside the labourforce, most likely these children were sitting at home doing nothing and occasionally helping the family adults in income generation activities. From the discussions with the children, we could gauge that the school attendance of the school going children was quite irregular, particularly at the time when the survey was carried out because of several factors like demolition, flooding etc. Most of these students went to the Municipal Corporation's school for their education. People said that in Mumbai, majority of Municipal schools offer education only till 7th standard and hence the children from the low income families are forced to discontinue after upper primary education. Thus, there are large number of children out of school and are either child labour or potential child labour.

We could not get good response from among the youth in age group of 15-25 years (65.4 per cent of them did not give any response). Neither they were studying nor were they working. Instead of stating that they did nothing, that is they were not able to get a job they desired, it is likely that they chose not to respond to the query. Thus, two in every three youth in the surveyed slums, were non-workers, deciding to remain so out of choice or because of lack of options of employment. In our field work, we always found large number of young men on the slum sites, typically what we would call 'hanging around' doing nothing particularly, while the young girls would be in their houses engaged in housework.

Table 12.6: Employment Pattern

Economic activity	*% workers*
Non-household manufacturing	1.0
Household manufacturing	2.0
Repairs	6.0
Construction	10.0
Personal services	20.0
Hawkers	4.9
Petty business	5.4
Clerical services	2.9
Blue collar services	1.0
Rag pickers/recyclers	17.0
Labour services	28.0
Any Other	1.8
Total	100.0

Only 19 per cent of those employed were in the secondary sector, which consisted of manufacturing, repairs and construction (Table 12.6). Just 3 per cent of the total workers were in manufacturing. Significant proportion of them were in construction (10% of the total) and then in repairs (6% of the total). The 2 per cent of the workers that have been classified as household manufacturing are the carpenters working out of home. A vast majority of the workers, 81 per cent of them, worked in the tertiary sector; 20 per cent in personal services like driver, housemaid, paper deliveryman, *poojari* (priest), tailor etc, 17 per cent as rag-pickers and waste recyclers and 28 per cent in petty labour services. These are highly vulnerable population in terms of their employment status. This vulnerability is also because 40 per cent of them have migrated to Mumbai in last 10 years as discussed later (Table 12.8). Majority of women worked as domestic servants and few were hawkers.

The CRH (2005: 4-5) reports finds that the population in the demolished slums are very productive and have an average of 2.1 earners per family. Our survey findings are somewhat different than the CRH findings on this regard. At the city level, based on the processing of National Sample Survey (NSS) data, which included households in Mumbai Municipal Corporation and Thane Municipal Corporation, Mahadevia (2005: 11-15) finds that 67.39 per cent of workers were employed in Mumbai in 1999-00. Further just 35.5 per cent of employed males and 20.7 per cent of the employed females were in secondary sector in 1999-00. Given that only 1 per cent of employed males and employed females were in primary sector, all the rest were in tertiary sector, see chapter 2. Thus, there is much higher tertiarisation of employment in the surveyed slums than in the whole of the city.

Table 12.7: Slumwise Type of Employment

Sl. No	*Name of the Slum*	*Secondary*	*Tertiary*	*Total*
1.	Annabhau Sathe Nagar	9.43	90.57	100.00
2.	Mandala	26.78	73.22	100.00
3.	Rafi Nagar	4.55	95.45	100.00
4.	Bharat Nagar	21.67	78.33	100.00
5.	Ambjwadi	21.57	78.43	100.00
6.	Rathodi Gaon	5.36	94.64	100.00
7.	Azmi Nagar	14.58	85.42	100.00
8.	Total	18.83	81.17	100.00

It is very important to see that most of the people are engaged in informal activities on daily wage basis. There are hardly any labour laws valid in this kind of temporary arrangement and people are always under the anxiety that they could be thrown out at any time both from the house and also from the work place.

Table 12.7 shows that in Mandala slum, about 27 per cent of the households were employed in secondary activities, which was 8 percentage points higher than the figure for all the slums together. Here the main secondary activity was construction. In Rathodi Gaon and Rafi Nagar the workers engaged in secondary were around 5 per cent. In both the places majority of the people are engaged in rag picking and recycling.

In Rafi Nagar people are engaged in different activities involved in garage sorting and recycling. We could find few people involved in collection of metal scraps, some collecting plastics and few others leather. Comparatively the demand for metal scraps is high and people involved in the collection are highly vulnerable .We found that the corroded metal pieces were being handled with bare hands. These people were spending three-fourth of their day inside the garbage dumping ground and hence were highly susceptible to all infectious diseases.

Table 12.8: Migration Details

Sl. No	Year	Number	%
1.	Upto1975	63	8.1
2.	1976-80	73	9.3
3.	1981-85	99	12.7
4.	1986-90	127	16.2
5.	1991-95	161	20.6
6.	1996-2000	105	13.4
7.	After 2000	48	6.1
8.	Born in Mumbai	64	8.2
9.	No Response	42	5.4
	Total	782	100.0

Of the surveyed households 66.9 per cent stated that they had come to Mumbai before 1995; another 8.2 per cent stated that they were born in Mumbai. This means that 75.1 per cent households were unfairly targeted in this spate of slum demolitions, which were to be for only those who had come to Mumbai after 1995. If the election promise of the Congress and the NCP is taken into account then those who could have been legitimate target of evictions were just 6.1 per cent of the households. All the studies carried out after 2004-05 demolitions showed that a large majority of the slum households were unfairly targeted by the demolition squads (YUVA 2005; CRH 2005), and that there was much more to the demolitions of 2004-05 than just plain implementation of Slum Clearance Legislation[6].

Demolition Impacts

Impact on Livelihoods and Assets

We then looked at the effects of the demolition on various aspects of the lives of the affected population. As expected, most respondents had lost a considerable number of workdays—because they were busy trying to protect or salvage their belongings during the course of the demolition, trying to recover from the effects of physical assault or to extricate themselves from the police and legal nets that they found themselves trapped in, or were simply afraid to leave their families alone at home to face further demolition while they were themselves away at work. Many lost their old jobs because of this irregularity of attendance or took time to restart work because they had lost the tools of their trade.

Over 70 per cent of the people interviewed reported changes in their employment terms or patterns after the demolition. The largest number of individuals (76%) in our survey lost between two weeks and three months of productive work-time (Table 12.9). Just 8 per cent of the workers in the affected households reported no loss of work. About one-third of them reported that they had lost work for a period ranging from 2 weeks to 1 month and another one-third stated that they had lost work for a period ranging from 2 to 3 months. For the poor households this means significant income loss.

Table 12.9: Loss of Workdays (Total) (%)

Sl. No	*Category*	*Male*	*Female*	*Total*
1.	No loss	7.96	9.26	8.15
2.	1 day to 1 week	5.41	9.26	5.98
3.	2 weeks to 1month	36.78	24.07	34.92
4.	2 to 3 months	32.64	35.19	33.02
5.	4 to 6 months	9.24	15.74	10.19
6.	> 6 months	5.57	3.70	5.30
7.	Stopped working	2.39	2.78	2.45
	Total respondents	628	108	736

For why they had stopped to work after the demolitions, 67 per cent stated that they had done so because of uncertainties caused due to loss of house (Figure 12.1). Another 20 per cent stated that they had stopped working because of injuries caused during demolitions. Rajendra's leg was hurt by the bulldozer and had plaster for two months and till then he couldn't resume the work. 5 per cent of them stated that they did not go to work as they had joined protest movement. In Ambujwadi we met Raju, Satheesh, Sable and Deepak, who all worked before the demolition but became active members of NAPM, busy in organising people to protest against demolition after demolitions. In few cases females have mentioned that they had to stop working to take care of their children who were under trauma because of the demotions. While few other stopped working as they were terminated by the employer because of their irregularity during the demolition period. When our survey was carried out in the later half of 2005, about six months after the demolitions, around 215 people had not yet restarted their work since demolition.

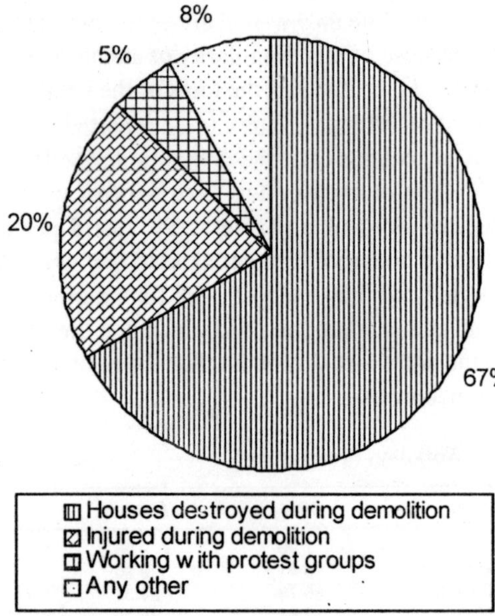

Figure 12.1: Reasons for Discontinuing Work

Table 12.10: Loss of Assets (Total Community)

Sl. No	*Item lost*	*Households*	
		Number	*%*
1.	Utensils	683	87.3
2.	Furniture	497	63.6
3.	Documents/Ration card	269	34.4
4.	Electric & Electronics Equipment	432	55.2
5.	Livelihood equipment	194	24.8
6.	Domestic Animals/Birds/	63	8.1
7.	Clothes/books	632	80.8
8.	Any Other items	618	79.0

As expected, asset loss was heavy. Table 12.10 shows that about 87 per cent of the households had some or the other asset lost. More than 80 per cent households had lost their clothes and utensils; about 64 per cent had lost furniture, more than half had lost their electrical and electronic goods and 34 per cent had lost all their documents such as ration cards.

In all the communities except in Rathdoi Gaon the police did not allow the people to collect their possessions but also set fire to the debris soon after the bulldozing. As a result, evicted people could not collect their belongings after the demolition. In Ambujwadi, people mentioned that the police threw away cooked food. For families that had gone out of Mumbai for vacation, demolition in this period caused maximum damage. When they retuned they could find only fenced land and they couldn't even recognise the location of their houses. Muhammed Khureshi of Ambujwadi was engaged in poultry business and he lost around 300 hens and his three goats were crushed by the bulldozer. Maithri Devi in Mandala was alone at home as her husband is a truck driver and he was out of Mumbai. During demolition she fainted out of fear and lost everything including photo-pass that was the proof of their residence in Mumbai prior to 1995.

Table 12.11: Community-wise Estimated Average Damage Incurred (Rs. per hh)

Community	*Average (Rs)*
Annabhau Sathe Nagar	13304.5
Mandala	19442.6
Rafi Nagar	14931.4
Bharat Nagar	18147.2
Ambujwadi	17715.6
Rathodi Gaon	14285.7
Azmi Nagar	7964.0
Total	15113.0

Table 12.11 shows that the demolition resulted in the loss of Rs. 15,000 per household. The total estimated cost of damages faced by the surveyed community is Rs. 543.6 millions. The figure of Rs. 15,000 per household damage tallies with the figure put forward by YUVA survey of Rs. 10,000 loss per damaged house and Rs. 5,000 loss for land filling (IPTEHR 2005). It is estimated that around 94,000 homes were demolished as part of 'Mumbai Make-over Plan' (IPTEHR 2005). Hence the total cost of damage resulted by demolition is estimated as Rs. 1,410 million (US$ 32.41 million) or 0.2 per cent of the city's GDP. The MCGM spent Rs. 84 Crores on demolitions. The average cost of damage was highest in Mandala and followed by Bharatnagar.

However the table on investment in housing shows that the amount invested in housing per hh was around Rs. 20,000 in Mandala (Table 12.15). Even in Rafi Nagar the average amounts spend on housing were around Rs. 24,000, but the estimated cost of damage is around Rs. 15,000.

However while responding to questions related the cost of damage the households were referring to the cost of damage to the household items and not the cost of house itself. In that case, the per household damage would be loss of house and household goods, which would be Rs. 39,500 in Mandala, Rs. 36,000 in Annabhau Sathe Nagar, Rs. 39,000, in Rafinagar Rs. 39,000, in Bharatnagar Rs. 36,300, in Ambujwadi Rs. 39,200, in Tathodi Gao Rs. 20,200 and in Azminagar Rs. 20,000. The total loss then would go up to Rs. 2,350 millions, which is a colossal amount.

Table 12.12: Distribution of Evicted HHs by Value of Asset Damage Sustained

Sl. No	*Amount in Rs.*	*Frequency*	*% Hhs*
1.	1 to 5,000	147	18.80
2.	5,001 to 10,000	157	20.08
3.	10,001 to15,000	171	21.87
4.	15,001 to 20,000	120	15.35
5.	20,001 to 25,000	54	6.91
6.	>25,000	109	13.94
7.	NR	24	3.07
	Total	782	100.00

About 36 per cent of the households had suffered damage of more than Rs. 15,000 whereas about 19 per cent of households had suffered damage of less than Rs. 5,000 (Table 12.12).

It is very obvious that the demolition would have direct impact on work and income of the slum dwellers. During the period of demolition and resuming of normalcy, people cannot either be at home or go to their place of work. Being forced to stay on the open ground after demolition and subsequent time and energy spend on protest, negotiations and resettling ultimately resulted in loss of workdays. This we have discussed earlier. The impacts on livelihoods are given in Table 12.13. It can be seen that around 60 per cent of the people had to change their employment and 89 per cent of those who had to change their employment were men. Some people mentioned that they had to completely change their employment. For example, Salim of Annabhau Sathenagar mentioned that he was a machine mechanic before demolition, but, because of loss of all his equipments during the demolition and lack of finance to restart the work, he started to work as a waiter in a small tea shop.

In Mandala people mentioned that the demolition resulted in increased demand for rag picking job mainly because it assures job for 365 days of year. Initial investment is minimal or nil. Importantly they could manage their time; many of them worked with the activist groups during the day time and in the evening went for their work. At the same time, the people who have shifted from Rafi Nagar and Sanjay Nagar to Mandala found it difficult to cope with the timing of their work, as most of them were involved in garbage sorting and recycling at their original place of work and had to go back there to carry out their employment. Since there is no public transport system that connects Rafi Nagar and Mandala they remained on their work site for the whole day without food and water.

Table 12.13: Impact on Livelihood

Sl. No	*Name of the slum*	*Number of persons*		
		Male	*Female*	*Total*
1.	Change in the Employment	497	56	553
2.	Livelihood equipment damaged in demolition	229	41	270
3.	Working from home	142	43	118
4.	Loss of clients	132	37	216
5.	No of people who are working from home lost the clients	77	21	98
6.	Stopped working	166	49	215

Nearly one third of the working population mentioned about damage to their livelihood equipments. Especially in Bharat Nagar and Ambujwadi, the motor work shops, flour mill, small health clinic, etc. were totally destroyed during the demolition. During our visit to Mandala we happened to meet a doctor inside the slum. He took us to his clinic; we could find only a chair, table, a torch and a pot to keep the water. As he said, he was running a clinic with all the basic facilities. But the demolition spared nothing, lost his stethoscope, thermometer, blood pressure measuring equipment and lots more; estimated cost of damage was around Rs. 1.5 lakhs.

Francis Xavier of Rathodi Gaon had another story. He is from Goa and reached Mumbai in 1998 with a dream of setting up his own hotel. Unlike other slum dwellers he speaks English fluently. He owned a mobile vending stall—a "*larry*"—in which he sold fast food at night and returned home only in the morning. On the day of demolition he was sleeping after long work hours. When he woke up by the roaring sound of the bulldozer, he found that his *larry* was totally destroyed. He now works as waiter in a restaurant in Malad.

In Ambujwadi, Zubaida was an agent to a 'big' company that was producing artificial jewellery. The company gave her the raw materials (small beads) to make bangles, chains and earrings every month. About hundred women were working under her and she distributed the beads at beginning of the month and collected it at the end of the month. During the demolition she managed to save the jewellery that she had, but she failed to recover the raw materials from others. Though the commodities were worth around Rs. 3,000 according to her, she was forced to pay a penalty of Rs. 10,000 and the company terminated her from work. Later after a long discussion she could restart her work.

Impact on Shelter

The scale of loss also needs to be viewed in the context of what these people have: apart from Bharat Nagar in Bandra (E), which is in a more settled and serviced part of town, these slums are in remote wastelands on the outer edges of the city, with virtually no civic services and very little apart from garbage-sorting in terms of employment in the immediate neighbourhood. Table 12.14 detailing materials used in the construction of houses prior to the demolition, and with luck, again after the abatement of the first wave of eviction, shows that the majority of homes had walls, floors and roofs all created with plastic sheeting or cardboard scavenged from discards near construction sites and industrial areas. The job of finding housing construction material of this kind is often that of the children: one family we visited told us proudly that their little girl of about eight and boy of about four or five found all the plastic sheeting that formed the only protection the family had from the slushy soil during the monsoon. The two children were now spending their spare time looking for bits of tile and granite from building sites, which could eventually be used to reinforce the flooring. This job is, of course, a never-ending one because everything is lost to the bulldozer at the time of each demolition.

At the time of our survey, all the households in the demolished slums were living in temporary shelters. It has been observed in Mumbai that the legal or authorised slums have a better physical appearance, with concrete walls, tin roofs and cemented floors whereas the illegal slums have houses with floor, roof and wall made out of plastic and other temporary material. This is quite in consonance with the international literature that argues for giving of land tenure to the urban poor to induce them to invest in their housing. Plastic is of help especially in the time of very high rains. Thus, these demolished slums had houses constructed out of such temporary materials before the demolitions and remain in the same condition after demolition.

Table 12.14: Distribution of Households by Materials Used for Construction

Sl. No.	*Indicators*	*I*	*II*	*III*	*IV*	*NR*
1.	Wall	2	114	587	65	14
2.	Roof	38	23	670	40	11
3.	Floor	19	126	576	49	12

Building material key

1. *Floor*

Cement floor/Concrete/Tile—I
Earth/mud—II
Plastic sheet—III
Others—IV
No Reply—NR

2. *Wall*

Asbestos sheet/Brick/Concrete—I
Plastic sheet/Paper—II
Wood/sticks—III
Others—IV
No Reply—NR

3. *Roof*

Asbestos/GI Sheet—I
Tile—II
Plastic/Paper—III
Other—IV
No Reply—NR

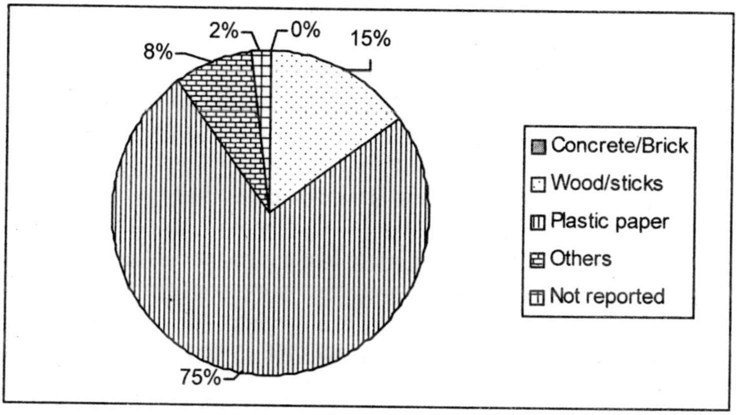

Figure 12.2: Presently Used Wall Materials

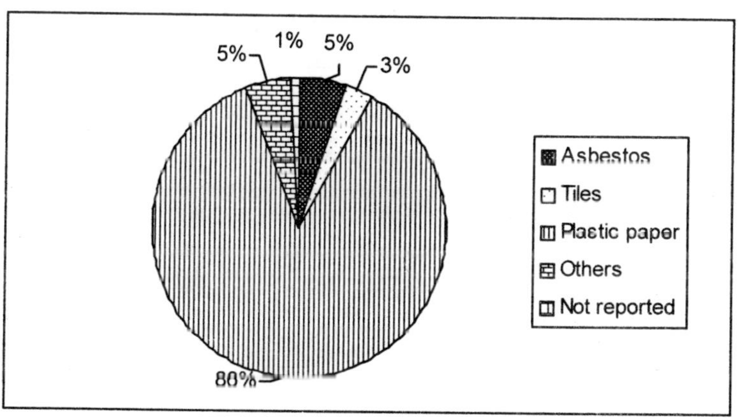

Figure 12.3: Presently Used Roofing Materials

These plastics sheets are regenerated from plastic sacks. Post demolitions, none of these houses had proper doors or ventilation. During the field visit we experienced unbearably high temperatures inside these houses. Though these plastics act as partition and restrict the direct entry of sunlight to the rooms it transmits the heat. It is obvious that these will have a direct impact on the physical condition of the people residing in these houses. In Annabhau Sathenagar and Mandala people have used plastic sacks while in Ambujwadi use of jute sacks were noticed. Interestingly most of these were cement sacks and irony is that the waste material generated during the construction of high rise buildings have turned out to be the building material for the houses of labourers involved in the construction of those buildings. Tsunami, cyclone or earthquake is not required to destroy these houses but a mild wind or a drizzle is enough to make these people homeless.

What has changed with regards to the housing conditions is the area of their house. The demolition has resulted in reduction of average area of houses from 212 sq ft to 191 sq ft, which is a reduction in size by 9 per cent. The area of the houses varied from 80 sq ft to 400 sq ft. In Ambujwadi and Rathodi Gaon slums, average area of the dwelling unit is more than 200 sq ft. whereas in Mandala it is 173 sq ft. and in Bharat Nagar is 163 sq ft (Table 12.15). It is also important to mention that in Ambujwadi and Mandala there were petty shops, hospitals, workshops etc. along with the dwelling units in the slum area. In Ambujwadi, the average area of a house has reduced from 232 sq ft to 204 sq ft (by 12.06%). But, nonetheless, the houses were not so small, and the average across all the slums came very close to the average size provided under the SRS.

Table 12.15: Community-wise Average Size (in sq ft) and Average Cost of Dwelling Unit

Sl. No	*Name of the Slum*	*Present Shelter*		*Previous Shelter*	
		Average size (sq. ft)	*Average investment (Rs.)*	*Average size (sq. ft)*	*Average investment (Rs.)*
1.	Annabhau Sathe Nagar, Mankhurd	193.4	1,406	203.3	22,271
2.	Mandala, Mankhurd	173.0	3,776	198.5	20,135
3.	Rafi Nagar, Govandi	199.0	2,755	214.0	24,011
4.	Bharat Nagar, Bandra (E)	162.5	1,541	175.0	18,326
5.	Ambujwadi, Malwani	204.7	2,738	232.3	21,523
6.	Ali Talao and Rathodi Gaon, Malwani	204.9	1,050	222.0	6,522
7.	Azmi Nagar, Malwani	199.6	2,379	237.0	20,038
8.	Total	191.0	2,235	211.7	18,975

Photo: Riby Rachel Mathew

Photo 12.1: Annabhau Sathenagar after Demolition, Mumbai

Photos: Erhard Berner

Photo 12.2: Demolition at Ambujwadi, Mumbai

After each successive wave of demolition, the quality and cost of freshly constructed housing necessarily deteriorates, both because the disposable income of the house-builder is eroded and because there is the fear that too much expenditure on house-building might be a waste because everything might be lost once again. Thus, successive demolitions push people to lower and lower levels of social well-being, as Table 12.15 demonstrates. It can also be seen that except Ali Talao and Rathodi Gaon in Malwani, in all other slums demolished, people had invested about Rs. 20,000 per dwelling unit. Post demolition, they have invested less than Rs. 3,000 in most of the cases. In fact, the expenses were incurred only on creation of some basic structure for protection. The demolition has caused colossal loss of investments and resources of the poor. This goes on to show that in every demolition, there is massive financial loss for the slum dwellers and then they begin investing once again, among the uncertainties how long the new investment would be safe. In other words, slum dwellers continue to invest in housing amidst the expectation of future demolitions.

The CRH (2005: Tables 3.2 & 3.3) study mentioned earlier shows that the average additional cost of damage and construction of temporary shelter was nearly Rs. 5,600 per household and not so as what we find in our study. The report further states that the 15 per cent of households have borrowed money from various sources while 43 per cent households constructed their temporary structure with materials saved after demolition; 26 per cent households had used their self-savings for the purpose. Then, the loss to the households because of demolitions would go up further than our estimates. Demolitions would therefore not only repeatedly lead to loss of financial assets of the dwellers but also put them in a situation of perpetual debt.

It is also understood that in Mandala and Ambujwadi while rehabilitating the people, the NAPM coordinators had taken maximum care to allocate same location and also same size of space for all the houses. However, a few people were lucky to get comparatively larger space after the demolition while few were unfortunate to get much lower area. This had resulted in minute disputes among the people. Although in some instances, as narrated in the beginning of the paper, slumlords or the middlemen were trying to push some of their own people in the survey of households carried out by NAPM for the rehabilitation purposes, on the whole the work of allotments went on well.

Impact on Basic Services' Availability and Access

When it comes to basic infrastructure, the abysmal living conditions of these communities is particularly, starkly apparent. This is actually one area in which there is very little difference before and after the demolitions, since the areas where our surveyed groups live never had very much in terms of civic services. For instance, Bharat Nagar is the only surveyed slum that has a 'pucca' or paved approach road, and this is because this community came up as a strip along a major road link near the Bandra-Kurla Complex in Bandra (E). All the other communities are strung out along main arterial roads too, but only on their outermost edge. Once away from the main road, individual homes are generally approached by winding paths of beaten mud that turn into (adult) knee-deep slush in the monsoon. The more settled areas that show signs of municipal services have narrow, open drains running along in the middle of the lane between huts, and the paved edges of these drains are the only stable surfaces in times of rain.

Table 12.16: Distribution of Households by Distance to Drinking Water Source

Name of the Slum	*Percentage distribution of households by distance in meters*						*Av. distance in meters*
	0 to 250	*251 to 500*	*501 to 750*	*751 to 1000*	*>1000*	*Total*	
Annabhau Sathenagar	0.0	47.5	41.3	11.2	0.0	100.0	535
Mandala	2.0	8.6	15.4	56.3	17.7	100.0	801
Rafi Nagar	0.0	22.9	26.7	50.3	0.0	100.0	694
Bharat Nagar	100.0	0.0	0.0	0.0	0.0	100.0	126
Ambujwadi	0.0	2.6	23.3	64.7	9.4	100.0	732
Rathodi Gaon	15.0	85.0	0.0	0.0	0.0	100.0	339
Azmi Nagar	0.0	35.4	63.2	1.4	0.0	100.0	541
Total	7.7	13.0	26.6	44.3	8.4	100.0	697

None of these slum households have bathrooms of their own, and most do not have a water connection anywhere near the home, leave alone a private water supply source. Water is bought and transported through hose-pipes or, more commonly, in plastic cans or '*phuggas*' from the handful of people in neighbouring 'legal' slums who have proper water connections or who have been able to poach on the municipal corporation water lines. Our survey showed that 44.3 per cent of the respondents sourced drinking water—indeed, any water at all—from locations that were 751-1,000 metres away (Table 12.16) and paid hefty sums of money for the privilege. This situation had worsened after temporary housing had been constructed post demolitions, but it had always been difficult. Only Bharat Nagar was able to get water from a public municipal tap reasonably close at hand. Expenditure levels varied widely, based on how much water-sellers were able to extort in each area, especially after the first set of demolitions, but some families spent over Rs. 480 a month, which is twice as much as many urban upper-middle-class spend in India. This figure has to be further adjusted in terms of the fact that members of the urban elite pay for unlimited or generous water supply, while the communities surveyed in the study pay this amount for supply that includes just a few bucket—or plastic can-full—maybe just three or four—each day.

Ambujwadi had and has the worst water supply. Here, there was no legal or illegal water supply available within the site. The houses are widely spread and the site is almost a km from the MCGM's supply point, hence even the private distributors find it difficult to distribute water efficiently. The far end of the site is low lying and hence the pressure cannot be maintained in those areas. People meet their water requirements from nearby pond though the water inside the pond is not of satisfactory quality for domestic purposes. In some part of the site we could observe that the people own small tanks that could hold 5 to 6 buckets of water. During the visit the people have mentioned that there were around 60 to 70 such kind of tanks inside the community and officials destroyed most of these during the demolition. Now only 5 or 10 exist in which the people were storing water. Since the area was under the creek, the water table level is still high and water remains in the pond.

In Rathodi Gaon people met their water requirements from the nearby 'Ali Talao' and the drinking water is bought from the private suppliers. They spend around Rs. 10 to Rs. 15 for 25 litres of water and they are not sure about its quality other than its physical appearance. Interestingly, we found a major outlet of MCGM's water supply connection in front of the slums at Rathodi Gaon. However these people were not allowed to use the water from the source as it is meant only for the Rathodi temple. In Mandala, people were buying water from some households located on the main road and who had poached on the municipal corporation water supply line.

A few residents of Mandala had been able to use community toilets in the neighbouring 'legal' portions of the sprawling settlement. However, of the 15 per cent of the respondents who said they had availed of this facility before the demolition of 2004-05, almost half said they were no longer able to do so, since they were now too far from the toilet blocks. As for everyone else in Mandala and the other communities, a covered, formal toilet had been a dream before the demolition, and the chances of ever being able to use one diminished further after the demolition.

Similarly, every single respondent said there had been no solid waste collection system in place ever—either before or after the big wave of evictions.

Power supply is one infrastructural service that four of the seven communities analysed said they had never had. The other three had some power supply—but all of it illegal. Even illegal supply (residents can pay anywhere from Rs. 50 to Rs. 150 a month to be able to run one illegal electrical point a month) was affected by the demolitions: in Annabhau Sathe Nagar, 77 per cent of the respondents said they had power supply before the demolitions, but only 52 per cent said they were able to once again enjoy this service after they had rebuilt their homes once the demolitions had been temporarily stopped. Similarly, in Mandala, 80 per cent had power supply earlier, and only 52 per cent had it later. After the latest wave of demolitions in May 2006, even this supply collapsed. Forty-three per cent of the people in Ambujwadi had power supply earlier, but none had any after the demolitions.

Impacts on Vulnerable Groups

The survey then looked at the effects of demolition on the most vulnerable age groups in the community: the youth and the elderly. There were noticeably few older people around, though one does not know whether this was because the elderly had stayed behind in the pre-migration location in the first instance, or whether they had been sent back for their own safety after the demolition—like many of the children had been. However, an overwhelming number of the 86 people over the age of 60 mentioned by the respondents were said to have suffered trauma of some kind, almost half of them suffered physical injuries and well over half suffered in some way (Table 12.17).

Table 12.17: Communitywise Percentage of Elderly Suffering Various Impacts

Name of the slum	*Total population above 60*	*Trauma*		*Physical injury*		*Any other*	
		Number	*%*	*Number*	*%*	*Number*	*%*
Annabhau Sathenagar, Mankhurd	19	19	100.0	7	36.8	12	63.2
Mandala, Mankhurd	15	12	80.0	6	40.0	9	60.0
Rafi Nagar, Govandi	16	15	93.8	9	56.3	11	68.8
Bharat Nagar, Bandra (E)	7	7	100.0	5	71.4	7	100.0
Ambujwadi, Malwani	18	15	83.3	12	66.7	10	55.6
Ali Talao and Rathodi Gaon, Malwani	6	3	50.0	1	16.7	5	83.3
Azmi Nagar, Malwani	5	2	40.0	0	0.0	1	20.0
Total	86	73	80.0	40	46.5	55	64.0

The effects on the children were found to be among the most disturbing ones. About 21 per cent of the children (in the age group 6-14) in the surveyed households discontinued school altogether after the demolitions. The proportion of girls who discontinued school altogether was 27 per cent and proportion of boys who discontinued school was 15 per cent. The discontinuation of school was for a variety of reasons (Table 12.18). 56 per cent of them stated that they did not go to school because they had lost their house and hence their situation had become uncertain; 20 per cent stated that they had lost their books and other school material and hence did not go to school; 12.5 per cent stated that they were traumatised and another 5.7 per cent stated that schooling did not remain affordable for them any more.

Table 12.18: Distribution of Children by Reason for Discontinuing Schooling

Sl. No	*Reasons*	*%*
1.	Lost the home	55.6
2.	Trauma	12.5
3.	Damage/loss of study materials	19.8
4.	Not affordable any longer	5.7
5.	Any other reason	6.4
6.	Total	100.0

Just less than one per cent children of the respondents stated that they did not loose days of schooling post demolitions (Table 12.19). As mentioned earlier, 21.6 per cent just stopped going to school. Almost two-thirds of the surveyed respondents' children lost between four months and one year of schooling, before their lives stabilised enough for them to start going again (Table 12.19) and in this, more than one-third did not go to school for more than six months to a year. Negative impact on children's schooling due to demolitions has therefore been quite severe. This is hardly a way to pursue 'Economic Growth with Human Face'! In all probability, many more children will now never return to school. The State needs to think about this population of young people who will grow up without the benefit of education or job skills, and nothing but the bitterness of being repeatedly victimised and isolated by the State and the community.

More than two-thirds of the households reported that demolitions had some short term impacts on their children. Two thirds stated that their children fell ill (had cold and cough according to them after the demolitions (Table 12.20) and two-fifths had suffered short-term trauma. About one third households stated that atleast one child in their family had suffered long term impacts, such as change in behaviour (38%) and loss of interest in studies (34.8%). The impacts on the children because of demolitions were quite visible. Their education had suffered, they were traumatised, had lost interest in education and behaviour had changed. Who is responsible if such large number of children suffer post-demolitions?

Table 12.19: Percentage Distribution of Children by Loss of Days of Schooling

Sl. No.	*Time period*	*%*
1.	No loss	0.8
2.	1 day to 1 week	0.5
3.	2 week to 1month	3.7
4.	2 month to 3 months	7.4
5.	4 to 6 months	27.6
6.	7 months to 1 year	38.4
7.	Stopped going school	21.6
8.	Total	100.0

Table 12.20: Households Reporting Long sTerm and Short Term Impacts on Children

Indicator	*Impact*	*No of Households1*	*% of Households*
Short Term	Trauma	630	80.6
	Cold/Cough	518	66.2
Long Term	Change in Behaviour	296	37.9
	Loss of interest in studies	272	34.8

The effect on the 'youth' (individuals in the 15-25 age group) was also devastating. Out of the 415 people in this age group about whom survey information was received and analysed, 25 claimed sexual abuse and 166 claimed a perceived threat of sexual abuse after the demolition (Table 12.21). It is not just females who stated these impacts, but even males stated that they experienced sexual abuse and were bothered by the possibility of sexual abuse. Even if any of these allegations were ever recorded, there is certainly no indication of their having been investigated. Also very disturbing was the information that several people (253 of them from 415 or 61 per cent of the youth) had been accused by the police and other authorities of '*gundagardi*' (criminal activity) and jailed for various lengths of time. In these 58 young women stated that they were accused of criminal activity. This is a common enough occurrence during the process of demolition, where those seeking to protect themselves and their belongings are neutralised by being counter-accused of being themselves the aggressors. 68 per cent of them (283 of 415) stated that their marriage possibility had got adversely affected and they were forced to think of delaying their marriage due to the demolitions. All of them stated that they suffered some or the other form of injury or physical assault by the demolition squad during demolitions! 60 per cent of them stated that they had lost educational opportunity because of demolitions.

Table 12.21: Communitywise Distribution of Youths by Various Impacts

Sl. No.	Name of slum	I		II		III		IV		V		VI		VII	
		M	F	M	F	M	F	M	F	M	F	M	F	M	F
1.	Annabhau Sathe Nagar, Mankhurd	21	39	11	3	2	1	7	13	24	9	14	24	27	11
2.	Mandala, Mankhurd	31	64	20	7	2	3	14	32	39	18	28	39	42	7
3.	Rafi Nagar, Govandi	22	18	9	1	0	0	5	11	18	7	16	18	20	2
4.	Bharat Nagar, Bandra (E)	14	27	4	2	0	3	8	9	16	5	11	16	18	3
5.	Ambuj-wadi, Malwani	44	58	27	11	7	9	12	29	47	25	29	47	54	27
6.	Ali Talao and Rathodi Gaon, Malwani	17	19	8	2	0	0	4	9	11	7	5	11	11	5
7.	Azmi Nagar, Malwani	22	19	6	2	1	0	6	7	19	5	6	19	23	3
	Total	171	244	85	28	12	16	56	110	174	76	109	174	195	58

Key : Trauma—I; Injury/Physical Assault—II; Sexual Abuse—III; Perceived Threat of Sexual Abuse After Demolition—IV; Loss of Educational Opportunity—V; Delay of Marriage Possibility—VI; Accusations of Criminal Behaviour—VII

Repeated Internal Migration Due to Demolitions

An important area that we focussed on in the study was that of migration to and within the city. This is because most demolitions are carried out around the political artifice of the 'cut-off' date—a date that shifts forward at regular intervals, and on the basis of which a slum-dweller's right to legitimacy at a particular location is decided.

The most direct links between housing for the poor and the political process has developed over the creation of the so-called 'cut off date' system, first introduced in Mumbai in the mid-1970s. The Emergency years of 1975-1977 saw large-scale and extremely brutal demolitions of informal housing settlements in urban centres around the country, most notably in Delhi and Mumbai. At this time, the first official 'slum census' was conducted, as a measure to soften the impact of the demolitions, and 630,000 hutments in Mumbai were 'registered' and issued photo-passes[8]. In reality, this accordance of legitimacy turned out to be fragile, with no guarantee against further eviction and only the tenuous promise of another settlement location, typically without any assurance of tenure.

From then on, the practice of granting 'regularisation', which has since helped to turn the whole issue of slum growth, eviction, resettlement and management into an entirely and solely political activity, had been set in motion. On the eve of every national or state-level election, political parties—most often the Congress—would promise to 'regularise' or recognise the existence in the city of slum-dwellers who could show proof of their having lived in the same place prior to a given cut-off date. Even as the demolitions continued apace through the 1980s and the 1990s, the cut-off date was successively extended to 1985, 1990, 1995. As part of its pre-election promises of 2004, the Congress in Maharashtra promised to extend this cut-off date to 2000, but went back on this promise immediately after the elections and proceeded to demolish slum sites it described as being post-1995. And in any case, even the gaining of 'recognition' based on a cut-off date does not guarantee protection from eviction, as this study showns.

Table 12.22: Percentage Distribution of Households by Number of Movements within MMR and Year of Each Successive Move

Movement		Year							
		Upto 1975	*1976-80*	*1981-85*	*1986-90*	*1991-95*	*1996-00*	*After 2000*	*Total Moves*
MOVEMENT	I	7.2	8.7	10.8	14.1	22.6	30.2	6.3	100.0
	II	0.0	2.8	4.8	11.7	29.7	37.3	13.7	100.0
	III	0.0	1.8	4.3	9.2	28.8	44.2	11.7	100.0
	IV	0.0	0.0	0.0	6.5	33.9	46.8	12.9	100.0
	V	0.0	0.0	0.0	0.0	0.0	11.1	88.9	100.0
	Total	*3.7*	*5.6*	*7.6*	*12.3*	*25.9*	*34.8*	*10.1*	*100.0*

We found that only 25 per cent of those evicted had arrived in Mumbai after 1995, the last officially announced cut-off date (Table 12.8). Only six per cent had arrived after 2000, the cut-off date promised by the Congress on the eve of state elections and ignored during this particular series of demolitions. More interestingly, almost 40 per cent of the respondents had arrived before 1985, which suggests that they could have been very young children when they arrived, and 8 per cent were born in Mumbai. However, only 7 per cent of the over 800 families surveyed had never moved locations within Mumbai. (If we correlate this last figure with the date of arrival in

Mumbai, we would probably find that these families that had never moved were also the most recent in-migrants to Mumbai.) Almost 50 per cent had moved at least once, and almost 5 per cent had moved four times, a few moved even five times since their first arrival (Tables 12.22 and 12.23). And further, like most 'rational' movers in Mumbai, they moved to the suburbs: mainly northwards, or they moved laterally between Greater Mumbai and the north-eastern municipalities of Thane or Kalyan.

We didn't ask the respondents the reason for each move, but we can make some surmises based on other data collected. For one thing, people made clear distinctions between moves they considered 'voluntary' and those they saw as forced. In informal interviews, they offered the same reasons that at least one other study of informal housing (in this case, pavement dwellers) in Mumbai has yielded: they had broken off from joint families to set up nuclear homes; they had stayed with friends or relatives when they first arrived in Mumbai, and moved when they could afford to[9]; they went home during communal riots (mainly in 1992) and returned to find the old place lost to them.

Table 12.23: Percentage Distribution of Households by Number of Moves Based on Locations

Location	*No of moves*						
	No Displacements	*I*	*II*	*III*	*IV*	*V*	*Total*
A	100.0	0.0	0.0	0.0	0.0	0.0	100.0
B	0.0	90.9	9.1	0.0	0.0	0.0	100.0
C	0.0	60.8	39.2	0.0	0.0	0.0	100.0
D	0.0	44.4	52.8	2.8	0.0	0.0	100.0
E	0.0	41.9	50.5	7.5	0.0	0.0	100.0
F	0.0	46.3	29.7	15.8	6.9	1.2	100.0
G	0.0	39.6	34.6	15.7	8.9	1.2	100.0
H	0.0	62.2	28.6	7.1	2.0	0.0	100.0
I	0.0	84.6	15.4	0.0	0.0	0.0	100.0
J	0.0	91.5	8.5	0.0	0.0	0.0	100.0
Total	7.2	48.6	28.9	9.9	4.8	0.7	100.0

Key: A Eastern Suburb/Western Suburb
B Island City to Eastern Suburbs
C Island City to Western Suburbs
D Eastern Suburb to Western Suburb
E Western Suburb to Eastern Suburb
F Northwards Within Western Suburbs
G Within Island City/Within Eastern Suburbs/Within Western Suburbs
H Northwards Within Eastern Suburbs
I City to Thane/Kalayan
J Thane/Kalyan to City

As per the rules of the state government, only 7 per cent of the over 4,000 people we talked to qualified as 'regularised' 'Mumbaikars', even though 75 per cent had lived in the city since before 1995. To gain legitimacy, a slum-dweller in Mumbai has to hold on to one specific piece of land, and retain the proof of this effort through disasters 'natural' (such as the notorious Mumbai monsoon) and unnatural (i.e., demolitions motivated by violent state action, during the course of which it is often not possible to retrieve even valuable papers from the path of the bulldozers).

This brings into question the ephemeral nature of the entire issue of a person's legitimate right to exist in the city—simply because of a failure on the part of the State to provide legally purchasable habitation. The Table 12.22 and 12.23 have illustrated these issues relating to migration to and within the MMR.

Conclusions

Our own research at the sites demolished in the Mumbai Metropolitan Region (MMR) in 2004-05, for instance, has come up with several instances of extreme brutality, for instance:

- Sunita Sukhram Verma, 25, was seven months pregnant. When she refused to move out of her house, policewomen dragged her out and beat her up with lathis. She lost her child during this process. While Sunita was struggling to save herself and her child, her husband was brutally beaten up.
- Ravi Kumar 4, son of Ramdulari Gupta, fell into boiling water during the course of the confusion created by the demolition process.
- Mohammad Faisal (4), Nasim Banu Ansari's younger son, was thrown out of his home on to the road and suffered serious injuries as a result. His parents rushed him to hospital, and therefore could not stay to save any of their personal belongings, including important papers.
- Deepak (9 months old), son of Vamalwati Devi, was killed on the spot when a bulldozer went over him.
- Many of the men were picked up and incarcerated on various charges, and bribes of Rs. 4,000-5,000 had often to be arranged to free them. This took time, not least because it often took the families several days to locate the lock-up where their loved ones were being held. The men were often moved to different

police-station lock-ups on successive days, and this made the search doubly difficult, especially when everything else was also in disarray.

- Children were both emotionally and physically traumatised. Many told us they were terrified of going to school in case they returned to find their parents missing. Being exposed to the elements and to even poorer quality water than they had before made them vulnerable to diseases like cholera and jaundice.

Is there not a way to channel people's need-based choices into productive ways of both benefiting the city's economy and ensuring life and livelihood for everyone? Can a city not set aside infrastructurally serviced locations for every income level to inhabit as it moves up the job and food-chain? If the time, energies and expenditure expended on demolition and eviction are focussed on the creation of employment and shelter creation, the city might benefit both financially and in terms of a more peaceful living environment for all. It is hard to figure out what has been the point of creating such a distress among such a large number of poor households in Mumbai? And is this the way 'Human Face of Urban Development' is going to manifest in our globalising cities?

This study has gone into only the details of immediate impacts of a spate of brutal evictions observed in Mumbai during 2004-05. As stated in section 1, the demolitions are continuing to this date, while this article was being written. The present government in the centre was celebrating its two years in power with a very progressively written Common Minimum Programme (CMP), which would be the programme of any Welfare State, a very large section of the poorest population of Mumbai was under such dire situations, suffering from severe impacts of demolitions. The urban poor in Delhi and all other metropolitan cities are experiencing these processes of demolitions. Mumbai and Delhi are the worst among the lot in terms of scale and brutality; one is the commercial capital and the other is the administrative capital of a rapidly growing economy.

NOTES

. This chapter is based on research undertaken through IDPAD project.

. One of our research team member contracted dengue fever because of outbreak of this epidemic post July 2005 flooding of Mumbai city. The situation in which the slum dwellers are put into every monsoon because of flooding, and more so the sufferings of the residents of the demolished slums can be imagined.

3. Mandala area is one identified for rehabilitation of the dwellers of demolished slums (See Chapter 18).
4. NAPM had organised the slum dwellers for resistance and at the time of our survey, the organisation was engaged with preparing a list of households to be resettled on Mandala site.
5. Here a *pucca* house is referred to a house that has concrete/brick walls and asbestos/tin roof.
6. See Chapter 18 for discussion on reasons for demolitions.
7. The household where either one or more children, that is atleast one child had suffered.
8. Chaware, Dilip, 'Hutment units to be regularised', *The Times of India*, Mumbai, November 24, 1991.
9. Study by the College of Social Work, Nirmala Niketan, 1985.

13

WATER FOR A GLOBALISING METROPOLIS

Policies and Problems in Hyderabad

C. RAMACHANDRAIAH

Introduction

Hyderabad Urban Agglomeration (HUA), the capital city of Andhra Pradesh State in India, has a population of about 6 million. With an area of about 778 square kilometres, the HUA consists of the Municipal Corporation of Hyderabad (MCH) and the ten surrounding municipal towns as important components. It has registered a decadal growth rate of about 43 per cent, 67 per cent and 28 per cent during 1970s, 1980s and 1990s respectively. Much of the spatial expansion in the last two decades has occurred in the surrounding municipalities, which recorded a high growth rate of 70 per cent in 1990s.

Being located in an undulating topography of the Deccan Plateau, Hyderabad city and its environs were blessed with a number of natural and man-made water bodies locally known as *Cheruvus, Kuntas* etc. These water bodies acted as water storage reservoirs for irrigation, drinking and groundwater recharge, and have been an inalienable part of the urban ecology of the city. Gradually, while some lakes were encroached and replaced by concrete buildings several others got severely polluted with the domestic and industrial effluents. With the loss of water bodies and the consequent decline in groundwater table, long-distance and expensive water projects had to be taken up to provide water to the city. The rural population along these water projects felt left out and resented that their water was being taken to Hyderabad. This paper attempts to analyse some of the issues relating to the main sources of water (decline of the old and taking up of the new projects), access to water in the city and the surrounding municipalities, water contamination, rising cost of water etc. The information has been drawn from the Census, Hyderabad Water Board's website, Fever Hospital, media reports and discussions with the concerned officials.

Water Sources and Water Supply

The main sources of surface water are Osmansagar, Himayatsagar, Manjira Barrage, Singur Dam and Krishna water (Table 13.1). Osmansagar and Himayatsagar were constructed in 1920s. Most of the old city of Hyderabad has been dependent on these two reservoirs which, together with Hussainsagar and Mir Alam Tank (built in 1562 and 1908 respectively), supplied drinking water to the city during the first half of the twentieth century. The latter two got polluted over the years and are no more used as drinking water sources. Further, there has been a decline in water supply from the first two sources and, for the first time in about 80 years, both of them dried up in 2003. When full, these two sources were supplying 45 Million Gallons per Day (MGD) to the city. Himayatsagar has dried up again in November 2004 while the Osmansagar went dry in April 2005. There has been a progressive decline in the per cent of rainfall converted to inflows into these two reservoirs during 1961-96 period even though the rainfall pattern has not changed much. These two water bodies reached their full reservoir levels more times (10 times by Osmansagar and 11 times by Himayatsagar) in the first 18 years of 1961-96 compared to the second half of the period (only 5 times by Osmansagar and 6 times by Himayatsagar). Based on this trend, experts have concluded that these two reservoirs may dry up completely in future: Himayatsagar in 2036 and Osmansagar in 2040. Even if they do not dry up, they are likely to receive mostly polluted water resulting from the increasing urbanisation of the catchment area and would cease to be the sources of drinking water, unless proper remedial measures are taken (Rao and Rao 1998). Despite copious rains in Hyderabad and its surroundings during July-September 2005 and 2006, the inflows into these reservoirs have been very low. This is due to construction of check dams and other encroachments in their catchment areas. The total water in these two reservoirs thus accounts for only 1 Tmcft (Thousand million cubic feet) as against their storage capacity of 7 Tmcft[1]. An area of about 140 sq. km in their catchment areas has been identified as a 'dangerous zone' using the data available from the satellite maps[2].

In view of the importance of Osmansagar and Himayatsagar for drinking water needs of the city, the state government issued an order in 1996 prohibiting certain activities in their catchment areas.[3] In a judgment of far reaching importance on 1 December, 2000, the Supreme Court of India prohibited setting up of water polluting industries within 10 km radius of these two water bodies in view of their importance in meeting the drinking water needs of Hyderabad. The Court applied the 'precautionary principle' to protect these two water bodies, and ordered the closure or shifting of the existing polluting industries within their 10 km radius. The Supreme Court further held that access to clean drinking water is a fundamental right under 'right to life' in Article 21 of the Constitution of India and that the State is duty bound not only to provide adequate drinking water but also to protect water sources from pollution and encroachment.

Table 13.1: Main Water Supply Sources for Hyderabad

Source	*Osman-sagar*	*Himayath-sagar*	*Manjira Phase-I*	*Manjira Phase-II*	*Manjira/ Singur Phase-III*	*Manjira/ Singur Phase-IV*	*Krishna water scheme*
Year of commissioning	*1922*	*1927*	*1965*	*1981*	*1991*	*1994*	*2004*
River	Musi	Esi	Manjira	Manjira	Manjira	Manjira	Krishna
Name of the impoundment	Osman-sagar	Himayath-sagar	Manjira Barrage	Manjira Barrage	Singur Dam	Singur Dam	Nagarjuna-sagar*
Distance from Hyderabad (Km)	15	8.6	58	59	80	80	130

Source: www.hyderabadwater.gov.in except for the last column (accessed in March 2005).

Note: First phase of Krishna Water Scheme has been completed and the 2nd Phase was started in September 2005.

* Already existing.

For the last several years the Hyderabad Metropolitan Water Supply and Sewerage Board (HMWSSB) has been supplying water on alternate days for durations of up to only two hours. Uneven pressure in supplies has been a major problem in several localities. The low-income group colonies and slums have been complaining of low pressure and inadequate supplies. In addition to this, water lines laid decades back during Nizam's time, sometimes beside the drainage lines, seem to have rusted and developed pores. This has resulted in the water getting contaminated resulting in outbreak of water-borne illnesses and hospitalization of the affected people. It is worth noting that the National Commission on Urbanisation (NCU) had remarked that it is 'inequitable distribution which causes real problems' than the lack of water and that the 'water supply system is unequal and unjust, being highly biased in favour of the rich' in Indian cities (NCU 1988).

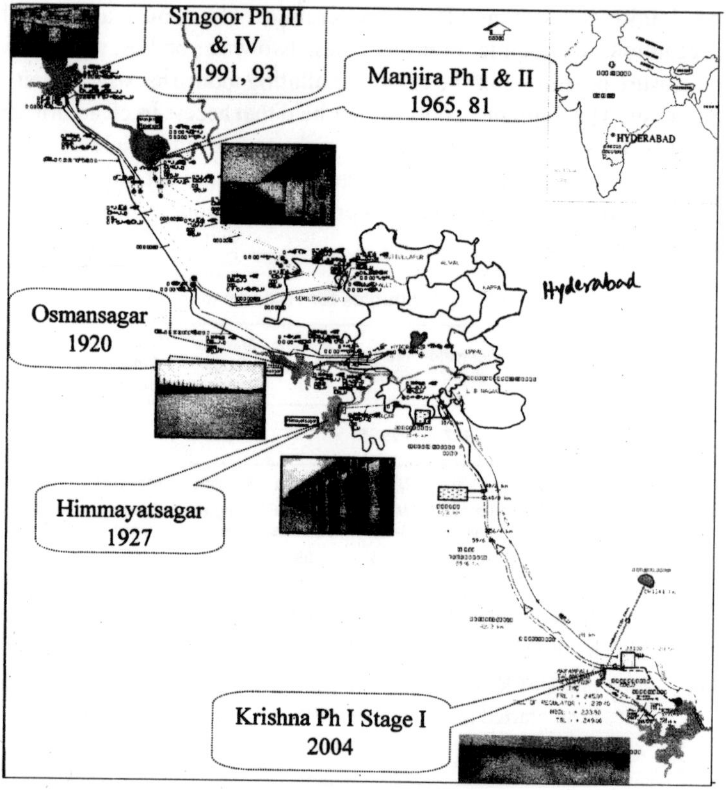

Map 13.1: Water Supply Sources, Hyderabad

Source: Based on presentation made by the Managing Director of HMWSSB on December 14, 2004 at Centre for Economic and Social Studies, Hyderabad.

How much water is being supplied by the HMWSSB daily? The recent figure puts the quantity at 220 MGD with Singur Dam supplying 120 MGD, Krishna 70 MGD and Osmansagar, Himayatsagar and Manjira accounting for the rest[4]. In May 2006, the total water supplied was 222 MGD with the supplies from Osmansagar (16 MGD), Himayatsagar (11 MGD), Manjira (45 MGD) (totalling 72 MGD from these three sources as against 30 MGD in September 2006), Singur (75 MGD), and Krishna (75 MGD). There has been some confusion on the quantum of water drawn from the Krishna scheme. While it is currently 75 MGD, the HMWSSB officials have been maintaining till recently that they are drawing 90 MGD from the Krishna scheme. It seems that the drawl from Krishna scheme was reduced in order to bring down the huge electricity cost to the HMWSSB[5].

The HMWSSB is responsible for providing water in the MCH limits. Over the years, however, its jurisdiction has extended to some of the surrounding municipalities and is expected to provide water to all the municipalities in the HUA in the coming years. The Census data for 2001 (Table 13.2) reveals that while tap is the principal source of water supply for 93 per cent of households in MCH area, the corresponding figure is only about 60 per cent and below in Alwal, Malkajgiri, L.B. Nagar and Rajendranagar municipalities. The location of the tap is outside the premises for a substantial proportion of households in several municipalities. For many families that depend on hand pump, the source is located outside the premises. The municipalities in the HUA are among those facing several acute water shortage in Andhra Pradesh (Ramachandraiah 2003). The completion of the ongoing Sahebnagar-Lingampally pipeline that connects Malkajgiri, Kapra and Uppal with the Krishna water system is expected to solve water problem in these water-starved municipalities where residents still get drinking water once in three to five days despite the comfortable water supply position this year. Completion of this pipeline system is expected to bring the entire city and the surrounding municipalities under the Krishna water scheme[6].

The second phase of Krishna project, when completed, is estimated to bring 90 MGD more into the city and total quantity may reach 320 MGD, making daily water supply a distinct possibility. There seems to be no infrastructure to store the water brought from the Krishna water scheme as of now. There are efforts to construct 12 new reservoirs of 100 million Litres Per Day (MLPD), including eight in the old city, and lay pipelines to take Krishna water to all areas. The new reservoirs will enable the HMWSSB store the huge volume of water. The board currently has 80 reservoirs with storage capacity of 200 MLPD[7]. Recently the HMWSSB has started to implement 24x7 water supply (24 hours, 7 days in a week) in a locality and has plans to bring the entire city into similar system.

Table 13.2: Water Supply by Source and Location at Household Level in Hyderabad and the Surrounding Municipalities

Hyderabad urban agglomeration	*Total and location*	*All sources*	*Source of water supply (%)*			
			Tap	*Hand pump*	*Tube well*	*Others*
Hyderabad (MCH)	Total	100.0	93.1	2.6	1.2	3.2
	Within Premises	83.9	87.8	29.8	67.0	
Serilingampalle	Total	100.0	70.9	13.1	9.4	6.6
	Within Premises	57.3	69.5	10.0	56.1	
Kukatpally	Total	100.0	85.1	6.8	5.3	2.7
	Within Premises	66.6	71.3	25.2	66.9	
Qutubullapur	Total	100.0	64.1	11.1	8.1	16.8
	Within Premises	53.5	74.3	10.3	34.7	
Alwal	Total	100.0	61.1	13.6	15.2	10.1
	Within Premises	59.5	70.4	27.6	55.3	
Malkajgiri	Total	100.0	49.4	12.8	20.2	17.6
	Within Premises	56.7	62.1	57.0	58.1	
Kapra	Total	100.0	67.4	7.9	8.4	16.2
	Within Premises	67.0	84.2	31.7	51.9	
Uppal Kalan	Total	100.0	82.3	4.3	6.1	7.3
	Within Premises	72.2	78.8	45.6	47.6	
Gaddiannaram	Total	100.0	95.6	1.6	1.8	1.0
	Within Premises	96.1	98.4	8.4	82.1	
L.B. Nagar	Total	100.0	60.7	9.2	22.4	7.7
	Within Premises	62.4	76.0	20.6	62.4	
Rajendranagar	Total	100.0	50.0	17.2	11.9	20.9
	Within Premises	37.0	59.5	13.8	33.2	

Note: The total number of households is 968,411.

Source: Census of India, 2001, Andhra Pradesh, Household Amenities.

Water Contamination and Disease

In several parts of the old city, contaminated water flows through rusted pipes, which were laid decades ago. Cement pipes and galvanized-iron (GI) pipes laid during Nizam's days (1920s, 1930s and even earlier) for water supply have depreciated and are known to have developed holes and cracks. Since these pipes are laid along side sewerage/drainage lines (open as well as closed), the drainage water can enter the water pipes and get mixed with drinking water. When the pressure of water in the pipes is low, due to alternate (or once-in-three days) supplies, extent of such mixing increases. This is a persistent problem in several areas and also in the slum localities. Thousands of people getting afflicted by diseases related to water contamination has become an annual feature. From 2003 onwards, after the drying up of Osmansagar reservoir and resultant low pressure in water supply, this problem has became worse and affected many areas.

To cite one instance, the then tourism minister had a first-hand experience of polluted water being supplied to people in the old city. At a place named Goshamahal, as water was released on the arrival of the minister; to everyone's shock the liquid (water) that trickled out of the taps was of black colour[8]. In another instance, the local people mobbed the water works office in Madannapet division to protest against supply of contaminated water. Several protests demanding an end to supply of such contaminated water and for supply of clean drinking water have been recorded. Even in areas that did not depend on Osmansagar reservoir, people have experienced similar problems. Though the problem is well known, and despite several protests, the authorities have attended to the problem temporarily by delivering water in tankers. The long-term need of the city of replacing the old pipelines with new ones has never been taken up seriously.

Apart from the MCH area, the neighbouring municipal towns of Malkajgiri and L.B. Nagar have also experienced similar problems. Improper sanitary conditions in poor localities compound the problem. To cite a few instances; the spectre of choked drains and overflowing *nalas* (small drains) haunt the people in the congested low-lying Amannagar area. This slum represents the seamier side of the state capital[9]. Conditions like *katcha* (unpaved) roads reduced to sewers and open patches turned to garbage dumping points with mosquitoes swarming everywhere have made hygiene the first casualty in most of the slums in the city. With basic facilities lacking, the contagious diseases reported at Ambedkarnagar, Muralidhar Bagh and Singagadikunta slums can be found everywhere[10].

As a consequence, thousands of poor people get affected by contaminated water and were admitted in various hospitals every year. One newspaper reported that in the first seven months of 2003, about 96,000 people were treated in the Fever Hospital for water and sanitation-related ailments[11]. In Fever Hospital alone, forty-five people died and several thousands were admitted due to diseases caused by polluted water and poor sanitary conditions (Table 13.3). The figures given in the Table 13.3 relate to seven diseases—Cholera, Infectious Diarrhea, Dysentery, Gastro-Enteritis, Enteric Fever (Typhoid), Acute Diarrhea Disease (A.D.D), and Urinary Tract Infection (U.T.I). Tens of thousands of people were treated as out-patients in this hospital. The numbers admitted and died in 2003 are more than double than those in 2002 for the same period. In Niloufer Hospital, during May-October 2003, about 10,500 persons were treated for just two diseases, acute diarrhea and enteric fever (typhoid), of which 22 died. As thousands of people were getting affected and hospitalized in several parts of the city, the chief minister declared a 'health emergency'. This has been happening even while the state government is projecting Hyderabad city as a 'health capital' in India because of the presence of large number of super-specialty corporate hospitals. And Hyderabad was awarded 'Clean & Green City' consecutively for four years from 1998 by the New Delhi-based Housing and Urban Development Corporation (HUDCO).

The large number of admissions (in-patients) and death of people due to water and sanitation-related diseases in the earlier years of 1995, 1996 and 1998 (Table 13.3) may, therefore, be attributed to the decline in water supplies from either or both Osmansagar and Himayatsagar reservoirs during those years.[12] The cause of disease and death of poor people in the low-income localities of the old city are thus directly linked to the availability of water from these two reservoirs. It may be recalled that supply of clean drinking water was responsible for significant decline in the number of cholera cases in Hyderabad's history.[13]

Table 13.3: Number of Patients Admitted and Dead in Fever Hospital, Hyderabad: 1995-2003

Year	*Number of In-patients*	*Number of Deaths*
1995	11722	44
1996	14018	76
1997	8973	31
1998	13353	86
1999	8189	32
2000	7147	23
2001	6647	17
2002	5936	20
2003	13473	45

Note: The data pertain to the seven diseases related to water and sanitation mentioned in the text.

Source: Fever Hospital, Hyderabad.

Loss of Water Bodies

It is estimated that there were 932 tanks in 1973 in and around Hyderabad which came down to 834 in 1996. Consequently the area under water bodies reduced from 118 sq km to 110 sq km. About 18 water bodies of over 10-hectare size and 80 tanks of below 10-hectare size were lost during this period in the Hyderabad Urban Development Authority (HUDA) area (EPTRI 1996: 23 and The Hindu[14]). Another study based on remote sensing data on 1:50000 scale reveals that the area under water bodies has reduced from 22.79 sq km in 1989 to 20.84 sq km in 1999 in the city and the surrounding municipalities. Micro level studies would indicate much higher reduction in the area under water bodies (Ramachandraiah 2002).

A notification by the HUDA[15] gives particulars of 169 lakes of 10 hectares and above, covering an area of approximately 90.56 sq km. As per this notification, the entire area falling within the full tank level must be kept free from any type of constructions, irrespective of the ownership or any land use or master/zonal development plans that may have been previously notified. Further, a buffer belt of 30 metre width on all sides of each lake must be kept free of any type of construction in the interest of prevention of lake pollution and allowing free flow of water into the water bodies. Sadly, one does not find any of these regulations being implemented for the lakes. Any sensible government would protect the existing water bodies and then look for additional sources to meet the growing demand.[16]

Pollution of Water Sources

In addition to encroachments, pollution of lake waters by untreated domestic sewage and toxic industrial effluents has been going on unabated over the years. Many lakes which provided drinking water earlier to the nearby population no longer serve the same purpose. Of the 38 lakes identified as potential sources of drinking water, bacteriological and chemical tests revealed that the water of only 6 lakes was in any usable condition[17]. Many of the industrial estates in and around Hyderabad are located in the foreshore areas of the lakes. Continuous discharge of untreated industrial effluents into the water bodies in total violation of the environmental laws has turned them into 'toxic ponds' almost devoid of any life. Due to seepage and infiltration from the polluted water bodies/ drains and other waste dumps, the water sources of many villages around Hyderabad have become highly polluted (Rao 2001: 24-26). The pollution control board has been ineffective to a large extent in penalizing the polluting industries despite the provisions of the Environment Protection Act, 1986. Rampant corruption and the industrialist-politician-bureaucrat nexus have played havoc on water bodies. The industrial lobby is so powerful that a sitting judge of the Andhra Pradesh High Court was transferred overnight for giving closure orders to the highly polluting industries in Patancheru area (Rao 2001: 46)[18].

Rising Cost of Water

With the growing water scarcity and the drying up, or not reaching full reservoir level of Osmansagar and Himayatsagar, the HMWSSB had to expedite the much awaited Krishna Water Project to transport water from Nagarjunasagar reservoir across Krishna river about 130 km away. This is an expensive water project because of the difference in altitude (about 1200 feet) between the source and the destination, which necessitates pumping of water to a higher level. In contrast, the cost of water from Osmansagar and Himayatsagar reservoirs is very low since the water flows by gravity into the treatment and distribution systems. The water from Manjira/Singur systems flows by gravity as well as. The cost per kilolitre (KL) of water from these systems is Rs. 2/- for Osmansagar/Himayatsagar and Rs. 3/- for Manjira/Singur sytem, whereas it is Rs. 18/- from the Krishna scheme[19]. The Phase I of the Krishna project was completed to bring about 45 MGD of water to the city. Implementation of this project entailed additional expenditure on the HMWSSB in the form of repayment of loan, interest and higher power consumption charges. The initial burden was estimated at Rs. 8 crore—Rs. 4 crore alone for power consumption and an equal amount towards debt servicing. To meet this financial crisis, to begin with, the HMWSSB increased the water tariff from Rs. 25.00 to Rs. 35 per KL for non-domestic and commercial users whose consumption is above 200 KL per month with effect from 1 October 2004. The stage II (of phase I) of the Krishna project was completed in April 2005 to bring an additional 35 MGD. With the additional drawl of water, the power bill had gone up to Rs. 8 crore per month, which amounted to 50 per cent of the expenditure of the HMWSSB. The debt servicing (repayment of principal and interest) puts an additional burden of about Rs. 10 crore per month. To ease the burden of power tariff, the District Review Committee appealed to the Electricity Regulatory Commission to allow a concessional tariff of Rs. 1.20 per unit (on the lines of lift irrigation projects) as against the present industrial tariff of Rs. 3.50 per unit as drinking water should be accorded top priority over and above irrigation[20].

To overcome these financial problems, the HMWSSB raised the water tariff again from 1 February 2005 for all categories of consumers except at the lowest level. A couple of changes announced in the revised tariff were: (a) 20 per cent reduction in the water tariff for hospitals and educational institutions run by the government; and (b) treating those companies which use water as a raw material for their business (soft drinks and bottled water) as a separate category and levying a higher tariff on them[21]. Even as the water tariff has been raised for the general public, the corporate sector's Indian School of Business (ISB) has been provided large quantities of water only at Rs. 15/- per KL as agreed by the

Government of Andhra Pradesh in the Memorandum of Understanding (MoU) signed with the ISB[22]. It has been reported that the forthcoming Fab City is also going to be provided with water at Rs. 15/- per KL. While there are 4.65 lakh connections, it is felt that there are still about 40,000 illegal connections in the city. Even when the connections are known, the amount of water drawn by each connection is difficult to measure since a large proportion of them do not have water metres. In the last few months the HMWSSB has launched special drives to encourage the consumers to fix water metres. With the phase II of the Krishna Project likely to be completed in near future, the water tariff is expected to be raised again.

Scope for Conflicts

The Government Order No. 111, dated March 8, 1996 mentioned earlier prohibited construction of several types of structures including check-dams in the catchment areas of Osmansagar and Himayatsagar reservoirs. There is, however, strong evidence of a number of such structures coming up in their catchment areas. Farmers are reported to have constructed a number of check-dams for water storage and recharge. As the land values have increased enormously in recent months, because of (i) urban sprawl, (ii) construction of the international airport close by, and (iii) the ongoing construction of the outer ring road, the catchment areas of the two reservoirs would also be subjected to construction activities on a larger scale. However, the government has shown little interest in implementing its own Order or practically found it difficult to do the same. As a consequence, these two reservoirs have not been reaching Full Reservoir Level (FRL) as discussed earlier. Despite heavy rains and large scale flooding in Andhra Pradesh during July-October 2005, these two water bodies did not reach FRL level even by 31 October 2005. Government's attempts to implement this Order may meet with resistance.

The HMWSSB takes about 7 TMC (thousand million cubic feet) of water from Singur system. In July 2005 the State government has decided to apportion 2 TMC of water from the summer of 2006 to the farmers of Medak district in which the water project is located[23]. With this reduction of 2 TMC from the available water in Singur system, the city's water supply could be in a tight-spot especially in a drought year[24]. It has been argued by an irrigation expert that it is unfair to divert water from one river basin which is already in deficit, Manjira in this case, before its needs are met to another basin, Hyderabad, which is located in the Krishna basin. In its Order dated 24 February 1990, the government has specified the water levels to be maintained in the Singur reservoir in each month. The danger to the farmers of Medak district with this Order is that except when the Singur reservoir is full or there is excess water, the water will not be released to the downstream farmers. The water is reserved for Hyderabad city to meet any contingency in anticipation of drought in the subsequent year. Thus, the farmers in the downstream are denied water for irrigation despite having a legitimate claim[25]. There have been many agitations by the farmers in Medak district, which is a backward district, for their legitimate share of water[26].

Along the 130-km Krishna water scheme, a number of villages in Nalgonda district are affected by high fluoride content in drinking water. The disease 'skeletal fluorosis' is widespread in these villages. There have been agitations by political parties demanding clean drinking water. Now that the Krishna water scheme is under execution (phase I completed, phase II continuing) the villages are demanding that their drinking water needs should be fulfilled before the water is taken to Hyderabad city. All the three situations outlined above have not resulted into direct conflicts as yet but have a potential of developing into tense situations. This is especially so since the Hyderabad city is poised to grow bigger in size resulting in a rising demand for clean water for which it has to depend on outside sources.

Conclusion

The decline of the traditional water sources (due to neglect, pollution and encroachments) has directly affected the water supply position of the city. As the city has grown, execution of long-distance water projects has become inevitable which has led to a rise in the cost of water in recent years. The situation in several of the surrounding municipalities is not encouraging in terms of access of households to tap water and also location of the water sources in the premises. Even as large quantity of water is brought into the city's water supply network, intra-city inequities in quantity and quality are causing a lot of water-related health problems among the poor. Replacing/relaying the worn-out pipelines in the Old City should receive a high priority. While the efforts are going on to link the entire water supply network with the Krishna water scheme, which is going to bring, when completed, more water into the city, emphasis has to be laid on reducing intra-city inequities in water supply.

NOTES

1. *The New Indian Express*, Hyderabad, 19 September 2006.
2. *Andhrajyothi*, Telugu Daily, Hyderabad, 23 July 2003.
3. Government Order No. 111, dated March 8, 1996, Municipal Administration and Urban Development Department (II), Government of Andhra Pradesh. This was an amended version of the then existing order No. 192 dated 31 March 1994. Also see Government Order No.50, dated January 28, 1989, Municipal Administration and Urban Development (A2) Department, Government of Andhra Pradesh.
4. *The Hindu*, Hyderabad, 29 September 2006.
5. *The Hindu*, Hyderabad, 19 May 2006.
6. *The Hindu*, Hyderabad, 26 May 2006.
7. *The Hindu*, Hyderabad, 19 December 2006.
8. *The Hindu*, Hyderabad, 10 April 2003.
9. *The Hindu*, Hyderabad, 15 July 2003.
10. *The New Indian Express*, Hyderabad, 5 July 2003.
11. *Andhrajyothy*, Telugu Daily, Hyderabad, 23 July 2003.
12. Drawl of water by HMWSSB in different years shows a decline from Osmansagar and Himayatsagar in those years. Any decline from these two sources directly affects the old city areas in Hyderabad.
13. For instance, it was reported that there was only one case of cholera in Hyderabad (including Secunderabad Cantonment) during April 1952 to March 1953 because of the improvement in drinking water supply (Report, 1954: 100).
14. *The Hindu*, Hyderabad, 25 January 1997.
15. Notification No. 3195/PR/H/2000 dated 4 May 2000 (*Deccan Chronicle*, Hyderabad, 6 May 2000).
16. Recently, the HUDA seems to have started fencing of the lakes, which is a positive feature (Source: Based on discussion with a top official in the HUDA).
17. *Andhrajyothy*, Telugu Daily, Hyderabad, 23 July 2003.
18. Justice Jeevan Reddy described this area as 'mini Chernobyl' and was about to issue closure order to Voltas (a pesticide unit owned by a powerful group), along with 12 other industries. The counsel (advocate) for Voltas asked for an additional day to produce evidence in their defense. By the next day, Justice Jeevan Reddy was transferred to Allahabad High Court (Gujarat) and was relieved even before the hearings started (Rao 2001: 46).
19. Based on a presentation made by the Managing Director, HMWSSB, at the Centre for Economic and Social Studies, Hyderabad on 14 December 2004.
20. *The Hindu*, Hyderabad, 30 January 2005.
21. The public institutions like government hospitals, educational institutions, student hostels etc. (non-domestic sector) have been placed on par with commercial sector in water pricing in Hyderabad. Some of these issues

were raised by representatives of some of the public/private institutions, civil society groups and researchers in a workshop on 'Cost and equity in water provision in Hyderabad' on 14th December 2004 and a Public Hearing on 'Drinking water at what price, to whom ? & Protection of Himayatsagar and Osmansagar' on 22nd December 2004 at Hyderabad.

22. Since the five-year term of the MoU has ended recently, the ISB is known to be paying the non-domestic tariff of Rs. 35/- per KL (Source: Based on discussion with a key official in the HMWSSB).
23. This seems to have been the understanding reached between Dr. Y.S. Rajasekhar Reddy, Chief Minister of Andhra Pradesh, and Mr. K. Chandrasekhar Rao, former union minister and president of Telangana Rashtra Samiti, a regional party demanding separate Telangana state (*Source*: Based on media reports).
24. *The Hindu*, Hyderabad, 29 July 2005.
25. Vidyasagar Rao, R. (2002) 'Hyderabad drinking farmers' tears?', *Vaartha* (Telugu daily), Hyderabad, 2 July.
26. Linking the entire water supply network with the Krishna water system is meant to reduce the dependence on Singur and Manjira so that the demand of the farmers of Medak district can be fulfilled by giving them Singur water (*The Hindu*, Hyderabad, 26 May 2006).

14

HANOI
A Case Study on Urban Development and Planning in Post-Reform Vietnam[1]

SHRAWAN KUMAR ACHARYA

Introduction

The Socialist Republic of Vietnam, with an approximate population of 80 million and 330,000 sq km area (Nguyen 2003a), is one of the fast emerging market economies in Asia. It's surging economic growth averaging 7.5 per cent per annum (p.a.) since 2000 is second only to China in the world (Lakhanpal 2005). The country divided into North and South during the cold war period was unified in 1975. The initial period was characterised by financial problems until the introduction of the economic reforms in 1986 by the 6th National Congress of the Communist Party of Vietnam. The economic reforms initiative known as "*Doi Moi*", (meaning renovation in English) is a policy, which introduced market mechanism and integration with the regional and global economy. The role of the private sector has considerably increased and foreign investments have become more significant. It is estimated that FDI in Vietnam was over 9 per cent of the GDP, much higher than China and Malaysia (Nguyen and Amin 2003). Urbanisation level has improved after the initiation of "*Doi Moi*" policy and today nearly 25 per cent of the country's population resides in 650 urban areas. It is estimated that by 2020, 40 per cent will be urban with the addition of one million urban inhabitants every year (Webster, 2003). *Doi Moi* has also reduced the overall poverty in Vietnam from 61 per cent in 1993 to 37 per cent in 1998[2].

The large cities such as Hanoi and Ho Chi Minh are witnessing significant changes in demography, morphology, environment and economy. Hanoi, the historic capital, has witnessed a large FDI flow, which has pushed up the population and even the densities, particularly in the historical districts, threatening the rich architectural heritage of the city. At the same time, lakes around the city have been degraded through water pollution as well as encroachments. Housing problems are also emerging with the increasing real estate prices. Efforts are being made now by the Vietnamese government and the international community to prepare urban development and conservation plans for Hanoi City to address these issues. This paper overviews the historical evolution of Hanoi, its morphology and planning tradition, the colonial and socialist impacts in the pre-reform period and address post-reform development issues.

Hanoi—An Introduction

Hanoi covers an area of 921sq. km. and consists of 9 urban and 5 rural districts. Hanoi's population has increased over ten times from the 1950s to reach nearly 3 million in 2004. Migration has played a very important role in the population growth after "*Doi Moi*" besides the incorporation of rural settlement into expanding urban system. It is estimated that nearly 36 per cent of population increase in Hanoi was contributed by migration during the 1994-99 period (General Statistical Office and UNDP 2001). Rural migration to Hanoi has substantially increased because of increasing inequality between urban and rural areas along with the relaxed household registration system[3]. According to the Hanoi Master Plan 2020, the population of core city is expected to reach 5 million by 2020, most of which is to be accommodated in satellite cities such as Xuan Mai, Ha Loc and Soc Son[4].

The Red River divides Hanoi into a northern and a southern part. The main concentration of inhabitants is in the southern part which accounts for only 28 per cent of the area but 69 per cent of the total population. The density is as high as 33,840 persons per hectare in the inner districts of the southern part.

Economically, Hanoi is the second most important city after Ho Chi Minh. Hanoi accounts for 0.28 per cent of the country's land area and 3.74 per cent of its population but accounts for 7.9 per cent of the national GDP[5]. Its GDP increased from 6 million in 1995 to 11 million Vietnamese Dong (VND)[6] in 2003. GDP growth, which was only 4.5 per cent during

1986-1990, has recorded a consistent growth of 12.5 per cent, 10.7 per cent and 11.1 per cent during 1991-1995, 1996-2000[7] and 2001-2003 periods respectively (Hanoi Statistical Office 2003). The Hanoi People's Committee (2004) intends to sustain the growth at 11 per cent during 2006-2020 period. Its per capita GDP increased from US$ 470 in 1995 to nearly US$ 990 in 2000 and by 2010 it is expected to reach around US$ 2,100 at the present growth rate (Nghiem 2001).

The share of industry, services and agriculture in the city GDP was 40 per cent, 58 per cent and 2 per cent respectively in 2004. In 2004 Hanoi' total export value was 2,164 billion as compared to 755 million USD in 1995. Its average export growth rate was 12 per cent per annum during 2001 to 2004 (Hong 2005). It received nearly one fourth of FDI flows into the country since 1988 (Nguyen and Amin 2003) and for the first time in 2005 captured more (US$ 1.6 billion) FDI than Ho Chi Minh City (US$ 738 million) reflecting its emergence as a major economic centre.

Hanoi has number of advantages as compared to Ho Chi Minh including lower wages, cheaper real estate and access to less congested port. Moreover, improving trade relations with China (Hoa and Nguyen 2005), proximity and improved access to South China, cheaper wage rates as compared to China and free trade agreement among the ASEAN member states have considerably enhanced the comparative advantage of Hanoi and the surrounding regions in the current decade (Johnson 2006).

In order to benefit from the comparative advantage and also to sustain 11 per cent growth, considerable emphasis is being given to modernise all the sectors of the economy in and around Hanoi (Science of Economic Association of Vietnam 2002). So far 9 old industrial zones, 5 new big zones and 16 small ones have been built. Five old industrial zones with 90 per cent FDI are located in the inner districts and the rest are being developed in the outer districts. Gia Lam, Dong Anh and Doc Son are the outer districts where large planned industrial zones are being developed. New sectors like Electronic, Footwear, Garments, Food Processing, IT, Telecom, Construction and Materials industry are being promoted in the new zones. More than two thirds of the FDI is from Japan, Singapore, South Korea, Hong Kong and Tiawan out of which the share of Japan is the highest (Nguyen and Amin 2003). Besides manufacturing, other services sector such as trade, finance, banking and tourism are being promoted (Governmental Price Committee 2001). In fact, service sector accounts for half of the FDI as compared to only one sixth in the manufacturing sector. In agriculture specialised area for organic farming, flowers, aquatic products and animal husbandry on industrial scale are being promoted.

Local and international experts have raised serious concerns regarding the threat posed by the rapid growth of the city in the post '*Doi Moi*' period, especially the changes in the demography, the morphology, the environment and the economy (Nguyen and Tran 2003) and the need to evolve appropriate planning strategies and institutional framework to resolve these concerns.

Morphology

Hanoi can be divided into four main areas in terms of its morphological characteristics and historical evolution. These include (a) the Citadel and the Ancient Quarters including the 36 streets[8] ; (b) French Quarters; (c) the Suburbs that developed mainly with the Soviet influence; and (d) modern Suburbs and Satellite Townships developed after 1986. Each one corresponds to particular ideological systems as prevalent during that historical period. The ancient city of Hanoi called Thang Long consisted of two parts: the Royal Citadel (*Hoang Thanh*) and the Civic Places (*Kinh Thanh*), known now as the 36 streets. The Citadel and the 36 Streets have a strong Chinese influence partly because of long, nearly 1000 years from 3 A.D to 938 A.D, Chinese rule and subsequent Confucian and Buddhist influence even after their departure. City morphology developed on the Confucian principle of space allocation based on hierarchical relations leading to the separation of the mandarins and the commoners. The Citadel was the fort and base of the authority whereas the 36 Streets, peopled by the commoners, outside the Citadel walls, developed as a trade and service centre catering to the needs of the aristocracy. The 36 Streets, with their multi-functional long and narrow "tube houses", guilds and living cultural heritage along the streets (Le 2003) are the most important physical and cultural landmark of old Hanoi. Historically, this area developed through the consolidation and urbanisation of many small villages. Each village had a specialised craft which developed into a guild over time and occupied a particular street. The guild-patterned street exists to this day though many of them have been destroyed and changed over time. The other important landmark in the area included the citadel, city wall, the dykes, communal houses (*Dinh*), religious buildings (*Chua*) like the Ba Da pagoda and the educational centres like *Van Mieu* (Temple of Literature).

PLAN DE LA VILLE DE HANOI

Map 14.1: The Old City of Hanoi

The French imposed other unique morphological characteristics known today as the French Quarters to the south of the Hoan Kiem lake and the Ba Dinh Quarters over the Citadel complex, where the French architectural style and urban planning principles were introduced. The morphological character includes wide, straight and tree lined streets, stately administrative buildings including governors' palaces, public building like the city hall, post office, municipal theatres, libraries, university and the residential villas. Though the French helped in creating a plural identity for the city it also led to the emergence of a dual city structure, one for the French and the other for the Natives and destruction of vernacular built fabric and cultural heritage of the city.

The Soviets introduced the strategy of decentralising the centre by developing satellite cities and industrial suburbs. Hanoi was characterised as a manufacturing city as a result of many production units being located in and around the city. During the period 1955-1975, the suburbs were also developed as mass standardised residential housing areas, based on "*Microrayan*" or "Living Quarter" equivalent to the housing estate concept. Each 'Living Quarter' was based on population standard of 60,000-70,000 people and which could support a viable senior high school. Large scale industrial activity was undertaken with this approach and reportedly 5,000 apartments were constructed between 1955 and 1960 (Dang 1985). Geometrical street patter, low-rise (five storey) walk-up residential buildings, broad central axis and abundant open spaces characterised the planned areas. Many of such structures are still found in and around the inner city districts of Hanoi.

The economic reforms and increasing global influences since 1986 have introduced a new character to the morphology of Hanoi. In the old city, these characteristics can be seen with respect to the construction of new residential and commercial structures and renovation and revitalisation of the old. In the suburbs, modern townships and shopping malls, being developed in collaboration with foreign firms, totally contrast the old style and architecture of Hanoi's suburban villages. New FDI-funded industrial estates like Thang Long and Gia Lam near the international airport result in different morphology than the old Soviet inspired industrial estates. Most of the industrial clusters are export oriented and reflect the global face of the old city. Another important trend post-1986 is the increasing concern for the culture and heritage of the city as a place-marketing strategy, which has led to resurrection and redefinition of old city spaces.

Changes and Problems in Peri-urban Areas

Urban development after the initiation of '*Doi Moi*' is characterised by rapid urban sprawl in the peri-urban regions exerting pressure on lands, traditional village communities, fragile ecology and governance structures here. Besides location of manufacturing activities and new township development as discussed above, there is speculative real estate development in Hanoi's peri-urban areas. The paddy villages surrounding the city have been replaced by new uptown housing colonies, industrial sites, haphazard low income migrant communities or shopping malls. Traditional flower villages like Ngoc Ha have disappeared[9]. New capital intensive flower villages have been developed by private entrepreneurs. Unlike in the past the nature of cultivation has changed and the community orientated approach has completely vanished. The shift to capital intensive floriculture practices involves money which many farmers do not possess. It is estimated that the urban peripheries account for 70 per cent of nation's economic output and employment and this share is bound to increase in the near future due to rapid rural-urban transition in Vietnam (Webster 2003). Activity patterns are changing along with the changes in social relations.

A footpath economy has emerged in the peri-urban settlements, that has provided earning opportunities to many but also enhanced vulnerability of certain groups like women to the market forces (Higgs 2003). Further, a strong family network, which characterises Vietnamese society (Turner and Phuong 2005) is weakening due to modernisation and integration of the household into the market economy (Norlund 2003).

Land and real estate development is also making villagers at the periphery vulnerable to uncertainty in the land market. Prices of agricultural land have increased which is leading many farmers to sell land either fully or in parts leading to changes in their life styles and also increasing their vulnerability to market forces due to loss of their fundamental assets. Increasing land prices has led to speculation and illegal conversion of agricultural and forest land into non agricultural uses. It is reported that in Soc Son district, around 10 per cent of the protected forest land was illegally transferred to residential land against Vietnam's land law (Thanh 2005).

The Asian Financial crisis which also affected Vietnam, led to suspension of many large scale land development projects, like the Ciputra West Lake City in the Tay Ho district near Hanoi. The uncertainty of the project and its withdrawal in 1998 adversely affected the large number of farmers and their economic decisions. After the crisis, many projects are being planned and developed in the suburbs and villages, causing land acquisition and hence relocation of the people. Adequate compensation[10] is a major cause of conflict and concern for the residents of peri-urban villages around Hanoi.

The evolution of the classical peri-urban region and its linkages with Hanoi reflect the contradictory processes of integration and detachment associated with globalisation processes. On the one hand, Hanoi's dependence on the periphery for certain resources like the perishable products has reduced but on the other its dependence on it for other resources including land for urban usage like housing, water and other products has considerably increased resulting in the creation of environmentally stressed zones with potential for social conflict (Douglass 1991). Appropriate policy interventions required are however lacking.

Housing and Real Estate

Due to a long period of instability, the physical condition of Hanoi deteriorated considerably and the condition was deplorable just before the initiation of "*Doi Moi*". Traditional built heritage, both Vietnamese and colonial, was decaying due to lack of maintenance and repair. On top of this new investment in housing was considerably lacking because the government did not have funds; the socialist policy did not permit private financing. In the socialist period, the State provided housing through the work units based on the philosophy of egalitarianism. Despite the philosophy of egalitarianism, access to housing was determined by position in the party and bureaucracy and those in the higher echelons got proper housing but, reportedly, in the early 1990s, only 30 per cent of the government officials and workers were provided proper housing whereas 70 per cent had to look for other alternatives in difficult conditions (Trinh and Nguyen 2001). Further, the housing quality deteriorated due to poor housing construction to begin with and then its poor maintenance.

It is reported (Vietnamese Architects Association 1991) that in the mid-1970s, nearly 100,000 people were living in temporary shelters called the tube houses in which lived 4-5 families instead of one. One French villa, on an average, accommodated 120 families. In the mid-1990s, nearly 50 per cent of the ancient quarter households were sharing a kitchen, 95 per cent a toilet and 100 per cent courtyard and corridors (Nguyen 1994). Housing scarcity led to increase in rental values. It was estimated that rental values in the city centre was US$ 600 per sq. m. p.a., comparable to the levels of Singapore, Tokyo and New York in early 1990s (Huus 1995). These have further considerably increased in the recent days[11] with annual increase in real estate price reported to be as high as 40 per cent in cities like Hanoi and Ho Chi Minh. Along with modern apartments and villas in the city and its periphery, new middle class urban housing—often the improvised version of tube house in the city centre—has emerged in an unplanned and haphazard manner.

Recent studies indicate that the problem continues. The proportion of households sharing a house is around 7 per cent. Though the average household size is only around 3.87 in Hanoi, the percentage of households with 6 or more persons is high mainly because of the fact that housing market is very tight and families have to share houses (General Statistical Office and UNDP 2001). This is very common phenomenon in the 'tube houses' in the old city area known as the 36 quarters. The housing pressure in the central part has also led to increasing suburbanisation, mostly of the rich, in Hanoi.

In order to improve housing situation, the government has opened up the housing sector for the private sector involvement since 1991. The State subsidised housing is being abolished and people are being allowed to build their own house and to buy State-owned houses. Today, nearly 70 per cent of housing is produced by the private sector. As a result, housing construction has increased. Total new residential construction, which was meagre 53 sq. m during 1991-1993, has drastically increased to 1.5 million sq. m and 3 million sq. m in 1996-2000 and 2000-2003 periods respectively; indicating major spurt in real estate activities in the city. By 2020 the city authorities expect the average housing area to increase from 6 sq. m to 9 sq. m (Pham 2004) in Hanoi.

Private housing consists of either individual construction on land acquired through use rights or on ownership basis, or through large-scale commercial housing projects. Commercial projects are mostly high-rise housing by the developers, mainly mass housing for low and middle income consumers. The problem, however, is that despite these measures, the overall housing condition is deplorably characterised by poor infrastructure and services, low technical and environmental standards, encroachment, haphazard development (Pham 2003) and low per capita built space. The old city tube housing and old Soviet flats in the city have degraded and there is increasing number of makeshift housing along the Red River bank and railway tracks. One can observe a mushrooming of "vertical tube or pole houses" all over the city which have mixed commercial and residential uses in order to optimise available space in the city. Also, maintenance of existing buildings is becoming a problem and its extent can be gauged from the fact that 434 multi-storey apartment buildings (4-6 storey) constituting 920,195 sq. m of area and housing 137,136 people in the city are in highly deplorable condition (Vu 2003).

On one hand, new governmental acts encourage private investment, both national and foreign investment, in housing construction and maintenance; on the other, there are restrictive housing and land related acts/rules, such as State land[12] ownership and short-lease period constraining private and foreign investments.

There is another limitation of the new market model in housing; majority of the developers belong to the public sector monopolies[13], which are often inefficient and corrupt, functioning through existing well-established networks. Multiple land ownership by different State bodies, work units, also creates problems for land transfer and development. This brings in the involvement of multiple agencies: Hanoi Peoples Committee, the district committees, and other government organisations. The World Bank estimates that land use rights have been issued for only 15 per cent of urban residential land (Thu 2005) because of poor land information system, lack of transparency and accountability in the administrative processes of land survey, land use zoning, certification and vested interest of the emerging capitalist class[14].

The private sector is constrained by limited access to long-term financing from the banks. Financial constraints hamper repairs and renovation leading to dilapidation and loss of housing stock.

The circumstances of demand outstripping the supply and continuing corruption, has adversely affected low-middle class and low-income households and unauthorised constructions and unplanned development. It is estimated that over 80 per cent of private construction in Hanoi is illegal—illegality defined as having 'no or not enough legal documents' (Leisch 2003). Housing construction without permit is common because of limited issuance of 'land use right' certificates. The problem is also compounded by frozen lands held by SOEs, which are not brought to the market and are often speculated upon. Many such lands are in the central areas and some in the peripheries. Lastly, there is large amount of illegal cash that gets invested in the speculative real estate ventures.

Artificial scarcity of land and housing has let to speculations in the housing and land markets. As there is no law setting limits on the amount of land that can be owned[15], few people have cornered the limited lands available. Data of the Hanoi Natural Resources, Environment and Land department indicates that a third of all the houses in Hanoi are speculative properties as 70 per cent of Hanoian cannot afford a house at the current level of income of around US$ 300 (4 million VND) per month (Thanh 2005). The land prices in Hanoi city have dramatically increased; reportedly these have tripled in some districts of Hanoi during 1991-2001 period and the market price was 5-7 times higher than regulated price in the centre and still about three times higher in the urban peripheries (Pham 2001). Thus, even the foreign entrepreneurs find land prices very high as compared to other competing cities of Asia like Bangkok where land values are half those of Hanoi (Moreau 2005). Formal housing has gone out of the reach of the urban poor increasing inequality between the rich and the poor[16]. To bridge the gap between the market and official price at which the lands on the city fringes are acquired, land acquisition law has been amended to permit land acquisition by the State agencies at market price. Consequently, the land acquisition prices on the fringes were set to increase from US$ 7 to US$ 57 per sq. m in 2006. This price excluded the expenses on compensation for assets on land and infrastructure (Ngoc 2005)[17]. Lastly, the private sector is catering to only the middle and higher income groups and the State is not in a position to provide affordable housing to the low income groups. Thus, *Doi Moi* has resulted in increasing inequality in the housing conditions in Hanoi. As a result, 'popular housing'[18] has emerged as a people's initiative in the city, which however is mostly illegal and with little regard for planning (Evertsz 2000: 171).

Basic Services and Infrastructure

The Hanoi Water Business Company is responsible for water supply in the urban districts. Over 84 per cent of the households in the inner city districts in Hanoi receive treated running water from a centralised water system (General Statistical Office and UNDP 2001). However, the supply is erratic because of 40 per cent physical and 30 per cent administrative loss (Pacific Consultants and Hokkaido Engineering Consultants 1996). Antiquated and fragmented pipeline network is a major problem. Poor water quality, contamination, absence of meters, illegal connections, non-refundable cost and the wasteful attitude of the local residents adds to the problem (MOC as reported in Nguyen and Amin 2003). The suburban districts do not get regular piped water supply and because of which the dependence on hand dug wells and surface water is high and hence are areas with high risk of water contamination.

Lack of underground drainage and sanitation is one of the major environmental issues in Hanoi. Combined storm and waste water drainage covers only one-eighth and proper sewer system covers only 35 per cent of the city area; both of which are poorly maintained (CRES and HSDC[19] as reported in Nguyen and Amin 2003). Only the central city and the newly planned high-income residential areas have proper sewerage and drainage facility. Even where the system exists, it works inefficiently because of poor maintenance and ensuing dilapidation. Thus, the use of unsanitary bucket and pit latrines is still widespread.

The drainage problems of the city are compounded by low lying areas in parts of the city and high water table in the Red River Basin. Also, Hanoi has many natural lakes and drains which act as a natural sink. But many of the natural water bodies have been reclaimed or encroached upon for real estate development, reducing the natural drainage capacity and thus to increased flooding. The suburbs discharge sewage directly into the natural water bodies, contaminating the surface water, on which a section of the urban population depends on for water. And so do the industries. The World Bank (1995) estimated that the annual discharge of untreated sewage and industrial waste was 120 million cubic meters in Hanoi in 1995 and this volume would be 10 times higher in the next 15 years. Aquaculture in the natural lakes has increased water contamination.

In 1997, around 1,848 tonnes of solid waste was generated per day in the urban districts of which only around 44 per cent was collected and all of it was dumped in improper and poorly managed landfill sites HURENCO[20] (as reported in Nugyen and Amin 2003). Waste management and collection has improved after the SARS and bird flu scare especially in the urban districts. The problem in the peripheries; of landfill sites and proper disposal still persists.

Traffic and Transportation

Traffic and transportation is a major problem in Hanoi, especially because of high number of two wheelers, poor public transportation system and less area allotted for roads in the city landuse. In 2004, there were 1,300,000 motorbikes, comprising 71 per cent of the total road traffic[21] and the numbers growing at the rate of 13 per cent p.a. Just 6.1 per cent of the city's area is under roads and another 1 per cent allotted for parking, when these figures for other countries are 25 per cent and 8 per cent respectively (Pham 2004). Efforts are being made to improve the system through efficient public transport system, road construction and traffic management. Hanoi already has 3 ring roads, 4th one is in the process of completion.

One of the biggest problems encountered in implementing urban infrastructure projects is related to land clearance and the compensation policy. Difficulty in getting land clearance, ownership and use rights is a major deterrent for many investors. The government acknowledges this and has decided to decentralise the powers for granting land use right certificate, approval of zoning plans and other administrative reforms (Ngoc 2005). The problems with regards to relocation and resettlements are that the compensation packages to the affected residents has not been standardised and there is lack of co-operation between different State agencies and also the different levels of the government such as the province, districts and the communes.

Urban Infrastructure Finance

Since 1997, the government has directed around 44 per cent of total State investment to infrastructure, resulting in infrastructure investment growth constantly outstripping the GDP growth and the infrastructure investment as a percentage of GDP reaching 10 per cent in 2003 (Xuan 2005). Despite this, infrastructural problems remain a major concern in the rapidly growing cities of the country. In order to address the issue, the Vietnamese government with the assistance of other countries is making sincere attempts and has internalised it as a part of the Comprehensive Poverty Reduction and Growth Strategy (CPRGS). The Socio Economic Investment Plan (Statistical Publishing House 2004) has acknowledged that the "urban infrastructure and services could not keep pace with the rapid urbanisation and high density is a big pressure on the city infrastructure" especially in the big cities like Hanoi. Poor resource base of the local, regional and state authorities and poor participation of the private sector is a major problem.

From 1991 to 1997, US$ 35 billion were mobilised for total capital investments in the urban infrastructure development for the whole of Vietnam. The funds came from the following major sources: (i) the State budget (21.9%), State Credit (6.6%), State Enterprise (13.6%), Private sector (31.1%) and FDI (27.3%). The new urban investment strategy, 2001 to 2005, for the whole of Vietnam estimated total fund requirement to be nearly 14 per cent[22] of total investment in the society. This being a substantial leap from the previous investments, the plan also specifies that around 62 per cent of the funds would be mobilised from sources other than the public investment programme. The financial requirement for Hanoi is estimated at US$ 19 billion (Pham 2004), a large part of which will be met through Overseas Development Assistance (ODA). Till 2002, Hanoi had received 54 projects valued at US$ 624 million (To 2002). Some projects are non-refundable and some are loan. In addition, other expected investments are for infrastructure (US$ 227 million), water supply and irrigation (US$ 177 million) and environment (US$ 41 million) totalling (US$ 445 million)[23]. 90 per cent of the committed capital was from bilateral donors and 10 per cent from multilateral donors. Japan has been the single largest donor accounting for nearly 83 per cent of the total assistance in the infrastructure component. Besides improving the internal city, the priority of the new ODA funded infrastructure projects is investments in the outer suburban districts like Cau Giay, Tay Ho, Gia Lam, Tu Liem, Dong Anh and Soc Son. In terms of development of urban infrastructure Ho Chi Minh City has moved ahead of Hanoi by floating municipal bonds and also by creating specialised State owned financial institution called the Ho Chi Minh City Investment Fund for Urban Development (Hiroaki 2004).

Corruption is also a major issue in big capital projects. The World Bank estimate indicates that up to 20 per cent of funds are lost in some sectors due to corruption and other administrative problems (Ba 2005). There are also fears that fast build up of foreign aid in recent years may lead to deterioration and misuse of resources especially when the budgetary systems are still opaque and lack discipline (Arkadie and Mallon 2003: 308). Many of the projects also suffer because there are no finances for maintaining the created assets. This is partly because of the fact that resource mobilisation from the beneficiaries is still low and procedures are in the nascent stage of evolution[24].

Heritage

Hanoi is designated as the heritage and cultural capital of Vietnam. Unlike Beijing, known for its monumental heritage structures—the Temple of Heaven and Imperial Palace—Hanoi's claim to heritage city is more because of its scale, the harmony between land, water, built structure and street activities. According to Logan (2000: 304) cultural symbolism makes this city distinct from other Asian city. Many aspect of this cultural richness, built and symbolic, was destroyed in the past and is under threat today due to the nature of developments taking place in the city.

The French introduced French colonial elements but in the process destroyed the traditional city structures like the Royal Kien Thien Palace, the Citadel, the Quoc Tu Giam, the Thi Huong Examination Hall and the Mot Cot Pagoda. Street pattern was changed and because of widening much of traditional residential structures were demolished. French-built structures replaced important Vietnamese buildings in many sites: for example, the Bao Thien Pagoda by the Catholic Church, Thao Dap Pavilion by the National Library, Bao An Pagoda by Government Administrative Building and Chua Tao Temple by Town Hall. This change and destruction was often justified on the pretext of modern town planning principles. During their rule, limited public housing for the poor was constructed (Ota 2003). But, the French allowed the poor to construct houses on self-help basis without technical guidance. Many of the old structures were thus replaced. Then came the war, then the freedom movement and then the socialist rhetoric in the later period, all of which destroyed the rich heritage of the city over time.

During the First Indo China war, 21 per cent of Hanoi's houses were completely destroyed (Logan 2000). Virtual absence of town planning and governance during the American war and also high degree of migration of rural people for housing and work also led to the deterioration of old houses in Hanoi (Thrift and Forbes 1985). It is reported that in the early 1990s only around 9 per cent of the existing houses were built before 1900, 9 per cent between 1900 and 1930 and 84 per cent were built after 1930 (Nguyen 1993).

For the communist government many of the traditional houses reflected the feudal past and therefore encouraged its proletarianisation by denouncing ownership rights and settling more people in the old city areas. This happened also in the French Quarters, which today forms an intrinsic and important part of the city heritage. The communist regime saw the French concessions and the built heritage, villas, as a symbol of oppression and capitalist exploitation. For them it was symbolically wrong and its colonial symbolic value had to be redefined and changed to represent the proletariat image. As a result colonial villas were taken over by the government for housing the officials and the workers. Many families were housed in one villa. Like the old city houses high density and poor maintenance have led to the deterioration of many of them.

Post-reform housing and real estate initiatives have also threatened the historic heritage of the city. Market-led reforms have created redevelopment pressure both in the Old Quarters and the French Quarters. With the appreciation of real estate values, there is increasing pressure to revitalise the central areas of the city and demolition and replacement of old properties is happening on a large scale. The first of such changes were observed in the

French Quarters, where old villas were purchased by the Australian embassy in the 1990s leading to relocation of nearly 60 families (Logan 2000). In 1993, the government evicted 1,000 families from the French villas and in 1998 a decision was taken to sell 398 State-owned villas to private individuals[25]. The process has continued since then and new commercial developments are coming up in the French Quarters area.

Similar post-reform changes are also visible in the old city area. But unlike in the French Quarters, most of the investment here is from locals, directed towards revitalisation and renovation of old residential housing for commercial use, mostly catering to tourists to Hanoi. Many of these developments are illegal because of the weak and contradictory land laws, high corruption, low fines and weak monitoring by the local authority. The change in the use of the property from residential to commercial, hotels, restaurants, bars, shops and boutiques has led to gentrification and subsequently to eviction and relocation of many original and marginal families. Very often, the changes are abrupt and affect not only the built structure and the occupants but also the thriving street activities (Higgs 2003). Numerous *nouveau* 'vertical tube houses' with kitsch architectural styles and shapes have mushroomed in the old city area, considerably destroying the physical aesthetic elements of the old city districts (Trinh and Nguyen 2001). Gentrification has led to the emergence of a new propertied class in the old city area. Inspite of ongoing destruction of the heritage buildings, the historical symbolism and culture have persisted, giving the city its distinctiveness and importance.

Conservation Initiative

'*Doi Moi*' has brought increasing pressure on land and at the same time it has also brought much needed investment in property development and maintenance as a result of which there is hope that the protection and conservation of historical and cultural heritage in the city could be pursued. At the same time, there is an increasing concern for the city heritage, especially at the local authority level and efforts are being made to enact appropriate rules and regulations. Foreign trained local architects and engineers are also getting interested in the protection and conservation of the heritage. Local, so-called "Vietnamese style", of buildings are now being built. There appears to be a concern for the roots. It is reported that in the recent years, 40 per cent to 60 per cent of the Graduate, Masters and PhD thesis in the Hanoi Architectural University have been related to heritage conservation (Nguyen and Tran 2003).

The concern for the heritage has also increased as a result of place marketing and promoting strategy. Vietnam has always enchanted visitors and Hanoi as a Francophone city with good environment and as the base of the Vietcongs during the war is a major attraction for the tourists. The fine balance between the built and the natural environment and the traditional character of the old city are added attractions. As a result, heritage is being promoted and thereby conservation and preservation have become important part of the local government's city development agenda.

International community has been very proactive in the post-reform period in protection and conservation of Hanoi's heritage. Foreign collaborations have brought much needed finances, research and new conservation ideas to Vietnam. It has also enhanced the technical capacity of the local people. Some of the important international initiatives in Hanoi are mentioned here. The first one is the cooperation between the French and the Hanoi city government in 1989 with emphasis on training, town planning and economic development. The French were trying to reinvent their colony and in way their heritage and legacy too. Hanoi also hosted the Francophone conference in the early 2000. The AUSAID carried out Planning and Development control project in Hanoi between 1994 and 1997. The UNESCO has also supported research, conferences and training program in this regard. Besides the government initiative, many private ones such as the Friends of Hanoi's Architectural Trust, the "*Amis du Patrimoine Architectural du Vietnam*" and universities and academics from France, Germany, Canada, Japan and Australia have been effective. Manpower training and capacity building for urban planning and management has been one of the important strategies in this respect (Le 2003, Do 2003, Nguyen 2003b). International cooperation has given wider universal perspective unlike in the socialist period where the emphasis was more preserving Vietnamese and indigenous cultural traits and not the colonial imprints like the French built heritage, which were not considered important. Today the conservation and preservation issue is inclusive of many colonial and foreign elements. But very often, the plethora of the foreign experts with their divergent and sometimes conflicting views[26] have created confusion with regards to arriving at a specific strategy for old city area conservation by the local authority.

The Hanoi People's Committee has also made efforts to address heritage issues through issuance of 'the Regulations on Construction Management and Conservation of the Old Quarters of Hanoi' and 'the 1984 Ordinance on 'Protection and Usage of Historical, Cultural and

Famous Places'. The Hanoi Master Plan approved in 1998 lays special emphasis on the conservation and preservation of Hanoi's cityscape (Ministry of Construction 1999: 52). Some of the provisions of the regulations are very clear and explicit. Private developers are required to seek permission for construction/demolition. Individuals are allowed to apply for renovations. Owners of classified buildings are eligible to receive financial assistance for repair and restoration. If relocation becomes necessary for restoration then there has to be adequate compensation. Further, restoration work also implies infrastructure improvement in the area but with due consideration to the original built fabric of the area. In this effort illegal, polluting and inappropriate buildings are to be removed. It explicitly adopts the Paris Plan which rules out high-rise buildings by enforcing strict building bylaws and heritage regulations in the heritage areas. In order to decongest and reduce the pressure on the old city the Master Plan intends to develop a new town on the north of the Red river. Hanoi Peoples' Committee has also established Hanoi Ancient Quarter Management Board and has involved the community in the movement. At the national level, national Architectural Research Institute has been established for training manpower and documenting heritage research.

One of the main problems faced in the restoration and development of the inner city area is the high density and number of families living in one house without clear property ownership rights. The latter creates a situation where the maintenance and restoration is nobody's responsibility. The former creates problems of effective relocation, rehabilitation and compensation.

Planning History

Western town planning was introduced in Hanoi after it became the French capital in 1883. Town planning and architecture service was established within the Public Works Department (PWD) in 1923 and the first Master Plan was prepared in 1924 with major emphasis on landuse zoning and traffic circulation. The 1924 Plan was only partially implemented but some aspect of it influenced later plans including the 1942 Master Plan of Henri Cerutti (Logan 2000). The head of the 1924 Plan, Ernest Hebard, significantly influenced Town Planning and Architecture. Unlike his predecessors he was sensitive to local environmental factors and tried to incorporate vernacular styles which led to the emergence of Indo-Chinese style of architecture and built forms.

Formal socialist planning became important in Hanoi after the Economic and Technical Co-operation Agreement of May 1955 signed between the Democratic Republic of Vietnam (North Vietnam) and the Soviet Union. Planning experiments undertaken in Russia and other socialist countries like Poland were replicated without due consideration to local culture and environment. The party and the State controlled the art, architecture and town planning to promote the socialist cause. Economic development and economic planning was considered important during the socialist era. As a result, town planning and urban development were closely tied to the country's five year plans. Some of the important planning initiatives undertaken during this time was the "Suggestive Plan for Hanoi" by a Polish Professor P. Zaremba in 1960; "Comprehensive Master Plan for Hanoi" by I.A Antyonov in 1962; and the Hanoi General Plan also called the "Leningrad Plan" under S.I Sokolov in 1973 (Logan 2000). On the whole, the socialist planning style was centralised, hierarchic, formal, very ambitious and ignored culture, tradition and vernacular styles.

A new era in planning started after the beginning of economic reforms in 1986. Economic compulsion due to war ravaged economy (war ending in 1975) and also the collapse of the Soviet Union forced Vietnam to look for resources and planning ideas from other countries like Japan, France and Australia (Ngo 1996: 65). Although the Communist Party still controlled the State, it was much more tolerant to new ideas than the previous regimes. The emergence of new society, view points, interest groups and foreign collaborations led to new ideas and innovations in urban planning.

Administration and Planning

Hanoi is directly administered by the central government. For administrative and planning purposes the city (*thanh pho)* has been divided into rural districts (*huyen)* and urban precincts/districts (*quan)*. The rural districts (*huyen)* are divided into villages or communes (*xu)* and townships (*thi xa)* and sometimes towns (*thi trun*). The city precincts are divided into wards (*phuong*). However, many of the political, social and sometimes administrative activities are performed at the neighbourhood (*cum*) and the lane level (*to*) with the community participation. Besides, there are mass organisations like the Fatherland Front, Youth Associations, etc. that are connected to the Communist party, are indirectly associated with administrative responsibilities[27] at the lower levels.

The Central Committee of the Communist Party of Vietnam (CPV) is the ultimate source of all policy and planning guidelines. All local economic and urban development plans are derived from the national plan. There is no distinction between Architecture and Planning in educational and professional structure in Vietnam[28]. The Ministry of Construction was formerly called the Department of Architecture and at present the Chief Architect's Office under the Ministry of Construction prepares the Town Plans. People's Committees at the city, district, ward and even at the smaller household group level represent the State. So all planning activities of the Chief Architects office operates under the direct control of the Hanoi People's Committee, which has responsibilities to implement and enforce central government laws. It is therefore apparent that planning and management is centralised and hierarchically arranged, even in the '*Doi Moi*' period.

Plan preparation is jointly carried out by the National Institute of Urban and Rural Planning (NIURP) and the local planning institute called the Hanoi Authority of Urban Planning and Architecture which is under the control of the Chief Architect of the Hanoi People's Committee. These institutes co-ordinate activities of other departments looking after the development of infrastructure, water supply, conservation, etc.

Urban planning is at four levels, (a) National, (b) Regional Zoning Plan, (c) Urban Development (Master) Plan, and (d) Detailed Plan. At the national level, the Ministry of Construction and its various technical departments has the responsibility to prepare a long term (20-25 years) urban development strategy. Regional Plan at the scale of 1:25,000 is the basis for planning of industrial development and residential areas, infrastructure development and environmental protection. This plan also addresses the question of regional inequality and appropriate settlement system. Urban Development Plans (Master Plans) are prepared at the scale of 1:10,000 in order to define orientations, improve whole urban area and its infrastructure and balance economic, political, cultural and national security requirements. These also address the issues of conservation of historical relics, natural landscapes, urban environment, densification of existing urban areas, new construction in the peripheries, establishment of sateliite and new towns and facilitate the urbanisation of rural settlements. Detailed plans at the scale of 1:5000 and 1:2000 are prepared to define and accurately implement the provisions of the Urban Development Plan (Japan Bank for International Development and Finance 1999; 157).

Three major Master Plans have been prepared since the economic reforms of 1986. The second last Master Plan was for 1990-2010, approved in 1992. In 1993, a plan for water, sewerage and drainage for the period up to 2010 was prepared with the assistance of Japanese consultants. The latest Master Plan is upto 2020, approved in 1998 and has been revised by the Japanese consultants in 2005. The plan emphasises multi-nodal decentralised structures, stipulates regional integration and environmental awareness. The new plan lays emphasis on the development of new towns in collaboration with the private sector—both domestic and foreign—for decentralising population and activities and proposes high-rise apartments as solution to the housing problem and also as a sign of modernity (Nguyen 2001). Unlike the previous plan that mainly focused on the urban districts, the new plan has a regional focus covering an area of nearly 8,000 sq. km with a radius of 30-50 kms.

Planning Issues

Despite the adoption of new planning ideology and process there are still inherent weaknesses which call for immediate attention[29]. The first one is, despite the initiation of reforms, the party and the State are still the dominant actors. Other actors such as the private sector, the NGOs and the CBOs are not adequately involved in the planning process, despite making the provision for public participation and consultation[30]. Planners have failed to address the problems of the common people especially the poor.

The second one is the lack of integration and proper sequencing of socio-economic and spatial planning. Under the law of construction, spatial planning is required for communes but many of them do not have socio-economic data which makes the preparation of spatial plans difficult and hence the Master Plan remains merely a physical and technical plan. Thus, the socio-economic aspects have not been internalised in the planning process. But, the landuse plan is seen as a constraint on the market economy. This conflict of regulation and control through landuse plan and play of market forces in the economy, which could have been resolved through bringing in socio economic aspects in physical planning have not been resolved. The third problem is, the conservation of historical and cultural heritage, environment and natural landscapes have not been paid adequate attention[31] in the Master Planning process.

Fourthly, planning has also become complex after the introduction of the reforms. Economic linkages with the surrounding regions and countries have considerably increased. Therefore, the need to coordinate with the surrounding regions has become important planning requirement. The spatial expansion of the economy and the change in the nature of the economy has also led to the creation of new departments which has further added to the problem of coordination. This has often resulted in haphazard and illegal developments leading to large scale corruption caused by a personalised governance system that allows for an extraordinary degree of negotiability, flexibility and accommodation, especially at the lower levels of administration[32].

Fifthly, the planning process takes far longer time than the rapid changes taking place in the economy and space, particularly since the reforms (opening up to market economy) in 1986. Further, the planning is based on not so skilled human resources and weak data base. The Plan preparation takes a long time; there is no mechanism to evaluate the Master Plan, no periodic or timely revision of the Plan and no audit system to verify planning activities (Duoang 2003). Financial feasibility of the plans is also not assessed properly. The available human resources lack skills required for modern planning techniques. The entire data base, demographic, economic and social is very weak and hence even the Plan projects are very weak (General Statistical Office and UNDP 2001). Particularly, the information of the rapidly developing fringe areas is not available[33].

Sixthly, lack of legal framework[34] is a major hurdle, though, compared to the pre-reform period substantial institutional improvements through legal enactments or administrative decrees have been attempted. Very often, documents related to construction and urban management such as the land laws, foreign investment laws, etc. are applied inappropriately in the master plan. Further, numerous laws and decrees which guide the planning system are "outdated, ambiguous and impractical" (Nguyen and Roberts 2001). In some cases, there are conflicts between the law and the provision of the Master Plan; as a result planners are not able to use the plan document as statutory structure plans for the benefit of the investors (Ngo 1996). Hanoi has witnessed substantial increase in ODA assistance in urban infrastructure. However the projects face problems because the process of ratification and approval of administrative procedures are still very complicated and urban planning remains unstable and lacks details (Viet 2000).

Another important reason for poor implementation of the Master Plan is the limited budget for urban development. Financing of development proposals is weak because there is no link with investment planning and there is no clear cut strategy to prioritise projects submitted by different departments, districts and wards. Coordination of the sectors or departments, as reflected in the case of the Ministry of Investment Planning and the Ministry of Construction has not been achieved mostly

Photo: Shrawan Kumar Acharya

Photo 14.1: Hoan Kiem Lake, Hanoi

Photos: Shrawan Kumar Acharya

Photo 14.2: Streetscape, Hanoi

Photo: Shrawan Kumar Acharya

Photo 14.3: Low Income Housing along the Railway Track, Hanoi

Photo: Shrawan Kumar Acharya

Photo 14.4: Open Drains, Hanoi

Photo: Shrawan Kumar Acharya

Photo 14.5: High Two Wheeler Density, Hanoi

Photo: Shrawan Kumar Acharya

Photo 14.6: Squeezed Existence of the Old, Hanoi

Photo: Shrawan Kumar Acharya

Photo 14.7: A Conserved Tube House, Hanoi

because the Master Plan has no power to coordinate sectoral spendings. Sector agencies, like construction, may have little commitment to the master plan, especially when the land is in short supply and the demand for real estate is high. As a result, conformity and coordination among different level of plans, the ward, the district and the city becomes problematic. Large number of organisations involved in investment process further complicates the matter. The government's decision to devolve authority to the local governments to decide projects, attract investment, promote development and GDP increase has created additional problems of varying capacities across the cities. As Hanoi is increasing linkages with the global economy, investment and planning decisions are becoming more prone to outside influences, resulting in increasing uncertainty. This makes planning more difficult than before.

Further, there are multiple organisations for plan implementation at the national and local level. For example, at the national level, the Ministry of Construction implements plans through companies like Vinaconex and Hanoi Construction Corporation. At the local level, the Hanoi People's Committee has its own construction department for different sectors like land and housing, transportation etc. Implementation is constrained by poor coordination and implementation of projects. Also, there is poor co-ordination and integration between sectors and departments; unclear distribution of power and responsibilities between different levels of the government hierarchy; ineffective system of project identification, preparation, appraisal and monitoring; limited understanding and skills required to the demands of market and inefficient use and management of information (Ngo and Schubeler 1998: 16) during planning and implementation phase. At times, reluctance on the part of the decision makers to entertain and accommodate criticism and feedbacks on the existing system also acts as a constraint (Centre for Human Settlements 1997) to improve the system.

Also, unlike China, the local governments in Vietnam have limited autonomy with regards to resource mobilisation and expenditure for projects. For example, Hanoi city government can only approve projects upto US $10 million[35] and for any larger project, central government approval is required (Thu 2005). This is accompanied by absence of resource transfer formulae at the national level. Lastly, in the whole of Vietnam as well as Hanoi, there is an absence of explicit urbanisation strategy. The Red River Basin, which has a very high growth, requires a regional planning strategy. There are also no strategies of absorbing large number of rural migrants to the cities.

Destruction of Lakes

Important planning failure in Hanoi is destruction of many of the existing lakes that characterise the city. It is reported that one-fourth of the 40 lakes existing in Hanoi have disappeared within 10 years (Giang 2000) and the West lake has decreased by one-fifth (Mclaren 1995: 66). Most of the lakes or their parts have been reclaimed for residential, commercial or agricultural development. The French colonial government started this process in 1904 by promoting new developments in a way that intervened with the natural drainage in the city and thereby destroying the interlinked system of the lakes[36]. Many of the prominent buildings like the University and the Municipal Theatre were constructed on the reclaimed land. Pressure on land and consequent expansion in the '*Doi Moi*' period intensified the destruction process, wherein the large corporations, even the government, rich Vietnamese individuals, villagers, squatters and small-scale vegetable and floriculture garden owners have encroached upon the lakes. Encroachments are visible everywhere including in low lying flood prone areas of the Red River.

Civil Society

One of the important developments in Hanoi after the '*Doi Moi*' has been the emergence of new forms of grassroots initiatives by civil society institutions, traditional and new, voicing their concerns regarding the city's growth and development. A middle class, which is better educated, aware and willing to voice its concerns have emerged in the cities and among them are also politicians willing to not follow the official line on certain issues (Logan 2000). Different civic organisations have emerged reflecting increasing diversification of social, economic and political practices in Vietnam (Wischermann 2001). This development is also due to the fact that despite centralised control of the Party-State, there is much political space in Vietnam, for people to protest and raise their voice against the State and its policies. This has been reflected in rural protest movements[37] as well as protests in urban areas like Hanoi on construction activities both in the city centre and in the suburbs. Two projects, namely, the Golden Hotel Project and the Twin Tower Plaza project in the old city were not implemented because of the protests from the civil society institutions (Agle 1998). Similarly, in May 1996 village in the periphery protested against the golf course being developed for foreigners by the Daewoo group.

The government has also initiated democratic reforms as reflected in the Grassroots Democracy Decree no 29, 1998, in order to promote participatory development (UNDP 2003: 69) which seems to be the response of the central government to challenge posed to the State authority at local level. But, even before this, the central government facilitated emergence of many non-governmental organisations in the field of research, consultancy and other services by legal pronouncements[38]. Many of the civil society initiatives are also the consequences of foreign aid. Increasing concern for equitable development, heritage and environment of the city is one positive contribution of these groups. They are acting not only as a watchdogs but also filling in the gaps created by the withdrawal of the State in providing civic responsibilities and also reflect the emergence of community politics which are grounded in the local and everyday experiences of the people (Thomas 2003) in post reform Hanoi. The emergence of civil society institutions are still in the formative stages lacking capacity to sustain themselves but with tremendous potential (Parenteau and Nguyen 2005) to play an active role in sustainable development of Hanoi.

Conclusions: Inclusion Exclusion Paradox in Hanoi

Hanoi is one of oldest and culturally rich settlement in South East Asia. The city has shown tremendous resilience and capacity to overcome death and destruction. It is not only the heritage city of Vietnam but also a symbol of resistance against oppression and colonialism. Its evolution has witnessed different ideological imprints resulting in a rich, diverse mosaic of built environment. Vietnamese, Chinese, French and Russian influences of pre-reform periods have been superimposed by post-modern global capitalist influences of the reform period. It also represents the cultural richness and diversity of Vietnam. Its post-modern symbol is that of an emerging global economic hub of South East Asia, with the city attracting more FDI and contributing more to the national GDP than Ho Chi Minh. Its economy has considerably diversified and is today known for manufacturing and service activities. It's rich culture and heritage has also made it a major tourist destination in South East Asia. This development can be attributed to the policies initiated after '*Doi Moi*' in 1986. However, reforms have also posed certain development challenges for the city.

High population growth due to migration is the major developmental issue confronting Hanoi. Urban centric development has increased rural-urban inequality after the reforms. Relaxation of household registration system has led to increase in rural-urban migration and consequently increased pressure on urban infrastructure such as water supply, sanitation, transportation, etc. Rapid growth of Hanoi city has caused environmental problems as reflected in the shrinking lakes and polluted water ways. The main constraint has been limited finance for infrastructure improvement. To overcome the problems, private sector participation is being encouraged, whose pace has not picked up because of lack of various necessary institutional reforms and fragmented nature of the projects. In this reform period, the planning authorities, which itself are with fragmented authority, are unclear about their role in a situation of a market economy. In absence of proper planning and its implementation on one hand and emerging speculative real estate market on the other, the low income groups have been forced to seek housing in the informal sector, particularly in lands that are vulnerable to flooding and on the periphery without proper infrastructure. There are severe housing shortages and per capita living space is very low. To top it all, the planning and housing problems are compounded by corruption.

But, there are many positive achievements as well, which are with regards to governance in the city. Unlike in the past, the city authorities are more open to ideas from outside the established political and administrative hierarchy. This has considerably increased the space for foreign governments and institutions and also civil society institutions both from within and outside the country to influence policy and its implementation. This is amply reflected in a number of collaborations, from within and outside the city, in the preparation of the Master Plans and Conservation Initiatives in the city. Though the Party-State is still powerful, city governance and planning process have become considerably transparent. The politicians and officials are aware of the benefits of the reforms but they are also concerned about the negative effects of the process and there is considerable urge to mitigate the negative and progress to catch up with other emerging Asian Cities in South East Asia.

The post-reform urban development trend in Vietnam demands clarifications regarding conceptual categories like 'inclusion' and 'exclusion'. 'Inclusion' and 'exclusion' are commonly understood with reference to 'equity'. It is referred to as a process which checks or enhances marginalisation by providing or restricting opportunities to different sections of the society. The contention here is that these concepts will have to be understood in a wider context mainly because the factors that determine 'inclusion' 'exclusion' are diverse and are place and time specific. During the socialist days, Vietnamese society was considered more 'inclusive'. The State was more responsible to the people and basic needs of citizens were taken care of. Inequality was limited. But this period 'excluded' large majority of the people to participate in gainful urban activities by restricting migration of the rural people. The regime also 'excluded' people from participating in civic organisations other than the ones prescribed or provided by the State. The ability of the citizens to dissent and actively participate in debates and policy matters were severely limited. Notions of heritage were narrowly described to include those that prescribed to the socialist cause. Moreover, during this period, Vietnamese State, 'excluded' all alternative economic ideas and innovations in order to protect the socialist cause. Such 'exclusion' had its own repercussion depriving the country of the much needed economic growth. It won't be a mistake to say that the socialist 'inclusive' growth model followed during the pre-reform period was pauperising the entire society and 'sharing of poverty was a common syndrome than sharing of wealth'!

This crisis forced the Vietnamese State to rethink its policies. It became more 'inclusive' by opening itself to alternative 'political', 'economic', 'social' and 'institutional' ideas which helped it overcome the economic crisis. Today, Vietnam is considered as an example for its poverty reduction strategy, the credit for which, to a large extent, goes to the adoption of market-oriented growth promoting strategies rather than dependence on 'exclusive' redistributive strategies of the pre-reform days[39]. It is also to be noted that the reformed Vietnamese State gives much more space to the people to move (rural-urban migration), organise and dissent (represented by emergence of civil society institutions) that have considerably enhanced their entitlements and capabilities. The idea of urban heritage itself became 'inclusive' by accepting the colonial, feudal, western art and architecture along with the socialist traditions. This change in perception has significantly widened the notion of heritage and also helped in conservation and preservation initiative.

But despite these inclusive trends, the Vietnamese experience of reforms has indicated emergence of new forms of exclusion; emergence of spatial and social inequalities. Increasing rural to urban migration, limited access to social services for the migrants, marginalisation of people and spaces at the peripheries, housing shortages especially for the poor after the dismantling of the government subsidised housing programmes, limited access to land and rental market, corruption and increasing presence of the FDI *vis a vis* local entrepreneurs indicates the 'exclusionary' development and potential for conflicts. It is interesting to note that many of these problems are the result of same policies which are commended for reducing poverty. It may be important here to contextually understand 'who gets excluded' 'why they get excluded' 'how many' and by 'whom' for evolving effective public policy. These contradictions also highlight the fact that to assume that there can be 'ideal inclusive public policy' is to ignore the difficulties in evolving appropriate policies for public action. There are costs involved in both the extremes and striking a balance between the two approaches is the real test of sound public policy. But despite these anomalies if public policy is 'the greatest good of the greatest number', than achievements of Vietnam in the reform period is commendable despite the aberrations that are emerging in the society. To a large extent these aberrations, besides other factors, can be, possibly attributed to the transitory nature of the State policies and institutions which are still evolving and are themselves mired in contradictions between the socialist past and the capitalist present and possibly the future.

NOTES

1. The present paper is part of the study undertaken in Hanoi between December 2005 to March 2006 at the Institute of World Economics and Politics, Hanoi, under the fellowship provided by the Asian Scholarship Foundation, Bangkok.
2. http://www.adb.org/Documents/ERD/Working_Papers/WP042.pdf.
3. Like China, Socialist Vietnam had introduced household registration system known as '*ho khau*' to regulate spatial mobility of the population.
4. Chief Architects Office, Hanoi, the figure however appears to be gross underestimation.
5. Vietnam Economic Review, March 2005, pp. 43-44.
6. Dong is Vietnamese currency (VND), 1 US $ = 15,000 VND approx. in 2006.
7. Slower growth during this period was due to the impact of Asian Financial crisis.
8. 36 Streets form part of the Ancient or Old Quarters of Hanoi. They are often used to denote the old city.
9. See www.tve.org/lifeonline.
10. Recently (in 2006) the government of Vietnam has brought two new regulations to curtail official involvement and direct involvement of private investors and land owners in land compensation. Under the first regulation the government will compensate land owners at the market rate in case of government taking over their land. Homes will also be compensated, cash

or new accommodation, at the prices of new homes. Such compensation package also involves vocational training of affected working age population. The government has also allowed investors to directly negotiate with land owners regarding land/ home and other compensation. The regulation also establishes land fund for speedy implementation of infrastructure projects which often gets delayed due to land and compensation issues.

11. In 2006, as per the Hanoi Association of Commerce and Industry (HACI), residential land in downtown area was priced at US$ 3,432 to US$ 7000 (100 million VND) per sq. m depending on the location. Prices of farm land at Soc Son district at the fringes of Hanoi was estimated to cost between US$ 42,000 (600 million VND) to US$ 70,000 (1 billion VND) per hectare. Land prices in townships being developed in Hay Tay bordering Hanoi was reported to be around US$ 300 (4 million VND) per sq m. Land for production/industries in rural areas was estimated at US$ 57 per sq. m and in urban areas at US$ 1,495. Rent structure in some of the industrial parks like Thang Long is US$ 77 a sq. m, Noi Bai US $ 13 to 17 a sq. m. Most local companies cannot afford these rates.
12. Most allocated land is in the hands of State Owned Enterprises (SOE) and often for an indefinite period of time. As a result, new rental and use contracts are limited. Most official new contracts go to SOEs. Albeit SOEs are not supposed to sublet or lease land, in many cases, private firms informally sublease land from SOEs at a negotiated rate which is much higher than the official leasing rate from the State. Such a system deprives the State of the resource and breeds corruption.
13. Of late Foreign consortium like the Ciputra groups are becoming active but the largely cater to high-income category.
14. Consisting of Government Officials, Local Politicians, Planners and Private entrepreneurs.
15. Like the Urban Land Ceiling and Regulation Act, 1976 in India, which however has now been repealed from all the states in India.
16. Hanoi is implementing a housing programme with 56 major projects and 140 smaller projects to create 10 million sq. m of housing for different income groups. In addition to this, as per the Hanoi Housing Development Managing Board, there were 440,000 square meters of housing reserved for low-income groups between 2001-2005. However, how much of it went to the actual needy remains a big question mark.
17. The new law is favourable to residents and can check undue eviction because of higher cost of land. But the problem is that many residents still do not possess proper land titles. Hanoi Natural Resources and Environment Department indicates that the city will have to issue more than 80,000 certificates to land title owners. The high cost of land will adversely affect the local investors whereas the big foreign investors will benefit due to their financial strength. A US$ 309 million residential and commercial

project by the South Koreans near the West Lake is estimated to cost around US$ 133 million in compensation and will clear more than 200 hectares of land, an amount very few local companies will be able to afford. This will have adverse effects on affordable housing supply for the middle and low income local residents since the big developers will cater to higher income segments only.

18. Popular housing indicates housing built by or on the initiative of individual residents. It includes luxurious villas, bamboo huts and everything in between these categories but the lower end represents the majority of popular housing.
19. CRES, Centre for Natural Resources and Environmental Studies and HSDC, Hanoi Sewerage and Drainage Company.
20. HURENCO, Hanoi Waste Management Company.
21. Ministry of Transport, 2004.
22. VND 122 trillion.
23. Information regarding finances especially urban infrastructure is sketchy and poorly organised and recorded therefore authenticity is doubtful. The figures here are indicative only.
24. Unlike in the past user charges have been introduced for services like water, solid waste, electricity etc.
25. Vietnam News, 29th June 1998, VNFORUM http://home.vnd.net/English/news/news.html.
26. Complete or partial restoration or redevelopment, rehabilitation, heritage not only as a built form but as a living and community heritage, etc.
27. Discussion with, Dr Le Thi Bich, Deputy Director, Institute of Architectural Research, Ministry of Construction, Hanoi.
28. Continuation of the French and Soviet legacy in Vietnam.
29. Issue highlighted in this section is based on the discussion with the following individuals, Mr Cuuong Duc Luc, Director, Centre for Research and Planning on Urban and Rural Environment, National Institute of Rural and Urban Planning, Ministry of Construction, Nguyen Mai Anh, Vice Director, Institute of Architectural Research, Ministry of Construction, Le Thi Huong, Consultant, Urban Rural Solutions, R. Dr Trinh Duy luan, director, Institute of Sociology, Vietnamese Academy of Social Sciences.
30. Draft plans are presented to the stakeholders and revised. Plans are displayed for soliciting people's comment. The Vietnam Urban Planning and Development Association (VUPDA) is the biggest non governmental planning association. They are basically involved in research to supplement the planning process or for formulating regulations. Most of the members are government officials and therefore do not represent the view of the common people. Involvement of organisations like the Father Land Front, vestiges of the Socialist era, is there but involvement of modern secular and non partisan civil society institutions in the planning process is still in the nascent stage.

31. With regards to heritage and conservation, international interest and support is forcing the local authority to pay increasing attention. Growing cultural tourism is another reason for increasing state interest in heritage conservation in Hanoi.
32. www.UNDP.org.vn.
33. Hanoi has not prepared Development Plan that covers all parts of the city. As per the Hanoi Planning and Architecture Department it has completed Zoning Plans for only 30 per cent of the land.
34. Enactment and implementation of the first city planning law was scheduled for 2005!
35. A new draft regulation intends to increase this limit to US$ 40 million for large cities like Hanoi and Ho Chi Minh.
36. To Lich and Hoan Kiem lake were interlinked in the past, today inflow in the To Lich has reduced and mostly carries household and other city waste water.
37. Protest movements in various provinces in 1997, especially in Thai Binh province, 80 kms south of Hanoi, against corrupt official, high taxes, land disputes, compulsory labour contributions to infrastructure projects and unjust rice prices.
38. Decision 35 of the Council of Ministers on the Management of Science and Technology, 1992 and Joint circular 195 of the Ministry of Science, Technology and Environment and the Government Commission for Organisation and Personnel Management, 1992.
39. But there is no denying the fact that the pre-reforms policy of investing on human capital like education, health etc. must have certainly played a favourable role in the post reform economic success story.

15

SECURITY OF HOUSING TENURE IN THE PEOPLE'S REPUBLIC OF CHINA
Background, Trends and Issues[1, 2]

DAVID G. WESTENDORFF

> *Conflicts caused by forced removals and demolitions are, as before, the main factor vexing social stability in Shanghai. A few private eviction companies' methods are wanton and vicious. Some companies employ thugs in the dark of night to destroy families' exterior stairs, doors and windows; secretly cut their electrical wires, break their water pipes ... to make it impossible to live a normal life, forcing them to move. Even more extreme, they commit crimes taking lives.*[3]

The historic problem of security of tenure whether to land or housing largely solved during the early years of the People's Republic of China has again become an issue of great concern. For anyone with a low or unsteady income in farming, manufacturing or service provision, in the city or the countryside, the fear of eviction is constant. Even economically better off residents may suffer eviction, but they are more likely to receive adequate compensation and/or better weather the negative consequences of forced eviction. This brief case study highlights the scale of the problem of insecure tenure to land and/or housing in China, the variety of forces that generate this insecurity and emerging policies and practices that may help reverse the current negative trends.

The groups of people in China most affected by insecurity of tenure include:

- Farmers, whose insecurity of livelihood in the countryside forces them to migrate to the cities in search of income earning activities. Lacking an urban residence permit, and in the absence of policies supportive to rural migrants, their security of tenure to shelter in the city remains tenuous, at best. Some 150 million migrant workers live in major metropolitan centres for a large part of the year.
- Former State sector workers who have been laid-off or paid-off[4] by their employers and are living in original 'welfare' housing that they bought from their employer during earlier housing reforms.[5]
- Non-state sector workers holding urban residence permits whose incomes do not allow them secure tenure to housing. These may be long-term inner-city residents who are/were employed in either collective or informal enterprises and who have been renting or subletting affordable housing from private parties or local authorities.
- Registered and non-registered urban residents of informal/illegal settlements, dangerous/dilapidated housing (*weijiufangwu*) and residences that are illegally constructed or non-compliant to the housing code *(weifaweiguifangwu)*.
- All other residents of property demolished under force of eminent domain[6].

The paper is divided into the following sections. The first describes the transition from insecure pre-communist tenure systems in the countryside and the city to collective tenure systems in force until roughly the beginning of the 1980s. These assured adequate access to land and housing in the countryside and to a spartan if egalitarian allotment of housing in the cities. The second section describes briefly how tenure insecurity first began reappearing in cities with the advent of rural workers entering the cities looking for cash income in the late 1970s and early 1980s. Section three then discusses forces that began to push rural workers off their land in ever larger numbers, exacerbating livelihood concerns in the countryside and increasing the pressure on urban centres to house those leaving the countryside for work in the cities. The fourth section examines the relationship between housing reform in urban areas and increasing insecurity of tenure for the previously securely housed workers of the State and collective sectors. The final section before the conclusion discusses the role of China's burgeoning informal settlements that provide housing to low-income groups in and around many of the country's growing cities.

Post 1949 Security of Tenure (1949–Early 1980s)

It is not surprising that a low-income country with as huge and diverse a land mass and population and a history of tumultuous political and economic change would be afflicted with problems stemming from insecure tenure. It is nonetheless surprising how quickly China has evolved from a country with relatively secure tenure for all during most of its post-1949 history to the opposite during the last decade.

China's largely successful transition to a highly globalised mixed economy from a minimally open command economy in the years since Deng Xiaoping announced the Four Modernisations in 1978 has much to do with this: land has become a scarce commodity. Prices now more accurately—if still incompletely—reflect the expected return on investment to alternate uses. Land prices have risen dramatically during the past decade, while the development of the legal and administrative infrastructure governing the allocation, transfer and conversion of rural and urban land has only just begun to adapt itself to existing and emerging economic pressures. As urban and industrial development have expanded westwards in the past decade, problems of insecure tenure that were originally found only in the fast growing coastal cities and their suburbs, can now be found throughout the country.

Among the first priorities of the Communist Party after taking power in 1949 was to reverse the age-old problem of insecurity of tenure in the countryside. Within three years, the government implemented an agrarian reform that redistributed rural land to peasants. In theory, former landlords and peasants were to receive the same land allocation; in many cases landlords got significantly less. The effect of the redistribution was to destroy the local landowning class power and replace it with that of the Communist Party. Depending on population density and the quality of land, the distribution ranged from 0.16 to 1.1 acre per capita. Almost as soon as land redistribution was complete in late 1952, the collectivisation of rural land into what were to become people's communes began. By the time this process reached fruition in 1957, the collectivisation had passed through three progressively integrated stages of agglomeration and cooperation: mutual assistance teams, semi-socialist agricultural producers' cooperatives, and cooperative farms. In the final stage of agglomeration, People's Communes grouped on average some 30 cooperative farms, comprising about 5,000 households or 25,000 persons. The Communes organised all economic and political activity within the territory occupied by its constituent farms, including the administration of villages, taxation, health, education, old age care, recreation, etc. The Communes also appropriated ownership of land, housing, livestock, etc. Single persons or childless couples lived in communal dormitories (Hsu 1976: 783-787).

In the cities, private property was gradually nationalised during the first half of the 1950s and redistributed for use by government offices, industrial departments, state and collective enterprises and residents. Investment in new housing remained minimal in most cities until the 1980s and often only kept pace with the need to take down dangerous or otherwise unsuitable structures serving as housing. Housing allocations were controlled by city housing offices and work units that were able to build housing or dormitories for their workers.[7]

For the large majority of city residents, possession of an urban household registration granted access to a welfare package that included employment, housing, health care, education and access to a minimum level of rationed goods. Either the local authority or the urban household registration holder's work unit (a state or collective employer) was responsible for arranging access to these goods.

Despite the emergence of reforms such as the family (individual) responsibility system in agriculture and the institution of employment contracts of limited duration in the urban state sector, rural and urban collectives tended to fulfil their established responsibilities to their members for ensuring access to land or housing throughout the 1980s. In the countryside, families or individuals contracted with the rural collective to lease a plot of land for a fixed price. Revenue received beyond the lease price remained in the hands of the lessee to apportion to taxes, production costs, investment, etc. The family's original housing entitlement remained unchanged.

In the cities, even if health and retirement benefits were among the first casualties of urban reforms, housing benefits tended to remain stable well into the 1990s. When urban labour contracts were not renewed, or only done so with a drastic reduction in real income, workers' housing entitlement was rarely affected. Top-level decision-makers perceived that adding homelessness on top of precipitously falling incomes among the traditional worker elite of the state sector was too great a threat to social stability to be considered.

Emerging Insecurity of Tenure in Chinese Cities (Late 1970s–Early 1980s)

The spread of the household responsibility system and the growing opportunities to market surplus grain and side crops in free markets during the early 1980s gave rural farmers incentives to work more efficiently on the land they tilled now. They realised that their income and individual effort were intimately linked. Many farmers found they could bring crops in with fewer hands than under the cooperative system. Excess labour initially flowed into township and village enterprises, creating additional wealth and consumption in the countryside and for a time helped diminish income inequality between the countryside and the cities (Selden 1993: 182-186).

Even with these positive changes, township and village enterprises could not absorb all the surplus labour in the countryside. By the mid-1980s, rural migrants could be found circulating in large numbers in Beijing, Guangzhou, Shanghai, Shenzhen and to a lesser extent in the other major port cities. Not only did migrant workers seek urban wages because these were higher than those that could be earned on the farm, but also, because they were paid largely in cash rather than in kind.

In the early phase of rural-urban migration (from the early 1980s), most migrants worked on construction sites, in small private restaurants, in homes as maids or nannies, on the streets as hawkers and short-term labourers, carpenters, masons etc. Much of the cash these migrants earned found its way back to the family in countryside to build new homes or expand the ones they occupied.

Because rural workers did not possess urban household registration cards, they could not legally live in the cities. This forced many into an uneasy 'clandestinity' by which housing provided by the temporary employer comprised implicitly a portion of the worker's wage. Hawkers slept under tables in the markets where they sold vegetables, maids on a sofa in the employer's home, carpenters in the rooms of the persons who hired them to build furniture or refit an apartment, construction workers on the work site, restaurant workers on the floor of the restaurants during closing hours, etc. (Wang 2000: 855; Solinger 1995: 134). Still, authorities did find workers sleeping in the open or wandering the streets looking for shelter, and many were incarcerated and then sent back to their hometowns. If they were lucky, these migrants could still return to the home on the piece of land in the countryside allotted to their family.

Urbanisation of Rural Land and Weakening Security of Tenure (Since 1985)

From the mid-1980s onward, large swaths of rural land in the near suburbs of major cities effectively entered the 'urban' land market, threatening peasants' security of tenure to land and housing (Cai 2003: 666). Between 1986 and 1996, 31 cities in China expanded their land area by some 50 per cent, absorbing a roughly equivalent amount of land classified as rural.[8] When this occurred, farmers were offered cash settlements or urban household registrations and employment as compensation for their lost farmland. Replacement housing or additional compensation were often part of the package if the house was lost in the transition (Selden 1993: 198-201). Not infrequently, promises of employment did not materialise or the employment offered yielded income lower than that obtained previously from farming. Village leaders' frequent manipulation of land use decisions for personal advantage often figured in such processes and led to numerous small and large conflicts with the local population.[9]

China's landmark 1992 legislation detaching land use rights from ownership of urban land, which by definition was held in 'state ownership', moved the foundation of the real estate market forward by allowing legal persons to transact land use rights. This legislation quickly brought government agencies, enterprises and service providers at all levels into the real estate market because it gave each an incentive to consider alternate uses for un- or underused land that they controlled.[10] During Deng Xiaoping's 'southern tour' that year, he urged southern provinces—and by extension the rest of the country—to learn from the example of the Pearl River Delta to be much bolder in their efforts to stimulate economic growth and development.

The combination of these events created a 'big enough' bang to unleash a sustained flood of domestic and foreign investment that kept China's GDP growth rate at approximately 9 per cent for the rest of the decade and to the present. These investments focused on infrastructure and amenities to attract and retain much larger flows of foreign investment and technology than were absorbed in the 1980s. Among them were:

- Power generating facilities (especially large dams), airports, train stations, ocean and river port facilities, subway and light rail systems, water and sewage treatment plants and intra- and inter-city highways;
- Full service industrial parks or economic development zones; and
- Urban renewal including, new urban streetscapes, grand plazas and parks, world class cultural facilities, hotels, apartment and villa complexes for expatriate workers.[11]

These new facilities required large quantities of land, much of it already occupied, whether for farming or housing in the peri-urban areas or in the city itself. In almost all cases, persons living on or around the areas affected by these projects had no choice but to move or be moved. Impacts on farmers and their families have been severe because in many cases their land was seized with little if any recompense. Box 15.1 lists some of the chief uses for agricultural land seized under these conditions.

Box 15.1: Causes for Large Scale Rural Land Seizures and Relocations

Hydropower projects: The Three Gorges Project is only the most famous among these, resulting in more than 1 million persons being relocated.[a] Farmers' compensation has often been much less than promised, whether in cash, in kind or employment, and resulted in worsening impoverishment for many. Long after the resettlement officially ends, tensions remain high in the regions where relocations for such projects have taken place.[b] New projects of a similar nature and projected negative outcomes based on past relocation experiences, find farmers swift to react: in November 2004, an estimated 100,000 farmers clashed with police in Hanyuan County in Sichuan Province because of the unacceptably low compensation they were being offered to make way for a new dam nearby. China's leaders had to impose martial law and send in paramilitary police to stabilize the situation.[c]

Economic development zones: Following Deng Xiaoping's urging during his 1992 inspection tour of China's southern provinces, urban authorities in many parts of the country set out to replicate efforts of Shenzhen, Xiamen, Shantou and other successful export processors' to attract foreign investment. This resulted in a massive investment in new 'economic development zones'. By 1996, within the areas requisitioned for construction of the zones, approximately 300,000 acres of land remained undeveloped for lack of investment. Roughly half was agricultural land, of which half could not be converted back to agricultural use. Proper compensation to the farmers was often ignored.[d] Still, the number of economic development zones continued to grow, exceeding 6,000 by 2003. Among these, 3,763 had already been ordered shut down after a series of investigations begun in the same year revealed they had been set up on illegally seized farmland.[e] More closures may result as investigations are pending for many of the more than 2000 remaining zones.

University cities: These are a recent variant of economic development zones in which local authorities and university officials take over suburban agricultural land for the construction of new educational and research facilities. For city officials who preside over the installation of such facilities, demonstrating that they are able to do things on a grand scale while significantly pumping up local GDP, are key to gaining promotions. For universities, the attractions include: economies of scale in shared educational facilities and urban networks; modernised physical plants; expanded enrollment capacity; and, typically, an opportunity to raise revenue through real estate projects within the zones. By the end of 2003, the 50 university

(*Contd.*)

cities already established occupied land surface equal to 89 per cent of the land occupied by all of the other universities in the country.[f]

Villa and golf course complexes: Exclusive residential complexes have sprung up in the suburbs of China's large cities. Many of the country's 320 golf courses are among their chief amenities. Indeed, the world's largest golfing complex, Mission Hills, is sited just outside the city of Shenzhen, adjacent to Hong Kong.[g] According to official sources, among the first 200 courses completed, only a dozen were built legally.[h] In November 2004, the Ministry of Land and Natural Resources classified golf courses among "*the five most egregious examples of illegal land seizures in China, noting that nearly a third of the land was taken improperly and that compensation had not been paid.*"[i]

Transportation infrastructure: In 2002, 84 per cent of the nation's 147 airports were losing money for lack of business; similarly, super-highways and ring roads outside the largest cities are quiet enough to be used for drying grain during the harvest season. Chinese economist Zhou Guangsheng attributes this phenomenon to overlapping and premature investments in transport infrastructure by cities that are too close together to each be served by three high-speed transport modes.[j] The rapid expansion of the high-speed (bullet-type) rail network will make matters much worse for the airports as passengers abandon air-travel for the cheaper and more comfortable trains. Today, despite five years of sustained high economic growth nationally, 33 per cent of all passenger arrivals and departures occur at the airports of Beijing, Shanghai and Guangzhou.[k] Meanwhile 75 per cent of the nation's other airports continue to lose money.[l]

Notes:

(a) Estimates of relocations from Three Gorges Project continue to vary, as does the fate of the migrants. However, an estimate of 1.13 million seems to be a middle figure (Jing 1997). The same source (p. 90) reports the finding of China's own Leading Group for Economic Development of Poor Areas that over 70 per cent of the 10.2 million persons relocated in other reservoir projects from the 1950s to the early 1980s live in extreme poverty.

(b) Jing (1997); Probe International. Updates are discussed occasionally on the website of Probe International www.threegorgesprobe.org.

(c) Bezlova (2004).

(d) Cai (2003: 671). Local governments also found outright sales or leasing of agricultural land a good source of income. These brought in between 30 and 70 per cent of local authorities income between 1987 and 1994 or totally about 242 billion Yuan. Peasants received about 10 per cent of this amount (Cai 2003: 072).

(e) Yardley (2004).

(f) Zou (2003). In one of the most egregious land grab cases of this kind, city and provincial officials of Zhengzhou acquired nearly 1,000 hectares of agricultural land without payment. They also hid their actions from the city office of the State Bureau of Land and Resources, from whom they were bound by law to seek approval of their planned action. Once caught in the fraud, Zhengzhou city officials directed the city office (of Land and Resources) to help cover up continuing efforts to bring their project to fruition. Within nine months of acquiring the land, city officials completed construction of the facilities and moved in five

(*Contd.*)

universities. Apparently local officials could count on success: three other university cities had already been built in Zhengzhou City (China Daily, 2006).

(g) Jenkins (2006).
(h) Chao (2004).
(i) Yardley (2004).
(j) Zhou (2005).
(k) Kahn (2003).
(l) ZJOL (2007).

Urban Housing Reform, Housing Markets and Security of Tenure

In the early 1990s when larger coastal cities began construction of new housing on a large scale and installing infrastructure and amenities to attract foreign investors, relocations rapidly grew to large scale. Residents that had to be moved were usually given replacement housing, though not always near their former residence. Few people objected as long as the new apartment was roughly as commodious as the former, and gave access to the kinds of amenities they were accustomed to in the previous residence. A marked reduction in commuting time from home to school or home to work might still trump the apartment's physical amenities. On the other hand, residents did complain bitterly when a new and larger apartment was not near a good school or lacked proper shopping facilities. Worse yet were apartments in new tall buildings where water pressure was low or elevators were slow or functioned erratically or markets for food and other necessities had yet to be established nearby.

The typical response to relocation remained nonetheless, much as it was in the 1980s: "*the country is trying to develop, we should cooperate*".[12] In any case, urban residents did not feel attached to their homes as long as they felt they could eventually trade up by moving elsewhere when a more attractive option opened up.

Compensation did not become an issue for city dwellers until later in the decade when the deepening of housing reforms, and specifically the abolition of welfare housing in 1998, encouraged large numbers of renters to buy the dwelling they inhabited. Employees of urban state-owned enterprises, government agencies and other state and better-off collective work units were among the first to take advantage of the policy change because they had little choice in the matter and their employers or the housing bureau were offering them advantageous terms.[13] With that transition, owners developed a keen sense of property rights. Almost as quickly, they began demanding compensation for anything that compromised the value or use of their property; especially if it was to be torn down to make way for new construction.

At the time, government regulations concerning eminent domain and eviction did not and still do not leave room for debate: if local authorities approve a project requiring land occupied by individuals or other public or private interests, the local authority has priority. The authority involved must follow established procedures concerning notification, waiting period, right to fair compensation and appeal in situations of disagreement on compensation or improper behaviour of the parties involved in removal/ eviction processes. Unfortunately for the dislocated party, failure to follow mandated eviction and removal procedures does not halt the eviction process to allow independent review of the case. Eviction and demolition can proceed legally before judgment is rendered.

It is difficult to estimate the number of forced evictions in cities across China. National and city statistical annuals do not provide detailed time series on relocations carried out under the use of eminent domain. Piecemeal data must be collected from press reports, specialist publications and internet debates of uncertain accuracy. Estimates of forced and violent evictions are even rarer. Case studies and research reports by Government offices and university researchers often do provide first hand data on the processes and scales of impact in specific cases.

In large cities undergoing urban renovation, expansion and reconfiguration, the numbers of relocations are almost always large. As mentioned earlier, highways and roads have to be installed to permit the flow of millions more motor vehicles than were on the road 10 years ago; subway and light rail systems need to be extended to move similarly large numbers of people. Preservation of historic neighbourhoods mostly entails moving low-income populations out and installing new residential and tourist amenities for a smaller but more comfortably housed urban elite. Decades of poor maintenance of older post-1949 buildings (15-50 years old) means they are more likely to be torn down than renovated. Prestige projects—museums, art galleries, opera houses, grand plazas, parks, parking facilities, etc.—also absorb large tracts of core city land formerly occupied by housing. Urban mega-projects like the 2008 Olympics in Beijing and the 2010 World Expo in Shanghai generate an even larger number of forced evictions and relocations. At the same time, they require substantial government investment in hardware and marketing that are justified more on their potential to catalyze economic and social transformation in the city and country rather than on the intrinsic economic or social benefit of holding the event in China.[14]

Tenure Security for Migrant Workers

The number of migrants workers[15] from distant and nearby rural locations reached somewhere between 85 and 120 million persons by the year 2000 (Yan 2005; Wu 2005). While this population contributed greatly to the refitting and expansion of Chinese cities in the 1990s and increased massively the number of persons in need of housing in or near the cities, the formal housing delivery system made no provision for them. But as Wu (2005: 15) has shown in Shanghai where policies towards migrants have been relatively progressive, neither steady nor lengthy employment tenure in the city had freed migrants from insecurity of tenure to housing by the new millennium:

> "It is no exaggeration to say that once in the city, migrants continue to be on the move. With substantially higher mobility rates than local residents, they experience much more residential mobility. But such mobility is not necessarily driven by the need for tenure or even amenity. Few migrants make the transition from bridgeheaders to consolidators after years of living in the city, a trend in migrant settlement seen elsewhere in other developing countries. Instead most remain trapped in the private rental sector or staying in dormitory housing. Home ownership is yet to become attainable for migrants, and self-help housing is largely absent because of the intolerance of municipal authorities."

Today the size of the floating population may be as high as 150-200 million and is expected to expand further with the migration to the cities of another 300 million rural residents by 2020.[16] With the rapid expansion of the migrant workforce, affordable housing options in the city centre or on work sites have become scarce. The overflow is now taking refuge in informal settlements. More and more, these resemble in size and form periurban settlements that characterised rapid urbanisation processes in other developing countries beginning from the 1950s. In China, the earliest of these developed in the 1980s on the peripheries of the faster growing major cities, i.e. Guangzhou, Shenzhen, Shanghai and Beijing. At first, when they grew large enough to draw the attention of local authorities, they were suppressed and eventually torn down.

Among the largest and most famous of these cases was *Zhejiangcun* (Zhejiang Village). Before its demolition in December 1995 at the insistence of local authorities, Zhejiang Village housed a population of some 100,000 persons, and thousands of enterprises. The village largely governed itself, establishing health clinics, water and sanitation systems, recreational facilities, schools using the Zhejiang dialect, etc. (Jeong 2002). It also proved itself to be a major boon to Beijing residents who rented land to the village and who bought the Village's prodigious output of low-cost fashionable clothing.

Today, Beijing's population of 16 million comprises roughly 3.6 million migrants.[17] Of the reported million plus people living in Beijing's 332 informal settlements, the 2002 census estimated that 80 per cent were migrants. Today the numbers are thought to be much larger, but according to officials, the flows in and out of informal settlements are so large it is impossible to be sure (Li et al 2006). More certain is that many cities around China are planning to suppress or redevelop informal settlements in the built-up or soon to be urbanised suburbs. In Beijing's case, the 2008 Olympics are adding urgency to this task. According to the plan for Olympic construction projects, the 171 informal settlements within the fourth ring road and surrounding the Olympic stadium site will be liquidated (Box 15.2). Between the end of the Olympics and 2010 another 61 informal settlements within Beijing's fifth ring road will be completely gone as well. The fate of the remaining 100 informal settlements in the municipality has yet to be announced[18]. Where the residents of the first 232 informal settlements demolished prior to 2008 will go remains unclear.

Box 15.2: Relocations Caused or 'Facilitated' by the 2008 Beijing Olympics

The Mayor of Beijing, Mr. Qisan Wang has said that some 300,000 people will be relocated from sites where facilities for holding the 2008 Summer Olympics are to be constructed.[a] This includes competition venues, the athlete's village, management facilities, green spaces, transport lines, hubs and amenities for visitors. However, if the standard for assessing the impact of the 2008 Olympics on relocations is widened to include urban development activities that were either speeded up, enlarged or facilitated by the politics of "holding the best Olympics ever", then the impact will be much larger.[b]

Among the projects 'helped along' by the Olympics are:

- the expansion of the capital's transportation network—including the airport, subway and light rail network, the extensive demolitions in the Qianmen quarter and it's planned reconstruction;
- the approval and construction of a CBD on the City's East Side;
- a new round of massive public contracts and investments in the high tech corridor of Zhongguancun;
- the clearance of old *danwei* (work-unit) housing in the central east corridor between the second and fourth ring roads to make room for

(*Contd.*)

high-end residential developments, luxury shopping complexes and entertainment districts; and

- large environmental remediation projects, including the rustication to Hebei Province of the main facility of the Capital Steel Factory.

An estimate made elsewhere of the number of persons directly affected by demolitions/relocations in the capital for the period 2000-2008 inclusive—the high tide of Olympic preparations—is 1.5 million. This would include Mayor Wang's estimate of those moved because of Olympic construction. By comparison, for the nine years 1991-1999, demolitions/relocations directly affected 640,000 persons, or roughly 70,000 persons annually. The average for the pre-Olympic period (2000-2008) is nearly 2.4 times larger, or 164,800 annually.[c]

Whether the some 400,000 migrant workers living in the informal settlements within the capital's Fourth Ring Road have been included in the Mayor's relocation estimate is unclear.[d] In all likelihood they have not, because very few of migrant workers own property legally in Beijing. Moreover, because they are renters in illegally constructed or dangerous buildings, they have virtually no protection against eviction or the right to a resettlement allowance. The total direct costs of holding the Games have been estimated at US$37 billion. The actual cost is likely to be considerably higher if losses to individuals are calculated.[e]

Notes:

(a) "*Dongqian*" meaning "relocation" is the term most frequently used in the Chinese press to describe the process of getting residents to move from their homes. Another term, "*chaiqian*" also appears frequently. This means to move because one's home has been torn down. Adjectives that are applied to "*chaiqian*" such as "*qiangzhixing*" and "*yeman*" mean "forced" and "savage". Formal/systematic data on these qualified forms of "*chaiqian*" do not exist in the public domain. As indicated in the opening quotation of this paper, however, public figures do admit that the scale of forced evictions amount to a serious social problem.

(b) Formal planning documents issued at the national and city level have emphasised that one of China's goals in holding the Olympics is to make the Beijing Games the best ever, thereby proving China is a first-rate country.

(c) Westendorff (2007).

(d) The Official Workplan for the 2008 Olympic Games calls for the eradication of 171 of the existing 332 informal settlements before the Games start. The number of migrant workers affected is a rough estimate based on the following calculation: Of the nearly one million persons living in Beijing's 332 informal settlements, 80 per cent are estimated to be non-residents (migrants), or about 800,000 persons. If the migrant population is distributed roughly equally among the *chengzhongcun*, then slightly more than half (171 of 332) would be affected by the pre-2008 Olympics demolitions.

(e) The costs of demolishing housing, removing debris and moving residents figure positively in the city's GDP, yet no accounting is made of the residents' losses of informal income, health, convenience or social networks.

Looking Forward

Between now and the year 2015/2020 China's urban population may increase by 300 million persons over the current level of approximately

550 million.[19] Most of this growth will come from rural residents moving into urban settlements. Already as many as 200 million persons of rural origin now spend the majority of their time working in cities. Many of these will not return to the countryside except to visit family members who have remained behind. Very few of these workers have secure tenure to their housing in the cities. Unlike registered urban residents, migrant workers do not typically need to find housing for their entire families, and are accustomed to moving in order to find work or more affordable accommodation.

Sample survey data from 2004 confirm that living conditions of migrant workers are crowded and rarely provide adequate sanitation and cooking facilities (Wang 2006). This should not be surprising given that 45 per cent of migrant workers surveyed earned less than 500 RMB (US$60) per month. Wages such as these in China's major cities make home ownership virtually impossible and rental of minimally adequate housing difficult.[20] Inadequate housing of migrants reflects their inability to afford secure tenure and the benefits deriving there from. Although systematic comparisons between Zhejiangcun of the early 1990s and the many informal settlements spread around Beijing today are impossible to make, anecdotal evidence suggests that migrants once could both afford and benefit from secure tenure, if only for a few years. There may be important lessons to learn from such comparisons where they may be found side-by-side today.

For many of the approximately 50 million urban low-income residents with urban household registration, neither security of tenure nor living conditions may be much better than for migrants. Those families that own a home or still live in a heavily subsidised apartment may rent out part or all of their homes to migrants, including foreigners, to cover expenses. But these homes, especially in central locations, are being demolished to make way for urban development projects, many of which are reconfiguring on a massive scale the social, economic and residential functions of the city. The current supply of state-owned or controlled low-rent housing can cover only a fraction of the demand, while the purchase prices for a subsidised apartment is far beyond the means of these families (*see* Box 15.3). The pressures are therefore building to find simultaneously a solution to the housing needs of both migrant workers and registered long-term low-income residents.

For the lowest income registered residents—those receiving government support in the form of a minimum income—open market rentals are also out of reach and ownership is unthinkable. Table 15.1 uses recent data from four coastal cities, Beijing, Shanghai, Guangzhou and Shenzhen to demonstrate the challenge the lowest income stratum in these cities face in accessing housing that may provide reasonably secure tenure. The cities chosen have greater resources and capacity to build low-income housing than any other cities in China. They also have relatively large and well-functioning secondary markets for both rentals and purchases of apartments for persons unable to access newly built accommodations.

Box 15.3: Urban Housing Programmes for "Low-income" Residents

Shanghai's low-rent housing (*lianzufang)* program is the country's largest and most developed. Yet, in 2006 0.5 per cent of households participated in it (21,460 households out of a city total of 426,000). To qualify, households must meet the city's requirements of being both income and housing poor.[a] The much larger publicly assisted housing programme, Economic Housing *(jingjishiyongfang)* receives government subsidies in the form of land contributions, and reduced taxes and fees to qualified purchasers. These subsidies can reduce the price of a similarly designed and situated commercial apartment by as much as 50 per cent.

Still, as a number of researchers inside and outside China have calculated, middle and low-middle income residents do not generally find them affordable. Households in these income categories need as much as ten years to accumulate the money needed for a down payment. Simulations using Beijing data have shown that mortgage options available in China today barely allow middle income families to cover their total costs of living in the subsidised (Economic) housing. For the next lower income category, simulations show low-middle income households running significant deficits.[b]

Aside from lack of affordability, the Economic Housing program suffers from other flaws, including high maximum income requirements, lax investigation of purchaser credentials and a high level of illegal sales that bring the apartments into the open market. Perhaps the program's most egregious flaw is the overabundance of large apartments (of more than 100 square metres and some as large as 250 square metres) it supplied instead of small apartments (between 70 and 90 square metres) as intended. The larger apartments effectively price low and middle income families out of the market and subsidise high middle income buyers who then frequently rent out the apartments on the open market.

According to Tomba,[c] by 2002 the open market purchase price of an average 80 square metres apartment in Beijing had already reached 33 times the average yearly family disposable income in the city. Even if appropriately sized Economic Housing were available, the lower two-thirds of the city's income distribution could not afford to buy one.[d]

Notes:

(a) Yang (2007).
(b) Duda et al (2005: 22-24).
(c) Tomba (2004: 20).
(d) Duda *et al* (2005: 26).

Table 15.1: Housing Market Challenges for the Very Low Income Group in Four Coastal Cities

City	*Purchase of 2nd hand housing*	*Monthly rental for ordinary apartment (by no. of bedrooms)*			*Social support per person per month*	*Total social support for family of 3*	*Months of total social support to rent 1 br*	*Months of total social support to buy 1.0 m²* of economic housing*
	Hsng/m²	*1 br*	*2 br*	*3 br*				
Beijing	8,916	1,550	1,987	2,487	290	870	1.78	5.1
Shanghai	12,774	1,844	2,267	3,464	290	870	2.12	7.3
Guangzhou	5,960	1,270	1,595	2,357	300	900	1.41	3.3
Shenzhen	9,645	1,642	2,076	2,632	300	900	1.82	5.4

Note: All prices are in Chinese Yuan (RMB).
br = bed room

Source: January 2007 Real Estate Index Monthly Report, http://www.sofun.com, Real Estate Portal, 14 March 2007, accessed 5 April 2007.

In each of the four cities, the minimum income payment is either 290 or 300 RMB (US$35 or 36[21]) per person per month. For a family of three, the maximum monthly payment would be 900 RMB (US$ 108). A family of this size and income would almost certainly rent a one-bedroom apartment in what is called a "common" apartment block. These would typically be in buildings left over from the era of mass produced, un-decorated apartments of the pre-housing reform era or even into the late 1990s. But they could have an independent kitchen and bathroom. Many multi-storey buildings would not have elevators, however. In each of the four cities, one month's rent exceeds the total family support from the government by a low of 140 per cent to a high of 210 per cent.

The prospects for purchasing a one bedroom apartment are even more dismal. To purchase 1 square meter of a low-end apartment in the second hand market, the price might be roughly one half of the overall average of second hand housing in a given city. In Guangzhou the ratio is most favourable: 3.3 months of the family's total government stipend would purchase one square meter. In Shanghai, the same square meter would require all the family's payments for 7.3 months. This analysis suggests that migrants and families on the government assistance are likely to be competing for the lowest end of the informal rental market as the remaining stock of publicly operated housing is privatised and/or torn down.

China's leaders recognise the seriousness of the problem of assuring adequate housing for all urban residents. The government is seeking to use the market and non-market methods to rein in the explosive increases in housing costs, to build or purchase from the market rental housing for the lowest income strata and to offer subsidised housing to help middle income families purchase their first homes. Low-income (rental) housing along with subsidised commercial housing will be located adjacent to the major mass transit arteries, as is being planned for Beijing and has been implemented to some extent in Shanghai. While such accommodations may be at some distance from the central city, the new communities are being designed to offer convenient access to full health, educational, commercial and recreational infrastructure. Expanding the coverage of the housing provident fund and instituting supports to help low-income families obtain mortgages, along with measures to fully integrate migrant worker housing needs into formal urban housing plans are recognised as important problems but have yet to see major policy initiatives taken up by lawmakers. Moreover, the supply of affordable housing being supplied to many urban markets through formal channels will fall far below the need for at least the next few years.

In the meantime, the principal focus of government policy, announced on 3 April 2007, is to rein in costs and prices of housing supplied through the Economic Housing program and the commercial housing market. The core of policy is to root out corruption in the planning, bidding, permitting, financing, land assemblage and clearance, construction, marketing and management of real estate projects. The assumption is that this will reduce the waste of public and private resources, diminish the impact of speculation, and allow a matching between the needs of consumers and quality of housing supplied by the market (Ministry of Construction, et al, 2007). Many of the concerns being targeted in the current initiative have been recognised for years. Responses were conceived by the responsible ministry, which then directed provincial and city level offices to implement the directive. As a whole, these initiatives have not been implemented effectively. The newly announced policy intends for close cooperation among eight ministries[22] in investigation of problems, implementation of corrective measures, and continuing monitoring of performance. However, even under the most optimistic scenario for implementing the policy and corrective measures, the near term housing problems of low-income households are likely to grow.

Concluding Remarks

For most of the China's history since 1949, families generally held secure tenure to land and housing. The picture is changed considerably today.

Peasants have been forcibly driven from their land by pollution, illegal land requisitions, large infrastructure projects and insecure livelihoods, among other reasons. As workers in the cities, migrants' wages and instability of employment rarely permit access to long-term housing. As a result, many migrant workers live in accommodations that are of the lowest quality, and not infrequently officially labelled as dangerous or illegal and earmarked for demolition.

While urban workers with stable formal sector employment have managed to purchase adequate housing, those who have lost their jobs or have retired on inadequate pensions or disability benefits cannot afford to buy apartments. Commercial rental options are also out of reach. These new urban poor are trapped in the remnants of the State-operated housing system in which rents are still heavily subsidised. These apartments, often located in core urban areas, have been allowed to become run down, and are prime targets for demolition. Forced evictions have occurred in significant numbers in these communities, very likely causing the families involved long-lasting distress. Migrant workers who house themselves in urban *chengzhongcun* and run-down low-rent apartments that are also targets for demolition are likely to form a large part of the demand for government sponsored low-rent housing. The supply of such apartments in the near term is far below the numbers needed.

Government efforts to induce the private sector to produce housing that will meet the needs of all but the most vulnerable members of urban society have fallen short of expectations, causing great uncertainty for low-middle income families. If recently announced policies to regulate the mainstream urban housing supply system do not have a strongly positive effect in the next few years, insecure housing tenure may well become the chief worry of the large majority of China's urban citizenry.

Despite the many prospective solutions being discussed at the highest level of government, it is unlikely that action can be taken in time to avert a housing crisis for the lowest income groups in many cities. Fast economic growth has produced a massive increase in the per capita residential housing space occupied by *hukou* holders in Chinese cities. At the same, however, the precariousness of tenure to housing for the lowest income decile of this group has risen sharply. Tens of millions of migrant workers and family members without urban *hukous* subsist in unhealthy and/or dangerous communities in both the centres and peripheries of China's largest and fastest growing cities. They will continue to do so for the foreseeable future.

NOTES

1. Final substantive revisions to this paper where submitted on 15 April 2007. The author would like to thank Daniel Abramson, H.B. Shin, and Weiping Wu for their generous comments on an earlier draft of this paper and to absolve them of any responsibility for errors and omissions that remain. These belong entirely to the author.
2. Many of the ideas discussed in this paper were included in the presentation made at the International Conference on 'Tackling Exclusion: Shelter, Basic Services and Citizen's Rights in Globalising Megacities of Asia', organised by Centre for Development Alternatives, Ahmedabad, Institute of Social Studies, The Hague, Institute of Human Development, New Delhi and CEPT University, Ahmedabad, June 1-3, 2006. Following additional research and revisions to the seminar paper, it was submitted as a background paper for the Enhancing Urban Safety and Security: Global Report on Human Settlements 2007. This background paper can be available from http://www.unhabitat.org/grhs/2007.
3. Shanghai Municipal Commission, Vice Secretary, Liu Yungeng, 3 February 2005. Reported in the Southern Weekend, 4 March 2005.
4. Laid-off (*xiagang*) state sector workers receive a minimum maintenance allowance and reduced access to healthcare and other welfare benefits. Paid-off (*maiduan)* workers have agreed to free the employer from any liability to the worker after payment of an agreed upon lump sum severance payment (Wang 2000: 848-849). Those unable to find new employment may apply for social support in the form of a minimum wage (*dibao*) of approximately 300 RMB/month (US$1.25/day) in the most expensive cities. In Shanghai disposable income of 15.5 per cent of the population in 2004 was at or below this level. (*SHTJNJ*, 2006: DigitalShanghai graph).
5. As many as 50 million urban residents were thought to be poor in 2000, and could thus be expected to have only a tenuous grip on adequate housing. Quoted from report cited by Solinger (2006).
6. Local and national authorities have broad powers to acquire legally occupied land deigned to be needed for advancing the public good. This 'eminent domain' power is frequently used to optimize—from the standpoint of either engineering or public expenditure—the installation of: infrastructure (whether for public transport, communication, sanitation, water supply, energy generation and delivery, etc); environmental remediation or protection; recreational or cultural facilities; public buildings and plazas; and removal of dangerous or illegal structures.
7. In its effort to protect key industries from attack, between 1965 and 1971 the government built or moved large-scale industrial plants to remote locations in the centre and far west of China. Construction of these 'greenfield sites' typically included dormitories for workers, many of whom vacated housing in the enterprise's original location.

8. In reality, the distinction between rural and urban land near large cities was often by that time purely administrative. Buildings housing township and village enterprises or the high density rural population already occupied land that had been farmed five years earlier. Ownership of the land remained, however, with the collective until the land was officially converted to 'urban'.
9. Cai (2003: 663). Cai describes the power imbalances between farmers and their leaders at the village and county level as the source of these manipulations. Leaders often commandeer farmland or other communal property and use it for their own purposes or rent the land to others without offering adequate compensation to the aggrieved farmers. Despite presenting hard evidence of misdeeds, farmers all too often found town or county officials from whom they sought redress disinterested in pursuing justice. Indeed, higher officials often participated in the illegal taking of agricultural land.
10. Implementation of land use fees in cities from 1988 began the process of getting occupiers of than to consider 'how much land they actually wanted to keep control over'.
11. See Yusuf and Wu (1997) for descriptions of investment strategies of Guangzhou, Shanghai and Tianjin during the 1980s and 1990s.
12. "*Guojia qiu fazhan, women yinggai peihe.*"
13. Urban housing reform spanned from isolated experiments the late 1970s and early 1980s to near universalization in the major urban centres today. The process comprised many different initiatives. The first consisted in raising rents in small increments to cover the costs of housing provided at minimal cost—estimated for 1991 by Zhang (2000 quoted in Duda et al 2003: 2) at about 1 per cent of the average worker's salary—to eventual full privatisation of financing, construction and ownership except for residual rental housing for very low income groups. For succinct descriptions of how this process worked for persons in the State sector prior to and after 1998 when welfare housing was abolished, see Plafker (2001) and Yu (2006).
14. Neither the Beijing Olympics nor the Shanghai Expo (2010) are likely to break-even during the course of the events. Nor are the long-term costs of sustaining the specially built facilities likely to be covered by subsequent uses. See Owen (2005) for Beijing and Asiaone (2006) for Shanghai.
15. Migrant workforce or 'floating population' (*liudongrenkou*). Other commonly used names for migrant laborers include *nongmingong* and *wailairenkou*.
16. In this scenario, China's total urban population will reach some 830 million persons (CCIDED 2005: 12).
17. Beijing Municipal Statistical Bureau, 2006 (referring to 2005 data, based on sample surveys).
18. Li, et al (2006). The guidelines for '*zhengdun*' of informal settlements are expected any time. The Chinese definition of "*zhengdun*" in the urban

context can mean any of the following: "consolidate", "clean-up" or "tear-down".

19. FN 17 provides one source of urban population growth. Johnson (2005) quoting World Bank projections states urban growth will grow to 850 million in 2015 from 520 million in 2005. In either case, these figures should be considered rough estimates.
20. A sample survey of migrant workers in six major cities found only 2.5 per cent purchased their own homes (Wang 2006). Although many migrants have permanent homes in the countryside, the combination of weakening tenure to these and the policy to encourage large numbers of rural residents to transfer to urban areas, one would expect growing numbers of migrant workers to seek secure(r) tenure for themselves and family members who are following them to the cities in greater numbers.
21. At the prevailing exchange rate in April 2007 of 1.0 RMB =0.12942 US$.
22. Construction, Development & Reform, Land, Tax, Finance, Audit, Legal Investigation, Industry & Commerce.

16

URBAN RENEWAL IN SHANGHAI
Issues, Strategies and Social Implications[1]

LIM POHIM

Introduction and Background

Shanghai is perceived as a thriving metropolis embedded in rich history and a culturally significant setting. The 'Urban renewal' framework in the city has evolved from the early on priorities in purist restoration and in social cohesion and then towards a more economically-driven, systematic and regulated urban redevelopment strategy under modernisation paradigm in the period of reforms. The city has managed to solve, to a great extent, the acute housing shortages, it has increased per capita living space whilst uplifting the living conditions of the city dwellers. Despite progress, urban renewal still faces vast challenges concerning the increasing cost of necessary investments, the arising social disparities and spatial disintegration in addition to the threat of losing the city's cultural identity. With the aim of stimulating economic development and in an effort to attract investments into the city, the city government has taken on an almost exclusive entrepreneurial role away from its traditionally regulatory and administrative responsibility. Many new strategies in the form of new set of laws, financial mechanisms and management structures have been set up to ensure the smooth running of the urban renewal process without compromising certain socio-cultural demands. This paper seeks to highlight and analyse several of these strategies and consider their wider social implications.

China has undergone a high rate of urbanisation in the last century especially during the so-called post-reform era. The long-awaited changes and new developments brought about by the reform and open door policy were much needed to rectify and rejuvenate the economy and the urban sector, which were damaged or put on hold due to civil wars, the Cultural Revolution and other turbulent events. Against the background of a transition era, from a self-reliant planned economy to a socialist market-driven consumer society, the country is experiencing an unprecedented rate of economic growth. A large part of it is manifested in the growth of big coastal megapolis such as Shanghai.

From the early decades of lilong[2] settlements and substantial areas leased out as Foreign Concessions, Shanghai has been a witness to various historical events that formed its socio-cultural history. In the late 1990s and early 2000s, Shanghai was given the additional role of future World City[3]. In embarking on the road to become a World City, Shanghai is tapping on the resources offered by its neighbouring cities and regions, under the 'One Dragon, Three Centres' policy. Shanghai is the 'Dragon Head' of a region that comprises Nanjing, Shanghai and Hangzhou. Recently, Shanghai has also been granted the challenge to host the World Expo in 2010. As a result, high-speed and mega-scale urban construction and development projects have been launched throughout the city. In line with aspirations to build a '*xiao kang she hui*' or 'small middle-income family' society, Shanghai has also embarked on strategies to improve the housing situation. The goal of achieving the per capita living space of 10 square meters (sq. m) by 2000 seemed successful with the average living space per person increased from 6.4 sq. m. in 1990 to 14.8 sq. m. in 2004 (Table 16.1).

Urban Renewal in Shanghai—Trends, Intensity and Approaches

In general terms, urban renewal in Shanghai can be divided into three phases. During the 1920s and 1930s the opening up of foreign concessions and huge influx of immigrants caused renewal efforts to be focused on removing the urban squatters living in wooden makeshift temporary settlements (*peng hu*) and various types of 'lilong[4]' houses then. Between 1949, after communists took over the country, and the late 1980s, China saw large-scale demolition of urban slums and the erection of workers' quarters or '*Gong Fang*'. The renewal effort in the 1950s and 1960s turned towards improving living conditions of the 'workers'. Some of the lilong housing also underwent rebuilding. Due to stagnation in urban construction in the late 1960s and 1970s, only a limited number of apartment buildings were built. The early 1980s saw the influx of workers returning to the city, causing acute urban housing shortage at that time. Many workers had to squeeze themselves in lilong houses or build makeshift temporary shelters. Due to the shortage of funds and the pressing need to relieve congestion in the city, rebuilding efforts were mainly concentrated on renovating the existing lilong housing with better facilities and living conditions. The 1980s also saw the beginning of proper city planning and the opening up of new lands for housing purposes. While in the early 1980s, redevelopment was mostly initiated by the government, participation of private entrepreneurs began only in the late 1980s.

The third phase began in the 1990s and runs up until today. In this period, Shanghai witnessed tremendous urban transformation characterised by more diverse property investments, development of old areas and the construction of modern multi-storey commodity housing (*Shang Ping Fang*). Similar to the decade of the 1980s, the early 1990s faced a tremendous task of resettling the growing urban population. However, in contrast the rate of resettlement had increased by 34 per cent as compared to early 1980s and in 2005, there were still 3,090,000 poor families waiting for assistance. Since the 1990s, urban renewal has been geared towards a 'whole scale redevelopment' approach (*cheng tao gai zhao*), which includes the setting up of the so-called '*jiu qu gai zhao pan gong shi*' (Redevelopment Offices). Renewal was carried out in terms of improving an entire area of housing, with coordinated planning and design, instead of piecemeal improvements. The 'whole scale redevelopment' or 'package redevelopment' approach also encouraged the demolition of entire neighbourhoods (*chai luo di*) and the construction of new apartment buildings imitated the architectural style of the old lilongs or European buildings. The lucrative financial returns from building higher-density housing have attracted investments from the private sector. However, the new housing with different designs and layout created different ways of social interaction and living habits while spirit of neighbourliness has diluted in the process.

Under the socialist-market economic model, the redevelopment of old areas in Shanghai has attracted enormous investments. Throughout the 1990s, the city managed to complete 3,650, 000 sq. m. of renewal, demolished various kinds of residential units totalling 27,870,000 sq. m., relocated 1,800,000 urban dwellers, as well as resettled and improved living conditions for 640,000 residents (Chen 2002). Although the city witnessed a tremendous influx of population, evident from the increased density, the average per capita living space has increased from 3.8 sq. m. in the 1960s to 6.6 sq. m. (1990) and to 14.8 sq. m. in 2004. Indeed, investment in residential housing has increased substantially, especially from 1990 onwards (*See* Table 16.1)

In order to stimulate the property sectors, a new strategy on land exchange (*tu di pi zhu*) was established. This was carried out by making use of differences in land costs in different city parcels, allowing land exchange as a means to create investment opportunities and profitability throughout the renewal process. The returns from this exercise are consequently used for resettling the residents and creating city infrastructure. This practice has improved the living conditions of many people and, to a certain extent, by allowing multi dimensional investments along the way, it has also resolved problems of funding. Some of these examples are Beijing Tong Lu 71 Streets in Huangpu District, Yao Sui Long in Putuo District, Tien Mu Xi Lu in Chapei District and other hotspots in the city centre (Fan 2004). The sporadic renewal process in the early 1990s, which sacrificed some of the traditional city character, prompted the government to do a review. In 1999, The Shanghai city government made modifications to the regulations and suggested that urban renewal process should strike a balance between "demolition, improvement and preservation" (*Chai, Gai, Liu*), more attention would be given to conservation and preserving the old characters of buildings.

Table 16.1: Investment in Residential Housing & Floor Space of Buildings Completed in Shanghai[5]

Year	*Floor space of residential housing completed (10,000 sqm)*	*Total household (10,000)*	*Dwelling Area per capita (sq. meter)*	*Average person per household*	*Density of population (person per sq. km)*
1960	67.04	234.14	3.8	4.5	1,787
1970	21.65	253.40	4.4	4.2	1,734
1980	304.32	303.87	4.4	3.8	1,854
1990	1,330.02	415.28	6.6	3.1	2,024
2000	1,724.02	475.73	11.8	2.8	2,084
2002	1,880.50	481.77	13.1	2.8	2,104
2003	2,280.79	486.06	13.8	2.8	2,116
2004	3,270.43	490.58	14.8	2.8	2,133

Policies and Regulation

In the early 1990s, Shanghai established the *Shanghai Historical and Cultural City Preservation Plan*, which designated eleven historical areas in the inner city and four historical towns in the urban fringes. The historical buildings were listed in three categories according to their national, municipal and district importance. In 1999, the city government approved again the *Shanghai Historical and Cultural Relics Preservation Plan (Historical Buildings and Streets)*. In 2002, Shanghai Municipal People's Congress approved the *Shanghai Historical and Cultural Relics and Historical Buildings Preservation Regulation*, which has been implemented since 1 January 2003. The Regulation sets forth standards, criteria, scope of preservation, planning requirements and management procedures. It also advocates a balanced relationship between preservation and redevelopment, effective utilisation of market mechanisms, and the importance of expertise input and consultation.

The new *Shanghai City Master Plan* (1999-2020) seeks to reduce the density of new development and to control the height of buildings. It has also embarked on related research, also in order to have better control on the density and height of buildings so as to improve the quality of the urban environment. It designated a total of 12 sq. km. of land, and 10 million sq. m. of buildings to be preserved, including 12 sites of historical or cultural significance, 234 streets of heritage significance, 440 sets of historical buildings. From the total of 20 million sq. m. of identified old buildings, nearly half of the old '*Shikumen*' (stone portal) lilong houses will be preserved in the effort to preserve the facades but improving their conditions in wholesome packages. The new master plan was based on the concept of sustainable development that, amongst other things, strives for better planning and management, urban design, proper dispersal methods for residents in the high-density old areas, as well as systematic and careful layout of high-rise buildings, towards its goal to make Shanghai a 'World City'.

One of the challenges in the renewal process has been how to resettle the populations affected by redevelopment. The Shanghai government came out with legislation and implementation guidelines to attend this problem. The first legislation concerning demolition and resettlement in China was created in 1991 when the *Shanghai City Housing Demolition and Relocation Administration Detailed Implementation Regulations* or '*Cheng Shi Fang Wu Chai Qian Guan Li Tiao Lie*' came into being. This ruling signified that the urban renewal process had reached at a significant milestone in China. Regulation specifies that the actual terms of relocation must be negotiated by the party carrying out the redevelopment process and by the affected household or unit. The terms of what constitutes appropriate compensation include a number of people to be resettled, an amount for compensation, a house area at a particular location, time for the process of transition and period of relocation as well as determining responsibilities and remedies for non-performance. During the decade of implementation, despite demonstrating traces of pre-reform socialist methods, this legislation has helped smoothen the process of redevelopment of the old precincts in the cities, improved urban living conditions and infrastructure, uplifted functional capacities and increased the value of properties.

Undoubtedly, this regulation has contributed tremendously to the rapid urban infrastructure development in the city. The regulation's Article 60 in Chapter 5 states that demolition and relocation should be guided by the principle of "vacate land first, then deal with disputes next". In the case for important projects, procedures pertaining to negotiations with affected parties can be suspended. Permission for demolition and relocation for important construction projects can be granted without negotiations between the municipal infrastructure agency and affected parties.

After ten years of implementation, despite substantial achievements, the old regulatory framework appeared to be outdated and not suitable to the current market forces and the legislative requirements. With evolving housing reform policies and diversification of home ownership patterns, emphasis has shifted from government or enterprise-owned properties to individual ownership. It has been estimated that the formerly government-owned quarters sold to individuals has reached 85 per cent and 99 per cent of the commercial housing (*shang ping fang*) is now under individual or private ownerships respectively (Zhang 2003).

Subsequently, new regulation was created in 2001 to address the needs of the current situation. The management aspects were shifted from administrative to a more legalistic approach. The new ruling has more details and thorough provisions on protecting the rights and benefits of all parties in the residential demolition and resettlement process. It spells out the rules of conduct for various parties including those of the private and government sectors in managing this process. The new ruling took precedence over other laws such as property, contract, administrative appeals and several other legislative procedures. This was to ensure that the socialist market economy functions under a regulated regiment. The new ruling emphasises an open and fair valuation process using market mechanisms to determine compensation. The valuation process is now based on market value of the residential units instead of the number of residents in the dwellings as prescribed in the old ruling. It also provides alternatives to choose the types of compensation, either by cash or property exchange, depending on location, usage and floor space of the units.

Lastly, planning legislation changes have been brought in for the inner city renewal purposes. First one is to do with permitting higher than normal densities in the renewal areas. This is to bring in the private developers, who would have to make large investments upfront for projects that might have long payback period. Government alone would not have so many funds. This policy originated from the System of Land Usage and Rewards. Other similar strategies, using the market-based tools, such as Land Readjustment Techniques, Bridging Subsidies Plan and 'match-making' the hotspots in the inner city with land designated for development, are designed as incentives for the private developers to take up redevelopment of the high density inner areas of the city. There is also a policy called "one city, nine towns" (*yi cheng jiu zheng*), which is for dispersal of population from the high-density inner city areas to the neighbouring suburbs. As incentives to the inner city residents to shift to the peripheral towns, they were exempted from taxes related to rental and housing purchase. The satellite towns are exempted from commercial property, land development and even individual income taxes, in addition to receiving heavy infrastructure investments to improve their quality of life and also being linked with good public transport system.

Social Implications

Urban renewal process is increasingly expensive, as the redevelopment process not only involves building new structures but also resettling the original residents. After several decades of renewal and low density areas of the inner city already been cleared out in the earlier phases, what have remained are high density areas of the "hard-core" problematic areas. Thus, the costs of redevelopment increases with, a possibility of the compensation amount and relocation costs going up to as high as 80 per cent to 85 per cent of the total costs of redevelopment, according to a source (*Shi Xuo Hui Huang Pu Fen Hui* 2003). With China's accession to the World Trade Organisation (WTO) will be increasing globalisation of local economy, which in turn would spur high income and high consumption patterns that would require construction of high-end properties. In such a climate, the costs of renewal efforts would go up or city may have to settle for lower quality of the new developments in that area. For these, number of planning legislation changes have been introduced as discussed above.

One of the emerging issues on the social aspects of renewal is the policy ambiguity about whether to relocate existing residents to the urban fringes or to encourage them to move back after renewal. On the one hand, the government is encouraging resettlement of urban residents to urban fringes because it is in line with the "one city, nine towns" policy, but at the same time, under the implementation of the New Regulation, the government also has a policy to encourage the existing residents to move back to their place of origin, by making various monetary or housing options available to them.

Resettling and encouraging private investments in the urban fringe is laudable as it can disperse the high-density inner-city population and at the same time, stimulate the growth of the urban fringes. The residents also enjoy higher quality of housing with bigger living space and better public amenities. However, relocating the old residents out of the city also causes social disintegration and creates a sense of dislocation in the residents, affecting their livelihoods and children's education, requiring them to adjust to longer commutes, and a loss of a sense of community. Encouraging the original residents to move back to the original place prevents the old areas in the city from being 'dead'. However, the realistic nature of these policies is questionable and may be difficult to implement. This is simply because the original settings and neighbourhoods no longer exist, and the prices of new houses are beyond the reach of the original residents.

Most of the affected residents prefer compensation in the form of housing rather than in monetary form. This is because, very often, the amount of compensation is not sufficient to purchase a 'second-hand' home in the 'not-so-prime' areas not too far from the city. Residents often need to fork out additional finances to top-up the purchase price, thus posing great difficulty to many of them.

Under the New Regulation, the amount of compensation is now based on the size of the buildings rather than the number of persons in the household. In high-density downtown areas such as Huangpu, Jingan and Luwan, where more than 50 per cent of the original residents are living under 10 sq.m. of space, it implies great hardship for the poorer households with large numbers. In tackling this issue, the Jingan Authority has implemented a minimum guaranteed size of space compensation (*bao di mian qi*) so that households with big family sizes can get a minimum living space of 16 sq. m. in Grade 5 and 6 lands in the suburbs.

The urban renewal process has shifted from the initial stages of piecemeal renewal (intended to improve living condition), to a more progressive approach, starting in the 1990s, with the '*chai luo di*' or tearing down and '*cheng tao gai zhao*' or whole scale redevelopment strategies. This has its benefits but at the same time, it came at the expense of bulldozing away cultural and historical heritage of the city. Many of the unpretentious Shikumen Lilong buildings have been the melting pot of the unique urban character today and they bear testimony to its glorious history. In the last decades especially, many old buildings in the prime areas were torn down to make way for urban development. Some of these old buildings were then 'recreated' elsewhere in the not-so-prime land. There have been attempts to captivate the nostalgic atmosphere by introducing old elements to the modern buildings, but the new developments failed to integrate with the old, hence destroying the unique urban character. Many traditional lilong neighbourhoods were torn down haphazardly and hastily.

On 10th October 2001, Shanghai announced the implementation of the new *Shanghai City Housing Demolition and Relocation Administration Implementation Detailed Regulation.* The new ruling advocated a market-based mechanism of compensation for housing demolition. Its major shift is from compensation based on the number of dwellers to calculations based on the size and quality of the dwelling units. Although the new ruling has spelled out what can be done and what is excluded as a part of demolition related relocation, the management process of demolition and relocation appears to be a huge grey area with loopholes for misuse of power and unfair treatment, especially in the process of arranging relocation and negotiating compensation. There are cases of falsification or of carrying out demolition without certificates and official approvals, etc. This is coupled by the lack of monitoring and enforcement expected from the city government to ensure that the demolition exercise follow the actual specifications laid out for valuing the properties to be demolished.

Throughout the 1990s, city governance was geared towards "*Zhen Fu Jing Ying Cheng Shi*" (Government as CEO of a city), local authorities were given additional roles to bring prosperity in their areas. In other words, the city governments were to induce economic growth. Thus one way was to embark on a more aggressive redevelopment of the old areas to attract investments and development. One of the factors for the fast-paced urban demolition and relocation in Chinese cities like Shanghai is that land in the cities belong to the government, so the government could 'buy-back' the land with low value and sell it for a higher price. General public awareness is still low concerning property and ownerships rights. The majority would resort to a compromise in order to make way for what seemed to be government's efforts in development and modernisation. The interchangeable roles of government appear to be an interesting subject to observe. The government can play the roles of regulator and arbitrator in one case and it can also become the project initiator/business eintity in another.

Conclusion

Urban renewal in China, specifically Shanghai, has reproduced the western experience in less than a decade. A large part of it happened after the post reform era, with aggressive rebuilding efforts, not so much as to rectify the "damages of the war" (as in the west) but as an answer to progress and modernisation. The rate, intensity and purposes of urban renewal have changed over the years according to the social, political and economic circumstances of different era. From the earlier decades of purely social objectives to improve the living conditions, it has transformed to become a vehicle to uplift the city rising to the challenges of globalisation and demands of the market economy.

Learning from the past and maturing over the years, Shanghai's renewal process now has new strategies and mechanisms being developed simultaneously for her new challenges. Through land exchange, whole scale redevelopment and other incentives, the government has managed to stimulate large-scale property development and improved the housing shortages. However, despite these new policies, regulation and financial mechanisms, there are still weaknesses in the implementation, especially in terms of enforcement and monitoring of the relocation/rehabilitation packages. Marginalised and displaced communities, issues of affordability due to rising home prices and loss of cultural heritage are some of the emerging issues. In adapting to current demands, the city and local governments have also taken on new role as "CEO of the city" under the concept of "government operates the city", with heavier charter to bring in investments and economic prosperity to the city. With the current scenario, it is suggested that more attention be given to balancing economic interests with social needs by focusing on long-term sustainable planning based on actual demand; stricter control on land available for development; more affordable and subsidised housing, and better monitoring and regulation of the property market.

NOTES

1. This paper is based on a research project sponsored by the Asia Scholarship Foundation (ASF). It was conducted between the periods between November 2003 to May 2004.

2. Traditional housing typology in Shanghai.
3. The term "World City" was coined by Jean Gottmann in his 1961 publication, *Megalopolis,* to denote an emerging phenomenon in the Asia Pacific region. The megalopolis concept stressed the development of supporting regions, creating an urban corridor to boost the economy of the region.
4. "Lilong" literally translated as "alley and lanes". Lilong types of houses refer to a style of housing emerged in Shanghai the 1920s to 1930s, combining western and traditional architecture elements and constructed in rows of two to three stories residential housing to cater for the high-density population in down town Shanghai. There are several kinds of lilong houses, e.g. 'terraced lilong' houses, 'garden lilongs' and 'apartment lilongs'.
5. Source: Shanghai Statistical Bureau (2004).

17

SINGAPORE'S EXPERIENCE IN HOUSING AND URBAN DEVELOPMENT

LIM LAN YUAN

Introduction

This paper describes the housing and urban development in Singapore over the last four decades during which it has emerged as a global city from being an under-developed city State. It highlights some of the key policies and experiences which have made the country one of the successful models in urban community development and public housing in Asia. It first provides the background of Singapore and then traces the different policy initiatives at different time points with regards to infrastructural development, public housing and urban management. These are in particular of interest in the context of dominant role played by the State in ensuring Housing for All, which goes towards forming of 'inclusive city', building a cohesive society and achieving liveable quality of environment for all her citizens. The Singapore model has been widely hailed as a success and is often studied by other countries which have yet to solve the housing problems of their urban population. She has been able to implement city-planning and urban-management policies that actually benefit the poor, and its housing programme has been successful and admired for producing low-cost, affordable housing on a mass scale. This paper is particularly of relevance for housing policy framing in Asian countries.

Background of Singapore

Singapore does not have a long history since she was founded in 1819. She is a multi-racial society with the forefathers of her citizens comprising largely migrants from South China, India and South-east Asia. Singapore has a land area of 697 sq km (MICA 2005) and a very small resident population of only 3.486 million (2004). She attained self-governing status in 1959 and independence in 1965. In the early 1960s, the city of Singapore was characterised by overcrowding, poor hygiene and sanitary conditions. Over 35 per cent of her population lived in squatter settlements (Lim 2000). Over the last four decades, Singapore has been transformed into an important financial hub with modern infrastructure and a rather clean and green environment. She has become an important economy in the Asia Pacific region.

An important achievement of the city today is that over 93 per cent of the households own their homes. Another feature of the city is that 84 per cent of the households live in public housing. This has been made possible through consistent national policies, some of which would be discussed in this article. Another critical factor in stupendous achievements in housing and urban development has been a stable policy regime and consistent direction for the development of Singapore achieved because of the dominance of the ruling party, the Peoples' Action Party (PAP), which has been in government for some 47 years. This party won the national elections once again in the recent general election held on 6 May 2006 with a strong mandate of 66.6 per cent to rule for another 5 years.

Overall Urban Development

One of the main focus of the government after Singapore's independence in 1965 was to cope with the massive housing shortage, poor infrastructure and communication facilities, and lack of industrial facilities. Driven by these circumstances, Singapore embarked on an ambitious national development plan which stressed on massive industrialisation, urban renewal and low-cost housing development. These development problems were dealt with by setting up a number of quasi-government agencies or statutory boards equipped with legislative powers and authority to implement policies. Industrial development was promoted by the Jurong Town Corporation (JTC) while housing was undertaken by the Housing and Development Board (HDB). Redevelopment of the central area was undertaken jointly by the Urban Redevelopment Authority (URA) and the private sector. A more detailed discussion of these various aspects of the development process is now given below.

Public Housing Development

Design and Planning of New Towns

The development of new town and public housing was undertaken by the HDB, a statutory board under the Ministry of National Development charged with the provision of low-cost housing and housing management services. In view of the limited land resources in Singapore, public housing development is typically high-rise and high-density in nature. They tend to comprise blocks of flats ranging from 100 to 200 units of different room types: from 1-room (33 sq m), to 5-room and executive apartments (125 sq m). Each of the new towns (ranging between 150,000 to 300,000 inhabitants) is self-sufficient. There are now twenty-three such new towns completed by the HDB having undergone four different phases of development. In the early 1960s, small isolated public housing estates were built as and when parcels of vacant State land were available. The priority then was to build as many dwelling units as possible in the shortest time and at the lowest cost. Many of these now old buildings have been either demolished or upgraded to modern standards.

In the mid-1960s, the towns were comprehensively planned with facilities for a target population and with a town centre. In 1973, new town development was undertaken more systematically with a prototype town model. Currently, the concept of 'precinct' is introduced to focus on community living and bonding. Flats in the older housing estates would, as far as possible, be reorganised into precincts, each comprising four to seven blocks with a total of 750 apartments. These blocks would share a common open space with landscaped gardens, playgrounds for children, and pavilions. Each precinct would have its own distinctive character and identity to give residents a greater sense of belonging, privacy and a pleasant living environment similar to those found in private condominiums.

Home Ownership

One of the most remarkable early achievements of the ruling PAP in Singapore was its housing policy. From the inception of its public housing programme, the purported aim of the government has been the creation of a nation whose people have homes they are proud to call their own. The underlying philosophy is: "if one owns an asset in the country, one would stand to defend it" (Wong and Yeh 1985: 231). Singapore's public housing programme is a symbol of pride, of nationhood, and of the political achievement of the ruling party (Pugh 1989). It has been directed towards achieving national development objective (Yeung 1973) and has to a large extent shaped the establishment of Singapore's urban community. Public housing is subsidised by the government. In addition, through the use of the Central Provident Fund (CPF), which was originally a retirement fund, citizens are encouraged to purchase and own flats.

The Housing Allocation System

As of now (2006), 84 per cent of Singapore's households live in public housing. This means that such housing is found all over the city and hence there are no neighbourhoods that could be classified as poor areas.

Further, a system of fair distribution of public housing units has been set up, which is based on a set of eligibility criteria. As public housing caters for the lower strata of the population and is subsidised by the government, only Singapore citizens of certain income category are eligible to apply. Other eligibility conditions include applicants' imperative to form a family nucleus, and to earn a gross household income not exceeding Singapore Dollar (S$) 8,000 per month. Another condition is that the allottees should stay for at least 5 years before they are allowed to sell their flat units. The main system of allocating flats to the applicants is on a first-come first-served basis. To ensure that completed housing units are not left vacant, the HDB has introduced a build-to-order system that requires some financial commitment from the household for the house. This is to replace the registration for flats system, which is the first-come first-served system in which all applicants have to just register. Only when some 70 per cent of the applicants have shown sufficient interest to purchase, will the HDB proceed to construct the blocks of flats.

Industrial Development

Singapore's industrial programme first started with the establishment of the Economic Development Board in 1961 which spearheaded the transformation of the city from a maritime trading nation into a modern economy, first an industrial one and then a service one. In the 1960s, labour-intensive industries were encouraged as a priority. By the early 1970s, when full employment was achieved, the emphasis shifted to the generation of higher-skill jobs and the production of quality products. In the late 1970s, industrial promotion focused on technology-intensive and high value-added industries and services. The focus in the 1980s was to develop Singapore into a global base for businesses, where firms and corporations could expand beyond manufacturing, to research and development, technical design, marketing, distribution and servicing. Subsequently, Singapore emerges as also a financial centre in Asia.

As part of the industrial programme, the Jurong Town Corporation was established in 1968 to take charge of the development and management of industrial estates in Singapore. This has, ever since, facilitated multi-national corporations in locating their manufacturing plants in Singapore. To date, the JTC has developed some 7,000 hectares of industrial land, four million square metres of space for some 7,000 companies.

Infrastructure Development

The successful implementation of housing and industrial developments as well as other forms of urban development requires provision of adequate infrastructure and communication networks. Each new town is planned to be self-sufficient with social, recreational and commercial facilities that support the modern urban lifestyles of the residents. These towns are linked with major commercial centres through the expressways and a comprehensive public transport network.

Singapore's transportation policies have been to control the growth of car population and to introduce traffic congestion control measures such as area licensing scheme and road pricing. This is done through implementing a long-term island-wide network of roads and rails coupled with an efficient public transport. A new light rail system has been introduced in addition to the Mass Rapid Transit. The LRT is an over-ground system connected to a public bus system for inter-regional travel. It also takes people to MRT stations and forms part of a highly integrated transport system. Pedestrianisation is being encouraged in the central area. There is a plan to convert parts of the central districts into pedestrian areas under the Pedestrianisation Plan, that would then provide various types of pedestrian linkages, plazas and open spaces in different parts of the central area identified in the Plan.

Urban Redevelopment and Conservation

The Urban Redevelopment Authority (URA) is responsible for the overall planning in the country and it is also in-charge of redeveloping the central areas in Singapore jointly with the public and private actors. The URA provides the guidelines and basic infrastructure to facilitate development while the private sector contributes with financial resources and entrepreneurial expertise. This is carried out through the 'Sales of Sites Programmes' which were first launched in 1967. By the end of 1994, the records indicated that some 22,000 units of private housing, 127 hectare of office space, 95 hectare of shop space, 41 hectare of industrial pace and 10,000 hotel rooms were constructed. The Sales Programmes were instrumental in facilitating Singapore's urban and economic growth.

The overall urban development in Singapore is guided by the Concept Plan which is a land-use and transportation plan designed for its long-term physical development. It was first published in 1971. Since then, three major reviews of the Concept Plan have taken place in 1980, 1991 and 2001.

The vision set out in the latest 2001 Concept Plan is of a thriving world-class city for the Twenty-first century. This Plan focuses on decentralisation to relieve the central areas of congestion and overdevelopment. Among the key proposals of this Plan are: development of a high rise city-living with creative designs, more choices for recreation, greater flexibility for businesses, and a global business centre. Singapore's potential as an international business centre has been increasingly recognised, and major initiatives have been taken to support this by creating needed basic infrastructure—telecommunications, business services, industrial and office space, and sea and air transportation. The aim of the Concept Plan 2001 is to create a distinctive city that is alive with heritage, character, diversity and identity.

With the maturing of the city centre, government has now shifted its focus to the conservation of the city heritage. Under an island-wide Conservation Master Plan introduced in 1986, more than 100 ha of old Singapore in the central area with significant historical and architectural value has been earmarked for conservation. This area includes the historic districts of Chinatown, Kampong Glam, Little India and the Singapore River. Planning Act has been amended for the purposes of the conservation of these districts. Any works carried out within the conservation area, such as any decorative painting on the buildings exteriors and renovation or building works that may affect the character or appearance of the building, are required to obtain a written permission from the Competent Authority designated under the Plan. Conservation is not only confined to the preservation of the building fabric but is also extended to retaining the rich history, architectural style and ambience of the entire areas or districts.

Protection and Greening of the Environment

With rapid urbanisation and industrialisation in the last four decades, it was realised that stringent measures will have to be taken to protect the population and the physical environment from the adverse effects of pollutants that enter the water or atmosphere. Hitherto, the control is effected by ensuring that land use proposals are compatible with the surrounding developments. The location of developments such as oil refineries, sewerage treatment plants, refuse disposal grounds and incinerators has to be carefully considered. In addition, the protection and improvement of the physical environment has also been carried out through landscaping and conservation of the nature reserves.

In 1990, a new statutory board known as the National Parks Board was formed to take charge of the conservation, management and improvement of the nature reserves and parks and gardens of Singapore. The original objective of the greening programme was to plant as many trees as possible within the city. With rapid urbanisation, buffer zones intended to serve as noise barriers with appropriate trees and landscaping are imposed on developments along major roads. The focus is to emphasize variety, colour and height to complement the high-rise buildings that dominate the landscape. The objective is to achieve a standard of 0.8 ha per 1000 population for public open space provision.

Urban Management

Town Management and Maintenance

Building modern infrastructure and housing stock, implies the need to manage and maintain such facilities and buildings whilst engaging with residents' participation in decisions upon their living environment. For this purpose, local self-governance was introduced in Singapore with the passing of the Town Councils Act in 1988. Prior to that, it was the HDB, which had constructed the largest number of housing buildings was itself managing the towns thus created. At one point, the HDB was managing the housing areas, through its own rules, for two million people. This was over-centralisation of management functions. Although the HDB had discharged its responsibilities admirably, it had done this at the price of uniformity and through the application of a rather inflexible set of rules. To overcome the problem of tying down of the HDB in town management, the Town Councils Act was passed. In elaborating on the concept of Town Councils at the second reading of the Town Councils Bill on 28 June 1988, the then First Deputy Prime Minister, Mr Goh Chok Tong, said that "it was never the original intention that the HDB should become the management corporation for over 80 per cent of the population of

Singapore". Town Councils provide residents the flexibility to decide on the kind of living environment they want and allow them to participate in the day-to-day running of their estates. The two main objectives of town councils are to transfer the responsibility of estate management from the HDB to local councils, and to allow participation of the HDB residents in policy formulation and decision-making on local estate matters (Lim 1995).

Although town councils in Singapore were conceived of and established as management agencies for public housing estates, they are also an important mechanism for building community bonding. Town councils were introduced in three phases. By March 1991, Town Councils had taken over the management of public housing estates in all constituencies. There are currently 17 such town councils managing all public housing estates in 84 constituencies.

Constitution and Organisation of Town Council

A town council is a corporate body, that is, it can sue or be sued in its corporate name. It has perpetual succession, meaning that it will continue to exist regardless of the particular people who happen to be residents of the town council at any particular time. It may appoint committees to carry out its functions and to deal with specific matters. These committees may be delegated with such powers, functions or duties of a town council. Depending on the needs of the individual town council concerned, committees may be appointed to deal with the following matters:

- To establish rapport with and obtain feedback from residents on the work of the town council;
- To disseminate information and promote the activities of the town council;
- To hold dialogue sessions with shopkeepers and market hawkers representatives;
- To improve the physical environment and supervise the provision of maintenance services;
- To assess and recommend improvement works for the estate; and
- To formulate financial guidelines and review the budget.

The Town Council is formed of Committees that play an important part in the management of the Town. They provide an additional avenue for residents to participate in the activities of the town council.

Functions and Powers of Town Council

Unlike the concept of Town Councils in other countries, the role of Town Councils in Singapore is largely confined to maintenance management. They are not empowered to perform many municipal functions such as levying and collection of taxes, approving planning and building applications, and other matters relating to health and social welfare. The Town Councils are, however, free to employ their own workers or to appoint a managing agent to manage their towns. Most town councils engage a managing agent to run their towns.

The main functions of town councils are to control, manage, maintain and improve the common areas of the residential and commercial properties in the public housing estates and to keep them in good repair and clean condition. Common areas are the open lands and common facilities including recreational or community facilities in the housing estates built for the use or enjoyment of the residents. To enable it to carry out its functions and duties, a town council is empowered to perform the following:

- To establish and maintain facilities for recreation, relaxation and other educational and cultural activities;
- To make improvements to the common property with the consent of the HDB;
- To acquire property for the performance of the town council's functions;
- To manage, by agreement, the HDB car parks and industrial or the government's market and food centres;
- To levy conservancy and service charges;
- To levy charges for the use of any facilities or services; and
- To enter any flat or property to carry out maintenance or repair work.

In addition, a Town Council may make by-laws for the purposes of exercising its powers and carrying out its duties. Essentially, such by-laws are made to regulate, control, manage, and administer use of the common property in the estates. Any person including a resident who commits a breach of any of the by-laws could be fined if found guilty. A Town Council is empowered to make by-laws to impose administrative fees for services provided by Town Council and penalties for late payment of conservancy and service charges. It can also introduce by-laws to collect deposits to secure payment for such charges and to regulate the parking of vehicles on common property.

Town Council Management

The two main functions of the Town Councils are the maintenance of the estates under their supervision and the management of the town funds (Lim 1998). Their main source of income is derived from the monthly service and conservancy charges they levy. And their main items of expenditure are in respect of maintenance, cleaning, utilities and management experiences. A Town Council is required to keep proper accounts and records of its transactions and to ensure adequate control over its receipts, payments, expenditure and assets. The annual accounts of a Town Council are required to be audited.

The main tasks and operations in maintenance management include undertaking daily conservancy and house-keeping, regular maintenance and repairs, and estate improvement and modernisation works. Conservancy and cleaning are house-keeping functions which keep the common areas clean and hygienic. The tasks include regular refuse removal and disposal, daily sweeping as well as the regular washing of common property and facilities within the estates.

Another major activity of the Town Council is the maintenance of the natural environment including horticulture maintenance. Grass-cutting works, pruning and cutting of branches and trees, minor planting, weeding of grass and turf areas and minor re-turfing are some of the common operations carried out. Its function also includes landscaping selected sites within the estates with flowering plants and shrubs as part of the estate improvement projects. Another equally important function of the Town Council management is to preserve and enhance the quality of the building structure and physical environment. The implementation of estate or town improvement projects helps to upgrade the living environment and create unique characteristics of the town.

At the outset, it should be noted that the efficient management of a town has never been an easy one. Unless there is also a strong sense of belonging and community spirit, no amount of quality improvements can create a vibrant town. Residents can play a useful role in establishing community goals and objectives and suggesting community projects which help to strengthen harmony and build rapport among the various groups living in the town.

Upgrading and Modernisation Programmes

In the 1960s and 1970s, many public housing estates and new towns were developed to meet the shortfall in accommodation. The design, layout and quality of materials of the flats improved along with each phase of the housing programme. This shift in emphasis from quantity to quality from the mid 1980s has resulted in great disparity between the flats built in the earlier phases and the recently completed ones in new towns of Sengkang and Ponggol.

The older flats, built about 40 years ago, have become less popular, particularly with the younger generation of Singaporeans. They have suffered physical deterioration and obsolescence. In order to satisfy the demand for improving the quality of existing housing, the government announced a S$[1] 15 billion upgrading programme in July 1989, for the next 15 to 20 years. The refurbishment programme covers improvement of three areas: flat interiors, the blocks and for the entire estate.

Improvements for the flat are generally confined to the additions of balconies, service yards, toilets, better wall and floor finishes and minor items replacements. This will not only increase the living space but bring the standard of design and layout closer to the newer flats. The improvements within the blocks are more visible as these have to do with the façades of the blocks of flats where additional architectural features are added to create individual character of the building, something that was absent from the earlier designs. The improvement in the housing estate is the most beneficial for the precincts and the entire community. These various upgrading programmes have helped to maintain the vibrancy and freshness in these neighbourhoods and the living environment which are necessary to maintain the standard of living and the quality of life.

Community-based Organisations

The government has also made extensive use of para-political community-based grassroots organisations to promote social integration and to service local residential areas, beginning with the Community Centres and continuing in the 1980s with Town Councils. It was not until the ruling PAP won the 1959 election that the political potential of Community Centres was realised. The government saw that under its control they could be employed as agents of socialisation, imparting value that would assist in nation building and lead to the emergence of an integrated urban community (Hill and Lian 1993).

The Citizens' Consultative Committees (CCCs) were set up in 1965 as part of the initiative to develop structures within which informal leaders could be identified and cultivated. They were modelled on a precedent established during the Japanese wartime occupation, when the village councils were formed to maintain order and to keep the Japanese administration informed of grassroots activities. Every constituency has a CCC which is nominated by the MP. Hence committee members have involvement in a wide range of political process. Below it are the Residents' Committees (RCs), which have been set up since 1978, and are specifically intended to promote neighbourliness, ethnic harmony and community cohesiveness, and are allocated local domains of activity throughout the HDB blocks. The RC members are appointed to represent their block or precinct in which they stay. Their function is to channel government policies to local residents and to provide feedback to the government.

Building Family Ties and Social Networks

Housing policy has also been used as an adjunct of social engineering and for promoting social integration and building close family ties. Various schemes have been introduced till now to promote family bonding. The Joint Balloting Scheme, begun in 1978, has enabled parents and married children to be allocated flats in close proximity. Other schemes include one permitting exchanges of flats to facilitate parent/children proximity, and a multi-tier family housing scheme encourage married children to stay together with their parents or grandparents in the same flats as an extended family.

In the initial years of the public housing programme the eligibility rules and income ceilings imposed targeted at lower-income and working-class families. By gradually increasing the family monthly income ceiling to S$ 8,000 and with the addition in 1971 of a large five room flats, the HDB housing was made accessible to wider income segments within the population.

Finally, the housing policy has played a significant part in assisting the process of ethnic integration. In order that different racial groups have the opportunity to mix together, an ethic integration limit is placed for each of the HDB block and the neighbourhood in accordance with the respective proportions of the racial groups in the population. For instance, Chinese residents must not exceed 87 per cent and 84 per cent of the total residents in a block and a neighbourhood respectively, and Malay residents must not exceed 25 per cent and 22 per cent respectively. No further resale of flats to a particular ethnic group is allowed if it increases the proportion of the affected ethnic group beyond the prescribed limit in the block or neighbourhood. This policy is applied consistently to all ethnic groups.

Conclusions

Singapore is often held out as a model of success, for her achievements in housing and urban development, and for being able to shift her position from a subordinate role to that of regional headquarters status in the intensely competitive interconnected global network of business. But what Singapore has found to be successful may be of limited application to other developing countries, as she stands out as an exception in a number of ways. First, she is a city State. As such, unlike other developing countries, national development is almost synonymous with urban development. Second, the trend of rural-urban migration, which has resulted in millions of urban homeless people in many other developing countries, is practically non-existent in Singapore. Third, her democratic socialist government, committed to nation-building through social reforms, has focused on public housing and urban development, and has consistently allocated a large proportion of the budget to this sector (Sim, Lim and Tay 1993).

Nevertheless, useful lessons can be drawn from the Singaporean experience. The relevant factors critical for the successful building of a quality urban environment may be summarised as follows:

(a) *Strong political leadership*: Strong political will and commitment is the main driving force for the successful introduction and implementation of the various policies described.

(b) *An inclusive vision*: The policies combine both political and economic considerations into a social rational. For instance, the push for public housing is based on the underlying philosophy that if one owns an asset in the country, one would have a stake in it and stand to defend it. Undertaking large-scale new town development and redevelopment is viewed as a major investment in social capital, with important ramifications on the national economy and significant multiplier effects on national income.

(c) *Comprehensive legislative support*: Effective legislation and enforcement has been available to undertake land acquisition and assembly. This has been coupled with a set of equitable resettlement policies to facilitate clearance of site for redevelopment. Strict laws and their compliance have helped to implement various initiatives in urban development.

(d) *Appropriate fiscal incentives*: Suitable fiscal incentives and concessions such as a reduction in property tax payable were offered under the Sale of Sites Programme. This has encouraged the involvement of the private sector to bid for the sites. Tax incentives are given to promote procreation and family formation.

(e) *Appropriate and integrated policies*: The adoption of appropriate policies at the right time is an important factor for success. The good working relationships and close liaison among the various government agencies have also contributed to the effective implementation of policies. The absence of a multi-level hierarchical administrative structure in government has helped in prompt decision making.

(f) *Efficient administrative structure*: An efficient and non-corrupt civil service has provided the support and push for the implementation of the policies and programmes for national development.

As a small country with limited resources, and faced with increasing competition from other developing countries much larger and better endowed than herself in terms of natural resources, Singapore had to develop strategies to be able to compete with these countries in economic and social development. After achieving independence in 1965, she needed to immediately establish herself as a politically stable economy which is self-reliant and vibrant to satisfy the basic needs of her citizens. It became an imperative to ensure basic infrastructure provision for sites for housing, industrial and other uses. Guided by an effective leadership and efficient administration, tremendous success was made in the provision of the basic needs of the population making her one of the most rapidly developing countries. The next stage consisted of shifting the emphasis from providing quantity to quality in development.

In anticipation of higher living standards and the growing expectations of the local population as the city advances economically, the 2001 Concept Plan has proposed a range of ideas to ensure a higher quality of life for Singaporeans. For instance, on urban density, it has proposed the reduction of high density housing from the present 83 per cent to 70 per cent of the total housing development with concurrent improvement of average living space from 20 sq m per person to 30-35 sq m per person.

The Singapore experience in housing development has shown that building of a cohesive and harmonious urban community can be achieved. However, a critical factor is the need for an enlightened (socialist) political leadership with a vision and ability to introduce programmes which are supported by citizenry and implemented efficiently to achieve the goal of nation building. The challenge for Singapore in the next decade is to further raise the quality of life by ensuring the efficient integration of physical and economic planning in order to promote sustainable economic growth and development (Lim 2001).

NOTE

1. Singapore Dollar.

PUBLIC ACTION

18[1]

SHANGHAING MUMBAI
Politics of Evictions and Resistance in Slum Settlements[2]

DARSHINI MAHADEVIA[2] and HARINI NARAYANAN

"On 9 December (2004)[3] my husband immolated himself to stop the demolition and subsequently passed away".

—Martha Shresth of Anand Nagar Society on Juhu Tara Road (Indian Peoples Tribunal on Environment and Human Rights—IPTEHR (2005: 18).

"I returned home at 10.30 pm and found our houses demolished. Some goons standing there asked us not to build anything there. ... We needed some place for our children to sleep. So we tried to build makeshift arrangement by using bamboos. ...Heated exchange of words soon resulted in physical blows. In that fight, a watchman from their side got hurt. They ... complained to the police. As a result, the commissioner summons us regularly to date although there is no information on the other party. .... We paid Rs. 20,000 to a goon for 10 × 20 ft home in Hari Omnagar. We did not have amenities, no water, no electricity, ... The goon whom we bought the house from did not give us anything in writing and that if we identified him he would say he did not know us".

—Deposition of Uma Shankar Jai Narayan Mishra from Hari Omnagar Seva Sangh, Hari Omnagar to IPTEHR (2005: 15)

"Bulldozers ran with two jeeps of police. Our houses were destroyed. Women were beaten. Children got burnt."

—Coordinator, Kadwi Wagari from Wagari Basti, in a deposition to IPTEHR (2005: 21).

"The next day they came again with bulldozers and took away all our belongings, including food items, utensils etc. ... An 8 year old girl and a 21 year old woman died due to cold."

—Ramzan Hasmat of Rafiq Nagar in a deposition to IPTEHR (2005: 24).

"They took my house away to turn Mumbai into Shanghai! Where is this Shanghai? Why, are there no poor people in Shanghai? At least in the next birth, I want to be born in Shanghai, where there is no BMC [Municipal Corporation of Greater Mumbai]".

—Renuka Naidu, Annabhau Sathe Nagar, Mankhurd, Mumbai, (IPTEH 2005).

"In the city, (poor) people find their role is to become human bulldozers. The poor squat on useless, rocky or marshy land; they level it and turn it into valuable real estate. When people started coming to Dharavi (the largest slum in Bombay) fifty years ago, land was forty paise a square meter; now it is 400 rupees a square meter. This is the hidden purpose of the poor in the city—to benefit the rich. No wonder they then try to criminalise the poor, say they're lazy and worthless. They want to get their hands on the urban land which the poor have improved and added value to."

—Seabrook: 1987, 149 quoting A. Jockin, then a social worker, now president of the National Slum Dwellers Federation and a recent winner of the Ramon Magsasay award.

"Nobody forced you to come to Delhi. Is there a right to live in Delhi only? Stay where you can.... Tomorrow you can come to the Supreme Court and settle here claiming a right... There has to be an end to this."

—Justices Ruma Paul and Markanday Katju, Supreme Court of India, 2006.

"We fully support the CM's drive on the demolition of illegal slums. ... If Mumbai has to be a World Class city then the slums have to go and for which strong and urgent steps need to be taken. Any encroachment of public property cannot be tolerated and must be dealt with according to the rule of law."

—Bombay First and Citizen's Action Group (CAG) comprising of prominent citizens[4].

"The UPA government commits itself to a comprehensive programme of urban renewal and to a Massive expansion of social housing in towns and cities, paying particular attention to the needs of slum dwellers... Forced eviction and demolition of slums will be stopped and while undertaking urban renewal, care will be taken to see that the urban and semi-urban poor are provided housing near their place of occupation."

—Common Minimum Programme, United Progressive Alliance (UPA), 2004.

Introduction

Series of statements that came up at the time of massive demolition drive launched in Mumbai by the Municipal Corporation with the directives coming from the state government, indicated the support for the demolitions as well its immediate impacts on those who suffered as a result of it. The statement by the Justices of the Supreme Court of India justify demolitions—something that has come up time and again (see Chapter 11 by Batra and Mehra)—but against the noble goals stated by the Common Minimum Programme (CMP) an agenda document based on which the coalition government at the national level is functioning. These statements sum up the contradictions within urban India, the contradictions between the haves and have-nots, those who have made it to the global India and those who have not. They also indicate the reality within which Indian politics is grounded and reality that Indian political parties have to recon with.

Mumbai, its political and business leaders hope, will be the driving force of India's global economic integration. Hence this comparison with Shanghai, which became the driving force of China's global economic integration from 1990s onwards (Yeung 1996). Since the development of the Pudong area in Shanghai, through foreign investments and the adopting special area development as a strategy to revitalise and redevelop old large cities, China's economic development strategy has shifted to encouraging real estate development (Yeh 1996). In transformation of Shanghai, real estate's contribution has been estimated to be 37.3 per cent in Pudong and 45.9 per cent in the whole of Shanghai in 1993 by Yeh (1996: 292). Further, since Shanghai was opened up for FDI, the per capita Gross Domestic Product (GDP) has accelerated in China (analysed from ADB document of key indicators of development).

The argument is powerful. To use real estate for city transformation, which in turn would spin-off rapid economic growth of the nation and in turn lead to decline in poverty and absolute deprivation. But, it is the transformation of Shanghai in short span is what has captured the imagination of the politicians, the planners and the business leaders in Mumbai. India, too, hopes that Mumbai, the commercial and finance capital of India, like Shanghai, would be such a driving force of Indian economy.

In order to kick-start this longed-for transformation, the state government apparatus felt the need to make dramatic demonstration of its ability to take difficult decisions and follow through with them even in the teeth of vehement opposition. Simply put, in Mumbai, between November 2004 and March 2005, 90,000[5] homes of slum-dwellers, located over 44 localities (IPTEHR 2005: 10), were demolished. Considering an average of five persons living in one slum home, 450,000 slum-dwellers were evicted by this concerted act of demolition. This means that about 8 per cent of the population living in slums within the jurisdiction of the MCGM—or in the Marathi form, Brihanmumbai Mahanagar Palika, or BMC, were evicted in the span of four months. The demolitions were observed with total helplessness by the slum-dwellers and concerned citizens for a while before the resistance gathered pace. By February 2005, the evictees' resistance movement to the demolitions gained strength and from then on, the history of the city's resistance is still being written.

Due to number of reasons, the slum evictions were halted. But, other forms of exclusions in the city, remained in the news. The first major exclusion since the idea of World Class City has gained ground is banning of dancing by girls in beer-bars (pubs) in the city. There are estimated 75,000 dance bar girls, as they are called, working in non-five star hotel bars[6]. Most of these girls come from families that are unable to find well-paying jobs in the city and the girls are important earning members and in some cases even the sole supporters of the family. Some of these girls do slip into prostitution while they are employed as dance girls in these bars and some of them take to it after retiring from the dancing profession, which is at a fairly young age. The state government's argument, made on its behalf by the Deputy Chief Minister (DyCM), Mr. R. R. Patil was moralistic; to protect the young generation from slipping into a moral abyss!

The other one, not so much reported event has been, banning of hawking in all but the designated hawking zones, a fallout of the Supreme Court order of December 2003 in response to a petition filed by a city-based NGO, City Space against hawking everywhere in the city. The Supreme Court order forced the BMC to take action, rather unsuccessful one, with strong resistance from the hawker union leaders[7]. Taken together, the slum demolitions, the removal of roadside hawkers' who peddle a variety of reasonably-priced wares to the city's middle—and lower-middle-income families, and the ban on dancing in the beer bars amounts to an attempt to remove economic activities and habitats that appear not to fit in with a particular vision of a 'World Class City'[8], which is popularly called Shanghaing Mumbai. In this article we have dealt with only the issue of slum demolitions in Mumbai.

Demolitions a Way of Planning in Mumbai

Every new 'Vision' or 'Dream' or what is now called 'Makeover Plan' for Mumbai has been accompanied by indiscriminate and brutal force used against the city's slum dwellers. There is an amazing similarity of narrations of the evicted slum dwellers over time; for example, between narrations in the document titled 'Forced Evictions' prepared by Indian People's Tribunal (IPT) in 1994 and a recent 2005 one titled 'Bulldozing Rights' by Indian People's Tribunal on Environment and Human Rights (IPTEHR). For the slum dwellers of Mumbai, history keeps repeating itself. It is as if the city is sending a message to her slum dwellers: "You are not wanted. Leave the city or we would continue to destroy your lives and you." It is a war of attrition. Every demolition leads to a proportion of affected slum dwellers leaving the city. Tenacious ones, hang on, fight, and get something out of their political patrons. The cycle goes on.

Historically, since the textile mills came up, migrants streamed into the city to work and informal housing developed, the relationship between the State, capital and the residents of these informal housing units has been tense and attritive. And the same trend has continued. The very first piece of legislation on slums in Maharashtra, the Slum Areas

(Improvement and Clearance) Act, 1956, "viewed slums as a law and order problem" (Nambiar 1999:43). The literature produced by the SRA in Mumbai indicates that the only official view of the slums till 1970 was these as settlements set up by illegal squatters and therefore needed to be removed[9]. Nambiar says, "The State, with the help of police and [the] mafia, [forces] the poor out of their homes. Demolition squads not only demolish hutments but also confiscate or destroy the belongings of slum dwellers. Evictions carried out are ruthless most of the time. They take place even in the night or in the middle of [the monsoon]. They also take place because of pressure from private parties... Demolitions represent an attempt on the part of the government to gain some control over a situation that has gone out of its hands. Civic authorities confronted with the problems of congestion, sanitation, waste management, pollution and obstruction to vehicular and pedestrian traffic see eviction as a solution," (Nambiar 1999: 40-41).

Thus, first large-scale evictions were conducted in 1958, a year after the second state-level elections in what was then the Bombay State in the newly-independent India. The now-familiar pattern of brutal evictions and resettlement—which amounted to little more than dumping on barren or waterlogged scrubland—was employed; 4,000 families were picked up from all over Mumbai and left to fend for themselves in the mangrove marshes of Mankhurd, in what was then in the very remote north-eastern suburbs that had only skeletal transport links with the city. This was in Janata Colony, which had emerged a decade earlier as one of the first state government-created slums in the MMR. Groups from various parts of the city were dumped in Janata Colony through the 1960s (after the old Bombay State was reorganised into the states of Gujarat and Maharashtra). Later, during the national political Emergency in 1976, around 40,000 of its residents were moved further north-east to Cheetah Camp, in Turbhe (Trombay)[10].

Cheetah Camp was created in the early 1950s by removing the pavement dwellers from central city areas. Then in 1967, after the national and state level elections in which the Congress Party won elections at both levels, Morarji Desai, who had earlier been the Chief Minister of Bombay State and was now Deputy Prime Minister of the country, decided he wanted to make Bombay like Paris, perhaps inspired by the latter's large-scale demolition, cleansing and reorganising by Baron Hausmann. This led to shifting of slum dwellers from central parts of the city to the margins in ward M, where the Cheetah Camp was. Over time, the slum dwellers built up their own colony by developing the site. But, they were re-evicted in 1976 because it was realised that they were near the Atomic Research Station, Turbhe. "We formed an action committee, we said we would resist. Well, it took 12,000 police to evict us in 1976. They evicted 70,000 people. In our place they accommodated 3,000. But of course, they were scientists and officials" (A. Jockin quoted by Seabrook 1987: 150). The evicted slum dwellers were pushed to a site only two to three kilometres from the earlier location of Cheetah Camp, once again on a land in low lying area, close to the sea that got flooded in times of high tide (Seabrook 1987: 154). The process goes on; once the slum dwellers fill up the land, it gets noticed by the planners, developers and builders and then the slum dwellers are evicted again.

By the 1970s, the authorities began to realise that slums—or informal settlements of the urban poor—were going to be a persistent feature of rapid and uneven economic development and urbanisation, and also that they were going to develop into a politically sensitive entity, given that they were going to house so many of the city's voters. Around this time, some policies to 'improve' or 'upgrade' the quality of infrastructure in these shanties were started, with such thrust also coming from the World Bank (Mahadevia 2003b), though the demolition of slums as a means of clearing land for economic or upper-income residential uses continued alongside.

The Emergency years of 1975-77, when then Prime Minister Indira Gandhi temporarily suspended a range of constitutional rights and freedoms in the name of perceived internal threat to the smooth running of the Nation State, saw large-scale and extremely brutal demolitions of informal housing settlements in urban centres around the country, most notably in Delhi and Mumbai. At this time, the first official 'slum census' was conducted, as a measure to soften the impact of the demolitions, and 630,000 hutments in Mumbai were 'registered' and issued photo-passes[11]. In reality, this accordance of legitimacy turned out to be fragile, with no guarantee against further eviction and only tenuous promise of another settlement location, typically without any assurance of tenure.

From then on, the practice of granting 'regularisation', which has since helped to turn the whole issue of slum growth, eviction, resettlement and management into entirely and solely political activity, had been set in motion. On eve of every national or state-level election, political parties—most often the Congress—would promise to 'regularise' or recognise the existence of slum-dwellers who could show proof of their having lived in the same place prior to a given cut-off date. After the election, there would be a period of intense and large-scale demolition, either preceded or followed by the issuance of the ordinance promising protection up to a given cut-off date—which slum-dwellers grew to realise would be extended at the time of the next election. Thus, after 1980, when the Congress-I party won in both the national and state-level elections, the cut-off date was extended to the year 1980.

A year later, in 1981, A.R. Antulay, the Congress-I CM of Maharashtra state at the time, decided that all residents of Mumbai who lived in informal settlements or squatted on the roadside pavements of major roads, and did not possess photo-passes had to 'return to their native places' 'voluntarily'. In July 1981, the MCGM evicted 10,000 people and another 90,000 would have been evicted if Bombay High Court had not given the stay order (Economic and Political Weekly 1982: 801). Several thousand such individuals were packed into buses and dropped off in the wilderness outside city limits and asked to find their way back 'home', even though for most of these people, the home was Mumbai and most family links were within the city. Again, in a pattern that has since become familiar, this extreme attempt to demonstrate State power was met with widespread public censure and an overt reminder from locally elected politicians that it was the all-important 'vote-bank' that had been disturbed and uprooted so unceremoniously.

However, the demolitions continued apace through the 1980s. After the Supreme Court order of 1985 which said, among other things, that slum units could not be demolished during the rains and also without adequate notice, the MCGM and the Government of Maharashtra (GoM) formulated 'Operation Demolition' Plan, Phase-I according to which around 15,000 families were to be evacuated (Singh 1986: 684). Instances have been documented of repeated demolition of a slum if the dwellers have resettled on the evacuated site. In 1985 alone, Sanjay Gandhi Nagar in Bombay, located between Cuffe Parade and Nariman Point, the posh commercial district of the city, was demolished 44 times (Singh 1986: 685). *Teen Dongri* slums in Bombay were demolished four times in 1981 and three times in 1985 (Singh 1986). Amar *Zopadpatti* located near Mahalakshmi racecourse for 20 years, was demolished in 1986 and residents deported to Dindoshi resettlement colony (sites and services project). Another slum, named Mori Road *Zopadpatti*, established in 1960 with 1,500 huts near Mahim station in the heart of Bombay (island city), was demolished in March, 1986 (Singh 1986).

Slowly, there was a move towards the recognition that if slum-dwellers were to be evicted, they had to be provided with alternative sites—even if only to squat on new lands pending the next round of displacement. In the 1980s, land was occasionally given on lease to slum-dwellers and soft loans were extended for what came to be known in the official parlance as 'upgradation' projects. Such projects could only be implemented on land that the State had gained control of through land-acquisition legislation like the Urban Land Ceiling and Regulation (ULCR) Act of 1976, and only if the land had not been reserved under the Development Plan for some other purpose.

In 1985, the World Bank offered an aid package of Rs. 282 crores for the city to help 'upgrade' 80,000 slum units, and also to provide 'sites-and-services' plots to another 65,000 families that needed to be resettled following eviction.

This year was a landmark year for the Mumbai slum-dweller in many ways. It was a year that marked significant political developments in the city and the state. It was the first time that a government other than and completely unrelated and unsympathetic to the Congress-I party gained control of the municipal corporation (MCGM)—it was the year that marked the gaining of office by the Shiv Sena party. To show that he meant business, Bal Thackeray, the leader of the Shiv Sena, ordered a comprehensive cleansing of all the city's estimated 500,000 'pavement dwellers' and several million slum-dwellers, declaring that "there was no question of showing any humanity", and that the city of Mumbai was not "the country's orphanage"[12]. This action left the Congress-I party, which was still in power at the state and central levels and was preparing to celebrate the centenary year of its existence with a huge public event in Mumbai, in a delicate position. The party had always been caught between its state-level legislators, who wanted to cleanse Mumbai of its migrant population, its representatives in the city who had won their positions by promising local slum-dwellers protection, and its national-level leaders who also wished to follow the party's stated policy of looking after the country's poor. Local Congressmen had been burnt by Antulay's 1981 evictions and did not want the Sena-controlled corporation's demolition plans to go through. They took the matter to the country's Supreme Court and got the mass demolition stalled just in time for the party celebration. During the celebration, then Congress-I President and national Prime Minister Rajiv Gandhi pledged Rs. 100 crores of his office's discretionary funds to Mumbai's slum upgradation efforts, especially in Dharavi, the city's largest and most visible slum—in what came to be known as the 'Prime Minister's Grant Project'.

At the time, a report produced by Rudolf C. Heredia for the Committee for the Right to Housing, titled 'Settlements and Shelter:

Alternative Housing for the Urban Poor in Bombay', made the following impassioned observations:

> "[S]lums are seen to be places festering with filth and fetid odours, unfit for human habitation. And so they must be demolished and eradicated, removed far away or hidden from sight. They are an eyesore that embarrasses us before our foreign tourists. [Slumdwellers] are dismissed as depraved, criminals, trespassers, a problem for the police, undeserving of our care. Here slums are perceived as an 'aesthetic' problem and the sensitivity to our foreign image allowed to outweigh any civic concern for our fellow citizens.
>
> "... how do we provide shelter for those whose labour is bought so cheap they are unable to afford conventional housing? This demands a more creative response than the bulldozer! ... But slums are illegal! Legality is a convenient stick which the sophisticated and privileged use to beat the simple and the disadvantaged. [W]e all know how building regulations, zoning laws, floor-space indices and the whole facade of legislation can be manipulated, changed and made flexible enough to 'legalise' powerful interests willing to pay a price. [A]lmost everyone who buys or rents conventional housing must pay for a large proportion of the transaction in 'black' money. Does not this make almost all of us living in conventional houses, law-breakers? It may be dictated by the compulsions of the market, but is it any the less illegal than what the slumdweller does out of necessity? Where does the greater moral justification lie? ...
>
> "The Government has had the power to acquire land for public purposes since the Land Acquisition Act of 1894. According to one study ... some 8,000 hectares of vacant land [out of a total Greater Bombay area [of 40,000 hectares] could be declared surplus and acquired... The direct economic returns on housing the urban poor are so low that neither the market nor even the Government are inclined to allocate available land for it. In spite of the dire human need for shelter, urban land lies vacant because there are larger profits waiting to be made with it in other ways... [M]iddle class stereotypes can be unsympathetic and harsh. Squatters are seen as unemployed parasites, criminals, depraved, without any drive to self-improvement. If they are given better housing, they sell it and go back to where they were. ... The profile that emerges [from a cited slum census]

> presents a rather different picture ... In an average household of 4.38 persons, 1.47 were workers... [S]lumdwellers were not very differently employed than the rest of the city population, except for markedly white-collar [professions] like financing, insurance, real estate and business services. A recent census of pavement dwellers covering 20,293 families ... showed [that] only 3 per cent of the families had no earning member... This data is far from supportive of the middle-class stereotypes... Yet these persist because such stereotyping conveniently distances us from the social realities of the slumdwellers and from any moral responsibility for them..."[13]

Even today, there is not much change about the perceptions about the slum dwellers and the same legalistic argument used to deny them their rights in the city.

Predictably enough, this period of upheaval was followed by a government circular declaring that all slum-dwellers in Mumbai would be 'regularised' at their current locations upto a cut-off date at the end of 1985. Soon thereafter, the People's Union for Civil Liberties (PUCL) produced a report in which it included a note prepared by the state government's Additional Collector for Bombay stating that there were over 6,000 acres of vacant lands available in just three neighbourhoods in the suburbs of Andheri, Borivali and Kurla where over six million people could be housed. Simultaneously, talk of contracting out this job of providing housing for the poor to the private sector, and of making it attractive by allowing a part of it to be sold at market rates, started gaining ground. The MHADA, with the support of World Bank funding, proposed what it referred to as a 'cafeteria approach'—a mix of slum 'improvement', 'upgradation', 'reconstruction' and 'relocation' schemes that would benefit a little less than 2,000 slum colonies with over three million inhabitants.

Even as many of these comparatively benign policies were being implemented, demolitions and evictions continued apace. Apart from political motivations on the part of the local State, and administrative decisions taken by the local bureaucracy, the judiciary too played its part in the whole exercise. An interesting, if bizarre and often tragic case is the one triggered by the demolition notice served in 1979 on a godown (store-house) owned by a certain Syed Zubair Hyder Akbar Mian in the eastern suburb of Ghatkoper. Akbar Mian formulated a proposition that his structure ought to be legalised since the same had been done in the case of lakhs (millions) of people in Mumbai who had encroached on public lands. After the city civil court threw his case out, Akbar Mian went to the state-level High Court, where, in mid-1990, Justice Sharad Manohar wanted to know if the state government really had such a policy of regularisation and whether such a policy was constitutionally valid and further, on his own initiative, called several municipal and state government bureaucrats to testify in this respect. While the case was still pending, Manohar then took—by his own admission—almost unprecedented step of calling a press conference and declaring that he wanted a debate on the subject of slum-dwellers and unauthorised constructions in Mumbai and whether the problem could be dealt with through a combination of blocking further in-migration and the rehabilitation of some of those who were already in the city[14]. The judge then went on to convert the individual's petition into a public-interest and delivered an order directing the state government to issue demolition notices to all 'encroachers'—whom he defined as people who could not prove their presence in the city before the most recently issued cut-off date of 1985[15].

The State machinery immediately took the opportunity to demolish over 600 huts before a division bench of the same High Court quashed Judge Manohar's order, stating that he had no right to use an individual case to give the state government carte blanche for demolishing homes all over the city[16]. Subsequently, protection was extended to all slum-dwellers until a revised cut-off date of 1990. Surely not by coincidence, 1990 was an election year in which the Shiv Sena gained control of the state government, while retaining its hold over the municipal corporation.

The following year (1991) marked a turning point in the country's economic history, when a newly elected Congress-I government at the national level publicly abandoned its decades-old socialist rhetoric and embraced a policy of economic liberalisation and globalisation. From then on, the goal was first to be like Singapore and later, as China emerged as a global economic giant, like Shanghai.

As mentioned earlier, one of the first ways in which the local State could demonstrate its preparedness for the new economic order—with the support of the local business elite as well as the bulk of that section of the middle classes that expected to benefit the most from the economic changes—was by engaging in highly visible and sustained campaign of slum demolition. Throughout the 1990s, this campaign was kept up, even as the state introduced the concept of the SRS whereby the private sector redeveloped slums in return for extra buildable capacity that it could sell on the open market. This scheme was later on renamed Slum Redevelopment Scheme (SRD).

Table 18.1: Yearwise Slum Demolitions in the 1990s, Mumbai[17]

Year	*Slum Dwellings Demolished*
1994	55,784
1995	62,385
1996	84,681
1997	108,322
1998	49,154

A newspaper report sums up the history of slum demolition in Mumbai in the 1990s (Table 18.1). It goes on to add that till 1998, the local corporation had managed to demolish an average of 50 units every day. By February 1999, it was doing away with 500 hutments a day, and still the end was nowhere in sight—primarily because the authorities were not doing very much with the demolished land and many of the evictees had simply rebuilt their homes on the original sites—only to have them broken down again and again in subsequent attacks. The morbid futility of this kind of brutality does not seem to be something that bothers local authorities.

One of the most shocking examples of sustained criminal violence against alleged squatters in Mumbai, prior to the 2004-05 demolitions is the clearance of settlements in the Sanjay Gandhi National Park in suburban Mumbai. Though the biggest sustained orgy of demolition activity committed against the over 400,000 people living in this area occurred in 2000, this focused act of aggression still continues intermittently. In a context where there are several areas of doubt and dispute, including the fact that the park's boundaries are unclear, that several of the settlements existed prior to the notification of these boundaries and some of them are old, tribal villages, and finally, that there is confusion over where the evicted people who are considered eligible for resettlement might be resettled, given that an environment group, the Bombay Environmental Action Group, is resisting most of the most viable proposed locations, the one thing that is unambiguous is the extremely brutal nature of the demolitions. As an example, here is the description of the demolition of one of the settlements in the National Park, quoted from the report of the Indian People's Human Rights Tribunal on these demolitions (IPHRC 2000:57-58):

> "Bhimnagar is a large basti of over 5,000 households claimed by the forest department to be on the land of the Sanjay Gandhi National Park. It borders the Otis Company and the Mahindra and Mahindra factory. The old slum is supposedly protected by the 1995 policy of

the Maharashtra government [to assure protection from eviction to slums in existence prior to 1995]. The state government has also passed a order—vide a notification of the Housing Department dated June 5, 2000 signed by Deputy Secretary R.D. Salvi—staying demolitions till September 30, 2000. But the forest department, armed with a High Court order, claims that a majority of the people had not paid the 'rehab' fees of Rs 7,000 and were thus not eligible for protection. The slum was demolished in the months of April and May this year [2000], after which a majority of the people paid the Rs 7,000 fixed by the High Court. However, no alternative rehab sites have been given to the people as yet, and most Bhimnagar families were forced to eke out a living at the old demolished sites.

"It is in this background that the forest department officials, accompanied by a company of policemen of the Samata Nagar Police Station came for a second round of demolitions on Saturday, July 22 at around noon. Pleadings by the people that the government itself had passed an order stating that demolitions would be suspended during the monsoon fell on deaf ears. Thereafter there was stiff resistance to the demolition operation. The police fired two rounds in the air and tear gas was freely used. In retaliation, several local boys used the rubble on the site to throw missiles at the police. Ultimately, the police and the forest department officials together with the demolition labour beat a retreat without being able to conduct much demolition. It was in this melee and chaos that Asha Pandey [a resident] had a stroke and died, residents reported.

"Almost acting in revenge, the police and forest department wrecked havoc on the residents of the basti the next day—Sunday, July 23. The local police reinforced by a battalion of the SRP first surrounded the basti at about 11.00 am. In order not to alert the people they left their vehicles near the highway and entered the area through the compound of the neighbouring Mahindra and Mahindra company. After cordoning off the slum, the forest department officials entered the basti demolishing existing houses and beating all those they could lay their hands on. The brutality of the police was unprecedented. Old women, small children and even pleading women were not spared the lathi blows. Simultaneously, the demolition workers along with two bulldozers pushed the people's household goods and building material into neat mounds and set them on fire so that they could not build again. The burning and beating operation continued till 6.00 pm in the evening. Around 45 people were arrested including the local corporator Ms Bharti Pandagale. At least a dozen people suffered broken limbs and were admitted in serious condition to the local municipal hospital in Borivali. Many were turned away despite serious injuries, residents complained." [Several of the victims of this series of demolitions were permanently incapacitated or killed as a result of the brutal physical assault by the police.]

The rhetoric remains the same, though the ideal to be emulated changes from time to time, depending on current socio-economic and political goals. If Mumbai wanted to be Paris in the 1950s and 1960s, New York in the 1970s and 1980s, it wanted to be Singapore in the first phase of liberalisation in the 1990s and then Shanghai in the 2000s. And so, at the end of 2004 and in early 2005, once again large-scale demolitions took place. Shanghai, without her knowledge, became the motivator of demolitions in Mumbai. Every time, it has been the state government's decision to carry out the demolitions and every time, it is the municipal corporation that carries out the demolitions. It is not the mayor of the city but the municipal commissioner who is the state government's representative, who is in charge of the demolitions.

Every new economic opportunity brings possibility of increase in property prices. Every increase in property prices in Mumbai, also leads to rash demolition drive. In the immediate wake of reforms, from 1992-95, property prices increased drastically in Mumbai. In 1994, there was a large-scale demolitions in Mumbai. In 2004-05, the property market has picked up with the expectations that lands in the middle of the city would be made available for real estate project. It resulted in slum demolitions.

The Process and Prognosis of Recent Demolitions

The last spate of demolitions of 94,000 homes is part of what is called the 'Mumbai Makeover Plan'[18] or 'Shanghaing Mumbai'. The demolitions were carried out on 44 sites. An estimated 288.80 acres of land was cleared of slums (IPTEHR 2005: 10). Of this, 272.8 acres belong to the GoM and 16 acres to the MCGM. The other available estimates of lands cleared are: (i) 216 acres cleared of slums, of which 16 acres belong to the MCGM and 200 acres to the GoM's various departments by the *Mid Day*[19] (a daily of Mumbai, and (ii) 306 acres by the MCGM (Table 18.2), in early January, 2005. We accept the MCGM's figures.

As mentioned above, 5.8 million population (48.5%) of the total 11.91 million population of the BMC lived in slums in 2001 (population census data). Of this, 450,000 were evicted, that is 7.8 per cent of the slum population was thrown out. Newspapers have called it 'Operation Shanghai'[20].

In the last week of November 2004, the Deputy Chief Minister (DyCM) of Maharashtra called a meeting to set up a committee comprising heads of government departments owning land in Mumbai, to prevent further encroachments on public lands in the city. The important ones who attended the meeting were: the MCGM, the MHADA and the MMRDA. The committee's agenda was to chalk out an action plan to save the government lands from encroachment, mainly referring to slums. The DyCM issued a warning in this meeting to the government employees that any one found issuing fake photo-passes to slum-dwellers would be punished.

Table 18.2: Extent of Lands Cleared of Slums and Their Ownership and Proposed Use[21]

Plot Location	*Area (acres approx.)*	*Ownership and use*
Ambujwadi, Malvani	25	Government land, reserved for non development zone (NDZ)
Land near Asmita Nagar, Marve road	25	Government land, reserved as NDZ (creek land)
Ali Talao, Marve Road	20	Government land, reserved as NDZ
Shataram Talao, on W.E Highway, Kurur	5	Government land, recreation ground/playground
Muttumari Nagar	8	BMC land, Recreation ground/playground and road
Shivaji Nagar	15	BMC land, road and dumping ground
New Mandala, Govandi	50	Government land, reserved as NDZ
Sathe Nagar, Deonar	25	Government land, development plan road and housing for dishoused
Maharashtra Nagar, Mankhurd	20	Government land, reserved as NDZ
Suman Nagar, Chembur	3	BMC land, secondary school and recreation ground (Fencing already sanctioned)
Netaji Nagar, Ghatkopar	100	PWD, proposed public housing
Laxmi Nagar, Goregaon	10	Private recreation ground, garden and parking
Total Land	306	

The last cut-off date for issuance of photo-passes to the slum dwellers was set at 1995. This was done through the amendment of Maharashtra Slum Areas (Improvement, Clearance and Redevelopment) (Second Amendment) Act, 2001. This amendment made encroaching a cognisable offence, in which the encroacher, the abettor and the competent authority are all liable for appropriate action if found guilty. This was ostensibly a warning to the lower rungs of officers in the administration to refrain from taking bribes from the slum dwellers to turn a blind eye to the encroachments.

Further, the DyCM also instructed to set up encroachment removal squads, each squad comprising of an assistant municipal commissioner, a police officer, junior civic engineer and police constables. The squad was given a digital camera to photograph illegal slums as proof and powers by the civic body to immediately take action against the illegal slum after lodging a complaint. "It's good news as most of our time is wasted in lodging complaints. Now that action can be taken on the spot, the encroacher will not get a chance to move court", an assistant municipal commissioner said.[22] Every ward[23] office was asked to prepare a list of illegal slums in their ward for the purpose of removal. The determination of the DyCM was strong. The Municipal Commissioner, the state government nominee as administrative head in the Municipal Corporation, co-ordinated the demolitions. The DyCM says, "I have asked police officers to charge those who build new slums under MCOCA[24]." The instructions were also to not let political interference (from municipal corporators), to stop the demolitions[25]. The state government prepared to bypass the local elected representatives to carry out slum demolitions.

From the beginning of December 2004, the demolitions of hutments that came up after 1995, started. Whether only those huts that came after 1995 were demolished or not is contestable, but, the BMC then claimed that it was so. When the facts came out, it was found that with the illegal hutments, even the legal ones got demolished. Everyone in a targeted settlement, whether had a photo-pass or not, suffered eviction.

The BMC also came up with the idea of seeking 'citizen's participation' in the demolition drive[26]. Contact phone numbers were given out where 'citizens' could inform the authorities about encroachments. Thus, people's participation was being sought for removal of slums and slum dwellers from the city and not in improving governance, stemming corruption and improving the basic living conditions in the city!

A group of 'prominent citizens' indeed formed a Citizens Action Group (CAG) to carry forward their support for slum demolitions and to act as a pressure group in the city in favour of demolitions. The members of the CAG, like the DyCM, were apprehensive of the likely intervention by local political leaders (the municipal corporators) to stop demolitions, as in the past. Thus, they gave a statement to the tune that they would support the CM and the DyCM in this matter even if the latter two were under the pressure from their own political parties to halt demolitions. The members of Bombay First (or Mumbai First) group, that calls itself an NGO and behind the Mumbai Makeover Plan, also joined the CAG. The CAG sought an appointment with Sonia Gandhi, the President of the Congress-I to impress upon her not to halt the ongoing slum demolition drive[27] fearing that as a Party President of the Congress-I, she might just do that.

Bombay First's executive officer said: (i) they fully supported the CM's drive on illegal slum demolitions; (ii) if Mumbai has to be a World Class City, the slums have to go and for which strong and urgent steps were needed to be taken; (iii) any encroachment of public property should not be tolerated and had to be dealt in accordance with rule of law[28] . The position that the Bombay First's executive took was quite in tune with the vociferous opinion of the several middle-class (in effect the elite) opinion makers. The proof of this is; when the *Indian Express* newspaper, an English daily, conducted an opinion poll putting the question, "Do you back the Maharashtra government's slum demolition drive in Mumbai?" over 84 per cent of respondents said 'yes', less than 2 per cent said they couldn't say, and just under 14 per cent said a firm 'no'[29]. The readers of *Indian Express* are certainly not the slum dwellers or the low income groups, and are generally the English speaking elites.

The displaced slum-dwellers were not welcomed anywhere else in Mumbai or towns/cities in the Mumbai Urban Agglomeration (MUA). The residents of Thane, another corporation in the MUA, did not allow the Mumbai's evicted slums dwellers to settle down in slums in Thane[30]. The Thane Municipal Corporation had set up three squads to keep vigil and monitor developments in its slums[31]. The Thane Corporation is ruled by Shiv Sena—BJP combine and hence was all the more vigilant not to let Mumbai's slum dwellers resettle in their jurisdiction. The situation this time was quite different than the previous demolitions when the slum dwellers could move on to the city periphery and resettle on the marginalised lands.

The brutality of the demolitions has been captured in the depositions of the slum dwellers as presented to the Indian Peoples Tribunal on Environment and Human Rights (IPTEHR 2005). Some other examples besides the one stated at the start of the chapter:

On December 9, the second day of demolition, a slum-dweller burnt himself to death in the hope that the act would stop the bulldozers from razing his home of 10 years, an 800-sq-ft. room in a slum in Pereirawadi, opposite the five-star Tulip hotel in Juhu, north-west Mumbai. Such protest had helped in the past, but not this time. The plot on which the slum was located was earmarked for a car park, as per a plan of beautification of Juhu beach approved by the High Court. The 40-year-old person was allowed to burn. No one was allowed to come near him to save his life. The wife and the son of the person were occupied with salvaging their belongings unaware that the man was burning outside.[32]

Narendra Panigrahi of Sathe Nagar, Mankhurd said (IPTEHR 2005: 20-1) that he had seen demolitions 5-6 times in his life. "But there is no precedence to this demolition. Earlier, despite demolition, we managed to stay, but this time we are not even allowed to stay after demolition. If we request to stay, we are tortured. Police often call and beat us. They come late at night, around 12 or 1 and enquire about who was providing us with water and other facilities. They forcibly take people to the police station and release them in the morning. Not a single house is left. No one can rent another house."

Ramzan Hasmat of Rafiq Nagar said (IPTEHR 2005: 23-4): "On 30 November 2004[33], we were served notice directing us to vacate our houses within 24 hours. On December 1, our houses were demolished... We removed our belongings. BMC bulldozers demolished houses. Then, they also removed us from the place where we had kept our belongings. .... The next day they came again with bulldozers and took away all our belongings, including food items, etc. Now people do not even have a glass to drink water. Two people died ... an 8 year old girl and a 21 year old women due to cold."

Deepak Kumar Roy from Indira Nagar—3, Maharashtra Nagar, Mankhurd (IPTEHR 2005: 25): "We have been staying there since 1990. ... we had filed an application with DM against the demolition of 1993. We have voter ID cards and Ration cards also. But, defying all documents, houses were demolished as if we were beggars and we do not count at all. ... We were told to run away with our belongings or face legal action. ...On 1 December, the police came with the BMC and demolished all houses. Still we would not go anywhere. We are staying in a makeshift arrangement there only. ... from 2-5 January, they cleared our houses totally. We are framed with cases and on the other side our houses are demolished also. ... We met our Corporator, ... for a solution. But we were told to keep away from the police and from protesting as they are helpless. ... The police tell us to catch any train and go back."

The target for demolition was 44,000 hutments. Of that, 39,000 were flattened in 18 days' time[34]. But, in the end, more than 90,000 hutments were demolished. The DyCM, to balance hutment demolition, asked the

BMC to prepare a list of illegal constructions by builders and shop keepers. But this, the Municipal Commissioner acknowledged, was not going to be easy as this category of encroachers would have to be served notices before demolition—notices which would immediately be challenged in court[35]. In some cases, this happened. The BMC's plan to demolish illegal bungalows on Madh island, used for film shooting and owned by the rich and powerful, and not very far from Malvani, could not be carried out as the bungalows' owners obtained an injunction from the court[36].

Some of the people affected by this demolition have faced repeated evictions in the past. Besides the statement of one of the affected persons above, other examples are: in 1994, a Bandra slum was demolished and families were shifted to Ambujwadi in Malvani, Malad. In 2004, Ambujwadi was demolished and the same people became homeless[37]. This settlement was one of the first ones to be demolished (IPTEHR 2005: 10). In an interview to Indian Express reporter Kavitha Iyer, on January 9, 2005[38], Dalit[39] leader Ramdas Athavale acknowledges that there were many supporters of his Republican Party of India in the Ambujwadi slum. Many of them were living in Bandra's Lal Mitti slum till 1994, and were moved to Ambujwadi in 1994, after he convinced them to move.

People had shifted from slums in Worli after the 1993-94 evictions to some slums in Malvani. In the IPT report of 1994 (IPT 1994), the case of the Mahakalinagar demolition is mentioned, which states that most of the persons residing in this slum had earlier been residents of Sidharthnagar in Worli. When Sidharthnagar was demolished in 1964, they were shifted to a site along a *nullah* (ditch, canal or rivulet) in Mahakalinagar. The authorities were aware that it was not safe to reside on the *nullah*. As a result, in 1993, a part of the *nullah* collapsed, 200 houses collapsed, and some 5 people died. Those affected were relocated at Oshiwara (Goregaon), 20 kms away. In 1994 June, another 500 houses were demolished (pp. 7-8), after giving notices and offering an alternate accommodation at Malvani. People were expected to pay between Rs. 5,000 to Rs. 10,000. At this new site (Malvani) the land was leased to the residents with the provision that it would be returned to the government whenever the government required. There was to be no security of tenure. And that is what happened. In 2004-05, people who had shifted from Worli and Bandra in the previous demolitions to Ambujwadi, were evicted again, as the state government wanted the land back.

In the communal riots of 1992-93, when Shiv Sena cadres went after the Muslims, the affected population left for Muslim-dominated areas.

Some of them (coming from all over Mumbai) moved to the site of the Azimnagar slum in Malvani and resettled there. The Bombay *Aman* (Peace) Committee rehabilitated 6,000 people in Azimnagar, after giving them documents of their residence. Azimnagar has now been demolished and the residents have became homeless again. The *Aman* Committee had given half the amount and the other half of Rs. 10,000 for a 150 sq ft room was given by the affected people.[40]

YUVA (Youth for Voluntary Action and Unity) immediately carried out a primary survey in 28 slums to assess whether the claim of the MCGM that only huts built after 1995 were demolished and to estimate the cost of demolition found that 2,405 (6%) houses of the total 41,900 demolished in 28 surveyed slums had come up before 1995 and the rest 39,495 had come up between 1995-2000. If the cut-off date had been extended to 2000, as promised by the election manifesto of the ruling party, then none of the houses demolished would have qualified for demolition! Further, one slum with 1,205 houses was demolished once before; 14 slums with 17,688 houses were demolished 2-5 times and 6 slums with 15,660 houses were demolished more than 5 times.

If the total value of a single demolished house is considered to be modest Rs. 10,000, then the total value lost would be Rs. 41.90 crores (Rs. 419 million or US$ 9.63 million[41]) in these 28 slums. If Rs. 5,000 spent by each household for land-filling on the site was added then the total value added by the slum-dwellers in the 28 slums would come to Rs. 628.5 million (US$ 14.45 million). If this figure is extrapolated to cover 94,000 units, this demolition amounted to a loss of Rs. 1,410 million (US$ 32.41 million) or 0.2 per cent of the city's GDP. The absolute figure is large, but, not so large in comparison to the city's economy for the city to care. The per unit loss of Rs. 15,000 is on the lower side. If average of Rs. 20,000 to Rs. 25,000 is considered to have been invested by the slum dwellers than the total loss would come to about 0.5 per cent of the city's GDP. The MCGM has also spent financial resources on the demolition drive, estimated to be Rs. 84 Crores (Rs. 840 million or US$ 19.31 million) (IPTEHR 2005: 28-9).

The Fight Back and Policy Formulation

The slum-dwellers and housing and human rights activists have given a fight back to this spate of demolitions. Initially, the slum dwellers had dispersed from the site, but, then they came back on the site and stayed on. Some did return to their villages. Some have tried shifting to places like Thane where, as mentioned earlier, they were prevented from settling. But, large numbers of affected have, subsequently, decided to erect semblance of shanties in the same place. For example, in Maharashtra Nagar in Mankhurd, the residents did not go scouting around for rented accommodation, they did not fill tempos with their household goods and did not move. People salvaged whatever they could from the debris and re-erected their houses on the old spot[42]. Newspapers have also cited that people remained on the demolished sites till a long time. For example, on January 23, 2005's *Indian Express* found that people were still living at Maharashtra Nagar, Mankhurd; Ambujwadi Malvani; Ganesh Murti Nagar, Cuffe Parade and Azimnagar Malad[43]. Large numbers of people did not leave the city like the authorities had hoped they would but hung on the site as they have no place to go.

Returning back to the demolished sites, in cases where the slum dwellers had dispersed also happened in many places. From the first week of February onwards, people started rebuilding their huts on the lands where they were squatting. They also resisted the bulldozers. In Worli, for example, people fought the bulldozers till the bulldozers returned. In Mulund, in Rafiqnagar, slum dwellers broke the barbed wire fence and entered the slum plot[44]. Women took a lead in many places; they marched to their original sites and put up their huts. Medha Patkar led the *morcha* (procession) in Vikhroli[45]. The same was the case with Ambujwadi in Malvani, where, women had re-erected their huts, as already discussed before. It was the women who picked up bamboo and tarpaulins to rebuilt threads of their demolished lives. Along with Medha Patkar, other human rights activists and organisations and some NGOs joined the resistance.

On February 1, the MCGM said that 200 acres of lands that were cleared of slums were reoccupied by the slum-dwellers. Since there was no plan and no protection for the vacated plots, and since the plots were to be developed by the MMRDA, which also did not have any plans for development, land was reoccupied. A February 11, 2005 newspaper report (*Times of India*, Mumbai) states that officials of the MMRDA expressed their unhappiness with the fact that 18 of the 21 cleared sites were re-encroached upon by the slum dwellers when MMRDA went to survey them.

Medha Patkar met the CM on Feb 1, 2005 with a delegation of slum dwellers, under the *Zopadi Bachao Sanyukta Kruti Samiti*, with the demand to immediately stop the demolition drive, rebuild the demolished huts, provide compensation for the damages suffered and regularise the huts that came up before 2000[46]. The affected slum-dwellers then registered their protests publicly in many peaceful but visible ways. For instance, they took to the streets in a demonstration on Feb. 2, 2005. Then on Feb 9, they protested in front of the Mantralaya (state legislative assembly building), when they were arrested[47].

Resistance came from some other quarters as well. As early as December 30, 2004, Maharashtra Minorities Front, through their lawyer, sent a legal notice to the CM asking why the CM was not fulfilling the election promise of extending the date for photo pass to 2000. The slum-dwellers whose huts were erected between 1995 and 2000 voted for the current government, but now they faced demolitions.

Some of the Congress-I members of Legislative Assembly (MLA) and members of Parliament (MP) elected from Mumbai raised their objections to the ongoing demolitions[48]. Some of them had intervened to stop the demolitions in the past[49] had also spent the development funds available with them for slum development. One MP, the film star Govinda and one MLA met the Municipal Commissioner after they were accused of not doing anything[50].

Together, they represented to the Congress-I party's national President Sonia Gandhi, about negative fall out of the demolitions. The CM, as early as the third week of December 2004, agreed to stall demolitions of slums constructed before April 2000 and made an unofficial announcement to this effect[51]. Sonia Gandhi summoned the CM, Vilasrao Deshmukh and Congress-I Party chief of Maharashtra unit to Delhi on February 16, 2005 to ask for an explanation of the decision to demolish and to find out what the plans of the state government were there to take care of the negative fallout of the demolitions[52].

A delegation of slum dwellers led by Medha Patkar also met Sonia Gandhi in New Delhi. On face of slum dwellers' resistance and also resistance from within Congress-I party, Sonia Gandhi wrote to the CM that the evicted slum dwellers must be allowed to return to their original plots till the state government found alternative sites to rehabilitate them. She further asked the state government to quickly carry out a survey in collaboration with the affected people and the NGOs to record how many were evicted and who among them came before 2000. She also suggested immediate withdrawing of cases against the slum dwellers. On June 6, 2005, the state government sent instructions to the MCGM to stall demolitions during the monsoon on humanitarian grounds.

Margaret Alva of Congress-I, who came in as emissary of Sonia Gandhi after the demolitions opined that the slum demolitions were against the Common Minimum Programme (CMP) of the United

Progressive Alliance (UPA). "Make everything for the masses and not for the classes," she said at a panel discussion at the Indian Merchants' Chamber on converting Mumbai into an international city[53]. This statement was also in reaction to the projection of ongoing road projects by the Chamber as development. She further added that instead of talking of just trans-harbour link and flyovers, the state government pay attention to buses and trains by which 90 per cent of Mumbai's population travel. In essence, the message was clear, the present 'City Makeover Plan' was not acceptable to the Congress-I's central leadership. With local pressure and also from the Congress-I's national President, the CM agreed to discuss modalities of legalising slums upto 2000 on February 16, 2005.

After directions from Sonia Gandhi, the CM came up with the idea to not just extend the cut-off date of 2000 for legalising slums but also a promise to rehabilitate them in case the slum lands were required for development projects. Implications of that are that post-2000 slums would still be demolished.

In April 2005, the slum-dwellers decided to register their protest against the demolitions and the continuing state of flux in their lives by taking out a procession in downtown Mumbai, near the seat of state government and police headquarters. After an orderly march lasting several hours under continuous police supervision, around 8,000 men, women and children from demolished sites all over the city and suburbs reached Azad Maidan, an open ground in South Mumbai that is commonly used for public protests. Since there were already several groups inside the ground, protest leaders including Medha Patkar asked the group to sit down outside the ground while they negotiated for space with the police authorities present. Suddenly, the police officer in charge ordered his men to attack the crowd with their batons (*lathi*). Many oral as well as visual—on-camera records—confirm that the attack was entirely unprovoked and conducted with no prior warning. In the ensuing melee, several protestors and outside observers, as well as members of the media and activists who were recording the event were severely injured, and one infant died. The IPHRC (Indian Peoples' Human Rights Commission) later requested retired Justice R.B. Mehrotra and J.B. D'Souza former Chief Secretary of Maharashtra to hold an unofficial judicial enquiry into the attack by the baton wielding Mumbai police. Around 80 individuals, including several of those affected and independent observers who had recorded the course of events testified before the commission.

The Commission's Report States:

"Was the demonstration on April 6 at any stage unlawful? We have carefully considered each of the five criteria listed in Sec 141, I[ndian] P[enal] C[ode], but find that none of them could characterize this demonstration. It was a demonstration aimed entirely at calling the attention of the state government and the public of Mumbai to the plight of the dishoused slum people, There was no force whatever, criminal or otherwise; there was no resistance to law or legal process; there was neither mischief nor trespass. The police had escorted the morcha all the way from August Kranti Maidan to Azad Maidan. Had the objective or the means of demonstrating been illegal it was surely the duty of the police to prevent the procession to south Mumbai...

"And as to their conduct on arrival outside Azad Maidan, we have the evidence of independent witnesses, evidence that has emphatically convinced us that there was no truth at all in the claim by A.N.Roy, Police Commissioner, later that day, that the lathi charge was a response to stone throwing. The films shot by [documentary film-maker Anand] Patwardhan and others show no rocks or stones lying on the street after dispersal of the demonstrators. Even the Times of India report on the next day on the incident, ends with a contradiction of his claim. It is disgraceful that a senior officer of the Indian Police Service should descend to fabrication and falsehood to defend the indefensible...

"We are satisfied, on the basis of the oral statements before us, the written statements we received, the films and newspaper cuttings we were shown, photographs and a floppy produced by Dave Ron [a Canadian journalist who was beaten twice by the police], that there was no provocation whatever of any type by the demonstrators which could excuse such brutal and inhuman lathi charge as occurred.

"[T]o give the police an opportunity to establish their version they were invited to appear before us. They did not. If they have an explanation of their conduct, they were not prepared to share it with us, for reasons that we can well understand... We also asked the Deputy CM, who is the Home Minister, to let us meet him. There was no response...

> "There is no justification for the police to have jumped straight to a lathi charge in their decision to disperse the slum dweller's morcha. And when they did so, they did it in the most brutal fashion, thrashing children and women with babes in arms or after they had fallen in flight, accompanying their assaults with obscene abuse, of which witness after witness complained... Altogether, the police did everything wrong; they broke the law, they were barbarous, cruel and deceitful..."[54]

Since neither the police nor the government apparatus chose to respond to this report, the enquiry continues to remain one-sided.

Subsequently, the State of Maharashtra went to the High Court with an application saying that it wanted to extend the cut-off date for slum regularisation to January 1, 2000, and that since it was considering this extension, it wanted to provide temporary accommodation to those who were likely to benefit from this extension at two locations: Ambujwadi, Malad in the western suburbs and Mandala, Mankhurd in the eastern suburbs. The court took upon itself to advise the state government to develop a long-term policy to provide cheap housing to its poor, taking into account the needs of the slum-dwellers, as well as the city's need for open spaces and so on. The judge also asked the state government to take the help of NGOs to conduct a fresh survey of all those affected by the 2004-05 demolitions to base its temporary and long-term relief measures on.

This survey has since been completed and fresh orders were awaited at the time of writing this article. Those involved in the case on behalf of the slum-dwellers, however, point out that the state government has no need to seek sanction in a court of law to extend demolition cut-off dates or offer those affected temporary relief, that both these activities are administrative ones, that the state government is well within its rights to conduct on its own at short notice and that, in fact, it has done so many times in the past. The suggestion is that the act of taking the matter to court—significantly in May, during the court vacation, and several months after the main phase of the demolition had been stalled—is just a means of stalling and buying time until the matter has receded from public memory and administrative decisions are put in place. However, in the course of hearing, the High Court asked those involved on behalf of the slum dwellers to suggest a comprehensive housing policy for Mumbai so that the matter of demolitions do not come up over and again[55].

Meanwhile (at the time of writing this article), Medha Patkar and others had taken to court a separate case, which argues that the whole notion of cut-off dates is wrong and that the State must acquire land under the ULCR Act to build cheap houses for the poor. The State, argue the petitioners, can start by simply acquiring those plots that are already available under the city Development Plan for 'housing the dishoused'. They also argued that if the State creates housing stock that is cheap, easily available and given on some form of license basis, the poor would pay for it and probably improve upon it. The petition further demanded that any big project should be required to incorporate housing for those displaced by it, and this factor should be added as a component of the project cost.

Explaining Slum Demolitions within Democratic Politics

Explanation of the recent slum demolitions lies in city's and state government's politics, politics of specific interest groups around the issue of urban land and changing development ideology in the context of globalisation. The large context of these politics and development ideology is the Indian electoral democracy, where the poor in particular, come out in large numbers to make their voices heard in times when the politicians and the bureaucrats are turning increasingly elitist. The 2004 May elections of the national Parliament and Maharashtra State Assembly are an indication of this.

The then ruling alliance at the centre, the National Democratic Alliance (NDA), led by the BJP, the right wing Hindu Party, as it is called, ran a campaign of 'India Shining', buoyed by the alliance's Prime Minister, Mr. Atal Bihari Vajapayee's immense popularity, nearly completing the full term—elections were called after four and a half years—and perception that India was doing economically very well. But, the India shining campaign did not go well with the common people, particularly with the rural population when farmers were forced to commit suicide. The NDA combine lost the elections. Even the two Chief Ministers with an image of being IT industry supporters—that of Andhra Pradesh and Karnataka—were rejected by the voters. A new centrist alliance, calling itself the UPA, came to power at the national level with support of the left parties from outside. The alliance policies were put out through the CMP document. The CMPs' position on the slums has been stated at the beginning of the chapter. A National Advisory Council (NAC) was set up, drawing known personalities, particularly those working with the poor and the marginalised, as members to monitor the implementation of the CMP. Sonia Gandhi, the President of Congress-I, herself an elected

Member of Parliament, who had declined her nomination as the Prime Minister of India, assumed the role of Chairperson of the NAC. With that, the NAC assumed great power. There was a distinct turn towards a welfare model, a relief from the Hindu communal politics played by the NDA government.

Maharashtra state also went for state legislative assembly elections in May 2004 along with the national Parliament elections, inspite the ruling combine, the Democratic Front (DF) government, comprising of Congress-I and NCP had a risk of facing anti-incumbency. And the DF won again, against the Shiv Sena—BJP alliance. The Shiv Sena is a regional chauvinist party, portraying itself as the party of the 'Sons of the Soil', who also runs anti-Muslim campaigns in general and against Bangladeshi migrants in particular. The Congress-I party did particularly well in constituencies in Mumbai, because it ran its campaign on the promise to cut-off date for slums to 2000.

Within six months of coming to power, the DF government faulted on its election promise and ordered massive demolitions of hutments that had come up after 1996. The DF government played smart politics. At the time of demolitions, the previous amendment of the Slum Act was valid, which set the cut-off date as 1995. To extend the cut-off date to 2000, a new amendment in the law was necessary and before that was done, the CM and DyCM ordered demolitions. The CM holds the urban development portfolio and the DyCM holds home portfolio that has law and order charge and hence it was easy.

By then, Mumbai Vision Plan, 2010, prepared by McKinsey and funded by the Bombay First group was out. To implement the plan, land is required for infrastructure and real estate projects. Also, since half the city's population lives in slums, the latter are visible wherever one goes, when one lands by air in the city, when one comes out of the airport, when one travels on the western express way on the way to the airport, when one goes to Bandra Kurla financial centre, and so on. But, instead of clearing lands in the places where infrastructure would have come up, 140 acres (45.75%) of the 306 acres of land cleared (Table 18.2) were under the NDZ, on the periphery and another 125 acres (40.85%) were meant for public housing or housing of the dishoused! Why were the NDZ lands, largely on the creeks and in the ecologically fragile parts of the city were cleared? There was therefore much more to the demolitions than the forces of globalisation acting on the city and there are many explanations for the need of such massive demolitions.

The first explanation cited, and which is quite a cynical view of Indian electoral politics is to do with the internal political competition in Congress-I in Maharashtra. It was widely stated that the CM does not come from the city and the city voters were not his constituency. On coming to power, he wanted to reduce the popularity of the MLAs elected from Mumbai city and hence he ordered demolitions of slums inspite of the poll promise. It was also argued that Vilasrao Deshmukh had an image of being a weak CM—he was removed from the position in his last stint as CM—and he wanted to prove his capability of taking tough decisions such as slum demolitions.

The second widely cited explanation emanates from another popular understanding that the builder-politician nexus in the state is very powerful and that the political parties take funds from the builders before the elections and release the lands under various reservations to the builders after the elections. Since, the contributions by the builders to the political parties are unaccounted amounts, individual politicians can also rake in money. Hence, there have been many demolitions in the past after the elections.

On one demolished slum site, Ambujwadi at Malvani, which is quite inaccessible in a way, at the end of a peninsular extension into a creek, 'in the jungle' as the local residents described the site, we were told by the slum-dwellers that one major builder of the city had interest in the land. This was because the same builder has developed massive real estate properties on the other side of the creek (on the mainland) and a link road between the mainland and the Malvani peninsula was to be constructed. The Ambujwadi site is state government land and in the NDZ. The NDZ would be freed of development restrictions ('released from the NDZ', in local parlance) in due course. Any such act of 'releasing land' involves exchange of 'under the table' money and the minister who presides over the exchange stands to make a fortune out of it. Hence, for more than a decade, every CM of Maharashtra has kept the urban development portfolio with himself.

This nexus between the builder and the politician, mediated with the support of the underworld, has existed in Mumbai for some time. Chandrashekhar Prabhu (2005), the president of the MHADA; Chairman, Advisory Committee, Department of Housing, GoM, and adviser to the GoM has, in a recent article penned in a news magazine, bluntly says:

> "At every opportunity, more land is created in Mumbai city, mainly by reclaiming the coastline or creeks, to be allotted to the builders

and more money made (for the builders and for the minister). There are well-established practices (bypassing the policies) to get the natural area converted into an NDZ and then into a developable area, either through organising the squatting of slum-dwellers or by selling it to a builder for real-estate projects. A number of NDZ areas have been opened up for urbanisation by different CMs over time. Even plots earmarked for gardens and playgrounds have been dereserved within the city."

"Chief Minister Sharad Pawar dereserved 285 plots; Manohar Joshi 300 plots; and Narayan Rane, in his eight-month rule, dereserved about 180 plots, one of which covered 660 acres (264 ha) in Mankhurd (an area that was severely affected by flooding with water rising to 12 feet). Vilasrao Deshmukh continued the trend. Sushilkumar Shinde de-reserved 67 plots. All these put together would perhaps amount to almost 50 per cent of the space for amenities. .... When a plot is reserved, it has no commercial value since nothing can be built on it. Its price is zero. But when it is dereserved, the price shoots up to the level of land price prevailing in the area. It is a major source of income for politicians. When more FSI (buildable capacity) is given on that plot, its worth increases further. So with an investment of a lakh of rupees, you can make Rs. 20-50 crores."

Take another example. Mr. Manohar Joshi, whose name appears in the list of the CMs who de-reserved open plots, has become a builder himself. He was a school-teacher before he gained ascendancy in the state and then the national politics. His son has set up a realty firm called Kohinoor projects. This firm, in partnership with Matoshri Realtors, which is headed by Raj Thackerey, the nephew of Shiv Sena leader Balasaheb Thackerey, bagged a prime site of 4.8 acres from a nationalised textile mill named Kohinoor 3 for a sum of Rs. 421 crores (Rs 4,210 million or US$ 96.78 million). The cost of land would therefore be Rs. 15,000 per sq ft. There were just three final bidders from among the 35 representatives of different developers who had turned up for the pre-bid meeting. A *Times of India* report states: "Many in the property market were expecting a dog-eat-dog fight among builders for this lucrative real estate. But ... when the bids were finally opened, ... it turned out that only three developers were in the fray".[56] The report alludes to the fact that if there are such powerful bidders, small bidders do not enter the fray. Further, the same report states that the Kohinoor Group is one of the most prominent real estate developers in the area around the plot that it bid for successfully. The politicians not only have nexuses with builders, they themselves have become builders.

Slum demolitions therefore have been taken up time and again, post-elections, to fulfil pre-elections commitment made to select builders after taking contributions from them[57]. To the electorate, only promises have been made in the manifesto and the electorate cannot do anything once the government is formed that would stay on for five years. Electorate have very weak bargaining power vis-à-vis the political leaders whereas the builders can dictate terms with the politicians. Politicians from all the political parties, exceptions are few, are part of this builder-politician nexus and hence none oppose slum demolitions of such kind. Any occasion to push the cause of the builders, like the idea to develop Mumbai into a World Class City like Shanghai that would lead to building of large real estate projects, is not missed out by the politicians.

The third explanation is increasing bias against the urban poor in the urban planning and management. Shiv Sena, the one that held power in the state government and one that held power in the MCGM, has a very clear position on pre-1995 slums, unlike ambiguous position held by the Congress-I on the issue. It views slum demolitions as legitimate way of expelling 'illegal Bangladeshis' from Mumbai city. Thus, both, BJP and Shiv Sena supported the CM on the demolition as that was expelling the Bangladeshis from the city[58]. Balasaheb Thackerey, the leader of Shiv Sena, said that demolition of hutments was a good move and that the CM and DyCM had taken a bold decision that has checked the deterioration of Mumbai. Further, he blamed the influx of illegal Bangladeshi migrants to the problem of slums in Mumbai[59]!

After Sonia Gandhi intervened to stop the demolitions, the MCGM, where Shiv Sena held power at the time of demolitions, said that it would continue with the activity. Narayan Rane[60], then the leader of the opposition in Maharashtra Assembly backed this position by his statement in the Assembly[61]. He further said that if the state government tried to protect post-1995 slum dwellers, Sena would invite people from rural Maharashtra to come and squat in Mumbai[62], implying that slum dwellers are non-Maharashtrians and also illegal Muslim migrants, not wanted in Mumbai that belonged to Maharashtrians and Hindus.

Further, the MCGM went to the extent of suggesting that the election commissioner delete the names of the evicted slum-dwellers from the electoral list[63]. Before the 2004 May elections, some prominent citizens of the city had filed a Public Interest Litigation (PIL) in the Mumbai High Court, demanding that the election commissioner disenfranchise any person staying in unauthorised structures, evidently referring to the slum dwellers. The argument was that if they were living illegally, they could not be considered legal citizens of the city and therefore could not be eligible to vote. A known film personality, Sadashiv Amrapurkar was one of the 11 'prominent Maharashtrians[64] ' who had filed this petition[65]. The Shiv Sena, under its *Mee Mumbaikar* (I, the resident of Mumbai) campaign in 2003-04, had categorically asked for the denial of voting rights to slum dwellers. Sainath[66] argues that it is curious to disenfranchise demolished slum-dwellers when India is considering giving voting rights to the NRIs (Non Resident Indians) and PIOs (People of Indian Origin) who do not even live in the country any more.

The Congress-I corporators, elected from the city, and are in contact with the day to day issues of their wards, did a vanishing act when the demolitions were going on, none picking up their mobiles[67]. One of the slum dwellers' deposition quoted before, too mentions their local corporator's advice to them to cooperate with the MCGM in the demolitions and not fight them. Some Congress-I corporators also supported the demolition drive, saying that Mumbai could not take on everyone's responsibility[68] in much the same was as a campaign of *Mee Mumbaikar* run by the Shiv Sena. One Samajwadi Party corporator fully supported the demolitions and went to the extent of saying that their goods must be confiscated[69]. The political party ideology was blurred as far as granting citizenship rights to the slum dwellers was concerned.

In India some of the recent events point to increasing intolerance of the upwardly mobile middle class to the legitimate demands made by the poor on the State. Intolerance to the squatting by the poor is presented forth as an issue of law enforcement. But, the incongruity in this position held by the city's middle class gets exposed when they do not express the same level of intolerance to the violation of other laws such as criminal laws by the underworld, black marketeering, and so on except in private conversations. The argument about the violation of law is a euphemism for intolerance towards the poor. As mentioned earlier, the NGO named CAG comprising of Mumbai's corporate sector fully came out in support of the demolitions.

The economic reforms of the 1990s, argue many scholars, have ideologically justified the pursuit of individual wealth as never before (Corbridge and Harriss 2000: 121), what Pavan Varma (1999: xii) observes about the Indian elite and middle classes as one that is imperviousness to the travails of one's own countrymen, this inability to see beyond the neon lights advertising one more object of desire, this absolute conviction that there is little in common between the possibility of the good life and the state of deprivation of the vast majority, and finally this *acceptance* of poverty and destitution for one set of Indians, even as another, much smaller segment celebrates the 'heady possibilities' released by the reform process—it is this attitude which has become pervasive aspect of middle-class thinking" (1999: 185). Rajni Kothari had already observed in the 1980s that the poor would be considered responsible for their own fates and viewed as a drag on the rest (Corbridge and Harriss 2000: 121).

Even the political class has become intolerant to the demands made by the poor on the State. It is summed up in what DyCM R.R. Patil had to say after returning from China (Shanghai); he was quite impressed by the development in China in general and Shanghai in particular, he liked it that government decisions cannot be challenged in China and felt that unfortunately, Mumbai could not be Shanghai since the government in India was not as powerful as the one in China[70] was.

If this were to stop at just hatred then there would not be much harm done. But it gets extended to the allocation of public resources. Hence, land can be taken away from the poor, denying them housing rights, but it can be allotted to most esoteric or luxurious uses such as water parks and for entertainment. There is little public finance for, say, basic services such as water supply and sanitation, which have to be passed on to the private sector, but funds can be easily allotted to the building of flyovers from which there is no cost recovery. There is an endless list of changing priorities in city planning, in Mumbai and in other cities, most of these priorities set by the vocal middle class, whose opinions are taken by the media and various opinion polls and then splashed as 'Gobblesian truths' which are picked up promptly by the policy-makers and labelled as the priorities of the people, followed by policy changes.

A human rights lawyer explained that the demolitions had no real economic sense, since the lands thus cleared had no immediate use for the city. Frequent and brutal slum demolitions are a way of demonstrating to the urban poor that they were not wanted in the city, but, could live so either under the patronage of politicians on humanitarian grounds and not through constitutional right and they had to obey the dictates of the government concerned about the city's and by that national development!

We suspect that there is also some unstated motive beyond this. If the large-scale infrastructure projects such as roads and freeways are to be implemented, somewhere or the other, slums are going to come in the way. Mandatory rehabilitation would be required for such slums, as per the norms of most bilateral funding agencies such as the World Bank, the ADB, etc. Thus, rehabilitation would increase the project costs on one hand and cause delays in project implementation as rehabilitation takes time. The best thing under the situation is to cut the problem at the root, deny citizenship rights to the poor and by that stop them from staking rehabilitation claims and thus claims on city resources. Demolitions are also a message to the other slum-dwellers that if they do not fall in line, that is, they do not agree to whatever rehabilitation package is offered to them, they would suffer the same fate as that of the evicted slum dwellers[71]. Thus, even if development-funding organisations such as the World Bank have rehabilitation policies built in as a part of the financing package, the government can bypass these conditions in this manner. What happens outside the ambit of their project would not be the concern of the funding agencies.

More sinisterly, demolitions destroy the evidences that the poor have about their legitimate existence in the city, the photo-pass given by the municipal corporation and the ration card given by the state government. To get them back, the government machinery at the lower level has to be greased, that is, the poor have to pay bribes to lower order government personnel to have these documents reissued. Till these documents are made, the police can harass them and extract money. Many slum dwellers have said this in their depositions to the IPTEHR (2005). Demolitions from time to time benefit those at the lower end in the administrative machinery.

Slums are on the axe; if the city has to beautify and convert herself into something else or to attract investments, if there is a natural disaster, if there is buoyancy of the property market and if there is pressure from middle class citizens groups to de-criminalise or detoxify the city. Slum demolitions take place after the elections, when the promises made during the elections have not to be kept and when money has been taken from the builders lobby for the elections. Lastly, slum demolitions have to continue forever to keep telling the slum dwellers that they are illegitimate residents. This is the ideology of development in Mumbai, which has got strengthened by the unfolding processes of globalisation in Mumbai City.

The populations thus made redundant, however, have not remained passive recipients of whatever comes their way. They have decided to chart their own course of democracy, to send message to the formal democracy in the country to heed to their minimum demands of existence. Such a space for poor to make their voices heard still remains in the

Indian political system, which the poor of Mumbai have used, with the assistance of the human rights and housing rights activists. The Indian Constitution, which is in a way inclusive in nature, has provided scope for judicial interventions in support of Mumbai's poor. But, it looks like that the battle of the poor to survive in the megacities such as Mumbai would continue and will have to be against the formidable alliance of the land related nexus and the aggressive middle classes largely concentrated in the cities.

Indian electoral democracy and politics has created some democratic space for those getting excluded. But, the space is not large enough to push for their long-term development aspirations. The poor in India in general and in particular in cities such as Mumbai, do not dream beyond minimum existence. They are not allowed to dream beyond minimum existence. They fight for minimum inclusions. This time, unlike in the past, this fight is veering towards formulation of a long-term housing policy for the poor in the city. It is hoped that this would lead to formulation of 'inclusive politics' and 'inclusive policies' even in cities such as Mumbai.

The Epilogue—The Drowning of the Shanghai Dream

Unprecedented rainfall in Mumbai of 944 mm on July 26, 2005, coupled with a high-tide level in the sea, led to the whole of north Mumbai and the cities of Thane, Kalyan-Dombivali, to the north of greater Mumbai totally flooded, with water as high as one storey (10 ft to 12 ft) in some places and the city coming to a grinding halt. Ground floor dwellings were fully submerged in many places. Telecommunication lines were snapped; arterial roads were jammed; the airport was closed and public transport came to a grinding halt—the three suburban train networks, the lifelines of the city, could not operate for close to 36 hours, stranding an estimated 150,000 people. Many people were stranded on the roads for two days, many spent two days away from their homes, many walked back home, trudging 12-15 hours on the road. Almost 15,000 children were stranded in schools without food and water. Once again, the entire nation's attention was on Mumbai. According to the state government, 736 people died in Mumbai and 191 died in neighbouring Thane (Katakam et al 2005). Post denudation, epidemics of leptospirosis and dengue broke out, which resulted in several deaths; by 2nd week of August, 66 people had died and 1,062 were admitted in the hospitals due to outbreak of leptospirosis and dengue epidemics[72].

Three main reasons for this inundation are: land reclamation in the existing waterways, creeks and river flowing through the city; a poor and insufficient drainage system, and garbage not being picked up regularly from the streets, which then goes into the drains and clogs them. It is a case of bad governance coupled with greed for land in the city. The reclamation is done by the public agencies to create new land for construction activities that they may either sell for their own profit (as the main land development agency, the MMRDA, has done to create BKC) or give it away at low cost to the builders. The builder-politician nexus has resulted in administrative attention being showered more on activities such as slum demolitions than on maintaining the city's sanitation and drainage systems. This disaster did not spare anyone, the slum dwellers, the film stars, the rich, and or anyone else in Mumbai. Normally, natural disasters disproportionately damage the poor. In Mumbai, the slum—dwellers faced mayhem.

The slum-dwellers who had their homes demolished, and whose fates were hanging in balance while the local administration pondered its future course of action, were badly affected. For instance, Annabhau Sathe Nagar in Deonar, in the north-eastern suburbs of Mumbai, is a vast slum built on soft, recently filled land that runs along a treacherously open drainage ditch (*nullah*) and which is impossible to traverse without getting one's legs mired in clay nearly up to the knees even after the lightest rainfall. After it had been demolished early this year, its defiant inhabitants put back makeshift structures and carried on living on the site, to the extent that some members of the municipal corporation—not willing to admit total failure in this case—now claim they never demolished the slum, says *Nirbhay Bano Andolan* (become bold struggle) activist Shakeel Ahmed. As a result, the structures and infrastructure here are more fragile than usual, and in the deluge of late July, the *nullah* was completely flooded. The entire area was waterlogged and all the makeshift houses were destroyed once again. To add to the tragic irony, there is a large campus of high-rise low-income housing units just across the ditch from Annabhau Sathe Nagar: it is one of the 'SRS' projects built by MHADA and currently lying locked and unused due to procedural delays. The desperate residents of Annabhau Sathe Nagar, when took shelter in the hallways and corridors of these buildings after their temporary homes collapsed, were promptly harassed and driven out of these buildings.

Another example of this kind of cruel, pointlessly perverse irony occurred in nearby Mandala, where 8,000 units were broken during the last demolition spree, and which location had subsequently been proposed by the local State as one of the two potential rehabilitation sites for eligible recent evictees. Mandala has become a socially and politically sensitive location because Medha Patkar and other activists have focussed much of their relief-related struggles here. It has, therefore, been better fenced and policed than many of the other demolition sites. At least half its former residents, who had been dispersed in the aftermath of the demolitions, have been going back defiantly, again and again, and attempting to rebuild their homes. When the deluge took over the site in late July, the Mandala evictees who had clustered in and around the site, hastily put up a large canvas tent and set up a community kitchen in a desperate effort to survive the forces of nature. This tent was torn down and the kitchen destroyed under civic authority orders, and two women were hurt in the process.

Now one more threat looms over the slum-dwellers who have encroached upon the banks of the river Mithi that flows through Mumbai. An estimated 6,000 hutments are there on the riverbank. It is expected that these slums will face evictions in the near future[73]. While vested interests including the political nexus that sees Mumbai as a ground to make unlimited money have destabilised Mumbai's ecology on the one hand and created a situation of lack of access to housing for more than half the population on the other, those who have been at the receiving end of all these past actions will once again be under the threat of eviction. In all of this, the one positive aspect is that a discussion on appropriate city development policies, focussed on basic civic services, housing for the poor, safe public transport systems, and good governance has come to the fore in light of this latest disaster—one for which the city clearly did not have any plan of management.

An activist from Mumbai told one of the authors, "the issues we have been raising in the context of slum demolitions are now in the mainstream of discussions in the city, and those who had supported or kept quite about the slum demolitions are also raising issues about an appropriate path to Mumbai becoming a World Class City or Shanghai."

NOTES

1. This chapter is based on research undertaken through IDPAD project.
2. The authors wish to acknowledge the contribution of Deepika D'Souza (Indian People's Tribunal for Environment and Human Rights) for sharing both ideas and information; Mihir Desai for information on the Public Interest Litigation (PIL) in the Mumbai High Court; Amrita Goswami of YUVA for past slum demolition data; Dr. Amita Bhide, Tata Institute of

Social Sciences, Mumbai, for sharing her study of the Slum Rehabilitation Scheme; Mr. Shakeel Ahmed for information on and access to the struggle in particular, as well as all activist friends in Mumbai for discussions on Mumbai.

3. Year in the bracket by the authors.
4. Based on the newspaper reports: *Times of India*, Mumbai, December 12, 2004; *Times of India*, Mumbai, December 26, 2004 and *Times of India*, Mumbai, February 16, 2005.
5. There are different estimates on number of homes demolished, the estimates varying between 88,000 and 95,000 homes.
6. Faleiro, Sonia, 'Girls interrupted', *Tehelka*, The People's Paper, April 30, 2004.
7. Faleiro, Sonia, 'Hawkers fight for space in City of Dreams' *Tehelka*, The People's Paper, April 30, 2005
8. Term coined by Bombay First, (a group that calls itself an NGO), by putting forth a document called "Vision 2010"—Converting Mumbai into A World Class City.
9. From the SRA website, http://www.sra.gov.in/HTMLpages/History.htm.
10. Jathar, Dnyanesh V., *The Week*, August 13, 2000: 67-69
11. Chaware, Dilip, 'Hutment units to be regularised', *The Times of India*, Mumbai, November 24, 1991.
12. Editorial 'Future of Bombay' in *The Statesman*, November 24, 1985.
13. Quoted by Dilip D'Souza in a posting on http://dcubed.blogspot.com/2005/02/still-same.html, February 21, 2005.
14. 'Stop influx and halt slum boom: judge', *Times of India*, Mumbai, May 25, 1990.
15. Mass demolition order set aside', *Times of India*, Mumbai, July 11, 1990.
16. 'Division bench to hear slum demolition case', *The Daily*, Mumbai, July 11, 1990; 'Mass demolition order set aside', *Times of India*, Mumbai, July 11, 1990.
17. Khapre-Upadhyay, Prasanna 'BMC to involve residents in fighting encroachments', *Indian Express*, February 20, 1999.
18. The English language newspapers in Mumbai, have been giving the information on the slum demolitions, and infrastructure development matter on under the title of 'Mumbai Make-Over'.
19. *Mid Day*, Mumbai, June 7, 2005.
20. For instance, *Mid Day*, Mumbai, December 6, 2004.
21. BMC as in *Indian Express*, Mumbai Newsline, January 4, 2005.
22. As per a report in *Indian Express*, Mumbai, November 30, 2004.
23. Ward is an administrative unit below the Municipal Corporation. Mumbai has 24 wards. As per 74th Amendment of Indian Constitution, ward level committees have been given powers for certain ward level development activities.
24. Maharashtra Control of Organised Crime Act.

25. As per a report in *Times of India*, Mumbai, December 6, 2004.
26. *Mid day*, Mumbai, December 6, 2004.
27. *Mid Day*, Mumbai, February 17, 2005.
28. *Times of India*, Mumbai, February 16, 2005.
29. From an opinion poll attached to a posting by expressindia of the *Indian Express* Group, on the site http://www.expressindia.com/fullstory.php?newsid=42079, posted online on Thursday, February 17, 2005.
30. *Indian Express*, Mumbai Newsline, December 18, 2004.
31. *Times of India*, Mumbai, December 20, 2004.
32. *Mid Day*, Mumbai, December 23, 2004 and IPTEHR (2005).
33. Bracket by the authors.
34. *Indian Express*, December 27, 2004.
35. *Indian Express*, December 27, 2004.
36. *Indian Express*, Mumbai Newsline, January 15, 2005.
37. *Times of India*, Mumbai, December 31, 2004.
38. *Indian Express*, Mumbai Newsline, January 10, 2005.
39. Dalit is a term used to refer to marginalised communities. It is also a term used to represent Scheduled Castes (SCs) that have affirmative action protection under Indian Constitution.
40. Singh, Navneeta, "'93 riot victims homeless again", in *Mid Day*, Mumbai, January 18, 2005.
41. At the currency conversion rate in 2004-05.
42. This land was a swamp some six till 1997-98, where the dwellers invested in trucks-full of mud and dirt to firm up the land on which they had erected their houses. Besides, they had also invested something between Rs. 30,000 and Rs. 40,000 in their houses. In this slum settlement, there are people who have migrated to the city in the early 1980s and came to live here from central Mumbai from where they were evicted (*Indian Express*, Mumbai Newsline, December 29, 2004).
43. *Indian Express*, Mumbai Newsline, January 23, 2005.
44. *Times of India*, Mumbai, February 4, 2005.
45. *Indian Express*, Mumbai Newsline, February 6, 2005.
46. Press trust of India, February 2, 2005.
47. *Times of India*, Mumbai, February 10, 2005.
48. *Times of India*, Mumbai, December 10, 2004.
49. For example, Kripashankar, MLA of Santa Cruz halted the slum demolitions on airport land in about 2003, as that was his constituency. Naseem Khan another Congress MLA did the same in the end of 2004 (*Times of India*, Mumbai, May 18, 2005).
50. *Mid Day*, Mumbai, December 22, 2004.
51. *Indian Express*, Mumbai, December 21, 2004.
52. This news was in all the papers and was reported in all the electronic media. See *Indian Express*, Mumbai, *Times of India* Mumbai and *Mid Day* Mumbai, of February 15, 2005. A television news channel, NDTV, also took up a

discussion on this subject in their prime time slot of 10.00 to 10.30 in the evening, in that period. The anchor of the programme was trying to put these developments as a case of Congress central leadership interfering in the state affairs, against the principles of federalism in Indian Constitution.

53. *Indian Express*, Mumbai, February 15, 2005.
54. Report of the Enquiry into the *Lathi* Charge on the Demonstration by Dishoused Slum Dwellers on 6th April 2005 in Mumbai: report available with the IPHRC.
55. That policy is being finalised at this moment, when this article is being written, through a consultative process.
56. *Times of India*, Ahmedabad, July 22, 2005.
57. An article by Nauzer Bharucha 'City builders pump Rs. 50 Crore into polls' in *Times of India*, Mumbai, October 7, 2004 (http://www1.timesofindia.indiatimes.com/cms.dll/articleshow?msid=876250), states that although it is impossible to estimate the amount, inquiries with city-based builders and property market watchers reveal that the contribution from this lobby alone to all parties for this election could be anywhere between Rs. 15 crore and Rs. 50 crore. Some say it could be even more than that. "Of course, this does not include the kickbacks many have paid the powers that-be for favours such as facilitating builders to buy government land at throwaway prices, selectively increasing the FSI, dereserving large tracts reserved for public purposes and unlocking land under the Urban Land Ceiling Act," says a developer. According to him, Congress-NCP candidates have got about 70 per cent of the donations, the Sena-BJP about 20 per cent and independents 10 per cent. "The sitting MLA has also to be taken care of," he says.
58. *Times of India*, Mumbai, April 17, 2005.
59. *Indian Express*, Mumbai, January 22, 2005 and *Times of India*, Mumbai, January 22, 2005
60. Ironically, Rane joined Congress in beginning of August 2005 after being thrown out of Shiv Sena of course not on the issue of any public concern such as slum dwellers' rights or so but on personal reasons, where he had become quite ambitious.
61. *Indian Express*, Mumbai, February 18, 2005.
62. *Indian Express*, Mumbai, February 18, 2005, *Free Press Journal*, Mumbai, February 18, 2005.
63. *Times of India*, Mumbai, January 22, 2005.
64. Residents of Maharashtra state.
65. *Times of India*, Mumbai, January 23, 2005 and IPTEHR (2005).
66. Sainath, P. "The unbearable lightness of seeing", *The Hindu*, February 5, 2005.
67. *Mid Day*, Mumbai, December 22, 2004.
68. *Indian Express*, Mumbai, January 22, 2005.
69. *Indian Express*, January 22, 2005.
70. *Times of India*, Mumbai, May 18, 2005.

71. It need be mentioned that 58,000 housing units are under construction (some already constructed) to rehabilitate slum dwellers displaced under MUTP and MUIP (Mumbai Urban Infrastructure Project), funded by the World Bank (*Indian Express*, Mumbai, January 24, 2005).
72. http://www.hindu.com/2005/08/12/stories/2005081205321300.htm.
73. As per an NDTV (New Delhi Television) discussion on August 10, 2005 (10.30 to 11.00 pm show of Mumbai Live).

19

DYNAMICS AND CONTOURS OF RESISTING DISPLACEMENT IN MUMBAI

AMITA BHIDE

Introduction

Displacement of the poor has emerged as an almost inevitable accompaniment to development in Mumbai. As the 'urban' assumes significant space in discourses of development, the emphasis on cities to be globally competitive paves the way for transformation of cities in ways significantly different from those thought earlier. This transformation of the city in lived, imagined and expressed space has profound implications for the poor and the slum dwellers in cities—mostly displacing. Mumbai is no exception to this.

Given the significant numbers of these sections; resistance to displacement and assertion of right to the city by the poor is inevitable. The recent past has witnessed a stronger resurgence of these struggles. The current paper is an attempt to map some of the dynamics and contours of these struggles and outline the challenge ahead.

Displacement Marathon in Mumbai

Displacements are not a new phenomenon in Mumbai. They have been a regular, almost invisible, facet of the city's administrative response to poor migrants' space even in the 1970s when policies towards slums shifted from clearance towards tolerance and acceptance. The Janata Nagar[1] evictions of 20,000 slum dwellers in 1972 and then en masse shifting of all pavement dwellers to the outskirts of the city in 1986 are two particularly known instances. Evictions have been particularly forceful when campaigns and discussions on beautifying the city have been launched.

Evictions have however, acquired a vicious edge since the late 1990s; their scale, occurrence, form are in many ways unprecedented. The eviction of 85,000 slum dwellers form the Sanjay Gandhi National Park[2] in multiple phases from 1999 to 2001 represents one of the largest and inhuman demolitions in the recent times. This was followed by evictions in Daulat Nagar[3] and Bhabrekar Nagar[4]. While all of these evictions were in response to public interest litigations and court decisions, the new wave of evictions in October-January 2004-05 which affected between 65,000-86,000 slum homes was not spurred by judicial decisions but by administrative determination. A pending court case in response to these evictions and Ms. Sonia Gandhi's intervention to keep up an electoral promise of extending tolerance date of slum dwellers to 2001 have put some deterrents in this newfound determination to do away with slums repeatedly expressed both by state government and the corporation of Mumbai. However, these deterrents have done little to stop the evictions on all major roads as well as every ward in Mumbai being carried out by both the Municipal Corporation and the MMRDA. Several projects in the pipeline—Mithi River Development, Airport Development, drainage, etc. pose threats to scores of slum dwellers in these areas. Displacement is thus, acquiring an enormity of scale.

Work spaces of the poor are similarly under threat. The closing down of mills and manufacturing industries in the city have resulted in the increase of number of people working in the informal sector. In the decade from 1980-90, the proportion of manufacturing employment to total employment reduced from 36.0 per cent to 28.5 per cent and the percentage of informal sector workers rose to 98 per cent in Mumbai (MMRDA 1996). For workers seeking refuge in the informal sector, the confinement of hawking spaces and stopping the issue of new licenses pose distinct threats.

There are also several invisible forms of displacement; these include rehabilitation schemes that compel households to move out of economically unsustainable arrangements, the formalisation of public service delivery and its restriction to paying citizens and the shrinking of spaces that are not fixed in use. Invisibility in data (poverty lines, eligibility lists) is another form of displacement which makes the city an increasingly difficult terrain for the poor. The scale and the form of displacement are however, only expressions of wider and much deeper assault on the poor which resistance has to contend with. An analysis of the sources of this assault is therefore, necessary.

Multi-Quartered Assault on the Poor

Development Planning

The poor and the slum dwellers always had a negligible place in developmental planning of cities, conventionally. The 'development plan' wave which was unleashed in India in the 1960s was dominated by visions of beautiful, use-segregated and planned cities. Slums had no place in this vision. However, as most plans were characterised more by non implementation than execution; public lands often became spaces for unauthorised occupation by the poor. Simultaneously, private land owners allowed slums to emerge on their lands to counter the threat of state intervention through the Urban Land Ceiling Act (Narayanan 2003). In Mumbai, currently, 43.1 per cent of slums are on public lands, 47.2 per cent are on private lands (YUVA 2001).

The planning regime has changed considerably in the last decade. In Mumbai, the planning body, the MMRDA has taken considerable initiative and amassed resources through execution of projects. Schemes for slum and old-buildings' rehabilitation are creating more mixed uses and floor space indices. The state government is taking keen interest in promoting Mumbai as a globally competitive city through setting up of a task force which has a considerable influence of private actors. The central government promises to back up through resources under the JNNURM and there is also the prospect of garnering international funding for the same.

This shift from a legislatively mandated, grand vision with very little execution potential to project-led, private-initiative based and resource-backed missions has considerable implications for spaces of the poor. The losing of the land regulation regime has opened up many more lucrative uses for private land owners than allowing lands to be encroached. The designated uses for public land have received a new sanctity and the new lands being contemplated for development (e.g. salt pan, mill lands) are dominated by a profit-led exploitation of potential. Thus, both the current spaces occupied by the poor and availability of such spaces in the future are threatened.

Administrative Vigour

Lackadaisical administrative styles depending on the limitations of regulations and resources are giving way to a vigorous, active administration, at least at the top level. This vigour is being demonstrated in the MMRDA which now views slum rehabilitation as secondary to the actual project. The MUIP funded by its own resources which focuses on widening and consolidation of road networks has to date followed the principle of 'project and displacement' first, 'rehabilitation (if any) later' approach. The Municipal Commissioner, not to be left behind, has carried out a consistent demolition campaign in the last first four months of 2006 and taken punitive actions against officials found to be negligent in their duty of carrying out demolitions[5].

Citizen Voices

The 'voice' of the upwardly mobile middle and elite class citizen has emerged as one of the most significant changes in the Indian urban landscape in the last decade. It has taken the form of projects partnering with the local government, of setting new planning agendas and obtaining resource backup, of initiating new forms of accountability of the administration and of advocacy of certain issues. The anti-slum agenda is an implicit part of several of these initiatives. For instance, in Mumbai, Advanced Locality Management (ALM) groups were created around the theme of public participation in solid waste management. However, as a study of ALMs in Mumbai (Zérah 2007) point out, removal of encroachments and hawkers was the *raison de etre* for most ALMs. PIL—a tool evolved for the use of vulnerable and weaker sections of society has acquired an anti-poor edge with the significant increase in PILs lodged by middle class citizens (Adenwala 1998). The citizen voice is also an important element of new visions of the city. This new citizen, who wants Mumbai to be Shanghai, is non-cognizant of her relationship with the poorer classes and would prefer them to be invisible. She thus, constitutes a major threat to the existence of the poor.

Judiciary

The jurisprudence in India has taken a distinct shift in the last few years. From a liberal interpretation of right to life as life with dignity necessitating fulfilment, of basic needs[6]; the judiciary has now begun treating slum dwellers as pick-pocketeers[7]. The series of judgments with respect to the Sanjay Gandhi National Park are a case in point. The manner in which the Mumbai High Court responded and hitched onto the issue of environmental restoration with a total disregard for slum dwellers residing on the land, its orders for execution of the demolitions (these included the use of Special Reserve Police Force, use of helicopters) and for ensuring protection from future encroachment, are examples of increasing insensitivity of the higher courts to the plight of the slum dwellers. The Mumbai High Court, in its order on Sanjay Gandhi National Park also mentioned that to prevent further encroachments, a fenced boundary along the periphery should be erected; no permission for schools, ration shops, dispensaries in the park be given and also no permission for holding of public meetings by the people eligible and awaiting rehabilitation be given. This judgement underlined and indicated a new trend of intolerance towards unauthorised actions of the poor. This trend has since been witnessed in several other judgments.

Media

A comparison of the coverage of evictions in October-January 2005 with the demolitions in Ulhasnagar[8] early 2006 tells its own story. The stance vis-à-vis the former was congratulatory, supportive of long-pending administrative action against illegal, unauthorised residence while that vis-à-vis the latter was cognizant of the complex nexus between developers, administrators, politicians and planning regimes and sympathetic to the plight of the residents. A large section of the media is devoted to the cause of the re-'visioning' and remaking of cities; the slums are obviously viewed as an impediment to this. Imagery of this kind is abundant both in print and electronic media.

City Politic

The right to vote enjoyed by the slum dwellers is their card in hand. Slums have been cultivated as vote banks by politicians as the 1970s and 1980s were characterised by withdrawal of middle class and active participation of the poor in electoral politics. In all the electoral constituencies in Mumbai, slum dwelling population is in majority. The politician is intricately connected both to the slum development as well as its perpetuation as a den for undignified living. The politics of the city has changed with the rise of the 'citizen voice'. The manifestos of all major parties vis-à-vis the city in the last *Lok Sabha* (National Parliament) elections had almost uniform agendas—i.e. making Mumbai globally competitive. The Members of Parliament across parties lobbied with the ex-Prime Minister Mr. Vajpayee to back up the Mumbai Vision

Plan. Slum rehabilitation through commercial development of land and massive infrastructural development has emerged as consensual priorities.

Politics needs to be minimally responsive to the concerns of the majority of the electorate; however, this responsiveness is unevenly balanced with a priority to converting Mumbai to Shanghai through a complex and multilayered network.

Housing Rights Struggles in Mumbai

The earliest struggles for resisting displacement in Mumbai were the housing rights struggles. These were para-political or away from mainstream politics. Thus, some trade unions and some political parties initiated mobilisational efforts in slum and pavement dwellings. These efforts however tended to be sporadic and lacked continuity.

In 1980s, the massive deporting of slum dwellers launched by the then Chief Minister—Mr. A. R. Antulay[9] saw the advent of new actors in housing rights struggles. On one side of the spectrum were the political parties who began to organise slum wings. These efforts were more effective in terms of outreach and scale. However, they were marked by inconsistency and arbitrariness and in many ways, perpetuated the existence of the slum as a slum. This period also saw the emergence of voluntary groups who increasingly realised a need for engagement with development issues. Networking and advocacy became the buzzwords of the time. These groups saw a role for themselves in organising slum dwellers so as to participate in development efforts and partake of its benefits. A comprehensive demand for basic right to housing was articulated at the city and national level. There were also attempts to build international coalitions.

The NGO efforts were effective in terms of qualitative improvements in awareness and capacities of local communities and leaders. They sought to define slum dwelling as a self-help effort and bring in an understanding of housing as a human right, often through international intervention—several forms of people's associations and institutions were created through these efforts.

The NGOs efforts were effective in terms of qualitative improvements in awareness and capacities of local communities and leaders. They sought to define slum dwelling as a self-help effort and bring in an understanding of housing as a human right, often through international intervention. The NGOs became important institutions in their own right; at least two

NGOs in Mumbai became important institutions in their own right and acquired the stature of international NGOs with several nationwide as well as international affiliations. Their role as expressing the concerns of the poor began to be increasingly recognised by Governments (Bhide 1999).

The changed economic and political landscape of the post-1990s, however, saw a tremendous change in the role of NGOs. Several erstwhile struggle-oriented organisations sought to partner with the state and private sector; several began to engage with public service delivery (Ramnath 2005). Whether it was the limitations of a struggle-oriented approach or the need to preserve their own existence or a search for a more befitting response to the new politico-economic environment; the emergent fact was that the interventions did not lead to significant and sustained grassroots mobilisation around the issue of housing. As Justice Krishna Iyer (former Chief Justice of India), points out in 1999; this lack of grassroots mobilisation proved to be the undoing of the national networks which became associations of the NGOs than people. The momentum of the housing rights movement in the 1980s could not be sustained; several networks fell apart. The articulation of housing as a broad right began to fall short of contesting the multi-quartered assault on spaces of the poor ranging from residential and work spaces, cultural and expressed spaces as well as other forms impinging on lived environment. The extremely differentiated realities of slums where datelines had ensured fractured constituencies, access to amenities was widely varying and the threat of displacement was often not active also deterred mobilisation efforts and exposed the limitations of an articulation based in housing rights. The ironic aspect of these developments is euphoric celebration of people's participation in almost every governmental policy and programme; according an integral place to involvement of NGOs. An atmosphere of apolitical, sporadic, localised mobilizations devoid of conflict has emerged and been in place for the last decade. Organisations in Mumbai had pioneered and been at the forefront of the National Campaign for Housing Rights (NCHR). However, by early 1990s, the city-level networks of NGOs had become inactive though the NGOs themselves were active or had even become bigger in stature. Several NGOs were engaged in projects in partnership with the government. Representation in governmental committees and other bodies was increasingly being monopolized by Big International Non-Government Organisations (BINGOs). The space for smaller organisation and struggles steadily decreased.

The impact of the processes outlined above was demonstrated in the response to evictions in late 1990s. The *Nivara Hakk Suraksha Samiti* (NHSS) (Committee for the Protection of Housing Rights) engaged in a grassroots as well as judicial struggle against evictions in the Sanjay Gandhi National Park, found itself waging an isolated, losing struggle and gradually was compelled to restrict itself to rehabilitation of 1,200 households considered eligible. Subsequent mobilisation contesting the legality of eviction and land acquisition by a political party was quashed in the *Lok Sabha* elections. In Daulat Nagar, the local CBO found few supporters. Joint actions of NGOs were sporadic. Voices of dissent were few and weak. The initial response to the massive and widespread evictions in October 2004 was one of shock and passive acceptance. One of the most important factors affecting the initial passiveness and lack of resistance was the fractured nature of slum dwellers as a constituency. People whose homes were not threatened were apathetic to the cause of the recent residents. They too used the term 'unauthorised' '*jhopdiwalas*' (hut-dwellers) in relation to the evicted populace. The evictees themselves had internalised their commission of illegalities and therefore, reacted through helplessness rather than anger. As the initial shock wore off and the demolitions continued unabated; there was a resurgence of civil society actions. It is this resurgence which holds a promise for the future.

In January 2005, nearly two months after the onset of evictions; several civil society actions were initiated. These actions saw alliance building between several actors: political parties, trade unions, NGOs, CBOs and sympathetic individuals. The involvement of trade unions that had hitherto confined themselves to the formal sector represents an attempt to redefine themselves in a changed employment landscape. Some political parties too joined hands with NGOs, adding a new dimension to the struggles. The People's Tribunal organised in January 2005 helped a public expression of anger and distress caused by the evictions. This was subsequently followed by an emergence of resistance on the ground. People started rebuilding on their lands; women took a lead and marched upto their original sites and put up their huts. Such was the case in Vikhroli, Mankhurd, Malad, Worli[10] and other places. Bulldozers were stopped and fences were broken into. By the end of February, 18 of the 21 sites cleared were re-encroached upon.

Build-up of political pressure on the state government to fulfil the electoral promise of extending the tolerance date to 2001 resulted in an agreement to do the same in February 2005. The subsequent filing of an affidavit by the state government to this effect and the Mumbai High

Court orders for formulation of a comprehensive housing policy put temporary deterrents in the demolition drive. The massive flooding in Mumbai in July 2005 exacerbated the difficulties faced by slum dwellers; however it also presented an opportunity to reclaim the cleared lands.

These claims have not been formally recognised; evictions and threats for the same are an ever present reality for the slum dwellers. However, communities have begun to resist and articulate their concerns in a few places. Currently, some of the alliances built up after 2005 demolitions have weakened; however there is a new willingness to join hands on issues expressed by all actors concerned.

Challenges Ahead

A critical challenge faced by the struggle is countering the internalisation of illegal occupancy and willingness to accept punitive action on one hand and asserting a right to the city on the other. The numerical and geographical strength of the struggle has grown manifold since 2005; several communities have spontaneously come forward to redress threats faced by them.

In projects like the MUIP where only sections of communities are displaced, assertion has been difficult vis-à-vis evictions effecting entire communities. The limited outreach of existing mobilisations and dependence on these are also impediments to a wider assertion of right to the city.

In many ways, the struggle has been able to connect disparate issues. This includes bridging of the divide between residential and work spaces. A proposed concept for recognising slums as service guilds is a step in this direction. It has also been able to forge connections between the evictees ineligible for rehabilitation and evictees getting rehabilitation and resettlement. Attempt to link issues of small and big cities, of rural distress, migration and urban displacement have been made through a nationwide consultative process. A process to redefine the nature of urban development emphasising sustainability and equity has been launched. It has been articulated in demands arising through the consultation and petitions made subsequently. However, this redefinition is fraught with internal contradictions and complexities, which are not easily reconcilable. The process of reconciliation requires much further debate.

This process may be compromised in the heat of responding to several impending threats of displacement. However, alignments based on this rushed process may not be tenuous. The multilayered nature of actions required to contend with the multi-quartered assault on the poor is another challenge faced by the struggle. Balancing the grassroots mobilisation with public demonstrations, court battles, advocacy attempts at the state and the national level, and media representations is a tightrope walk; especially given the fact that organisations have little preparedness for prolonged struggles as they have been well settled in 'developmental' work for a long time.

The biggest challenge to the struggle however, remains the fractured nature of the constituency. It needs to be acknowledged that the slums and the informal sector are widely differentiated. They are divided by datelines for tolerance, by their ethnic, religious and caste compositions, access to basic services; land ownership and geophysical locations. The systems of tenure and 'ownership' are also complex, often multi-tiered. Forging unity in this fractured constituency is perhaps, not an impossible but an uphill task. An equation of slums with poverty and slum dwellers with exploited is not realistic. Binaries can lead to easy, momentous mobilisation but can slip into being iniquitous labels themselves.

Slippery Terrains

There is a definite multi-directional assault on the poor in cities in India. Mumbai as the commercial capital of the country is ideally positioned for gaining global competitiveness. The demands for becoming competitive have meant vigorous, continuous actions against spaces of the poor. The resurgence of civil society actions from a NGOised, isolated, hierarchical situation demonstrates the vibrant potential of several organisations in the country and their essential rootedness in their respective realities. It evokes hope and promise. However, a mapping of the contours of this struggle demonstrates the uphill task confronting the struggle. It also demonstrates slipperiness of the terrain and the challenge therein.

NOTES

1. These evictions were one of the largest demolitions in the city at that point. These settlements were evicted to make way for quarters of Atomic Energy Officials. The slum dwellers had to wage a struggle to get rehabilitated.
2. Sanjay Gandhi National Park is located in the Northwest suburb of Borivali. The evictions in this case were a response to a public interest litigation filed by an environmental group in Mumbai.
3. Daulat Nagar was located in Santacruz, now an elite Western suburb. This

eviction too was in response to a public interest litigation filed by the residents association to restore their rights to a planned neighborhood.

4. Bhabrekar Nagar is a settlement in the Western part of the city suburbs. Its demolition was brutal and in the midst of monsoons. The State Government agreed to rehabilitate eligible settlers after a fact finding inquiry by civil society organisations.
5. *Mumbai Mirror*, May 17, 2006, page 1.
6. M/s Shantistar Builders *vs*. Narayan Totame, 1990.
7. Amitra Patel *vs*. Union of India 2000.
8. Ulhasnagar corporation is located towards the north of Mumbai Metropolitan region. In response to a PIL filed by a two citizens it was revealed that over 90 per cent of constructions in the city were illegal. The court ordered these to be removed. After a few such actual demolitions, the State Government regularized these through a resolution.
9. Mr. Antulay was well known for his closeness to the then PM for whom he also stated a special foundation; a lot of funds were routed to the foundation by developers who sought enhanced cement quotas. He resigned in the wake of a public exposure of this scam.
10. These are all various places in the city. Worli is in the city, Vikroli and Mankhurd are eastern suburbs while Malad is a western suburb.

20

SLUMS AND CIVIL SOCIETY
The Limits of Urban Activism[1]

SUPRIYA ROYCHOWDHURY

Introduction

The literature on urban poverty in recent times has offered rich insights into the scale and depth of urban poverty alongside escalating wealth in cities, as well as the political-institutional factors that have underlined the neglect of the urban poor. In contrast, there has been relatively less scholarly attention on what seems to be an equally important dimension: the large and expanding number of groups engaged in addressing the multiple dimensions of urban poverty. These of course are what are commonly known as the NGO sector, or civil societal organisations. While there are indeed valuable studies at the micro level on the work of particular NGOs in specific sectors, there is an absence of effort to address the question of the limits and potential of such activism. For example, given the proliferating number of NGOs/civil society organisations, an important question, but one which is never posed would be: is there a common, anchoring, framework which defines NGO urban activism? A second important question would seem to be, since welfare and redistribution, are essentially political issues, is there a possible way in which we can define the politics of NGO/civil society organisations? Finally, it would seem that the centrality of civil society as the agent of welfare has emerged in the background of the near total disappearance of the agency of class in welfare politics. At the same time, however, there is little attempt to provide the theoretical foundations of civil society activism as an alternative to class-based activism. At some level, the highly disparate functioning of civil society organisations in the realm of urban poverty could be related to this lack of theorisation, or at least to the absence of any substantive attempt to understand what could be the central underpinnings of this activism, its limits and possibilities. These and related issues underline the tentative considerations in this paper.

The question of poverty in Bangalore city has attracted much attention in recent years. In the era of globalisation, Bangalore has been rapidly catapulted to the status of a city on the high growth path, driven by cutting edge sectors like the IT and the BT. The concomitant expansion of wealth amongst the city's upper classes, as also the poverty of many deprived sections has been commented upon.

The scholarly literature on Bangalore's poverty has sought to establish links between globalisation/liberalisation policies and the city's poor, as also to the changing profile of governance that has led to the neglect of the underclass. Thus scholars have pointed to the implicit bias in urban governance and institutions—in patterns of master planning, in the emerging role of parastatal agencies, as well as in the growing impact of corporate thinking on urban governance that has led to a definition of urban development along lines of infrastructure development—roads, airports, by passes and bridges—that benefit the urban upper class rather than the underclass[2].

Despite this emerging scholarly attention to Bangalore's poverty profile, the fact that the city's underclass have not benefited from this change, remains a subscript, rarely featured in the public domain. It is, however, also a script that is the daily engagement of the large number of civil society groups which perceive themselves as advocating and acting for the rights of the urban poor. Given the scale of urban poverty, and the large number of groups that are in fact engaged in work to relieve the conditions of the poor in the city, it is somewhat ironical that poverty and poverty-related NGO work is largely invisible, and absent from the public or the political imagination. For the most part, NGO/civil society activism related to urban poverty is about lobbying and negotiating with government agencies, organising funding of different activities, organising grassroots work like teaching of schools in slums, and to a limited extent, advocacy directed towards policy changes (for example, over legislation related to unorganised workers' rights). Such advocacy, however, takes place mostly in committee rooms, and very occasionally in *dharnas* and public meetings. Thus the low visibility of urban poverty related issues is possibly a function of the way in which civil society organisations, working on urban poverty, have chosen to define their activities. This activity takes place by and large in NGO offices, these may range from a one room office equipped with a single computer, to fairly large organisations employing perhaps 50 to 60 persons. The work occurs simultaneously from these offices and from the grassroots levels, that is, in slums and related areas. But rarely are the issues projected into the public domain. While lobbying with government agencies is an important part of NGO activity, this is most often in the patron-client format. Influencing policy remains in the realm of advocacy and rarely becomes a part of the nitty gritty of political bargaining.

This is significant because the whole issue of urban poverty is, after all, necessarily a political issue. The self conscious distancing of NGO activism from political parties (discussed in greater detail in section 3) would be a point to note. There is also of course the fact that in Bangalore the influence of the left, either in terms of political parties, that is the CPI (M) or other leftist parties and that of trade unions, is fairly low. The recent resurgence of naxalite activities in Karnataka would seem to indicate that some political mobilisation around issues of economic deprivation linked to globalisation policies is indeed occurring, but these activities so far have remained confined to rural themes and outlying areas. The question of urban poverty has not found a political/intellectual anchoring in any explicit understanding or critique of broader policy issues that provide the context of urban poverty.

It is in the background of this broad characterisation that this paper seeks to look at urban poverty in Bangalore from the perspective of activities of civil society organisations. The paper is organised in the following manner: in section 2, I raise some theoretical issues around the question of civil society initiatives in the realm of urban poverty/welfare. In section 3, I present some information, drawing partially on an ongoing project on slums in Bangalore. This section is concerned primarily with the activities of civil society organisations in slums, and an attempt to understand the modalities of their activities, the impact, the potential and the limitations. In the light of the theoretical questions raised in section 2, the empirical data are reviewed in section 3 and tentative analysis is made in section 4.

Class and Civil Society: Problematising Political Action

While the market is perceived to be indifferent to welfare, the State is seen to be increasingly disinterested or disinclined towards welfare and redistribution related issues. Civil society has gained much centrality as a domain where these values are prioritised. This paper raises the question of the efficacy of civil society as a political agency. While the State may be disinterested in welfare, nevertheless welfare and redistribution remain, primarily, political issues. In other words, the context for welfare is essentially one of contestation over policy, over resource allocation, implementation and so on.

Thus although civil society is largely seen, and celebrated, as an arena distinct from the State, it is somewhat, paradoxically, actually in the site of politics—and in continuous dialogue and interaction with the State and its agencies as well as other politically defined entities—that the practical context of civil society functioning is constituted. It is therefore relevant to raise the question both of what constitutes the politics of civil society, as well as, in what sense can we talk of political agency in the context of civil society. In the following I attempt to outline the main contours of these questions.

Historically, the struggle for welfare and redistributive rights has been pitched, both theoretically and in practice, in terms of the rights of workers, specifically, (or broadly in terms of a redefinition of property rights, as in land reforms). The protagonists of such struggles, as is well known, have been trade unions and social democratic parties, (peasant movements, radical political parties,) and so on. In the present era, the capitalist structure of production has changed from centralised production to increasingly decentralised and unregulated systems, which underlie the emergence of "informality" in employment structures. The widely dispersed and diverse nature of the informal sector workforce, as well as the multiplicity of issues that characterise the informal sector, would render the task of constructing a sharply defined politics or theory of class obviously difficult. Informality thus poses serious challenges both to the theorists and the practitioners of class politics.

An obvious consequence of this has been certain dissolution of working class political agency in the politics of welfare, and the disappearance of class related issues from the welfare discourse. Civil society has become central in the activism around issues of inequality, redistribution and welfare. In this domain of activism, the issues of deprivation and rights that affect the urban poor/informal sector workers have been addressed by focusing on themes of community/neighbourhood/slum development rather than on the workplace, and on broad themes of basic amenities rather than on employment/income. Thus, the focus is on the citizen, rather than on the worker, and on citizens' rights rather than on workers' claims. The shift, then, is from class to community, both as a recipient of welfare and as agency in the struggle for welfare.

(This shift is noticeable in the rural context as well. The new focus of rural welfare is no longer land reforms, which, typically, pit the landless and marginal peasantry against landlords or kulaks. For both governments and activists, the focus is on development projects—which affect the rural community as a whole—and on local government, which define the entire village in terms of a community as an agent of change rather than focusing on class cleavages along land ownership issues).

How does one theorise political action in the context of this shift? As a concept, civil society, compared to class, provides a much broader basis of activism: NGOs, community based groups, grass-roots organisations. While these are studied extensively both in Political Science and in Sociology, there is relatively little active theorisation on the problem of what is the constitutive ingredient of such activism, politically defined.

Multiple issues, ideas, funding sources, and methodologies, characterise the domain of civil society activism. There is also the absence of an unifying or anchoring identity. In principle, there is nothing wrong in a large number of diverse groups engaged in an ever widening range of activities over numerous issues, and what is lost in terms of coherence and unity of action would be gained in terms of the variety of issues covered, and the richness of participation. This indeed is the image of civil society activism that has inspired a whole generation of scholars and activists. And yet, a deeper examination of the concepts highlights that there is a reluctance to engage with the need to define the politics of activism.

First, understandably, the nature of political alignments in civil society is varied (that is, it may range from nil to intense) and shifting, at the level of practical activities. There is also of course the consideration that much of welfare related social activism is self-consciously non-political. It is not clear to what extent we can call this apolitcal in nature, or in what sense, being distanced from politics, that is, from any single political party/parties, itself constitutes a kind of unnamed political space. But whether civil society activism is nebulously connected to the political mainstream, or is seeking an alternative political space, the question of political agency is one that remains unaddressed or inadequately addressed in the scholarly literature, and is approached entirely in the spirit of ad hocism in practice.

Secondly, while activists are engaged at various levels, there is no one single developmental model that anchors this diverse activism around the multiple issues of urban poverty. A large number of civil society organisations are struggling with a diversity of issues: street children, adult literacy, slum development, provision of basic services to the urban poor, health, environmental issues, credit availability and so on. Yet there is little to bring these groups together. While many of these groups are visible in large, anti-globalisation fronts, such as the World Social Forum, and so on, their stand on economic reforms and related policies, on an every day basis, is not known. Such groups may well depend upon international funding generated from countries and from agencies which are pro-marketisation or they may be drawing upon government funding from State agencies and ministries which are at the same time responsible for enacting marketisation policies. The point, however, is not only that this duality is present in the functioning dynamics of many civil society associations, but that most such associations do not necessarily perceive the need to develop a clearly articulated stand either on economic policy, or on their own politics.

Third, while community has replaced class, how does one theorise political action in the context of communities? We know of course that communities can and do act as powerful political agents in given circumstances. But particularly in the context, for example, of urban poverty, and the diverse ways in which poverty affects the ethnic, religious, gender and other divides, there has been little scholarly thinking on the issue of what could be a unifying platform for political action on the basis of community identities.

Finally, in the shadow of this largely unaddressed question lies a second one: while class is no longer central in the context of political subjectivity, yet economic deprivations remain an enduring and underlining issue in the rhetoric and practices of many civil societal organisations working on developmental/poverty related themes. But, the question, specifically, of a politics of need, is not addressed. Or perhaps it is more correct to say that the politics of need is entirely fragmented, surfacing to political visibility at times over the struggle for urban land, at times for the rights of children, at other times over livelihood issues such as the right to use pavements for selling goods. Consequently, the issue of political agency or subjectivity gets linked to the question of economic deprivation in an ad hoc, case by case manner, but not in a substantive sense.

A more specific way of stating this would be that the concern with issues of poverty and inequity are not placed within a paradigm of conflicting or competing interests. This position, firstly, shapes the selection of issues around which the activist discourse on poverty is articulated. For example, urban activism has made a definitive turn towards issues of basic amenities, away from income and employment. Basic amenities have a flavour of collective sharing, (thus, admitting more numbers to the enjoyment of certain rights without displacing or reducing the rights enjoyed by others), and also can be seen under the broad umbrella of human/citizens' rights (rather than the rights of a specific class or category of the population, typically pitted against the claims of other categories). A basic amenity, as a concept, also lends itself well both to State responsibility as well as to the notions of public-private partnerships and so on which now dominate the developmental jargon. In other words, the debates around basic amenities occur within the accepted framework of developmental and policy discourses and regimes. While these debates reflect differences, they do not reflect zero sum options. On the other hand, questions such as employment go to the heart of policy options (privatisation, large-scale, capital-intensive technologies versus small-scale, labour-intensive technologies, the scope of FDI, and so on) and questions of wages and income are at the rough edge of thorny dualities of profit/investment/efficiency versus welfare/redistribution/ social insurance and justice.

The space of urban activism is today occupied by a large number of groups working on slums, the physical habitation of the urban poor, rather than in the factory, workshop, or construction site where the poor work. This choice of site shapes and at the same time is shaped by a politics that treads a pragmatic, functional path, which does not address questions of competing or conflicting interests. Thus, the questions of primary education for children in slums, or providing toilets to slum dwellers are welfaristic but non-conflictual issues. Even where slum dwellers see themselves in conflict with the interests of private urban land owners, this conflict, as it has been defined by civil societal associations, is entirely mediated and structured through State agencies, rather than involving any direct confrontation or even dialogue with land owners.

But what is the broader politics, which shapes this strategy? Tentatively one could say that civil society associations actively engaged in slum development do have a criticism as well as a systematic understanding of the broader forces of globalisation. For example, escalating urban land prices are directly related to private sector and multinational entry into the domain of urban real estate. However, the activism around slum land does not relate to this understanding or critique. In other words, this critique remains latent, while activism is focused on methods that are largely in the nature of lobbying with government agencies for a particular piece of land, and occasional movemental impulses such as taking out a procession, or holding a public meeting in front of a state government office, and so on. The point is that in this context activism around issues of land, relating to the urban poor, is rarely, if ever, able to connect the struggle at the micro level to either a macro struggle or to a broad policy challenge. While particular policies or directions taken in a globalising economy may be critiqued by activist groups, there is no attempt to take this forward towards the formulation of a generalised political position on the question.

NGOs and Slums in Bangalore[3]

While there is some debate about the exact number of slums in Bangalore, there is a general consensus that the number of sums and of slum dwellers has increased in the city (Schenk 2001). The debate itself reflects a lack of clarity on the definition of slums, whether one should count as slums only the officially declared slums or the large number of undeclared slums, squatter settlements and so on. There is also the question that all of the city's poor do not necessarily live in slums. Be that as it may, one could proceed with a rough conception of slums as the habitation of the largest number of the city's poor, reflecting varied, but generally highly inadequate access to basic resources of life.

Slum dwellers in Bangalore are employed in a wide range of economic activities in the informal sector, be it in manufacturing (small factories), services (auto/bicycle repairing, small eateries) or in self employment (push cart vendors, street side/traffic light sellers) rag pickers and so on. While there is considerable deprivation linked to these given forms of employment, emerging from inadequate incomes, lack of health and other insurance, and complete absence of security of employment, NGOs and civil society organisations are focused, almost exclusively, on the issues of housing, basic amenities (water, sanitation, street lights, electricity), and education. In a limited number of cases, there has been some effort to address work related questions, such as in the case of rag pickers and construction workers.

Drawing partially from an ongoing project on slums in Karnataka, I describe below the nature of activism around slum issues. Chamrajpet is an important commercial area located in the heart of Bangalore near Lalbagh road. There are twenty three slums in this area, out of which this project did a survey of twelve slums. While the details of this survey are not presented here, I draw partially from the survey in order to address the questions raised in this paper.

The main problem, as articulated by people living in the slum as well as by slum leaders, relate to land. While the majority of slums in this cluster were "declared", in each of the slums there was a complete absence of adequate housing. Houses were in the form of temporary, make-shift structures. Basic amenities were highly inadequate, although in a few of the slums in this cluster, public toilets and taps had been built through the initiative of the local MLA or the councillor.

The predominant, shared concern in the slums was the question of land rights. It was clear that this issue had crowded out other issues such as livelihood and education. In each of the slums, the common context was that the land in question remained legally in the name of a private owner, and therefore, in the eyes of law, the slum dwellers, although living in a declared slum, were encroachers in some sense. The land occupied by the slum dwellers can become rightfully theirs only if the private land-owner is willing to transfer the ownership rights. There appeared to be a whole range of complex questions around this issue. The question of land acquisition by the government is of course tied to the question of the interests of different stake holder: private land owners, government officials, politicians, interested real estate developers, and the slum dwellers themselves. In this particular case, successive governments appeared to have little or no interest in land acquisition and in negotiating and enforcing an acceptable rate of compensation. Government officials, in collusion with private owners, foot drag and stall the settlement of the ownership and compensation question, even as real estate values soar rapidly and land prices in this prime area are pushed up every year.

In each of these slums, despair and hope both are focused on the land question. In this particular area, there has been no significant NGO intervention. Slum dwellers had for long pinned their hopes on the MLA of the Congress party for whom they have voted in four recent assembly elections except the last by-election, in 2004. The Congress MLA, R.V. Devraj, has brought some basic amenities to each of the slums, through the MLA fund. On the question of land, however, long promised action has never materialised. Inspite of this, Devraj continues to have some kind of hold on the slums, mediated through slum leaders.

Each of the slums surveyed had a slum committee. While the committees themselves appear to be in a moribund State, the leaders of the committees are fairly articulate on the question of slum development. These committees were originally linked to the National Slum Federation, through the Karnataka Slum Federation. However, in the course of time, local slum leaders in this area grew increasingly disenchanted with the

National Slum Federation. Over the last few years, they have broken away from the National Federation, and formed the Bangalore Slum Federation, covering 153 slums in the central areas of the city.

The formation of the Bangalore Slum Federation reflects the fractures and factions within the national and state level slum activism. More interestingly, however, the operational dynamics of the Bangalore Slum Federation reflect some of the central dilemmas facing grassroots peoples' movements. While linked closely to the Congress MLA and the Congress Councillor, leaders of the federation also seek to carve out a space for themselves. In doing so, they have given themselves a time frame beyond which they will not wait for Devraj to help them. A new committee has been formed with representatives from each of the slums in the Chamrajpet area. The singular characteristic of this committee seems to be that anyone with any party affiliation can be part of the committee. The single unifying theme is the question of land rights. And land rights is the single agenda of the Bangalore Slum Federation, as well as the Committee.

The Committee thus occupies an autonomous political space in their imagination. This theme of autonomy is significant, as it reflects the urban poors' disenchantment with established institutions, which include both the political parties and the NGOs. Despite the proliferating number of NGOs in the city, this pulsating space has not attracted too much NGO attention. While the Congress has promised action for a long time, nothing has happened. In the 2004 elections, the long time MLA, Devraj yielded his constituency to the former Chief Minister S.M. Krishna. Although Krishna was widely known for an elitist bias in his urban policies, he nevertheless won the seat, which he gave up almost immediately after being appointed Governor of Maharashtra. In the subsequent by—election, while Devraj contested again, a Muslim member of the Janata Dal (S) won by a narrow margin. The defeat of the long time Congress candidate, to whom many of the slum leaders are connected, has only increased the distancing of these persons from political institutions. In fact, the alienation of the slum leaders from political representatives is fairly deep. The most significant example of this seemed to be in their approach to information. "We don't get to know any budget allocation or what has been happening for the development of the slums. There is no information that comes to us by any source. If at all we want to know about the budget or the government policies and approach the MLA or the Councillor for implementation of those activities, we will be seen as a threat to their position and they will start ignoring us. We don't want to lose their favour. The government calls only the NGOs and political party members to decide the policies".[4]

The decision to form a Committee in an autonomous space reflects their distrust of political structures, and their deep disappointment with the lack of results on the land question. However, this fledgling initiative appeared to be unanchored in two significant ways. In the first place, Bangalore's real estate situation represents a highly charged, intensely competitive environment, with its complex links to the world of officialdom and politicians cutting across party lines. There would be no way to evolve an alternative space in this context of power, money and corruption, without political alignments on the basis of which an alternative power block could be constructed. In principle such political resources could be provided by radical, leftist parties, and/or by the sheer weight of numbers where thousands of slum dwellers, pursuing their land rights, could come together. But for the weight of the political establishment to shift in their favour, such an uprising would necessarily have to be *political.* The visibility of leftist parties is low in the city, and I have already mentioned the fractured character of the Slum Federations at national and state levels, which prevents the coming together of large numbers of slum dwellers.

Secondly, while members of the Committee are aware in an approximate manner of the politics of land in the city, their understanding of the land question is not based on an understanding of the overall policy context. Economic policies, pursued by successive governments in the last two decades, have created the context in which land prices have soared, and where the State's interest in acquiring land for slum dwellers has obviously diminished[5]. A peoples' movement to get land rights for slum dwellers is unlikely to achieve its objectives unless this broader policy context is at the same time understood and challenged. But there appeared to be little basis for thinking that the kind of activism reviewed here would evolve towards a broader challenge to existing power and policy regimes.

In the case reviewed briefly above, the initiative around the question of land rights has shifted, albeit partially, from a tenuous dependence on the local MLA to the formation of an autonomous slum federation, which has risen, organically, so to speak, from the slums. What happens when the land question is mediated by a NGO/civil society organisation? Drawing again partially from the surveys made in the project, I review briefly the activities and impact of NGOs. Most NGOs enter slums with the idea of developmental activities. Given the predominating preoccupation of slum dwellers themselves with the question of land rights, NGOs typically become involved in this issue. The Karnataka Koligeri

Nivasa Sangathana (KKNSS) has been engaged with a wide range of issues related to the urban poor for over two decades in Karnataka. In Bangalore, in recent years, activists of the organisation have been increasingly drawn into the battle for land. Here I summarise a single case where the KKNSS has successfully led the people of a particular slum to gain their land rights.

In 1975 when NGEF (New Government Electric Factory) was being constructed, a large number of construction workers were engaged and were provided with living space inside the construction ground. After some time a shed was put up as makeshift housing. In 1987 KKNSS began work in the slum, with the first objective of getting the slum declared. From the beginning, NGEF, although a public sector company, adopted a hostile approach towards the issue of the slum dwellers' rights. After a few years of struggle, the slum was declared.

At this time, the slum dwellers, under the leadership of the KKNSS, staked a claim to the land. The argument was that they had invested years of work in constructing NGEF and had developed some interests in the surrounding area. In response, The NGEF issued a letter to each household in the slum declaring them to be illegal occupants and ordering them to vacate the area within seven days. The negotiations that followed took on the colour of a movement, under the leadership of the KKNSS. The refusal to grant the land was made on the ground that the fact that NGEF had turned out to be a loss-making unit. Finally, as the struggle moved towards a crescendo, the government agreed to formally transfer the land from NGEF to the KSCB, and each household was given a possession certificate. After the land transfer, houses were constructed with loans from HUDCO and a grant from Rotary.

An NGO called Maithri has been working in slums in the southern and eastern parts of Bangalore for close to twenty years. Maithri's main focus in the initial years was to provide pre-primary support and education. In the course of working in slums, the NGO has been drawn into the land question, and other issues of community development. In Bharatmata slum, the NGO had successfully negotiated for land rights, and subsequent to this, with a loan from HUDCO and a subsidy from the state government, houses have been built for the slum dwellers.

Thus, in both NGEF and Bharatmata slums, under the leadership of two different NGOs, slum dwellers had succeeded in obtaining some permanency of status on the land, and permanent houses. In Bharatmata slum, however, the houses had no water or electricity supply, no sewerage connections and no system of garbage disposal. Most of the slum dwellers spoke with a sense of complete helplessness of the lack of response from the local councillor and the local MLA on these issues. Other than the land question, one central activity of Maithri has been to provide education and to pull children away from the streets (mainly rag picking). In the slum there are 53 children who are still working as whole time workers. Around 20 children were seen attending a newly set up school within the slum. A few were in the age of 2-6 years. Of the rest who were in the age group of 7-15 years, several were working part time in domestic work or as waste pickers. In spite of the newly constructed houses, the slum bore a look of dirt and degradation. Young adults are all drop outs after class 7 or 8. Some of them appeared to be employed, in a variety of informal sector jobs, such as electrician, plumber, cycle repairing. However, no one has work or a full six days of the week.

In the NGEF slum, households had electricity, regular water supply and sanitation. What stood out starkly in this slum, particularly in the context of its relatively better infrastructure, was the lack of work amongst the majority of the men and women. Most of them were construction workers, who got work irregularly, and had no access to any kind of social insurance. In both these cases, the gaining of land rights appeared to have done what a critique of housing projects has appropriately pointed out: "put a roof over their poverty" (Satterthwaite :2002).

Deshianagar is another slum in which Maithri has been engaged for 18 years. This slum is composed of 150 huts; each of these had a tarpaulin roof, supported by some kind of poles. The land on which these constructions have come up used to be a grave-yard. As such the land belongs to the BMP. Thus, although in principle the transfer of land rights should have been easier where a public agency is the owner, this has not been so in this case, and the land rights remain elusive for the people. The slum represented an image that was far away from the time and space in which Bangalore city is located. Of the 150 households, men are astrologers, that is, persons who sit on pavements, or go from house to house, and read peoples' fate. The women are beggars at road sides and traffic lights. The average income of households was reported to be Rs. 1,000 per month. Although located in a central part of Bangalore, no government programme or project had reached the slum. Maithri had been instrumental in building toilets, and in making arrangements for a weekly medical clinic. But other than this, two decades of its engagement had left no perceptible impact on what appeared to be a picture of complete darkness, dilapidation and hopelessness.

Conclusions

As mentioned at the outset, new forms of urban activism have replaced the traditional struggles of the less privileged, typically waged by trade unions and left-leaning parties. The literature on urban movements, as also the shifting modalities of urban activism, reflects the search for new instruments and objects of struggle as well as a search for agency. Indeed, within Marxist scholarship itself, the response to the numerical shrinking and the changing face of the formal sector workforce has been to acknowledge the need to shift the struggle from wages to a broad spectrum of rights of citizens. But within Marxist scholarship there has been relatively little theorisation on the political agency of this new welfarism. Are the new protagonists of welfare going to be those employed diversely in the informal sector, but seeking a common platform of rights, or are they going to be members of communities, defined diversely in terms of their physical habitat, gender, ethnicity, and so on?

While the literature on civil society is both large and rich, the question, specifically, of political agency, has not been problematised. As a possible direction, one could look, for example, at Partha Chatterjee's notion of political society (Chatterjee 2004). According to Chatterjee, civil society represents associational forms of the westernised elite, which typically do not include members of the underclass. On the other hand, as a result of both democratisation and of the availability and possibility of a large number of developmental and welfare provisions, this mass of citizens obviously occupies an increasingly politicised space. Distinct from the so-called "modern" politics of elite civil society organisations, and perceived by the State frequently to stand at the margins of legality, these political mobilisations, often transitory in nature, constitute what Chatterjee terms "political society". In the absence of class politics, and where civil society is seen to be representative only of a narrow, "modernised", social elite, political society is the third side of the triangle that embodies the promise of a wider democracy.

There is a definite sense in which political society is sought to be given the characteristic features of a community. Thus a slum association, when it is fighting for basic rights, draws not only upon the government's stated responsibilities, but also appeals to the moral rhetoric of a community. Secondly, from Chatterjee's perspective, many of these associations frequently occupy the terrain of illegality: slum dwellers occupying unauthorised land, vendors selling their wares under makeshift pavement constructions. Therefore the State's relationship with these organisations, as well as the State's recognition of their claims, is necessarily only of a contingent nature, depending upon the particular nature of political configurations at any given time. There is, in Chatterjee's text, an explicit mention that the State's recognition of these groups' claims is a measure of how far the rules can be bent in a given moment. Finally, there is a definite sense in which civil society and political society are seen to be at opposite ends of the spectrum. The project of modernisation is one that is imposed from the top downwards, and in this the modernisers (that is, the elite, those who are in the civil society) encounter much resistance which is facilitated by the activities of political society.

If one could take the Bangalore Slum Federation as an example of political society, how would one, then, examine the political efficacy of such examples of political society? The other question, of course, is: in what sense can we, realistically speaking, think of political society as community? Community, as we know, is defined by a sense of collective identity, sustained, and this is important, over time. Where the acquiring of permanent rights over land is the only and single objective, it is not clear in what sense a slum association, or a number of associations, pursuing a single objective, can qualify to be a community. And indeed, studies of slum activism have shown that this kind of activism, focused upon a single slum or a set of slums frequently dissipate not only into multiple groups, ostensibly pursuing the same objectives but in a competitive manner. Such organisations also very soon lose their sharpness and direction as they become co-opted by diverse political parties/other organisations (Smith 2001). Beyond the immediate objective defined by a specific issue there is little to hold such associations together over a period of time or to extend their activities to diverse sources of deprivation that affect people living in slums. In that sense, there is little to qualify them as a community except in the most transitory or latent sense. Perhaps more importantly, the element of political representativeness or agency that is the defining question of this paper, is found in such collectivities in a sporadic, transient, and unsystematic manner.

The other more urgent questions with regard to such formations would be, occupying, as they do, a grey area between the terrains of the legal and the unlawful (seeking ownership rights over a piece of land which may be morally theirs but legally belong to someone else), defining a collective identity only in terms of this single objective, unanchored in a wider world view or vision, and perhaps most importantly, lacking any substantive links with the structures of political power (via parties, or other established political lobbies), in what sense can one speak of political society as a substantive agent of political action in the struggle for welfare?

Civil society associations, of the kind reviewed above, function in a sphere of legality and are endowed with sophisticated organisational features and more sustained pattern of community developmental action. Both KKNSS and Maithri would fit into the category of civil society organisations. There are, however, two basic questions that can be raised in connection with the nature of activism which is consciously delinked from questions of income and employment. First, one could take the example of activism around slum development. Slums indeed represent in the ultimate physical form the misery of the urban poor. It would be difficult to contest the claim that improving living conditions in slums would make a significant impact on the poor in terms of reducing their misery. Whether or not the physical improvement of living spaces could have an impact on the basic situation of poverty, or whether such physical improvement can be sustained in a context where there is no perceptible improvement in employment opportunities and in income, these are important questions which have somehow not featured in the overall conceptualisations of civil society organisations of their own work.

The second dimension to this question involves the workplace itself. If indeed activism is to be centred around questions of well-being delinked from the work situation, there would indeed be no way, within this paradigm, to address workforce related issues at the workplace. It needs to be underlined here that the world of informality encompasses not only those who are self employed—a class of persons who may have some control over their working lives, if not over the income that they generate—but also an expanding number of the workforce who are employed with unregulated wages and working conditions. The vulnerability of such workers arises from the way in which labour is increasingly being organised in certain sectors: minimum or below minimum wage rates, absence of employment security, regulated working hours, and social insurance. In other words, while work and welfare are not always and in every instance linked together (as in unemployment insurance policies, food stamps, and so on), at the same time it could be argued that the question of welfare cannot be addressed in any substantive manner unless the question of work and wages is simultaneously addressed.

Economic rights have rarely, if ever, been the gift of governments. Economic rights are most frequently the result of sustained struggles, hard bargaining and negotiations, social movements and political activism. What would be the political modalities and instruments through which such a struggle would be conducted in the current context? To what extent would political society/civil society address this question[6]?

The struggles of a whole range of activists indicate possible answers to this question. While activists are engaged at various levels, there is no one single developmental model that drives activism around the multiple issues of urban poverty. But this orientation also sets the limits of urban poverty policies and activism by closing off the possibilities of a more broad ranging debate over urban poverty, and the formulation of more comprehensive policies that would include vital dimensions of citizens' lives.

Secondly, the discourse and activism around livelihood rights and projects on basic amenities such as housing, water, sanitation, and so on, are relatively non contentious issues. On the other hand, any engagement with questions of employment and income would involve activists in larger questions of the structure of the economy and the broad direction of economic policies. Thus, a single most important cause of urban poverty is indeed the increasing informalisation of the industrial economy. But, it is somewhat easier to address questions that represent the symptoms of poverty, such as housing, slum development and so on, rather than confront the content of economic policies that underlie much of current forms of urban poverty.

Finally, given the multiplicity of the many communities as well as the diversity of the issues being addressed, activism is organised around small groups lobbying over specific issues, rather than collective questions. This positioning obviously rules out the question of larger mobilisations for political purposes, and sets its own limits to the impact that such activism can have over broader questions of economic policy. At the theoretical level, this question has not been addressed systematically. There is always an effort to bypass the question of the political subjectivity of the workforce in the informal sector, both by noting their extreme heterogeneity and by somehow pushing the agenda of welfare past work and income related issues.

NOTES

1. This is a revised version of a paper presented at a conference entitled "Tackling Exclusion: Shelter, Basic Services and Citizen's Rights in Globalising Megacities of Asia", New Delhi, June 1-3, 2006, and at a second conference on "Indian State and Globalisation" National Foundation of India, New Delhi, October 6-8, 2006. The author is grateful to participants

at both conferences for useful comments. The research on this paper was made possible by a grant from the National Foundation of India under the project "Globalisation and the Indian State". The author is particularly grateful to Prof Neera Chandoke and Prof Pratap Bhanu Mehta, coordinators of the project, for their useful insights and suggestions on the project on Karnataka as well as on the present paper.

2. *See*, for example, Benjamin (2000) Ghosh, (2005) Pani (2006).
3. This section draws from an ongoing project ("Local Welfare in a Global Context: Slums and Urban Welfare in Karnataka's Development") being funded by the National Foundation of India, New Delhi. The project involves a survey of 30 slums in Bangalore and two other districts. The analysis in the present paper draws only on case studies of four slums in Bangalore city, and the activities of three NGOs.
4. Meeting with slum leaders in the Chamrajpet area, 15 February, 2006.
5. Governmental non-attention to the urban poor could be attributed to certain emerging structural features of the economy rather than to the inclinations and activities of particular government agencies or officials. This becomes particularly clear in the dynamics of land sale to multinational IT companies, and in government acquisition of land for mega projects that are clearly designed to support the part of Bangalore city which is closely aligned to the global economy. There are currently three mega projects being pursued by the government that were offered major concessions in the purchase of land. Land for the 138.6 sq km of IT Corridor to the east of the city was acquired under the single window clearance scheme of the Karnataka Industrial Area Development Board (KIADB) from small farmers in the area at low rates. Several landowners in the area have challenged in the High Court the acquisition of their land at rates which are alleged to be well below the market value. The IT Corridor has been provided with high grade infrastructure facilities, and will include not only IT offices, but also high end housing projects.

   The second major project for which the government has acquired 4,000 acres of land is the proposed new international airport at Devanhalli, to be constructed at a cost of Rs.1,355 crores. Around 40 per cent of the total area will be allotted for real estate development to fund the public-private partnership that will build the airport. Here too land was acquired from farmers at relatively low rates. The third major project is the Bangalore-Mysore Infrastructure Corridor (BMIC), a six-lane, 111km highway connecting Bangalore and Mysore. The KIADB notified 29,000 acres of land to be acquired on behalf of the private company which is constructing the BMIC (See Menon 2005)
6. For an examination of a civil society association engaged with workers' welfare, see RoyChowdhury (2005). In a study of women garment factory workers in Bangalore, it was found that CIVIDEP, an NGO, focused primarily on SHGs, awareness raising and so on, rather than on wage and work related issues.

REFERENCES

Acharya, S.K. (2002). "Slum Networking in Ahmedabad: An Alternate Approach", in A. Kundu and D. Mahadevia (eds.) *Poverty and Vulnerability in a Globalising Metropolis: Ahmedabad*, Manak Publishers, Delhi, pp. 349-72.

Acharya, S.K. and A. Parasher (2008). *Managing Waste in a Peri-Urban Locality: Vejalpur*, in D. Mahadevia and J. Wolfe (eds.) *Solid Waste Management in Indian Cities: Status and Emerging Practices*, Concept, New Delhi, pp. 312-28.

Adenwala, M. (1998). "Evicting the Right to Shelter", *Lawyer's Collective*, September.

Agle, R. (1998). "Wait for It: Foreign Contractors Have Been Loosing the Battle to Meet Construction Deadlines", *Vietnam Economic Times*, January, pp. 24-5.

Ahmedabad Urban Development Authority (1997a). *Revised Draft Development Plan of AUDA-2011 AD - Survey, Studies and Analysis, Part–I*, Ahmedabad Urban Development Authority, Ahmedabad.

Ahmedabad Urban Development Authority (1997b). *Revised Draft Development Plan of AUDA – 2011 AD - Policies, Proposals, and Programmes, Part II*, Ahmedabad Urban Development Authority, Ahmedabad.

Amis, P. (1997). "Indian Urban Poverty: Where Are the Levers For Its Effective Alleviation?" in *IDS Bulletin*, 28 (2).

Arkadie, B.V. and R. Mallon (2003). *Vietnam: a Transition Tiger*, Asia Pacific Press, Australian National University

Asian Development Bank (2001). *Poverty in People's Republic of China*, ADB, Manila.

Asian Development Bank (2004a). *Poverty Profile of the People's Republic of China*, Asian Development Bank, from the website.

Asian Development Bank (2004b). *Outlook 2004*, Oxford University Press for the Asian Development Bank, New York.

Asian Development Bank (2007). *Inequality in Asia - Key Indicators 2007 Special Chapter Highlights*, ADB, Manila. (Source: http://www.adb.org/documents/books/key_indicators/2007/pdf/Inequality-in-Asia-Highlights.pdf).

Asiaone (2006). *Shanghai Expo Aims to Break Even*, http://www.trade.gov.cn//php/show.php?id=3368 (accessed 24 April, 2006).

Association of Metropolitan Development Authorities (2003). *Land Policy for Development in the National Capital Territory of Delhi: 2001 - Considering Various Alternative Techniques of Access to Land*, Delhi Development Authority, Delhi.

Ba, T. (2005). "Time to Get it Right", *Vietnam Economic Times*, February, pp.14-6.

Badami, M. G; G. Tiwari and D. Mohan (2007). "Access and Mobility for the Urban Poor in India", in A.A. Laquian, V. Tewari and L.M. Hanley (ed.) *The Inclusive City – Infrastructure and Public Services for the Urban Poor in Asia*, published by Woodrow Wilson Centre Press Washington DC and distributed by The John Hopkins University Press, Baltimore, pp.100-21.

Bahl, Roy (1999). *Fiscal Policy in China – Taxation and Intergovernmental Fiscal Relations*, The 1990 Institute, San Francisco.

Balagopal, K. (2002). "Reflections on 'Gujarat Pradesh' of Hindu Rashtra", *Economic and Political Weekly*, 37 (22), pp. 2117-9.

Banerjee Guha, S. (1995). "Urban Development Process in Bombay: Planning for Whom?", in S. Patel and A. Thorner (eds.), *Bombay: Metaphor for Modern India*, Bombay. Delhi. Calcutta. Madras: Oxford University Press, pp. 100-20.

Baranovitch, N. (2003). "From the Margins to the Centre: The Uyghur Challenge in Beijing", *The China Quarterly*, pp. 726-50.

Batra, B.J. (2007). "Entitlement to Services and Amenities in JJ Clusters, JJ Relocation Colonies and Other Non-planned Settlements in Delhi: An Overview", in R. Sudarshan and S. Pande (eds.) *Ensuring Public Accountability through Community Action: A Case Study in East Delhi*, Institute of Social Studies Trust, New Delhi, pp. 54-76.

Baviskar, A. (2003). "Between Violence and Desire: Space, Power and Identity in the Making of Metropolitan Delhi", *International Social Science Journal*, 55, pp. 89-98.

Beall, J. (2002). "Globalization and Social Exclusion in Cities: Framing the Debate with Lessons from Africa and Asia", *Environment and Urbanization*, 14 (1), pp. 41-52.

Beijing Municipal Bureau of Statistics (2003). *Beijing Statistical Yearbook, 2003*, China Statistics Press, Beijing.

Beijing Municipal Bureau of Statistics (2004). *Beijing Statistical Yearbook, 2004*, China Statistics Press, Beijing.

Beijing Municipal Statistical Bureau (2006). *Beijing Statistical Yearbook, 2006*, Beijing Municipal Statistical Bureau, Beijing.

Benjamin, S. (2000). "Governance, Economic Settings and Poverty in Bangalore", *Environment and Urbanization*, 12 (1), April.

Benjamin, S. (2004a). "Urban Land Transformation for Pro-Poor Economies", in S. Oldfield (ed.) *Differentiation in South Africa and Indian Cities, Geoforum*, 35 (2), pp. 177-87.

Benjamin, S. (2004b). *From Income to Urban Contest in Global Settings: Chronic Poverty in Bangalore*, Working Paper No. 4 CPRC-IIPA, New Delhi.

Benjamin, S. (2005). "Touts Pirates, and Ghosts" in *SARAI Reader 05: Bare Act,* Sarai, New Delhi.

Benjamin, S. (2007). "Lifestyling India's Metros: The Elite's Civic Reform", in Ratna Sudarshan and Suchi Pande, (eds.) *Public Accountability Through Community Action – A Case Study in East Delhi,* Indian Institute of Social Science Trust, New Delhi, pp. 179-208.

Benjamin, S. and R. Bhuvaneswari (2001). *Democracy, inclusive governance, and poverty in Bangalore*, Working Paper No.26, International Development Department, School of Public Policy, University of Birmingham UK. Source: www.idd.bham.ac.uk/research/urban-governance/case_studies/wp%2026%20bangalore.pdf.

Benjamin, S.; R Bhuvaneswari, P. Rajan and Manjunatha (2005). *Bhoomi: 'E-Governance', Or, An Anti-Politics Machine Necessary to Globalize Bangalore?* A CASUM Working Paper, CASUM, Bangalore, January.

Berner, E. (2001). "Global Citadels and Ghettos: The Dynamics of Inclusion and Exclusion in Metro Cebu", *Philippine Quarterly of Culture and Society*, 29, pp. 211-25.

Bezlova, A. (2004). "China: Petition System in Danger Even as Public Unrest Grows", *Global Information Network*, New York, Nov 9, p. 1.

Bhide, A. (1999). *Whose City Is It Anyway*?, Unpublished paper presented at the International Conference On Human Rights And The Law, Panchgani.

Bhide, A., P.K. Shajahan and S. Shinde (2003). *Utilisation of Slum Rehabilitation Scheme—A Study Conducted for the Slum Rehabilitation Authority, Mumbai, Volume II*, Tata Institute of Social Sciences, Mumbai, December.

Bhowmik, S. (2000). "A Raw Deal?", *Seminar*, Source: http://www.india-seminar.com/2000/491/491%20s.k.%20bhowmik.htm.

Bhowmik, S. (2006). "Social Security for the Street Vendors", *Seminar*, Source: http://www.india-seminar.com/2006/568/568_sharit_k_bhowmik.htm.

Birdi, H.D. (1995). *Slum Law and Urbanisation,* Vidhi Publishing, Delhi.

Bombay First – McKinsey (2003). *Vision Mumbai – Transforming Mumbai into a World Class City, A Summary of Recommendations*, Bombay First, Mumbai and McKinsey and Company, Mumbai.

Breman, J. (2002). "Communal Upheaval as Resurgence of Social Darwininsm", *Economic and Political Weekly*, 37 (16), pp 309-48.

Bunsha, D. (2006). "Zone of Conflict", *Frontline*, 23 (12). Source: www.hinduonnet.com/fline/fl2312/stories/20060630003711300.htm, (accessed on September 10, 2007).

Cai, J. and V.F.S. Sit (2003). "Measuring World City Formation – The case of Shanghai", *Annals of Regional Science*, 37, pp. 435–46.

Cai, Y. (2003). "Collective Ownership or Cadres' Ownership? The Non-Agricultural Use of Farmland in China", *China Quarterly*, pp. 662–80.

Calderia, T. (1996). "Fortified Enclaves: The New Urban Segregation." *Public Culture*, pp. 303-28.

Cartier, C. (2001). "Zone Fever, the Arable Land Debate and Real Estate Speculation: China's Evolving Land Use Regime and Its Geographical Contradictions", *Journal of Contemporary China*, 10(28), pp. 445-69.

Castells, M. (1998). *End of Millennium*, Blackwell, Oxford.

CCICED (China Council for International Cooperation on Environment and Development) (2005). "Sustainable Urbanization in China", Summary *Record of the Fourth Meeting of the Third Phase*, Kempinski Hotel, Beijing, November 18–20, http://www.harbour..ca/dlam/summary%20record %2005.htm.

Centre for Human Settlements, School of Community and Regional Planning (1997). "Strengthening the Capacity for Urban Management and Planning in Hanoi" *Second Workshop,* September 23-4th October, University of British Columbia, Vancouver.

Centre for Monitoring of Indian Economy (2004). *Infrastructure Report*, CMIE, Mumbai, March.

Chao, J. (2004). "Land Grabs Ruin China Farmers" Livelihood, Developers Often Illegally Gain Control, Offer Little Recompense" [Home Edition], *The Atlanta Journal – Constitution,* Aug 22, p. A.7.

Chatterjee, P. (2004). *The Politics of the Governed: Reflections on Popular Politics in Most of the World*, Columbia University Press, New York.

Chen, G. (2004). "Chaoyang Develops Modern Service Sector", *China Daily*, June 30. Source: http://www.chinadaily.com.cn/english/doc/2004-06/30/ content_344047.htm.

Chen, Y.W. (2002). "*Jiu cheng gai zao yu ke chi xu fa zhan*" ["Redevelopment of the Old City and Sustainable Development"], *Gui Hua Shi* [*The Planner*], 3 (18), (in Chinese).

China Daily (2006). "Combating Land Seizures", *China Daily*, (North American ed.). New York, Sep 29, p. 4.

China Development Research Society and United Nations Development Programme (2005). *China Human Development Report 2005*, CDRS and UNDP, Beijing.

China, Ministry of Construction (2003). *China Urban Construction Statistics Yearbook, 2002*, China Architecture and Building Press, Beijing.

China, Ministry of Construction (2005). *China Urban Construction Statistics Yearbook, 2004*, China Architecture and Building Press, Beijing.

China, Ministry of Construction (2006). *China Urban Construction Statistics Yearbook, 2005*, China Architecture and Building Press, Beijing.

China, National Bureau of Statistics (1995). *China Statistical Yearbook, 1995*, China Statistics Press, Beijing.

China, National Bureau of Statistics (1996). *China Statistical Yearbook, 1996*, China Statistics Press, Beijing.

China, National Bureau of Statistics (1997). *China Statistical Yearbook, 1997*, China Statistics Press, Beijing.

China, National Bureau of Statistics (1998). *China Statistical Yearbook, 1998*, China Statistics Press, Beijing.

China, National Bureau of Statistics (1999). *China Statistical Yearbook, 1999*, China Statistics Press, Beijing.

China, National Bureau of Statistics (2000). *China Statistical Yearbook, 2000*, China Statistics Press, Beijing.

China, National Bureau of Statistics (2001). *China Statistical Yearbook, 2001*, China Statistics Press, Beijing.

China, National Bureau of Statistics (2002). *China Statistical Yearbook, 2002*, China Statistics Press, Beijing.

China, National Bureau of Statistics (2003). *China Statistical Yearbook, 2003*, China Statistics Press, Beijing.

China Research Society of Urban Development (2003). *The Yearbook of China's Cities, 2002*, The Yearbook of China's Cities Publishing House, Beijing.

China Research Society of Urban Development (2006). *The Yearbook of China's Cities, 2005*, The Yearbook of China's Cities Publishing House, Beijing.

China Statistical Press (1991). *China City Statistical Yearbook, 1990*, China Statistical Press, Beijing.

China Statistical Press (1992). *China City Statistical Yearbook, 1991*, China Statistical Press, Beijing.

China Statistical Press (1996). *China City Statistical Yearbook, 1995*, China Statistical Press, Beijing.

China Statistical Press (1998). *China City Statistical Yearbook, 1997*, China Statistical Press, Beijing.

China Statistical Press (2001). *China City Statistical Yearbook, 2000*, China Statistical Press, Beijing.

China Statistical Press (2002). *China City Statistical Yearbook, 2002*, China Statistical Press, Beijing.

China Statistical Press (2003). *China City Statistical Yearbook, 2002*, China Statistical Press, Beijing.

China Statistical Press (2005). *China City Statistical Yearbook, 2004*, China Statistical Press, Beijing.

China Statistical Press (2006). *The Yearbook of China's Cities, 2005*, China Statistical Press, Beijing.

Choate, A. (1998). *Local Governance in China, Part II – An Assessment of Urban Residents Committees and Municipal Community Development*, Working Paper No., 10, The Asia Foundation, Beijing.

Chongqing Municipal Bureau of Statistics (2006). *Chongqing Statistical Yearbook, 2006*, China Statistics Press, Beijing.

Chreod (2000). *Urbanizing Regions in China's Yangtze Basin – Development Trends and Key Priorities*, for the World Bank, Chreod, Shanghai.

Chua, B-H. (1998). "World Cities, Globalisation and the Spread of Consumerism: A View from Singapore", *Urban Studies*, 35(5-6), pp. 981-1000.

Clammer, J. (2000). "The Global and the Local: Gender, Class and Internationalization of Consumption in a Tokyo Neighbourhood", in M. Ashkenazi and J. Clammer (eds.) *Consumption and Material Culture in Contemporary Japan*, Kegan Paul International, London, pp. 249-83.

Clammer, J. (2003). "Gobalisation, Class, Consumption and Civil Society in South-east Asian Cities", *Urban Studies*, 40(2), pp. 403-19.

Committee for Right to Housing (2005). *Demolitions: Driving Urban Poor to the Edge - Impact Assessment Study of Demolitions in Mumbai 2004-05*, CRH, Mumbai.

Concerned Citizens Tribunal – Gujarat 2002 (2002a). *Crime Against Humanity—An Inquiry into the Carnage in Gujarat, Volume I: List of Incidents and Evidence*, Citizens for Peach and Justice, Mumbai.

Concerned Citizens Tribunal – Gujarat 2002 (2002b). *Crime Against Humanity—An Inquiry into the Carnage in Gujarat, Volume II: Findings and Recommendations*, Citizens for Peach and Justice, Mumbai.

Contractor, Q.; N. Madhiwalla and M. Gopal (2005). *Uprooted Homes Uprooted Lives – Key Findings of a Study of the Impact of Involuntary Resettlement of a Slum Community in Mumbai*, CEHAT, Mumbai.

Cook, S. (2000). *After the Iron Rice Bowl: Extending the Safety Net in China*, IDS Discussion Paper 377, IDS, Sussex.

Corbridge, S. and J. Harriss (2000). *Reinventing India – Liberalization, Hindu Nationalism and Popular Democracy*, Oxford University Press, New Delhi.

Cox, K.R. (1995). "Globalisation, Competition and the Politics of Local Economic Development", *Urban Studies*, 32, pp. 213-24.

D'Monte D. (2002). *Ripping the Fabric - The Decline of Mumbai and Its Mills*, Oxford University Press, New Delhi.

D'Monte, D. (2006). "Turning Mill Land to Mall Land", *InfoChange News & Features*, March, source: http://www.infochangeindia.org/analysis120.jsp.

Dang, H.T. (1985). *Hanoi's Architecture in 19th and 20th Century*, Nha Xuat Ban Xay Dong, Hanpi (Hanoi), pp. 46 (Vietnamese).

Das, P.K. (2003). "Slums. The Continuing Struggle for Housing", in S. Patel and J. Masselos (eds.) *Bombay and Mumbai – The City in Transition*, Oxford University Press, New Delhi, pp. 207-34.

DDA (1990). *Master Plan of Delhi 1962*; DDA, New Delhi.

DDA (1999). *Master Plan of Delhi: 2001*, Aklank Publications, Delhi.

DDA (2004). *Annual Administration Report 2003-2004*, DDA, New Delhi.

DDA (2005). *Draft Master Plan for Delhi 2021*, DDA, New Delhi.

Department of Urban Society and Economic Statistics, National Bureau of Statistics (2006). *China Urban Life and Price Yearbook, 2006*, China Statistics Press, Beijing.

Deshpande S. and L. Deshpande (1991). *Problems of Urbanisation and Growth of Large Cities in Developing Countries: A case study of Bombay*, Geneva Population and Labour Policies Programmes, Working Paper No. 177, International Labour Organisation, Geneva, October.

Dewan, Ritu (2005). *Gender Budget Perspectives on Macro and Meso Policies in Small Urban Manufacturies in Greater Mumbai*, Discussion Paper Series 12, Human Development Resource Centre, UNDP, New Delhi.

Dharmakumar (2001). *Colonialism, Property and the State*, Oxford University Press, New Delhi.

Dick, H. W. and P. J. Rimmer (1998). "Beyond the Third World City: The New Urban Geography of South-east Asia", *Urban Studies*, 35 (12), pp. 2303-21.

Do. H. (2003). "Short term Training an Important Solution for Capacity Building for Urban Authorities in the Process of Urban Development Control", paper presented at the *International Congress of Asian Planning Schools Association*, Hanoi, September, 12-14.

Dongguan Municipal Land Resource Administration Bureau (2003). *Report on the General Plan of Land Use of Dongguan City*, Hand out prepared on November 6.

Dongguanshi Tongjiju Bian (2003). *Dongguan Tongji Nianjian, 2003*, China Statistical Press, Beijing. [Dongguan Municipal Bureau of Statistics (2003). *Dongguan Statistical Yearbook, 2003*, China Statistics Press, Beijing].

Douglass, M. (1991). "Planning for Environmental Sustainability in the Extended Jakarta Metropolitan Region" in N. Ginsburg, B.Koppel and T.G. McGee (eds.), *The Extended Metropolis: Settlement Transition in Asia*, University of Hawaii Press, Honolulu, pp. 239-74.

Douglass, M. (2000). "Mega-urban Regions and World City Formation: Globalisation, the Economic Crisis and Urban Policy Issues in Pacific Asia", *Urban Studies*, (37)12, pp. 2315-35.

Dowrick, S. and M. Akmal (2003). "Contradictory Trends in Global Income Inequality: A Tale Of Two Biases, a paper presented at UNU / WIDER Conference on Inequality, Poverty and Human Well-being", Helsinki, May. Source: http://www.wider.unu.edu/conference/conference-2003-2/conference%202003-2-papers/papers-pdf/Dowrick%20and%20Akmal%20150503.pdf, (accessed on October 6, 2007).

Dubey, A. and D. Mahadevia (2001). "Poverty and Inequality in Indian Metropolises", *The Indian Journal of Labour Economics*, Vol. 44, (2), pp. 223-42.

Dubey, A. and S. Gangopadhyay (1998), "Occupational Structure and Incidence of Poverty in Urban Sector by Size Class of Towns" in M. Agarwal, A. Barua, S. K. Das, and M. Pant (ed.), *Indian Economy in Transition*, Har-Anand Publications, New Delhi, pp. 92-106.

Dubey, A., S. Gangopadhyay and W. Wadhwa (2000), "Occupational Structure and Incidence of Poverty in Indian Towns of Different Sizes", *Review of Development Economics*, 5(1)

Duda, M., X. Zhang, and M. Dong (2005). *China's Homeownership-Oriented Housing Policy: An Examination of Two Programmes Using Survey Data from Beijing*, W05-7, July, Joint Center for Housing Studies, Harvard University.

Duoang, Q.N. (2003). "Issues Facing Urban and Rural Planning in Vietnam", paper presented at the *International Congress of Asian Planning Schools Association*, Hanoi, September, 12-14.

Dupont, V. and U. Ramanathan (2005). "The Courts and the Squatter Settlement in Delhi – Or the Invervention of the Judiciary in Urban Governance", a paper presented at the *IDPAD seminar on New Forms of Urban Governance in Indian Mega-Cities*, held at Jawaharlal Nehru University, New Delhi, 10-11 January.

Dutta, S. (2002). "Partnerships for Urban Poverty Reduction: A Review Experience", in A. Kundu and D. Mahadevia (eds.) *Poverty and Vulnerability in a Globalising Metropolis: Ahmedabad*, Manak Publishers, Delhi, pp. 237-67.

Economic and Political Weekly (1982). "Expensive Housing, Cheap People", *Economic and Political Weekly*, 17 (20), pp 801-2.

EPTRI (1996). *State of Environment for Hyderabad Urban Agglomeration*, Environment Protection, Training and Research Institute, Hyderabad.

Evertsz, H. (2000). *Popular Housing in Hanoi*, Cultural Publishing House, Hanoi.

Fan, W.B. (2004). *Shang Hai Li Nong De Bao Hu Yu Geng Xin* [Conservation and Renewal of Lilongs in Shanghai], *Shang Hai Ke Xue Ji Shu Chu Ban She* [Shanghai Scientific Technology Press]), Shanghai (in Chinese).

Fasenfest, D. (1993). "Cui Bono? Corporate Feeding from the Public Trough, in *Grand Designs, Corporate Strategies and their Effects on Unions, Workers and Communities*, Cornell ILR Press, Ithica, New York, pp. 119-37.

Frankel, F. R. (1978). *India's Political Economy 1947-1977, The Gradual Revolution*, Princeton University Press, New Jersey.

French, H. W. (2004). "Boomtowns Change Path of China's Growth", New York Times, July 28. Source: http://www.chinadaily.com.cn/english/doc/2004-07/28/content_352452.htm.

Friedman T. (2005). *The World is Flat*, Penguin, London.

Friedmann, J. (1986). "The World City Hypothesis", *Development and Change*, 17, pp. 69-84.

Friedmann, J. (1988). *Life Space and Economic Space: Essays in Third World Planning*, New Brunswick (USA) and Oxford (UK) Transaction Books.

Friedmann, J. (2000). 'Where We Stand: A Decade of World City Research' in: P. Knox and P. Taylor (eds.). *World Cities in a World System*, Cambridge University Press, Cambridge, MA.

Friedmann, J. and G. Wolff (1982). "World City Formation", *International Journal of Urban and Regional Research*, 6, pp. 306-44.

Fuller, C. J. and V. Benai (2002). *The Everyday State and Society in Modern India*, Social Science Press, New Delhi.

Galsze, G., C. Webster and K. Frantz (eds). *Private Cities—Global and Local Perspective*, Routledge, London and New York.

General Statistical Office and UNDP (2001). *Census Monograph on Internal Migration and Urbanisation in Vietnam*, General Statistical Office and UNDP, Hanoi.

Ghosh, A. (2005). "Public-Private or a Private Public: Promised Partnership of the Bangalore Agenda Task Force", *Economic and Political Weekly*, Nov. 19.

Giang M. (2000). "Hanoi Sees Red as Its Green Lungs Are Choked by Squatters" *Vietnam News*, 11th January, p.5.

Gillion, K. (1968). *Ahmedabad: A Study in Urban History*, University of California Press, Berkeley.

Girior, G. (2006). "The Purple Jade Villas (Beijing) – A Golden Ghetto in Red China", in G. Galze, C. Webster and K. Frantz (eds) *Private Cities – Global and Local Perspective*, Routledge, London and New York, pp. 142-69.

GNCTD (2001). *Economic Survey of Delhi*, Planning Department, GNCTD, Delhi.

GNCTD (2002). *Socio Economic Profile of Delhi 2001-02*, Planning Department, GNCTD, Delhi.

Goodfriend, D. (1989). "The Tyranny of the Right Angle: Colonial and Post-Colonial Urban Development in Delhi", in P. Singh and R. Dhamjia (eds.) *Delhi: The Deepening Urban Crisis*, Sterling Publishers, New Delhi, Bangalore.

Gopalakrishnan, S. (2007). "Negative Aspects of Special Economic Zones in China", *Economic and Political Weekly*, (42)17, pp. 1492-94.

Government of Maharashtra (2004). *Transforming Mumbai into a World-Class City—First Report of the Chief Minister's Task Force*, Government of Maharashtra, Mumbai, February.

Governmental Price Committee (2001). *Hanoi Economy: At the Threshold of the 21st Century, Nha Xuat Ban*, Hanoi.

Guangdong Provincial Bureau of Statistics (2003). *Guangdong Statistical Yearbook, 2003*, China Statistics Press, Beijing.

Gupta, R. G. (1995). *Shelter for Poor in the Fourth World (Vol. 2)*, Shipra Publications, Delhi.

Habib, I. (1995). *Essays in Indian History: Towards a Marxist Perspective*, Tulika, New Delhi.

Haidar, M. and M. G. Badami (2007). "Balancing Efficiency and Equity in Public Transit in Pakistan", in A. A. Laquian, V. Tewari and L. M. Hanley (eds.) *The Inclusive City – Infrastructure and Public Services for the Urban Poor in Asia*, published by Woodrow Wilson Centre Press Washington DC and distributed by The John Hopkins University Press, Baltimore, pp.122-43.

Haila, A. (2000). "Real Estate in Global Cities: Singapore and Hong Kong as Property States", *Urban Studies*, 37(12), pp. 2241-56.

Hall, T, and P. Hubbard (1998). *The Entrepreneurial City*. Wiley, Chichester.

Hanoi, Ministry of Construction (1999). *Preserving Hanoi's Architectural and Landscape Heritage*, Construction Publishing House, Hanoi.

Hanoi Statistical Office (2003). *Hanoi Statistical Year Book, 2003*, Hanoi Statistical Office, Hanoi.

Haribhakti, S. (n.d.). "IMC's Development Vision: A Clean, Green, Vibrant Mumbai" in Indian Merchants' Chamber (ed.) *Development of Mumbai City MUMBAI... PAST PRESENT AND FUTURE*, Indian Merchants' Chamber, Mumbai, pp 165-66.

Harris, N. (1996). "Introduction", in N. Harris and I. Fabricius (eds.) *Cities and Structural Adjustment*, UCL Press, London, pp. 1-12.

Harvey, D. (2002). *The New Imperialism*, Oxford University Press, Oxford.

Hayakawa, K. and Y. Hirayama (1991). "The Impact Of The Minkatsu Policy on Japanese Housing and Land Use", *Environment and Planning D: Society and Space*, 9, pp. 151–64.

Hazards Centre (2006). *List of Demolitions (in Delhi). Last 5 Years*, Unpublished Pamphlet.

Heitzman, J. (2004). *Network City – Planning the Information Society in Bangalore*, Oxford University Press, New Delhi.

Higgs, P. (2003). "Footpath Traders in a Hanoi Neighbourhood", in L. B. W. Drummond and M. Thomas (eds.) *Consuming Urban Culture in Contemporary Vietnam*, Routledge Curzon, London, pp. 75-87.

Hill, M. and K. F. Lian (1995). *The Political of Nation Building and Citizenship in Singapore*, Routledge, London.

Hill, R. C. and J. W. Kim (2000). "Global Cities and Developmental States: New York, Tokyo and Seoul", *Urban Studies*, 37(12), pp. 2167-95.

Hiroaki, S. (2004). *International Experience on Sub- Sovereign Financing for Infrastructure Investment*, workshop presentation, The World Bank, March 18.

Hirway, I. and D. Mahadevia (2005). *Gujarat Human Development Report, 2004*, Mahatma Gandhi Labour Institute, Ahmedabad.

Hoa, H. L. and N. T. Nguyen (2005). "Role of Hanoi in the Two Vietnam-China Economic Corridors", *Vietnam Economic Review*, August, pp 39-44.

Hong, Q. (2005). "Restructuring Hanoi's Export", *Vietnam Economic Times*, 16 March.

Housing and Land Rights Network - Habitat International Coalition (2002). *Restructuring New Delhi's Urban Habitat: Building an Apartheid City*, Habitat International Coalition, Housing and Land Rights Network, SARP, New Delhi.

Hsu, I. C.Y. (1976). *The Rise of Modern China,* Oxford University Press, New York.

Huang, Y. and D.L. Yang (1996). "The Political Dynamics of Regulatory Change: Speculation and Regulation in the Real Estate Sector", *Journal of Contemporary China*, 5 (12), pp. 171-85.

Hussain, A. (2001). *Draft Report on Poverty Profile and Social Security in China*, Asia Research Centre, London School of Economics, London.

Huus, K. (1998). "Boom and Busted", *Far Eastern Economic Review*, April 13th, pp. 48.

IL&FS Ecosmart Limited (2006). *City Development Plan, Delhi*, Report submitted to Department of Urban Development, Government of India, New Delhi.

India, Office of the Registrar General & Census Commissioner (2005). *Slum Population Series-I, India, Census of 2001*, Office of the Registrar General & Census Commissioner, New Delhi.

Indian Peoples Human Rights Tribunal - IPHRT (2000). *Crushed Homes, Lost Lives: The Story of the Demolitions in the Sanjay Gandhi National Park*, IPHRC, Mumbai.

Indian People's Tribunal—IPT (1994). *Forced Evictions*, IPT, Mumbai.

Indian People's Tribunal on Environment and Human Rights – IPTEHR (2005). *Bulldozing Rights—A Report on the Forced Evictions and Housing Policies for the Poor in Mumbai*, IPT, Mumbai, June.

Jacobs, J. (1984). *Cities and Wealth of Nations*, Random House, New York.

Jain, A. K. (1990). *The Making of A Metropolis: Planning and Growth of Delhi*, National Book Organisation, New Delhi.

Japan Bank for International Cooperation (1999). *Urban Development and Housing Sector in Vietnam*, Research Paper No. 3, Tokyo.

Jenkins, A. (2006). "Fine Green China", *Travel+Leisure Golf*, http://travel.msn.com/Guides/.aspx?cp-documentid=375741.

Jenks, M. (2003). "Above and Below the Line: Globalization and Urban Form in Bangkok", *Annals of Regional Science*, 37, pp. 547–57.

Jeong, J-H. (2002). "Shifting Central-Local Relations in Post-Reform China," *Development and Society*, 31(1), pp. 23–51.

Jessop, B. and N-L Sum (2000). "An Entrepreneurial City in Action: Hong Kong's Emerging Strategies in and for (Inter)Urban Competition", *Urban Studies*, 37(12), pp. 2287-2313.

Jing, J. (1997). "Rural Resettlement: Past Lessons for the Three Gorges Project", *China Journal*, No. 38 (July), pp. 65–92.

Johnson, K. (2006). "Waking up the North", *Time*, May 1st, pp. 34-6.

Johnson, T. (2005). "In China's Dash to Develop, Environment Suffers Severely", *Knight Ridder Washington Bureau*, July 25, http://www.enn.com/today.html?id=8322.

Joshi, R. (2002). "Integrated Slum Development: Case of Pravinnagar-Guptanagar", in A. Kundu and D. Mahadevia (eds.) *Poverty and Vulnerability in a Globalising Metropolis: Ahmedabad*, Manak Publishers, Delhi, pp. 268-308.

Kahn, J. (2003). "China Gambles On Big Projects For Its Stability" *New York Times*, 13 January.

Katakam A. (2003). "A Blueprint for Mumbai", *Frontline*, November 22 to December 5.

Katakam, A., L. Bavadam and D. Bunsha (2005). "High Water and Hell",

Frontline, from website: http://www.hinduonnet.com/fline/fl2217/stories/20050826006000400.htm.

Kenny, J and S. Chatterjee (1999). "Creating a New Capital: Colonial Discourse and the Decolonization of Delhi", *Historical Geography*, 27, pp. 73-99.

Knox, P. and P. Taylor (2000). *World Cities in a World System*, Cambridge University Press, Cambridge, MA.

Kohli, A. (2003). "Introduction", in A. Kohli, C. Moon and G. Sørensen (eds.) *States, Markets, and Just Growth: Development in the Twenty-first Century*, United Nations University Press, Tokyo, New York, Paris, pp. 1-6.

Kohli, A. and R. D. Mullen (2003). "Democracy, Growth and Poverty in India", in A. Kohli, C. Moon and G. Sørensen (eds.) *States, Markets, and Just Growth: Development in the Twenty-first Century*, United Nations University Press, Tokyo, New York, Paris, pp. 193-226.

Krugman, P. (1996a). "Making Sense of the Competitiveness Debate", *Oxford Review of Economic Policy*, 12, pp. 17-25.

Krugman, P. (1996b). *Pop Internationalism*, MIT Press, Cambridge, MA.

Kundu, A. (2001). "*Development in Practice*, Vol. 11 (2 & 3), pp. 174-89.

Kundu, A. and D. Mahadevia (2002), "Globalisation, Poverty and Vulnerability" in A. Kundu and D. Mahadevia (eds.) *Poverty and Vulnerability in a Globalising Metropolis: Ahmedabad*, Manak Publishers, Delhi, 2002, pp. 1-29.

Lakhanpal, G. (2005). "Vietnam: Rags to Riches Story", *The Financial Express*, 14th May, p.7.

Le, D.T. (2003). "Training Planning Architects with the Works of Construction Planning and Urban Management", paper presented at the *International Congress of Asian Planning Schools Association*, Hanoi, September, 12-14.

Leftwich, A. (2002). "Forms of the Democratic Developmental State—Democratic Practices and Development Capacity", in M. Robinson and G. White (eds.) *The Democratic Developmental State—Politics and Institutional Design*, Oxford University Press, New York, pp. 52-83.

Leisch, H. (2003). "Urban Planning and Development in Hanoi and Jakarta", paper presented at the *International Congress of Asian Planning Schools Association*, Hanoi, September 12-14.

Lever, W. (1997). "Economic Globalization and Urban Dynamics—II", in F. Moulaert and A. J. Scott (eds.) *Cities, Enterprises and Society on the Eve of the 21st Century*, Pinter, London and Washington, pp. 33-53.

Lever, W. F. and I. Turok (1999). "Competitive Cities: Introduction to the Review", *Urban Studies*, 36 (5-6), pp. 791-3.

Li, P., Q. Zhang and J. Wu (2006). "The Future of Beijing's 332 Chengzhongcun: Renovation Plan Points the Dagger at the Floating Population", *Economic Observer*, http://news.hexun.com/detail.aspx?id=1842620 (accessed on 24 Sept. 2006) (in Chinese).

Li, Z. (2001). *Strangers in the City: Reconfigurations of Space, Power, and Social Networks Within China's Floating Population*, Stanford University Press, Palo Alto.

Li, Z. (2004). "Lightening the Load", *Beijing Review*, July 8, 47 (27). From the website: http://www.bjreview.com.cn/200427/Cover-200427(A).htm

Lim, L.Y. (1995). *Marine Parade Town Council*, School of Building & Estate Management, Singapore.

Lim, L.Y. (1998). "Town Council Management in Singapore", *Facilities*, 5 & 6.

Lim, L.Y. (2000). "Urban Development in Singapore and its Relevance to Africa", in *Regional Development Policy and Practices in Africa and Asia: A Comparative Study*, United Nations Centre for Regional Development, Nairobi.

Lim, L.Y. (2001). "Quality of Life Case Studies for University Teaching in Sustainable Development", *International Journal of Sustainability in Higher Education*, 2 (2), pp. 127-38.

Linebaugh, P. and M. Rediker (2000). *The Many-Headed Hydra*, Verso, New York.

Lo, F-C and P. J. Marcotullio (2000). "Globalization and Urban Transformations in the Asia Pacific Region: A Review", *Urban Studies*, 37 (1), pp. 77-111.

Lo, F-C and Y-M Yeung (eds.) (1996). *Emerging World Cities in Pacific Asia*, United Nations University Press, Tokyo.

Logan, W. S. (2000). *Biography of a City*, UNSW Press, Select Publishing, Sydney.

Ma, L.J.C. (2002). "Urban Transformation in China, 1949-2000: A Review and Research Agenda", *Environment and Planning A*, 34, pp. 1545-69.

Mahadevia, D. (1998). "State Supported Segmentation of Mumbai: Policy Options in the Global Economy", *Review of Development and Change*, 3(1), pp. 12-41.

Mahadevia, D. (2001). 'Sustainable Urban Development in India: An Inclusive Perspective", *Development in Practice*, 11, No 2 & 3, pp. 242-59.

Mahadevia, D. (2002a). "Changing Economic Scenario: Informalisation and Increased Vulnerability" in A. Kundu and D. Mahadevia (eds.) *Poverty and Vulnerability in a Globalising Metropolis: Ahmedabad*, Manak Publishers, Delhi, pp. 30-79.

Mahadevia, D. (2002b). "Interventions in Development: A Shift towards a Model of Exclusion" in A. Kundu and D. Mahadevia (eds.) *Poverty and Vulnerability in a Globalising Metropolis: Ahmedabad*, Manak Publishers, Delhi, pp. 80-132.

Mahadevia, D. (2002c). "Urban Poor's Access to Land and Basic Services: Rhetoric, Reality and Dilemmas", *Nagarlok*, 33 (1), pp. 66-85.

Mahadevia, D. (2002d). "Communal Space Over Life Space: Saga of Increasing Vulnerability in Ahmedabad', *Economic and Political Weekly*, 37 (48), pp. 4850-58.

Mahadevia, D. (2003a). "From Utopia to Pragmatism: The Paradoxes of Urban Development in India". *Review of Development and Change*, 8, July-December, pp. 171-220.

Mahadevia, D. (2003b). *Globalisation, Urban Reforms and Metropolitan Response: India*, Manak Publishers, Delhi.

Mahadevia, D. (2005). "The Megacity Should Work on Rational Projects", in *The Times of India*, Ahmedabad, December 12.

Mahadevia, D. (2006a). "Urban Infrastructure Financing and Delivery in India and China", *China and the World Economy*, 14 (2), March-April, pp. 105-20.

Mahadevia, D. (2006b). "NURM and the Poor in Globalising Mega Cities" in *Economic and Political Weekly*, 41 (31), pp. 3399-3403.

Mahadevia, D. (2006c). "The Lessons of Urban Deluge 2005", *Nirnay*, 13 (1), pp. 66-72.

Mahadevia, D. (2007a). "Urban Infrastructure Financing and Delivery in China", *Economic and Political Weekly*, 42 (11), pp. 964-972.

Mahadevia, D. (2007b). "A City with Many Borders – Beyond Ghettoisation in Ahmedabad", in Annapurna Shaw (ed.) *Indian Cities in Transition*, Orient Longman, Hyderabad, pp. 341-89.

Mahadevia, D. (2007c). *Urban Land Market and Access of Poor, India*, a paper presented at the Workshop on Urban Poverty, held by Jawaharlal Nehru University, at Nainital, July 13-14.

Mahadevia, D. (2008). "Inclusions and Exclusions", *Economic and Political Weekly*, February 2, 2008, pp. 42-4.

Mahadevia, D. and V. Bhatt (2002). "Economic Liberalisation and Urban Land Market: Trends from Ahmedabad", in F. Hesselberg (ed.) *Issues in Urbanisation—Study of Ahmedabad City*, Rawat Publications, Jaipur and New Delhi, pp. 128-64.

Mahadevia, D. and A. Mukherjee (2003). *Municipal Finances and Development in Small and Medium Towns: Comparing of Gujarat, Punjab and Andhra Pradesh*, Working Paper No. 18, Institute of Human Development, New Delhi.

Mahadevia, D. and A. Parashar (forthcoming, 2008). "Dynamics of High Tech Urban Spaces: Case of Pune", C. Ramachandriah, C.R. G. Westen and S. Prasad (eds.) *Dynamics of High-Tech Urban Spaces – Asian European Perspectives*, Manohar, New Delhi.

Mahadevia, D. and B. Pharate (2008). "Multiple Partnerships: Mumbai" in D. Mahadevia and J. Wolfe (eds.), *Solid Waste Management in Indian Cities : Status and Energy Practices*, Concept, New Delhi, pp. 212-56.

Mahadevia, D. and S. Sarkar (forthcoming, 2008). *Unequal Urban System, India—Poverty, Employment and Development in Small and Medium Towns*, Institute of Human Development, New Delhi.

Mahadevia, D. and C. Singh (1998). *Liberalisation and Urban Real Estate—Case of Mumbai*, Working Paper No. 8, School of Planning, CEPT, Ahmedabad.

Mahadevia, D. and J. Wolfe (2008). "Introduction", in D. Mahadevia and J. Wolfe (eds.) *Solid Waste Management in Indian Cities: Status and Emerging Practices*, Concept, New Delhi, pp. 1-23.

Mahadevia, D., J. Wolfe and A. Parashar (2008). "Solid Waste Management in Indian Cities—An Overview", in D. Mahadevia and J. Wolfe (eds.) *Solid*

Waste Management in Indian Cities: Status and Emerging Practices, Concept, New Delhi, pp. 24-84.

Maitra, S. (2006). *Delhi: the City and the Capital, A Status Report*, submitted to the Delhi Government by Institute for Human Development, New Delhi.

Maitra, S. (forthcoming, 2008). "Dynamics of High Tech Urban Spaces—Lessons from IT Sector Expansion in the National Capital Region", in C. Ramachandriah, C.R., Guus Westen and Sheela Prasad(eds.) *Dynamics of High-Tech Urban Spaces—Asian European Perspectives*, Manohar, New Delhi.

Majumdar, I. (2005). *Emergent Contradictions: Globalisation and Women Workers in India*, Unpublished manuscript.

Marcotullio, P.J. (2003). "Globalisation, Urban Form and Environmental Conditions in Asia-Pacific Cities", *Urban Studies*, 40(2), pp. 219-47.

Marcuse, P. and R. van Kempen (2000). "Introduction", in Peter Marcuse and Ronald van Kempen (eds.) *Globalizing Cities—A New Spatial Order?*, Blackwell Publishers, Oxford, pp. 1-21.

Marvin, S. and S. Graham (2003). *Splintering Urbanism: Networked Infrastructures, Technological Mobility and the Urban Condition*, Routledge, London.

Massey, D. (2005). *For Space*, Sage, London.

Mathur, O.P. (2000). *Study on State and Municipal Finances*, unpublished report prepared for the Twelfth Finance Commission, National Institute for Public Finance and Policy (NIPFP), New Delhi.

Mclaren, F.T. (1995). *The French Colonial Quarters in Hanoi, Vietnam: A Preservation Approach*, Unpublished Master of Environmental Design (Planning) Thesis, University of Calgary, pp. 66.

MEDC (2000). *Fact book on Mumbai*, Published by Bombay First.

Mehta S. (2004). *Maximum City -- Bombay Lost & Found*, Penguin/Viking, New Delhi.

Menon, P. (2005). "The Two Bangalores", *Frontline*, 22 (22), Oct. 22-Nov. 4.

Menon-Sen, K. (2006). "Better to Have Died Than Live Like This: Women and Evictions in Delhi", *Economic and Political Weekly*, pp. 1969-73.

Ministry of Environment and Forests, Government of India and Planning Department, Government of National Capital Territory of Delhi (2001). *Report on Delhi Urban Environment and Infrastructure Improvement Project*, Ministry of Environment and Forests, Government of India and Planning Department, Government of National Capital Territory of Delhi

Ministry of Information, Communications and the Arts (MICA) (2005). *Singapore Facts and Pictures*, MICA, Singapore.

Mitra, S. (2005). *TDR as a Tool for Slum Rehabilitation—Geography and Experience in the Context of Mumbai*, unpublished Master's Dissertation, School of Planning, CEPT University, Ahmedabad.

MMRDA (1996). *Regional Development Plan for Mumbai Metropolitan Region, 1996-2011*, MMRDA, Mumbai.

Moreau, R. (2005). "The Last Asian Tiger?", *Newsweek*, May 2nd, pp. 32-34.

Mukhija, V. (2003). *Squatters as Developers? Slum Redevelopment in Mumbai*, Asgate, Aldershot, England.

Nair, J. (2005). *The Promise of the Metropolis: Bangalore's Twentieth Century*, Oxford University Press, New Delhi.

Nambiar, A. (1999). *Mumbai: From a Fishing Hamlet to a Polyglot Megalopolis*, Documentation Research and Training Centre (DRTC), Justice and Peace Commission, Mumbai, March.

Narayanan, H. (2003). "In Search of Shelter: The Politics of the Implementation of the Urban Land (Ceiling and Regulation) Act of 1976 in Greater Mumbai", in S. Patel and J. Masselos (eds.) *Bombay And Mumbai The City in Transition*, Oxford University Press, New Delhi, pp. 183-206.

NCRPB (1999). *Delhi '99: A Fact Sheet*, Government of India, Delhi.

NCU (1988). *Report of the National Commission on Urbanisation*, Vol. II, National Commission on Urbanisation, New Delhi: Government of India.

Nghiem, X.D. (2001). "Hanoi's Economic Development Strategy during 2001-2010 Period", *Vietnam Economic Review*, December, pp. 39-42.

Ngo, H.T. (1996). *Improving the Role of Master Plan in Urban Development of the Costal Cities of Vietnam, Case Study Halong Bay City*, Unpublished Master Thesis, Institute of Human Settlements, Rotterdam, Netherlands.

Ngo, T.H. and P. Schubeler (1998). *Strengthening the Capacity for Urban Management and Planning in Hanoi*, Hanoi People's Committee and UNDP, Hanoi.

Ngoc, S. (2005). "Land Issues Persists", *Vietnam Economic Times*, January, pp. 24-26.

Nguyen, B.H. (1994). "*L'Arrondissement Hoan Kiem avec ses'rues Antiques*" paper presented at the UNESCO, Government of France and Vietnam *Symposium Politique Urbaine et Protection du Patrimonie Architectural du Vietnam*, Hanoi and Hue, March (in French).

Nguyen, C.V. (1993). "Old Quarters of Hanoi: an S.O.S" seminar paper, *Friends of Hanoi Workshop*, Hanoi, November (in Vietnamese).

Nguyen, H. (2001). "Development Direction for Planning and Architecture in Hanoi", Proceedings of the Symposium, *Institutional Arrangement for Urban Planning and Development in Vietnam and Japan*, Vietnam Urban Planning and Development Institute and Infrastructure Development Institute Tokyo, pp. 29-32.

Nguyen, H.T. and Q.T Tran (2003). "Cities in Vietnam - Distinctive Values and Experience Values", paper presented at the *International Congress of Asian Planning Schools Association*, Hanoi, September, 12-14.

Nguyen, L.T. (2003a). "Regional Classification in Vietnam for Urban and Regional Research", paper presented at the *International Congress of Asian Planning Schools Association*, Hanoi, September 12-14.

Nguyen L.T. and B.H. Roberts (2001). "Challenges in Reforming the Planning System in Vietnam" paper presented to *World Planning Schools Congress*, 11-15th July, Shanghai.

Nguyen, M.T.B. and N. Amin (2003). "The Role of Foreign Direct Investment in Urban Environmental Management: Some Evidence from Hanoi, Vietnam", paper presented at the *International Congress of Asian Planning Schools Association*, Hanoi, September 12-14.

Nguyen T.H (2003b). "Training Urban Planner-Architects in the Present Conjuncture of Socio-Economic Development", Paper Presented at the International Congress of Asian Planning Schools Association, Hanoi, September 12-14.

Nolan, P. (2004). *Transforming China—Globalization, Transition and Development*, Anthem Press, London.

Norlund, I. (2003). "Social Capital or Social Capitalism: Diversification of the Vietnamese Rural Scenery" Paper Presented at the International Conference *Modernisation and Social Transformation in Vietnam: Social Capital Formation and Institution Building*, Munich Institute for Social Sciences and Hanoi Institute of Socio Economic Development Studies, Hanoi.

Ohame (2001). "How to Invite Prosperity from The Global Economy into a Region", in A.J. Scott (ed.), *Global City-Regions: Trends, Theory, Policy*, Oxford University Press, New York, pp. 29-43.

Oi, J.C. (1992). "Fiscal Reform and the Economic Foundations of Local State Corporatism", *World Politics*, 45, pp. 99-126.

Oi, J.C. (1998). "The Evolution of Local State Corporatism", in A.G. Walder (ed.) *Zouping in Transition: The Process of Reform in Rural North China*, Harvard University Press, Cambridge, MA, pp. 35- 61.

Oi, J.C. (1999). *Rural China Takes Off: Institutional Foundations of Economic Reform*, University of California Press, Berkeley, CA.

Ota, S. (2003). "The Housing for the Poor in Vietnam under Colonial Rule", paper presented at the *International Congress of Asian Planning Schools Association*, Hanoi, September 12-14.

Owen, J.G. (2005). "Estimating the Cost and Benefit of Hosting Olympic Games: What Can Beijing Expect from Its 2008 Games?", *Industrial Geographer*, Fall.

Pacific Consultants International and Hokkaido Engineering Consultants (1996). *The Study of Hanoi Water Supply Systems*, Japan International Cooperation Agency (JICA).

Pangotra, P. (1998). *City Monitor*, Ahmedabad Management Association, Ahmedabad.

Pani, N. (2006). "Icons and Reform Politics in India: the Case of S.M. Krishna", *Asian Survey*, March/April, Vol. 46 (2).

Parenteau, R., Q.T. Nguyen (2005). "Environmental Rehabilitation - Role of Civil Society in Urban Environmental Rehabilitation: A Case Study of Thanh Xuan District, Hanoi Vietnam", *Environment and Urbanisation*, 17, April, pp. 237-48.

Patel, G. (2002). "Narendra Modi's One-Day Cricket Match", *Economic and Political Weekly*, Vol 37, No. 48, pp. 4826-37.

Patel, S. (2003). "Bombay and Mumbai: Identities, Politics and Populism", in S. Patel and J. Masselos (eds.) *Bombay and Mumbai—The City in Transition*, Oxford University Press, New Delhi, pp. 3-30.

Peng, Z-R. and Y. Zhu (2007). "Urban Transport in Chinese Cities: The Impact on the Urban Poor", in A.A. Laquian, V. Tewari and L.M. Hanley (eds.) *The Inclusive City—Infrastructure and Public Services for the Urban Poor in Asia*, Published by Woodrow Wilson Centre Press Washington DC and distributed by The John Hopkins University Press, Baltimore, pp.144-70.

People's Union for Democratic Rights – PUDR (1982). *The Other Face of Asiad 82*, PUDR, Delhi.

Peterson, G.E. and P.C. Annez (eds.) (2007). *Financing Cities – Fiscal Responsibility and Urban Infrastructure in Brazil, China, India, Poland and South Africa*, for the World Bank, Sage Publications, Los Angeles, London, New Delhi and Singapore.

Pham K.T. (2001). "Land Administration for Urban Development in Vietnam", Proceedings of the *Symposium, Institutional Arrangement for Urban Planning and Development in Vietnam and Japan*, Vietnam Urban Planning and Development Institute and Infrastructure Development Institute Tokyo, pp 79-86.

Pham, L.T. (2003). "Structures of Housing Provision and Residential Landscape in Hanoi City", paper presented at the *International Congress of Asian Planning Schools Association*, Hanoi, September 12-14.

Pham, L.T. (2004). "Hanoi Today and in the Future" Workshop Presentation, *Swiss Vietnamese Clean Air Programme*, December 3rd, Hanoi.

Pieterse, J.N. (2000). "Shaping Globalization" in Jan Nederveen Pieterse (ed.) *Global Futures: Shaping Globalization*, Zed Books, London. New York.

Pinto, J. and N. Fernandez (2003). *Bombay Meri Jan, Writings on Mumbai*, Penguin Books, New Delhi.

Plafker, T. (2001). "Home Ownership: The New Chinese Dream" *Urban Age*, World Bank, http://www.worldbank.org/html/fpd/urban/urb_age/chinamort.htm.

Planning Department, Delhi Government (2005a). *Mid-Term Appraisal of Tenth Five Year Plan*, Planning Department, Delhi Government, New Delhi.

Planning Department, Delhi Government (2005b). *Annual Plan 2005-2006, Vol. (IV, VI)*, Planning Department, Delhi Government, New Delhi.

Planning Department, Delhi Government (2006). *Economic Survey of Delhi*, Planning Department, Delhi Government, New Delhi.

Planning Department, Government of National Capital Territory of Delhi (2002). *Tenth Five-Year Plan, 2002-07*, Planning Department, Government of National Capital Territory of Delhi, New Delhi.

Porter, M.E. (1995). "The Competitive Advantage of the Inner City," *Harvard Business Review*, May/June, pp. 55-71.

Porter, M.E. (1996). "Competitive Advantage Agglomeration Economies and Regional Policy", *International Regional Science Review*, 19, pp. 85-90.

Prabhu, C. (2005). "Why Mumbai Choked", *Frontline*, 22 (17), August 13-26, from: http://www.hinduonnet.com/fline/fl2217/stories/20050826004601700.htm.

Prasad, S. and C. Ramachandraiah (forthcoming, 2008). "The Makeover of Hyderabad—The "Model" IT City?" C. Ramachandriah, C.R. G. Westen and S. Prasad (eds.) *Dynamics of High-Tech Urban Spaces—Asian European Perspectives*, Manohar, New Delhi.

Przeworski, A. (1990). *The State and Economy under Capitalism*, Harwood Academic Publishers, Chur, Switzerland; New York.

Pugh, C. (1989). "The Political Economy of Public Housing" in K.S. Sandhu and P. Wheatley (eds.). *The Management of Success: The Moulding of Modern Singapore*. The Institute of South East Asia Studies, Singapore.

Punwani, J. (2003). "My Area, Your Area': How Riots Changed the City", in S. Patel and J. Masselos (eds.) *Bombay and Mumbai – The City in Transition*, Oxford University Press, New Delhi, pp. 235-64.

Purcell, M. (2002). "Politics in Global Cities: Los Angeles Charter Reform and the New Social Movements", *Environment and Planning A* 2002, 34, pp. 23-42.

Qian, Y. (2002), *The Institutional Foundations of Market Transition in the People's Republic of China*, ADB Institute Working Paper 9, ADB Institute, Tokyo.

Ramachandraiah, C. (2002). *Location and Land use Characteristics of Hyderabad*, paper prepared for the WHO-NIUA project on Healthy Cities, Centre for Economic and Social Studies (mimeo), Hyderabad.

Ramachandraiah, C. (2003). "Urbanisation and Urban Services", in Hanumantha Rao, C.H. and S. Mahendra Dev (eds.) *Andhra Pradesh Development: Economic Reforms and Challenges Ahead*, CESS, Hyderabad.

Ramachandran, R. (1989). *Urbanization and Urban Systems in India*, Oxford University Press, Delhi, New York.

Ramanathan, U. (2004). *Illegality and Exclusion: Law in the Lives of Slum Dwellers*, Working Paper 2, International Environmental Law Research Centre, New Delhi.

Ramnath, R. (2005). *From Conflict To Collaboration—A Study of Nongovernmental Organisations and Their Strategies for Local Control of Slum And Squatter Housing in Mumbai*, Unpublished PhD Dissertation, Virginia Polytechnic and State University, Blacksburg, Virginia.

Rao, G. (2000). "Indian Fiscal Federalism: Major Issues", in S. Mundle (ed.) *Public Finance—Policy Issues for India*. Oxford University Press, New Delhi, pp. 224-258.

Rao, K.A. (2001). *Patancheru-A Hell on Earth (A Saga of a People's Struggle Against Industrial Pollution)*, A.V.R.R. Memorial Charitable Trust, Hyderabad.

Rao, V.B. and N.S. Rao (1998). *Influence of Urbanisation Over the Nearby Catchments of the City—A case Study of Hyderabad (India)*, Hyderabad: JNT University (mimeo).

Rao, V.R. (2002). 'Hyderabad Drinking Farmers' Tears?', *Vaartha* (Telugu daily), Hyderabad, 2 July.

Retail Real Estate (n.d.). *Malls in India.*

Risbud, N. (1999). "Policies for Tenure Security in Delhi", a Paper Presented at a Workshop on *Tenure Security Policies in South African, Brazilian, Indian and Sub-Saharan African Cities: A Comparative Analysis*, IFAS and Development Works, Johannesburg, 27-28 July 1999.

Robinson, M. and G. White (2002). "Introduction", in M. Robinson and G. White (eds.) *The Democratic Developmental State—Politics and Institutional Design*, Oxford University Press, New York, pp. 1-13.

Robinson, R. (1998). "The Emergence of the Middle Classes in Southeast Asia and the Indonesian Case", in J. Dragsbaek Schmidt, J. Hersh and N. Fold (eds.) *Social Change in Southeast Asia*, Longman, Harlow, pp. 60-77.

Robinson, R. and D. Goodman (eds.) (1996). *The New Rich in Asia: Mobile Phones, McDonalds and Middle Class Revolution*, Routledge, London.

Roy, D. (2004). *From Home to Estate*. Source: http://www.india-seminar.com/2004/533/533%20dunu%20roy.htm.

RoyChowdhury, S. (2005). "Labour Activism and Women in the Unorganised Sector: Garment Export Industry in Bangalore", *Economic and Political Weekly*, 40 (22 & 23), May-June.

Saito, A. (2003). "World City Formation in Capitalist Developmental State: Tokyo and The Waterfront Sub-Centre Project", *Urban Studies*, 40(2), pp. 283-308.

Sassen, S. (1991, 2001). *The Global City: New York, London, Tokyo*, Princeton University Press, Princeton, NJ.

Sassen, S. (1999). "Global Financial Centres", *Foreign Affairs*, 78, pp. 75-87.

Satterthwaite, D. (2002). *Reducing Urban Poverty, Some Lessons*, IIED Working Paper on Poverty Reduction in Urban Areas, IIED, London.

Savitch, H.V. (1996). "Cities in a Global Era: A New Paradigm for the Next Millenium", in M.A. Cohen, B.A. Ruble, J.S. Tulchen and A.M. Garland (eds.) *Preparing for the Urban Future – Global Pressures and Local Forces*, published by Woodrow Wilson Centre Press Washington DC and distributed by The John Hopkins University Press, Baltimore, pp. 39-65.

Savitch, H.V. (2002). "What is New About Globalisation and What Does it Portend for Cities?", *International Social Science Journal*, 172, pp. 179-89.

Schenk, H. (ed.) (2001). *Living in India's Slums*, Manohar, New Delhi.

Schumpeter, J.A. (1934). *Theory of Economic Development: An Enquiry into Profits, Capital, Credit, Interest and the Business Cycle*, Harvard University Press, Cambridge, MA.

Science of Economic Association of Vietnam (2002). *General Planning of Vietnam's Socio-Economic Development, Section I*, National Political Publishing House, Hanoi.

Scott, A.J., J. Agnew, E. W. Soja and M. Storper (2001). "Global City Regions", in A.J. Scott (ed.) *Global City-Regions: Trends, Theory, Policy*, Oxford University Press, New York, pp 11-30.

Seabrook, J. (1987). *Life and Labour in a Bombay Slum*, Quartet Book, London.

Selden, M. (1993). *The Political Economy of Chinese Development*, M.E.Sharpe, New York and London.

Sen, A. (2005). *Argumentative Indian*, Allen Lane an imprint of Penguin, London.

Sender, H. (1997). "Bubble Vision: Unprecedented Liquidity Send Asset Price Soaring," *Far Eastern Economic Review*, 3, July, pp. 66-7.

Shachar, A. (1997). "Economic Globalization and Urban Dynamics—I", in F. Moulaert and A.J. Scott (eds.) *Cities, Enterprises and Society on the Eve of the 21st Century*, Pinter, London and Washington, pp. 18-32.

Shah, G. (2002). "Caste, Hindutva and Hideousness", *Economic and Political Weekly*, 37(15), pp. 1391-93.

Shang Hai Shi Fang Chan Jing Ji Xue Hui (2002) *Fan Rong Yu Fa Zhan—2002 Nian Shang Hai Fang Di Chan Jing Ji Li Lun Yan Jiu* [Prosperity and Development – Year 2002 Research Results of Economic Theories on Property Development in Shanghai], Shanghai.

Shanghai Statistical Bureau (2004). *Shanghai Tong Ji Nein Jian 2004* [*Shanghai Statistical Yearbook 2004*], Zhong Guo Tong Ji Chu Ban She [China Statistical Press], Beijing (in Chinese and English).

Shanghai Tongji Nianjian (SHTJNJ) (2006). *Shanghai Statistical Yearbook 2005*, China Statistics Press, Beijing.

Sharma, K. (2000). *Rediscovering Dharavi—Stories From Asia's Largest Slum*, Penguin, New Delhi.

Shaw, A. (forthcoming, 2008). "High Tech Development in Kolkata Metropolitan Area: Locational Dynamics and Impacts", C. Ramachandriah, C.R. G. Westen and S. Prasad (eds.) *Dynamics of High-Tech Urban Spaces—Asian European Perspectives*, Manohar, New Delhi.

Shi Xue Hui Huang Pu Fen Hui (2003) "*Zhi Xing Xin Chai Qian Xi Zhe*" ["Issues in Implementing the New Regulations of Demolition and Relocation"], *Fang Di Guan Li* [*Shanghai Property*], No. 1, pp. 41-5.

Silver, C. (2003). "Do the Donors Have it Right? Decentralization and Changing Local Governance in Indonesia", *Annals of Regional Science*, 37, pp. 421-34.

Sim, L.L., L.Y. Lim, and K.P. Tay, (1993). "Shelter for All: Singapore's Strategy for Full Home Ownership by the Year 2000", *Habitat International*, 17 (1), pp. 85-101.

Singerman, D. (1995). *Avenues of Participation: Family, Politics, and Networks in Urban Quarters of Cairo*, The American University in Cairo Press, Cairo.

Singh, G. (1986). "Bombay Slums Face Operation Demolition", *Economic and Political Weekly*, Vol. 21(16), 684-7.

Sivaramakrishnan, K.C., A. Kundu, and B.N. Singh (2005). *Handbook of Urbanization in India: An Analysis of Trends and Processes*, Oxford University Press, New Delhi and New York.

Smith, M.P. (ed.) (1984). *Cities in Transition*, Sage, London.

Solinger, D. (1995). "The Floating Population in Cities: Chances for Assimilation?",

In Deborah Davis, et al (eds.) *Urban Spaces in Contemporary China: The Potential for Autonomy and Community in Post-Mao China*, Woodrow Wilson Centre Press, Washington, pp. 113-39.

Solinger, D. (2006). "The Creation of a New Underclass in China and Its Implications" *Environment and Urbanization*, 18 (4), pp. 177-93.

Sorensen, A. (2003). "Building World City Tokyo: Globalization and Conflict over Urban Space", *Annals of Regional Science*, 37, pp. 519-31.

Statistical Publishing House (2004). *Strategies-Plans-Programmes of Vietnam Socio-Economic Development Investment to the Year 2010*, Statistical Publishing House, Hanoi.

Stockholm Environment Institute with United Nations Development Programme (2002). *China Human Development Report 2002: Making Green Development A Choice*, Oxford University Press, New York.

Stubbs, J. and G. Clarke (1996). *Megacity Management in the Asian and Pacific Region, Volume—I*, Asian Development Bank and United Nations/World Bank Urban Management Programme for Asia and Pacific, Manila.

Sudarshan, R. (1990). "In Quest of the State: Politics and Judiciary in India", *Journal of Commonwealth and Comparative Politics*, 28(1), pp 44-69.

Suri, P. (1994). *Urban Poor: Their Housing Needs and Government Response*, Har-Anand Publications New Delhi.

Tarlo, E. (2000). "Welcome To History: A Resettlement Colony in the Making" in V. Dupont, E. Tarlo and D. Vidal (eds.) *Delhi: Urban Space and Human Destinies*, Manohar, Delhi.

Thanh, H. (2005). "Land of Milk and Honey", *Vietnam Economic Times*, February, pp. 21-22.

The Committee for the Right to Housing (1994). *The Indian People's Tribunal on Environment and Human Rights, the Fifth Report* in Collaboration with the Committee for the Right to Housing, CRH, Bombay.

Thomas, M. (2003). "Spatiality and Political Change in Urban Vietnam" in L. B.W Drummond and M.Thomas (eds.) *Consuming Urban Culture in Contemporary Vietnam*, Routledge Curzon, London, pp. 171-88.

Thrift, N.J. and D.J. Forbes (1985). "Cities Socialism and War: Hanoi, Saigon and the Vietnamese Experience of Urbanisation", *Environment and Planning: Society and Space*, 3, pp. 279-308.

Thu, H. (2005). "Handling Land", *Vietnam Economic Times*, January, pp. 26-27.

Tianjin Municipal Bureau of Statistics (2002). *Tianjin Statistical Yearbook, 2002*, China Statistics Press.

Tianjin Municipal Bureau of Statistics (2006). *Tianjin Statistical Yearbook, 2006*, China Statistics Press.

To, X.D. (2002). "Evaluation of ODA Projects of Hanoi Social-Economic Development", seminar paper *Regards croises sur Hanoi- Transition, Specificite Urbaine et Choix de Developpement*, November 12-14 (in French).

Tomba, L. (2004). "Creating an Urban Middle Class: Social Engineering in Beijing", *The China Journal*, (51), pp. 1-26.

Town and Country Planning of India—TCPO (2007). *Evaluation Study of DMA Towns in National Capital Region*, TCPO, Ministry of Urban Development, Government of India, New Delhi.

Town and Planning Organization—T & PO (1973). *Review of Master Plan for Delhi*, Akalank Publications, New Delhi.

Trinh, L.D. and V.Q. Nguyen (2001). *Socio-Economic Impacts of "Doi Moi' on Urban Housing in Vietnam*, Social Science Publishing House, Hanoi.

Turner S. and A.N. Phuong (2005). "Young Entrepreneurs, Social Capital and *Doi Moi* in Hanoi, Vietnam", *Urban Studies*, September, pp. 1693-1710.

United Nations (2006). *World Population Policies 2005* (ST/ESA/SER.A/254), Population Division, Department of Economic and Social Affairs, United Nations, New York.

UNDP (2003). *Country Evaluation: Assessment of Development Results, Vietnam, Vol 11*, UNDP, New York.

UNDP (2005). *Human Development Report, 2005*, Oxford University Press, Oxford, for UNDP

UN-Habitat (2003). *The Challenge of Slum – Global Report on Human Settlements, 2003*, Earthscan, London and Sterling.

UN-Habitat (2007). *State of the World's Cities, 2006/7*, Earthscan, London.

United Nations Conference on Trade and Development (2007). *World Investment Report, 2006—FDI from Developing and Transition Economies: Implications for Development*, United Nations, New York and Geneva (from the website: http://www.unctad.org/en/docs/wir2006_en.pdf, accessed on August 1, 2007).

United Nations Population Fund (2007). *State of World Population, 2007—Unleashing the Potential of Urban Growth*, UNFPA (from the website).

Van Der Linden, J. and J.W. Schoorl (1983). *Between Basti Dwellers and Bureaucrats*, Pergamon Press, New York.

Van Grunsven, L. (2000). "Singapore: The Changing Residential Landscape in a Winner City", in P. Marcuse and R. van Kempen (eds.) *Globalizing Cities—A New Spatial Order?*, Blackwell Publishers, Oxford, pp. 95-126.

Vandenhole, W. (2000). "Book Review: People, Law and Justice; Supreme Court on Public Interest Litigation: Cases and Materials, vol 1-4". *Human Rights Quarterly*, 22, pp. 1111 14.

Varma, P. (1998). *The Great Indian Middle Class*, Viking, Delhi.

Varshney, A. (2002). '*Ethnic Conflict and Civic Life: Hindus and Muslims in India*', Oxford University Press, New Delhi.

Verma, G.D. (2002). *Slumming India—A Chronicle of Slums and Their Savriours*, Penguin, New Delhi.

Viet, C. (2000). "Hanoi, a Promising Market, 990 Year Old Thang Long, Hanoi", *Special Supplement of International Affairs Review*, September, 47.

Vietnamese Architects Association (1991). "Residential Architecture and Construction by Individual Residents Investors" *Kien Truc*, 32, pp 17-22 (Vietnamese).

Vliet, W. van (2002). "Cities in a Globalizing World: From Engines of Growth to Agents of Change", *Environment and Urbanization*, 14 (1), pp. 31-40.

Vora, R. and S. Palsikar (2003). "Politics of Locality, Community, and Marginalization", in S. Patel and J. Masselos (eds.) *Bombay and Mumbai—The City in Transition*, Oxford University Press, New Delhi, pp. 161-82.

Vu, A.K. (2003). "Rehabilitation of Old Apartment Living quarters—A Contribution for Sustainable Development of Hanoi City", A paper presented at the *International Congress of Asian Planning Schools Association*, Hanoi, September, 12-14.

Wang, G. (2006). *Characteristics and Livelihood Status of China's Floating Population* (In Chinese) (*Danggin 'Woguo De Liudongrenkou Tedian Yiji Shengcun Zhuangquang*) http://cangzhou.china.com.cn/chinese/renkou/.htm.

Wang, J.J. and C. Chan (2007). "Public Transit in Hong Kong: Does It Help the Poor?" in A.A. Laquian, V. Tewari and L.M. Hanley (eds.) *The Inclusive City – Infrastructure and Public Services for the Urban Poor in Asia*, The published by Woodrow Wilson Centre Press Washington DC and distributed by The John Hopkins University Press, Baltimore, pp.171-96.

Wang, S. and K. Jones (2002). "Retail Structure of Beijing", *Environment and Planning A*, 34, 00. 1785-1808.

Wang, Y. (2000). "Housing Reform and its Impacts on the Urban Poor in China", *Housing Studies*, 15 (6), pp. 845–64.

Wassall, G. and D. Hellman (1985). "Financial Incentives To Industry and Urban Development", *Policy Studies Review*, 4, pp. 626-40.

Webster, D. (2003). "Identifying Strategies Priorities for Urbanisation in Vietnam", Paper Presented at the *International Congress of Asian Planning Schools Association*, Hanoi, September 12-14.

Wei, H. (2002). *Dynamics of FDI Location after China's Entering WTO*, a paper presented at Hong Kong Economic Association (HKEA) Second Biennial Conference, 16-17 December, Hong Kong.

Westendorff, D. (2007). *New Beijing, New Olympics: Urban Transformation at What Cost?*, Unpublished Manuscript, COHRE, Geneva.

White, G. (2002). "Democratic Developmental State", M. Robinson and G. White (eds.) *The Democratic Developmental State—Politics and Institutional Design*, Oxford University Press, New York, pp. 17-51.

Wischermann, J. (2001). "The Relationship between "Civic Organizations" and "Governmental Organizations" in *Vietnam: Selected Findings of an Empirical Survey, Vietnam's Socio-Economic Development*, Autumn, pp. 19-34.

Wong, A.K. (1985). *Housing a Nation: 25 Years of Public Housing in Singapore*, Singapore, Maruzen Asia.

Wong, C. (1998). *Municipal Finance in China: The Development of Extra-Budgetary Revenues*, paper presented at the International Municipal Finance Forum organised by The World Bank, Washington DC, April 15-16.

The World Bank (1994). *China Urban Environmental Service Management*,

Report No. 13073-CHA, December 31, East Asia and Pacific Regional Office of the World Bank; (from the website).

World Bank (1995). *Vietnam Environmental Program and Policies Priorities for a Socialistic Economy in Transition*, Report No. 13200-Vn, February, 1995.

The World Bank (1999). "Creating Cities that Work in the New Global Economy", *World Bank Policy and Research Bulletin*, 10 (4), pp. 1-4.

Wu, F. (2002). "China's Changing Urban Governance in the Transition Towards More Market-oriented Economy", *Urban Studies*, 39 (7), pp. 1071-93.

Wu, F. and A.G.O. Yeh (1999). "Urban Spatial Structure in A Transitional Economy: The Case of Guanzhou, China", *Journal of the American Planning Association*, 65, pp. 377-94.

Wu, W. (1996). "Economic Competition and Resource Mobilization", in M.A. Cohen, B.A. Ruble, J.S. Tulchen and A.M. Garland (eds.) *Preparing for the Urban Future—Global Pressures and Local Forces*, published by Woodrow Wilson Centre Press Washington DC and distributed by The John Hopkins University Press, Baltimore, pp. 123-54.

Wu, W. (2005). "Migrant Settlement and Urban Transformation in China: The Case of Shanghai", *World Bank Third Urban Research Symposium, Brasilia*, Brazil, 2-4 April.

Xiao, L. (2004). "2008 Games Mean Golden Commercial Opportunity", *China Daily*, April, 19. (from http://www.chinadaily.com.cn/english/doc/2004-04/19/content_324348.htm).

Xuan, S. (2005). "Meeting the Need", *Vietnam Economic Times*", February, pp. 18-9.

Yadav, C. (2005). *Impact of Bonds on Finances of Ahmedabad Municipal Corporation*, Unpublished Master's Dissertation, School of Planning, CEPT University, Ahmedabad.

Yan, H. (2005). *Emerging Urban Poverty in China*, Report of the National Commission on Development and Economic Reform. State Council, China.

Yang, B. (2007). *Where is the Fix for Shanghai's Housing Guarantee System?* (*Shanghai Zhufang Baozhang Zhidu De Chulu Hezai?*) (In Chinese) http://www.lrn.cn/landmarket/landpolicy/200701/t20070117_23235.htm.

Yardley, J. (2004). "A Troubled River Mirrors China's Path to Modernity", *New York Times*, 19 November.

Yeh, A.G.O. (1996). "Pudong—Remaking Shanghai as a World City", in Y.M. Yeung and Y-W Sung (eds.) *Shanghai—Transformation and Modernization under China's Open Door Policy*, The Chinese University Press, Hong Kong, pp. 271-98.

Yeh, A.G.O. and X. Xueqiang (1996). "Globalization and the Urban System in China", in F-C Lo and Y-M Yeung (eds.) *Emerging World Cities in Pacific Asia*, United Nations University Press, Tokyo, New York—Paris, pp. 219-67 (from the website http://www.unu.edu/unupress/unupbooks/).

Yeung, Y.M. (1973). *National Development Policy and Urban Transformation in Singapore*, University of Chicago Press, Chicago.

Yeung, Y.M. (1996). "Introduction", in Y.M. Yeung and Y-W Sung (eds.) *Shanghai—Transformation and Modernization under China's Open Door Policy*, The Chinese University Press, Hong Kong, pp. 1-23.

Yixing, Z. and L.J.C. Ma (2003). "China's Urbanization Levels: Reconstructing a Baseline from the Fifth Population Census", *China Quarterly*, pp. 176-96 (from the electronic version).

Yu, Z. (2006). "Heterogeneity and Dynamics in China's Emerging Urban Housing Market: Two Sides of A Success Story From The Late 1990s", *Habitat International*, 30, pp. 277-304.

Yusuf, S. and W. Wu (1997). *The Dynamics of Urban Growth in Three Chinese Cities*, Oxford University Press for the World Bank, New York.

YUVA (2001). *A Survey of Slum Settlements in Mumbai—A Study for Mumbai Sewerage Disposal Project*, Municipal Corporation of Greater Mumbai, Mumbai.

YUVA (2005). *The Mumbai Evictions (December 2004 onwards)—An Analysis of Impact in Twenty-Eight Communities*, Monograph, YUVA, Mumbai, January.

Zérah, M.-H. (2007). "The Rise of 'Middle-class' Neighbourhood Associations as Political Players in Mumbai", *Economic and Political Weekly*, 42 (47), pp. 61-9.

Zhang, Hao (2003). "*Xin Xing Shi Xia Fang Wu Chai Qian Yu Fang Wu Jia Ge Wen Ti De Si Kao*" ["Thoughts on Issues of Housing Costs, Demolition and Relocation under the New Trends"], *Shanghai Fang Di* [*Shanghai Property*] (in Chinese).

Zhou, G. (2005). *Prevent the Waste of Resources in Overlapping Transport Projects*, [*Fangzhi Zhi Jiaotong Shangcongfu Jianshe Ziyuan Langfei*] (In Chinese), http://news3.xinhuanet.com/zhengfu/2005-09/23/content_3530728.htm.

ZJOL (2007). "Yang Yuanyuan: Ninety of China's Smaller Airports are Losing Money" (*Yang Yuanyuan: Zhongguo 90 Duoge Xiaoxing Feijichang Jiben Chuyu Kuisun Zhuangtai*), *Zhejiang Online News Service* 26 January, www.zjol.com.cn (accessed 14 March 2007) (In Chinese).

Zou, J. (2003). "Investigation of the University City Phenomenon: Land Policy Gets a Red Light, Higher Education in Crisis", *China Economic Times*, 12 December (In Chinese).

INDEX